Carolina
Encyclopedia

Carolina Beach Music Encyclopedia

Rick Simmons

McFarland & Company, Inc., Publishers
Jefferson, North Carolina

LIBRARY OF CONGRESS CATALOGUING-IN-PUBLICATION DATA

Names: Simmons, Rick, author.
Title: Carolina beach music encyclopedia / Rick Simmons.
Description: Jefferson, North Carolina : McFarland & Company, 2018. |
Includes bibliographical references and index.
Identifiers: LCCN 2018022610 | ISBN 9781476667676 (softcover : acid free paper) ∞
Subjects: LCSH: Popular music—North Carolina—Encyclopedias. | Popular
music—South Carolina—Encyclopedias.
Classification: LCC ML106.U4A C335 2018 | DDC 781.6409757/03—dc23
LC record available at https://lccn.loc.gov/2018022610

BRITISH LIBRARY CATALOGUING DATA ARE AVAILABLE

ISBN (print) 978-1-4766-6767-6
ISBN (ebook) 978-1-4766-3153-0

© 2018 Rick Simmons. All rights reserved

*No part of this book may be reproduced or transmitted in any form
or by any means, electronic or mechanical, including photocopying
or recording, or by any information storage and retrieval system,
without permission in writing from the publisher.*

Front cover images of record labels from
author's collection *background* © 2018 iStock

Printed in the United States of America

*McFarland & Company, Inc., Publishers
Box 611, Jefferson, North Carolina 28640
www.mcfarlandpub.com*

Table of Contents

Preface   1

Introduction   5

The Encyclopedia   15

Barbara Acklin	15	Bruce Channel	63
Arthur Alexander	16	The Checkers	64
The Artistics	18	Dee Clark	65
The Astors	19	Doug Clark and the Hot Nuts	66
The Bad Habits	20	Tony Clarke	67
Razzy Bailey	21	Judy Clay & William Bell	69
Lavern Baker	22	The Clovers	70
Hank Ballard and the Midnighters	23	The Coasters	72
The Band of Oz	25	The C.O.D.s	73
Darrell Banks	26	Bob Collins and Fabulous Five	74
Gene Barbour and the Cavaliers	27	The Commands	75
Chris Bartley	29	Cornelius Brothers & Sister Rose	76
Fontella Bass	30	The Corsairs	78
William Bell	31	Clifford Curry	79
Archie Bell and the Drells	33	Tyrone Davis	81
The Blenders	34	Otis Day and the Knights	81
Bob and Earl	35	Bill Deal and the Rhondels	82
Earl Bostic	36	Harry Deal and the Galaxies	84
Calvin Boze	37	The Delfonics	84
Bradford & Bell	38	The Dells	85
Jan Bradley	39	Varetta Dillard	87
Jackie Brenston and His Delta Cats	41	Floyd Dixon	88
Buster Brown	42	Ernie K. Doe	89
Maxine Brown	43	Patti Drew	90
Ruth Brown	45	The Drifters	92
James Brown and the Famous Flames	47	The Drivers	95
The Buckinghams	48	The Du-Droppers	96
Solomon Burke	49	Champion Jack Dupree	97
Jerry Butler	50	Donnie Elbert	98
Cannonball	52	The Elgins	100
The Capitols	53	The Embers	101
The Cardinals	54	The Esquires	103
Carl Carlton	55	Betty Everett	104
Clarence Carter	56	The Falcons	105
The Catalinas	57	The Fantastic Shakers	107
The Chairmen of the Board	59	The Fantastics	108
Gene Chandler	61	The Fiestas	109

Table of Contents

The Five Du-Tones	110	Major Lance	172
The "5" Royales	111	Barbara Lewis	173
Eddie Floyd	112	Jimmy Liggins	174
Frankie Ford	113	The Love Committee	175
The Formations	114	Carrie Lucas	176
The Foundations	115	Barbara Lynn	177
The Four Jacks	116	The Magic Lanterns	178
The Four Tops	117	The Main Ingredient	179
Little Frankie	119	The Manhattans	180
The Friends of Distinction	121	Martha and the Vandellas	182
The Futures	123	The Marvelettes	183
Don Gardner and Dee Ford	124	Cash McCall	185
Marvin Gaye	125	Gene McDaniels	186
Barbara George	126	Stick McGhee	187
The Georgia Prophets	128	Clyde McPhatter	188
Jim Gilstrap	131	Mel and Tim	189
The Globetrotters	132	Harold Melvin and the Bluenotes	190
Rosco Gordon	133	Bob Meyer and the Rivieras	191
The Happenings	134	Amos Milburn	192
Harmonica Fats	135	Percy Milem	194
Peppermint Harris	136	Garnet Mimms and the Enchanters	195
Wynonie Harris	137	The MOB	196
Wilbert Harrison	138	The Monzas	198
Leon Haywood	140	Jackie Moore	200
Bobby Hebb	141	Bobby Moore and the Rhythm Aces	201
Eddie Holland	142	New York City	202
The Impressions	143	Billy Ocean	204
The Intrigues	144	Lenny O'Henry	205
The Intruders	145	The O'Jays	206
The Isley Brothers	146	The O'Kaysions	207
Paul Jabara	148	Patty & the Emblems	209
Chuck Jackson	149	Freda Payne	210
Deon Jackson	150	Teddy Pendergrass	211
J.J. Jackson	151	The Penguins	212
Millie Jackson	151	The Platters	213
Etta James	153	The Poets	215
Jimmy James and the Vagabonds	154	Tower of Power	216
Janice	155	Lloyd Price	218
Jay and the Techniques	156	Louis Prima and Keely Smith	219
Jewell and the Rubies	158	James & Bobby Purify	220
The Jewels	159	The Radiants	221
The Jive Five	161	Lou Rawls	223
Little Willie John	162	Jimmy Ricks and the Ravens	224
Robert John	163	John Roberts	225
Ben E. King	164	Smokey Robinson and the Miracles	226
The King Pins	166	Rose Colored Glass	227
Robert Knight	166	Jackie Ross	229
Gladys Knight and the Pips	168	Diana Ross and Marvin Gaye	230
Bob Kuban and the In-Men	169	David Ruffin	231
The Lamplighters	171	Jimmy Ruffin	233

The Sandpebbles	234	Willie Tee	268
The Sanford Townsend Band	235	The Tempests	269
The Sapphires	236	The Temptations	270
Boz Scaggs	237	The Trammps	272
Peggy Scott and Jo Jo Benson	238	Doris Troy	273
Shades of Blue	240	Big Joe Turner	274
The Showmen	241	The Tymes	276
The Skyliners	242	The Van Dykes	278
Percy Sledge	243	The Videos	279
Soul Inc.	244	Jr. Walker & the All Stars	280
The Spaniels	246	Billy Ward and the Dominoes	281
Benny Spellman	247	Dionne Warwick	283
The Spinners	248	Dinah Washington	284
The Spiral Starecase	252	Mary Wells	285
Edwin Starr	253	The Whispers	287
Billy Stewart	254	Wild Cherry	288
Sunny and Phyllis	256	Lenny Williams	290
The Supremes	258	Maurice Williams and the Zodiacs	291
The Swallows	259	Jackie Wilson	292
The Swingin' Medallions	261	The Winstons	294
The Tams	262	Robert Winters and Fall	295
Tavares	266	Brenton Wood	296
Gloria Taylor	267		

Works Cited 299

Index 305

Preface

In the late 1980s and early 1990s I wrote more than a dozen articles for various magazines about culture and history relating to life in South Carolina and the surrounding areas, principally the Grand Strand where I lived for so many years. Writing was, and I suppose still is, just a hobby, but like all hobbies, sometimes life takes precedence over entertainment. Though I was gainfully employed and had a family I decided I wanted to pursue an academic career, so I started graduate school in 1992 in pursuit of a Ph.D. in English literature. As a result, my research and writing about South Carolina history, folklore, and music was relegated to the background for a while. As a college professor, one of the requirements for tenure is publication about issues in one's field of academic expertise, so after my appointment as an assistant professor in 1997 I spent the first 10-plus years of my career publishing articles and a book related to 19th-century British literature. But after securing tenure and promotion to associate and then full professor, I decided it was time to write about the things that I had pushed to the background in pursuit of an academic career.

My first two books, *Defending South Carolina's Coast: The Civil War from Georgetown to Little River* (2009) and *Hidden History of the Grand Strand* (2010), grew from my interests in Grand Strand history and folklore, and after their publication I decided I wanted to write a book based on my love for beach music. *Carolina Beach Music: The Classic Years* (2011) was well received and became a finalist for the 2012 Excellence in Historical Sound Research Award in the category of "Best Research in Rock and Pop Music" by the Association for Recording and Sound Collections (ARSC), which was a whole lot more than I expected for a book I had written just for fun. I was encouraged enough to write a second book, *Carolina Beach Music from the 60s to the 80s: The New Wave* (2013). Both of these books focused on a select number of individual songs and the stories behind them based on interviews with the artists.

But what was apparent then and is still apparent now was that beach music really did not have its own reference work, one solid reliable source where someone could go to find out something about this music and the diverse array of the artists who recorded it. As I researched my first two books about beach music in broad reference works such as *The Encyclopedia of Popular Music*, *The Encyclopedia of Rhythm and Blues and Doo Wop Vocal Groups*, and *The All Music Guide to Soul: The Definitive Guide to R&B and Soul*, or more narrowly focused works such as *Kansas City Jazz: From Ragtime to Bebop—a History*, *South to Louisiana: The Music of the Cajun Bayous*, *A House on Fire: The Rise and Fall of Philadelphia Soul*, and *Chicago Soul*, I became more and more convinced that there was a market for a similar work about Carolina beach music. Rock, R&B, pop, punk, new wave, new age, reggae, country, classical, rockabilly, and so on have all had multiple reference works written about their genres, so why not beach music?

I'm not forgetting Greg Haynes' *The Heeey Baby Days of Beach Music*, which is quite

1

good, but by design the book's focus has a regional flavor, and concerns itself primarily with homegrown groups such as The Prophets, Bill Deal and the Rhondels, The Embers, and others. I felt like there was a need for a work that incorporated information about well-known and little-known groups on a national scale whose music has been appropriated by beach music audiences, as well as those home-grown artists from Florida, Georgia, Virginia, and the Carolinas whose time in the national spotlight was brief, if it existed at all. True, there have been a few works about beach music that have dealt with some of this, but most have been self-published and do not qualify as definitive reference works. In fairness, they weren't designed to do anything more than sell books for audiences eager for anything written about beach music, so I'm not faulting them. There is value in those books, and a paragraph or two about a beach song is generally more than could be found anywhere else previously. I just felt that something more scholarly was needed.

Once I'd made up my mind what I wanted to do I had to find someone who'd publish it if I wrote it. The problem was that the publisher I was with for my first two beach music books did not publish books of the magnitude that I knew this work would have to be. For their books they wanted a word count in the 45,000 to 50,000 range, and I knew the work I was proposing was going to be a lot bigger than that. Even at that, I knew my focus wasn't going to be on *every* aspect of beach music, but instead my project was going to be a reference work containing detailed information about artists and songs in the Carolina beach music oeuvre, including biographical information about the artists, information about the record labels, and whether or not the recordings made the national charts. Futhermore, as I'll explain below, rather than try to do that for the last 80 years, I decided to limit my focus to the music from the early, or "classic" years of beach music. In short, the focus was to be on recordings made between 1940 and 1980 that are generally considered beach music, as well as the artists who made them. As a result, we have the *Carolina Beach Music Encyclopedia*, a painstakingly researched work that should be able to provide all the information you need about classic beach music.

Let me say a word about the scope of the work. The music that can be called "beach music" is often hard to define, which is not surprising since people even argue about when the term first came into use. Some of the artists themselves have given me conflicting accounts, some swearing that some of the songs were being called beach music as early as the mid 1960s, while others say they never heard the term until the early 1970s. To be honest, I don't think it is as important to know when it came to be as it is to know what it is and how the definition of beach music has changed over the years.

One thing I do know is that up until about 1980, it wasn't all that difficult to determine what was and what was not beach music. As I'll address in the introduction, it was after 1980 that the somewhat dichotomous relationship between what was beach music and shag music developed. I'd argue that they are not the same thing, but again, I'm not sure that question existed until the 1980s. Because the pre–1980s releases provide a pretty safe zone, and because it's in my wheelhouse because I was listening to beach music right up through the '70s, I decided to set the limits for this book at 1940 to 1980. There is plenty to cover there, and although I'm sure some people will be upset that some of their favorites (perhaps songs such as "Brenda" by O.C. Smith or "Lady Soul" by the Temptations) came after that, I had to draw the line somewhere. That early, classic period is fairly easy to define, and it's the period I know best, so that's how I decided to limit this work.

Despite those very clear-cut lines, there is nevertheless one more issue, which is the trickiest and most debatable of all. What if a song existed before 1980, but wasn't really "discovered" or adopted as a beach song until after 1980? Unfortunately, there are a number of these, and this brings us back to the difference between beach music and shag music that I'll address in the introduction. But by the early 1980s I think DJs, record collectors, and beach music compilation album producers were listening to a lot of old music that beach music audiences had either missed altogether or forgotten about, and so there came a broadening of the roster of songs that could be marketed as beach music. There's nothing wrong with that in principal, and in fact it brought to light some pretty fine tunes that maybe we'd all missed the first time around or forgotten about over time. By way of example, from the 1950s, the Drivers' "Smooth, Slow, and Easy," Champion Jack Dupree's "Rub a Little Boogie," and the Four Jacks' "Last of the Good Rocking Men" are all songs I really don't remember hearing prior to 1980, although they'd been around more than 20 years at that point. I would not say that no one *ever* listened to those songs in beach clubs or called them beach music during that period, and it is quite possible that they were popular at one time but then faded away as a lot of songs do. But I think I could argue that none of those songs would have made anyone's top 50, 100, or maybe even 200 beach songs prior to 1980 because they just weren't on the radar. However, at some point they were back in the mix, so the way I approached those songs was as follows: if it were a song that that was recorded in the '40s, '50s, '60s, or '70s that would have fit nicely as a beach music song during any of those decades, I included it even if it only became popular later.

Unfortunately, we keep coming around to the difference between shag music and beach music, and so here I will add that a number of older songs that probably *didn't* belong were "shoehorned" into the beach music genre during the 1980s, '90s, and 2000s. There are principally two types of songs that fit this category, the first of which were disco-type songs from the 1970s. I can confidently say that songs such as Tina Charles' "I'll Go Where the Music Takes Me" or Candi Staton's "Victim" were not considered beach music when released, and were only so-designated later. I have not included songs such as these in this book unless I know for a fact they were being listened to and danced to by beach music audiences during the 1970s. The same goes for a number of songs such as "Begin the Beguine" by Johnny Mathis, "A Nightingale Sang in Berkeley Square" by Bobby Darin, or "My Baby Just Cares for Me" by Nina Simone. While these are fine songs, they were not considered beach music at the time they were released, nor (in my opinion) should they be now. These were also late additions introduced, again, for people looking for shag music as opposed to music that adhered to the spirit of beach music.

Those distinctions aren't going to make everyone happy, but again, the rule of thumb is that if you played the song for a fairly knowledgeable fan of beach music in 1980, and he or she said, "yes, that's beach music" or "it should be beach music," then it's in. Otherwise, it is not.

Now that I've made an attempt to explain what has and has not been included here, an explanation of the listings is in order.

Listings, Labels and Chart Positions

The entries in this book are organized alphabetically by the artist's last name if an individual, alphabetically by the last name of the featured artist if a group with the singer's name listed (for example, Hank Ballard and the Midnighters can be found in the B's), or by the first word listed in the group's name, save for the "the" (for example, The Chairmen of the Board can be found in the C's). This is followed by the "beach music discography," a listing of *only* the singles that have found an audience with beach music lovers, regardless of how many singles the artist released or how many of the artist's records have charted. Generally though, mention will be made in the chapter of other significant recordings by the artist even if they are not considered beach music. For example, although Marvin Gaye's "Stubborn Kind of Fellow" peaked at #46 on the pop charts, it is discussed in this book because it's considered beach music, while 1973's "Let's Get It On" is not although it went to #1 and was a much bigger hit nationally.

Information about the record follows the song title, starting with the label of release. If a single came out on a regional label, but was later released on a national label, in the chapter headings it is listed by its original release if the record never charted, or the national label if it did chart. For example, "Kidnapper" by Jewell and the Rubies was first released on La Louisianne 8041, then picked up and released by ABC on ABC Paramount 10485. Since neither record made the national charts I have listed the original La Louisianne release in the chapter heading. To illustrate the opposite point, "Double Shot" by the Swingin' Medallions was released first on 4 Sale 002 before being picked and released on Smash 2033. The Smash recording made the national charts, so that version is listed in the chapter heading. This is followed by the year of release if the song did not chart, or the year it reached its peak position if it did chart. Finally, this is followed by the highest position the record reached on the Billboard Pop Charts. If it did not make those charts, it will say "Billboard Pop Did Not Chart," followed by the listing on the Billboard R&B charts if it made those charts. Taking William Bell's "Easy Comin' Out (Hard Goin' In)" by way of example, since it did not make the pop charts but did make the R&B charts, it says "Billboard Pop Did Not Chart, R&B #30." If a record did not make either chart it will say simply "Did Not Chart." In the body of the entry I have usually included the artist's place of birth, though not their birth date. This is usually followed by the artist's early experiences in music, any groups he or she may have been with at any time, the artist's recordings (focusing of course on beach music). In some cases, if the artists went on to record for a number of years yet produced no more music that fits the beach music genre, single releases and chart history will only focus on any big hits. Finally, when applicable, if the artist is deceased, the year of his or her death will usually be noted. Sadly, death is the one thing in this book that is not static, and as of this writing at least half a dozen artists have passed away since I've been working on this book.

What I think you'll find in these pages is a useful guide to songs that were recorded and included in the beach music genre between 1940 and 1980. While I can't claim to have included every single song that someone, somewhere, at some time, has considered beach music—despite my best efforts—I can't imagine I've missed much. I hope you find this guide useful, and as enjoyable to read as it was for me to write it.

Introduction

I grew up in Florence, South Carolina, a town about 70 miles from Myrtle Beach. As early as junior high school I had some idea of what beach music was, or at least enough to know that it wasn't California beach music by groups such as the Beach Boys or Jan and Dean. I knew just enough to know that in my area of the country it was mainly R&B-based music people heard at the beach, and as an untutored teenager, that meant music by groups such as The Drifters and The Tams, though somehow even early on I was also aware of Willie Tee and the Georgia Prophets—though don't ask me how. It was not necessarily the type of music that I liked best as a pre-teen, but I have to admit it appealed to me on some level. When I was growing up my mother loved Motown, so I knew and often heard the music of the Supremes, Four Tops, Temptations, and other groups, and so what passed for beach music was close to the music I heard playing in the house when I was a child.

Then, around 1974, I was in one of those once-ubiquitous shops you used to find near the boulevard in Myrtle Beach that sold bootleg 8-track tapes. I'm not sure what I thought those tapes were at the time, but I knew they weren't original releases because they were cheap, had no (or generic) pictures on them, and didn't sound all that great. But for a high school kid on a budget they were a bargain, and as I thumbed through the racks of cheap tapes, for some reason my attention was drawn to a tape called "Beach Music Hits" that, as best I can remember, contained the following tracks:

"Gimme Little Sign"—Brenton Wood
"Kidnapper"—Jewell and the Rubies
"I Dig Your Act"—The O'Jays
"39-21-40 Shape"—The Showmen
"Anna"—Arthur Alexander
"Mixed Up, Shook Up, Girl"—Patty & the Emblems
"Opportunity"—The Jewels
"Thank You John"—Willie Tee
"The Entertainer"—Tony Clarke
"Across the Street"—Lenny O'Henry
"A Quiet Place"—Garnet Mimms
"California"—Georgia Prophets
"Michael, the Lover"—The C.O.D.s
"Together"—The Intruders
"If We Had to Do It All Over"—Sunny and Phyllis
"Hey! I Know You"—The Monzas

As you can see, that's a real strong list of beach classics, and it was with this tape that I think my love affair with beach music really began. I'm not even sure why I bought it, and

I certainly wasn't familiar with all of the songs on the tape, but I know for a fact that was the day that changed my life.

Maybe in retrospect the exceptional collection of songs on the tape made me a bit of a purist, and perhaps in my mind a prerequisite for "real" beach music was that it should principally be '50s and '60s rhythm and blues—period. I broadened my horizons just a little when I entered Clemson University in the fall of 1976. I joined Kappa Alpha Order at Clemson, and not surprisingly I was in an organization whose members had many of the same interests I did, and beach music was one of those interests. We were the preppy, khakied, button-down collared, Weejun and Topsider wearing frat, a bit of anachronism at a time when every other fraternity was into silk shirts, stacked heels, and leisure suits. In that sense, the music fit who we were, and that was the next big step in my development.

As a KA I learned a lot more about the music from older guys in the chapter, and it was at that point that I also learned that there were some pretty fine newer beach recordings too, and so I became aware of songs such as "You Keep Tellin' Me Yes" by Cannonball, "I Dig Everything About You" by the MOB, and "Something Old, Something New" by the Fantastics for the first time. I've read in places that songs such as "Summertime's Callin Me" and the Tymes' "Ms. Grace" really didn't take off with beach music audiences until the late '70s or even the early '80s, but I assure you they were on the jukebox at the KA house by 1976 when I arrived on campus. Of course, if you were a KA at Clemson you had to know how to shag, and so by that time the circle was complete. This is when I started collecting records that were also exclusively beach music. As time went on, with nothing more than the authority of having a pretty decent collection of 45s, I started occasionally working as a beach music DJ at parties. I already worked at the beach every summer, and after my freshman year in college a friend was talking to a bar manager who had decided he wanted to play beach music in his bar one or two nights a week. This led to my friend suggesting me for the job, which led to a stint playing beach music part time for a couple of summers in Litchfield Beach at the Litchfield Inn, in the hotel bar which was then known as "Big Daddy's Bottom." During those years I was also able to see a lot of the beach bands that played in the area, including The Tams, The Georgia Prophets, The Catalinas, The Embers, and even acts with a broader national appeal such as the Cornelius Brothers & Sister Rose and even the Four Tops. Needless to say I also visited a variety of beach clubs and bars, including The Spanish Galleon, Fat Jacks, Crazy Zacks, and sometimes even places like the Afterdeck had beach bands as well. If you love beach music and think this all sounds pretty much like a perfect life for a beach music fan, it was.

By the early '80s I was finished with college and had moved to the beach to live full time, and during this period I was married, we had children, and eventually I was off to grad school to get a Ph.D. in English. I was offered a job and we moved to Louisiana in 1997, and of course part of being employed as a professor involves publishing. As I mentioned in the Preface, I eventually turned from academic writing to writing about my personal interests. Had I known there would be more than one book, I probably would have done one book about the beach music grounded in the '40s and '50s, one about the '60s, and then one about the '70s and early '80s; in other words, something with the type of parameters you find in this book. However, I didn't *know* there would even be more than one book when I wrote the first one, so the first one spanned all of those decades, then the second one was about the period from 1965 on. Consequently, that left a lot of songs, especially from pre–1965 period, that didn't get covered at all.

Working on those books, and especially after having left the job unfinished, it was apparent that beach music really did not have its own reference work, one solid reliable source where someone could go to get reliable information about this music. It's generally easy to find out information about chart hits by well-known groups, but what about some of the lesser lights, at least in terms of chart success in the annals of popular music? There have been a few works that have dealt with some of the music, but sadly most were not designed or researched enough to serve as definitive reference works. Consequently, I felt it was time for a definitive, library-quality research work about beach music.

Earlier I mentioned growing up and then going to college in the '70s, and while by the 1980s I still listened to beach music, I was no longer active on the club scene and that was certainly true as I got married and we moved first to Columbia and then Louisiana. This is all to say that for me, beach music was basically frozen in time around 1980. As it relates to my writing, and the material in this book, I think that's okay because as this book proves, there was plenty of music recorded that qualified as classic beach music prior to 1980. That music doesn't need to be defended nor does it need to be justified in order to make it legitimized as beach music. After roughly 1980, I'm not so sure that's the case.

Classic Beach Music and "New" Beach Music

Saying beach music—what it was, what it meant, and what it included—was frozen in time for me around 1980, may need some elucidation. It requires an explanation of how it was changing, what the "newer" or "new wave" of beach music was, and the rise of shag music as opposed to beach music. But before I can do that, perhaps it's a good idea to talk about the foundation of it all—classic beach music.

Put 10, 20, 30—or even 2—people in a room and ask them to define beach music and you're sure to get number of different answers that will probably equal the number of people responding. No one has ever come up with a definition that fits it perfectly, and in all honesty to some degree I'm depending on readers to come into this book already having a pretty good idea of what beach music is. Words and phrases used to define it often relate it to music about sand, the surf, salt air, spring break, summer vacation, The Pad, the Ocean Drive Pavilion, the Myrtle Beach Pavilion, girl watching, regional R&B bands, Labor Day Weekend, beach parties, the boardwalk, young love…. I could probably come up with 100 words that connect with what beach music is about and I'd still miss some things. Most people reading this book will know a lot of early beach music was R&B by black groups that, in the 1940s and '50s, was played only on jukeboxes at the beach, often at pavilions and "juke joints" where it was okay to play "race music" long before white radio stations would play it. A lot of those old Atlantic, Federal, King, and Chess releases qualified, but they weren't the only labels releasing it. This music by black artists started to appear on jukeboxes in the area around Myrtle Beach and eventually all along the coastal bars, pavilions, and dancehalls of North and South Carolina, Georgia, and Virginia.

The old story goes that people would hear this music at the beach and go home and talk about that "beach music"—the music they heard played at the beach. When in the '50s and '60s more and more local bands started to pop up all over the Southeast they knew that one of the best ways to please the crowds was to play that beach music that fans had a hard time listening to anywhere but along the coast. As Ammon Tharp of Bill Deal and the Rhondels told me, "We played down in the Carolinas, and during the summer of 1968 people kept requesting [Maurice William's] 'May I.' We did it live on stage, and they went crazy down there. We were there the rest of the week, and we'd get requests to do it two or three times a night. We came back home to Virginia Beach and said, 'Wow—we really gotta record this damn thing.'" Certain bands became identified with this sound and type of music, and in my interviews I've had a number of band members tell me quite pointedly that though they may have forayed into other types of music at one time or another, eventually they decided to be a beach band. They'd play those old classics they knew, throw in some original stuff that fit that loosely-defined beach music template, and they were on their way. If they were good, and could bring something special to those covers, they could be successful even if they never had a hit on national radio. Many of them did have a few national releases, and some of them—such as Bill Deal and the Rhondels with their Top 40 covers of "May I," "I've Been Hurt," and "What Kind of Fool"—actually had national hits with them.

During the mid– to late 1960s, much of the music from Motown and Stax fit the beach music template, though of course by that time what was once considered race music was being played on radio stations and in clubs everywhere, and was no longer relegated just to jukeboxes and local bands playing on the coast. Since the dance people had been doing along the coast for decades, the shag, was danced to beach music, beach music started to diversify in the late '60s and early '70s, and in some cases became whatever music could be shagged to, though it still primarily consisted of soul and rhythm and blues. Consequently, more pop music started to work its way onto beach playlists across the South, and not surprisingly, by the mid–1970s with the rise of disco, some of that music worked its way onto beach playlists as well. In addition, many well-established and enormously successful national groups who had been considered solid soul/R&B/beach music acts such as the Four Tops, The O'Jay's, The Intruders, and even The Drifters expanded their repertoires in order to keep up with music's new directions and keep their music relevant. This led to a very different sound for some of these groups, but it also meant that many of the songs they recorded were accepted much more quickly as part of the beach music canon than would have otherwise been the case.

But perhaps the most dynamic change, and what truly changed beach music forever, was that groups whose sole purpose was to find a localized audience in the Carolinas started to produce self-reflective and self-aware beach music beginning in the mid– to late 1970s. This principally started after The Catalinas' 1975 recording "Summertime's Callin' Me" became a huge regional favorite. Here was a song written about the beach, by a group from the Carolinas, and even though the group had released a record on a national label (Scepter) in the 1960s, by the 1970s the group apparently had nothing more ambitious in mind than having a song that was a hit on the beach music circuit. It eventually became just that, and consequently claims on The Catalinas' website that note that "the song's popularity was the main catalyst that kicked off the modern day beach music renaissance" are true without a doubt: certainly, after the regional success of "Summertime's Calling Me," beach music would never be the same again. By the late '70s, established acts who had recorded classic era hits but principally played the beach music circuit by this point, such as The Tams, The Chairmen of the Board, Clifford Curry, The Embers, and others, also started to record songs about the beach geared for a beach music, as opposed to a national, audience. They recorded regional hits such as "Shag with Me," "On the Beach," "I Love Beach Music," and others, and so these well-established acts lent credibility to those beach-music-about-the-beach songs that might otherwise have been slow to gain acceptance. This left the door open for newer acts in the late '70s and early '80s who were able to break onto the scene without a national recording of the type that lent them instant credibility as had, to some extent, previously been the case. Whereas groups such as those mentioned above had recorded with national labels and paid their dues, groups such as The Band of Oz, The Fantastic Shakers, Bradford & Bell, and others began to break onto the beach music scene without having had that big national release. While it's true that not all of the groups with classic-era hits had had national releases, it certainly wasn't for lack of trying, but in many ways, by the late '70s a recording contract with a national label, no matter how briefly it ran, was no longer a pre-requisite for being taken seriously as a major beach music act.

In many ways it was inevitable that this had to happen. As the Chairmen of the Board's General Johnson later wrote of his founding of Surfside Records with Mike Branch in 1979, "Our objective was to record new music to revitalize the identity of a thriving [beach] music market that was slowly being recognized as too dependent on old recordings." Certainly, it's true that a few hundred solid classic era beach music hits couldn't carry the industry forever. As acts and individuals grew older and passed on, it would mean that every beach music song one heard performed live would be a cover version and that certainly would have relegated beach music to an amateurishness which the genre perhaps could not have survived.

Nevertheless, as the 1970s came to an end, beach music was still pretty easily definable. There were those old R&B songs from the '40s, '50s, and early '60s that had always fit the mold of classic beach music, some Motown, Stax and the like, releases by regional bands, some of which had charted nationally, newer recordings by older classic groups, and self-aware beach music recorded to be beach music from the mid–1970s on. Am I forgetting anything? Probably, but nevertheless, if you were compiling a list of great beach songs around 1980, while you might debate what did and didn't belong on the list due to how popular the song was as a beach music hit, you wouldn't necessarily have debated whether it was actually beach music or not.

As the music had become popular there was a growing market for people who wanted to read and learn more about it, and in 1979, Chris Beachley started *It Will Stand Magazine*, a publication about beach music that, in my mind, has never been surpassed. It featured interviews with beach music artists, discographies, news on beach concerts, shag contests, and all other things concerning the beach music scene. One especially important thing it did was run a poll during its first year in print, and subsequently offered a list of the top 50 beach music hits of all time:

1. Billy Ward & The Dominoes, "Sixty-Minute Man" (1951)
2. The Tymes, "Ms. Grace" (1974)
3. Willie Tee, "Thank You John" (1965)
4. The Catalinas, "Summertime's Calling Me" (1975)
5. The Showmen, "39–21–40 Shape" (1963)

6. Jimmy Ricks and The Ravens, "Green Eyes" (1955)
7. Garnet Mimms and The Enchanters, "A Quiet Place" (1964)
8. Barbara Lewis, "Hello Stranger" (1963)
9. The Clovers, "Nip Sip" (1955)
10. Tony Clarke, "The Entertainer" (1964)
11. The Platters, "With This Ring" (1967)
12. Maurice Williams and the Zodiacs, "Stay" (1960)
13. The Clovers, "One Mint Julep" (1952)
14. Doris Troy, "Just One Look" (1963)
15. The Tams, "I've Been Hurt" (1965)
16. Willie Tee, "Walking Up a One-Way Street" (1965)
17. The Platters, Washed Ashore (On a Lonely Island in the Sea)" (1967)
18. The Embers, "Far Away Places" (1969)
19. The Tams, "Be Young, Be Foolish, Be Happy" (1968)
20. The Georgia Prophets, "I Got the Fever" (1968)
21. The Temptations, "My Girl" (1965)
22. Lenny O'Henry, "Across the Street" (1964)
23. Bruce Channel, "Hey! Baby" (1962)
24. Marvin Gaye, "Stubborn Kind of Fellow" (1962)
25. The Embers, "I Love Beach Music" (1979)
26. The Trammps, "Hold Back the Night" (1975)
27. Billy Stewart, "I Do Love You" (1965)
28. The Drifters, "Under the Boardwalk" (1964)
29. The Chairmen of the Board, "(You've Got Me) Dangling on a String" (1970)
30. The Platters, "I Love You 1,000 Times" (1966)
31. The Georgia Prophets, "California" (1970)
32. The Artistics, "I'm Gonna Miss You" (1966)
33. The Drifters, "I Got Sand in My Shoes" (1964)
34. The Coasters, "Zing! Went the Strings of My Heart" (1958)
35. Jackie Wilson, "(Your Love Keeps Lifting Me) Higher and Higher" (1967)
36. The Checkers, "White Cliffs of Dover"(1953)
37. The Radiants, "It Ain't No Big Thing" (1965)
38. The Showmen, "It Will Stand" (1961)
39. Deon Jackson, "Love Makes the World Go Round"(1965)
40. Mary Wells, "My Guy" (1964)
41. The Globetrotters, "Rainy Day Bells" (1970)
42. Billy Stewart, "Sitting in the Park" (1965)
43. The Chairmen of the Board, "Everything's Tuesday" (1970)
44. Wynonie Harris, "Good Rockin' Tonight" (1948)
45. Maurice Williams and the Zodiacs, "May I" (1965)
46. Hank Ballard and the Midnighters, "Work with Me Annie"(1954)
47. The Four Tops, "I Just Can't Get You Out of My Mind" (1974)
48. The "5" Royales, "Think" (1957)
49. Archie Bell and the Drells, "I Can't Stop Dancing" (1968)
50. Billy Stewart, "Fat Boy" (1962)

I will tell you quite frankly that my personal list, whether it was compiled then or now, would not differ from this list much at all. There might be about five songs that would make my top 50 list that aren't here, but the songs I'd replace would still be in the top 100 or so. And all of the songs on my list could have been on this list in 1980—they were all around then too.

In creating this book, then, I took the circumstances surrounding the *It Will Stand* list as the baseline. If it could have made that list in 1980, it will be covered in this book. If it could not be on the list because it had not been recorded or "discovered" yet (by discovered, as I explained in the Preface, I mean those songs that were recorded during the pre–1980 period, but perhaps did not come to the attention of beach music audiences until much later), it would not. I was inflexible in regard to the 1980 recording date, but the tricky part was the discovered songs. By way of example, Marvin Gaye's "Come Get to This" has been included. This song wasn't a blip on the radar of beach music when it came out in 1973, nor at any time prior to 1980 as far as I know, no matter how much people may like it today. That doesn't mean no one heard nor even shagged to it prior to 1980, but it was not considered beach music in the decade following its release no matter how much of a favorite it may be now. However, since Marvin Gaye had a preexisting beach music repertoire I have included "Come Get to This" in this book. On the other hand the Mills Brothers' "A Donut and a Dream," also released in 1973, is not included. Neither the song nor the Mills Brothers were under the beach music umbrella prior to 1980 (with good reason I think), and in fact, this song wedged its way onto playlists in the 1990s because people were desperate for songs to shag to. In my mind it is not nor ever will be a beach music song, which brings us to the difference between "shag music" and "beach music"—and they are not the same thing.

The Curse of "Shag" Music

A few years ago, I was at the O.D. Pavilion talking to the late H. Lee Brown, and as we talked about the state of beach music, he said something to the effect that he almost feared for the music, and was worried that maybe younger generations might not carry on the tradition. But as I listened to the music coming across the speakers on the dance floor, I had a thought I've had many times since then: no one really knows what beach music is anymore, and we've increasingly blurred the lines between shag music and beach music. Now more than ever they are not the same thing.

The first time I really became aware that what passed for beach music was changing was in the 1990s when I saw a Ripete compilation CD with Grand Funk's "Bad Time" on it. I think beach music lovers owe a debt of gratitude to Ripete because they made hundreds of songs available on vinyl and CDs that were nearly impossible to find after their original release. Before the advent of MP3s, there weren't a lot of choices if a record was out of print, so Ripete can take a lot of credit for saving some of that old music from obscurity. However, they had a business to run, and you can't get very far recycling the same 200 or 300 songs over and over in new packaging. Also, often the terms or the rights and royalties changed, so something had to give. I'll admit I loved Grand Funk when I was in junior high, and "Bad Time" truly is a great song, and technically one you can shag too. But it's not beach music no matter how you cut it. I use this as an example that's sure to provoke a knee jerk response, because the image of a longhaired, shirtless (as he often performed) Mark Farner singing lead on a beach music song defies imagination. I've interviewed Mark Farner, and he is a wonderful man and a devout Christian; I just can't consider anything by Grand Funk beach music no matter how hard I try. But I think the inclusion of "Bad Time" on a beach music CD shows just how desperate things were by the 1990s, as people in the beach music *business* sought to keep it a viable industry.

The solution seems to have been to start calling anything you could shag to beach music, which to me really violates the spirit of what that music was up until the early 1980s. But quality "new" beach music, and new music that could be adopted as beach music, wasn't produced at a pace that was likely to keep shaggers satisfied, and so in my mind things changed to the point where beach music and shag music had become two different things—which I think they have and are. I've seen lists purporting to be "Beach Music Top 40s" containing songs by the Bee Gees, Eric Clapton, Van Morrison, Cher, Bob Segar, John Fogerty, Rod Stewart, and many others. I'm not sure that people who would call songs by those artists beach music really understand what beach music is, and I think they need to recognize that shag music is not exactly the same as beach music. While it's clear that when I grew up they were the same thing, it's just as obvious that today they are not. Those two things took different paths long ago. I understand people want different music to shag to, and I know DJs need something to play beyond a few hundred classic songs, but I resent having something that is clearly in no way beach music being shoved down my throat and told it's the same thing. It is not.

Then there's the newer beach music, which is generally new homegrown beach-music-about-the-beach. Sonny Threatt of the duo Sunny and Phyllis once told me, "I hear so many repos and soundalikes it makes me sick. Songs ABOUT beach music insult the intelligence of anyone who really loves the real thing." There are a considerable number of people who would certainly agree, though obviously there is a thriving industry out there based on the modern beach music sound and whose supporters would beg to differ. The superb beach music DJ Charlie Brown explained to me his theories on why he thought this happened, noting that perhaps the difference is that instead of simply being about the music like it once was, some individuals are selling beach music, shagging, and so on as a lifestyle package more so than just being about great music. For these people, apparently those old classics are great songs, but they are no longer an essential part of the modern beach music scene, the "Carolina beach music" scene, as it is now known. There's a whole new catalog of music for those people. I understand this as well, but just because a group covers "Thank You John," or writes and records a new song about being at the beach, don't expect me to embrace it.

Finally, it's not just modern music that seems to be bleeding over, but older music as well. As I mentioned in the Preface, from the 1980s on, a lot of old songs were "discovered" or "rediscovered." Unfortunately, though, a number of older songs that probably *didn't* belong were "shoehorned" into the beach music genre during the 1980s, '90s, and 2000s, and the most egregious of these were songs not considered beach music at the time they were released, nor (in my opinion) should they be now. These were also late additions introduced, again, for people looking for shag music as opposed to music that adhered to the spirit of beach music. Just because you can shag to Van Morrison's "Brown Eyed Girl," that doesn't make it beach music.

As a result of all these factors, though beach music has always been hard to define, I think that's true now more than ever. Rather than negotiate the minefields of what is beach music as opposed to maybe just shag music, and rather than try to write a book about a post–1980 period I admit I know very little about, I played it safe in this book and dealt with a period I *do* know a whole lot about as a native South Carolinian who grew up listening to that old, classic beach music. In this book I have written almost exclusively about the songs I consider indisputable beach classics, although I admit there's always room for discussion. I've tried to be pretty inclusive here, and if you were to ask me if I really think there are more than 400 great beach music songs I'd be inclined to say perhaps not, but it is probably better to be inclusive than not. My job, as I saw it, was not to simply include what *I* think are the best beach songs, but what are more or less universally hailed as beach songs of merit recorded and recognized prior to 1980.

I realize I've probably missed a few, and there are some songs I ended up leaving out at the last minute because I was on the fence about whether or not to include them. To be honest, a lot of R&B recorded in the 1950s and early '60s could qualify as beach music in some way, and there are obviously a lot of songs from the period you can shag to. Even now there are songs here that I'm not 100 percent sure are the best examples of beach music, but if we shagged to them and considered them some form of beach music back in the day, I erred on the side of caution and included them.

I hope you enjoy this reference guide that was so many years in the making. For me, it was truly a labor of love.

The Encyclopedia

Barbara Acklin

BEACH MUSIC DISCOGRAPHY: "Love Makes a Woman" (Brunswick 55379, 1968: Billboard Pop #15); "Am I the Same Girl" (Brunswick 55399, 1969: Billboard Pop #79).

Born in Oakland, California, Barbara Acklin's family moved to Chicago when she was five, and after graduating from high school she worked as a secretary at Chicago's St. Lawrence Records while waiting for her big break. She did get the opportunity to record an early side under the name Barbara Allen on the Special Agent label, though it failed to chart. Acklin also stayed active in the business by doing back-up work for Etta James and Fontella Bass, and by 1966 she had moved to the larger and better-known Brunswick records to work as a receptionist while still trying to land a contract as a singer. She was also writing music, and along with her friend David Scott she co-wrote a song called "Whispers" and took it to Brunswick's biggest act, Jackie Wilson. At the time Wilson hadn't had a Top 20 hit since 1963, but after he recorded "Whispers" in 1966 it hit #11 on the pop charts and his career was rejuvenated (see the entry for Jackie Wilson). In *Chicago Soul*, Bob Pruter notes that Acklin said Wilson appreciated what she had done for him, and told her "'If there is anything I can do for you let me know.'" Acklin asked Wilson to tell Brunswick to give her the opportunity to cut a record of her own, and in turn Wilson persuaded Brunswick to give her a shot; "About three weeks later I was in the studio" Acklin told Pruter.

Her first solo efforts, "Fool, Fool, Fool" and "I've Got You Baby" didn't do much, but Brunswick labelmate Gene Chandler had heard her sing and decided it might be a good idea to record a couple of duets with her. "Show Me the Way to Go" went to #30 on the R&B charts, while "From the Teacher to the Preacher" went to #57 on the pop charts and #16 on the R&B charts. In between those two releases was another solo effort, the beach standard "Love Makes a Woman," and it became her first big hit. The song went to #15 on the pop charts, #3 on the R&B charts, and would win a Broadcast Music Inc. (BMI) award.

Acklin's next single, "Just Ain't No Love," did moderately well, and though her next release, "Am I the Same Girl," was her lowest charting record of those listed so far, it probably had the potential to be her biggest hit. Acklin sings backed by the in-house Brunswick studio musicians, and listening to it today it's obvious it should have charted and done well. Unfortunately, Brunswick didn't like the finished product and refused to release it as it was. Instead, the label removed Acklin's vocal track and added another piano section to the song, re-titled the song "Soulful Strut," and released it as being by Young-Holt Unlimited (though neither Young nor Holt actually played on the track). The instrumental release went to #3 in the U.S. and #1 in Canada in 1968 and sold two million copies. Brunswick finally released Acklin's original version in 1969, but by that time audiences were probably tired of what they heard as "Soulful Strut" with overlaid vocals; Acklin's version stalled at #79 on the pop charts.

Acklin would have a few more moderate hits on the R&B charts, but would never make a substantial mark as a singer. As a songwriter, however, she would be hugely successful, and would co-write several of the Chi-Lites' hits including "Have You Seen Her," which was #3 on the pop charts and #1 on the R&B charts. Her own solo career would eventually wind down, and she would go on to sing backup for acts such as the Chi-Lites and Tyrone Davis before passing away in 1998.

Arthur Alexander

BEACH MUSIC DISCOGRAPHY: "You Better Move On" (Dot 16309, 1962: Billboard Pop #24); "Anna" (Dot 16387, 1962: Billboard Pop #68); "Every Day I Have to Cry Some" (Buddah 492, 1975: Billboard Pop #45).

Arthur Alexander, Jr. (called "June" by his friends in reference to Jr.) was born in Florence, Alabama, and as a teenager his first success in the music business came when his group the Heartstrings sang on a few radio shows. He came to attention of Florence resident Tom Stafford, who along with Billy Sherrill and Rick Hall opened the Florence Alabama Music Enterprise in Muscle Shoals, which is now better known as FAME studios. Alexander spent time in the studio and co-wrote a song called "She Wanna Rock," which was recorded by Amie Derkson in 1959. A year later, recording as June Alexander, he recorded another song he co-wrote, "Sally Sue Brown," on the tiny Judd Records label. Though the record was not a commercial success, it would later be recorded by Bob Dylan. By then Alexander was married, a father, and working part time as a bellhop and selling bootleg liquor to make ends meet. It was at this point he wrote another song that would become his second recording, "You Better Move On." It was recorded at FAME studios and when it was released under his given name in 1962 on Nashville's Dot label the record finally brought him some notice. The song was based on Alexander's relationship with girlfriend (and later wife) Ann, and how her wealthy former boyfriend tried to win her back. Alexander's advice to boyfriend to "move on" was one of many songs he would write and record about troubled relationships, and it seemed to resonate with listeners. The song went to #24 on the charts and got Alexander a booking on *American*

Arthur Alexander circa 1962 (photograph courtesy Richard Younger).

Bandstand. It was the first national hit recorded in the state of Alabama, and the studio's first hit of the many to follow. Like many of Alexander's recordings, it would be also be covered by multiple artists, including the Rolling Stones, the Hollies and Chuck Jackson, among others.

After releasing the excellent but somewhat underappreciated "Soldier of Love," which would be covered by the Beatles and eventually Marshall Crenshaw and even Pearl Jam, his next recording was 1962's "Anna," written about his wife and their doomed relationship, which would ultimately end in divorce. Alexander later noted that while in reality his wife had not been unfaithful, he believed she was starting to regret not going with that other guy who had "moved on." "Anna" went to #68 on the pop charts and was reportedly one of John Lennon's favorite songs. Consequently, the Beatles recorded it and in 1963 released their own version on the album *Please Please Me*. The Beatles would eventually cover two other Alexander recordings, "A Shot of Rhythm and Blues" and "Where Have You Been," and with those and "Anna" and "Soldier of Love," it was clear, as Paul McCartney later said in a 1987 interview with Mark Lewisohn, that if the early "Beatles ever wanted a sound, it was R&B … we wanted to be like Arthur Alexander." Despite the influence of his music, "Anna" was his last record in the 1960s to make the pop charts, and by the end of the decade he was playing smaller venues. His friend Clifford Curry told me in an interview that the two of them "did a few gigs together in the Carolinas in the late 1960s," including the Beach Club in Myrtle Beach, and that Alexander was surprised at how popular his music still was among the beach music crowd. "He was really pleased by that," Curry said.

While his older songs were adopted as beach music on the coast, in the music industry Alexander's heartfelt recordings would continue to inspire others, and the likes of "Burning Love" would be covered by Elvis Presley. Another song Alexander wrote, "Every Day I Have to Cry Some," was first recorded by Steve Alaimo in 1962, then Dusty Springfield, the McCoys, The Bee Gees, Johnny Rivers, and others before Alexander's own version went to #45 in 1975.

On a personal level, however, Alexander's life was not so successful. Alexander divorced Ann, and his behavior became increasingly erratic. He often had to be tracked down in bars to perform, and on one occasion he walked off stage in the middle of a performance for no apparent reason. In 1975 he recorded the very fine "Every Day I Have to Cry Some" which reached #45 on the charts, but the next recording, "Sharing The Night Together," did nothing until covered by Dr. Hook and the Medicine Show in 1978 when it peaked at #6. In the late 1970s he inexplicably decided he was through with music and simply dropped out of sight. Alexander moved to Cleveland and spent most of the rest of his life working as a bus driver and janitor, and Alexander's co-workers had no idea who he was until 1993, when he recorded his comeback album, *Lonely Like Me*. Shortly thereafter, he suffered a fatal heart attack and died at the age of fifty-three.

Keith Richards of the Rolling Stones said, "When the Beatles and the Stones got their first chances to record, one did 'Anna,' and the other did 'You Better Move On.' That should tell you enough." Ultimately, Alexander is perhaps the only performer to have his songs covered by Bob Dylan, Elvis, The Beatles, and the Rolling Stones—and of course many others. Considering his many contributions to his own catalogue as well songs he wrote and/or recorded and others covered, it isn't hard to see that Alexander was an underappreciated genius often laboring in relative obscurity.

The Artistics

BEACH MUSIC DISCOGRAPHY: "This Heart of Mine" (Okeh 4-7232, 1965: Billboard Pop #115); "I'm Gonna Miss You" (Brunswick 55301, 1966: Billboard Pop #55).

Formed in Chicago in 1958, Aaron Floyd, Curt Thomas, Laurence Johnson and Jesse Bolian made up the original Artistics, and the group got their first opportunity to play a big venue at the Democratic National Convention in 1960. Thereafter they were joined by new lead vocalist Robert Dobyne, and soon they came to the attention of Major Lance, who in 1962 had signed with Okeh records as a solo act. For Major Lance's second recording on Okeh in August 1963, he enlisted the Artistics as backup singers on "The Monkey Time," which peaked at #8 on the Billboard charts. Okeh gave them their own recording contract, and they recorded "I Need Your Love" in 1963 before problems within the group forced Dobyne out and Charles Davis, formerly of the Dukays, took over in his place. Davis was eventually replaced by Marvin Smith, who had been a member of several groups including the Four Eldorados and the Tempos. Smith sang lead for "Get My Hands on Some Lovin'," which was recorded in January 1964.

Their next recording for Okeh was 1965's "This Heart of Mine," written by Barrett Strong of "Money (That's What I Want)" fame. Strong, who by 1965 had moved more towards writing than performing, gave the group their first real hit, and even though "This Heart of Mine" rose no higher than #115 on the pop charts, it did go to #25 on the R&B charts. They followed this with their album *Get My Hands On Some Lovin,'* but after several more recordings in 1965 and 1966, internal struggles at Okeh resulted in several artists leaving the label and going to Brunswick with producer Carl Davis. Brunswick, which was or would be the home of Jackie Wilson, Gene Chandler, Lavern Baker, and others, signed the Artistics as well, and their first recording was the Marvin Smith-led "I'm Gonna Miss You." Though not a big hit—it only climbed to #55 on the pop charts and #9 on the R&B charts—it was nevertheless a step in the right direction, and at long last the Artistics seemed poised to break out. On the strength of that record they played the Apollo Theatre in New York, the Uptown in Philadelphia, the Royal in Baltimore and the Howard in Washington, among others. But yet again, changes in the lineup would affect the group's continuity. Smith had left for a solo career (he had already recorded "Time Stopped" backed by the Artistics in 1966), and Tommy Green had now come onboard as the lead vocalist while Bernard Reed also joined the group. Oddly enough, even though Smith had left in 1967,

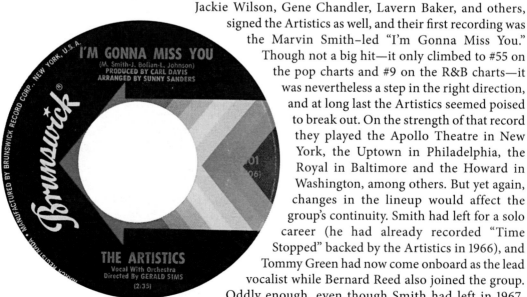

Brunswick continued to releases singles and two albums he performed on throughout 1968 and 1969. In the meantime, Green left and was replaced by Fred Pettis, who only recorded one single with the group. Reportedly Pettis' stage presence was so bad he was let go as well.

The Artistics would release one more single that they thought had potential, "Make My Life Over," with old member Robert Dobyne back on lead. It also failed to chart, the group changed leads again (Morris Williams) and at this point they asked Brunswick to release them from their contract because they felt they were being ignored by the label. Brunswick wouldn't comply, and rather than stay with the label the group disbanded in 1973.

The Astors

BEACH MUSIC DISCOGRAPHY: "Candy" (Stax 170, 1965: Billboard Pop #63).

Curtis Johnson, Eliehue Stanback, Sam Jones, and Richard Harris formed the Duntinos while schoolmates at in high school in Memphis, Tennessee, in the late 1950s. Along with Richard Griffin, the group had been organized by piano player Herman "Red" Arnett, and initially they picked up gigs singing the types of doo-wop tunes that were popular at the time. Rufus Thomas, who would later have a hit with "Walking the Dog," took the group under his wing and they went on the road with Thomas for a while until they were out of high school. Eventually they decided to live with Johnson's relatives in Buffalo, New York, figuring it would put them closer to the heart of the big time in New York City. But soon they were back in Memphis, working as backup singers for artists such as Carla Thomas at a new company called Satellite records—soon to become Stax.

Starting afresh, the group changed their name to the Chips and recorded their first record as a featured act in 1961 on Stax 105, a song called "You Make Me Feel So Good." The song did nothing, Griffin left the group and Johnson joined the Air Force, but like William Bell (see the entry for Bell), who was also at Stax, Johnston continued to record for the label while on leave. By 1963 they had changed their name to the Astors, and that year released "What Can it Be?" a song written by guitarist Larry Lee, who would later work with Jimi Hendrix at Woodstock, and even later, with Al Green. That song failed to chart as well, and so after three name changes and three singles, and having worked with a number of famous or soon-to-be famous artist and writers, the group looked destined to join the hundreds of other groups around the country who had had a small taste of success but not enough to sustain them.

Their big break came when guitarist Steve Cropper of Booker T. & the M.G.s and Isaac Hayes, who would later be a superstar in his own right, wrote the group a song called "Candy," which was recorded and released in 1965. At last the group had a taste of the success they had been looking for, as the song went to #12 on the R&B charts and #63 on pop charts. Suddenly the Astors were in demand, and performed with a number of notable acts such as The Coasters, The Impressions, Booker T. & the M.G.s, and James Brown. They not only played the Apollo Theater, but they also appeared on *Where the Action Is, Hollywood A-Go-Go*, and performed at nightclubs on the Sunset Strip in Hollywood.

Yet like many groups before and after them, the magic was fleeting, as they failed to follow up their first effort with another hit. Their next release (which Hayes also co-wrote), "In the Twilight Zone," failed to chart. Harris left the group, and after cutting one more non-charting record for Stax, 1967's "More Power to You" (with another Hayes co-writing credit), members started to go their separate ways. Harold and Curtis joined the group Brothers Unlimited, and Curtis Johnson went to work for Mercury Records. A few sides they had recorded at Stax were later released on Ace records, but none charted and by that time the group had disintegrated.

The Bad Habits

BEACH MUSIC DISCOGRAPHY: "Night Owl" (Paula 327, 1970: Did Not Chart).

Debby Folse (often credited as Debbie Folse or Debby Falls) came from a musical family of six children (her father Pott is a member of the Louisiana Music Hall of Fame), and when she was just 11 she recorded her first single backed on the piano by Mac Rebennack, who would later gain fame as Dr. John. She recorded "You Shouldn't Have" and "Hurry Hurry" as Debbie Falls on the Virgil label out of New Orleans, and while still in high school she joined a band called the Lads, which eventually became Debbie and the Ladds. This group won a number of singing competitions and ended up winning a Battle of the Bands contest in Louisiana, ultimately heading to New York City for national competition. They continued to play clubs and concerts in Louisiana and at one point opened for Herman's Hermits and also appeared with The Who and the Blue Magoos in Baton Rouge. They recorded a single, "Dear Lord Above" on the local Ladd label, and in 1969 after she graduated from high school, Debbie and the Ladds—now consisting of Debbie Folse, Pershing Wells, Rick Folse and Ronnie Plaisance—signed a contract with Stan Lewis's Paula Records in Shreveport and changed their name to The Bad Habits.

For their first single the group covered "It's Been a Long Time Coming," a song that Delaney and Bonnie Bramlett had released as a single in 1968. The song was well suited for Debbie Folse's vocal range as she sounded somewhat like Bonnie Bramlett, and so for the B-side they did a throwaway called "Night Owl." The song was a cover of "Nite Owl," a 1955 release by New Orleans group Tony Allen and the Champs on the Specialty label, which had been covered by the Righteous Brothers in 1965 and Paula labelmates John Fred and the Playboy Band for an LP in 1966. When the Bad Habits went into the studio in Tyler, Texas, to record the song there was a difficult solo that guitarist Pershing Wells couldn't work out, so manager Gene Kent asked Mouse and the Traps guitarist and Tyler resident "Bugs" Henderson to step in and play. When finished, the song was relegated to the flip side of the record, but perhaps because of composer Tony Allen's Louisiana connection, New Orleans DJs flipped the record and "Night Owl" ended up getting the airplay. Reportedly the song was a #1 hit in some regional markets and was listed by Billboard as a regional breakthrough song, though it never made the Billboard or *Cash Box* Top 100.

The group released two more singles on Paula in 1970 and 71, but by then Debby Folse was married and had a child. The group decided to go their separate ways, and because they were a popular regional act Kent decided to form a new group behind Rick Folse to capitalize on their name. Folse and Bob Fell, Sonny Williams (and later Nick Pratt), Ron DiIulio and Fred Engelke, most of whom had recorded as Noel on Tower Records, emerged as the new Bad Habits. The group recorded three singles on Paula in 1971 and 1972, none of which charted. Debby Folse (Chiasson) eventually returned to the music business when Debbie and the Ladds reformed briefly, and over the years appeared with groups such as the Pott Folse Family Band, the Country Sunshine Band, the Breeze Band, the Down Home Band, and others.

Razzy Bailey

BEACH MUSIC DISCOGRAPHY: "I Hate Hate" (MGM 14728, 1974: Billboard Pop #67).

Born Rasie Michael Bailey in Lafayette, Alabama, Bailey's first experience singing was in high school as a member of a Future Farmers of America band. After high school he turned his love of music into a career playing small clubs in Alabama and Georgia, writing songs all the while and eventually signing with Atlanta promoter Bill Lowery. He cut his first record, "9,999,999 Tears," backed by an all-star combo of then relatively unknown artists including Billy Joe Royal and Joe South. The song did nothing, but Bailey continued to record sides and a couple of albums on regional labels for the next few years. Around 1972 he recorded a song he had written, "I Hate Hate," for Bobby Smith's Boblo records based in Macon, Georgia, and the label credits it to "Razzy" Bailey. Though it is unlikely that most people have ever heard this rather rare version, it is perhaps the best version of the three recordings of the song which would ultimately be released. Recorded in mono as opposed to the later stereo releases, this song has regular back-up singers (not the "neighborhood kids"), no strings or piano, and is much more soulful with a strong bass line and drumbeat. Many listeners have compared it to Archie Bell and the Drells' "Tighten Up" in an instrumental sense, and its raw unadulterated sound sounds like many of the beach songs released in the 1960s.

Despite the song's high quality it languished for two years before being re-recorded on Nashville-based Aquarian records in 1974. This cut is credited to Razzy Bailey and the Neighborhood Kids, and Bailey is backed by his group the Aquarians while preschool children sing the chorus to the song and clap in the background. This version was recorded in stereo, and despite the merits of the song, this is clearly a case where well-enough should have been left alone; the result is an over-produced mess which many listeners have described as "screeching" or "screaming" kids in the background. Considering that social activism was at its peak in this country in the early 1970s, having a studio full of children sing about how they "hate hate" probably seemed like a good idea at the time. Surprisingly, this is probably the cut that many beach music lovers first heard in the Carolinas, as the Aquarian version sold half-a-million copies in the South.

After the popularity of the Aquarian version, MGM picked it up for national distribution. In this version, which is simply credited to "Razzy," the children's voices were mixed down and only become intrusive during the last 30 seconds of the record. There is a little clapping, and the strings are more prominent in this version. Though the song is clearly preferable to the Aquarian version, it still lacks the soulful feel of the Boblo release. This recording of the song made the national charts, peaking at #67 on the pop charts in May 1974.

Even given the record's limited success, Bailey still hadn't found his proper milieu, and it wasn't until Dickey Lee released his own version of Bailey's "9,999,999 Tears" in 1976 that people started to really notice Bailey as a prominent songwriter and then a singer as well. Bailey signed with RCA in 1978, and over the course of the next decade he released more than 30 songs which made the country charts, and thirteen of them would make the Top 10 and five of them would go to #1. The result of Bailey's massive chart success was that the soulful sound heard on "I Hate Hate" would be relegated to the background. Nevertheless, for a brief moment in time, Bailey was a star in beach music circles even before he would go on to take the world of country music by storm.

Lavern Baker

BEACH MUSIC DISCOGRAPHY: "Tweedle Dee" (Atlantic 1047, 1954: Billboard Pop #14); "You're the Boss" (with Jimmy Ricks) (Atlantic 2090, 1961: Billboard Pop #81).

Delores Lavern Baker was born into a musical family and sang in her church choir, and so it was no surprise when at age 17 she began singing on the Chicago club circuit. The five-foot-tall Baker was billed as "Little Miss Sharecropper" and dressed like a farmhand, but despite the fact that Baker disliked the gimmick she had an extremely popular act. She recorded some unreleased sides under that name in the late 1940s, and by 1947 she had relocated to Detroit, gotten married, and finally released a few singles on RCA and National under the Little Miss Sharecropper stage name. None of these sides charted, and by 1951 she had dropped the Little Miss Sharecropper tag (though the name would follow her for a while) and started working as Bea Baker. In 1952 she finally started recording as Lavern Baker.

In 1952 and 53 Baker recorded a few records, toured with a group in Europe, and then returned to the U.S. and signed with Atlantic Records. Her first two records did nothing, but the third, 1954's "Tweedlee Dee," was a hit on both the R&B charts (#4) and the pop charts (#14) at a time when crossover hits by black artists still were not all that common. What was common at the time was that white artists would cover songs by black artists for "white" radio, and in this case Georgia Gibbs did what was basically a note-for-note cover version for Mercury that even used the same backup singers and most of the same musicians that that Baker's version had used. Gibbs' version went to #1 on the pop charts, and an infuriated Baker unsuccessfully tried to get Congress to make that type of duplication illegal. Though it was precedent setting, the suit failed and the bill did not pass.

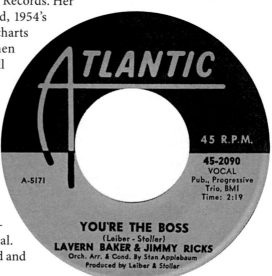

Baker would follow "Tweedlee Dee" with several Top 10 R&B songs before recording "Jim Dandy," which topped the R&B charts for 18 weeks and also went to #17 on the pop charts. The recording sold more than a million units and earned a gold record, and Baker was now firmly entrenched as an up-and-coming rock and roller. She appeared in the several rock films, toured, and continued to have records on both charts, including "I Cried a Tear," which made the pop and R&B Top 10. In 1961 she recorded a song considered a seminal beach hit, "You're the Boss" with Jimmy Ricks. Ricks had been the lead singer and co-founder of the Ravens of "Green Eyes" fame (see the entry for Jimmy Ricks and The Ravens), but had been working, largely unsuccessfully, as a solo act for a number of years. The Jerry Leiber and Mike Stoller penned tune only made it to #81 on the pop charts.

Eventually Baker left Atlantic for Brunswick, where she recorded an odd duet with Jackie Wilson called "Think Twice" in 1966. Though the "clean" version made the R&B charts at #37 and the pop charts at #93, it was her last chart record to break the Top 100 on either chart.

Baker was performing for U.S. troops during the Vietnam War when she developed pneumonia and had to be hospitalized in the Philippines. She ended up staying there for two decades, performing and working as the entertainment director at a military nightclub on the Subic Bay Naval Base. She eventually returned to the U.S. and started performing again, and in 1991 became the second solo female artist indicted into the Rock and Roll Hall of Fame after Aretha Franklin. A diabetic, later in life she had both legs amputated due to medical complications; she passed away from heart disease in 1997.

Hank Ballard and the Midnighters

BEACH MUSIC DISCOGRAPHY: "Work with Me Annie" (Federal 12169, 1954: Pre-Billboard Pop Charts—R&B Charts #1); "Annie Had a Baby" (Federal 12195, 1954: Pre-Billboard Pop Charts—R&B Charts #1).

In 1950, Charles Sutton was singing at an amateur show in Detroit when he met Freddie Pride, Sonny Woods, Alonzo Tucker, and Henry Booth, all of whom wanted to form a singing group, The Royals, in the mold of the Orioles or the Dominoes. Soon they were entering amateur contests singing cover tunes, but after just a few months Pride was drafted. He recommended Lawson Smith, who joined the group in his place, and in 1951 the new line-up won an amateur contest at Detroit's Paradise Theater. Singer Johnny Otis was playing there that week, and he told the group he wanted to manage them and that he could get them a contract with Federal Records. The Royals agreed to his terms and Otis got them signed to Federal, and although Lawson Smith was soon drafted, they were able to get a few songs recorded before he left for active duty. Once again down a member, they added a friend of Woods' named John Kendricks, who changed his name to Hank Ballard, using a family surname.

The group released a half dozen singles in 1952 and 1953 before they hit with "Get It," which climbed to #6 on the R&B charts. The song had suggestive lyrics and was banned in some markets, but this would come to be a hallmark of the group's records throughout the decade. In 1954 they were working with A&R man Ralph Bass who had an idea for a record, or at least a partial lyric: "work with me." He sat down with Ballard and they wrote the classic, "Work with Me, Annie." Ballard told Andrew Edelstein in an interview for Goldmine that they chose Annie to go with the "work with me" phrase simply because "It was just a good commercial name. You know, 'Annie Get Your Gun,' 'Little Orphan Annie.'.. It's just a catchy name. It could have been 'Work with Me Mary' or 'Work with Me Sue.'" Despite being banned by some stations for its suggestive lyrics, "Work with Me Annie" became a hit almost overnight, reached #1 on the R&B charts and crossed over onto the pop charts climbing to #22. While Federal clearly had a successful act on its hands, trouble was brewing in the form of another group, the "5" Royales, with whom the Royals were often confused. Federal told its group they had to change their name to The Midnighters, and so while early copies of "Work With Me Annie" were released as being by the Royals, even as the record was riding the charts it was being released by the Midnighters as well.

The group's next big release was "Sexy Ways," a record no doubt designed to cement their standing as a group who sang risque music—which was clearly what the public really wanted, despite the fact that the group's records continued to be banned. The record went to #2 on the R&B charts, and was followed by "Annie Had a Baby," which passed "Sexy Ways" and went to #1 on the R&B charts. A perhaps apocryphal story about the song was that before the record existed a DJ on the West Coast made an off-hand comment to the effect that if listeners thought "Work With Me Annie" was scandalous, wait till they got a load of "Annie Had a Baby." Apparently listeners were calling record stores asking for the single, and so Federal quickly wrote it, had the group record it, and got it out there. This second Annie hit opened the door for a legion of imitators, including "Annie Pulled A Hum-Bug" (the Midnights), "Annie's Answer" (Hazel McCollum & El Dorados'), "I'm The Father Of Annie's Baby" (Danny Taylor), "My Name Ain't Annie" (Linda Hayes & Platters), and "Annie Kicked The Bucket" (the Nu-Tones)—and those were just in 1954. Even the Midnighters got in on the act again, recording "Annie's Aunt Fannie" which went to #10 on the R&B charts.

It was at about this point that Sutton was forced to leave the group for medical reasons, and ultimately the Midnighters moved on without him. At first it seemed as if Sutton got out at the right time, as from 1955 to 1959 the group didn't have a single release make the charts, and that included 1958's "Baby Please," which had some play in the beach clubs. Then in 1959 they changed their name to Hank Ballard and the Midnighters, went to Federal's parent label, King, and their first release was "The Twist." The song had been written by the Sensational Nightingales, but because it was somewhat suggestive they shopped it around and finding no takers finally Ballard agreed to record it. It was actually released as the B-side of the record but nevertheless went to #6 on the R&B charts in 1959, then to #28 on the pop charts and #6 on the R&B charts again when re-released in 1960. The best known version was Chubby Checker's cover, which reached #1 on the pop charts in 1962 and 1963, making it the only song to hit #1 in two different years through two different releases.

The 1959 release of the "The Twist" would kick off a period of the group's greatest chart success, although their later recordings were not as popular in beach clubs. Hits such as "Finger Poppin' Time," "Let's Go, Let's Go, Let's Go," and others would chart through 1962. The group released records up through 1968, and Ballard went solo that year. Ballard was inducted into the Rock and Roll Hall of Fame in 1990, while the Midnighters were inducted as a group in 2012. Ballard, who was the cousin of Florence Ballard of the Supremes, died in 2003.

The Band of Oz

BEACH MUSIC DISCOGRAPHY: "Shaggin'" (Mega 18830, 1978: Did Not Chart).

The Band of Oz got their start in Grifton, North Carolina, in the late 1960s as The Avengers, and the core of the group consisted of Johnnie Byrd, Buddy Johnson and Keith Houston. By 1970 they had changed their name to the Band of Oz, added horns and expanded their playlist as they played the party and club circuit. By the mid–1970s their line up consisted of Chuck French, Bob Lynch, Ronnie Forbes, Shep Fields, Freddy Tripp, Billy Bazemore, David Hicks, and Keith Houston, and they performed across the South. After "playing full-time traveling all over the southeast" for several years but "tired of being on the road," Houston said the group decided to go back to their roots, and specialize by playing what was known in the Carolinas as beach music. "We figured ... we could go back to North Carolina and do

The Band of Oz, circa 1978 (photograph courtesy Keith Houston).

that type of music again. The disco era was fading, and so we came back home started playing the old beach music that we used to play. It was actually getting big then, and new beach music was being written as well."

That new music, in the form of songs such as "Summertime's Callin Me" by The Catalinas, "I Love Beach Music" by the Embers, and "Myrtle Beach Days" by the Fantastic Shakers, was extremely popular and the Band of Oz decided to offer up their own contribution in the form of "Shaggin" in 1978. "Billy Bazemore was our lead vocalist, and he came in one day and said 'Look, I gotta set of lyrics here, I've written a song'" Houston told me. "Well, he pulls out *four pages* of lyrics—it was probably three or four songs! I took it and edited down and put the music to it. And though we had two or three songs worth of lyrics, we did get one real good hit out of it." They tested it out by playing it in their act, and after "playing it live before we ever made the record … we decided to record it. It was the first time our band had actually been in the studio." The band went to Mega Sound in Bailey North Carolina and recorded the song with Bazemore singing lead. "You never know what's going to happen when you make a record" Houston said, "but we got a good response. We started pushing it at the radio stations. All the beach jocks started to play it, and it got a lot of airplay. Then when Ripete records came in and put together that first Beach Beat album, and it had 'Shaggin' on it along with 'Myrtle Beach Days,' 'I Love Beach Music,' and a lot of national releases, it locked it in as a beach music hit."

At first, nothing they did could really follow up "Shaggin'" as far as audiences were concerned, and even though "We recorded another song about that time, 'Song of my Life,' it never did anything, because "Shaggin' overshadowed it." There were a few more personnel changes, and in 1982, another big hit came along—actually one that was even bigger—when they recorded "Ocean Boulevard," which was written and produced by General Johnson and Warren Moise. That song went on to win song of the year at the Carolina Beach Music Awards and the accolades have followed the Band of Oz almost nonstop over the years since. They've done so many songs since "Shaggin'" that Houston says "we don't play 'Shaggin' all that much now. Even though it was one of the biggest selling things we did, we only play it once in a great while. We get more requests for 'Shama Lama Ding Dong' and 'Over the Rainbow' than 'Shaggin' and 'Ocean Boulevard.' But you know, I think it's one of those things that if we did it every night, we'd be indoctrinating another group of kids, because most people are more familiar with the newer stuff. But they are still great songs." And even though they might not play those older hits as much as they used to, they still stand as seminal beach music songs that came out as the genre was making its transition from a collection of national releases appropriated for use as beach music, to a genre that was increasingly creating songs all its own. Houston and the band continue to perform today.

Darrell Banks

BEACH MUSIC DISCOGRAPHY: "Open the Door to Your Heart" (Revilot 201, 1966: Billboard Pop #27).

Darrell Banks grew up in Buffalo, New York, and like many young men who sang R&B in the 1950s and '60s, he got his start singing with gospel groups before he turned his talents to solo musical pursuits. He would often play at the Revilot Lounge in Buffalo, and there his friend Donnie Elbert wrote a song for him called "Baby Walk Right In"—the actual working title of "Open the Door to Your Heart." The song would take Banks off the lounge circuit and put him in a studio in Detroit to record the song, which went all the way to #27 on the Billboard Hot 100 and to #2 in the R&B listings. Suddenly, Banks was a hot singing commodity and Elbert had written a hit song.

However, when the record came out, Elbert noticed that Banks, and not he, was credited with writing the song. Willing to give Banks the benefit of the doubt, Elbert attempted to correct what he assumed was a clerical error but was shocked to learn that the song's rights had been given to Banks not because of an error but because Banks had told the record company (and indeed had filled out documents saying) that he alone had written the song. After a protracted legal battle, Elbert was at last able to get himself listed as co-songwriter but only as a co-writer because apparently Banks had made some minor changes, such as speeding up the tempo, so Banks was given 50 percent authorship. Perhaps it's indicative of the injustice of Banks's perfidy that while Elbert would go on to write well more than one hundred songs, "Open the Door to Your Heart" is the only song for which Banks would ever receive a songwriting credit.

Banks stayed with Revilot for one more single, "Somebody (Somewhere) Needs You," which hit #55 that same year. Banks moved to Atco and then Cotillion, where none of his releases would chart. Stax records signed him to its Volt subsidiary on for a couple of singles, though chart success would elude him there as well. Plagued by personal and professional demons, while waiting at his estranged girlfriend's house one afternoon in February 1970, he saw her return home in the company of another man. An infuriated Banks pulled a gun on him, despite the fact that the man identified himself as off-duty policeman Aaron Bullock. Faced with being shot himself, Bullock shot Banks in the neck and the chest; he was declared dead at the hospital at the age of thirty-two.

Gene Barbour and the Cavaliers

BEACH MUSIC DISCOGRAPHY: "I Need a Love" (Hit 101, 1966: Did Not Chart).

Gene Barbour and The Cavaliers started as simply The Cavaliers, and when they got together in 1963, they were Charles Aycock, Walt Jones, Paul Mattox and Donald Hobson, all of whom were in the band at Dunn High School in Dunn, North Carolina. The band started out like many others, playing high school gigs whenever they could get them. Feeling that with a little direction they could improve their sound and bookings, they hired Jones' uncle Harry Driver to be their manager. Driver brought in Tommy Ralph to play bass, and with Aycock singing lead, the group became a successful local act. Next Driver found Gene Barbour, who had his own group called Gene Barbour & The Shakedowns, and he was added as lead singer. Billy Wellons then joined, and the pieces all seemed to be in place.

Driver had the group record a song Mattox and Barbour had co-written titled "Nobody." Though the record is now a collector's item, the original recording only sold "probably 100 units or so" according to Hobson. Nevertheless, in the summer of 1966 Driver decided to take them to Bill Lowery's studio in Atlanta to record once again, and one of the songs they recorded was "I Need a Love." Produced by Ted Hall's Charlotte-based *Hit Attractions*, the song, which the Impressions had released as the single "I Need You" in 1965 (Billboard #64),

28 Gene Barbour and the Cavaliers

Gene Barbour and the Cavaliers, 1966 (photograph courtesy Donald Hobson).

"sold pretty well regionally but nothing really significant," Hobson said. The group always thought that the song was retitled by the Cavaliers management, but Hobson discovered that the release of their single "I Need You," the Impressions released their 1966 LP "Ridin High," which contains the exact song that charted *except* that on the LP it had a new title—"I Need a Love." This is the song that Hobson's group would record—word for word, title and all—in 1967. As a result, the mistake was on the Impressions album, and not a change made by the Cavaliers' management.

 The group would become one of the most popular bands in the Carolinas and played with and opened for groups including the Four Tops, Martha & the Vandellas, the Platters and Smokey Robinson & the Miracles. Yet despite their success, like many groups performing in the late 1960s, several members of the group were eventually drafted or enlisted. By the early 1970s, the Gene Barbour & The Cavaliers group that had recorded "I Need a Love" was no more. The group did reunite as the original Men of Distinction, but they never cut a song with the staying power that "I Need a Love" has had.

Chris Bartley

BEACH MUSIC DISCOGRAPHY: "The Sweetest Thing This Side of Heaven" (Vando 101, 1967: Billboard Pop #32).

Harlem-born Chris Bartley began his performing career in the late 1950s as a member of a group called the Soulful Inspirations, who would change their name and personnel several times before settling on the name The Mindbenders. While searching for a label, they auditioned for songwriter, producer, and singer Van McCoy (who would later become well known for 1975's "The Hustle"). Though McCoy was not interested in signing the group, he was impressed by Bartley, and signed him to a solo contract group with the new Cameo subsidiary label Vando, owned by McCoy and Douglas Henderson (VAN and DOug). The label's first release on Vando 101 was Bartley singing "The Sweetest Thing This Side of Heaven," a song McCoy had written. The song sounds very much like a Motown/Smokey Robinson release, and perhaps as a result the song went to #10 on the R&B charts and #32 on the pop charts.

Over the course of the next year Bartley would release four more singles and an album on Vando, all written, accompanied, and produced by McCoy. But despite this promising beginning and constant touring, nothing else would chart. The Vando label folded after just seven single releases, but McCoy had enough faith in Bartley that he facilitated his signing with Buddah Records. For Buddah he recorded two singles, "Baby I'm Yours," his cover of the Barbara Lewis song that McCoy had also written, and "I Know We Can Work It Out," which was a re-recording of "Sugar Baby," a McCoy-penned song from his Vando album. Neither single was successful, and not long afterwards Bartley briefly retired from the music business to look after his ailing mother. He started recording again in 1971, signed with Musicor for one unsuccessful single, and then released his last single in 1975 on the Right-On label, which was only available in England. He later joined the Ad-Libs, and in the '80s even re-recorded "The Sweetest Thing This Side of Heaven," but he would have no further chart success. Bartley died of kidney failure in 2009 at the age of 52.

Fontella Bass

BEACH MUSIC DISCOGRAPHY: "Rescue Me" (Checker 1120, 1965: Billboard Pop #4).

Fontella Marie Bass was born in St. Louis Missouri, and both her grandmother Nevada Carter and her mother Martha Bass were gospel singers. Fontella's mother had sung with a gospel quartet under the guidance of Willa Mae Ford Smith, and had also been a member of the Clara Ward singers, and so Fontella was immersed in gospel from a very early age. She began singing in the church choir when she was six, learned to play the piano and organ, and by the time she was nine she was touring and singing with her mother. As a teen, however, Fontella became interested in secular music, and after graduating from St. Louis's Soldan High School she auditioned for a singing job with the Leon Claxton Carnival. She won the job and after performing for two weeks she decided to go on the road with them. Even though Fontella was 18 her mother refused to let her go, but her appearances with the carnival had come to the notice of R&B singer Little Milton and his bandleader, Oliver Sain. They hired her to back Little Milton, but on one occasion Little Milton was late for a gig and Sain asked Bass to take the stage in his stead. This led to solo appearances in Milton's show, as well as single releases on Sain's Bobbin Records and working with Ike and Tina Turner and the Ikettes as well as singles on Turner's Prann label. None of the releases charted, however.

In 1964 Bass and her husband, saxophonist Lester Bowie, moved to Chicago and she signed with Chess Records. Chess had her record two singles with Bobby McClure, and both "Don't Mess Up A Good Thing" (#33 pop, #5 R&B) and "You'll Miss Me When I'm Gone" (#91 pop, #27 R&B charted) were released on the Checker subsidiary. Her first solo release on Checker was 1965's "Rescue Me," a record that would not only be a national chart success but would generate interest with beach music audiences as well.

On the recording Bass was supported by several later-notable singers and musicians, including Maurice White, later of Earth, Wind and Fire, who played drums on the track, and backing vocalists included Leonard Caston, later a member of the Radiants who sang on "Voice Your Choice" and co-lead on "It Ain't No Big Thing," as well as Minnie Riperton, who would come into her own as a solo artist a decade later. Reportedly the lyric sheet fell off of the music stand when they were recording, and so Bass hummed her way out of the song instead of singing the song as written while her manager Billy Davis went around the room tapping the musicians on the shoulder one at a time to get them to stop playing. Chess decided to use the cut, impromptu or not, and the song went to #1 on the R&B charts for 11 weeks and made it to #4 on the pop charts. It surpassed a million units in sales, and was the first million seller the label had had since Chuck Berry's 1955 hit "Maybelline." Though many people have compared Bass's singing on the track to Aretha Franklin, Franklin was little known in 1965, and wouldn't have a Top 10 pop or #1 R&B hit for two more years.

The label followed the single with an album,

The New Look, as well as a follow-up single, "Recovery," but neither performed particularly well and the single only went to #37 on the pop charts and #13 on the R&B charts in 1966. "Recovery" would be her last pop Top 40 hit, and just three more R&B Top 40 songs would follow; by 1967 her time on the charts had ended.

Ironically, Bass would always claim that the success of "Rescue Me" was to some extent responsible for derailing her career. Chess staff writers and Carl William Smith and Raynard Miner were credited as the songwriters, but Bass apparently made significant contributions to the track and expected to receive label credit. She did not, but said she was told by her manager that even though it wasn't on the label the record company paperwork listed her as a co-writer. When she received her first royalty check for the song she realized it was so small that she knew she'd been lied to, and reportedly tore the check up on the spot. Her relationship with Chess became contentious, and she left the label the next year. It was only through continued litigation that she finally received due credit for the song in the late 1980s, but even at that point she still had to fight to protect her artistic rights. As late as the 1990s she had to sue American Express for the unauthorized use of the song in a commercial.

Even before the 1980s and '90s however, fighting for her rights cost her dearly, and she had been tagged with a reputation as a troublemaker due to the controversy over 'Rescue Me" in the 1960s. She always felt Leonard Chess had her blackballed in the industry, and certainly after she left the label nothing she recorded charted. She and her husband moved to France until 1972 and then came back to the States, and after raising her children she concentrated on jazz and also gospel music. She occasionally performed with her mother as well as her younger brother David Peaston, who himself had a half dozen R&B chart hits between 1989 and 1991. In 1995 her gospel album *No Ways Tired* was nominated for a Grammy, and she continued to record until her health no longer permitted it. In 2012 Bass died from complications from a heart attack and several strokes that she had suffered towards the end of her life.

William Bell

BEACH MUSIC DISCOGRAPHY: "Easy Comin' Out (Hard Goin' In)" (Mercury 73961, 1977: Billboard Pop Did Not Chart, R&B #30).

William Bell's career as an entertainer had a promising start when he won a talent contest in in his hometown of Memphis as a teenager. In addition to a $500 cash prize, Bell (who was born William Yarborough) was invited to go to Chicago and do a weekend gig with the Red Saunders Band at Club Delisa. Saunders was impressed with the young man and recommended him to a man named Phineas Newborn, who let Bell sub in as a vocalist on and off for the next few years. Bell also became a member of the Del Rios along with Harrison Austin, Melvin Jones, and David Brown, and in the late '50s along with the group recorded a couple of singles for the Meteor and Bet T labels. By the early '60s Bell had signed with Stax, scoring a minor hit with a song he had written called "You Don't Miss Your Water." The song reached #95 on the Billboard Hot 100, and it would be the first of many successful sides Bell would record for the label in the 1960s.

Bell served in the Army from 1962 to 1966, but he was able to record enough material while on leave to enable Stax to release new singles throughout his service in the Army. None of them were very successful, but after his enlistment was up Bell had a couple of R&B hits before "Everybody Loves a Winner" crossed over to the pop charts in 1967. He was also writing material for other artists, including "Born Under a Bad Sign" (which would also be covered by Cream) for Albert King, and a song he wrote for himself and recorded in 1968, "I Forgot to Be Your Lover," would be recorded by Billy Idol in 1986 as "To Be a Lover" and go to the #6 position on the pop charts.

Perhaps the most notable recording to come out of his Stax years was 1968's "Private Number," a duet with Judy Clay (see the entry for Judy Clay and William Bell). But after Stax's biggest star, Otis Redding, died in 1967, Stax was in trouble. The label lost their distribution deal with Atlantic Records in 1968, and Stax started to make some poor financial decisions, including borrowing heavily against their brand and projected sales of future releases. As Bell said,

> The downfall of Stax was kind of systematic deflation of the label by the powers that be. When you say you'll release 50,000 records for a new William Bell single, and then once you get into that borrowed money you only release 5000 records instead, automatically your earning potential has diminished. A lot of people don't realize it, but we had two or three hit records on the charts when Stax folded. But the thing about it was that we weren't selling as many records. We were forced out of the business because we had to make monthly payments on these huge loans, and with the diminishing numbers of pressed products, if it wasn't pressed, we couldn't sell it, so we were forced to file bankruptcy.

Bell briefly retired at that point—"I decided I wasn't going to record anymore and I was going to do something else"—but his old friend Charles Fach, who was now with Mercury, called and coaxed him out of retirement to record a few sides for the label. Bell's first release was a song he'd co-written, "Trying to Love Two," and would go on to be his biggest hit. It climbed to #10 on the pop charts and #1 on the R&B charts, and though his next Mercury release wasn't spectacular his third release was "Easy Comin' Out (Hard Goin' In)." Bell says, "The song was written during the disco era, which was a wild period. It was kind of adopted at Studio 54 in New York, and just really turned out to be a double entendre type thing even though it was written just as a clean-minded, clean-cut song; but it turned out to be a good record for us." The song peaked at #30 on the R&B charts, the third Mercury single in a row to chart.

Bell thinks the record might have done even better, but just as forces at the record company beyond his control had affected his production at Stax, it was déjà vu all over again at Mercury. "Right about that time there was some corporate upheaval at Mercury and Charles left. When I found out, I realized that there was nobody there who really knew what I was about with Charles gone, and I knew then the writing was on the wall." Bell told Mercury he was leaving, and at that point he says it was clear to him that Mercury quit pushing "Easy Comin' Out" even as it was moving up the charts. "After I asked for my release, within about three weeks the record dropped completely off the charts. That shows you what was going

William Bell, circa early 1970s (photograph courtesy William Bell).

on in the collective effort from a corporate standpoint there." Bell would continue to record for several labels and his songs would continue to chart right up until the mid–1990s. Despite the fact that "Easy Comin' Out" was not a major chart success, today he still performs it in his shows and it's "one of my biggest songs now and one of the staple songs in my repertoire. I can't leave the stage without performing it, and if I don't perform it, I'm in trouble. It's very popular."

Bell continues to perform today, and was inducted into the Beach Music Hall of Fame in 2004.

Archie Bell and the Drells

BEACH MUSIC DISCOGRAPHY: "Tighten Up" (Atlantic 2478, 1968: Billboard Pop #1); "I Can't Stop Dancing" (Atlantic 2534, 1968: Billboard Pop #9); "There's Gonna Be a Showdown" (Atlantic 2583, 1968: Billboard Pop #21); "Girl You're Too Young" (Atlantic 2644, 1969: Billboard Pop #59); "My Balloon's Going Up" (Atlantic 2663, 1969: Billboard Pop #87); "Dancing to Your Music" (Glades 1707, 1973: Billboard Pop #61); "I Could Dance All Night" (T.S.O.P 4767, 1975: Billboard Pop DNC, R&B #25).

Archie Bell, James Wise, Willie Parnell, and Billy Butler first formed their group in 1966, and in 1967 they recorded a couple of sides for the Ovide label, including "Tighten Up." But soon Bell was drafted, and just as he was being inducted into the Army, the record with its lead-off that proudly proclaimed they were "Archie Bell and the Drells from Houston Texas" took off in the South. The record sold several hundred thousand copies regionally before being released by Atlantic, and upon its national release it climbed all the way to #1 on the Billboard pop charts and earned a gold record in 1968. Everyone was shocked, and no one more so than Bell. "We never thought 'Tighten Up' would be as big as it was," he said. "It was a real surprise to everybody." Even more surprising is that other than Bell's lead, there was almost no participation by the rest of the group on the record. The backbone of the song is the instrumental work of a Texas group, the TSU Tornadoes, and other than some hand clapping and whistling, the Drells didn't contribute much else.

The group needed to follow up their big record, and fortunately, the Army was liberal with Bell's time after "Tighten Up" became a hit and frequently allowed him to go home for a few days and perform. "We were in Longside, New Jersey, in a bar called Lauretta's Hi-Hat. Kenny Gamble and Leon Huff came into the dressing room, and told me 'We've got a song for you.'" That led to their first collaboration, 1968's "I Can't Stop Dancing." Actually Bell didn't know who Gamble and Huff were at the time, and asked Atlantic Records if it was okay to work with them. The label agreed, but by then Bell was back in Germany. Gamble and Huff sent Bell a demo of the song, which he flew back to record while on a three day pass. Though he recorded the lead vocals, the Drells weren't in town, and so Gamble and Huff did backing vocals so that's them, not the Drells, heard on the recording. The song was another hit and went to #9 on the pop charts, perhaps because it closely followed the same formula as their previous hit. "If you listen to 'Tighten Up' and 'I Can't Stop' they have almost the same riffs, tempo, and everything, except 'Tighten Up' was a jam" Bell told me. "It turned out to be another big, big number for us." They followed that with "There's Gonna Be a Showdown," another Gamble and Huff composition, which was based on "dance competitions [where] they'd have this thing called a 'showdown.' They'd form a big circle, and put money in a hat and the one who ended up winning would win the pot. Well every time you would win you'd put a notch on your shoe. That's why the words to the song say 'I got ten notches, on my shoes'—that's where that came from." The song peaked at #21 for their third big hit of 1968.

In 1969 Bell would finally be mustered out of the Army, and the group would also release two more songs that would go on to be beach music favorites, "Girl You're Too Young" and "My Balloon's Going Up." "Girl You're Too Young," which would peak at #59 on the pop charts and #13 on the R&B charts, "was a song I wrote about a young lady I was interested in, but she was little bit too young" Bell said. "My Balloon's Going Up," another Gamble and Huff composition, "was about a guy who is losing his girlfriend. The balloon was his love, going up, getting away from her." Though it peaked at #87, Bell says it was big with beach music audiences because "It was danceable, and it's the type of song you can shag to easily. What we called the old soft shoe."

The group left Atlantic in 1972, and signed with the Miami-based Glades label. Despite the fact that the group found the label unorganized and somewhat unprofessional ("I told my manager 'This is not going to work' Bell said), their biggest song for the label, "Dancing to Your Music," was "a great song, one of my favorites." Despite Bell's enthusiasm it only went to #61 on the pop charts and #11 on the R&B charts, and would in fact be their last entry ever on the pop charts. Soon they were looking for a new label, and signed with Gamble and Huff's TSOP subsidiary of Philadelphia International. They were given another song in the dance-mode genre, 1975's "I Could Dance all Night," a "disco era" song with a fast beat. Though the song didn't make the pop charts, it did rise to #25 on the R&B charts, and was a good start for their time at TSOP.

Over the next four years they had R&B chart hits twice more on TSOP, and then four times on Philadelphia International. In 1977 they also released a song admired by some beach music enthusiasts, "Old People," but it did not chart and in 1979 they decided to call it quits as a group. As of this writing Bell is touring again, playing his classic hits throughout the country.

The Blenders

Beach Music Discography: "Don't F**k Around with Love" (Jay-Dee 780, 1973 Re-Release: Did Not Chart).

In 1948, Henry Oliver Jones (known as "Ollie"), who had been a member of the Ravens and later the 4 Notes, decided to form a new group, The Blenders, along with James DeLoach, Tommy Adams, Abel Decosta and Herman Flintall. Jones turned to his friend Jimmy Ricks for help getting started, and Ricks brought them to the attention of Al Green at National Records. They recorded a few sides for National in 1949, but after meeting Lee Magid, who agreed to manage them, they jumped to Coral/Decca in 1950.

Though they made a number of recordings in the ensuing months, none of them charted, and both Adams and DeLoach left the group to be replaced by Dick Palmer and Raymond Johnson. Although the group continued to record and continued to get airplay, still nothing charted, and inevitably Decca dumped them in late 1952. They got a new manager (Rita Don), group members started to change, and in 1953 Don took them to producer Joe Davis, who was about to start his own label, Jay-Dee records. He had them record a few songs that he sold to other labels, but held back just two for his own label: "You'll Never Be Mine Again" and "Don't Play Around with Love."

Recorded at a time when R&B music was rife with innuendo and double entendre, some songs, such as the Clovers "Cocksuckers Ball," pushed the envelope too far to receive any airplay whatsoever. While "Don't Play Around with Love" was a fairly solid doo-wop song, after it had garnered some attention in the northeast Davis had the group record a "special" version called "Don't Fuck Around with Love" that he planned on sending to DJs as a party record not for airplay. While it never graced the airwaves, as an underground recording it stayed in play for a couple of decades. Actually, the "explicit" version of the record is far superior in sound to the original "clean" version, though at times it's obvious that the group has to struggle to remember which lyrics they are supposed to sing on the risqué recording (there's a point at roughly 2:10 on the record where a couple of the background singers sing "play around" while the others do not). The song made the rounds for years before the record was released on the Kelway label in 1971, and then in 1973 Davis released it on his own label. It still didn't receive any airplay of course, but did find its way on to more liberal jukeboxes, and was played at a lot of fraternity parties throughout the South.

The Blenders wouldn't release another record until 1955, but it was an old recording because by that time the group had folded. Jones worked more as a songwriter thereafter and sang backup as well, though he would later form the Cues with Decosta, and as a studio group under different names they would back up Atlantic artists such as Ruth Brown, Big Joe Turner, Lavern Baker, and Ivory Joe Hunter. As a result, The Blenders would have the strangest track record of any group in this book. They never had a record make any chart under the Blenders name, and the principal members of the group would be most successful backing up other acts. But that one song that made the rounds in beach music circles a full 30 years after it was recorded—and it was a pretty memorable record indeed.

Bob and Earl

BEACH MUSIC DISCOGRAPHY: "The Harlem Shuffle" (Marc 104, 1964: Billboard Pop #44).

Bob and Earl were Fort Worth, Texas-born Bobby Byrd and Lake Charles, Louisiana, native Earl Nelson, former Hollywood Flames members whose group had taken their single "Buzz Buzz Buzz" to #11 on the pop charts in 1957. Byrd had also recorded "Little Bitty Pretty One" as Bobby Day and with Nelson on backup the song charted at #57; Thurston Harris would take his version of the song to #6 later that year. Despite the fact that his own version misfired, Byrd would write other successful songs, such as "Over and Over," for the Dave Clark Five (#1, 1965), and he would also find solo success as a singer with "Rockin Robin" (#2, 1958). In 1960, he teamed up with Nelson to form the initial pairing of Bob and Earl, and they'd have a minor hit with "Gee Whiz" (#103), but by 1962 Day decided to go solo again, so Bobby Relf joined Nelson. Relf had been a member of several moderately successful groups, and one contribution he made to the new duo was that he brought along a young keyboard player named Barry Eugene Carter—later to perform as Barry White.

The first record by the new incarnation of Bob and Earl, "Don't Ever Leave Me," would be a local hit in Los Angeles, but their second release, 1964's "The Harlem Shuffle," recorded on the fledgling Marc label, went national. Relf and Nelson co-wrote the song while loosely adapting a song called "Slauson Shuffletime" by Round Robin, and the song was about a street in L.A. But in order to make it nationally appealing, they changed to locale to the better-known Harlem area of New York, with Bob and Earl singing the revamped tune and with White on keyboards. The song referenced a number of dance songs popular in the early '60s, such as "Hitch Hike," "Shake a Tail Feather," "The Monkey Time" and others, and it went to #44 on the Top 40 pop charts. While the group would record other singles, their biggest subsequent hit would be "Baby It's Over," which went to #26 in 1966. Again, however, limited success led to the group's breakup, so Nelson started singing as Jackie Lee and had his own dance-based hit, "The Duck," in 1965. Relf, meantime, began recording as Bobby Garrett and saw some success as well. Then, in 1969, "Harlem Shuffle" became a hit all over again when released in England; in fact, it outdistanced its American release by climbing to #7 on the charts. Sensing an opportunity that had largely eluded them for several years, Relf and Nelson re-teamed once again as Bob and Earl to tour.

The reunion was short-lived, however, and by the early 1970s they had gone their separate ways again. Relf went back to working with Barry White (and wrote "Bring Back My Yesterdays" for him in 1973) and produced for the Love Unlimited Orchestra and Gloria Scott as well. Nelson continued to tour and record throughout the '70s and '80s. Yet despite the ever-changing and transitory nature of the duo, the song "The Harlem Shuffle" would surpass anyone's expectations and would be covered by groups as diverse as Booker T. & the M.G.s, John Fred and his Playboy Band and, most famously, the Rolling Stones, who took it all the way to #5 in 1986. The group House of Pain sampled the song on their #3 single "Jump Around" in 1993, and George Harrison claimed that Bob and Earl's version of "The Harlem Shuffle" was his favorite all-time song. The British newspaper the *Daily Telegraph* ranked the song #23 on its list of the top fifty duets ever recorded. Nelson, Byrd, and Relf are now all deceased.

Earl Bostic

BEACH MUSIC DISCOGRAPHY: "Flamingo"(King 4475, 1951: Did Not Chart, R&B #1); "Night and Day" (King 4765, 1955: Did Not Chart); "I Hear a Rhapsody"(King 4978, 1956: Did Not Chart).

Tulsa, Oklahoma born Eugene Earl Bostic played the saxophone and the clarinet in high school, then attended Xavier University where he earned his degree in music theory. After considerable experience playing with bands in the late '30s he moved to New York City where he played with Cab Calloway and Don Redman. Over the next two decades he would play and sometimes arrange for some of the biggest names in music, including Lionel Hampton, Gene Krupa, Louis Prima, Charlie Parker, and many others, often playing what was then called "be-bop" music. He first signed with the Gotham label in 1946 and recorded a cover of Erskine Hawkins "Trippin In," bringing a new swing to the music that would lead to his playing what would soon be categorized as "jump blues" as popular music transitioned into rock and roll. After a number of recordings on Gotham, including the popular "Temptation" which broke into the Top 10 on the R&B charts in 1948, the larger and better known King label picked up Bostic's contract in 1948, and thus began the most prolific period of his career. His first big hit for the label was 1951's "Sleep," which peaked at #6 on the R&B charts.

Bostic's second big hit for King was the Ted Grouya and Edmund Anderson penned song "Flamingo," a cover of Herb Jefferies' and Duke Ellington's 1941 hit, which Bostic would take all the way to #1 on the R&B charts. By now his stature was such that he was touring constantly to packed venues, and he began recording even more frequently which would eventually result in his releasing more than 80 singles on King. In 1955 he would cover another old standard, the Cole Porter-penned "Night and Day." Originally written in 1932 for the musical *Gay Divorcee*, Fred Astaire's version had been a #1 hit, and many artists recorded the song over the years including Frank Sinatra, Bing Crosby, Doris Day, and others. Bostic would bring his own twist to the song and the up tempo beat has made it a favorite with shaggers, though the record never charted. In 1956 Bostic would record another cover, "I Hear a Rhapsody." Written in 1941, it had reached #1 for several artists, including Jimmy Dorsey and Dinah Shore; Bostic's version did not chart.

Bostic's music falls into the category of shag music more so than pure beach music, as his saxophone-driven, vocal-less recordings were never particularly popular among collegians and are more for the dance clubs. In terms of his broader appeal, although Bostic only had three chart records in his career he was a popular performer and recording artist from the late 1940s until the early 1960s. In addition to the more than 80 singles he released with King, Bostic would release more than sixty extended play records and 25 albums, making him King's most prolific recording artist second only to James Brown; only Elvis Presley would record more albums.

Bostic was already having health problems in his 40s, and after a stroke in the late 1950s his health would continue to decline. He died of a heart attack in 1965.

Calvin Boze

BEACH MUSIC DISCOGRAPHY: "Safronia B" (Aladdin 3055, 1950: pre–Billboard pop charts, R&B charts #9).

Native Texan Calvin Boze got his start playing trumpet in his high school band, and in college he played with the Prairie View Collegians, then worked as a singer with the Marvin Johnston Orchestra, and still later became a member of the Milton Larkins Orchestra. After the World War II he moved to Los Angeles, where he was signed by Aladdin Records in 1949. He cut a few early sides such as "Workin' With My Baby," "Satisfied," "Waitin' and Drinkin'," and "If You Ever Had the Blues," but none of the recordings did much nationally. Boze formed the Calvin Boze Combo in 1950 (soon to become the Calvin Boze All-Stars), and in January 1950 Boze and his band recorded "Safronia B," a jump blues song Boze had first recorded as "Saffronia Bee" on the G&G label under the name "Calvin Boaz" while with the Marvin Johnson Orchestra in 1946. This time around the Boze played trumpet and handled the vocals, while Maxwell Davis, Marshall Royal, Don Wilkerson, and Willard McDaniel provided the accompanying instrumentation.

Released on Aladdin in May 1950, by June the record had climbed to #9 on the R&B charts. Though the band's personnel started to change soon after the record charted, the widespread exposure the group got from their single led to increased touring, and they played with the likes of the Ravens, Dinah Washington, and others. They performed at New York's Apollo Theatre, the Uptown in Philadelphia, D.C.'s Howard, and almost every other famous R&B venue open in the 1950s.

"Safronia B's" stay on the charts was short lived, however, and it was to be the only national chart record Boze would ever have. Boze continued to record, releasing tunes such as "Beale Street on A Saturday Night," "Baby You're Tops with Me," "I've Got News For You," and others, but nothing matched the popularity of "Safronia B." Released in 1952, "Looped" was mildly popular, as was "Hey Laudie Miss Claudie" (which predated Lloyd Price's more famous retitled version), but it failed to sell well. He apparently stopped recording altogether after 1952, opting instead to become a session musician in the Los Angeles area. Boze later became a social worker and then a schoolteacher before passing away in 1970.

Bradford & Bell

BEACH MUSIC DISCOGRAPHY: "(They Call It) Mr. Dollars" (Spirit 101, 1980: Did Not Chart).

Bill Bradford noted that when he was a child he loved music, and he'd respond to "anything that had a beat." It was in the third or fourth grade when he caught on to R&B. "I just gravitated towards it" he said. "I don't really have an explanation for that interest, and it astonished my parents. But that somehow was a bit of hardwiring I developed at an early age." Though he played the piano, at that point he wasn't pursuing a musical career, though he did collect records. "I remember listening to records and listening *through* them to try and understand how they did what they did and got the sound they did and how they balanced the instruments and all that. I don't know where that came from but that was a real interest I had." As he finished college and settled down, "about 1975 I started to think I could write music, so I bought a 4 track recorder and set up a little studio in my apartment. It's almost like somebody decides they want to paint, and sets up a studio and experiments by themselves. That's what I did for three or four years."

Bradford was friends with keyboard and blues harp player Sandy Bell, and they started talking about putting together a record label. They thought that "beach music might be our wedge into a market," but they didn't have a song or even much of an idea at that point, until one afternoon when Bell started playing with the makings of a song about going to Charlotte hotspot and beach club, Johnny Dollars: "Johnny Dollars was popular beach club in Charlotte in the late 70s," Bill Bradford told me. "One Sunday Sandy Bell and I were in my apartment, and he was noodling at the keyboard and started singing about going down to Johnny Dollars because we were going there and get a beer later that afternoon. I said 'Whoa, you might have something there. So I ran over and got my handheld cassette recorder and let him play into it, and I said 'Lets comeback to that later on. We might have an idea.'"

After recording their initial idea that Sunday, "we went down and had a nice afternoon at the club. In the weeks after that we really thought that it might be a good idea to develop it into a song and see if the club owner would allow us to put it on his jukebox." Though they were limited by the old equipment they had, the flipside was that "the equipment we had was about what a well-equipped Atlantic records studio might have had about 1955. Since a lot of the classic beach music had that sound—the Clovers, Coasters, Drifters—we decided to give it a try. We said, 'Let's try to produce the best classic 50s R&B sound that we can, because we've got the means to do that, and have this song sound like something you might have heard in 1959 or 1960.' So the sound of the tune was intentional in that way." With Bradford singing lead, they completed the song, pressed some demos, and arranged a meeting with Bob Whitman, who owned Johnny Dollars. They hoped to at least get him to put the record on the club's jukebox, and so one night after the club closed they played the song for him. Whitman loved it, and he said "Yeah, I'll put it on my box." They had 500 copies pressed, took Whitman a copy for his jukebox, and at the club the record seemed to play nonstop. It was popular, which "showed we had a good sound and a record that people would respond to, and along with all the other stuff on the jukebox it would be a seamless transition and people would keep dancing—which was important to us." The song's popularity was not without its faults, however; "At one point it played so much the employees were sick of it, and Bob said they had to take it off the box!"

Knowing that they had a good record, Bradford says the next step was to get the record out to more than just the club. "We got the boxes of records and threw them in the back of my car and Sandy and I both took a week off and went to Myrtle Beach, and from there to all of the major cities in South Carolina that had radio stations that played beach music." Before long the song was a regional hit, and within a very short time it was even included on beach music compilation albums alongside those classic tunes by The Drifters, the Clovers, and other groups whose sounds they had tried to emulate.

Bradford says he and Bell still play the song occasionally though neither of them are full-time members of a band now. Bradford & Bell still own Spirit Records, which continues to record and produce other artists to this day.

Jan Bradley

BEACH MUSIC DISCOGRAPHY: "Mama Didn't Lie" (Chess 1845, 1963: Billboard Pop #14).

Byhalia, Mississippi born Addie "Jan" Bradley was discovered singing with a group called the Passions at a high school talent show in Chicago. Manager and producer Don Talty felt she had the talent to make it as a solo artist, although initially Bradley's parents resisted Talty's desire to work with her. Bradley's parents insisted she finish school before attempting to embark on a career in music, and when Talty finally had the opportunity to work with Bradley he was able to get Curtis Mayfield of the Impressions to write a few songs for her to try out. Mayfield had been working with Jerry Butler on some of his early solo hits, and Talty hoped he would be the perfect writer to maximize Bradley's potential as well. The first song Mayfield wrote for her, "We Girls," was released on Talty's Formal records in 1962, and though the song did well regionally it wasn't picked up nationally. After recording singles such as "Whole Lot of Soul" and "Behind the Curtains," neither of which was successful, her next recording was 1963's "Mama Didn't Lie."

Mayfield had written "Mama Didn't Lie" and had taken the song to Bradley, and she recalled that he said, "'Okay, this is what I've got that I think will work for you. Take a listen.' I heard 'Mama Didn't Lie' and I thought, 'I love his style, I can do this, I really like this!' When 'Mama Didn't Lie' came around and started getting airplay, it got a lot of interest from major record companies, and Chess pursued us too. We had tried to get them interested in 'We Girls' because they were a big label here in Chicago, and they specialized in R&B. They had passed on 'We Girls,' but they wanted 'Mama Didn't Lie' and took it. The national promotion they were able to provide made it a really big hit." "Mama Didn't Lie" was a smash, going all the way to #14 on the Billboard charts and #8 on the R&B charts in 1963. Bradley readily admitted that Mayfield's writing was the perfect complement for her voice, and Bradley seemed poised for a string of successes as long as Mayfield was writing for her. Unfortunately, Chess demanded that Mayfield sign over the rights to his music, and to increase the pressure on him they told him that Bradley wouldn't be able to record any more of his songs unless he did so. Feeling betrayed, an incensed Mayfield departed the label, and as a result of Chess's ultimatum Bradley's first big hit written by Mayfield would also be her last; Bradley and Mayfield never worked together again. In the meantime, Mayfield had hopped over to ABC Paramount where he produced a competing version of "Mama Didn't Lie" for the Fascinations. Their record was released just as Bradley's broke into the Top 40, although the Fascinations version stalled at #108.

Bradley says that as these events were occurring she was surprised to see that side of the music business. "I was sincerely seeking to break into this business, and of course, being so young, I didn't know a lot about what was going on out there. I was very sad and disillusioned when I could no longer record Curtis's material. Other writers tried to come up with songs for me, and they just didn't work out too well." Without Mayfield writing for her the material she was asked to record wasn't clicking. Her next three singles failed to chart, and so Bradley says she decided to start writing for herself. It got her back on the charts, as her self-penned song "I'm Over You" went to #24 on the R&B charts and #93 on the Top 100. After that, however, none of the singles she recorded did anything on the Top 100 charts, and after her contract with Chess ended she recorded for several smaller labels but nothing she did made the charts. By the end of the 1960s, Bradley was ready to call it quits. "I had started college right after high school, but my musical career interests just took over. Then later on, after my musical career was at a point where disenchantment was setting in, I decided to finish college." She completed her undergraduate degree and earned her master's and became a social worker in Chicago. She got married and started a family, and has had a long successful career out of the public eye. "Do I miss the music business? Sometimes I do, sometimes I don't," Bradley told me. "It's always there," she said, "and because that's your first love, you start thinking about how much you enjoyed it. But overall, if I had to say one way or the other, I don't miss it. Music is moving, it's soothing, it means a lot to most people. So it still has a big place in my life—but I don't miss the business."

Jackie Brenston and His Delta Cats

BEACH MUSIC DISCOGRAPHY: "Rocket 88" (Chess 1458, 1951: Pop Did Not Chart, R&B #1).

Jackie Brenston was a saxophone player from Clarksdale, Mississippi, who teamed up with another Clarksdale product, Ike Turner, when Turner was putting together a band in the late 1940s. Turner's band, the Kings of Rhythm, was apparently so good that B.B. King heard them and hooked them up with Sam Phillips in Memphis, where King himself was recording at the time. Legend has it that the band had a hard time getting to their recording session due to vehicle trouble, rainy weather, a speeding ticket, and—as it turned out most importantly—because some of their equipment fell off the top of the car. Ultimately the band arrived too late for their scheduled session and they were bumped until the subsequent day.

When the band was ready to record the next day, the amp that had fallen off the car and had taken on rainwater during the trip was clearly damaged. Sam Phillips decided to allow guitarist Willie Kizart to use the distortion-producing amp anyway (Phillips later said they stuffed some paper in it to fix it), and by actually emphasizing and over-amping the distortion instead of mixing it down, Phillips used a technique that would be featured on a number of recordings in the decades to come. The first two sessions featured Turner singing and Brenston on sax, then for the next two numbers Brenston took over lead vocals. The second song Brenston did was "Rocket 88."

There seems to be some disagreement about where the song "Rocket 88" came from and how it came to be chosen. Phillips said the band had never performed the song or even rehearsed it before that day, while Turner later said that Brenston more-or-less wrote the song the day before, after seeing a Rocket 88 (the 1950 Hydra-Matic Drive V-8 Oldsmobile 88) on the highway. The song was based on a 1947 song by Jimmy Liggins called "Cadillac Boogie," and in fact it sounds very similar although the words have been changed. "Rocket 88" is a song not only about a fast car, but women and drinking too. With Turner pounding the boogie-woogie piano, and Raymond Hill playing a wailing sax, the song they produced was a sure-fire winner, and Sam Phillips knew it.

Phillips hadn't yet started Sun Records, so he sold the master tapes to Chess Records, who released the song as being by Jackie Brenston and his Delta Cats—even though that was not the name of the group and it was

Turner's group, not Brenston's. The song shot to the top of the R&B charts and remained there for five weeks, and Brenston was suddenly famous as a lead singer of a Delta Cats group that did not even exist under that name; predictably this led to acrimony Turner and Brenston. Turner was reportedly livid about the Chess label credit—he had expected the song to be released as being by Ike Turner & His Kings of Rhythm featuring Jackie Brenston—and now Brenston, and not he, was a star. The inevitable break-up, Brenston later admitted, was the worst thing that could have happened; Brenston didn't know how to lead a group or manage his money. After starting his own group and making several largely unsuccessful recordings he rode the fame of "Rocket 88" for two years. Then, broke and a borderline alcoholic (about the only thing he had left was a battered Oldsmobile Rocket 88 GM had given him for the free publicity he gave them), he went back to work for Turner as a session musician. Turner of course would marry Anna Mae Bullock, who would later come to be known as Tina Turner, and he would go on to some fame as a singer, and later an even greater level of infamy. A frustrated Brenston would eventually give up music, work as a truck driver and then later succumb to alcoholism and was reportedly homeless at the time of his death.

Sam Phillips called "Rocket 88" the first rock and roll recording, and though there is some basis for that claim, the song it is in fact probably too derivative of several other important songs to be considered *the* seminal rock record. On the other hand, although in future year groups such as the Beatles would often use guitar distortion in their songs, "Rocket 88" appears to have been the *first* song ever to purposely incorporate distortion. It was the first song recorded at Phillip's Sun studios (even though it wouldn't officially bear that name until a year later), where Elvis Presley, Johnny Cash, Jerry lee Lewis, and many others would eventually record. For all these firsts, the song was a solid early beach music and boogie woogie hit whose importance goes far beyond the shag clubs of Georgia, Virginia, and the Carolinas.

Buster Brown

BEACH MUSIC DISCOGRAPHY: "Fannie Mae" (Fire 1008, Billboard Pop #38, 1960); "I'm Going—but I'll Be Back" (Fire 507, Did Not Chart, 1961).

Many of the details of Buster Brown's early life are confusing. Most sources note that he was born in 1911 in Cordele, Georgia, and in fact the Georgia census of 1920 shows a 9 year old African American male named Buster Brown living in nearby Rochelle, Georgia. Considering that Rochelle was a town of only a few hundred people in 1911, and Cordele had about 6000, it is not unlikely that Cordele would have offered the closest medical facilities and doctors, and hence may have been the place of his birth even if he lived in Rochelle. Some older reference works say that he was born Waymon Glasco, but more up-to-date sources refute this by saying that Glasco was his manager who bought Brown's catalog after his death and the confusion arose when reissues of Brown's songs bore Glasco's name. In addition, it was once believed that Buster Brown was a stage name the singer had taken from the cartoon character who represented the shoe company of the same name. However, the character had existed since the 1890s so it would not be unheard of for the Browns to have given their son the name Buster because they simply liked the name. In any event, a boy with the birth name Buster Brown was in fact born to Ciela [sic] and William Brown in or near Cordele in 1911, one of five children they would have by 1920. For more than 40 years Buster remained in Georgia, and census records show his occupation listed as "agriculture" in some of the ensuing years. He apparently did play part time gigs in the 1930s and '40s, and then, as later, he would be known for playing the harmonica. As the book of *Blues and Gospel Records 1890-1943* notes, he also played at a folk festivals including one at nearby Fort Valley College in March 1943.

It wasn't until the 1950s that he decided to make the move to New York and pursue a career as a professional entertainer. Between picking up small local gigs and working in a restaurant to make ends meet, he auditioned for Bobby Robinson, who owned the Fire and Fury record labels. Robinson had just released Wilbert Harrison's #1 record "Kansas City" in March 1959 on Fury, and while looking for the label's next big hit he had Brown come in for an audition. Brown sang an acapella version of a song he had written himself called "Fannie Mae." Robinson liked what he heard and had quickly assembled some of his regular studio musicians as well as guitarist "Wild" Jimmy Spruill, who had not only played on "Kansas City," but who over the next two years would play on hits such as Bobby Lewis' "Tossin' and Turnin'," and the Shirelles' "Dedicated to the One I Love." After just two takes, they had a recording that Robinson felt was good enough to release, and indeed it would eventually go to #1 on the R&B charts though it would only just break into the pop Top 40, stalling at #38. Brian Wilson later stated that the song was influential for the Beach Boys and in particular "Help Me Rhonda."

Brown released an album on Fire in 1961, *The New King of the Blues*, but other than two singles, 1960's "Is You Is Or Is You Ain't My Baby" (#81, Pop) and 1961's "Sugar Babe" (#19 R&B, #99 Pop), further chart success eluded him. The flip side of "Sugar Babe" was a song that became mildly popular in the beach clubs, "I'm Going—But I'll Be Back." Like "Fannie Mae" the song was Harmonica driven and written by Brown but it failed to chart. During the 1970s it received a fair amount of airplay from beach music DJ Billy Smith, who actually included it on his second (but unreleased) *Billy Smith's Beach Party Volume 2* album, where it was labeled "Billy's Closing Theme."

Brown would leave Fire shortly thereafter, and a series of singles during the 1960s on labels such as Gwenn, Serock, Nocturn, and even one on Chess, his last recording would be in 1972 on Astroscope, when he drew on his biggest hit with the follow-up "Fannie Mae's Place." The record failed to chart, although his music reached a new generation of listners when "Fannie Mae" was on the *American Graffiti* soundtrack in 1973. No new recordings followed, however, and Brown passed away in Brooklyn in 1976.

Maxine Brown

BEACH MUSIC DISCOGRAPHY: "Oh No Not My Baby" (Wand 162, 1964: Billboard Pop #24).

Kingstree, South Carolina-born Maxine Brown began singing as a child, and by the late 1950s she had moved to New York where she performed with several gospel groups. She signed her first recording contract with the Nomar label in 1960, and her very first release was a song she had written called "All in My Mind." The song peaked at #19 on the pop charts and #2 on the R&B charts, and her next release, "Funny," went to #25 and #2 on the R&B charts. It seemed apparent Brown was about to make a major breakthrough, so ABC-

Paramount picked up her contract in 1961. She subsequently released eight singles for ABC over the next year, and only "After All We've Been through Together" (#102), "I Got A Funny Kind Of Feeling"(#104), and "My Time For Crying"(#98) even made an impression on the charts. ABC gave up on her at that point, and she signed with the Scepter subsidiary Wand in 1963. Her first two releases for Wand, "Ask Me"(#75) and "Coming Back To You"(#99) performed about as poorly as her ABC efforts had, and the sum total of her efforts since leaving Nomar had been ten singles, none of which had come anywhere near the Top 40.

Just as it looked as if Brown was destined to be yet another talented artist with unrealized promise, she lucked into the opportunity to record a song Carole King and Gerry Goffin had written for the Shirelles called "Oh No Not My Baby." At the time the Shirelles were one of the hottest acts in music, having recorded nearly two dozen charts records, one of which was the #1 Goffin and King composition "Will You Still Love Me Tomorrow." Goffin and King had written "Oh No Not My Baby" for them as well, but the group's recording was reportedly a disaster, with each member of the group alternating the lead. With a solid song on their hands but an unreleasable recording, Scepter head Stan Greenberg asked Brown to do something with the mess. She was given a demo of the Shirelles recording and told to do the best she could with it. Brown told David Freeland in *The Ladies of Soul*, "it sounded like everybody wanted to do their own thing … because they were so far off in taking their own lead, no one knew anymore where the real melody."

Brown said she took the song home, put her speakers in her window, turned it on and went out to sit on her front porch. She listened to the song, trying to find the hook, the real melody beneath the Shirelles' haphazard recording. She says she thought, "Oh, my God, how am I am gonna get through this?" when she had help from an unexpected quarter: some neighborhood children. "The kids were skipping rope, and after a while the kids kept singing 'Oh no, not my ba-by' … in time with the skipping of the rope." Brown said it hit her then that "'I know a hook when I hear it. Time to go to work!' I left the porch, and I went back in the house and I found a melody in no time.… I knew we had a hit."

With Brown's solid lead, a piano intro by Carole King and backing vocals by Dee Dee Warwick, Brown's version of "Oh No Not My Baby" stayed on the charts for seven weeks and went to #24. Scepter didn't completely scrap the original Shirelle's recording though, and Brown's, King's, and Warwick's parts were added over the same musical tracks that the Shirelles had recorded—their vocals were simply removed. "Scepter did a lot of that in those days," Brown told Freeland. "It saves money from going back to pay the musicians."

Unfortunately, though Brown would have nine more Top 100 charting singles, none would break the Top 40, and 1969's "We'll Cry Together" was her last song to make the pop charts at #73. Eventually she moved into stage work and worked the club scene, and by the 1990s, she was inducted into the R&B Hall of Fame. "Oh No Not My Baby" has often been recorded since Brown's original charter; Merry Clayton earned a Grammy nomination for her rendition in 1972, Rod Stewart's 1973 version charted and the song has also been recorded by Cher, Linda Ronstadt and others. Nevertheless, it's Maxine Brown's original version that stands above the others as a beach music classic.

Ruth Brown

BEACH MUSIC DISCOGRAPHY: "Teardrops from My Eyes" (Atlantic 919, 1950: Billboard Pop Did Not Chart, R&B #1); "5–10–15 Hours (Of Your Love)" (Atlantic 962, 1952: Billboard Pop Did Not Chart, R&B #1); "Mama (He Treats Your Daughter Mean)"(Atlantic 986, 1953: Billboard Pop #23).

Portsmouth, Virginia-born Ruth Alston Weston was one of seven children of mother who was a domestic worker and a father who was a dock laborer who also worked in maintenance and retail. She got her start singing in the Methodist church, encouraged by her father Leonard who was a choir director and sang and played the piano. When she was eight years old she got paid a few dollars to sing at a wedding, and from that point on she decided she wanted to be a professional singer. When she was 15 she was singing in amateur shows in nearby Norfolk, and inspired by singers such as Billie Holiday and Ella Fitzgerald she decided to follow a career in secular music despite the misgivings of her father. When she was 16 she took a bus to New York on the pretense of visiting an uncle, when in truth she was going to sing at the amateur contest at the famed Apollo Theater. Singing "It Could Happen to You" she won first prize, and soon she was singing in a number of different venues. At one of these, the Big Track Diner in Norfolk, she met her future husband Jimmy Brown, who was moonlighting playing the trumpet while still in the navy.

Once she was 18 and had graduated from high school, she began to pursue opportunities farther afield, and while playing Detroit's Frolic Club she was spotted by orchestra leader Lucky Millender, who offered her a job. She only worked with him a month when a misunderstanding led to her being fired while the band was in Washington, D.C., but fortunately she was able to get a job at Washington's Crystal Caverns jazz club run by Blanche Calloway, Cab Calloway's sister. Despite the fact that she took the job in desperation after being fired, it was pivotal in her personal and professional life. Her old acquaintance Jimmy Brown was in the house-band there, and they would soon be married; Blanche Calloway would agree to become her manager, and would serve in that capacity for the next decade; Duke Ellington and Sonny Til and the Orioles would catch her act there one night, and would call Atlantic Records founder Ahmet Ertegun and tell him to see Ruth perform. He did, and offered her a contract with his fledgling Atlantic label.

Blanche Calloway got Brown a booking at the Apollo, and Calloway and Brown set out to New York to sign her contract and perform backed by Dizzy Gillespie's band. They never made it, however; an automobile accident in Chester, Pennsylvania would see Brown hospitalized for the better part of a year. Eventually she'd sign her contract in the hospital instead of New York, and after her release in May 1949 while still on crutches she recorded her first record for Atlantic, "So Long." It went to #6 on the R&B charts, and became the label's third hit record (Stick McGhee's "Drinking Wine, Spo-Dee-O-Dee" and Frank Culley's "Cole Slaw" were the others). It was in 1950 however that her new, more upbeat sound debuted, when she recorded "Teardrops from My Eyes," a song written by Rudy Toombs, who would also write The Clovers' "One Mint Julep" and Amos Milburn's "One Bourbon, One Scotch, One Beer." Most of Brown's songs up to that point had been slower torch songs, but "Teardrops" was upbeat although inititially Brown was not sure she wanted to go in that direction. Ertegun convinced her that it would be a good move, and his instincts would prove to be correct; the song would be #1 for a total of eleven weeks. Perhaps more importantly, it became the label's first million-seller, and was the second 45 rpm record the label would release (Joe Morris' "Anytime, Anyplace, Anywhere" was the first).

Brown followed "Teardrops" with successive Top 10 R&B hits, before releasing "5–10–15 Hours" in 1952. Another Toombs composition, it was #1 on the R&B for charts for seven weeks, and Brown considered it one of her best recordings. The song was originally called "Five-Ten-Fifteen *Minutes*," but Brown told Toombs that considering that the Dominoes' "Sixty Minute Man" had already topped the charts, this song needed to be about *hours*, not minutes. The sax work by Willis "Gator Tail" Jackson is especially notable because she'd marry him after she divorced Brown.

By now her sound had elevated her to an impressive level of success. She'd acquired the name "Miss Rhythm" after Frankie Laine saw her perform, and the newly-succesful Atlantic Records was being called "The House That Ruth Built." She was on an impressive run of hits that would see her stay on the R&B charts for 149 weeks with five #1's. Her next #1, in fact, would be her biggest, the 1953 Johnny Wallace and Herb Lance composition "(Mama) He Treats Your Daughter Mean." The songwriters supposedly heard a blues singer on a street corner in Atlanta singing for change, and he dropped the line into one of his songs (it's possible the singer was singing "Last Dime Blues" as sung by Blind Lemon Jefferson). Wallace and Lance wrote a song around the line, and originally composed as a slow ballad, the arrangement was altered to make it another uptempo song to fit Brown's new style. Nevertheless, Brown did not like it, and told author Chip Deffaa she thought it was "the silliest mess I'd ever heard." She only agreed to record it because the two songwriters were friends and she was hoping to help them out. Although they did the song in just two takes, it would be her biggest hit, and went on to actually crossover onto the pop charts where it hit #23.

Brown would have seventeen more R&B hits through 1959, and two of them hit #1. She'd also have two more songs crossover to the pop charts, as the Jerry Leiber and Mike Stoller penned "Lucky Lips" would hit #25, and "This Little Girl's Gone Rockin'," written by Bobby Darin and Mann Curtis, would go to #24. Brown left Atlantic in 1961 and signed with Phillips, which resulted in just two recordings that barely broke into the Hot 100. She then jumped to Decca and Mainstream, and after that she basically retired from music to raise her family. She had been divorced a number of times, and once she was out of the music business at one point she even became a bus driver to earn money to raise her children. By the 1970s she started recording again although her music did not result in any chart hits, she did start acting and appeared as a semi-regular on the 1979 sitcom *Hello, Larry*. She appeared on Broadway in *Amen Corner* in 1983, in *Staggerlee* in 1987, and in the 1988 film *Hairspray* as well as others. In 1989 she won a Tony Award for her performance in *Black and Blue* on Broadway, and won a Grammy in the category Best Jazz Performance, Female, for the album *Blues on Broadway*.

Her career having come full circle, she became an advocate for musicians' rights and royalties. She was largely responsible for the formation of the Rhythm and Blues Foundation in 1989, and was inducted into the Rock and Roll Hall of Fame in 1993. She passed away in 2006.

James Brown and the Famous Flames

BEACH MUSIC DISCOGRAPHY: "Don't Let it Happen to Me" (Federal 12361, 1959: Did Not Chart).

Born in Barnwell, South Carolina, James Brown was raised in extreme poverty and was without parental guidance of any type for most of his early life. He lived in Elko, South Carolina, then moved to Augusta, Georgia when he was around five. There he lived with an aunt in a brothel, and between working odd jobs and the time he spent on the streets, school was not a priority for him and he dropped out in the sixth grade. He committed armed robbery when he was 16, and was sentenced to three years in a juvenile detention center.

Despite this less than ideal beginning, Brown had already exhibited an interest in music. At 13 he had been part of the Cremona Trio, and while finishing up his sentence in detention he came to the attention of Bobby Byrd. When released he joined Byrd's group the Gospel Starlighters (who also went by the name the Avons), though between gigs they often ran moonshine across state lines. Brown played piano and the drums at times, as well as handling vocals, and by the time they changed their name to the Flames they were picking up regular bookings, including opening for Little Richard. In the fall of 1955 the group had come up with a song called "Please Please Please," and recorded it at a Macon radio station. It started to get local airplay, and came to the attention of Ralph Bass, a talent scout and producer for King Records who was in the Atlanta area when he heard it. Bass signed the group to a contract for $200 on the Federal subsidiary, and at their first recording session in February 1956 they did a more polished version of "Please Please Please" and three other songs. Released as being by James Brown with the Famous Flames (the top billing was apparently unexpected by the group members), the record made the top five on the R&B charts and sold more than a million copies. Despite this success, for the next two years none of Brown's singles charted and consequently most of the original Flames had quit and gone back to Georgia. Then he released his eleventh single, "Try Me," in 1958, and it went to #1 on the R&B charts and broke into the Top 50 on the pop charts. The singles that immediately followed did okay, with "I Want You So Bad" going to #20 on the R&B charts. The single after that, "Good Good Lovin,'" did not chart, but its flip side "Don't Let it Happen to Me," was picked up in the late 1970s by beach music audiences who found the song to be a good shag tune, and an unusual song for Brown in that it was neither a slow, pleading ballad nor the type of funk-infused songs that would follow in the '60s. The song did not chart, however, its popularity largely being limited to the Carolinas, Georgia, and Virginia.

At this point Brown's releases diverged from anything that could be realistically considered beach music, although he did do a faster, jazzier cover of the "5" Royales "Think" in 1960 which went to #33 on the pop charts and #7 on the R&B charts, two spots higher that the "5" Royales original release in 1957. Throughout his career he'd release nearly 120 chart records, best known among them being songs such as "Papa's Got a Brand New Bag," "I Got You (I Feel Good)," "It's a Man's Man's Man's World," "Get Offa That Thing," and many others. Brown was one of the first inductees into the Rock and

Roll Hall of Fame in 1986, and he received a Lifetime Achievement Award from the Grammys, a Rhythm & Blues Foundation Pioneer Award, a star on the Hollywood Walk of Fame and many, many other distinctions. He died from congestive heart failure on Christmas Day, 2006.

The Buckinghams

BEACH MUSIC DISCOGRAPHY: "Susan" (Columbia 4-44378, 1967: Billboard Pop #11).

Dennis Tufano and George LeGros were members of a Chicago-area group called the Darcells when John Poulos of the Pulsations asked them to join his group, who played well but were in dire need of vocalists. The Pulsations mainly played dragstrips and car shows, but because the name "Pulsations" sounds *exactly* like a band that played car shows—and nothing else—as they became more popular Tufano says they felt the need to change their name "to something more English because of British invasion." Oddly enough, a security guard overheard them talking and one possibility he suggested was "The Buckinghams, which stood out because there's a beautiful fountain in Chicago called Buckingham Fountain. We felt that would be a great name because while it sounded English at the same time we wouldn't be selling out Chicago." Over time the group evolved to include Carl Giammarese, Nick Fortuna, and later Marty Grebb, but when LeGros was drafted Tufano says "I became the lead singer by default." The group became extremely popular in the Chicago area, and their manager Carl Bonefetti knew Jim Holvay, lead and songwriter for the MOB (see the entry for the MOB). Bonefetti asked Holvay to come hear the group and see if Holvay had any material the group could record. Holvay liked the band's sound, and gave the group a song he had written that wasn't right for his band, but that he felt would work for the Buckinghams. Tufano says, "the song was 'Kind of a Drag.' We got it arranged and recorded it, and that's when everything changed for us."

The group had recorded "Kind of a Drag" in their first session for USA records, but the song was the last single by the group the label released just as their contract ran out. They were only signed with USA through 1966, and so at the end of the year the group appeared to be done. Their keyboard player quit, and even Bonefetti gave up on them. "No label, keyboard player, no manager" Tufano says. "We were sitting in Nick Fortuna's basement and John Pullos comes down and has Billboard magazine and plops it on the table and says 'Open it up. Open it up!' We open it to the Hot 100 and 'Kind of a Drag' is #1. We have a #1 record but no manager, keyboard player, or label." But a #1 record changes a lot of things, and they found a manager in Jim Guercio and signed with Columbia Records. They got Holvay and his bandmate Gary Beisbier to write them more songs, and the result was a string of Top 40 hits after "Kind of a Drag"—"Don't You Care" (#6), "Mercy, Mercy, Mercy" (#5), and "Hey Baby (They're Playing Our Song)" (#12). In 1967, Billboard declared The Buckinghams "the most listened to band in America," and based on their chart success that year it would be a hard claim to dispute. Their last hit of 1967 was a song well suited for beach music audiences, "Susan."

Tufano says "Jim had been working on 'Susan' for a while before he finished it, because I think he was stuck on the bridge, which Gary eventually added and which tied it all together." It was a beautiful song as written, but unbeknownst to the songwriters and the group, after it was recorded, Tufano says "Guercio had this crazy idea to insert this backwards tape thing like the Beatles did on "Day in the Life.' We didn't know about it, and we were out on the road when we heard it for the first time—and we didn't like it." What the group learned though was that they weren't alone—almost no one liked the weird interlude Guercio had added. "Most radio stations cut it out anyway. We'd be doing an interview and they'd say 'hey, we cut that part because we didn't like it and when that's playing people change the station.' We said 'we agree' and 'thank you very much!' But Guerico had the last word, and for a long time the

Buckinghams could do nothing about his production of the song, even though they did not include the psychedelic portion in their performances. Eventually the edited version became widely distributed, and it's that version that beach music audiences adopted. "It's great song," Tufano says. "Like all of our songs, it's about 'you broke my heart but I still love you.' Every one of them. But that's kind of the universal theme of life."

1967 was the high-water mark for the group, and after that they had just one release that charted, "Back in Love Again," and it wouldn't even break into the Top 40. Eventually the group broke up, and today Carl Giammarese and Nick Fortuna tour as the Buckinghams. Dennis Tufano tours solo now, singing many of those Buckingham classics on which he sang lead the first time around.

Solomon Burke

BEACH MUSIC DISCOGRAPHY: "Cry to Me" (Atlantic 2131, 1961: Billboard Pop #44).

Philadelphian James Solomon McDonald was born to a single mother who married Vincent Burke, when Solomon was nine, and his name was then changed to Solomon Vincent McDonald Burke. Born into a religious family where his grandmother claimed she had been told by God that he was coming twelve years before his birth, young Solomon was destined to hold a place in the church and in fact he gave his first sermon at age 7; by the time he was 12 he had a radio ministry and also a travelling ministry. When he was 14 he wrote a song for his grandmother who gave him a guitar and told him it was through music that he must now reach out to others. His grandmother passed away the next day, and soon Burke formed a group called the Gospel Cavaliers. It was when Burke performed solo at a talent show that he was discovered when he was spotted by the wife of Philadelphia DJ Kae Williams, who introduced him to Apollo Records' Bess Berman who signed him to a contract in 1955. He was not successful with Apollo, and in fact none of his ten releases (including two as "Little Vincent") were hits. He broke his contract with Apollo when he felt he wasn't receiving the royalty payments he should have, and later claimed they had him blackballed from the industry for a while. Indeed, he could not find work as a singer and he worked in a funeral home and was homeless for a while.

By 1959 Burke was recording once again, though two singles for Singular failed to chart. He then signed with Jerry Wexler at Atlantic Records in 1960, and though his first single, "Keep The Magic Working" did not chart, his second, "Just Out Of Reach (Of My Two Empty Arms)," climbed to #24 on the pop charts. It was at this point that Wexler asked him to record some songs Bert Russell (later Bert Berns) had written. Berns, who would go on to produce and write for some of the '60s biggest artists including The Drifters, Van Morrison, The McCoys, Garnett Mimms, Otis Redding, The Isley Brothers, and Ben. E. King, offered Solomon two songs he had written. The first was "Little Bit of Soap," which the Jarmels would later have a hit with, and then "Hang on Sloopy," which would become the McCoys signature hit. Burke refused both, but when offered his third and final chance for a Russell song, he accepted at Wexler's urging. That song was "Cry to Me."

As written, "Cry to Me" was a slow ballad about loneliness, but on his own Burke made the decision to sing, play, and record the song a bit faster. As a result, the song became a massive success: "Cry to Me" peaked at #44 on the pop charts and #5 on the R&B charts, and led to an appearance on American Bandstand. It later became famous once again for its inclusion as the background music for the pivotal dance scene in 1987's *Dirty Dancing*.

After the success of "Cry to Me," Burke would go on to record more than two dozen more singles for Atlantic, though the most successful of them on the pop charts would be 1965's "Got to Get You Off My Mind" at #22, and would also hit #1 on the R&B charts. In fact, Burke's greatest success would come on the R&B charts, where "If You Need Me" (#2), "You're Good for Me"(#3), "Goodbye Baby (Baby Goodbye)" (#8), "Everybody Needs Somebody to Love"(#4), "The Price"(#10), and "Tonight's the Night"(#2) would all break into the Top 10. Having failed to maintain any long term success on the pop charts, and now seen as a second tier Atlantic act due to a roster that featured artist such as Aretha Franklin, Wilson Pickett, and Otis Redding, in 1968 he jumped to Bell Records, then in 1970 to MGM. Though a few songs did chart, no major hits followed, and the next two decades saw Burke record for a number of labels. Though lacking the quality of some of his earlier recordings, his 1987 release on the Rounder label, "Love Buys Love," did find an audience in the beach music community. Ultimately after having had several Grammy nominations over the years, he finally received one for his 2002 album *Don't Give Up on Me*.

Burke passed away in 2010, and although his reputation never reached the heights of contemporaries such as Otis Redding, Wilson Pickett, or James Brown, Wexler was quoted as saying he was "the best soul singer of all time." He was inducted into the Rock and Roll Hall of Fame in 2001.

Jerry Butler

BEACH MUSIC DISCOGRAPHY: "I Dig You Baby" (Mercury 72648, 1966: Billboard Pop #60); "Never Give You Up"(Mercury 72798, 1968: Billboard Pop #20); "Hey Western Union Man" (Mercury 72850, 1968: Billboard Pop #16); "Only the Strong Survive" (Mercury 72898, 1969: Billboard Pop #4); "Moody Woman" (Mercury 72929, 1969: Billboard Pop #24); "What's the Use of Breaking Up" (Mercury 72960, 1969: Billboard Pop #20); "(I'm Just Thinking About) Cooling Out" (Philadelphia International 3656, 1978: Billboard Pop Did Not Chart, R&B #14).

Mississippi-born Jerry Butler's family moved to Chicago when he was three, and as a teenager he performed sporadically with a several different groups before landing with the Roosters along with co-members Curtis Mayfield, Arthur and Richard Brooks, and Sam Gooden. After singing with the Vee-Jay label they changed their name to the Impressions, and their first recording was a song by Brooks and Butler called "For Your Precious Love." It peaked at #11 in 1958, but after their next six singles failed to chart, in 1960 Butler decided to go solo. Known as "the

Iceman" for his smooth and cool delivery, almost immediately Butler had a solo hit with "He Will Break Your Heart" (#7), followed by others such as "Moon River" (#11, 1962) and "Make It Easy on Yourself"(#20, 1962). While he would go on to have almost twenty Top 100 hits with Vee-Jay between 1960 and 1966, but after Vee-Jay filed for bankruptcy in August 1966 Butler signed with Mercury for what some might say was the third and most consistently productive phase of his career.

His third release for Mercury was 1966's "I Dig You Baby," a smooth soulful song that, though it would only peak at #60, would also go on to become a very big song on the Carolina beach music scene. "The original version was done by Lorraine Ellison and produced by Jerry Ross, and he produced mine too," he said. Some reports have claimed Butler doesn't like to sing the song, but he clarified that it was only because the song was somewhat dated. "That happened because of the etymology of the song," he said. "The expression 'I dig you baby' connotes the hip-ness of being. But I was performing it and a boy said 'That's so square!' because the youth had moved beyond that expression. Because of that I think I was intimidated and for a long time I didn't want to sing it anymore!"

Butler asked Mercury if he could work with two up and coming songwriters, Kenny Gamble and Leon Huff. One of the first songs they all wrote together was "Never Give You Up," which went to #20 on the pop charts and #4 on the R&B charts, followed by another Gamble, Huff, and Butler composition called "Hey Western Union Man." "Kenny, Leon, and I were not only the writers, but they produced, did the background vocals, and just about everything that was needed" he said. "I tell people all the time that 90% of the arrangement was in the way Leon Huff plays piano." The recipe was successful, as the song went to #16 on the pop charts and #1 on the R&B charts in the fall of 1968. Butler's next release was "Only the Strong Survive," "a song that everybody seemed to derive their own personal meaning from—everybody heard whatever message they wanted to put into it." It was a song that many people felt strongly about, and the anthem-like nature of the song saw it go to #4 on the pop charts and #1 on the R&B charts.

While the three Gamble and Huff collaborations appeared on Butler's album *The Ice Man Cometh*, which spawned four Top 40 singles on the pop charts, the first single off the next album, *Ice on Ice*, was "Moody Woman," "a play off of being married" Butler said. It went to #24, and was followed by "What's the Use of Breaking Up," "which dealt with people who are always going through some conflict or another, and then after getting the steam out they go back to being what they were before," which went to #20. But not long afterwards "Kenny and Leon decided that they weren't going to produce any outside artists anymore and they were going to concentrate on building their own label," and since Butler "was under contract with Mercury and couldn't leave," the collaboration was over. Unfortunately, without Gamble and Huff, Butler's music seemed to languish. After more releases on Mercury and then a few on Motown, he re-joined Gamble and Huff, but this time on their label Philadelphia International. "Because of our relationship as friends, they said 'let's go back into the studio, and see if we can recapture what we did at the very beginning.' We went up to this resort up in the Pennsylvania mountains and sat down, and just started talking about just cooling out, getting away, taking a break from the routine. The idea is you need to just slow down because you're moving too fast. And that's how the song's title came about—so the song was about what it's like to 'cool out.'" Though "(I'm Just Thinking About) Cooling Out" did not make the pop charts, it did hit the R&B charts at #14, and was his strongest entry in the beach music milieu.

Butler continued to record until the early '80s then became successful first in business, and then as a politician in Illinois and served as a commissioner for Cook County. In 1991 he was inducted into the Rock and Roll Hall of Fame as a member of the Impressions.

Cannonball

BEACH MUSIC DISCOGRAPHY: "You Keep Telling Me Yes" (Blast 101, 1973: Did Not Chart).

In the mid–1960s Joe Clinard was a member of Calvin Lindsay and the Hysterics, a regional band from High Point, North Carolina, who were popular on the beach club circuit and recorded a nice cover of the Poets' "So Young (And So Innocent)" and the Radiants' "Ain't No Big Thing" on the Greensboro-based Jokers Three label around 1966. Clinard left the group in 1967 for basic training and then joined The Impacts (elements of which would later become Grand Impact). Eventually, there would be some changes and the band would become Flagstone, soon to change their name once again and become the eight piece horn band Cannonball. Clinard says they changed the name because he felt they needed to in order to get some airplay, and as they were becoming a bit more of a beach music band they needed to forge a new identity. In 1972 Cannonball first recorded a cover of the Wildweeds' 1967 Chess release "No Good to Cry," which is an uptempo beach-like number. "Danny Pierce did the vocals, and we recorded it at Reflection Sound studios in Charlotte" Clinard said. "Tommy Witcher from the original Georgia Prophets helped me produce it, and it made its way to several charts around the Carolinas." The flip was an early Clinard and Ted Bacon composition called "Sunny Day Today."

Clinard soon became the band's manager, and by this time the group consisted of Clinard, Chris Miller, Jack Atchison, Jerry Hutchens, Bucky Cherry, Paul Craver and Phil Garrett. The group often played at a bar over the Idle Hour Arcade near the Pavilion in Myrtle Beach, first called the Tail of the Fox, then "Dr. Generosity's, which later became the Castaways," Craver said. Clinard says they played there with bands such as "The Showmen, Dr. Hook, and Nantucket, to name a few." In 1973 the group recorded their second single, the beach music classic "You Keep Telling Me Yes," written by Cherry, Hutchens, and Clinard, and recorded it at Reflection Sound studios in Charlotte in 1973. On that song the group worked with producer Duke Hall, who had also produced the Platters' hits "With This Ring," "Washed Ashore" and "I Love You 1,000 Times." Clinard says, "Hall not only produced the song, he also did horns and strings. Chris handled lead vocals, and I played the Sax solos."

Released on the group's own Blast label, the song was instantly popular on the beach music circuit, selling thousands of copies at the beach, where "it became #1 on the beach charts" Craver says. Unfortunately, as is the case with many regional hits, that didn't translate to national sales, so the success of the group's big moment was confined principally to the Carolinas. However, a measure of the song's enduring popularity was that the single was so much in demand that bootlegs started to come out—which is almost unheard of for a regional release. "Blast was our label," Clinard said, "but then the record showed up on the Reflection label, and then Shadow. As is often the case, I'm not sure what happened to the royalties from sales through the years, because I only saw some in early 70's." The song was in fact so popular that it was included on the very first Ripete beach music compilation album.

Despite the record's solid sound, the group's makeup changed very quickly, and though Clinard tried to hold the group together, it was becoming more and more of a problem. "I was trying to sing songs that I hadn't sung lead on originally, and I didn't feel good doing that. I think we were booked on a show with Cornelius Brothers & Sister Rose and about the third day of the gig I called the guys together back stage and told them 'I can't do this anymore.' I never did walk on a stage again." Clinard left the music business and became a successful businessman, and known today as "Bikini Joe," he owned and founded a number of enterprises including Cheap Joe's, Texas Jeans, and AQUA Boutiques.

Craver eventually put back together a later version of the O'Kaysions, who for legal reasons changed their name to the Kays. Craver found considerable fame in several other groups such as Shagtime, the Kruze Band and the Men of Distinction, and he has also received a number of accolades for his solo work. A number of band members got out of the music business altogether, though Atchison is still a singer and drummer for Brice Street.

The Capitols

BEACH MUSIC DISCOGRAPHY: "Cool Jerk" (Karen 1524, 1966: Billboard Pop #7).

The Capitols were a Detroit group who started in 1962, and performing at different times as The Caps and the Three Caps they consisted of Samuel George, Don Norman Storball, and Richard Mitchell McDougall. Barbara Lewis's manager Ollie McLaughlin saw the group when they were on the bill with Lewis at a Detroit-area gig, and signed the group to his newly-formed Karen label. As the Capitols they recorded 1963's "Dog and Cat" which was the group's and the label's debut release, but the record stiffed. The group broke up not long afterwards.

In the early 1960s the Jerk was one of the hottest dance crazes in America, fueled by the popularity of songs such as "The Jerk" by the Larks and "Come on Do the Jerk" by the Miracles, and its mention in songs such as Chris Kenner's 1963 release "Land of 1000 Dances" (and again later when Wilson Pickett's cover went to #1 on the R&B charts in 1966). Apparently this gave rise to a derivative version of the dance called the "Pimp Jerk," which was popular in Detroit clubs. Reportedly its name came from the fact that area pimps were too "cool" to dance the more prosaic Jerk, and thus created their own dance which consisted of suggestive hip thrusting and grinding. Storball decided to write a song about it, and the Capitols re-formed and reestablished their connection to Ollie McLaughlin and Karen Records. Now carrying the more radio-friendly title "Cool Jerk," McLaughlin set up a recording session at Ed Wingate's Golden World Studios, arguably Detroit's second most famous studios after those at Motown. Unfortunately some of the musicians hired to play on the Capitols' session did not show up, so McLaughlin called on Motown's notoriously underpaid musicians the Funk Brothers, who would moonlight from time to time even though it was against Berry Gordy's wishes (see the entry for Edwin Starr).

Between working on sessions for the Supremes' "Love Is Like an Itching in My Heart" the Funk Brothers made the crosstown trip and laid down the tracks for "Cool Jerk," contributing to its distinctly Motown-like sound. Released with a the odd pairing of a cover of Barbara Lewis' "Hello Stranger" on the flipside, "Cool Jerk" peaked at #7 on the pop charts and #2 on the R&B charts; it was nominated for a Grammy for Best Rhythm and Blues Group Performance.

The group followed "Cool Jerk" with two albums in 1966, one of which, *Dance the Cool Jerk*, broke the Top 100. They also released two more singles that year, "I Got to Handle It"(pop #74) and "We Got A Thing That's In A Groove" (pop #65). One more single, "Soul Brother, Soul Sister," made the lower reaches of the R&B charts in 1969, but it wasn't enough to sustain the group and after two more singles that year they disbanded.

The Cardinals

BEACH MUSIC DISCOGRAPHY: "Come Back My Love" (Atlantic 1067, 1955: Did Not Chart).

The Baltimore–based Cardinals were a talented ensemble who were one of a number of bird-named groups popular in the 1950s and included the Ravens, Swallows, Wrens, Robins, Crows, and others. The quartet of Leon Hardy, Meredith Brothers, Donald Johnson, and Ernie Warren began in the late 1940s as the Mellotones, and after adding Jack Aydellote they played the club circuit before landing a recording contract with Atlantic in 1950. They changed their name to the Cardinals due to the many groups performing as the Mellotones at the time, and initially recorded four sides including "Shouldn't I Know," which in 1951 went to #7 on the Billboard R&B charts. After releasing two more singles, "I'll Always Love You," and "Wheel of Fortune," which went to #6 on the R&B charts, Warren was drafted and Aydelotte left the group. Luther MacArthur replaced Warren and Leander Tarver replaced Aydelotte, but Tarver only stayed around for one single, "The Bump," before leaving and being replaced by James Brown (not *that* James Brown), who also soon left, and then Aydelotte returned.

Despite the fluctuating line-up, the group was popular on the club circuit, but even though they had landed a couple of chart hits Atlantic was releasing their recordings at a snail's pace, and there was a nine-month period between the release of "The Bump" and their next release "You Are My Only Love." The next release came a year later, and was an early recording by the group featuring Warren, "Under a Blanket of Blue." It did nothing, and it was clear that Atlantic wasn't fully behind the group, though whether it was because they were awaiting Warren's return from the Army or because Atlantic was putting all of their promotional power behind labelmates The Drifters and the Clovers is unclear. In 1954, Warren, who had been sitting in with the group occasionally, saw the end of his term of service and rejoined the Cardinals. They soon recorded "The Door is Still Open," and when released in 1955 the record was hugely successful, going to #4 on the R&B charts. This resulted in an appearance at the Apollo as a headline act and extensive touring. That July they released their eighth single, the beach music favorite "Come Back My Love." The song had been recorded by the New-York based Wrens in 1954, and although the song did not chart for that group many consider it the Wrens' best recording. The Wrens version is a bit slower and more of a ballad, whereas the Cardinals version has a peppier doo-wop feel. Although the Cardinals version failed to chart as well, it solidified their popularity at the time and led to even more touring and shows. However, the group's next two releases didn't sell well, and after releasing "I Won't Make You Cry" later that year the group decided to call it quits. Not long after that Atlantic released their final recording "One Love," and it too sunk without a trace.

After less just a dozen releases, the Cardinals were done, though in 1957 Warren attempted to reform a new Cardinals lineup that folded in 1958 after just three recordings. Warren then tried to get some of the original group together once again, and joined by Johnson, Brothers, and two new members, the lineup toured for a few years before dissolving for the last time.

Carl Carlton

BEACH MUSIC DISCOGRAPHY: "Everlasting Love" (Back Beat BB27001, 1974: Billboard Pop #6).

Detroit-born Carl Carlton grew up singing in the church, but even as a child his siblings recognized the power of his voice and would sneak him into nightclubs to sing for tips. He reportedly took his first step towards being a professional singer when he and some friends were playing baseball in the street and a neighbor told them to turn the radio down because the music was too loud. After being told it wasn't a radio playing and that it was simply Carl singing, supposedly the neighbor arranged for Carl to visit the offices of Detroit's newly-formed Lando Records to pursue a recording contract. At the time "Little" Stevie Wonder was recording for Berry Gordy's Tamla label, and his "Fingertips" had gone to #1 on the pop and R&B charts in 1963; perhaps envisioning a similar record of success for young Carl he signed with Lando and was billed as "Little Carl Carlton." In 1964 and 1965 he had a couple of releases on Lando, and recording as "Carl Carlton the 12 Year Old Wonder" he had a Golden World release in 1965 as well, but none of the records made the charts. Don Robey's Back Beat Records heard about him and signed him, and his first release for the label, 1968's "Competition Ain't Nothing," became his first chart record, going to a respectable #36 on the R&B charts and #75 on the pop charts. Several more disks by "Little" Carl followed (and one that billed him as "Little Carl Carlton the 14 Year Old Sensation"), and though a couple of them did well on the R&B charts, none made the pop charts.

The last "Little Carl Carlton" disk appeared on Back Beat when he was 17, and now recording as simply Carl Carlton he had two releases on Back Beat in 1971 and 72 and one on ABC in 1973, and none made the Top 40 on either chart. It was at about this time that Carlton asked to record "Everlasting Love," and song written by Buzz Cason and Mac Gayden and recorded in 1967 by Robert Knight (see entry for Robert Knight). Knight's well-known version had peaked at #13 on the pop charts, but oddly enough it wasn't Knight's version but a cover by David Ruffin on 1969's *My Whole World Ended* album that brought the song to Carlton's attention. Recorded in Nashville in Cason's studio, the record was produced by "Papa Don" Schroeder (who had also produced James and Bobby Purify's "I'm Your Puppet" and "Wish You Didn't Have to Go") and Tommy Cogbill (who played bass on Dusty Springfield's "Son of a Preacher Man" and Wilson Pickett's "Funky Broadway"). Originally slated to be the B-side of "I Wanna Be Your Main Squeeze," when the song started getting airplay in 1973 Back Beat rereleased it as the A side in 1974. With its updated and suitable for dancing sound, it was a hit in discos as well as beach clubs. It went to #6 on the pop charts and #11 on the R&B charts.

While the success of "Everlasting Love" should have kick started his career at long last, it didn't as it turned out. Robey had sold Back Beat to ABC in 1972, and this led to a complicated series of legal entanglements involving royalties that actually kept Carlton from recording at all for a couple of years. Eventually he was free of ABC and signed with Mercury, which led to just one single and no hits, and then finally he signed a record deal when his friend Leon Haywood (see the entry for Haywood) got him signed with 20th Century Records, with whom Haywood was signed as well. He released a cover of Haywood's "This Feeling's

Rated Xtra" which made the lower reaches of the R&B charts before releasing 1981's "She's a Bad Mama Jama (She's Built, She's Stacked)" which went to #2 on the R&B chart, #22 on the pop charts, and won him a Grammy nomination in 1982.

Once again, success was fleeting, as Carlton would continue to record but he would never have another big hit. He started singing gospel again, and in 2011 was nominated for a Detroit Music Award for "Outstanding Gospel/Christian Vocalist." He continues to perform to this day.

Clarence Carter

Beach Music Discography: "Slip Away" (Atlantic 2508, 1968: Billboard Pop #6).

Calvin George Carter was born in Montgomery, Alabama, and although born blind he was able to get an education by attending the Alabama School for the Blind starting when he was six years old. He took music lessons and learned to play the guitar and piano in school, and he went on to Alabama State College and earned a degree in music. He was playing in nightclubs on the weekends, and though his goal had been to be a teacher he formed a band instead. He did back up work for artists such as Otis Redding and Gene Chandler, and he teamed up to create an act with his friend Calvin Scott, who was also blind. While working the Alabama club circuit as Clarence & Calvin and later as The C&C Boys they recorded several sides on Fairlane and Duke and one on Atco, though none of the singles charted. The Atco single, "Step by Step," had been recorded at Rick Hall's Muscle Shoals based FAME Studios, and after Scott was injured the duo broke up and Carter returned to Muscle Shoals to pay to record some songs by himself. Hall heard him singing, and eventually Carter would record several songs on Hall's own Fame label, beginning a working relationship that would last a number of years. The first of these singles was 1967's "Tell Daddy," which became Carter's first hit, going to #35 on the R&B charts. Etta James would cover the renamed song as "Tell Mama" later that year at those same FAME studios using many of the same musicians, and her song would break into the pop charts.

Carter signed with Atlantic, and in 1968 he had his first hit for the label, "Slip Away." By this point Carter was known for his anguished songs of heartbreak and lost love, and the song resonated with audiences, going to #2 on the R&B chart and #6 on the pop chart in 1968 and earning a gold record. Like much of the soul coming out of Muscle Shoals at the time, it has an earthier sound than many traditional beach songs had up to that point, but nevertheless it found an audience with shaggers. His follow-up single, "Too Weak to Fight," also went gold, and was immediately followed by the risqué "Back Door Santa," with themes he'd explore again in the 1980s. By the late '60s Candi Staton was one of his backup singers, and they'd get married in 1970 though they'd divorce in 1973.

In 1970 Carter would record "Patches," which would go on to be his biggest hit at #4 on the pop charts. The song was written by Chairmen of the Board frontman General Norman Johnson, and his group recorded it for their eponymous first album, and later released it as the B-side of the beach hit "Everything's Tuesday." Apparently Atlantic Records discovered the song deep on the Chairmen of the Board album and decided they wanted some of their artists to record it and they would release the version they felt had the most commercial appeal. Hall asked Carter to record it when he arrived at FAME studios straight off a redeye flight from a gig. Even though he was tired and didn't know the words—apparently one of the studio's engineers whispered the words in Carter's ears as they recorded—the song was another million seller. Though not a beach song, after the song's meteoric rise General Johnson began performing the song live during the Chairmen's shows and consequently it received a lot of play in the Carolinas.

Carter would never have another hit as big as "Patches," as his type of music wouldn't fare as well during the disco age. He would continue to record with Atlantic for a few years before going back to Fame Records, then he'd record for ABC, Venture, and a few other labels. He'd sign with the Atlanta based Ichiban label in the 1980s, where he would be most famous for the off-color single "Strokin.'" Though never played on the radio, the record company created an audience for the record putting it on jukeboxes and having it played in clubs.

Carter is a member of both the Alabama and Georgia Music Halls of Fame.

The Catalinas

BEACH MUSIC DISCOGRAPHY: "You Haven't the Right" (Scepter 12188, 1967: Did Not Chart); "Summertime's Calling Me" (Sugarbush 114, 1975: Did Not Chart).

Originally formed in 1958, The Catalinas are one of the longest-lived beach music groups in the Carolinas, and as a result there have been a massive number of line-up changes as well. The group was started when Buddy Emmerke and Wayne Donaho merged with O.C. Gravitte of a Charlotte group called the Kingbees (they later added member Bob Meyer as well) and added members Pam Kopp, Butch Gallagher, Judy Westmoreland, John Soldati, Frank Everett as well. They settled on the name The Catalinas, and though their membership in the late 1950s and early '60s was constantly changing, they quickly became popular playing fraternity parties and dances in the Carolinas. They eventually graduated to playing the Myrtle Beach Pavilion, reportedly drawing the some of the largest crowds that venue ever saw. In 1961 the group recorded four songs in Memphis, though only Emmerke, Gravitte, Meyer, Tommy Black and Johnny Wyatt made the trip. From this session they released "Wooly Wooly Willie" on Rita Records, and their signature song "Hey Little Girl" was eventually released on Zebra Records. Neither record was a national hit, though "Hey Little Girl" received a fair amount of airplay in the Carolinas.

Over the next few years the group remained popular in the Southeast though predictably the lineup changed frequently, and by 1967 the group consisted of Tom Black, Jack Stallings, Sidney Smith, Johnny Edwards, Tom Plyler, Tommy Garner, Rob Thorne and Johnny and Gary Barker. The group had worked with high school classmate Ted Hall and his booking agency Hit Attractions, and Hall arranged to have the group go to Nashville and record some songs, among them "You Haven't the Right" and "Tick Tock." Gary Barker told me, "'You Haven't the Right' was written by Tom Plyler in 1966, and The Four Seasons were really hot back in those days and we had a lead singer, Tom Black, who sang a lot like Frankie Valli, so we—kinda unintentionally—patterned the arrangement after the Four Seasons." The song was released on the Scepter label, and although it well in some regional markets, especially in the South (and oddly enough in San Diego), it didn't sell nationally. The group recorded some other tracks for the label, but none was ever released, so the group carried on, its lineup ever changing, still waiting for that hit that eluded them. They changed their sound at one point to mirror some of the popular horn bands in the late 1960s and early '70s, but by about 1973 they had moved back to the beach music sound.

In 1972 Bo Schronce had become the group's lead, and there were other personnel changes as well. Johnny Barker was still the group's keyboardist, and he wrote "Summertime's Calling Me" one night on the way to Boone, North Carolina, to play a gig. "I was trying to come up with an idea for a song," Barker told the author:

Two lines—"I want to sit there in the sand," "and watch those golden tans go walking by"—came to me. After trying for a while to come up with something that everyone could relate to, especially the

The Catalinas, circa mid–1960s (photograph courtesy Gary Barker).

college crowds, I came up with "I know it isn't fair, cause you might really care, but it's different now, that summertime's callin' me." I mean, after all, we all can't wait for the end of winter's misery and that first real summer vacation, and so I thought I had what we in the music business call a good "hook" for a song at the very least. Well, I was driving alone, but knew for certain I had to write this down. So I found a matchbook cover in the car and carefully scribbled the chorus down. I knew the rest of the story would come in time.

When the song was completed the group recorded it and added it to their repertoire, but much to their disappointment it didn't catch on at first. Gary Barker noted "We were really excited about it and started performing it everywhere we went, but nothing happened and nobody seemed interested. Finally, we even kinda quit playing it." The hope had turned into another disappointment.

"And then something very strange happened during one of our jobs at a sorority party at Wofford College," John Barker said:

> We introduced "Summertime's Calling Me" as our latest recording, and stood there amazed at what we saw next. All of the girls in the sorority lined up and performed for us while we played. Not only did they know all of the words to our song, but they had their own version of a line dance they had created for each line of the song. I remember Gary and I looking at each other in disbelief at what was going on. From that night forward, "Summertime's Calling Me" grew quickly in popularity, mainly on college campuses in Georgia, North Carolina, and South Carolina. It became an anthem for getting out of town, heading for the beach, and most of all, for having fun.

"Summertime's Callin Me" has since come to be regarded as the first "new" beach song, as it pre-dated other now-classic regional beach hits such as "I Love Beach Music," "Myrtle Beach Days," and "Carolina Girls." Before "Summertime's Calling Me" songs now regarded as beach music were written to get air time, to sell records, and hopefully, to make the Top 40 on *national* radio. But many artists looked at the regional popularity of the record, started to write songs like it as a result, and so "Summertime's" started a new trend, the composition and marketing of songs about the beach *designed* to be beach music. Within a few years bands all over the South were recording songs about beach music itself, about sitting on the beach, about summertime, and any and all associated areas of beach music. Though The Catalinas have had a frequently-changing roster over the last fifty-plus years, Gary Barker is still with the group and his brother is performing with them once again as well. Though still known for the quality of their performances, ultimately their legacy will always be as the group who recorded "Summertime's Calling Me" and thus started the emergence of original beach music that continues to this day.

The Chairmen of the Board

BEACH MUSIC DISCOGRAPHY: "Give Me Just a Little More Time" (Invictus 9074,1970: Billboard Pop #3); "(You've Got Me) Dangling on a String" (Invictus 9078, 1970: Billboard Pop #38); "Everything's Tuesday" (Invictus 9079, 1970: Billboard Pop #38); "Pay to the Piper" (Invictus 9081, 1971: Billboard Pop #13); "On the Beach" (Surfside 800414, 1980: Did Not Chart); "Carolina Girls" b/w "Down at the Beach Club" (Surfside 800902, 1980: Did Not Chart).

General Norman Johnson got his start in the music business as a member of Humdingers in the early 1950s, a group that eventually became the Showmen and signed with Minit records (see the entry for the Showmen). He left that group in 1968 to work for the famed songwriting team of Holland, Dozier, and Holland, who by that time had decided to leave Motown and form the Invictus label. Though the original idea was that the group, consisting of Johnson and Danny Woods, Harrison Kennedy, and Eddie Curtis, would share lead vocal duties, very quickly it became apparent that Johnson's voice was the most unique, and his vocal on "Give Me Just a Little More Time" confirmed that. The song, with instrumental backing by the famous Funk Brothers of Motown, went all the way to #3 on the pop charts and #2 in England. The record sold more than one million copies, and the group was awarded a gold record by the Recording Industry Association of America.

The Chairmen of the Board would go on to have three more Top 40 hits in rapid succession. "You've Got Me Dangling on a String" would go to #38 and #5 in England, "Everything's Tuesday" would also go to #38 on the U.S. pop charts and #12 in the UK and the group's first 1971 release, "Pay to the Piper," would go to #13 and #34 on the UK charts. Having had their first four singles sell extremely well, the group appeared ready to make a run on the charts that would last for years to come. In the meantime, Johnson was writing hits for other artists as well, and he wrote "Patches," which Clarence Carter recorded in 1970 and which won Johnson a Grammy award and contributed to his distinction of being named BMI songwriter of the year. He also wrote "Bring the Boys Home" for Freda Payne, the million seller "Somebody's Been Sleeping" for 100 Proof Aged in Soul, and the #1 million seller "Want Ads" for Honey Cone and many others.

But all was not well for the Chairmen, and after "Pay to the Piper" few of their singles charted. Johnson was also having differences with Invictus, because as one of the most successful singer/songwriters of the early 1970s, he felt he should be compensated more appropriately but Invictus did not agree. Johnson eventually left to pursue a solo career at Arista,

The Chairmen of the Board, circa late 1970s (photograph courtesy Ken Knox).

but because there he didn't feel he had enough artistic control, he left that label and re-formed the Chairmen of the Board with original member Danny Woods and former back-up member Ken Knox. Knox says Johnson told the group, "'We're gonna go down to the Carolinas, and do this music they have called beach music. I'm going to write some songs about the culture, where all the kids go down to the beach and places like the Pad.'" Johnson himself later said, "For the first time in eight years, I enjoyed performing music without the depression of the music business. I found an independent music industry that was still free of monopoly, politics and categorization." In 1979, Johnson and Mike Branch formed Surfside records in an effort to revitalize a beach music industry they felt was "too dependent on old recordings." They felt that the genre couldn't survive based only on classic recordings, and so a whole new era began for the group, kicked off by 1980's "On the Beach." "General said 'I'm going to write a song called "On the Beach"'" Knox told me. "He wrote 'Cool water at my feet, ice cold beer in my hand…' I mean, because that's the way it was, and that's what people were doing. The song was perfect—it gave you a scenario of what Carolina beach music was all about … that song kind of summed it up." The song became an instant hit in the Carolinas, although there was one element of the song that, to this day, causes some confusion. One of the lines says "Everybody loves to ball," and many fans seem to think this refers to one of those elements many beach music songs deal with in addition to the sand, suds, and surf—sex. "No, no" Knox said. "It means everybody likes to party … it's like when the kids get away from their parents and come to the beach they let their hair down and party till daylight. It wasn't a reference to sex."

Next up were the back-to-back hits "Carolina Girls" and "Down at the Beach Club." "Everybody has always talked about and sung about California girls, but nobody had really sung about the Carolina girls" Knox told me. "Well, the General really knew what people would like to hear about, and he said 'I'm gonna write about the girls here.' And what the song did was to give pride to the women of the Carolinas—so much pride that you saw 'Carolina Girls, Best in the World' on license plates, t-shirts, and stickers everywhere. Because of that song, every generation will be proud of the culture; being a Carolina girl means you're the best in the world." In many ways the song was unlike any beach music song, ever. It is a recognizable brand, the slogan has been on the lips of thousands, and it has become a real symbol of pride in the Carolinas. People who don't know a thing about beach music, or the Chairmen, or much about the culture at all, may well know that song, arguably the most significant work of Carolina beach music ever recorded. The flipside of the single held another powerful song, "Down at the Beach Club," because it certainly could have been a hit single in its own right. "General said 'Let's do one about the beach club. If you're at the beach you go down to the beach club, or if you're inland you say 'Yeah, we're going down to the beach club tonight to see the Chairmen of the Board.' The way he wrote it you can see it, you can hear the music—and it doesn't have to be our music—you heard the music of the Tams, the Embers, the Band of Oz, or whoever. The DJ was always playing beach music at the beach club, so that's where the record came from."

The Chairmen would go on to record a number of new beach tunes throughout the '80s, and would keep right on performing until General Johnson passed away in 2010. "I feel very fortunate to have been with him for 37 years" Knox said. "When General passed I received probably a couple of thousand emails from people saying 'Please keep the band going, keep the legacy going.' General's family and the fans wanted me to keep it going, and thank God they stood behind me." Today Knox carries the torch as he still performs those classics. The group was inducted into the North Carolina Music Hall of Fame in 1999.

Gene Chandler

BEACH MUSIC DISCOGRAPHY: "Duke of Earl" (Vee-Jay 416, 1962: Billboard Pop #1); "Nothing Can Stop Me" (Constellation 149, 1965: Billboard Pop #18); "Groovy Situation" (Mercury 73083, 1970: Billboard Pop #12); "Let Me Make Love to You" (Chi-Sound 2451, 1980: Did Not Chart).

Chicago-born Eugene Dixon formed his first group, the Gaytones, while a student at Englewood High School in 1955. By 1957 he was a member of the Dukays along with James Lowe, Earl Edwards, and Ben Broyles, but he was drafted that same year and served overseas in the Army until 1960. When his enlistment was up he rejoined the Dukays and they added his cousin Shirley Johnson just before the quintet signed with the Nat label. In 1961 they recorded "The Girl's a Devil," which reached #64 on the Hot 100, and "Nite Owl," which reached #73. For their third release Dixon wanted to do a song the group had recorded "Duke of Earl," a song that originated from the Dukays warming up sessions when they'd sing "do-do-do-do" and Dixon would sing "duke-duke-duke." To this "duke" sound Dixon added Edwards first name to come up with the name "Duke of Earl," filled out the rest of the song, and they recorded a demo and asked Nat to release it. Nat didn't agree about the song's quality and passed, so Dixon shopped the record and the Vee-Jay label decided to release it. Changing his last name to Chandler to avoid contractual problems (and because he liked the sound of actor Jeff Chandler's last name) he released it as Gene Chandler on Vee-Jay where it hit #1 on the pop charts in February 1962. The Dukays folded soon afterwards, and Chandler went forward as a solo act.

At this point Chandler made the somewhat unusual decision to play on the popularity of "Duke of Earl" by dressing in a cape, monocle, and top hat while performing under the name The Duke of Earl. While this did result in one low charting song ("Walk with the Duke," #91), it resulted in a loss of credibility to some extent as some viewed him as a novelty act. However, after three singles as the Duke, Chandler seemed to realize it had played out and released "You Threw a Lucky Punch," an answer record to Mary Wells' "You Beat Me to the Punch." "Punch" came in at #49 on the pop charts, but it was the flip side that Chandler preferred, a song called "Rainbow." That song charted also, going to #47 in 1963. He'd have three more releases for Vee-Jay before heading to Constellation, a new label founded by Bunky Sheppard and Ewart Abner. While there Chandler had nine records make the pop charts, mostly the lower reaches, though most fared better on the R&B charts. The best of these, by far, and his most successful single since "Duke of Earl," was 1965's "Nothing Can Stop Me."

While a record such as "Duke of Earl" was a hit in its own right that worked as a shag song, the Curtis Mayfield-penned "Nothing Can Stop Me" was a mid-tempo song that was beach music to the core like other mid 60's Chicago soul by acts such as the Radiants, Tony Clarke, and the Artistics. When Constellation folded both Checker and Brunswick released his songs, but by the late '60s he was starting to branch out in to areas besides just performing. He formed two production companies, served as President of Bamboo records (and discovered Mel and Tim), and founded his own Mr Chand label. He signed with Mercury in 1970 and hit gold once again with "Groovy Situation." Written by Russell Lewis and Herman Davis, the song was one Chandler had produced on Mel and Tim's *Good Guys Only Win in the Movies* album on Bamboo in 1969. Their version was never released as a single, so Chandler decided to issue it as his first Mercury single. It sold more than a million copies and went to #12 on the pop charts and #8 on the R&B charts, and so once again Chandler had a big hit. But performing, producing, and being a label owner was too much for Chandler, and both Bamboo and Mr. Chand folded within three years. He signed with old pal Curtis Mayfield's Curtom label next, but no hits resulted and he was out at Curtom by 1973.

Between 1973 and 1978 he had just one release on the obscure Marsel label, and without a record contract his career hit a low point, punctuated by a 1976 drug arrest and prison sentence.

Most singers' careers would have been over at this point, but when released from jail in 1978 he signed with Carl Davis's Chi-Sound label. With just his second release, 1978's disco offering "Get Down," he was back in the spotlight, as the single went to #3 on the R&B charts, his highest soul charter since 1966. Chi-Sound had a distribution deal with 20th Century, so Chandler's next seventeen releases through early 1982 alternated between the two labels, though most were on Chi-Sound. One of these, 1980's "Does She Have a Friend?," did well on the soul charts, going to #28 and bubbling under at #101 on the pop charts. When DJs in the beach clubs flipped the record they found a delightful song, "Let Me Make Love to You," which came at time when shaggers were struggling to find new songs to dance to. Though it never charted, it was extremely popular in the Carolinas.

Chandler continued to release singles into the mid-1980s, and had his last minor R&B chart hit, "Lucy," in 1986. He is a member of the Grammy Hall of Fame and the Rhythm and Blues Music Hall of Fame.

Bruce Channel

BEACH MUSIC DISCOGRAPHY: "Hey! Baby" (Smash 1731, 1962: Billboard Pop #1).

Born Bruce McMeans in Jacksonville, Texas, Channel got his start playing with a group called the Little Gentlemen in his home state in the 1950s. As his reputation began to grow, he played the *Louisiana Hayride* radio show, which featured up-and-coming performers such as Elvis Presley, Hank Williams, Johnny Cash and others, and it was at about that time that he took his mother's maiden name "Channel" because he was told the name McMeans didn't have "marquee value." Instead of pronouncing it "channel" (like a television channel) it was to be pronounced like the perfume, Chanel No. 5. Channel had been writing songs since he was a teenager, and one of those early compositions came about in 1959 when he says he "wrote 'Hey! Baby' with a friend of mine named Margaret Cobb." Though not a published songwriter, Cobb had apparently written hundreds of songs, and working together Channel says they wrote "Hey, Baby!" in about 30 minutes. Channel said he had been playing the song in clubs for a while, and in 1961 he played the song for Fort Worth producer Bill Smith who had the Le Cam label. Smith liked the song and booked studio time, and when Channel arrived at the studio he met Delbert McClinton and his band, the Straightjackets, and they recorded "Hey, Baby!" in just a few takes. The song sounds much less like a country song than it does R&B, and McClinton's harmonica unifies the song. The record took off, and Smash picked it up for national distribution. It shot to #1 on the Billboard charts by March 1962 and stayed at #1 for three weeks, and it also went to #2 in the UK. The song sold over one million copies and was awarded a gold record, and Bruce Channel and "Hey! Baby" were international sensations.

"That began a career of touring with names like Fats Domino, Brook Benton and Curtis Mayfield and the Impressions," Channel told me. "While touring England with Delbert McClinton, we did some shows with the Beatles in their early days when Pete Best was their drummer." Indeed, Channel was the headliner for that show, and a young John Lennon was a fan of Channel's and was fascinated by McClinton's harmonica playing and how Channel had incorporated it into "Hey! Baby." Reportedly, this was what led to Lennon's harmonica use on "Love Me Do," which would go to #1 for the Beatles in 1964 and would encourage the instrument's use on many other early Beatles songs, such as "I Should Have Known Better," "Thank You Girl," "I'll Get You" and others. As many have pointed out, Channel's "Hey! Baby" therefore had a major formative effect on rock-and-roll.

Over the next few years Channel continued to have records chart, such as "Number One Man," "Come on Baby" and "Going Back to Louisiana." He never had another big chart hit that could match "Hey! Baby," and over the ensuing decades dozens of artists have covered the song. But by the late '60s Channel was tired of touring and decided to call it quits as a full-time performer. Today he works as an active songwriter and publisher in Nashville who has written award-winning songs for John Conlee, Janie Fricke and T.G. Sheppard. But he'll always be identified with "Hey! Baby," the song that was not only a #1 hit and is a beach music staple but inspired the Beatles as well. He's proud that "After all these years, 'Hey! Baby' still has legs." It's a beach music classic and a seminal rock-and-roll hit as well.

The Checkers

BEACH MUSIC DISCOGRAPHY: "The White Cliffs of Dover" (King 4675, Did Not Chart 1953); "Over the Rainbow" (King 4719, Did Not Chart 1954); "Don't Stop Dan" (King 4710, Did Not Chart 1954); "I Wasn't Thinkin, I Was Drinkin" (King 4751, Did Not Chart 1954).

The Checkers got their start when Charlie White and Bill Brown left Billy Ward's Dominoes in 1952. Brown had sung lead on the Dominoes "Sixty-Minute Man," which was voted the year's #1 record and #1 on the R&B charts, where it was in the Top 10 for months and sold more than one million records. But even with this success, all was not well within the group, and some members resented Billy Ward's control over most aspects of their lives. So White left (ostensibly to join the Clovers), and then Brown left too, with the idea of forming a new group.

According to Marv Goldberg, Brown knew a singer whose name has come down to us only as Joe who had been with Brown in the group the 5 International Gospel Singers of South Carolina. Brown, White, and "Joe" met Irwin "Teddy" Williams and his friend John Carnegie, who were members of a local group called the Checkers (so named in honor of the Dominoes). As the Checkers they got a contract with King, and though they cut several records in 1952 none of them charted. Perhaps because of the lack of success the group was having, or the promise of a chance to join the Clovers (which he did), Charlie White left the group. Perry Heyward was brought in, after one release he left and was soon replaced by David Baughn, who had been with the first, short-lived incarnation of The Drifters in May of 1953. In September, Brown, Irwin, Baughn, and the mysterious "Joe" went into the studio to record again, and it was from this session that "White Cliffs of Dover" emerged.

Originally released a decade earlier as "(There'll Be Bluebirds Over) The White Cliffs of Dover," the song was made popular by British singer Vera Lynn during World War II. Written in 1941, the song referenced the beautiful white cliffs of Dover where German and British pilots often engaged in aerial combat, and the song was a tune of hope for the times. The Checkers went to a lot of trouble to remove the original lyrics which were certainly much more specific to World War II with the mention of bombs and angry skies, and much more melancholy. With Brown and Baughn trading lead the Checkers' version is one of the finest vocal productions of the early 1950s. Nevertheless, while Lynn's song had been a major hit in England, the Checkers' version fell flat other than in some local markets.

While one can see how a song about a war in the not-too-distant past might not have been a hit, it's really hard to understand how their next release, 1954's "Don't Stop Dan" wasn't a smash. Released in April, the song reprised Brown's "lovin' Dan" persona from the Dominoes' smash hit "Sixty Minute Man." Brown was of course the lead singer on both tunes (which no doubt further confused listeners concerning the rumors that the Dominoes and the Checkers were actually the same group), and the subject matter was more of the same risqué, double entendre that had populated the Dominoes' hit. The saga of "Dan," whose female friend tells him not to stop because he has 59 minutes to go, did well in many large regional markets, but inexplicably it did not chart nationally, despite its high quality and the ties to its #1 ranked predecessor by the Dominoes.

In June of that year the group released "Over The Rainbow," another cover of a song released more than a decade previously. The song had been written for the 1939 film *The Wizard of Oz*, and though Judy Garland's version would be ranked the number one song of the century by the Recording Industry Association of America, the Checkers version did not chart despite superior vocal performances by the group. Perhaps what makes the song's failure all the more surprising is that several artists would score chart hits with the song in subsequent years. Perhaps feeling they were going nowhere after another dud, all except Brown apparently left to join other groups, so he recruited several new members including Eddie Harris, David Martin, and James Williams. This group recorded four new songs in October 1954, including the fine "I Wasn't Thinking, I Was Drinking," which incorporated the boisterous drinking scenario made popular by performers such as Peppermint Harris, Jimmy Liggins, Stick McGhee, and the Clovers. This song did nothing as well, and the group disbanded in early 1955.

There were a few more releases credited to the Checkers in the late 1950s, but none of those singles were by the Checkers group detailed in these pages. Apparently someone felt the name was a valuable commodity and issued these sides giving them credit, but after that, a reissue or two was all that was released in the group's name, primarily, as Goldberg notes, "for the Carolina 'Beach Music' crowd." Only in the Carolinas have the Checkers gained the recognition that is so richly deserved.

Dee Clark

BEACH MUSIC DISCOGRAPHY: "Raindrops" (Vee-Jay 383, Billboard Pop #2 1961).

Born Delectus Clark in Blytheville, Arkansas, as a child his family moved to Chicago. He was encouraged to sing and eventually he joined a group called the Hambone Kids, and in 1952 the group recorded "Hambone" on Okeh when he was just 14. Soon thereafter he joined the Goldentones, who changed their names to the Kool Gents and recorded two singles and two more as the Delegates before Clark went solo on Falcon (a subsidiary of Vee Jay) in 1957. His first three recordings on Falcon didn't chart, but the fourth, on Abner (another Vee-Jay subsidiary), "Nobody but You," went to #21 on the pop charts in 1958. He followed that with "Just Keep It Up" (#18), the very fine "Hey Little Girl" (#20), and four more Top 100 singles over the next two years. He toured with Little Richard's backup band, The Upsetters, and in 1961 he finally hit it big with "Raindrops."

Though "Raindrops" isn't about the weather, the song utilized the sounds of rain and thunder similar to the way the Tymes' "So Much in Love" and the O'Jays' "Lonely Drifter" used the sounds of the ocean two years later. Clark's wailing falsetto and plaintive cries propelled the record up the charts, as it reached #2 on the pop charts, #3 on the R&B charts, and went to #1 in New Zealand and made the Top Ten in a number of countries around the world. It would later be covered by a number of pop artists, Narvel Felts would have a Top 40 country hit with it in 1974, and even Clark himself would redo it in 1973.

After the peak he had reached with "Raindrops," his fall was precipitous and steep indeed. Of the next eight singles he released over the next two years, only "I'm Going Back to School" and "Crossfire Time" charted, disappointingly at #52 and #92 respectively. More surprising still, these were his last American chart records of any type. Though he recorded eight singles on Constellation between 1964 and 1966, from 1967 to 1975 he recorded on a variety of well-known labels such as Columbia, Wand, Liberty, United Artists, and Chelsea but he never again had a song make the American charts. His 1975 single "Ride a Wild Horse" did chart in England, reaching #16 during the Northern Soul boom when many soul acts were scoring hits overseas, but that was his last hit in any country.

Once his recording career was over, like many artists of the '50s and '60s who did not earn substantial songwriting royalties, he would find himself struggling to make ends meet financially. By the 1980s he was reportedly living on welfare, and due to his financial situation his only appreciable income was earned from playing occasional oldies shows. Despite the mild paralysis that was the result of a stroke in 1987, he performed up until his death of a heart attack in 1990 when he was 52.

Doug Clark and the Hot Nuts

BEACH MUSIC DISCOGRAPHY: "Baby Let Me Bang Your Box" (Jubilee 5536, Did Not Chart 1966).

Doug Clark and the Hot Nuts began as the Tops in Chapel Hill, North Carolina, in 1955. Formed by Doug Clark, his brother John, and several other students from Lincoln High School, the group was put together in an effort to earn money playing fraternity parties at UNC. They broke up and reformed the next year as the Doug Clark Combo, and continued as a party band over the next few years. Before long one of the most popular songs in their repertoire was the bawdy "Hot Nuts," which cemented their reputation not only as a party band, but a "blue" band who sang sexually suggestive songs as well.

In order to capitalize on the popularity of the song, they changed their name to Doug Clark and the Hot Nuts, and over the ensuing years the band cultivated their reputation during their live performances by telling dirty jokes, calling out members of the audience, and singing songs like "He's Got the Whole World by the Balls," "Big Jugs," "The Bearded Clam," and many others. Their reputation soon brought them to the attention of the well-established R&B label Jubilee, who, although seeing a potential for record sales, was reluctant to have them record their brand of music on the label. Jubilee's answer was to establish a subsidiary, the appropriately titled Gross label, and there the group was able to record their off-color music without casting aspersions on Jubliee, whose name never appeared anywhere on any of their albums. Their first album on Gross was 1961's *Nuts to You*, and by this time the ever-changing line-up of the band consisted of Doug Clark, June Bug, "Big" John Clark, William "Chicken" Little, and Prince Taylor. Among the album's tracks were "Let's Have a Party," "Gay Caballero," "Hot Nuts" (part one and part two), and "Two Old Maids," and if the track titles left any doubt, the album was labeled "For Adults Only" and had a picture of Clark flipping the bird on the cover.

This was the first in a series of albums of party songs and "blue" music, most of which focused on the college party and fraternity market and were titled as such. *On Campus* (1963), *Homecoming* (1963), *Rush Week* (1964), *Panty Raid* (1965), *Summer Session* (1966), and *Hell*

Night (1967) all played on the college theme, and the pictures on their covers did likewise. *Summer Session* included a song originally done by the Toppers called "Baby Let Me Bang Your Box," and for the first time Jubilee released a Hot Nuts' song as a single under their own imprint. Though not a shag song, it is a beach music party record in the mold of the Swingin Medallions "Double Shot" or The Five Du-Tones' "Shake a Tail Feather." The record did not chart, although it was popular (predictably) on the southeastern college circuit. A second release, "Milk the Cow," was their second and last 45 on Jubilee, and did not chart either. But even on the fraternity party circuit things were beginning to change by the late 1960s, the group's next two albums, *Freak Out* (1968) and *With a Hat On* (1969), broke away from the frat house party antics in favor of broader appeal. Unfortunately Jubilee and their sister label Josie went bankrupt in 1970, and the band's recording contract was voided with the collapse.

Less than a decade later, when retro-music became popular in late '70s films such as *American Graffiti, Big Wednesday, American Hot Wax*, and others, *Animal House* featured a raucous party band called Otis Day and the Knights, and Doug Clark believed that the Hot Nuts were the inspiration for the group in the film. He claimed that not being acknowledged as such or being chosen to play the role was a great disappointment, one of greatest in his life. In the February 1992 issue of *Penthouse* magazine, whose cover said "The Hot Nuts: The Most Outrageous U.S. Rock Band," Clark said, "If the band they had in that film wasn't modeled after us, I don't know who it could have been."

Despite never having been a successful recording act on the national scene, Doug Clark and the Hot Nuts were one of the most popular bands on the college party circuit in the 1960s. Though Doug Clark died in 2002 the group performs today as Doug Clark's Hot Nuts, and still packs in the crowds with their raucous party rock and blue music, a throwback to the nostalgic times when their special brand of music was as much a part of the college scene as draft beer, panty raids, and freshman beanies.

Tony Clarke

BEACH MUSIC DISCOGRAPHY: "The Entertainer" b/w "This Heart of Mine" (Chess 1924, Billboard Pop #31 1964).

Many things about the man who is remembered in music history as Tony Clarke are debatable and shrouded in mystery. He was probably born in New York City as Ralph Thomas Williams, though some sources suggest that in fact his name may have been Ralph Ferguson or Ralph Clarke. He was raised in Detroit, and he was training to be a chef when he decided to pursue a career in music instead. He first recorded "Hot—Rod—Car" as Tall Tonio with the Mello-Dee's for Stepp in 1960. The record was not a hit, nor was his next single, "Cry," which was recorded on the Fascination label in 1962 under the name Tony Clarke.

Clarke had begun writing music as well, and in 1963 two of his songs charted for Etta

James, "Pushover" (#25) and "Two Sides to Every Story" (#63). Clarke was also writing for other artists, such as the Vibrations, and he also co-wrote "Mr. Bus Driver" for David Ruffin on Check-Mate in 1962. He was also apparently writing under pseudonyms such as Tony Lois and even Thelma Williams as well. Clarke was still trying to make it as a recording artist, and he signed with Chess and released "(The Story Of) Woman, Love and a Man" and "Ain't Love Good, Ain't Love Proud" in 1964, neither of which charted.

His third Chess release was "The Entertainer," and it went big. With an organ-played introduction from "I Got Plenty O' Nothing" by way of George Gershwin's *Porgy and Bess*, the single rose to #31 on the Billboard Top 100 and went into the Top 10 on the R&B charts. The backup singers for "The Entertainer" were another Chess group, the Radiants, who that same year would have a hit with "Voice Your Choice" as well as "Ain't No Big Thing." "The Entertainer" was backed with "This Heart of Mine," and for that single the backing vocals were by The Celebrities (Lloyd Robinson, Thomas Pennington, Scott Snowden, Norman Dixon and Mike Hemp). The flip was a good song that probably should have been a single release in its own right.

The success of "The Entertainer" made Clarke a star-of-the-moment, and he earned top billing at several engagements in Detroit such as the Rooster Tail and the Twenty Grand, went on tour with James Brown and even appeared on the Dick Clark Revue. He reportedly leveraged his success into buying the Brute label from LeBaron Taylor, and is listed as composer and producer on the Brute releases by the Tokays ("Baby, Baby, Baby") and Buddy Smith ("When You Lose the One You Love"). In regard to his own recordings he had two more non-charting singles on Chess in 1965, and then recorded his final Chess single, "Landslide," in 1967. Though it too failed to make the U.S. charts, it found an eager listening audience in England and it was a huge Northern Soul hit in the '70s, coming in at #15 of Kev Roberts's list of the Top 500 greatest Northern Soul hits of all time.

Clarke moved to Hollywood, and there he was co-founder with Roger Spotts of his own company, Earthquake Productions. He recorded "Ghetto Man" on Chicory, and even appeared in the Sidney Poitier film *They Call Me Mr. Tibbs*, where he had a bit part as a detective. He never seemed to be able to resist the pull of Detroit however, mainly because his children lived there with his mother and ex-wife. On one trip home he signed with M.S. Records, and in 1968 released another non-charter "They Call Me a Wrong Man," which is also a highly regarded Northern Soul disk. While he continued to write music, "Wrong Man" was his last single release. In 1971 Clarke broke into his wife's house and during a domestic dispute reportedly pushed his mother aside as he tried to hit is wife with a tire iron. She claimed she shot him in the arm in self-defense, but the bullet ricocheted into his chest and killed him. He was 31 years old.

Judy Clay & William Bell

BEACH MUSIC DISCOGRAPHY: "Private Number" (Stax 0005, 1968: Billboard Pop #75).

Judy Clay was born Judith Grace Guions in St. Paul, North Carolina, and was raised by her grandmother in Fayetteville, North Carolina. She started singing in church as a child, and after moving to Brooklyn in the early 1950s she sang with the choir at Faith Temple in Harlem. There she came to the attention of Lee Drinkard Warwick of the gospel group the Drinkard Singers. Lee was Cissy Houston's sister and Dionne Warwick's mother, and Judy was soon involved in the group with them, as well as with Dionne's sister Delia, who who later go by the name Dee Dee Warwick. Clay moved in with the Drinkards in East Orange, New Jersey, and sang lead vocals on several numbers during an appearance by the group at the Newport Jazz Festival in 1957 when the group came to the attention of RCA and landed a recording contract. Judy eventually went solo, changing her name to Judy Clay (although Amanda Knight was first suggested) and signing with Ember Records in 1961. Singles on Ember and then Lavette failed, and when Lavette was bought out by Scepter a series of five singles between 1964 and 1966 all failed to chart.

Frustrated by a lack of chart success made more pointed by the accomplishments of her adopted sisters Dionne and Dee Dee Warwick, she signed with Atlantic, and there recorded two duets with Billy Vera. In 1967 "Storybook Children" hit #20 on the R&B chart and #54 on the Hot 100, and in 1968 "Country Girl–City Man" did even better, charting at #36 on the pop charts and #41 on the R&B charts. Her next single would also be a duet, with Stax recording artist William Bell. Bell had his first recordings as a member of the Del Rios in the late 1950s, and would eventually sign the newly formed (and renamed) Stax records. His first single, "You Don't Miss Your Water," would only reach #95 on the Billboard Hot 100, but it was the beginning of a long, productive career that would see Bell regarded as one of the label's top draws and would produce a number of hits (see the entry for Bell). "I happened to be in the studio when Judy was doing a session and she didn't have enough material" Bell told me:

> Her producer asked me if I had anything that she could record. Well, this song "Private Number" was a song that had been kicking around in my head for a while, but I only had one verse and a chorus written. I told him I'd finish it and have it ready the next day and Judy could record it then. Well, as luck would have it, she had to leave the next morning and go back to New York for some business. So Booker (T. Jones, of Booker T. & the M.G.s) and I finished up the song that night and went back into the studio and did a demo of it. On that, I sang the entire song. We sent the tapes to New York for Judy to hear so she could learn the song and then put her voice on the tapes. Somebody—it might have been Jerry Wexler—had the bright idea that this would be a great duet. They kept my verse and chorus and they put Judy on the second verse and on the choruses singing harmony with me. It turned out great.

"Private Number" was a modest hit, going to #75 on the pop charts, but was even bigger on the R&B charts, peaking at #17. The song was even more successful overseas, and went all the way to #8 in the UK. "It's strange when you think about it though," Bell said. The two of us were never together in the studio singing—even though it sounds like we were—but it was a big hit. We were really proud of it because it was kind of a fluke. We did eventually get a chance to perform it together three or four times live on stage together, but never in the studio."

Clay and Bell would go on to do one more duet for Stax, 1968's "My Baby Specializes," but it would be much less successful and would only make the R&B charts. Clay would return to Atlantic for another duet with Vera, and would have a few solo efforts during the next decade but without much chart success. She would go on to a career largely as a backup singer then move to gospel music before dying in 2001. Bell would stay at Stax until 1974 then sign with Mercury where the greatest success of his career awaited him with "Trying to Love Two," "Easy Comin' Out (Hard Goin' In)" and other recordings.

The Clovers

BEACH MUSIC DISCOGRAPHY: "One Mint Julep" (Atlantic 963, 1952: Billboard Pop Did Not Chart, R&B #2); "Your Cash Ain't Nothing but Trash"(Atlantic 1035, 1954: Billboard Pop Did Not Chart, R&B #6); "Nip Sip" b/w "If I Could Be Loved by You" (Atlantic 1073, 1955: Billboard Pop Did Not Chart, R&B #10); "Drive It Home" (Atlantic 2129, 1961: Did Not Chart).

The Clovers started out as a group Hal Lucas formed around 1946 at Washington, D.C.'s Armstrong High School along with Billy Shelton and Thomas Woods. They were soon joined by John "Buddy" Bailey and became the 4 Clovers. In 1948, Matthew McQuater replaced Shelton, and at about that same time bass singer Harold Winley replaced Woods. In 1950 they met Lou Krefetz, who agreed to manage them and soon got them a recording session with Rainbow Records in New York. They recorded two songs, and a cover of Eddie Cantor's "Yes Sir, That's My Baby" was released as their first single though it was not a hit. Not long afterwards they added Bill Harris to the group, and Krefetz was able to get them an audition with Ahmet Ertegun of the up-and-coming Atlantic label. In February 1951 they signed with Atlantic, and their first two single releases, "Don't You Know I Love You" and "Fool, Fool, Fool," both went to #1 on the R&B charts and collectively sold something in the neighborhood of three quarters of a million copies. By now the group was in great demand, frequently playing the Apollo and even appearing on the cover of *Cash Box*.

In December 1951 they recorded some new songs at Atlantic studios, among them "One Mint Julep," which was released in March 1952. Recorded with Buddy Bailey singing lead, its release followed Stick McGhee's "Drinkin Wine Spo-Dee-O-Dee" by a few years but was the first of a somewhat sustained series of "drinking-story songs" that would hit the airwaves in the early '50s. As the story of a man who ended up married all because of "One Mint Julep," it's a humorous take on the evils of drink. The man and a girl he meets have a few "nips," but then he kisses her and one thing leads to another. Later Bailey tells us getting frisky has saddled him with six extra children, so the dangers of drink are all too apparent. "One Mint Julep" was a hit, peaking at #2 on the R&B charts. The song would be covered by other artists including Louis Prima, and in 1961 Ray Charles's version would go to #8 on the pop charts and #1 on the R&B charts.

After "One Mint Julep" the group would release six more singles from 1952 through 1954, and every one of them—"Ting-A-Ling," "Hey Miss Fannie," "Crawlin'," "Good Lovin'," "Comin' On," and "Lovey Dovey," would make the Top 10 on the R&B charts. The group was widely recognized as one of the biggest acts in the music business, and by April 1953 they had topped two million in record sales. The group did this while dealing with personnel changes once again, as Buddy Bailey was drafted and replaced by John Phillip, and Charlie White was let go and replaced by Billy Mitchell. It was with this line-up that they went into the studio in December 1953 to record several songs including "Your Cash Ain't Nothin' But Trash."

New member Billy Mitchell sang lead on the group's first recording of "Your Cash Ain't Nothin' But Trash," but this was not the version released as a single, although it was later released on some albums. The version most listeners know was recorded in April 1954 and released that June. Another storytelling/drinking song, it peaked at #6 and was a featured song in the 1955 movie *Rock 'n' Roll Revue.*

Buddy Bailey rejoined the group that year, but despite their hot streak of their next three single releases only "Blue Velvet" would chart and it would be their first release not to make the Top 10. They bounced back with the iconic beach song "Nip Sip," which was released in August 1955. Backed with another fine song, "If I Could Be Loved By You," "Nip Sip" went to #10 on the R&B charts, but it was one of the last drinking songs to perform well as those types of releases had run their course. The group would have three more Top 10 hits in 1956, but they'd suddenly go into a tailspin that would see them have no chart records at all in 1957 or 58. They'd leave their long-time home Atlantic Records for United Artists, and in June 1959 they'd record the Leiber and Stoller–penned semi-novelty song "Love Potion # 9." Done in a style similar to the songs Leiber and Stoller were producing for Coasters, it would be their highest-charting pop record and their best-selling single, going to #23 on the pop charts. But like the Coasters, the Clovers would see that the story-song market was drying up quickly, and in fact, "Love Potion #9" would be their last chart record.

The group disbanded in 1961, and almost immediately Harold Lucas and Billy Mitchell would form a new Clovers group with James Walton and Robert Russell. In October 1961, they returned to the Atlantic Studios to do four songs, including "Drive It Home" with Billy Mitchell singing lead. "Drive It Home" was released in December on Atlantic, and was a remake of a much more subdued 1953 song by Hal Paige also on Atlantic. The song did not chart, and soon the group was moving around for one-offs on different labels before becoming essentially an oldies act with a fluctuating membership. Unlike the other Clovers songs mentioned above "Drive it Home" found its greatest audience in beach music circles, so much so that in 1988 a Clovers group consisting of Harold Lucas along with Steve Charles, Johnny Mason, and John Bowie re-recorded "Drive It Home" for South Carolina's Ripete Records.

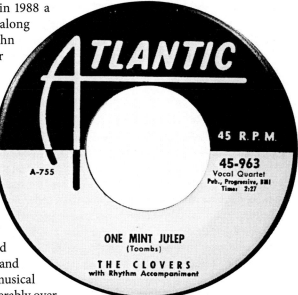

The Clovers had had an astounding twenty-one chart records and a legacy as a seminal rock and R&B group. From the earliest days of beach music, the Clovers' recordings have been an essential part of the beach music canon. The first two beach music compilations albums ever produced, Atlantic's 1967's *Beach Beat* and 1968's *Beach Beat Vol. 2,* now seen as prototypical examples of classic beach music albums, each contained selections by the Clovers, "One Mint Julep" and "Nip Sip" respectively. In a genre where musical tastes and standards have fluctuated considerably over

The Coasters

BEACH MUSIC DISCOGRAPHY: "Brazil" (Atco 6073, 1956: Did Not Chart); "Zing! Went the Strings of My Heart" (Atco 6116, 1958: Did Not Chart).

The Coasters had their origins in the 1940s in a variety of groups with ever-changing memberships. The A-Sharp Trio became the 4 Bluebirds, who became the Robins, who added solo artist Bobby Nunn, who sang as Mel Walker and the Bluenotes and as Maggie Hathaway and the Robins, with Johnny Otis, as the Nic Nacs, and as The Drifters, all of which occurred by 1955. The Los Angeles–based Robins—which included Carl Gardner, Bobby Nunn, Ty "Terrell" Leonard, Billy Richards, Roy Richards and Grady Chapman—had recorded a Jerry Leiber and Mike Stoller song called "Riot in Cell Block #9" with Richard Berry singing lead. The song was released on the Spark label, and didn't have an impact on the charts, but the Robins released a few more singles on Spark before Leiber and Stoller sold the label to Atlantic. At that point the group fractured, with Gardner and Nunn going to Atlantic. They were joined by vocalists Billy Guy and Leon Hughes, and guitar player Adolph Jacobs, and together they formed the Coasters and were signed to Atlantic's then new Atco label.

They first charted with "Down in Mexico," which went to #8 on the R&B charts, followed by "One Kiss Led to Another," which charted at #73 on the Billboard Hot 100. The flip side of "One Kiss" was "Brazil," a song composed by Ary Barroso in 1939. The song had been previously recorded by Xavier Cugat and the Jimmy Dorsey Orchestra, and is often considered the most famous Brazilian song ever written. Though the Coasters version did not chart, it no doubt inspired other versions, as Frank Sinatra recorded it the next year, followed by Bing Crosby, Paul Anka, and others. Though not a chart success, it would become a beach music classic, as would a 1980s version by the Poor Souls. But it was their next release, "Young Blood," that kicked off a long string of chart hits, going to #8 in 1957, while its flip side, "Searchin'," did even better by charting at #3.

After a few more releases, the group decided to leave Los Angeles and head to New York. Nunn and Hughes opted to stay in California, so the group added new members Will "Dub" Jones and Cornell Gunter. Their first effort was "Yakety Yak," which was a solid #1 smash in 1958. While "Yakety Yak" was wowing crowds, some listeners flipped the 45 over and found an excellent version of "Zing! Went the Strings of My Heart." Another cover of an old tune, the song had been written by songwriter James Hanley in 1935, and Judy Garland's 1939 recording was probably the most famous version, though notable artists such as Frank Sinatra and Dinah Shore had recorded it as well. The real anomaly concerning the record, though, is that it is so unlike the Coasters' hits up to that point. The three songs the group charted with in 1957, the year before "Zing!" was released, were "Young Blood," "Searchin'" and "Idol with the Golden Head," and clearly what audiences expected from the Coasters were the "novelty" or "storytelling" hits for which they were famous. This may explain why a quality recording such as "Zing!," with Jones and Gunter sharing lead vocals, went unnoticed by many listeners at the time, in that perhaps this love song with a doo-wop feel was so atypical for Coasters listeners that it just didn't register. Producers Leiber and Stoller reportedly considered it the greatest doo-wop song ever recorded, but even Coasters member Carl Gardner didn't think a lot of the song, telling the author only that the song's appeal was due mainly to the bass singing of "Will (Dub) Jones, who was one of the best."

After "Yakety Yak" and "Zing!," the group scored again with "Charlie Brown" (#2), "Along Came Jones" (#9) and many more chart hits over the next few years. Yet the novelty songs that had made them successful were by the early '60s somewhat passé, and so after 1961 they only charted twice more. There was nothing wrong with the quality of the music, but with the British invasion, the Vietnam War and psychedelic rock, by the late 1960s the world had changed, and the Coasters were seen as a link to a simpler, and perhaps by then irrelevant, past.

The C.O.D.s

BEACH MUSIC DISCOGRAPHY: "Michael, the Lover" (Kellmac 1003, Billboard Pop #41 1965).

The C.O.D's were Chicago residents Larry Brownlee, Robert Lewis and Carl Washington, and in an interview with the *Chicago Defender* they said they "decided to do something for kicks, to form our group and sing." Though they wanted to be recording artists, they were rejected by "several companies as having no talent" before they were literally discovered in a park singing under a street lamp by Chicago entrepreneurs Ace Singleton and Harry Mitchell. According to Bob Pruter in *Chicago Soul*, Singleton and Mitchell rounded up a few more investors to form a record label to promote the act, and thus was born Chicago's Kellmac Records. Although the label would release singles by several artists including Ruby Stackhouse and the Vondells, The Combinations, Paul Bascomb, and Paul "Guitar Red" Johnson, the newly dubbed C.O.D's would account for nearly half of the fledgling label's mere dozen releases.

For their first effort, Kellmac asked the group to bring them a recordable song, and Brownlee, who would write all of the group's material, came up with "Michael, the Lover." According to the article in the *Defender*, there was actually "this guy in our neighborhood who [told] everybody he [was] Michael, the lover. We wrote it, practiced it, got it up tight and then recorded it." For that special "female" sound in the background they enlisted the help of labelmate Ruby Stackhouse (later Andrews), who herself recorded "Please Tell Me" for Kellmac in 1965 but would go on to greater R&B chart success with the Zodiac label in the late '60s.

"Michael" just barely missed entering the pop Top 40, stalling at #41, but it did even better on the

R&B charts in England, rising to #5. Based on the success of this first record, the future seemed promising, but four more Kellmac releases in 1965 and 1966 failed to chart, and the group broke up in 1967; the label folded that year as well, having been a huge loss for all parties involved. Brownlee would go on to join the group Lost Generation and write their signature song "Sly, Slick, and Wicked" and a number of other recordings for Brunswick between 1970 and 1974. He would then join Mystique, who recorded four singles for Curtom in 1977. A prolific songwriter, at the time of his death in Chicago in 1978 Brownlee would be credited with nearly five dozen titles, although he never had that one breakout hit. "Michael" would, however, go on to be fairly highly regarded, and was covered by the Mad Lads in 1966 and jazz saxophonist Paul Bascomb actually recorded it on Kellmac immediately following the C.O.D.s' recording and actually used the same backing tracks laid down by the C.O.D.s.. It is often erroneously reported that the Jackson 5 recorded it, but that version is actually a different tune, "Some Girls Want Me for Their Lover," whose name was changed to "Michael the Lover" to capitalize on Michael Jackson's first name.

Bob Collins and the Fabulous Five

BEACH MUSIC DISCOGRAPHY: "If I Didn't Have a Dime (To Play the Jukebox)"(Jokers Three Productions 1498, 1966: Did Not Chart); "Inventory on Heartaches"(Main Line 1367, 1967: Did Not Chart).

Summerfield, North Carolina native Donny Trexler started performing before he was 10 years old, and he formed his first band, Donny and the Blue Jets, when he was 14. In 1959, "Chuck Tilley and I started a band known as The Six Teens" Trexler said. "All of us were 16 when we formed the band, but when we turned 17 in 1960 we could still call it the Six Teens because we were still six guys all in our teens." They added 19-year-old Bob Collins to play drums, and when he turned 20, "the 'Six Teens' name was no longer accurate and we changed the name to 'Chuck Tilley and the Fabulous Five.' Chuck was the lead singer, I was the guitar player, and Bob played drums" Trexler said. Eventually Tilley left and when Collins moved up front in 1962 the group's new name became Bob Collins and the Fabulous Five.

In 1964 the group—then consisting of Trexler, Collins, John Cook, David Hamilton, Dick East, and Tommy Tucker—heard a song called "If I Didn't Have a Dime" by the Los Angeles based Furys. "If I Didn't Have a Dime" had been written by Bert Russell and Phil Medley, who had also written songs such as "Twist and Shout" and "A Million to One," and it had first appeared as the flipside of Gene Pitney's 1962 smash "Only Love Can Break a Heart." The Furys single hadn't sold—they had only one chart record, a version of "Zing! Went the Strings of My Heart" that went to #92 on the pop charts in 1963—but apparently their cover made enough of an impression that the group decided incorporate the song into their act. "We put it together and the college kids really loved it" Trexler told me. "We played a lot of fraternity parties and they always wanted to hear it. The song was so popular that we went to Arthur Smith studios in Charlotte and recorded it in late 1964, but we didn't like the recording. In the meantime we were playing it live and people were going crazy for it. Fans were saying 'God, you've got to record that song!' Finally we re-recorded late in the summer of 1966 in Greensboro at Copeland Sound Studios." In order to bring the energy and enthusiasm that accompanied those live performances at clubs and fraternity parties across the South, "we took the recording to a club in Greensboro called The Jokers Three. We played the song and acted like we were singing it, and we got the people to carry on and we recorded the audience and the background noise. What you hear there on the song is exactly what we heard and what it sounded like when we played it at parties and in clubs. People went crazy over it. The fans were great, and we wanted the recording to sound the way they liked the song to sound."

Although the single only sold regionally, the song's popularity contributed to the group's renown and led to them playing with the Four Tops, Martha Reeves and the Vandellas, Major Lance, and many other acts, some of the biggest names of the decade. Consequently, one would have expected them to follow that success with another recording, and they almost did. "When we recorded 'Jukebox' we also recorded 'Lonely Drifter' by the O'Jays, and I sang that too." But the group delayed putting it out, "and Pieces of Eight released it and it hit the charts." The South Carolina–based Pieces of Eight version was released on A&M records in 1967 and climbed to #59 on the pop charts. Having missed that opportunity, the Fabulous Five's next release was a song Trexler had written called "Inventory on Heartaches." They recorded it with Collins on lead and Trexler playing guitar and singing backup while arranging the song as well. Oddly enough though, by the time the single was released, Trexler was no longer with the group. He says that after the group delayed releasing "Lonely Drifter" and let the Pieces of Eight get the jump on them, he realized they weren't taking advantage of their opportunities or thinking big enough, and "I decided it was time to move on." Because the group had gotten some money up front from Mainline Records to record the song, they released it even though Trexler had by then joined Ted Carrol and the Music Era. Like many regionally-recorded songs "Inventory on Heartaches" didn't make an impression on the charts, and owes its subsequent success not only to its popularity on the beach music circuit but also the Northern Soul scene.

Bob Collins and the Fabulous Five disbanded not long after Trexler left the group, while Trexler joined the O'Kaysions for a while and became their lead singer when Donnie Weaver left the group in 1969. He eventually had a band called Swing from 1972 until 1986, then began performing with his wife Susan and since then the two of them have both gone on to be two of the biggest names in Carolina beach music. Trexler, who still owns the rights to the name Bob Collins and the Fabulous Five and their recordings, won a CAMMY Award for "Lifetime Achievement" in November 2000 and was inducted into the South Carolina Rhythm and Blues Hall of Fame, among other accolades.

The Commands

BEACH MUSIC DISCOGRAPHY: "No Time For You"/"Hey It's Love" (Dynamic 104, Did Not Chart 1966).

The Commands formed in 1964 when Sam Peoples, Jack Martinez, Dan Henderson and Emmanuel Gracey were stationed at Randolph Air Force Base in San Antonio, Texas. Peoples, the group's leader and principal songwriter, worked long hours as an air traffic controller, which provided him with enough down-time to write the songs the group would perform as they played local gigs. A true singing group as opposed to a band, they appeared in trademark

76   Cornelius Brothers & Sister Rose

white gloves backed by area combos as they played VFWs, nightclubs, and sockhops in the area.

With a smooth sound that successfully bridged the gap between the waning doo-wop scene and the emerging R&B sound of the mid–1960s, by 1965 the group was enough of a regional draw that they came to the attention of San Antonio visionary Abe "Abie" Epstein, who would be known as the creator of the "West Side Sound." "The West Side Sound" featured groups who had a good doo-wop and R&B sound, which Epstein infused with reverb vocals, harmonies, and a touch of rock and roll. Epstein had The Commands go into his studio and record a haunting song Peoples had written called "No Time For You." Pressed on the Dynamic label, the song features Peoples and the group's plaintive vocals backed by the Dell-Tones (Roger Ruiz, Pete Granato, Johnny Zaragoza, and Victor Montez) over a simple, yet effective, beat. The flip side was a song that would also go on to be well known in beach music circles, a mid-tempo track Henderson had penned called "Hey! It's Love." This track featured Henderson in the lead, again over sparse instrumentation by the Dell-Tones.

"No Time For You" was a regional smash, and soon came to the attention of Don Robey in Houston, owner of the national label Back Beat, a subsidiary of Duke Records. In the 1960s the Back Beat stable included artists such as Roy Head and O.V. Wright, and would in 1974 have one of its biggest hits with Carl Carlton's "Everlasting Love." With the exposure the label could deliver it seemed a certainty that "No Time For You" would be a national hit as well. But despite the fact that a number of copies made it as far as the shag-haunts of the Carolinas and were played seemingly non-stop, the song did not chart nationally. The O'Jays apparently liked the song so much that they would cover it on Imperial in 1966, but that version, too, would fail to chart.

The group would record several more singles for Dynamic, and one for Back Beat, but mainstream success would remain elusive for all involved. The group disbanded in 1967 when the Air Force stationed Peoples in Thailand; they never recorded as The Commands again.

Cornelius Brothers & Sister Rose

BEACH MUSIC DISCOGRAPHY: "Treat Her Like a Lady" (United Artists 50721, 1971: Billboard Pop #3); "Too Late to Turn Back Now" (United Artists 50910, 1972: Billboard Pop #2); "Don't Ever Be Lonely (A Poor Little Fool Like Me)" (United Artists 50954, 1972: Billboard Pop #23); "I'm Never Gonna Be Alone Anymore" (United Artists 50996, 1972: Billboard Pop #37); "Let Me Down Easy" (United Artists 208, 1973: Billboard Pop #96); "Big Time Lover" (United Artists 377, 1974: Billboard Pop Did Not Chart, R&B #88); "Since I Found My Baby" (United Artists 534, 1974: Billboard Pop Did Not Chart, R&B #59).

Carter, Eddie, and Rose Cornelius were born in Dania, Florida, near Fort Lauderdale.

Their mother would have thirteen children in all, and of those Carter, Eddie, Rose, John, and Billie Jo formed the Split Tones, a singing group popular in the Fort Lauderdale area. Rose would be the first to find success outside of the Fort Lauderdale area as a member of the Gospel Jazz Singers, allowing her to perform in Las Vegas and on the Ed Sullivan Show in 1967. Eventually, however, Eddie and Carter and their friend Cleveland Barrett (who would die in an automobile accident before the group became successful) decided to form a group and their mother asked Rose to return to Florida and join them. The group came to attention of record producer Bob Archibald after being recommended by recording engineers at Criteria Studios in Miami, and Archibald agreed to manage them and signed them to his own tiny Platinum record label. In May 1970 they released "Treat Her Like a Lady." The regionally successful record was picked up for national distribution by United Artists, and with its funky, upbeat sound, the record connected with listeners and went to #3 on the Billboard charts, was a million-seller and earned a gold record.

With such significant initial success, the group added another sister, Billie Jo, who was on board for their next single release, 1972's "Too Late to Turn Back Now." The song went a spot higher on the Billboard charts, to #2, #5 on the R&B chart, and #1 on the *Cash Box Top 100 Singles* chart; it also sold one million copies and earned a gold record. Subtly, the song was different and more indicative of the songs that would come rather than of the formula that "Treat Her Like a Lady" had followed. Instead of a funky, fast beat, "Too Late" featured lush orchestration and anguished lyrics describing the pitfalls of unrequited love and loving too much and too soon. However, it was this sound that made it a beach music classic and a perfect shag tune as well. Subsequent singles were in a similar vein: "Don't Ever Be Lonely" (#23), "Never Gonna Be Alone Anymore" (#37), and "Let Me Down Easy," which peaked only at #96, their lowest chart performance up to that point. It appears that the group had come to be pegged as romantic balladeers, which apparently wore thin with listeners, as each single charted lower than the release before it. After the four charting singles from the first album, by the time their second album was released, 1973's *Big Time Lover*, audiences seemed to have lost interest, despite the fact that the cut "Big Time Lover" may actually be one of their finest tunes. It failed to make the pop charts at all, though it did go to #88 on the R&B charts. That same year they released "Since I Found My Baby," and although it did a little better than "Big Time Lover," making the R&B charts at #59, it was their last chart record of any kind.

With their popularity waning, the group split up in 1976. Nevertheless, for a moment in time, Cornelius Brothers & Sister Rose was one of the biggest romantic soul acts on the planet, and while those soft sounds and romantic leanings meant that the group's popularity was not very enduring in the 1970s, it's that very element that has made their songs Carolina beach music favorites, and continues to resonate with listeners as even today.

The Corsairs

BEACH MUSIC DISCOGRAPHY: "Smoky Places" (Tuff 1808, 1962: Billboard Pop #12).

The Corsairs were a family act from La Grange, North Carolina, who got their start in the 1950s. Brothers Jay 'Bird' Uzzell, James Uzzell, Moses 'King Moe' Uzzell, and their cousin George Wooten started as the Gleems, a name chosen as an homage to their high school glee club. After taking advantage of just about every performing opportunity possible in the La Grange area, they decided to move to New Jersey in 1961 in order to be close to the explosive New York music scene. There they were discovered by Abner Spector, an A&R man for Chess records who had his own label, Tuff records. Spector (no relation to Phil Spector) offered to manage the group and sign them to a contract, and one of his first moves was to rename the group the Corsairs. They first recorded two songs James Uzzell had co-written, "Time Waits" and "It Won't Be a Sin" as the A- and B-sides of Tuff 102, but the single did nothing when released in August 1961. Spector decided that the group should next record a song he had written about people meeting for a secret rendezvous, "Smokey Places." With Jay Bird Uzzell singing lead and lyrics that described two lovers hiding in the darekend corners of bars during a clandestine affair, the record's sophisticated and somewhat exotic sound—almost hypnotic with the rhythm of the bongos pierced by an occasional blast of falsetto wailing—the song came together and was an obvious winner. Even with the misspelled title (it was released as "Smoky Places"), the song went to #10 on the R&B charts and #12 on the Billboard Pop charts. The Corsairs were suddenly a hot national act.

But as was the case with many groups in the 1960s, the follow-up didn't do quite as well as its predecessor, as "I'll Take You Home" only went to #68 on the pop charts and #26 on the R&B charts. At this point Spector started experimenting with different sounds, and Jay Warner notes that he even tried using "mandolins on 'Dancing Shadows' and vibraphones on … 'While'" in 1962. These efforts to try and recapture the magic the group had with the exotic "Smoky Places" did not work, nor did follow-ups such as 1962's "At the Stroke of Midnight," or 1963's highly-regarded "Stormy." The group added Landy McNeil (real last name McNeal), billed themselves as Landy McNeil and the Corsairs, but nothing changed and 1964's "The Change in You" changed nothing either. With the rise of Motown, and the demise of doo-wop, the group seemed a bit of an anachronism, and perhaps a victim of having never really had a definitive sound they folded in 1965 without ever having another hit.

Spector would write another song that would become a big hit on Tuff, 1963's "Sally Go Round the Roses" by the Jaynetts, which would go to #2 on the pop charts. Like the Corsairs, however, the Jaynetts would never be a sustained chart presence either. While Spector would, however, ultimately have more success, including his stint producing Willie Dixon's acclaimed *I Am the Blues* album in 1970, the Corsairs simply faded from sight.

Clifford Curry

BEACH MUSIC DISCOGRAPHY: "She Shot a Hole in My Soul" b/w "We're Gonna Hate Ourselves in the Morning" (Elf 90002, Billboard Pop #95 1967); "Shag With Me" (Woodshed 001, Did Not Chart 1980).

Clifford Curry, 1967 (photograph courtesy Clifford Curry).

Clifford Curry started his musical career as a member of the doo-wop group the Five Pennies, but despite landing a recording contract with Savoy records, the group was unable to produce a successful single. In 1959 Curry decided to go back home to Tennessee pursue a solo career, and after recording a few singles for Excello he joined the Bubba Suggs Band as their featured singer. The group landed a number of back-up gigs supporting the likes of Solomon Burke, Wilson Pickett, Joe Tex, Little Willie John and others, but by 1963 Curry decided to go back to Knoxville and joined a local band who played parties. Curry also decided to try recording a few songs on his own, and because his friend Rob Galbraith worked at WNOX, Curry said "we'd go out there after midnight and record our songs on tape." The amateur recordings and local touring paid off, and on one trip to Nashville he met producer Buzz Cason, who liked Curry's voice and decided to give him the chance to record a couple of songs—"She Shot a Hole in My Soul" and "We're Gonna Hate Ourselves in the Morning."

First Curry and his band recorded "She Shot a Hole in my Soul," and the consensus from the band at the time was that "we felt really good about it, and we believed it was going to chart." Their intuition was correct, and after being released on Elf records, the song reached #95 on the Hot 100 and #45 on the R&B charts. The flip side of the record was a tune Arthur Alexander had co-written, "We're Gonna Hate Ourselves in the Morning," and though at the time it didn't do much it has become a well-known song too. But Cason and even Curry thought the B-side was just a throwaway. "We didn't have any idea it was going to be a hit. We had the horn arrangements written out for the horn players to play, and Buzz decided not to use them. He figured it was just a B side so he sent the horn players home to save some money." And though the side didn't chart nationally, in the Carolinas it was big, and airplay there got both songs noticed. "I had no idea the songs were going to fit into the beach music thing like they did. I was just a singer trying to have a hit."

Suddenly, Curry was in demand in the Carolinas. "Robert Honeycutt had a club in North Carolina called Williams Lake…. That was my first gig, and Robert was the one who got me to the Carolinas. I played that week, and he had a friend in Myrtle Beach named Cecil Corbett who had the Beach Club. He hired me the next weekend, Easter weekend, when the kids were out on school break. Those two weeks were the best two weeks I ever had in my career. That's what got me into beach music."

Curry didn't follow-up with any recordings as big as those first two however, and admits "I had a career lull after 'She Shot a Hole' and those songs I did with Buzz. Buzz just wasn't familiar with the whole beach music thing like I was, and we were doing things that just weren't being recognized in the Carolinas. It wasn't beach music. I was playing and writing and traveling but the songs weren't being played." Thereafter Curry recorded for several labels, but since none were targeted towards beach music audiences his songs didn't seem to be catching on. But by the late '70s he had hooked up with his friend Archie Jordan, who "had written

'What Difference You Made in My Life' for Ronnie Milsap and 'The Drifter' for Sylvia—both #1 songs on the country charts—and he wrote a song specifically for me." Jordan, who had been born in South Carolina and had played guitar for The Tams, had roots in beach music, and so he gave Curry a new song he had written, "Shag with Me."

"We cut that record in 1979 and it came out in 1980, right about the time all the regional beach music songs were coming out, and it was a comeback song for me" Curry said. Though the record didn't chart nationally, it did get a lot of airplay in the Carolinas. Though they followed "Shag with Me" a year later with another Woodshed release it didn't catch on. Jordan soon moved on to other projects, and so he and Curry never duplicated the magic of their previous release. Nevertheless, Curry was one of only a few performers not only to have hits during the early classic years of beach music, but during the late '70s "new wave" of beach music as well. Curry passed away in 2016.

Tyrone Davis

BEACH MUSIC DISCOGRAPHY: "Can I Change My Mind?" (Dakar 1452, 1968: Billboard Pop #5); "Turn Back the Hands of Time" (Dakar 616, 1969: Billboard Pop #3).

Born Tyrone Fettson in Greenville Mississippi, at age 14 he moved to Saginaw, Michigan, where his father was a minister. In 1959 when he was 19 he moved to Chicago, and there he got his first brush with the music business as a chauffeur and valet for blues artist Freddie King, and he also came into contact with blues artists such as Otis Rush and Mighty Joe Young. He was encouraged to develop his voice and audition for singing gigs, and he managed to land a number of gigs in small Chicago clubs throughout the early 1960s. He was "discovered" by pianist Harold Burrage, and recording as "Tyrone the Wonder Boy" he released several unsuccessful singles on the Four Brothers and Sack labels in 1966 and 1967. In 1968 Carl Davis signed him to the Dakar label, had him drop the "Wonder Boy" moniker, and adopt Tyrone Davis as his stage name. His first release for the label was 1968's "Can I Change My Mind," though it was originally designated as the B-side. The record sold more than a million copies, went to #1 on the R&B charts and #5 on the pop charts, and Davis was a star.

Davis recorded four more singles in 1968 and 69, although only one "Is It Something You've Got," made the pop (#34) or R&B (#5) charts. Then in 1970 he released "Turn Back the Hands of Time," which soared to #3 on the pop charts and #1 on the R&B charts. The song was very similar to "Can I Change My Mind" in that one of the two songwriters, Jack Daniels, had also written his first hit, and that most of the same musicians played on both recordings. The result was another million-seller, and earned Davis another gold record.

From there Davis would go on to have close to a dozen pop chart records and 40 more R&B chart records, including another R&B #1, "Turning Point" in 1975. He would change labels several times over the years, recording for Columbia, Future, Ocean Front, and others. His records would chart right up through the late 1980s, and in 1998 he was awarded the R&B Foundation's prestigious Pioneer Award for his work. Davis had a stroke in 2004, and passed away due to complications in 2005.

Otis Day and the Knights

BEACH MUSIC DISCOGRAPHY: "Shama Lama Ding Dong" (Soundtrack cut from the film *Animal House*, Did Not Chart, 1978).

There really was no band called Otis Day and the Knights—at least not at first—as they were a group simply created for the 1978 movie *Animal House*. The movie centers around the exploits of the Faber College fraternity Delta Tau Chi, and twice in the film the band Otis

Day and the Knights appear: once at a toga party at the Delta fraternity house where the band plays a cover of the Isley Brothers' "Shout," and later at the Dexter Lake Club where they play "Shama Lama Ding Dong." Though certainly the inclusion of "Shout" in the movie brought it to the attention of a whole new generation of party-goers who hadn't been around in 1959 when the Isley Brothers took the record to #47 on the pop charts, nor in 1962 when the song re-charted briefly (#97), but "Shama Lama Ding Dong," on the other hand, was an original song written for the film. Despite the similarity of the song's name to the Edsels' 1961 hit "Rama Lama Ding Dong" (#21), and the fact that both songs have a doo-wop feel, the song in the movie is not a cover of the Edsels' song. Otis Day's "Shama Lama Ding Dong" was written by Mark Davis, who had worked with artists and producers such as Curtis Mayfield, Minnie Riperton, Norman Whitfield, Berry Gordy, Diana Ross, Marvin Gaye, and many others. In the late 1970s he was hired by Universal Pictures to work on film soundtracks, and wrote "Shama Lama Ding Dong" specifically for *Animal House*. The man chosen to sing the song (and "Shout") was Lloyd Williams, who recorded the two songs for the soundtrack.

However, the producers of the film decided they wanted Otis Day to have an outrageous look for the film (and apparently felt the suave looking Williams didn't have that look), and so they hired actor Dewayne Jessie to play Otis Day on screen. Though as time has proven Jessie could in fact sing capably—his brother Young Jessie had been with the Coasters and sang on songs such as "Young Blood"—that's Williams' voice we hear in the film as Dewayne Jessie lip syncs to it. As one of the film's few original songs "Shama Lama Ding Dong" struck a chord with audiences, and though never released as a single it nevertheless made its way onto a lot of DJ's playlists at beach clubs and frat parties throughout the South. In the meantime, the two Otis Day songs were so popular that within a few days of the film's release Jessie was contacted about having his "band" perform at a gig in Rhode Island. Though he did not book that performance, the demand for Otis Day and the Knights was so great that before long Jessie did form a band (the band in the film, which included young blues guitarist and now five-time Grammy winner Robert Cray, was made up of studio musicians and was not a real group) and hit the road. Today Jessie's Otis Day and the Knights perform several gigs a month, and "Shout" and "Shama Lama Ding Dong" are of course the mainstays of their act.

The song has certainly had legs. John Cougar Mellencamp recorded it in 1987, and the Band of Oz was smart enough to seize on the song's appeal and record a version which in 1995 won Song of the Year at the Carolina Beach Music Awards. But for many purists, it's the original film recording of the song not really sung by the band that didn't really exist that's the best and most favored version, despite the cover versions that have followed.

Bill Deal and the Rhondels

BEACH MUSIC DISCOGRAPHY: "May I" (Heritage 803, 1969: Billboard Pop #39); "I've Been Hurt" (Heritage 812, 1969: Billboard Pop #35); "What Kind of Fool" (Heritage 817, 1969: Billboard Pop #23).

Bill Deal and Ammon Tharp formed their group in 1960 and were happy playing the club circuit in the Carolinas and Virginia, performing old R&B and soul songs. As the '60s progressed, audiences in the Carolinas were clamoring for "beach music," although the Virginia Beach natives didn't quite yet know what that was. Since audiences were often requesting the old Zodiacs tune "May I" as an example of beach music, they made the connection. Deal, however, created his own uptempo version of "May I," and the song was instantly a crowd favorite. "May I" did well when pressed and came to the attention of Heritage Records. The group landed a recording contract, and the single took off. "May I" entered the Hot 100, and then the Top 40, before it stalled at #39.

Bill Deal and the Rhondels, circa late 1960s (photograph courtesy Ammon Tharp).

"Then we did 'I've Been Hurt'—I don't really know why we chose it next, but Deal just had an insight on how to do those songs in our style," Tharp said. "We were doing Tams songs in our set and liked the songs, but thought, 'Let's change it up for a national audience.'" Their remake of The Tams' 1965 single would do a little better than its predecessor, stalling at #35—and would even be voted song of the year in Mexico. Next they'd next release a remake of another song in their act, the 1964 Tams' hit "What Kind of Fool," and it would surpass both previous releases, going all the way to #23. In just one year, with their updated versions of the Carolina beach music sound, the group had become a solid national act.

But with success came constant touring, and the time in the spotlight was taking its toll. "We were going to New York every week promoting and doing TV and radio, and traveling and playing," and when they played Madison Square Garden with Neil Young, Deep Purple and Crazy Elephant, "we realized, 'We're in the wrong place here.' We're a bunch of short-haired, Ivy League–looking guys doing Motown and having to play with these rock bands, and we weren't into the rock thing, which was coming on really strong. Every time we played up there we'd go against a rock band, and while they loved our records, they'd come on and blow our ass away with their rock-and-roll." So as the touring got old, and since "we were making decent money, but we weren't getting rich, we thought, 'You know, we could do this at home and just play the Southeast.' We were kind of homebodies—we loved Virginia Beach—and we figured financially we could do just as well and not be gone all the time. So we said bye-bye. We thought success was fine—but 'nah.'"

The group took it home, and though they still played the clubs and toured, by removing themselves from the national spotlight and focusing on more regional venues, they were able to maintain some semblance of normality in their lives. It served them well, and they were popular for many years in the Carolinas and Virginia, always playing to packed houses. Though Bill Deal passed away in 2003, Ammon Tharp continued to perform those great standards until his death in 2017.

Harry Deal and the Galaxies

BEACH MUSIC DISCOGRAPHY: "I Still Love You"(Eclipse 1001, 1970: Did Not Chart); "She's Got it All Together" (Eclipse 1007, 1975: Did Not Chart).

Founders Harry and Jimmy Deal started the group in Taylorsville North Carolina in 1959, along with band members Frank Barber, Stan Bumgardner, and Tony Harrington. Their early appearances were doing gigs such as the Beta Club convention in Asheville, and regional shows such as 4-H Club contests, but perhaps most notable were their appearances at the Myrtle Beach Pavilion starting in 1960, where they reportedly set attendance records at the time. Their regional popularity interested record companies in the mid 1960s, and after their first release on the obscure Petal label in 1964, "Smacky Mouth," they next recorded "Bad Girl" for the higher profile Jubilee label in 1966. Despite successive recordings on the Laurie, Jubilee, SSS International, and Atlantic labels over the next four years, none of their records made the national charts. In 1968 they founded their own Galaxie III studios in Taylorsville, and by 1970 they had founded their own label, Eclipse. Their first release on Eclipse was a song then-keyboardist Glen Fox had written called "I Still Love You." Though not a national hit, it was hugely successful in the southeast, as was "She's Got It All Together," released on Eclipse just a few years later. In the 1970s they released covers of beach classics such as "Stay," "Ms. Grace," and "Hey! Baby" on Eclipse as well and occasionally saw releases on labels such as T.K. and Supreme also.

The group's membership has fluctuated a great deal during the 50+ years they have been in existence, and at one time included influential Catalinas members Johnny and Gary Barker, as well as a number of Deal family members. Harry Deal and the Galaxies were inducted into the Beach Music Hall of Fame in 2007.

The Delfonics

BEACH MUSIC DISCOGRAPHY: "La-La-Means I Love You" (Philly Groove 150, 1968: Billboard Pop #4).

As teenagers, Philadelphia natives William "Poogie" Hart and his brother Wilbert formed The Four Gents along with Ritchie Daniels and Samuel Edlightoon. That group became the Orphonics in high school and added Merfhab Isvardsoon and Randy Cain, and it was this group who caught the eye of record store owner Stan Watson. Watson called a young up-and-comer working at Cameo-Parkway named Thom Bell, and asked him to audition the group. Bell did, and decided that Poogie should be the featured lead singer. They went to Cameo studios and as the Del Fonics recorded "He Don't Really Love You," but Cameo-Parkway declined to release it so Watson saw that it was released on the tiny Moon Shot label in 1966. The record had moderate local sales, and at about this time Isvardson and Lightoon quit the group and Daniels was drafted; the Harts and Cain moved forward as the Delfonics. Though "He Don't Really Love You" had only been a regional hit, Cameo was impressed enough by its local success to ask Bell to work with the group again. They released "You've Been Untrue" on Cameo in 1967, and despite a strong regional following the record did not catch on nationally, largely due to the fact that the Cameo label was failing and its promotional efforts were faltering. The label would in fact shut down later that year.

Even though the label was folding and no one knew what would happen to the group next, Poogie Hart and Bell had written a song that he, Watson, and Bell felt was a sure winner, "La-La-Means I Love You." As Bell had done on earlier releases he had produced, he played all of the instruments and overdubbed and combined the tracks, adding backing vocals in the process. Without a label, however, there was no way to get the song out there, but once again Watson came to the rescue, forming the Philly Groove label. The record was the label's very first release in early 1968, and was a national smash, going to #4 on the pop and #2 on the R&B charts. It sold a million copies, and netted the group a gold record.

The group's next six releases during 1968 and 1968 had differing degrees of chart success, and "Ready or Not Here I Come" not only went to #35 nationally but recieved some play time in the beach clubs. Their next big hit was "Didn't I Blow Your Mind This Time," which went to #3 on the R&B charts and #10 on the pop charts and won a Grammy for best R&B group performance.

It was at about this time that Randy Cain left the group, and the group brought in Major Harris, who'd later have a #5 solo hit with "Love Won't Let Me Wait" in 1975. Unfortunately, it was at this time that Thom Bell also stopped working with the group, having moved on to work with the Stylistics and eventually the Spinners. As a result, after 1970 the group had no more Top 40 pop hits and disbanded in 1975. As has been the case with many groups, this resulted in splinter groups and acrimony between factions. Both Poogie and Wilbert Hart tour with competing groups today; Randy Cain and Major Harris are now deceased.

The Dells

BEACH MUSIC DISCOGRAPHY: "There Is" (Cadet 5590, 1967: Billboard Pop #20); "Wear It on Our Face" (Cadet 5599, 1968: Billboard Pop #27).

The Dells were originally Chuck Barksdale, Michael McGill, Marvin Junior, Lucius McGill, Verne Allison, and Johnny Funches, a group of friends who attended Thornton Township High School in Harvey, Illinois, a Chicago suburb. They formed a group in 1952 known as the El Rays, and under that name they recorded "Darling I Know" for the Chess subsidiary label Checker. The record did not chart, and McGill left the group and joined the Marine Corps. Because Chess had a group named the Rays and Vee-Jay had the El Doradoes, they dumped the name El Rays and renamed themselves the Dells, signed with Vee-Jay Records, and released "Tell the World" and "Dreams of Contentment" in 1955, neither of which charted. Their next Vee-Jay release however, 1956's "Oh What a Nite," would be big indeed. It peaked at #4 on the R&B singles chart and eventually sold over a million copies. Other than that single though, their time with Vee-Jay was a disappointment, and their next ten singles on the label would do nothing. On the way to a performance in 1958 the group was in an automobile accident and injuries sidelined most of the group for a while, to the point that they decided to quit performing temporarily. Barksdale joined the Moonglows briefly, and by the time the guys decided to come back together Funches opted to quit the group for good. He was replaced by former Flamingos singer Johnny Carter, and they spent the next period as backup singers for Dinah Washington, who actually encouraged them to stay together and pursue another recording contract.

In 1962 they signed with Chess's Argo subsidiary. This period with Argo was not productive in terms of record sales, and they had no chart hits; they did, however, sing on Barbara Lewis's "Hello Stranger" in 1963 (see the entry for Lewis), providing the "chew-bop, chew-bop, my baby" background vocals on the record. They once again returned to Vee-Jay in 1964 for a few releases, and in 1965 they released "Stay in My Corner," their first chart record in almost a decade. It went to #23 on the R&B charts and bubbled under at #122 on the pop charts, but even this moderate success must have felt like a step in the right direction. Unfortunately, Vee-Jay filed for bankruptcy in 1966, and without a recording contract they returned to singing back up, this time for Ray Charles.

The group signed with Chess once again, this time on the Cadet subsidiary, and after their first couple of singles sank without much interest it must have seemed as if the group would simply never break big. However, Leonard Chess had the group start working with songwriter-producer Bobby Miller and arranger Charles Stepney in 1967. The two of them decided to use the Dell's voices in more nontraditional ways and arrangements, and one of the first of these was "There Is," a song written by Miller and Raynard Miner. Alternately featuring Junior's, Carter's, and Barksdale's voices, it was a very new sound for a group long identified with slow ballads and doo-wop. It was so different in fact that at first the group decided they didn't want to record it because it was too fast. Even once it was released it was as a B-side to "O-O I Love You," but as it so frequently happens, disk jockeys found "There Is" to be the hot side and started playing it. As a result Cadet re-released the single with "There Is" as the A-side, the song raced up the charts to peak at #11 on the R&B charts and #20 on the pop charts in 1968, and it became their first Top 40 pop hit.

Miller and Stepney also oversaw the group's next hit, "Wear It On Our Face." Their tendency to experiment with the group is evident from the first notes of the odd piano and steel drum intro, through the powerful brass backing, to Junior's screamer-style vocals that could be favorably compared to Wilson Pickett or Otis Redding. Though not as big nationally as its predecessor—the song peaked at #27 on the R&B charts and #44 on the pop charts—it was popular among the beach music crowd. Due to the success of these two singles Chess had Stepney go work with another group whose career seemed to have stalled, the Radiants, and their 1968 release "Hold On" in fact sounds like a Dells song as well (see the entry for the Radiants).

The group's next release, "Stay in My Corner," was, like "There Is" and "Wear it On Our Face," from the group's album *There Is*. It was a remake of their 1965 Vee Jay release of the same name, and went to #1 on the R&B charts and #10 on the pop charts, the same positions a remake of "Oh, What a Night! on Cadet in 1969 achieved. In fact, from 1967 through the end of the 1970s, the group would have nearly 40 chart hits, and another ten or so in the '80s and '90s. And despite all of the personnel changes of their early years, Junior, Allison, McGill, Barksdale and Carter stayed together from 1960 until Carter died in 2009, providing them with a consistency and solidity that most groups can only hope to match. One of the most successful groups in music, the Dells were inducted to the Rock and Roll Hall of Fame and the Vocal Group Hall of Fame in 2004.

Varetta Dillard

BEACH MUSIC DISCOGRAPHY: "Mercy Mr. Percy" (Savoy 897, 1953: Billboard Pop Did Not Chart, R&B #6).

Harlem, New York-born Varetta Dillard was born with a congenital spine condition that forced her to undergo frequent operations as a child and walk with the aid of crutches throughout her life. Despite her disability, she had the gift of tremendous voice, and she would often sing to the hospital staff to entertain them. With the encouragement of singer Carl Feaster of the Chords she began entering singing competitions as a teenager in the late 1940s. After two successive wins at the Apollo Theatre, in 1951 Dillard signed with Savoy Records, where she released "Please Come Back to Me," which faded without fanfare. Despite the fact that she was constantly touring and playing venues from the Apollo and the Howard to small clubs from New York to the Deep South, releases such as "Hurry Up," "A Letter In Blues," and "Them There Eyes" all failed to find much of an audience. One 1952 release however, "Easy Easy Baby," attracted enough of a following that it went to #8 on the R&B charts and was covered by the white artist Eileen Barton on Coral. Savoy even tried pairing her with blues singer H-Bomb Ferguson for "Tortured Love," but it didn't attract much notice either.

She continued to tour, and in 1953 her persistence recording finally paid off when "Mercy Mr. Percy" was released. "Mercy Mr. Percy" sold extremely well and rose to #6 on the R&B charts, and had the right beat that it was a hit on the emerging beach music scene in the South as well. Despite having had two Top 10 R&B hits in the space of a year, her next releases, "I Love You" and "I Ain't Gonna Tell" both failed to chart. She had only one Savoy release in 1954 due to her pregnancy and the birth of her daughter, and after a few more Savoy non-charters in 1954 she released "Johnny Has Gone" in 1955. The record was a tribute to recording star Johnny Ace, who accidentally shot himself between performances on Christmas Day 1954. It equaled the success of "Mercy Mr. Percy," reaching #6 on the R&B charts as well.

It was to be Dillard's last chart record, as even a follow up trying to capitalize on the success of "Mercy Mr. Percy" titled "Promise Mr. Thomas" failed to chart. Dillard left Savoy in 1956 for what promised to be greener pastures at the RCA subsidiary label Groove, though the change produced no chart records although another tribute record, "I Miss You Jimmy," attracted some attention due to the death of James Dean. After RCA discontinued Groove she moved to the main label in 1957, and despite a number of attempts to follow up on her earlier success by 1958 she left RCA when her contract was not renewed. She subsequently recorded for Triumph and Club with no further chart success, and had stopped recording as a solo artist by 1961. She went on to record gospel music with her husband's group the Tri-Odds, and eventually worked as a music therapist and in other jobs until her death in 1993 at age 60.

Floyd Dixon

BEACH MUSIC DISCOGRAPHY: "Hey Bartender" (Cat 114, 1955: Did Not Chart).

Marshall, Texas-born Floyd Dixon taught himself to play the piano as a child, but despite his musical abilities and love of singing, initially he didn't appear destined for a career in entertainment. His parents moved to Los Angeles when he was 13, and there he worked as a caddy and even considered a career in hotel management before winning a talent show in 1948. People thought he sang in the style of the popular blues singer Charles Brown, who as a member of the Three Blazers was extremely popular during the late '40s. Brown, who was also from Texas, was at the talent show that Dixon won, and acted as a mentor to the young singer for the next few years.

Dixon was able to first get a recording contract with Supreme Records, but it was his second attempt with Modern Records that would start to bring him fame. He recorded "Dallas Blues" in 1948, and by early 1959 it was #10 on the R&B charts. Despite the record's success, Modern wanted him to move away from his Charles-Brown-sound-alike recordings, and in the spirit of some of the more risqué R&B music emerging at the time they had him recording songs such as "Baby Let's Go Down to the Woods" and the very early Jerry Leiber-Mike Stoller composition "Too Much Jelly Roll" and others. He recorded some sides for Don Robey's Peacock Records, and he convinced Aladdin to pick up the contract and buy and release those masters. Consequently, when Charles Brown left the Blazers, who recorded for Aladdin, he replaced Brown for a while, and by now his reputation was such that the group's Aladdin sides were credited to Floyd Dixon and Johnny

Moore's Three Blazers (not the Johnny Moore of Drifters fame). He jumped to Specialty Records next, and there he recorded "Please Don't Go" in 1953, a song that had some life as a shag song though it has not endured as a beach song in the more traditional sense. By this point he'd had five R&B Top 20 singles, and his next stop was at the ever-growing Atlantic label, where he released some sides on the short-lived Cat subsidiary. Among these was "Hey Bartender," which did not chart, but would find a massive audience in 1978 with the Blues Brothers version on their album *Briefcase Full of Blues*. Because Dixon wrote the song, he made far more off of the royalties of the covers in the 1970s, and again in 1983 when country singer Johnny Lee took it to #2 on the country charts.

From the mid–1950s on, Dixon recorded for a variety of labels as his reputation including Combo, Pearl, Checker, Cash and others. In 1966 he recorded "Don't Leave Me Baby" on the Los Angeles based Chattahoochie label, which was another record valued more as a shag tune than as beach music. He retired from music briefly before touring in Europe in the 1970s, and he was commissioned to write a song for the Los Angeles Olympics in 1984. He began actively recording again in the 1990s, and received a Pioneer Award from the Rhythm and Blues Foundation in 1993. He recorded a well-received album in the 1990s on Alligator Records, *Wake Up and Live*, for which he won the 1997 W.C. Handy Award for Best Album of the Year by a comeback artist. He continued to perform and record, and after a bout with cancer he died from kidney failure in 2006.

Ernie K. Doe

BEACH MUSIC DISCOGRAPHY: "Mother-in-Law" (Minit 623, 1961: Billboard Pop #1); "Te-Ta-Te-Ta-Ta" (Minit 627, 1961: Billboard Pop #53); "Certain Girl" (Minit 634, 1961: Billboard Pop #71).

Born Ernest Kador, Jr., in New Orleans, like many R&B artists his first experience singing was in the church. As a teenager he went to Chicago to live with his mother (his father and mother were separated) and there he started singing in nightclubs. In 1954 he returned to New Orleans and joined a group called the Blue Diamonds, and with Ernie on lead they recorded one single, "Honey Baby," for Savoy. Eventually he had the opportunity to record a few solo sides, and he released "Eternity" as Ernest Kador on Specialty and "My Love for You" as Ernie Kado and again as Ernie K. Doe on Ember. In 1959 signed with Minit, where he had the chance to work for the now-legendary Allen Toussaint. His first single, "Make You Love Me," didn't do anything, though the next, 1960's "Hello Lover," generated enough regional interest that it reportedly sold 100,000 copies. His next release was the 1961 smash "Mother-in-Law."

"Mother-in-Law," written by Toussaint, was a playful tune in the vein of many of the Coasters hits. K. Doe later claimed (though Toussaint disputed it) that he found the song in a trashcan after Toussaint had thrown it away. K. Doe told the *Chicago Tribune*'s Dave Hoekstra that the song resonated with him because "my mother-in-law was staying in my house. I was married 19 years, and it was 19 years of pure sorrow. When I sang 'Satan should be her name,' I meant that." One thing that really made the song work was the contribution of backup Benny Spellman, who at the time was also a struggling artist for Minit. Spellman agreed to help out on "Mother-in-Law," and his bass voice can be heard echoing K. Doe by singing the words "mother-in-law" throughout the record. The other back-up vocals were provided by Calvin Lee and Willie Harper of the Minit group the Del Royals. Between K. Doe's playful lyrics and Spellman's resonating bass, the song hit #1 on both the pop and R&B charts. The song was so popular that it spawned a number of answer songs and knock offs, such as The Blossoms "Son-in-Law" and Paul Peek's "Brother-in-Law"; K-Doe himself would do the non-charter "My Mother-in-Law (Is in My Hair Again)" in 1964.

But the song's success caused a rift between Spellman and K. Doe. Deacon John Moore, who was a musician on the record, remembers that when K. Doe went out on a national tour when "Mother-in-Law" hit #1, "Benny was a little peeved at K. Doe because K. Doe didn't take him out on the road with him. Benny was upset because, he said, '"Mother-In-Law" wouldn't have sold if they didn't have my bass voice in there'—that's really what Benny thought sold the record. There was a little disagreement between them." The little disagreement became a big disagreement—and led to blows when K. Doe came back to town. "They went back to the studio to do a follow up to 'Mother-in-Law' with the same kind of line called 'Get Out of My House,'" Moore said. "Benny was there, and K. Doe and Benny were in the booth for the singers and you could just see the tension between the two of them. All of a sudden, K. Doe and Benny came tumbling out of the booth with their hands at each other's throats. They were rolling on the ground, fighting, and Allen Toussaint called off the session!" Moore said. "We assumed they were arguing about who made the record sell, over whether or not it was Benny's bass voice. Later on, I also heard it might have been over a woman!"

Though "Mother-in-Law" had made K. Doe a star, his next song, 1961's "Te-Ta-Te-Ta-Ta" wasn't a big hit—although over time it has come to be regarded as a beach music classic in its own right. "That was written because Ernie had his trademark style of singing where he'd go 'ah-ah-ah,'" Moore said, "and so Allen wrote 'Te-Ta-Te-Ta-Ta' to rhyme with that." Recorded at that same follow-up session with "Get Out of My House," "Te-Ta-Te-Ta-Ta" would go to #53 on the Top 100 and #21 on the R&B charts. "Certain Girl," released right after "Te-Ta-Te-Ta-Ta," is another favorite in beach music circles, though it only reached #71 on the pop charts. His next release, 1962's "Popeye Joe" (#99) was his last record on the pop charts, and by 1964 K. Doe had left Minit. In 1967 "Later for Tomorrow" and "Until the Real Thing Comes Along" would both make the R&B charts on the Duke label. Perhaps his biggest success story post–"Mother-in-Law" came when he released "'Here Come the Girls" in 1970. It failed to find an audience, but in 2007, a British pharmacy chain used the song in a commercial and K. Doe's version was re-released and went to #43 on the British charts. In 2008, the British girl group Sugarbabes released a cover version of the song called "Girls," which went to #3 in England, and nearly four decades after its initial release, K. Doe's music was in the Top 10 again.

After a career in radio in the 1980s, K. Doe opened the Mother-in-Law Lounge in New Orleans in 1994. He frequently performed there, often in a cape and a crown in his "Emperor of the Universe" persona. A flamboyant performer until the end, he died from liver and kidney failure in 2001.

Patti Drew

BEACH MUSIC DISCOGRAPHY: "Tell Him" (Capitol 5861,1967: Billboard Pop #85); "Workin' On a Groovy Thing" (Capitol 2197, 1968: Billboard Pop #62).

Patti Drew was born in Charleston, South Carolina, though her family moved first to Nashville, and then to Evanston, Illinois in 1956 when Patti was 11. There Patti and her sisters Lorraine and Erma sang in the choir at their local church. Patti's mother was a housekeeper for Maury Lathowers, the regional promotional manager for Capitol Records, and one Sunday she asked Lathowers to come to church to hear her daughters sing. Lathowers ending up booking a formal audition for the girls, and after playing the demo for Capitol exec Peter Wright they signed the group to a contract. For their first release they recorded a song Erma's future husband Carlton Black had written, "Tell Him." Black had previously been a member of the Chicago group the Duvals, and with Black singing bass he and the Drew girls called themselves the very similar sounding Drew-Vels. "Tell Him" was a huge regional hit in the Chicago area in 1964, though it only made it to #90 on the national R&B charts. The group performed with Chicago stars Gene Chandler and Major Lance at Chicago's Regal Theater, and although they released a few more singles none were successful and they decided to break up.

Before long, however, Wright and Lathowers came calling again, unwilling to let Patti's magnificent voice go unutilized. "About a year after the group broke up, Peter and Maury came to me and asked me if I'd like to be a solo artist" she told Bob Abrahamian in a 2008 interview. "I didn't want to do it without the girls, [but] they wanted to be housewives and mothers. I finally said yes [and] the first thing we recorded was 'Tell Him.'" With notable singers Fontella Bass and Jackie Ross on backup, and Carlton Black singing bass once again, this time the song went to #22 on the R&B charts and #85 on the pop charts. Drew's next charting effort was "Workin' on a Groovy Thing." Drew said she would sit around and listen to demos and try to pick good ones to record, and when she heard "Workin'" (penned by Neil Sedaka and Roger Atkins), "I thought 'Hmm, that's a catchy little tune–I'd like to do that one.'" It was a good choice, and would be Drew's biggest record, going to #34 on the R&B charts and #62 on the pop charts in 1968. It's clear Drew had a good ear for music, and also clear that maybe she wasn't getting the promotion she should have; a year later, a version by the 5th Dimension that most consider inferior to Drew's would go to #20 on the pop charts.

Although she'd had a couple of chart records and been on *American Bandstand* and *Soul Train*, several factors caused Drew's career to stall at this point. Her management didn't seem to know what kind of singer they wanted her to be—"Capitol couldn't decide if they wanted me to be another Aretha Franklin or another [jazz singer like] Nancy Wilson"—and as a result of not having a clear identity she was recording the wrong types of music, and a lot of cover tunes. The first single release from her second album, 1969's *I've Been Here All the Time*, was a cover of Otis Redding's "Hard to Handle" (which charted at #40 on the R&B charts), and the album also included covers of The Grass Roots' "Midnight Confessions," Ben E, King's "I Who Have Nothing," and The Drifters' "Save the Last Dance for Me." While a singer may score an occasional hit with a cover, frequently doing covers of other artists works are generally not a recipe for recording success. During this period Drew was on the road constantly playing the nightclub circuit—which also meant she wasn't in the studio developing new material. She was playing clubs around the country two weeks at a time, but said the travel was "brutal. I lived out of a suitcase, I was always alone, I traveled by myself—it was too much." She told author Bob Pruter that she also started taking drugs, and "completely lost contact with the people around me. I became militant, and finally my manager suggested I take some time off." Drew quit the music business temporarily in 1971, though she tried a disco comeback in 1975 and then performed with Black sporadically in the 1980s. By the 1990s she quit the music business for good, and still lives in Detroit today.

The Drifters

BEACH MUSIC DISCOGRAPHY: "Money Honey" (Atlantic 1006, 1953: Billboard Pop Did Not Chart, R&B #1); "Honey Love"(Atlantic 1029, 1954: Billboard Pop Did Not Chart, R&B #1); "Adorable" (Atlantic 1078, 1955: Billboard Pop Did Not Chart, R&B #1); "Ruby Baby" (Atlantic 1089, 1956: Billboard Pop Did Not Chart, R&B #10); "Fools Fall in Love" (Atlantic 1157, 1957: Billboard Pop #69); "Drip Drop" (Atlantic 1187, 1958: Billboard Pop #58); "There Goes My Baby" (Atlantic 2025, 1959: Billboard Pop #2); "(If You Cry) True Love, True Love" b/w "Dance with Me" (Atlantic 2040, 1959: Billboard Pop #33/15); "This Magic Moment" (Atlantic 2050, 1960: Billboard Pop #16); "Save the Last Dance for Me" (Atlantic 2071, 1960: Billboard Pop #1); "I Count the Tears" (Atlantic 2087, 1960: Billboard Pop #17); "Some Kind of Wonderful" (Atlantic 2096, 1961: Billboard Pop #32); "Please Stay" (Atlantic 2105, 1961: Billboard Pop #14); "Sweets for My Sweet" (Atlantic 2117, 1961: Billboard Pop #16); "When My Little Girl Is Smiling" (Atlantic 2134, 1962: Billboard Pop #28); "Up on the Roof" (Atlantic 2162, 1962: Billboard Pop #5); "On Broadway" (Atlantic 2182, 1963: Billboard Pop #9); "I'll Take You Home" (Atlantic 2201, 1963: Billboard Pop #25); "One Way Love" (Atlantic 2225, 1964: Billboard Pop #56); "Under the Boardwalk" (Atlantic 2237, 1964: Billboard Pop #4); "I've Got Sand in My Shoes" (Atlantic 2253, 1964: Billboard Pop #33); "Saturday Night at the Movies" (Atlantic 2260, 1964: Billboard Pop #18); "Come on Over to My Place" (Atlantic 2285, 1965: Billboard Pop #60); "I'll Take You Where the Music's Playing" (Atlantic 2298, 1965: Billboard Pop #51); "Kissin' in the Back Row of the Movies" (Bell 600, 1974: Billboard Pop Did Not Chart, R&B #83); You're More Than a Number (In My Little Red Book)" b/w "Do You Have to Go Now?" (Arista 78, 1976, Did Not Chart); "Closely Guarded Secret" (Arista 202, 1978: Did Not Chart); "Pour Your Little Heart Out" (Epic 7806, 1979: Did Not Chart).

To date The Drifters have sold more than 200 million singles and 100 million albums, and among the handful of groups with a half dozen or more beach music hits The Drifters have more than any other act. They recorded songs that appealed to beach music audiences for more than three decades, music that at different times exemplified '50s doo-wop, '60s pop, and even included those British Drifters hits of the '70s that blurred the lines between disco and beach music. During that period, the group had at least fifteen different lead singers and more than sixty group members, and more than four dozen songs that have made the U.S. pop charts, the R&B charts, or both. Many of those have qualified as beach music classics.

The Drifters got their start when Clyde McPhatter left Billy Ward and the Dominoes in 1953, and Ahmet Ertegun of Atlantic Records urged him to form his own group and record for Atlantic. McPhatter first assembled the members of a gospel group he had worked with, the Mount Lebanon singers. This group, consisting of James Johnson, William Anderson, Charlie White, David Baldwin, and David Baughan, recorded four songs for Atlantic, but

Ertegun was disappointed with the results and told McPhatter to put together an entirely different group. This time McPhatter recruited South Carolina-born Bill Pinkney, brothers Andrew and Gerhart Thrasher, Willie Ferbee, and Walter Adams. When this group emerged from the studio Atlantic was pleased with the results, and released "Money Honey" in 1953. The song, which the label credited to Clyde McPhatter and The Drifters, went to #1 on the R&B charts, and the group was on its way.

McPhatter sang lead on several more hits including the beach music classic "Honey Love," which topped the R&B charts and wen to #21 on the pop charts, before he was drafted and sold his controlling share of the group to manager George Treadwell. Johnny Moore joined the group—now consisting of Gerhart Thrasher, Andrew Thrasher, Bill Pinkney and Jimmy Oliver—and took over as lead singer. Their first recording with Moore as lead, "Adorable," went to #1 on the R&B charts and was followed by several chart records including the classic "Ruby Baby," which was Top 10 on the R&B charts and was their first collaboration with Jerry Leiber and Mike Stoller, who wrote the song. However, there was tension between the group and their manager, and after Pinkney asked for more money he was fired, and Andrew Thrasher quit as well. The group now consisted of Tommy Evans, Charlie Hughes, Gerhart Thrasher, and Johnny Moore. This group recorded "Fools Fall in Love" which in 1957 went to #69 on the pop charts and #10 on the R&B charts. Soon Moore and Hughes received their draft notices, and Bobby Hendricks stepped in to do lead vocals on their next hit, "Drip Drop," another song written by Leiber and Stoller. After "Drip Drop" there were more defections and more dissension, and ultimately Treadwell decided to start over afresh and fired the whole group.

Having had a string of chart hits, Treadwell and Atlantic knew that the name The Drifters was a valuable commodity that shouldn't be wasted. On one occasion when The Drifters had been performing at the Apollo, Treadwell had heard a young singer named Benjamin Nelson (later to become Ben E. King, see the entry for King) singing with his group the Five Crowns, and in order to keep The Drifters name alive Treadwell hired him and Charlie Thomas, Doc Green, and Elsbeary Hobbs of his group the Five Crowns to become the new Drifters. Their first release was "There Goes My Baby," which went to #2 on the charts and had the distinction of being one of the first rock records to incorporate strings. They were working with producers Jerry Leiber and Mike Stoller at this point, and this would be the most successful phase of the group's chart history. While the earlier Drifters' music had more of a doo-wop feel, the new Drifters music had a more elegant sound, and the #1 hit "Save the Last Dance for Me," written by the famous songwriting team Doc Pomus and Mort Shuman, seemed to confirm that they'd found the right formula.

Other songs from this period included "(If You Cry) True Love, True Love" (with Johnny Lee Williams stepping in to sing lead), "Dance With Me," "I Count the Tears," and "This Magic Moment," another Pomus and Shuman composition. But money issues arose once again, and King left for a solo career, and thus continued a cycle of an ever changing lineup and the use of a variety of singers doing lead duties. Johnny Lee Williams took over lead for a while, as did Charlie Thomas, and then Treadwell recruited Rudy Lewis, who took over lead vocals on "Some Kind of Wonderful," a song written by Gerry Goffin and Carole King. "Some Kind of Wonderful," "Please Stay," written by Burt Bacharach and one of his earliest compositions to make the charts, and "Sweets for My Sweet," another Pomus and Shuman composition, were all recorded during the same session. "Sweets for My Sweet" was one of the group's few hits from this period not to incorporate strings, and featured Dee Dee Warwick, Cissy Houston, Dionne Warwick, and Doris Troy singing back-up. "When My Little Girl Is Smiling" and "Up on the Roof" followed, the latter another Goffin and King (who also played piano on the recording) penned hit. Continuing to record songs written by the most notable songwriters of the 1960s, the group recorded "On Broadway," written by Barry Mann and Cynthia Weil with some additions made by Leiber and Stoller. One of the features of the song is a guitar solo by a then little-known musician named Phil Spector.

The group was on a roll and although "I'll Take You Home" and "One Way Love" weren't big chart hits, they received a fair amount of play in beach clubs. Their next release, however, not only went into the Top 5 on the pop charts, but also came to epitomize everything that beach music stood for. "Under the Boardwalk" was scheduled to be another song on which Rudy Lewis handled lead vocals, but sadly he died of a drug overdose the night before the song was recorded. Johnny Moore (who had returned to the group) took lead on the song, which was written by Arthur Resnick (who would later write "Good Lovin'" for the Rascals and "Yummy, Yummy, Yummy" for the Ohio Express) and Kenny Young (who would write "Arizona" for Mark Lindsay). The song was reportedly a bit faster and more upbeat originally than in the recorded version, but given the group's despondency that day it ended up having a slower, more melancholy sound. Moore also sang lead on the beach-themed follow-up, "I've Got Sand in My Shoes," another Resnick and Young song similar in style and sound to "Boardwalk." From then on, Moore handled lead duties on songs such as "Saturday Night at the Movies," the group's last Top 20 pop hit in the U.S., as well as low charters such as "Come on Over to My Place" and "I'll Take You Where the Music's Playing."

Their last song to make the U.S. charts was in 1966, and by the late '60s The Drifters were no longer a hot property. After numerous personnel changes they left Atlantic Records and headed to England, which was gripped in the Northern Soul boom. They signed with Bell Records, and their third release, 1973's "Like Sister and Brother," was a #7 hit in England. Though Moore was still the lead singer of the group, it was around this time that Clyde Brown joined them. "I was managed by Jimmy Evans in New York City, who also managed Wilson Pickett and a number of other artists," Brown said:

> Jimmy called and asked if I wanted to sing with the Drifters. At first I said I didn't know, but I met up with them in Jamaica, and later we played the London Palladium, the Middle East, South Africa, all over. Though I'd originally only signed a one-year contract, I played with them from 1974 to 1982. Brown had signed on just in time for their fourth release on Bell, 1974's "Kissin' in the Back Row of the Movies." I really didn't like that song for some reason. But our manager Faye Treadwell (George Treadwell had died in 1967) said to me, "It's gonna be a hit, Clyde—come and do the session." I said, "I don't like the song, and I don't feel like I can do the song justice, because I don't really like it." She said, "That has nothing to do with it, whether you like it or not. Go ahead and sing on it." So I sang on it—and sure enough, it was a hit.

The song went all the way to #2 in England, and The Drifters were officially back—though the record only reached #83 on the R&B charts in the United States (their last chart record of any kind in the United States).

This became the period known to beach music fans as the group's "British Years," and was marked by a number of personnel changes. This period produced hits not only on Bell but also later on Arista, such as "You're More Than a Number (In My Little Red Book)." Brown said "The song was written by Tony Macaulay and Roger Greenaway, and I sang co-lead with Johnny Moore on it. Johnny sang the hook—'You're more than a number in my little red book, you're more than a one-night date…' and so on. I sang the verses like, 'Oh baby, give us a chance/Don't let those small town rumors end our first real romance.' It was very successful in England, a top ten hit." It went all the way to #5, and the flip side, though not a chart hit, was another song beach music audiences have taken to, "Do You Have to Go Now." "Closely Guarded Secret" was another beach hit on Arista, although their next beach favorite, "Pour Your Little Heart Out," saw them on yet another label, Epic.

During this period the grind of performing had taken its toll on the group. "We performed every night, and we did so many shows. We did thirty-four nights straight one time, and some of the nights we doubled. We'd sing in one town, get back on the bus and go to another town and do another show the same night. It was terrible," Brown said. In addition to the constant traveling and performing, the group was also affected by the many lawsuits they had to file against all of the imitation Drifters groups, splinter groups consisting of one or more singers who had been with the group at some point, but who were no longer recording or managed by Treadwell. "I don't know if you know this, but we went to court about who owned the name because there were dozens of groups around the world claiming to be the Drifters. We went to court to straighten it out, but it was like opening Pandora's box. It was exhausting." With the stress of touring and litigation, Moore called it quits in 1978, and Brown a few years later, though both would return and leave again. Johnny Moore, who had been with the group through all of their major periods and incarnations in the '50s, '60s, and '70s, would rejoin yet again in 1987 and stay with the group until he passed away in 1998.

The Rock and Roll Hall of Fame inducted The Drifters in 1988, specifically naming the members with the group during their most prolific periods—Clyde McPhatter, Bill Pinkney, Gerhart Thrasher, Johnny Moore, Ben E. King, Charlie Thomas, and Rudy Lewis. Several of the members received Pioneer Awards from the Rhythm & Blues Foundation, and the Vocal Group Hall of Fame inducted both Clyde McPhatter's original group and the group from the Ben E. King years.

The Drivers

BEACH MUSIC DISCOGRAPHY: "Smooth, Slow, and Easy" (Deluxe 6094, 1956: Did Not Chart).

The history of the Drivers and their recording career is short, obscure, and shrouded in uncertainty. The members of this Cincinnati group—Willie Price, Charlie Harris, Leroy Harmshaw, Carl Rogers, and Leroy Smith—were supposedly truck drivers by day and singers by night. The group formed in in 1952 and first recorded a one-off on the Linn label, "A Man's

Glory/Teeter Totter" in 1954. Between 1956 and 1957 they recorded three singles for Deluxe, and the first of these was by far the best, a song written by Harris and Smith, "Smooth, Slow, and Easy." This recording is one of the most polished-sounding releases the group did, and like many R&B records of that period it is an innuendo-laden song that is supposedly about driving, but is most certainly about sex. As lead singer Willie Price sings, you better fill his body with "aka-hol" if you want his motor to roll. A mention of the song in *Billboard* in the April 28th, 1956 issue claimed "Deluxe's new group sells 'Smooth, Slow, and Easy,' a slightly spic[y] ditty, with verve and enthusiasm. The group is loaded with showmanship, and the lead singer is a particular standout." Despite subsequent sidebar ads in *Billboard* pushing the song in the ensuing weeks, the record failed to chart. They followed "Smooth" on Deluxe in 1957 with "My Lonely Prayer" and then "Dangerous Lips," neither of which charted either.

Over the next few years the group had a rotating line-up, as Paul McCoy, James Pate, and Edison Thompson later joined the group. They recorded a variety of sides for several labels over the next few years, including "Blue Moon" for RCA in 1957, and the recordings of "Ho Ho"/"Doe Doe" on Alton in 1959 and "Mr. Astronaut" for King in 1962 may be the same group as well. None of these singles charted and it appears the group faded from notice.

The Du Droppers

BEACH MUSIC DISCOGRAPHY: "I Found Out" (RCA 5321, 1953: Billboard Pop Did Not Chart, R&B #3).

The Du Droppers were formed in Harlem in 1952 by lead J.C. ("Junior" Caleb) Ginyard. Ginyard had been with the Royal Harmony Singers in the 1930s, which became the Jubalaires in the early '40s, and then he formed the Dixieaires in 1948. Willie Ray and Harvey Ray (who had been with the Southwest Jubilee Singers), and Eddie Hashaw filled out the remainder of the group when they formed in New York. They signed with Red Robin Records in 1952 and released "Can't Do Sixty No More," which of course was a response to the Dominoes 1951 hit "Sixty Minute Man." Oddly enough, though the titles are the same, this is not the same song the Dominoes would release in 1955 (see the entry for the Dominoes). The song has a gospel-like sound, but was not a substantial hit perhaps because it didn't have much in common with the original.

Not long after this Hashaw left the group and Bob Kornegay joined in his stead, and the group also left Red Robin for RCA. Their first release for that label, "I Wanna Know," went to #3 on the R&B charts, and suddenly the group was in demand. Then the group issued another follow-up record, only this time it was to their own hit, not someone else's. "I Found Out (What You Do When You Go 'Round There)" was a follow up to "I Wanna Know," and used some of the same lyrics as their previous hit. It, too, peaked at #3, and by the end of 1953 *Billboard*'s R&B charts rated "I Wanna Know" as the #13 hit of the year and "I Found Out" as #39. The Du Droppers were also ranked by *Rhythm And Blues Magazine* as the sixth most popular R&B group of 1953.

In 1954 the group began touring all over the U.S. and Canada as a result of their newfound popularity, but oddly enough, just when the group seemed to be hitting their stride, instead of reaching greater heights they started to fall apart. RCA had switched them to their new "Groove" subsidiary label, and though they released a number of singles none of them charted. They added a fifth member, Prentice Moreland, who only stayed with them a few months, and Harvey Ray left and also Joe Van Loan of the Ravens sang with the group on and off. There was legal wrangling about Van Loan's contract with the Ravens, and Charlie Hughes, who would later be with The Drifters, actually sang with the group a while. Ultimately the group broke up in 1955, having never had another hit after "I Found Out."

Champion Jack Dupree

BEACH MUSIC DISCOGRAPHY: "Rub a Little Boogie" (King 4706, 1954: Did Not Chart); "Let the Doorbell Ring" (King 4797, 1955: Did Not Chart).

When he was two years old William Thomas Dupree was sent to the Colored Waifs Home in New Orleans after his parents were killed when the Ku Klux Klan burned down their home. There Dupree taught himself to play the piano after getting preliminary instruction from a priest, and at age fourteen or fifteen he left the home to make a living playing piano in bars and New Orleans speakeasies. He honed his craft as a pianist under the tutelage of iconic bluesmen such as Tuts Washington, Willie "Drive 'Em Down" Hall, and Roy "Professor Long Hair" Byrd, and soon he was regarded as one of most promising boogie-woogie pianists in New Orleans. Exhibiting the restless spirit that would define him for the rest of his life, living as a hobo he took to riding the rails and eventually ended up in Chicago. There learned about boxing from Joe Louis, and he eventually fought more than 100 professional bouts and became the Golden Gloves and lightweight champion of Indiana, hence his nickname "Champion Jack."

Even when boxing Dupree continued to play music, and in 1940 he recorded "Warehouse Man Blues," the first of nine releases he would have on the Okeh through 1942. He was drafted during World War II and served as a cook in the navy, and after his ship was sunk in the South Pacific he spent two years in a Japanese prisoner of war camp. After the war Dupree returned to the U.S., where over the next ten years he recorded not only under his own name but also as Brother Blues and the Backroom Boys, Big Tom Collins, Blind Boy Johnson and His Rhythm, Duke Bayou and His Mystic Six, Meat Head Johnson and His Blues Hounds, and Willie Jordan and his Swinging Five. Often a member of these "groups" was Brownie McGhee, brother of "Stick" McGhee of "Drinkin Wine Spo-Dee-O-Dee" fame, and Stick McGhee himself even sat in on Dupree's 1954 release on Robin, "Drunk Again." As a result, Dupree recorded for a dozen labels during the 1940s and '50s, including Apollo, Red Robin, and King. It was on King that he would find his greatest commercial success, the height of which was a 1955 duet with Teddy "Mr. Bear" McRae called "Walking the Blues," which was on the R&B charts for 11 weeks. Prior to this release, he recorded two songs that have gained an audience in beach music circles with fans of boogie-woogie jump blues. 1953's "Rub a Little Boogie" was recorded in 1953 in New York City, and featured Dupree on vocals backed by Papa Lightfoot, Milton Batiste, Nat Perilliat, Edwin Maire, and Charles Connor. For whatever reason Dupree would have no recordings or releases in 1954, but in 1955 he would record "Let the Doorbell Ring," backed by Jerome Darr, Cedric Wallace, and Cornelius Thomas. Though the song was actually the B-side of the record ("Harelip Blues" was the A side), it would nevertheless be a latter day hit with shaggers, though it was not a hit commercially at the time.

Dupree became increasingly despondent about the racism he saw in America, and by 1960 he moved to Europe, taking up residence in West Halifax England by the mid–1960s. In the '60s he would record his music in London, Paris, Zurich Switzerland, and Copenhagen, Denmark, with an occasional foray into New York as well. Over time his reputation grew as one of the finest bluesmen who ever recorded, and he has been cited as an influence on performers from Eric Clapton to Fleetwood Mac. Despite a lifetime spent exiled from his native land, he returned to America to play the New Orleans Jazz and Heritage Festival in 1990, where he was enthusiastically received. Still recording into his 80s, he died at his home in Hanover, Germany, in 1992; he was inducted into the Blues Hall of Fame in 1993.

Donnie Elbert

BEACH MUSIC DISCOGRAPHY: "Where Did Our Love Go" (All Platinum 2330, 1971: Billboard Pop #15); "I Can't Help Myself" b/w "Love is Here and Now You're Gone"" (Avco 4587, 1972: Billboard Pop #22); "Come See About Me" (Avco 4598, 1972: Did Not Chart).

Born in New Orleans, Louisiana, Donnie Elbert and his family moved to Buffalo, New York, when he was three, and by the time he was a teenager he was already involved in music. He co-founded the Vibra-Harps in 1955, and along with Danny Cannon (who would later take the name Lenny O'Henry and record "Across the Street"), Charles Hargro, and Donald Simmons (some sources list Douglas Gibson as a founding member as well), the group recorded the group their first single, "Walk Beside Me," for the New York based Beech label in 1958. Apparently the group had a disagreement right before they recorded the song and Elbert opted not to sing on the record. Elbert soon left the group, and his first solo single, 1957's "What Can I Do," would make the lower reaches of the pop charts at #61. Over the next few years he would record nearly three dozen singles for a number of labels including Deluxe, Vee-Jay, Red Top, Jot, Jalynne, P&L, Parkway, Cub, Up State, and Checker, but not one would make the American charts. He signed with the small-brand Pittsburgh-based Gateway Records in 1964 and wrote a song called "Run Little Girl" which reportedly captured the attention of famed writers and producers Jerry Leiber and Mike Stoller. Apparently they offered Elbert $10,000 dollars for the rights to the song, but Gateway convinced Elbert to turn them down because he could make even more money if he retained ownership and Gateway released the record. He kept the rights, and Gateway failed to follow through. Not long afterwards Elbert wrote a song called "A Little Piece of Leather," which got the interest of Berry Gordy who wanted Elbert to record the song for Motown. Again Elbert listened to the wrong advisors, Gateway released it and it flopped. It would become a big Northern Soul hit in England, however, and would break the U.K. Top 30 in 1965.

While he was trying to break through as singles artist, Elbert was also writing music, and he wrote a song for his friend Darrell Banks called "Baby Walk Right In." Unbeknownst to Elbert, Banks would take the song, rename it, and record it as "Open the Door to Your Heart." The song would be huge for Banks, reaching #27 on the Billboard Hot 100 and #2 on the R&B charts. But when the record came out, Elbert noticed that Banks, and not he, was credited with writing it, and Elbert was shocked to learn that Banks had claimed sole credit for having written the song. After a protracted legal battle, Elbert was at last able to get himself listed co-writer, the lesser status being attributed to the fact that Banks had made some minor changes, such as speeding up the tempo and changing the name. Elbert's claims were validated by his actions: while Elbert would go on to write more than one hundred songs, Banks would never again receive a songwriting credit.

In late 1966 Elbert moved to England where he'd had his only chart success of late, and after a couple of singles (1969's Reggae hit "Without You" actually went to #1 in Jamaica) he moved back to the U.S. in 1970. His first hit back in the States was 1970's "I Can't Get Over Losing You," which climbed to #98 on the pop charts and #26 on the R&B charts, giving him his first American chart records in thirteen years. After two more releases that did not chart, he released a version of the Supremes' 1964 #1 hit "Where Did Our Love Go" that he had recorded in England in 1969. He offered it to a couple of American labels who declined it before he made a deal with the London label for release in the UK, but after the song hit #8 in England, All Platinum agreed to release it for American distribution. The song went to #15 on the pop charts and sold a million and a half records, and the bouncy beat helped it quickly become a favorite in the shag haunts of the Carolinas as well. He followed this with another Motown cover, a version of the Four Tops' #1 hit "I Can't Help Myself," because, as he said in a 1972 interview on British Radio, "it's within the same pattern, and I thought it would be the best follow up." It too charted, going to #22 on the pop charts and to #11 in England. The flip side, a cover of the Supremes' "Love is Here and Now You're Gone," may be one of the finest records he ever recorded, and in fact the 45 probably sold well on the basis of the recordings on both sides. 1972 also saw Elbert record his own version of another Supremes' hit, "Come See About Me." The song was not supposed to be released as a 45, but some copies were accidentally mispressed and labeled as "Ooo Baby Baby," though the recording is in fact "Come See About Me." It did not chart, and by 1972 Elbert was angry that he was being asked to do Motown covers almost exclusively. He'd have several more records make the R&B charts over the next few years, though none would surpass the success of "Where Did Our Love Go."

Elbert would once again become embroiled in a songwriting credit controversy in 1975. He was apparently shopping around a song he had written called "Shame, Shame, Shame" while at All Platinum, but without asking his label gave the song to a new group they had signed called Shirley & Company, featuring Shirley Goodman, formerly one half of the duo Shirley and Lee who had charted with 1957's "Let the Good Times Roll." "Shame, Shame Shame" was released by Shirley & Company crediting label co-owner Sylvia Robinson as the writer, and the song went to #12 on the pop charts, #1 on the soul charts, and #1 on the dance charts. Once again, Elbert had been denied the credit he deserved, but unlike the contention surrounding "Open the Door to Your Heart," Elbert was never legally recognized as the writer of "Shame, Shame Shame." Just as Darrell Banks never had another hit after recording "Open the Door to Your Heart," Shirley & Company would never reach the Top 40 again either.

After a few more releases, Elbert moved to the administrative side of the music industry as a director of A&R for Polygram's Canadian division. He would remain in that position just a few years, dying in 1989 after a stroke at the age of 53.

The Elgins

BEACH MUSIC DISCOGRAPHY: "Heaven Must Have Sent You" (V.I.P. 25037, 1966: Billboard Pop #50)

The Elgins had their origins in several groups such as the Sensations and the Five Emeralds, but by 1961 members Cleo "Duke" Miller, Robert Fleming, Norman McClean, and Johnny Dawson were recording as the Downbeats. While doing back-up vocals as session singers for the Lu Pine and UA labels, they had come to the attention of Berry Gordy, who was looking for a doo-wop type groups to sign to the labels he was forming. They signed with Motown, releasing the unsuccessful single "Your Baby's Back" on the Tamla label. At time Motown was also attempting to develop solo artist Saundra Mallett (later Edwards), and although she had already recorded "Camel Walk" backed by the Vandellas, the record's failure perhaps prompted Berry Gordy to suggest that Mallet join the Downbeats. Although this merger would seem to indicate there would be more releases, over the next three years no records were forthcoming until their first single, a Holland, Dozier, and Holland composition "Darling Baby," came out on Tamla in 1965. *After* the record was released, Gordy learned there was another group called the Downbeats, and Dawson thought they should call themselves The Elgins because he saw a sign advertising Elgin watches. Gordy approved the name, even though that had been the original name of the Temptations, who had changed it. The single was then re-released with the label denoting the single as being by the Elgins, and rose to #72 on the pop charts and #4 on the R&B charts.

This would be surpassed by their next release, another Holland, Dozier, and Holland composition and production, "Heaven Must Have Sent You," one of the finest Motown recordings not released by the label's bigger, more successful acts. With backing vocals augmented by Motown's Andantes, the song went to #50 on the pop charts and #9 on the R&B charts, and at the end of the year Billboard ranked it as one of the Top 100 R&B songs of the year. Compared to most Motown chart records it wasn't very successful, but the group was touring and enjoying some popularity, so an LP, *Darling Baby*, was released. Motown released one more Elgins single, "It's Been a Long Long Time," though it only rose to #92 on the pop charts. At this point the group started to splinter and change their line-up, and though they continued to record nothing else was released; more than a dozen recordings were left in the vaults, and would stay that way until 2007.

"Heaven Must Have Sent You," however, would prove to have a life of its own. Like many unappreciated and obscure American R&B recordings from the 1970s, during the English Northern Soul boom the record would be much more successful, and would shoot all the way to #3 on the English charts when re-released in 1971 (in fact, according to chronicler Kev Roberts it is among the greatest Northern Soul hits of all time). The group quickly reassembled for an English tour, but Mallet-Edwards apparently was not interested and was replaced by Yvonne Vernee-Allen. No further chart hits resulted, but the group would always have a following in England and toured there extensively in the early 1970s.

Oddly enough, the song would receive its greatest U.S. exposure by way of a funkier disco version released by Bonnie Pointer in 1979, which would go to #11 on the charts. However, the flipside of the original 45 release contained a traditional version by Pointer that matched the Elgins' style perfectly. While it was not released as an A side, not surprisingly the flipside found its way onto many jukeboxes in the Carolinas during the late 1970s and early 1980s.

Original members Allen, Dawson, and McLean got together again in England in the late 1980s and early '90s, resulting in the release of some mostly-new material in the 1990s. A few of the last living members of the group made a final tour after their unreleased tracks were made available on a compilation called *The Elgins: The Motown Anthology* in 2007, but after that they quit touring and the group dissolved.

The Embers

BEACH MUSIC DISCOGRAPHY: "Far Away Places"(MGM 14167, 1969: Did Not Chart); "I Love Beach Music" (eEe 1002, 1979: Did Not Chart).

Bobby Tomlinson, Jackie Gore and Blair Ellis founded the Embers in the '50s, playing fraternity parties and any other type of gig they could get. While they were mainly a rhythm and blues group, "because we played functions for older people too we also performed old standards," Tomlinson told the author. They became so successful that in 1965 they opened their own club in Raleigh and another in Atlantic Beach in 1968, and there they played with acts such as Jackie Wilson, Jerry Butler, and The Drifters. It was in Atlantic Beach one night that something happened almost by accident. "In 1968, Archie Bell had 'Tighten Up' out with that 'dut duh duh duh duh duh' rhythm and beat to it," Tomlinson said. "One night we were performing—there were probably had 1,500 to 2,000 kids in there—and we were playing 'Tighten Up.' We got into a grove, just jammin,' and Jackie then led right into and started singing 'Far Away Places,' and it went over. And it worked so well that we started doing it all the time." As one of those old standards they had cut their teeth on, "Far Away Places" had been written in 1948 and recorded by the likes of Bing Crosby, Perry Como and Dinah Shore. Though it was a well-known song at one time, setting it to that "Tighten Up" beat, allowed the Embers—now consisting of John Thompson, Durwood Martin, Johnny Hopkins, Ray Rivera, Bobby Tomlinson and Jackie Gore—to make it their own and were soon they were playing it for audiences throughout the area.

Tomlinson said agents and promoters used to come into their clubs, and eventually a friend heard them do "Far Away Places," which ultimately led to a contract with MGM Records. "We made a tape, sent it to [Bob Crewe], and he signed us to a contract. They did the music out there with professional musicians, and then they flew two producers out and it the vocals were recorded here. They released it and it was doing great, and we thought we were on the way," Tomlinson said. "It was being played everywhere, and we heard it was played in Vietnam all the time. Then Bob Crewe was fired from MGM, and every act he'd just signed went out with him. They pulled the plug on us." As a result, the record stopped getting airplay and never quite became the hit many thought it would be.

The group continued to perform, and a decade later they'd have another big song,

The Embers, circa mid–1960s (photograph courtesy Bobby Tomlinson).

arguably one of the most important beach music recordings ever. "They started calling that old rhythm and blues 'beach music' in the late '60s, because these kids would go to the beach and hear all that kind of music being played," former Embers lead singer Jackie Gore told me. "Then they'd go home and want to hear that music they heard on the beach during the summertime—that 'beach music.' Well, in 1979, we'd had a lot of young people who were following us around as we played beach music, and my wife said, 'Why don't you write a song for the young people about beach music?' So that's what I did—I sat down at my kitchen table one morning and came up with the 'I Love Beach Music' melody." He says he figured one good way to make the song relevant was to "mention about seven or eight of the most popular beach music songs of all time. I just linked them together and made it all fit." Consequently, listeners heard references to songs by the Dominoes, Willie Tee, The Drifters, the Tymes, the

Showmen, The Tams, and even their contemporaries The Catalinas—with a few chords of the Embers own "Far Away Places" thrown in. The song came out and was an instant beach music hit.

But the song would find its greatest audience as a commercial jingle in the early 1980s. "I did the song at a beach music concert," Gore said, "and instead of singing 'I Love Beach Music,' I started singing 'I Love Budweiser,' and the crowd went wild. Budweiser wanted us to record a commercial for them right then. It became a national commercial for them, and that's where the song made all of its money, through the association with Budweiser, not just as a song itself. It went on for a couple of years, we recorded several other commercials for Budweiser and we started playing their national events all over the country." But once the commercials stopped running, the resilience of the song really became apparent, and it became, and has remained to this day, beach music's anthem. It is probably the most recognizable song ever written about beach music, and with its ties to the old classics and standards, it serves as a bridge between the classic years and the revival years for beach music that would follow the song's release.

Though Gore is no longer with the Embers, he still performs "I Love Beach Music" today. "I am truly not tired of singing it," Gore says. "We can stand up there and play all night long, and there won't be that much dancing, but when we play 'I Love Beach Music' the floor fills up with people every time. I'm very proud of it, very proud of what the song has done for me and my groups over the years, and I never get tired of performing it."

The Esquires

BEACH MUSIC DISCOGRAPHY: "Get On Up" (Bunky 7750, 1967: Billboard Pop #11); "And Get Away" (Bunky 7752, 1967: Billboard Pop #22).

Birmingham, Alabama-born Gilbert, Alvis, and Betty Moorer were raised in a home where music was a daily part of life; their father sang in the gospel group the Friendly Five, and their mother who played the piano. The family moved to Wisconsin, and while at North Division High School in Milwaukee Gilbert, Alvis and Betty formed Betty Moorer and the Esquires in 1957 with the help of brothers Perry (who played saxophone) and Charles (who played trumpet). The group would go through a number of personnel changes between 1957 and 1966, most importantly the departure of Betty, who as Betty Moore would record the single "Long Hot Summer" on the Cuca label with her brothers singing backup. By 1966 they were known as the Esquires, consisting of Gilbert and Alvis as well as Sam Pace (who joined in 1961) and Shawn Taylor(who joined in 1965), and they left Milwaukee for the burgeoning Chicago soul music scene. In Chicago they tried to get a contract from Curtis Mayfield, who was running the Windy C and Mayfield labels, but he reportedly didn't like their sound because he felt they sounded too much like his group the Impressions. They continued to line up auditions until they tried out for Bill "Bunky" Sheppard at Constellation Records by doing a song called "Get on Up" that Shawn Taylor and Gilbert Moorer had written. Sheppard liked the song, but rather than have the group record it he turned them into a studio group and had them sing backup on a series of releases by Mill Evans, none of which charted.

Constellation folded and Sheppard established his own label, Bunky Records, and for the label's first release he finally decided to issue the Esquire's "Get on Up." Arranged by Thomas Washington, who would later work with Earth, Wind & Fire, The Dells, and the Chi-Lites, the song was similar in content to many of the songs in the 1960s that dealt with the politics of dancing, as the vocalist implores his girl to get up on the floor and dance some of the most popular dances of the day such as the Monkey and the Philly Dog. However, according to Mill Evans, Sheppard felt that something wasn't right about the song, and called in Evans to determine what that was. In an interview with Bob Pruter, Evans said he told Sheppard, "They're singing 'get on up' and then there's a big hole there! I worked on it and came up with the bass parts for the song. It was to fill the hole." With Evans singing that catchy bass addition, the song shot to the top of the local charts, and then climbed the national charts, lodging at #11 on the pop charts and #3 on the R&B charts. The group, now with Evans as a permanent member, started touring the country, quickly filling seats wherever they played, including the Apollo Theater in New York, the Uptown in Philadelphia, and the Howard in Washington. Unfortunately, Shawn Taylor was repeatedly late for performances and Sheppard fired him.

Now a quartet, to follow the success of their debut single, they next recorded what was an answer record to "Get On Up" called "And Get Away." The song is much like its predecessor though brassier, while some of the lyrics are similar and the refrain of "get on up" even sounds basically the same. In spite of this—or perhaps because of this—when released in 1967 it too performed well, reaching #9 on the R & B charts and #22 on the pop charts. An album followed, and the future looked quite bright for the group. Yet even though the group released three more singles in 1968, none of them made the Top 100 of the pop charts. They signed with Wand and had two more semi-successful records in 1968 and 1969, "You've Got the Power (#91 Pop, #29 R&B) and "I Don't Know" (did not chart Pop, #37 R&B). They changed labels again, and hit the lowest reaches of the charts on Lamarr. At this point the personnel changes were coming fairly frequently, and other than a 1976 release of an updated version of "Get On Up" called "Get On Up '76" for Ju-Par Records (#62 R&B), their charting days were over. Eventually the group moved back to Milwaukee and played the oldies circuit with Gilbert and Alvis Moorer as the mainstays of the group; when Gilbert Moorer passed away in 2008 the group ceased to exist, though it was soon reorganized by some of the children of the original members. In addition to Gilbert Moorer, Alvis Moorer and Sam Pace have also passed away.

Betty Everett

BEACH MUSIC DISCOGRAPHY: "The Shoop Shoop Song" (Vee-Jay 585, 1964: Billboard Pop #6).

Betty Everett was born in Greenwood, Mississippi, and began playing the piano and singing gospel in the church when she was nine. When she was a teenager her family moved to Chicago, and she was spotted singing at the Hideaway Club which led to a contract with the small Chicago-based Cobra label. Between 1957 and 1959 she recorded three singles for them, none of which were successful, and so she followed with some sides for another small Chicago label, C.J. Two singles there in 1960 and 1961 also failed to connect with listeners, and frustrated by the lack of success at this point Everett considered returning to her gospel roots, but the label made it clear they were not interested in releasing religious music. Then she met Leo Austell, who was starting another small Chicago label, Renee, and the label's second release was Everett's "I'll Be There." Apparently the song showed promise and was picked up and re-released by another fledgling label, One-Derful. Although it did not chart, One-Derful also released two more tracks she had recorded for Renee, though the results were the same.

It wasn't until she signed with the better-established Vee-Jay label in 1963 that things came together for Everett. Though her first single, "Prince of Players," failed, her second, 1963's "You're No Good," took her music to the charts at last. The song was a Clint Ballard, Jr., composition (he'd get his first #1 with "Game of Love" by Wayne Fontana and the Mindbenders in 1965) and had originally been recorded by Dee Dee Warwick though the single failed. Calvin Carter of Vee-Jay secured the rights to the song intending it for Dee Clark, but Clark didn't want to record it and didn't. Everett did record it, and her version was a hit, going to #51 on Billboard's R&B chart. The song would go on to be recorded by a number of artists, and eventually Linda Ronstadt would take it to #1 in 1974.

The follow-up would do even better. "It's in His Kiss (The Shoop Shoop Song)" was written by Rudy Clark, and it, too, was a cover of an earlier version, this time by Merry Clayton which also had not charted. As had been the case with "You're No Good," Calvin Carter found the song in New York, and encouraged Everett to record this one as well. Apparently Everett was not convinced that the song was right for her, but recorded it anyway. Carter obviously knew what he was doing, because the song became her only million-seller, going to #6 on the pop charts in February 1964. This prompted the small Dottie label to re-release a couple of her old Cobra recordings, but her next new recording was 1964's "I Can't Hear You" on Vee-Jay; it only went to #66 on the pop charts.

After one more Vee-Jay release she recorded a song with Jerry Butler, "Let It Be Me." Another cover, the song was originally a 1955 Gibert Becaud song released in France called "Je t'appartiens," which had been covered by the Everly Brothers in 1960 and went to #7. Jerry Butler thought it would be good to redo the song, and he felt that Everett would be the perfect partner for a duet. Their collaboration went to #5 on the pop charts.

Everett was on a roll, but unfortunately Vee-Jay was foundering. She had two more low-charting singles before Vee-Jay folded, and after spending an unproductive year with ABC she signed with UNI. Three UNI releases made the charts, but only 1969's "There'll Come a Time" made the Top 40. After one final release on Fantasy in 1970 that inched into the Top 100, of her subsequent recordings just four more made the R&B charts, the last being on United Artists in 1978.

Everett quit recording in 1980. She moved to Wisconsin to live with her sister and reconnected with gospel music through the church and also worked for the Rhythm and Blues Foundation. In 1990 she had resurgence in popularity after "The Shoop Shoop Song" was used in the movie *Mermaids* and re-recorded by Cher, and Everett was subsequently coaxed into performing once again. However, after a few performances she seemed to tire of the grind of performing and after failing to appear for two scheduled appearances shortly thereafter she retired for good. Everett passed away in 2001; she was inducted into the Rhythm and Blues Hall of Fame in 1996.

The Falcons

BEACH MUSIC DISCOGRAPHY: "You're So Fine" (Unart 2013, 1959: Billboard Pop #17)

The Falcons originated in Detroit when jewelry store co-workers Eddie Floyd, who was black, and Bob Manardo, who was white, decided to form a singing group, which interestingly enough would make them one of the first notable interracial groups. While Floyd would go on to great success not only with the Falcons but also later as a solo performer, Manardo's singing career would be short lived; not long after Floyd and Manardo added Tom Shetler (who was also white) Arnett Robinson, and Willie Schofield (who were black), they cut just one record, 1956's "Baby That's It," before Manardo was drafted and Shetler volunteered for service. The group had hired Floyd's uncle Robert West to manage them, and with his connections to the Detroit music scene they were able to replace the departed members by holding auditions. They selected Joe Stubbs, the brother of Levi Stubbs of the soon-to-be-famous Four Tops, and his friend, guitarist Lance Fennie. Soon Arnett Robinson left, and after more auditions, he was replaced by Mack Rice, who in the mid–1960s, as Sir Mack Rice, would record as a successful solo act as well. With this line-up in place the group finally gelled and turned their attention to recording.

After failed singles on the Silhouette and Kudo labels, in 1959 they released a side with Stubbs on lead, "You're So Fine," on the Flick label. It was recorded at Jack and Devora Brown's Fortune Records studio, a venue known for using cheap equipment and for producing a "hollow" sound. Though the record sounded like it had been recorded in someone's basement, after it started to shoot up the local charts, Robert West got a United Artists subsidiary label, Unart, to release the song nationally. The song was a hit, going to #2 on the R&B charts and #17 on the pop charts, and has been referred to as the first true soul recording. Unfortunately none of their other Unart singles charted, though 1959 did see a song they had recorded for Chess, "Just for Your Love," make the R&B charts. After a third release with Joe Stubbs, he left the group and was replaced by Wilson Pickett, yet another member who would go on to greater fame later. Their third recording with Pickett had him singing lead on "I Found a Love," which would go to #6 on the R&B charts although it peaked at #75 on the pop charts. After this their make-up would shift constantly, as the group's members would start to come and go. They'd officially breakup in 1963, though a new Falcons group was formed by West and would perform for a few more years before the Falcons name was retired for good around 1970.

Individually, of course, most of the members of the group would be tremendously successful. Mack Rice would go on to write and record "Mustang Sally" in 1965, which would chart but which would be an even bigger hit for Wilson Pickett in 1967, going to #23 on the pop charts for him. As well-known as this version was, it was but a minor hit in Pickett's repertoire, as he would have nearly fifty chart records on the pop and R&B charts, including "In the Midnight Hour," "Funky Broadway," "Land of 1000 Dances," and many others. Joe Stubbs would sing with several groups, including the Contours and the Originals, before going on to his greatest success as the lead singer of a group founded by Holland, Dozier, and Holland, 100 Proof Aged in Soul. Their hit "Somebody's Been Sleeping" would go to #8 on the pop charts, sell more than a million records and receive a gold record in 1970. Finally, with nearly twenty chart records while at Stax, including the hits "Knock on Wood," "Bring It on Home to Me," and the beach favorite "I've Never Found a Girl (To Love Me Like You Do)," Eddie Floyd would be a superstar in his own right as well. As a result, while the Falcons are not today a household name like many of their contemporaries, and even though they had only one Top 40 pop hit, without a doubt the group counted among its membership more singers who would go on to find individual and/or group success than any other 1960s soul group.

The Fantastic Shakers

BEACH MUSIC DISCOGRAPHY: "Myrtle Beach Days" (The Fantastic Shakers 16256, 1978: Did Not Chart).

North Carolina native Jeffrey Lynn Reid started playing music at age 10 when his mother gave him a guitar. In 1973, he began his career as a professional musician when he joined the house band at the Shadow Club in Newton, North Carolina, and by 1975 he was working in Myrtle Beach playing an after-hours bar called the Army-Navy Club. "I was 20 years old, and played from midnight to five in the morning," Reid told me. "A lot of groups would come in after they finished at the clubs where they were playing, and sometimes they'd jam with us. I used to see groups like Wild Country—later known as Alabama—and others come in." One person who came into the club was Bo Schronce of the Catalinas, who sang lead on "Summertime's Calling Me." Schronce was a native of Lincolnton North Carolina who had been in several bands before The Catalinas, including Nobody's Perfect and Bo & The Fugitives. Reid got to know Schronce and eventually played him an original composition called "Myrtle Beach Days," based, oddly enough, on the Queen song called 'Killer Queen. "It originally sounded a lot like 'Killer Queen' in fact, with the piano—well actually, it didn't sound *that* good!" Reid says. Reid and his song made an impression on Schronce, and when he left The Catalinas to form a new band in late 1977 he asked Reid to join the group and he agreed. The new group, Blacksmith, consisted of Schronce, Reid, Dino Fair, Tim Faulkner, and Don Tetreault. Before long Blacksmith decided to become "a beach and R&B band," Reid said, and "Bo wanted to do Las Vegas–like shows. He saw a group called The Fantastic Puzzle who did floor shows, and there was also a local band called the Shakers who used to perform. He just put the two names together to come up with the Fantastic Shakers."

Just as The Catalinas had jumped to the forefront of the beach music scene with member Johnny Barker's "Summertime's Calling Me," Schronce knew better than anyone that the Shakers needed their own signature song. That's where "Myrtle Beach Days" came in. "Bo said, 'We ought to take that old song of yours, "Myrtle Beach Days," and make it a beach song'" Reid says. Despite the fact that it was modeled after a '70s rock song, Reid says the conversion wasn't all that difficult. "As written the chords were e to g, but after changing the chords we decided to record it. Well, in my version had I played all the instruments, and I'd never really worked on my lead vocal—I always did keyboards guitar, background vocals, and never really worked on lead vocals much. But Bo had the right type of voice—he has a great R&B voice—so that was the right way to go and he sang it." With Schronce's distinctive voice singing lead the song was a hit. "By 1980 when our album came out it was really big" Reid says. 1980 was in fact the year that classics such as "Carolina Girls," "On the Beach" and other local favorites were released, and it was also when songs recorded earlier such as "Shaggin,'" "I Love Beach Music," "Myrtle Beach Days" and others were all starting to peak as Carolina beach music was hitting full stride. "I remember playing in Columbia in 1980 at the stadium and there were six to eight thousand people there. It was quite a time." "Myrtle Beach Days" had become one of the biggest hits of the period: "I'm really proud of it" Reid says.

Reid stayed with the Shakers until 1994, when he decided to go out his own again, filling in with different bands from time to time, and recording as well. Even though he's not with the Shakers now, "when I play solo I play I still get asked to play 'Myrtle Beach Days' a lot. I'm glad it made the impression it made on so many people." Schronce still performs with the Shakers, who are members of the Beach Music Hall of Fame and the North Carolina Music Hall of Fame.

The Fantastics

BEACH MUSIC DISCOGRAPHY: "Something Old, Something New" (Bell 977, 1971: Billboard Pop #102).

The group began as the Troubadours, and by the time they changed their name to the Velours in 1956 the lineup consisted of Jerome Ramos, John Cheetom (sometimes recorded as Cheatdom), Donald Heywood, Kenneth Walker and Marvin Holland. They showed enough promise as an up-and-comer that they played the Apollo in 1956, and after two non-charting records on the Onyx label in 1956 and 1957, they recorded "Can I Come Over Tonight." The song—which Ramos had written for his girlfriend—would go to #83 on the charts in June 1957 and be their first chart record. They released "This Could Be the Night" next in 1957, and though it didn't chart, their next record, "Remember," did. Thus, with two of their three recordings charting in less than a year, the future looked promising.

But for whatever reason, the group had already reached its high-water mark. Over the course of the next ten years, they would jump from small label to small label, including Cub, High Keys, Studio, Gone, Gold Disc, End, Relic, and Rona. None of their records charted, and members came and left the group periodically. In 1968, the group—now consisting of Ramos, Cheetom, Heywood and Richard Pitts—decided to change their name to the Fantastics, perhaps deciding that the Velours name was too closely tied to the doo-wop tradition, a musical phase that had long since passed, not to mention that they hadn't really had any notable success with the name in more than a decade. After the name change, they moved to England and recorded five singles between 1968 and 1971, but at least they were now recording for better-known labels, including MGM and Deram. In 1971 they signed with Bell records, and they had the opportunity to work with English songwriter Roger Cook. Cook was the writer responsible for hits such as "Here Comes That Rainy Day Feeling Again" by the Fortunes, "I'd Like to Teach the World to Sing" by the New Seekers and "Long Cool Woman in a Black Dress" by the Hollies among many other songs, and in the early 1970s he was riding a tremendous wave of success. For their first Bell release Cook gave the group a song he had written with Tony Macaulay and Roger Greenaway called "Something Old, Something New." The group recorded the song on Bell in 1971, and though it is a fine tune, it struggled up the charts, just bubbling under the Top 100 at #102 in the United States. In the UK, however, the song went all the way to #9. Two releases later, they had their only charting record in the United States, 1971's "(Love Me) Love the Life I Lead," which went to #86.

Within a year, the group's lineup changed yet again, and after two more singles their recording career as the Fantastics was over. Cheetom became a member of a Platters offshoot group, Ramos moved back to the United States, and Heywood tried to keep the group going as the Fantastics for a while. The old Velours name was even resurrected later, so in truth the group existed as the Fantastics for only a short time in their long and storied career before fading from sight.

The Fiestas

BEACH MUSIC DISCOGRAPHY: "So Fine" (Old Town 1062, 1958: Billboard Pop #11); "Broken Heart" (Old Town 1122, 1962: Billboard Pop #81).

Newark, New Jersey residents Tommy Bullock, Eddie Morris, Sam Ingalls, and Preston Lane formed the Fiestas in 1958. Their first hit came about when the group convinced Jim Gribble to manage them, and add them to the stable of artists that he would represent that included the Passions, Mystics, and the Classics. The next step was to find them a label, and there are two very distinct stories about how the group's signing with Old Town records came about. One story says that after shopping around for a label for several months, the group cut a song called "So Fine," written, they thought, by Gribble, who pitched the song to Old Town records and the label signed them to a contract. A more apocryphal story exists that says Old Town co-owner Hy Weiss heard them singing in the bathroom next to his office, signed them on the spot, and then had them record "So Fine" at a total cost of $40. Whatever its origin, the song was recorded and released, oddly enough with and without a gospel-like piano intro (versions with the intro have the letters ZTSP on the label under the catalog number 1062). Whether or not the record had the piano intro probably didn't matter to Weiss, because he had decided that the flip side, "Last Night I Dreamed," should be the A-side, and tried to promote that as the playable hit. The record was out six months before it cracked the Top 100, and only then because DJs turned the record when word got out that "So Fine" was the better track. Ultimately, the song with its unique four-part harmonies went to #3 on the R&B charts, and #11 on the pop charts. The group had their first hit, and Old Town had just its second national hit record.

The label credited Gribble as the songwriter and international versions listed the songwriters as Gribble and Weiss. The problem was, however, that neither of them had actually written the song, and there was ample proof to that effect. Johnny Otis had written the song and copyrighted it to Eldorado Music, and in 1955 Jesse Belvin's group the Sheiks had recorded it on the Federal label. When Otis heard the Fiestas' version, he filed a lawsuit against several people and entities including Old Town and the group, and eventually the suit was settled. Bullock claimed neither he nor anyone in his group had been aware of or heard the original version, and ultimately the brunt of the criticism fell on Gribble, who parted company with both the Fiestas and Old Town.

The group's next release in 1959 was "Our Anniversary," but neither that nor their next six releases on Old Town charted. Their lineup started to shift, but with the original lineup intact once again in 1962 "Broken Heart" became their second chart single. The song, written by Gene Redd (who arranged "Opportunity" for the Jewels) and R.G. Moseley, reached #18 on the R&B charts but peaked at #81 on the pop charts. The group stayed with Old Town through 1965, and while continuing to perform they recorded for a number of labels over the next decade and a half, including Checker, RCA, and Arista. They even tried their hand at disco in the 1970s, recording the Mack Rice composition "Tina (The Disco Queen)" in 1977. Like all of their other post–Old Town releases, it failed to chart. Over the years, "So Fine" has been recorded by a number of artists, including The Ventures, Paul and Paula, The Newbeats, The Everly Brothers, and Sonny & Cher. Ike and Tina Turner (1968), The Oak Ridge Boys (1982), Howard Johnson (1982), and Petite (1986) all charted with cover versions of the song as well.

The Five Du-Tones

BEACH MUSIC DISCOGRAPHY: "Shake a Tail Feather" (One-Derful 4815, 1963: Billboard Pop #51).

The St. Louis based Five Du-Tones formed in 1957 and were originally Robert Hopkins, LeRoy Joyce, Willie Guest, Oscar Watson and James West, though by the time they recorded their first side for One-Derful in 1963, "Please Change Your Mind," the group was based out of Chicago and consisted of Andrew Butler, Frank McCurrey, Guest, Joyce, and West. Their third release on One-Derful was "Shake a Tail Feather," a raucous dance song that also featured the talents of their back-up band, the Exciters (occasionally referenced as the X-Citers). "Tail Feather" peaked at #51 on the Top 100 pop charts and #28 on the R&B charts, and the group appeared to be on their way. Their lineup started to change when West died of heart failure in 1963 and was replaced by David Scott of the Exciters, and they also added the Du-Ettes, female back-ups Barbra Livesy and Mary-Francis Hayes.

Looking to repeat their initial success and perhaps thinking they had found their niche in the popular dance-music market, over the next few years the group released several dance-based singles such as "Monkey See—Monkey Do" and "The Cool Bird," and even a novelty tune, "The Chicken Astronaut." None of these songs charted, and by 1967 the group split up. Butler went on to join a latter-day versions of groups such as the Rivingtons, the Coasters, and the Robins, while McCurrey joined the South Shore Commission, an updated version of the Exciters (Sheryl Henry, Sidney "Pinchback" Lennear, Eugene Rogers, David Henderson and Warren Haygood) who recorded for Atlantic, Nickel, and

Wand throughout the early to mid 1970s. That group had three R&B charts hits, of which "Free Man" was the most significant, going to #9 on the R&B charts and topping the disco/dance music charts for a week in 1975.

Though not enormously successful as a group, the Five Du-Tones sole foray onto the pop charts did generate a rash of cover versions, the most notable being James and Bobby Purify's version in 1967 that reached #25. The song has also been covered by artists as notable as The Monkees, The Kingsmen, and Ray Charles as well.

The "5" Royales

BEACH MUSIC DISCOGRAPHY: "Think" (King 5053, 1957: Billboard Pop #66); "I Know It's Hard But It's Fair" (King 5191, 1959: Did Not Chart).

The Winston Salem, North Carolina–based "5" Royales began as the gospel group The Royal Sons Quintet in 1942. Brothers Lomond "Lowman" Pauling, Curtis Pauling, and Clarence Pauling, along with Johnny Tanner, William Samuels, and Otto Jefferies made up the group, and in 1943 Jimmy Moore replaced Clarence Pauling. In 1950 Obadiah "Scoop" Carter replaced Curtis Pauling, and the group, who were extremely popular on the gospel circuit in the Carolinas, signed with Apollo and went to New York to record a few sides. Apollo, however, was aware of the burgeoning R&B scene and was looking for a vocal group to score some chart hits, and as a result had them cut a few singles and released "Too Much of a Little Bit" in 1951. Though the record didn't chart, it did bring about a new focus for the group, and they changed their name to the Royals to differentiate themselves from the gospel group they had been. Because there were two other Royal/es groups there was confusion with bookings and recordings, so the North Carolina Royals would eventually change their name to the "5" Royales while the Detroit-based Royals, led by Hank Ballard, changed their name to the Midnighters. They used the "5" in quotation marks almost ironically, as there were actually seldom just five of them due to their constantly fluctuating lineup; by this point nine singers had already been members at one time or another.

After releasing "Too Much of a Little Bit," they'd release one more single before "Baby Don't Do It" topped the R&B charts in 1952. The song spent three weeks at #1 and would later be covered by Jaye P. Morgan. Their very next single, 1953's "Help Me, Somebody," would also hit #1, this time for five weeks, while the flipside, "Crazy, Crazy, Crazy," went to #5. "Too Much Lovin' (Much Too Much)" went to #4 that year, and it's flip, "Laundromat Blues," did not chart but would become a classic of risqué early '50s R&B. But after "I Do" charted at #6 in 1954, the group went through a transition period for the next three years. They jumped to the King label and recorded out of Cincinnati, and in 1954 and 1955 their recordings were being released on both King and Apollo. One of these, "Monkey Hips and Rice," did not chart but later gained some traction in the beach clubs. During this period they were performing regularly, but their records weren't selling in great numbers.

By this point Johnny Tanner's brother Eugene had joined the group, and the group consisted of Lowman Pauling, Johnny and Eugene Tanner, Jimmy Moore, and Obadiah Carter, with Otto Jeffries having moved into a position as the group's manager. The Tanner brothers were alternating lead on the songs, and Lowman Pauling's guitar work was becoming increasingly prominent; Booker T. & the M.G.s guitarist Steve Cropper would later declare Pauling one of the most influential of all the early rock guitarists. It wasn't until 1957's "Tears of Joy" that they'd have a record make the charts again (#9, R&B), and it was at this time that they also entered the most productive period of their career in terms of songs that have stood the test of time. Their next release, "Think," also went to #9 on the R&B charts, and was their first record to crossover to the pop charts at #66. Written by Lowman Pauling and punctuated by his guitar licks, "Think" is generally considered one of the Top 50 classic beach music hits of all time. It was so popular that James Brown recorded a version in 1960, and Brown's version made the pop charts as well. Other King recordings from this period include 1958's "Dedicated to the One I Love," which was co-written by Pauling and would go on to be a big hit for the Shirelles (#3, Pop) and the Mamas and the Papas (#2, Pop). Interestingly, the "5" Royales' version would make the pop charts three years later when King Records' Syd Nathan would rerelease it after the Shirelles had their hit, although the "5" Royales version would a barely break into the Top 100 at #81. Other recordings of note from that period included "The Slummer the Slum," which critic Dave Marsh named one of the 1001 best singles of all time in his book *The Heart of Rock and Soul* (he also gives "Think," "Dedicated to the One I Love," and "Baby Don't Do It" that distinction). Marsh also credits Pauling with the innovative use of guitar feedback years before groups such as the Beatles did it. Ray Charles would take another song from 1958, "Tell the Truth," to #13 on the R&B charts in 1960, while 1959's "I Know It's Hard but It's Fair" another Lowman Pauling composition, is enormously popular on the beach music circuit.

Unfortunately for all parties concerned, when Brown recorded "Think" in 1960 he was also with the King label, and when the group sued him for recording the song without their permission they ended up leaving King and signing with the Home of the Blues label out of Memphis. This began a series of label jumps and no hits with Vee-Jay, ABC, Savoy, Smash, Todd, and others. Although they had recorded more than one hundred songs, by the mid–60s members of the group started dropping out; the original group was essentially done by 1965.

Lowman Pauling ended up working as a janitor and passed away in 1973; his brother Clarence became Clarence Paul, a producer and songwriter at Motown. All of the members of the group have since passed away as well. The group was inducted into the North Carolina Music Hall of Fame in 2009 and the Rock and Roll Hall of Fame in 2015.

Eddie Floyd

BEACH MUSIC DISCOGRAPHY: "I've Never Found a Girl (to Love Me Like You Do)" (Stax 002, 1968: Billboard Pop #40).

Eddie Lee Floyd was born in Montgomery, Alabama, and when he was six weeks old his family moved to Detroit, Michigan. When Floyd was in his early 20s he and jewelry store co-worker Bob Manardo decided to form a singing group, and after adding Tom Shetler, Arnett Robinson, and Willie Schofield they became Falcons, one of the first interracial singing groups (Shetler and Manardo were white, Floyd, Robinson, and Schofield were black). The group would go through a number of personnel changes over the next five years, and included members who would go on to further success such as "Sir" Mack Rice, Wilson Pickett, and Joe Stubbs. Because Floyd's uncle Robert West owned the Lupine and Flick labels, his connections helped the group record singles on West's labels and others. The pinnacle of their success was "You're So Fine" in 1959 (see the entry for the Falcons); they disbanded in 1963.

After the group disbanded, Floyd released some solo recordings on Lupine, as well as on the Safice label, which he founded with his friend Al Bell. When Bell was asked to come to the Stax label to do promotion, Floyd and Bell both went to Memphis. Floyd took a job with Stax as a writer and producer, and though initially he was writing mainly for Carla Thomas and William Bell, eventually he'd write for all of the label's major acts, including Sam and Dave, Otis Redding, and Booker T. & the M.G.s. He often worked with Stax guitarist Steve Cropper, and together they wrote a number of songs, including "634-5789" for Wilson Pickett, and 1966's "Knock on Wood," which Floyd himself recorded. The song was intended for Otis Redding, but after Floyd did the demo the label decided to release it with Floyd's vocals after all, and it became Stax's third record to hit #1 on the R&B charts. Suddenly Floyd was a valuable commodity not just as a songwriter, but as a singer as well.

Over the next year Floyd reeled off three more Top 40 R&B hits, though none broke into the Pop Top 40 ("Knock on Wood" had only barely broken onto the pop charts, and then at just #28). His next release however, 1968's "I've Never Found a Girl (To Love Me like You Do)," would be the second biggest hit of his career. Written by Floyd, Booker T Jones, and Al Bell (whose songwriting credits were usually published under his birth name, Alvertis Isbell), the three finished composing the song about three in the morning and woke up Stax musician Al Jackson to get into the studio and lay it down while the sound was in their heads. Produced by Cropper, Jackson played all the instrumental parts except the drums, and also the string arrangements when they were added later. Probably due to the orchestration the song had a smooth, easy-going sound without the grittiness that characterized many of the Stax releases. The record peaked #2 on the R&B charts and #40 on the pop charts, and perhaps because of its uniquely atypical Memphis sound it succeeded in a way that few Stax releases did in that it became a favorite on the beach music circuit.

Floyd would continue to write for other artists, and he'd also continue to have chart as a solo artist, amassing nearly 20 charts hits in the U.S. He stayed with Stax until the label filed for bankruptcy in 1975, and not long after that he came to the attention of the public all over again when Amii Stewart covered "Knock on Wood" and her disco version went to #1 in 1979. Floyd has remained an active performer and recorded an album as recently as 2013.

Frankie Ford

BEACH MUSIC DISCOGRAPHY: "Time After Time" (Ace 580, 1960: Billboard Pop #75).

Frankie Ford was born in Gretna, Louisiana in 1939, and started performing in local shows when he was five years old. In high school he was with a group called the Syncopators, and as a pianist and vocalist he soon became immersed in the burgeoning New Orleans music scene. He eventually met the New Orleans distributor for Ace records, Joe Coranna, who offered him the opportunity to record with the label. Ford's first record, "Cheatin Woman," though successful regionally, was not a national hit. His next recording, "Roberta," was not a hit, though the B-side of the record would find an audience and *become* a national hit. That cut was "Sea Cruise," a song that New Orleans–like Huey "Piano" Smith and the Clowns had recorded backing Bobby Marchan. Coranna felt that Ford's voice and raucous style would make for a good marriage with the song, and so Ford recorded the vocals, they were overdubbed onto the previous recording's instrumentation by Smith and the Clowns, and the recording was designated the B-side of "Roberta." Once the record was flipped it took off, and "Sea Cruise" went to #14 on the charts. His next record on Ace, "Alimony," didn't fare nearly as well, going only to #97.

Ford next recorded an old standard, "Time After Time." The song had initially been written by Sammy Cahn and Jule Styne, and was introduced and performed by Frank Sinatra in 1947 for the film *It Happened in Brooklyn*. The song, as written and first performed, was a slow ballad, but due to Ford's bold voice his rendition is a peppier version. Interestingly enough, the record utilized the almost intrusive background singing by several unknown females, but when the Ace masters were released in 2008 the version without the background singers dubbed in proved to be popular too. Nevertheless, what listeners heard in 1960 was the version with the background singers chanting "yeah, yeah, yeah pretty baby...," and as recorded it went to #75 on the pop charts.

Despite the fact that other than "Sea Cruise" Ford hadn't yet had a big chart hit, Imperial signed him in 1960. There he recorded several singles, but only a very good cover of Joe Jones' "You Talk Too Much" (#87) and "Seventeen" (#72) charted. Before Ford was able to gain any real momentum on Imperial, however, he was drafted into the Army, where he spent the next few years primarily entertaining the troops. After the Army he continued to record, doing stints on a number of labels including Paula and ABC, and he also appeared in the movie *American Hot Wax* in 1978. Despite the fact that the man known as "The New Orleans Dynamo" and the "King of Swamp Pop" never had a national chart hit after 1961, he remained a cultural icon on the Louisiana music scene until his death in 2015.

The Formations

BEACH MUSIC DISCOGRAPHY: "At the Top of the Stairs" (MGM 13899, 1968: Billboard Pop #83).

When Victor Drayton, Jerry Akins, Ernie Brooks, Reginald Turner and Johnny Bellman started recording as the Formations in Philadelphia, they first existed as a backup group singing behind Marge Raymond in Margie & The Formations, who recorded 1965's "Sad Illusion" on the Coed label. Their first effort, post Margie, was the now-classic 1967 offering "At the Top of the Stairs," a song with a pedigree that one would think would have insured success. Written by Akins and Leon Huff—one half of the future Huff/Kenny Gamble team responsible for some of the finest Philly soul ever recorded—the single had a sophisticated sound that would almost guarantee success had it been released in the 1970s. Even in 1968 it was a smash in the Philadelphia area when released on the Bank label, but after being picked up by MGM for national release it didn't go very far, and climbed only to #83 on the Billboard charts.

Though not a bad showing for a first national release, the problem was that the Formations weren't able to duplicate even that level of success again. Their next MGM single, "Love's Not Only for the Heart," was produced by Gamble and Huff but did nothing, nor did their third single. Three unsuccessful singles led the group to take the rather unheard of step of changing their name in an effort to start over, a solution they would try again and again, going from The Corner Boys (Neptune label, 1969), to the Silent Majority (Hot Wax and Detroit Star labels, 1970–71), to Hot Ice (Heavy Duty, 1972, and Atlantic, 1974). Each time they kept the same lineup, and the results were always the same—records that failed to chart.

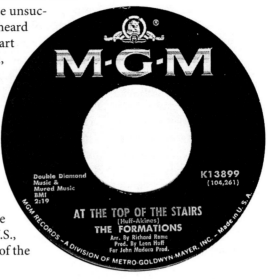

In 1974 the group finally called it quits, though in 1970 "At the Top of the Stairs" had been re-released on the Mojo label in England and charted all over again, rising to an impressive #28 on the charts there. In England and the U.S., "At the Top of the Stairs," would be the pinnacle of the Formations' success.

The Foundations

BEACH MUSIC DISCOGRAPHY: "Baby, Now That I've Found You" (Uni 55038, 1967: Billboard Pop #11); "Build Me Up Buttercup" (Uni 55101, 1969: Billboard Pop #3).

The Foundations consisted of Trinidadian lead singer Clem Curtis and Allan Warner, Eric Allendale, Pat Burke, Michael Elliot, Anthony Gomez, Peter Macbeth, and Tim Harris. The group's multinational and racial makeup contributed to their uniqueness, as in addition to Trinidadian Curtis among their members there were two Jamaicans, a Dominican and a mix of Brits. Perhaps as a result, unlike many of the most popular British groups during the 1960s, the Foundations were surprisingly soul-based. In 1967, the diverse group came to the attention of producer and songwriter Tony Macaulay, and although he had not yet become the hot property he would be in the 1970s after writing hits such as the 5th Dimension's "(Last Night) I Didn't Get to Sleep at All," David Soul's "Don't Give Up on Us Baby," Edison Lighthouse's "Love Grows (Where My Rosemary Goes)" and others, he was already becoming a prolific composer. According to John Kutner and Spencer Leigh in *1000 UK #1 Hits*, when Macaulay originally heard the Foundations, he thought they were terrible, but because he had a hangover he believed it was more his head than his ears that didn't like their sound, so he agreed to write for the group.

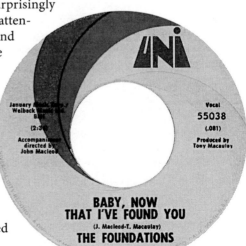

Lead singer Clem Curtis said Macaulay initially

offered the group two songs, one being "Let the Heartaches Begin," the other being "Baby, Now That I've Found You." Curtis said they decided to record "Baby, Now That I've Found You" "because I didn't think I could sing 'Let the Heartaches Begin' as well. 'Baby, Now That I've Found You' just seemed to be a better song for me." It was a good choice, and though initial sales were sluggish, eventually the record took off, benefiting from the English soul boom and interest in the Motown sound. Consequently, "Baby" raced to #11 in the United States and #1 on the UK charts, although Curtis admits, "I really had no idea it would be such a success." (Interestingly enough, the song the group refused, "Let the Heartaches Begin," would also hit #1 in England for Long John Baldry.)

As the first British band with a major soul hit, the Foundations were big, and their follow-up single, "Back on My Feet Again," hit #18 in the UK. But things weren't going well within the group. Despite the success of their first single, Macaulay admittedly didn't like the group's sound any better now than he had initially, and he was trying to push their output in a more pop-oriented direction. In the meantime, Curtis says he was feeling the need to go out on his own, and his friend "Sammy Davis Jr. had recommended that I come to the United States" because Davis felt that Curtis would be a draw there and he had the potential to be a huge solo act. "So, I was about to leave the group," Curtis told me, just as Macaulay told them he'd co-written another song he wanted them to record. Even though it wasn't enough to make Curtis stay, even as he left he sensed the song might be another big one. "It's true I had nothing to do with the song at the time, and then I realized I really liked it," he said. That song was "Build Me Up, Buttercup."

It's rare that a group can survive the departure of a lead singer, but the Foundations managed with new singer Colin Young singing lead on "Buttercup." It's a catchy, joyful-sounding tune, even though the lyrics are actually about a man who has been jilted repeatedly by the girl who is the love of his life. Listeners bought the record in droves and made the song one of the top hits of 1969; "Buttercup" went to #2 in the UK and to #3 in the U.S., and the Foundations were back on top once again. Their next single was another great Macaulay-penned song, "In the Bad, Bad Old Days," which was a UK Top 10 hit but only went to #51 in the U.S.

Macaulay parted ways with the group not long afterwards, and with the Foundations recording songs by other writers the magic was gone and they disbanded in 1970. Since then though, "Baby, Now That I've Found You" and "Build Me Up, Buttercup" have become classics. Curtis, who passed away in 2017, told me in 2010 that "'Baby, Now That I've Found You' is still a crowd pleaser, a song that is fun to do," and one he performed "because everyone in my age group and young people like hearing it too." "Over the past forty-three years I have sung these songs all over the world," and he agrees that "Buttercup," especially, is pretty much universally recognized. Both songs have been embraced in the Carolinas and are now considered beach music classics.

The Four Jacks

BEACH MUSIC DISCOGRAPHY: "The Last of the Good Rocking Men" (Federal 12087, 1952: Did Not Chart).

The Four Jacks were a short-lived recording group who had some brief notoriety, primarily on the Federal label, in the early 1950s. Founding member Ellison White had been a member of the gospel groups Wings Over Jordan and The Wingmen Quartet, and he would also perform with The Bombers and the Four Nuggets. White, along with Four Jacks members Bowling Mansfield, Buell Thomas, and George Comfort recorded "I Challenge Your Kiss" and "Careless Love" on the Allen label in 1949 before recording "I Cry My Heart Out" on Gotham in 1950.

By 1952 they had signed with Ralph Bass at Federal, and there they cut "Goodbye Baby," which did nothing. Federal then used them along with Cora Williams & Shirley Haven on "Sure Cure for the Blues" that same year. "Sure Cure" is fairly innuendo-laden, but not nearly as much as their next release, "The Last of the Good Rocking Men," also released in 1952. Because the Four Jacks were purely a vocal group, they were backed on the recording by the Johnny Otis Band, and all of the elements come together to produce an exceptional effort. However, though today the song is a highly regarded beach tune, at the time it did nothing chart-wise, and in fact was banned on many radio stations due to the sexual innuendo the song clearly contains. Using "rock" as a euphemism for sexual intercourse—as did many, many songs at the time—the singer suggests women try his red-hot lovin' and he has something strong and tan to rock any women who need it. Frankly, the song sounds no more suggestive than the comparable release of the previous year, "Sixty Minute Man" by labelmates The Dominoes, but whereas the Dominoes record went on to be hugely successful, "Good Rocking Men" flopped.

After just two failed singles, Bass apparently turned his energies to the Lamplighters (see the entry for the Lamplighters), and for the rest of the year relegated the Four Jacks to duties as Federal's primary studio backup group. They backed Lil Greenwood on two 1952 Federal singles, "Monday Morning Blues" and "Never Again," then backed by Shirley Haven on "Troubles of My Own." After recording at Federal for less than a year, it appears that the group's status as a feature act ended, and service as a Federal back-up act was at an end as well. The group continued to pop up occasionally doing backing vocals throughout the 1950s, recording on the Tops label behind Ben Zappa on several recordings (including a version of "Why Do Fools Fall in Love"), and they surfaced at Aladdin backing Mac Burney on "Tired of Your Sexy Ways" in 1955. All in all, however, the Four Jacks were no longer a feature act, which is unfortunate considering what "The Last of the Good Rocking Men" seemed to indicate in terms of their potential.

The Four Tops

BEACH MUSIC DISCOGRAPHY: "Could It Be You"(Chess 1623, 1956: Did Not Chart); "Baby I Need Your Loving" (Motown 1062, 1964: Billboard Pop #11); "Without the One You Love (Life's Not Worthwhile)" (Motown 1069, 1964: Billboard Pop #43); "Ask the Lonely" (Motown 1073, 1965: Billboard Pop #24); "I Can't Help Myself" (Motown 1076, 1965: Billboard Pop #1); "It's the Same Old Song" (Motown 1081, 1965: Billboard Pop #5); "Reach Out I'll Be There" (Motown 1098, 1966: Billboard Pop #1); "Bernadette" (Motown 1104, 1967: Billboard Pop #4); "I'll Turn to Stone" (Motown 1110, 1967: Billboard Pop #76); "Ain't No Woman (Like the One I've Got)" (Dunhill/ABC 4339, 1973: Billboard Pop #4); "I Just Can't Get You Out of My Mind" (Dunhill/ABC 4377, 1974: Billboard Pop #62); "Seven Lonely Nights" ABC 12096, 1975: Billboard Pop #71).

The Four Tops

Levi Stubbs (born Levi Stubbles) and Abdul "Duke" Fakir were friends at Pershing High in Detroit, while Renaldo "Obie" Benson and Larry Payton attended Northern High School. Stubbs first sang with Jackie Wilson in the 4 Falcons, while Payton was with the Thrillers along with his cousin, Roquel "Billy" Davis. Though the Thrillers released a couple of singles regionally, the group eventually broke up, as did the 4 Falcons. In 1954 Stubbs, Fakir, and Benson graduated from high school (Payton was a little younger), and they came together to form the Four Aims. They released "If Only I Had Known" on the Grady label in 1956, and sang behind Carolyn Hayes and then Dolores Carroll on singles on Château, but it wasn't until Roquel Davis sent a demo tape to Chess Records that the label signed them; it was at about this time that they changed their name to the Four Tops.

Their one and only Chess release was 1956's "Kiss Me Baby" backed with "Could It Be You," both written by Davis, and neither of which did anything on the charts. Over time, however, beach music audiences picked up on "Could It Be You" with its doo-wop sound and suitable-for-shagging beat; another song they recorded for Chess, "Woke Up This Morning" went unreleased at the time. For a few years after the Chess single they did back-up work, one single for Columbia and another for Riverside, but they got their big break in 1964 when they signed with Berry Gordy at Motown. Apparently Mickey Stevenson had spotted them singing a few years earlier and had in fact tried to sign them to Gordy's new Tamla label, but the group declined. By 1964 Gordy's labels were no longer new and were in fact racking up the hits, so the group signed. The dynamic Holland, Dozier, and Holland writing team was coming off a big hit for the Supremes, "Where Did Our Love Go?," and Gordy hoped they could do the same for the Four Tops. Their first pairing was "Baby I Need Your Loving," which went to #11 in 1964. The song, which would go on to sell more than one million records, was popular not only for the Four Tops but would also go on to be a hit for others, including Johnny Rivers. It was the Tops' version that was first and best, however, prompting *Rolling Stone* magazine to rank it as one of the "500 Greatest Songs of All Time." They followed this with "Without the One You Love" and "Ask the Lonely" before they released their first really big hit, "I Can't Help Myself."

With the Funk Brothers laying down the instrumentation, the Holland, Dozier, and Holland-penned song featured Stubbs's agonized voice singing (some have likened it to shouting) the "Sugar pie, honey bunch" catchphrase. In an interview with Pete Lewis for *Blues and Soul Magazine*, Stubbs said, "'I Can't Help Myself' ... I mean, we musta sung that song so many times I wake up in the NIGHT singing it! In a way it's our theme song!" That "theme song" went to #1 on the pop charts and the R&B charts, was the group's first single to chart in England, and made *Rolling Stone*'s "Greatest Songs" list as well. "I Can't Help Myself" was followed by an astonishing twenty-five more chart hits while at Motown, and nearly every one of their chart hits was suitable for shagging. Hits such as "It's the Same Old Song" (#5) and "Reach Out and I'll Be There" (#1) also found an audience in the Carolinas, as did many more of the group's songs and even "I'll Turn to Stone," the B-Side of "7 Rooms of Gloom." But "Bernadette" (#4) was their last Top 10 hit during the '60s and at Motown, largely due to the fact that Holland, Dozier, and Holland left Motown in 1967. As Levi Stubbs told Lewis, "We were hurt, shattered, and a bit confused. We still got hits, but suddenly we weren't getting all those songs custom-written for us." Then when Motown tried to lowball its bid for the group's new contract in 1972, they left for ABC-Dunhill.

Initially it seemed apparent that Motown had unwisely let the group go too soon. Their first release for ABC, "Keeper of the Castle," went to #10 in 1972, and in 1973 they followed up with "Ain't No Woman" (#4). The song had first been recorded by Hamilton, Joe, Frank, and Reynolds, and was the Four Tops' most successful ABC-Dunhill effort. The year 1974 brought a song that, though not a national success, is one of the best-loved beach tunes of all—"I Just Can't Get You Out of My Mind." Like "I Can't Help Myself," it is often known in beach music circles by another name, "Call Me," which alludes to the fact that the song begins with those two words. While many other Four Tops songs are beach music classics, perhaps it's "Call Me" that seems most distinctly to be a beach song, perhaps because like many other beach music cuts it wasn't all that popular outside of the Carolinas. It wasn't a big hit for the group; not only did it score low on the pop charts (#62), but it only made #18 on the R&B charts and it didn't chart at all in England. Another of their ABC-Dunhill sides, "Seven Lonely Nights," was only a moderate hit nationally (#71), but like "I Just Can't Get You Out of My Mind" with beach audiences it was as big as anything the group had done while at Motown. By the mid-1970s the ABC songs were no longer charting, and the group signed with Casablanca records where they had another song big on the beach circuit, 1981's "When She Was My Girl," which went to #11; it would be their last Top 20 pop hit.

Unlike many other groups that constantly changed over the years, only death could split up the group, which never varied its lineup once in forty-four years. Though Stubbs, Benson and Payton have all now passed away, Fakir continues to perform with a new group and sing those great classics. The group has achieved the highest standards of achievement in their industry, including induction into the Rock and Roll Hall of Fame (1990), the Vocal Group Hall of Fame (1999), the Hollywood Walk of Fame (1997), the Grammy Hall of Fame and a Grammy Lifetime Achievement Award (2009), a Rhythm and Blues Foundation *Pioneer Award* (1997), and others.

Little Frankie

BEACH MUSIC DISCOGRAPHY: "I Want to Marry You" (Smash 2067, 1967: Did Not Chart).

Newington, Georgia-born Roy C. Hammond moved to New York when he was 14, and his original aspiration was to be a professional boxer. While training at Stillman's Gym near Madison Square Garden, he was asked to spar with fighter Hurricane Jackson, who had fought eventual world heavyweight champion Floyd Patterson. Hammond took a punch to the face that convinced him that maybe a career as a professional fighter would not be his best career path, and after leaving the gym that afternoon he was waiting on a train when a member of the Doo Wop group the Genies heard him singing and asked him to join their group. Hammond joined Alexander Faison, Bill Gains and Fred Jones, and later Claude Johnson (who would go to fame later as one half of the duo Don and Juan), and the Genies practiced singing and searched for a record deal. Soon the group signed with Bob Shad, an A&R man for Mercury who liked the group's sound and signed them to a contract with a label he was starting, Shad Records. Though they only recorded one song for the label, that disk, 1959's "Who's That Knocking?" went to #71 on the Billboard charts. The group played several dates at the Apollo, and after recording several more singles on the Warwick, Hollywood, and Forum labels, they landed a contract with Atlantic although they broke up before they had an Atlantic release.

Hammond was drafted at this time and after serving he decided to try it as a solo artist. Recording as Roy Hammond, he scored with the classic "Shotgun Wedding" which he first released himself but which was later released as being by Roy C. on the Black Hawk label. The song went to #14 on the R&B charts in 1965. Like many 60's soul recordings, it was even bigger in England, going to #6 on the singles chart and then again to #8 when re-released in 1972. The single spawned his first album, 1966's "That Shotgun Wedding Man," and so at this a point Hammond's career was really starting to take off. He was writing songs, and even managing an act, and that's when 1967's "I Want to Marry You" came about.

Hammond had written "I Want to Marry You," but it wasn't for him. "What happened was that there was a singer known as Little Frankie, who I was planning to record. We were in the studio, and he just couldn't sing the song" Hammond told the author. Hammond became frustrated, and eventually, "I just stepped up to the mike and I did the song. I did the singing. I was his manager, and I'd written it, so when he couldn't get it right I did it instead. I just took over." After the recording was released the single got enough of a response that audiences wanted to hear it live. Hammond and the real Little Frankie thought they had it worked out so Little Frankie could perform it on stage, but the first time he was scheduled to sing it live, there was a problem again. "After I did it in the studio, I really hoped he could pick it up on the shows, but he couldn't do that either. We did a show in Philadelphia with Charlie Brown, and Little Frankie came out on stage and he blew it. He couldn't perform. He was nervous and messed up in front of 1700 people." So, Hammond said, "after that for a while I just took the name Little Frankie." He, and not the original Little Frankie, sang the song in live performances, and though the song didn't chart, it was popular nevertheless. But despite its popularity, Hammond had no interest in continuing to perform as Little Frankie. "After that I dropped the name, because I didn't want to continue using two names. For audiences it would be too confusing."

Hammond went on to record several dozen more singles over the years on several labels, and in the 1970s he'd make the R&B charts with singles such as "Got to Get Enough," "Don't Blame the Man," and "Love Me Til Tomorrow Comes." In 1973 his album *Sex & Soul* also made the R&B charts, and each of the more than a dozen subsequent albums had a loyal following as well. He later formed his own label and moved his headquarters to Allendale, South Carolina, which is roughly 30 miles from where he was born. He produced an album by Dennis Edwards of the Temptations among others, and in 1998 his song "Love Me, Love Me" was sampled in a song on the soundtrack of "How Stella Got Her Groove Back." He's still working today, and continues to record and produce new material.

The Friends of Distinction

BEACH MUSIC DISCOGRAPHY: "Grazing in the Grass" (RCA 740107, 1969: Billboard Pop #3); "Love or Let Me Be Lonely" (RCA 740319, 1970: Billboard Pop #6).

Texas-born Harry Elston began his singing career with Ray Charles' backup band, the Hi-Fis, who changed their name to the Vocals around 1960. Californian Floyd Butler joined the group as road manager before sliding into the role of bass singer, and in 1964 the Vocals recorded a couple of records for Charles' Tangerine label, "Lonesome Mood" and "Let No One Hold You Out." Neither of the songs charted, and eventually the group separated in a contract dispute. In 1965 group members Lamont McLemore and Marilyn McCoo formed The Versatiles, who would go on to considerable success under a name they adopted in 1966, "The 5th Dimension." Floyd would work out of music for a while before teaming with Elston around 1968 to form a new group along with two singers they'd known for a few years, Barbara Love and Jessica Cleaves. They initially called themselves The Distinctive Friends, though according to Elston, Love suggested they change the group's name from The Distinctive Friends to The Friends of Distinction.

The group was discovered and subsequently managed by football player Jim Brown, who arranged for them to sign with RCA records. Elston says the group chose RCA because they wanted to work with producer John Florez and Ray Cork, Jr., and they thought a good choice for a release would be a song Hugh Masekela had recorded and taken to #1 in 1968, an instrumental called "Grazing in the Grass." Though the music was right for Elston's purposes, a vocal group needed lyrics so Elston wrote those himself. "Well I first called it 'Flaking in the Grass' because I didn't know I could use the same title as the instrumental since I was changing the song and adding lyrics" he said. "But everybody was like, 'Get out of here!' so I came back with the same music and title and they loved it. We recorded it at RCA for our first album and from then things happened very quickly. We weren't teenagers, but we were pretty young, and not knowing how things worked we just rode the wave. We didn't know until later how big the song was." With Elston singing lead, the song spent 16 weeks on the pop charts and peaked at #3, 17 weeks on the R&B charts and peaked at #5, and sold more than a million copies. After "Grazing in the Grass," they charted again with "Going in Circles," which went to #15 on the pop charts and also sold a million records. At about that time Barbara Love got pregnant and had to take maternity leave. The group was too hot and too popular to go on extended hiatus, and needed to record and tour in order to stay in the public eye. Fortunately, Elston said, "Our bass player, Stan Gilbert, said he knew a girl in Milwaukee who would be great to fill in. So, we auditioned Charlene Gibson and brought her in."

The timing was good, because "we had a song, 'Love or Let Me Be Lonely,' that had been written by Skip Scarborough, Jerry Peters, and Anita Poree." Though none of the songwriters were well-established at that point, Scarborough would later write hits for Earth, Wind, & Fire, Bill Withers, and even win a Grammy for Anita Baker's "Giving You the Best That I Got," Peters would work with Aretha Franklin, Marvin Gaye, Diana Ross, and win a Grammy for co-writing "It's What I Do," and Poree would co-write songs such as "Boogie Down" and "Keep on Truckin" for Eddie Kendricks. "They gave us time off from touring to do an album, and we went to RCA's studio in New York and recorded 'Love or Let Me Be Lonely' there."

Any doubts they may have had about Gibson's abilities were quickly dispelled, as she took lead on the song "and she flat out tore it up" Elston said. Knowing that Love's absence could have spelled disaster for the group, Gibson's success meant they didn't miss a beat. "Charlene was a Godsend," he said. "She did lead on several songs, such as 'Crazy Mary,' and she was great on them all." "Love or Let Me Be Lonely" went to #6 on the pop charts and #13 on the R&B charts, and was very popular with shaggers during the 1970s.

The Friends of Distinction, circa 1970 (photograph courtesy Harry Elston).

At that point, Love returned to the group and Gibson bowed out, but then "Jessica split and went with Earth, Wind & Fire, and later Parliament Funkadelic." Gibson rejoined the group in her stead. Love left to concentrate on being a mother, and for a while Gibson, Elston, and Floyd performed until Gibson left for good. By this time, Elston says, "being on the road was tiring, and we felt like it was time to hang it up." Elston noted that RCA may not have really understood how to market the group either. "When you are putting out maybe three or four records a year, it has to be planned. RCA didn't have many black artists, and they didn't seem to know what to do with them. You had the R&B department fighting with the pop department, because there was crossover. So we kind of got caught in the middle of that stuff." Ultimately the group called it quits in 1975.

Since then their songs have been covered by a number of artists, resulting in chart hits for the Gap Band, Luther Vandross, and Paul Davis. Butler and Cleaves have passed away, while Elston performs with a new group as the Friends of Distinction today.

The Futures

BEACH MUSIC DISCOGRAPHY: "Party Time Man" (Philadelphia International 3661, Did Not Chart 1978)

The Futures were a Philadelphia group formed in 1968, and despite some early personal changes, the core members of the group were Frank Washington, Kenny Crew, James King and his brother John King, and Henry McGilberry. Their first single was the 1970 release on Amjo "Breaking Up," which did not chart (nor did a re-release on Avalanche in 1971). They then went to Kenny Gamble and Leon Huff's Gamble Records, where they released the single "Love is Here." Though it only went to #47 on the R&B charts in 1973, it appeared they were poised for a breakthrough under the tutelage of hitmakers Gamble and Huff.

It was at this point that the group probably made a major, career-altering mistake. Rather than stay with Gamble and Huff, who were developing the relatively new Philadelphia International label (home of the O'Jays, Harold Melvin and the Bluenotes, and others), the group apparently felt that the O'Jays were getting all of the label's attention and so they signed with Buddah, a label best known for bubblegum music, not R&B. Though they issued four singles at Buddah, only one charted, 1975's "Make It Last," which peaked at #35 on the R&B charts. When their contract with Buddah ended, they were without a label for several years, but in 1978 they were re-signed by Philadelphia International. The label had enough faith in them to issue their first album in 1979, *Past, Present, and the Futures*, and the leadoff song was "Party Time Man." Written by Sherman Marshall (who penned "Then Came You" by the Spinners and Dionne Warwick and "Lady Love" by Lou Rawls) and Ted Wortham (writer for the Spinners, Teddy Pendergrass, Dionne Warwick), the song has that bold Philadelphia International sound, the vocals are strong, and the beat was good enough was extremely popular in dance clubs at the time. In fact, a longer version, running

6:05 (the original 45 ran 3:43) was released as a "disco single," but despite some play, it never did better than #94 on the R&B charts.

The group released another album, and five further singles, but only a 1981 cover version of the Rays' 1957 hit "Silhouettes" made the R&B charts at #79. The group left Philadelphia International, and broke up soon after. Eventually, McGilberry would join the Temptations, and Washington would join the Delfonics and later the Spinners, in each case to replace to replace members who had departed.

Don Gardner and Dee Dee Ford

BEACH MUSIC DISCOGRAPHY: "I Need Your Loving" (Fire 508, 1962: Billboard Pop #20).

Philadelphia-born Donald Gardner got his start as a drummer in the late 1940s as a member of Harry "Fats" Crafton's band. An accomplished vocalist, at the age of 18 Gardner got his chance to record a few sides for the Gotham label. In the early 1950s he recorded with the Julian Dash Septet, Dickie Smith's Sonotones, and with Smith and Albert Cass as the Don Gardner Trio. By the late '50s he was recording simply as Don Gardner for the Cameo, Junior, Deluxe, and Kaiser labels. None of these efforts, however, were successful on the charts.

By the early 1960s Louisiana-born Wrecia Holloway (whose real name was actually Wrecia Mae Ford) was performing with Gardner. A talented keyboardist with a strong background in gospel, Holloway, who went by the stage name Dee Dee Ford, brought a different sound to Gardner's act as he became more firmly entrenched in and served the R&B market. Gardner released the gospelly-sounding "Glory of Love" in 1960 on the Val-Ue label, and though Ford doesn't receiving co-billing on the label and sings backup, her strong voice carries the song and it was apparent that she wouldn't be relegated to the background for long.

Gardner and his band were billed regularly as headliners at a New York club called Smalls Paradise, where they were seen by another artist, Arthur "Big Boy" Crudup. Crudup recorded for Bobby Robinson, owner of the Fire and Fury record labels, who counted among its artists Buster Brown, Wilbert Harrison, and the pre–Motown Gladys Knight and the Pips, and Crudup convinced Robinson to catch Gardner and Ford's act. Robinson saw them perform a screamer of a number Gardner had written called "I Need Your Loving," and signed them to the Fire label.

When performed live, "I Need Your Loving" would run as long as five or six minutes, with a long soulful buildup, which was really a very different song from the second part (often done as an encore) which kicked in right after Gardner hit "Wo-wo-wo-wo-wo-wo-wo!" nearly three minutes into the song. Though Fire had the group record a long version, they cut off the last two minutes and forty three seconds and issued that part of the song as a single in 1962. It reached #20 on the Billboard pop charts and broke into the Top 10 on the R&B charts. Their next side for Fire, "Don't You Worry," also went to the Top 10 on the R&B charts but only reached #66 on the pop charts, but after one more single for Fire, they left the label, perhaps due to Robinson's failure to pay royalties properly. Gardner and Ford recorded for Red Top and Ludix, and Gardner did some solo work for Jubilee, but none of the efforts charted. The two of them went to Europe and even cut a single there, but by 1965 they were back in the states and broke up the act.

Thereafter Ford (now as Wrecia Holloway) focussed on writing songs, including one for a former member and backup singer for the Don Gardner and Dee Dee Ford Review from their Small's Paradise days, Betty (later Bettye) Lavette. The song, "Let Me Down Easy," made the Top 20 on the R&B charts and "bubbled under" the pop charts at #103. Gardner continued to record, but other than a 1973 duet with Baby Washington, "Forever" (a cover of a 1963 Marvelettes release), nothing charted. As of this writing Gardner is still living; Ford left the music business and died in 1972.

Marvin Gaye

BEACH MUSIC DISCOGRAPHY: "Stubborn Kind of Fellow" (Tamla 54068, 1962: Billboard Pop #46); "Hitch Hike"(Tamla 54075,1963: Billboard Pop #30); "How Sweet It Is" (Tamla 54107, 1964: Billboard Pop #6); "I'll Be Doggone" (Tamla 54112, 1965: Billboard Pop #8); "Ain't That Peculiar" (Tamla 54122, 1965: Billboard Pop #6); "Too Busy Thinking About My Baby" (Tamla 54181, 1969: Billboard Pop #4); "Come Get to This" (Tamla 54241, 1973: Billboard Pop #21).

Marvin Gaye was born Marvin Pentz Gay, Jr., in Washington, D.C., as one of four children of a domestic worker and a father who was a minister. Like many prominent R&B artists he got his start singing in church as a child, and in high school he sang in several local groups before dropping out of school at age 17 and joining the Air Force. He found the military not to his liking and according to his service record was given a discharge after only eight months for being uncooperative and having no initiative.

Back in D.C., he and his friend Reese Palmer formed a group called the Marquees. Under the mentoring of Bo Diddley, the group released a one–off single on Okeh that went nowhere before being picked up by Moonglows founder Harvey Fuqua. Fuqua renamed his group Harvey and the New Moonglows, and as a later incarnation of Fuqua's doo-wop group the Moonglows, the group recorded some side for Chess and did back-up vocals for artists such as Chuck Berry. Fuqua later founded his own label and signed Gaye, and eventually Berry Gordy acquired Gaye when Gordy bought out Fuqua's Tri-Phi label. Initially Gaye did session work and played drums on Motown recordings, but in 1961 he released several singles which did not chart. He added the "e" to his last name at about this time, and his breakthrough finally came with 1962's "Stubborn Kind of Fellow." Co-written by Gaye and Mickey Stevenson and George Gordy, Gaye reluctantly made some changes to the song based on suggestions made by Berry Gordy, and backed by several then-unknown background vocalists including Martha Reeves, the song hit #46 on the pop charts and #8 on the R&B charts. His next hit, "Hitch Hike," had a very similar genesis, as once again it was written by Gaye and Stevenson, though this time with Clarence Paul. Martha Reeves along with Rosalind Ashford and Betty

Kelly (the Vandellas) again did backing vocals, and the record outperformed its predecessor, breaking the pop Top 40 at #30.

At this point his career took off, and over the next few years he charted more than two dozen times, on his own and singing duets with Kim Weston, Mary Wells, and Tammi Terrell. Among his many hits, the most popular with beach music audiences are generally considered to be 1964's "How Sweet It Is," written by Holland, Dozier, and Holland; 1965's "I'll Be Doggone," his first million seller and first R&B #1; 1965's "Ain't That Peculiar," his second million seller and another R&B #1 hit. Gaye was on a roll, and when he released "I Heard It Through the Grapevine" in 1968, it surpassed four million in sales and was the biggest selling song in Motown history up to that time. It hit #1 on the Billboard pop, R&B, and the British charts.

By the time he recorded "Too Busy Thinking About My Baby" in 1969 he was one of the biggest stars in the business, but the sound of his music was definitely changing. While during the previous two years he had charted with typical Motown-sounding songs such as "If I Could Build My Whole World Around You" and "Ain't Nothing Like the Real Thing" (both duets with Terrell), his solo efforts were developing a completely different sound. In that sense, "Too Busy Thinking About My Baby" is an anachronism, and sounds like it should have been recorded in the mid–60s when the more traditional Motown sound ruled the airwaves; there's a good reason for that. Actually, the song was a Norman Whitfield, Barrett Strong, and Janie Bradford co-written album-cut that the Temptations had recorded in 1966, and that Jimmy Ruffin had also recorded but didn't release in 1967. Everything about the execution of the song follows that mid–60s Motown sound as well. The music was by the Funk Brothers, and backing vocals were by the Andantes, who'd sung back up on classics such as Mary Wells' "My Guy," "I Can't Help Myself" by the Four Tops, and some of Gaye's previous hits such as "I'll Be Doggone," "Ain't That Peculiar," and others. It was Gaye's second biggest hit of the 1960s, reaching #4 on the pop charts, #1 on the R&B charts, and was the top selling R&B record of 1969.

It was one of the last throwback-sounding songs Gaye recorded. Soon more socially-conscious songs were his forte, and by 1971 efforts such as "What's Going On," "Mercy, Mercy Me (The Ecology)," and "Inner City Blues (Make Me Want to Holler)" represented his sound. His 1973 album *Let's Get It On* went in yet another direction with smoother, sexier sounds, and after "Let's Get it On" went to #1, and the second single from the album was "Come Get to This." Gaye wrote the song himself, and it was not a big hit, peaking at #21 on the pop charts and #3 on the soul charts. Likewise, during the 1970s, it was not considered a part of the beach music canon, but was re-discovered by beach music audiences post–1980 and has come to be quite well regarded due more to the influence of shaggers than pure beach music enthusiasts.

Gaye would have a number of chart hits thereafter, and his 1974 duet with Diana Ross, "My Mistake," would also become a beach music classic. Sadly, in 1984 Gaye was killed by his father during an argument. He was inducted into the Rock and Roll Hall of Fame in 1987, a Grammy Lifetime Achievement Award in 1996, and many other awards and recognitions in the years since his death.

See also Diana Ross.

Barbara George

BEACH MUSIC DISCOGRAPHY: "I Know (You Don't Love Me No More)" (A.F.O 302, Billboard Pop #3 1961).

Barbara George was born Barbara Ann Smith in New Orleans' 9th Ward, and like many Southern girls her first singing experience came in church. By the time she was sixteen she was married, and as Barbara George she was looking for a sustainable career in music. New Orleans R&B singer Jessie Hill discovered her and took her to New Orleans music guru Harold Batiste, who was starting the seminal New Orleans black music label, A.F.O. (All for One), and was looking for new acts to add to a stable that would eventually include beach legend Willie Tee.

The label's second release was a song George had written that Batiste reportedly didn't much care for, "I Know (You Don't Love Me No More)." George based "I Know" on the gospel tune "Just a Closer Walk with Thee," and in fact listening to the latter it is obvious that George based parts of her song on the hymn. Recorded when she was seven months pregnant, and on her first ever visit to a recording studio, "I Know" features Melvin Latiste's cornet solo, Marcel Richardson's piano and backing vocals, and of course George's strong, youthful, determined vocals.

The song was a hit in New Orleans, and then went national and by early 1962 it climbed to #1 on the R&B and #3 on the pop charts. A subsequent release on A.F.O., "You Talk About Love," went to #46 on the pop charts, and A.F.O. would also issue an album, *I Know*, featuring ten original George compositions. At 19 years old Barbara George had become a star almost overnight.

In what was one of the strangest twists in musical lore, this success indirectly brought about the end of the A.F.O label and the ruination of George's career. In a 1971 *Creem* magazine interview, Batiste told journalist Charlie Gilett that at that point Juggy Murray of Sue Records signed George right out from under A.F.O. "At first, we didn't realize it was happening, but we found out that when Barbara went to New York to sing at the Apollo, Juggy took her down town in a Cadillac to buy her mink coats and all of that kind of thing, using her royalty money to do it. But she didn't understand, and wanted to know why we hadn't been buying her all those kind of things." As Batiste explained it to interviewer John Browen in *Rhythm & Blues In New Orleans*, he tried to explain to George that she needed to be careful about falling for such an overtly commercial deception to get her to sign a record deal, but "fatherly advice is no good when you're fighting Cadillacs, fancy clothes and money." This led to a separation between Batiste and George, who told Gilett, "After that, running the company was never the same … somehow our hearts weren't in it after she left." Having lost its biggest star, A.F.O. would release a few more sides over the next couple of years before folding in 1963.

As for George, her first recording on Sue, "If You Think," would only "bubble under" the pop 100 at #114, and her next release, "Send for Me," would only go to #96 on the pop charts. Two further releases on Sue wouldn't chart at all, and so by 1964 her Sue contract and releases—and chart records—were all at an end. After this, her personal history is a bit spotty, and like many famous-overnight teenagers she apparently developed a drug problem as well. She would next record in 1967, and after a couple of late '70s recordings she would eventually leave the music business. Out of show business, she rededicated herself to her gospel roots and the church, and remained in Louisiana until she passed away in 2006.

The Georgia Prophets

BEACH MUSIC DISCOGRAPHY: "Don't You Think It's Time" (Jubilee 5596, Did Not Chart 1967); "I Got the Fever" (Smash 2161, Did Not Chart 1968); "For the First Time" (DoubleShot 138, Did Not Chart 1969); "California" (Capricorn 8006, Did Not Chart 1970); "Nobody Loves Me Like You" (Capricorn 8009, Did Not Chart 1970); "I Think I Really Love You" (Together 108, Did Not Chart 1971); "So Glad You Happened to Me" (3-P 36506, Did Not Chart 1974).

One of the most dynamic and influential figures on the Carolina beach music scene, Billy Scott was born Peter Pendleton in Huntington, West Virginia. After being discharged from the Army in 1964, he changed his name and with his wife, Barbara, worked singing backup vocals in the Augusta, Georgia, area. While in the studio in June 1965, Augusta musician Tommy Witcher happened to hear them singing and asked the two to join his band, the Scottsmen, which consisted of Witcher, Freddie Williamson, Walter Stanley and Jimmy Campbell. Soon the group changed their name to the Prophets, and eventually had the chance to cut their first record, "Talk Don't Bother Me," for Delphi in 1966. Jubilee picked up the single for national distribution, and though it didn't chart, Jubilee also decided to release their next Delphi single, 1967's "Don't You Think It's Time." This record failed to chart as well, but the group continued to play throughout Georgia and the Carolinas, and in 1968 Roy Smith wrote a song for them called "I Got the Fever." Billy Scott told the author, "Roy called me and said, 'You gotta come over to my house right now—I just wrote your next hit record.' So I drove over to his house, and I sat down beside him at the piano. He started playing, and the hooks in that song just threw me back—'I love you, I love you, I love you yes I do.' I went, 'Oh man!'

The Georgia Prophets, circa late 1960s (photograph courtesy Billy Scott).

I mean, you know, it got me right then. Then he started playing the verses. It went back and forth like that and I thought, 'Oh my God, this is going to be a great tune.'" Scott says they played it for Witcher, and he arranged for them to go to Atlanta and record it on the Smash label. Though the song didn't make the national charts, it did sell well in certain areas of the country, especially in the South.

Suddenly the group was bigger than ever, and that forced a change. "We changed our name to the Georgia Prophets in 1969 for several reasons. There was a group called the Prophets in Florida that threatened to sue us, and there were also several other groups named the Prophets, and it was confusing for fans. We'd be booked somewhere and people would call and be told the Prophets were playing, and they'd ask, 'Which Prophets?' Told it was us, people would say, 'Oh, you mean the Georgia Prophets.' So our fans really changed our name for us," Scott said. At about this same time Smith had written them a new song, a duet that emphasized the singing abilities of Billy and Barbara, "For the First Time." "[Roy] called up excited about the song saying 'I wrote you and Barbara a great song.' He asked 'Can I play some of it for you over the phone? You'll sing this part, Barbara sings this part, then y'all sing this part together' So I listened and then I got excited about it too. We'd been looking for a really good duet." They recorded the song, and it was impressive enough that they had a chance at their first really big break—Motown wanted to release the record. "But Tommy made all the decisions and negotiated the record deals, and we were just singers in the band at the time" Scott told me. "Tommy said, 'I offered this to Motown, and they want it, but there really isn't much money in it for us.' I said, 'Okay, you're taking care of business so whatever you decide is what we'll go with.'" Instead, Witcher sold the song to Double Shot records in Hollywood, and Scott said "Well, as bad as I wanted to go with Motown at the time, we were happy with Double Shot. I got a call from Irwin Zucker who was in charge of their promotions, and he let us know what a wonderful song it was, and that he was going to do everything he could to promote it."

Despite the song's potential, it didn't make the Billboard pop charts, though it did reach #36 on the Cash Box R&B charts. Zucker would later call Scott again, and tell him "Billy, I'm just taken aback with what's happening with this song. I don't understand it, it's a turntable record.' What he meant by that was that the DJ's loved the song, but it didn't sell like he wanted it to. Of course we were really disappointed because we knew that it was a great tune." Perhaps in retrospect, while Double Shot was a fine label, they were much smaller than Motown and perhaps Motown could have promoted the record better; no one will ever know.

At this point Witcher decided to add another female vocalist to the group, Janet Helm, and Helm brought the group a song she had written, "California." "Janet, who played the acoustic guitar, played it for us and sang, 'California is a callin' me, California is a where I should be, California 90023'" Scott said. "I said, 'What does 90023 mean?' And she explained, 'That's the zip code where I lived.'" Scott says Helm explained that she wrote the song because, "'I moved to

California, but didn't stay long, because things just weren't going right. But I just loved it out there and so on my way home I decided to write about it.' So she wrote it and offered it to us, the band rehearsed it and got it all together before we got to the studio, but we didn't work on the background vocals. So Barbara and Janet came up with the background vocals on the way to the studio, and I just sat there listening to them in the car on the way to Atlanta. We got there, put it all together, and recorded it in one take." The group was now signed to the Capricorn label, and although the song went on to be their most popular beach music song behind "I Got the Fever," once again the record didn't chart. Scott felt that "unfortunately Capricorn was most interested in promoting their Southern rock groups like the Allman Brothers, and so ['California'] wasn't promoted much nationally" Nevertheless, regionally the group was experiencing unprecedented levels of popularity.

"By then "Roy had to start writing songs for three people—me, Barbara, *and* Janet—as opposed to writing just for a solo artist or duet" Scott said, "but he was excited about the possibilities because he had heard what we'd just done on 'California.'"

Smith next wrote "Nobody Loves Me Like You," and "Janet helped us with vocal arrangements. Coming off of two regional hits such as 'For the First Time' and 'California' we were very much in demand in the southeast, and the songs helped because the compatibility of the three voices after 'California' was just phenomenal" Scott says. "Nobody Loves Me Like You' was what it was because of that third voice, because of Janet." Scott notes that in fact they liked the finished product so much that "we decided to have the horn and string arranger come back and put strings on 'Don't You Think It's Time,' which had been released originally in 1967, so we used it on the flip side."

Even though they were coming off a string of national single releases and regional hits, the group was splintering, and Scott says he, Barbara, and Janet felt like they were moving in one direction and the rest of the group was going in another. Ultimately Billy, Barbara, and Janet started their own group in 1971. Witcher owned the rights to the Georgia Prophets name, but Billy, Barbara, and Janet "didn't want to lose the name Prophets and lose our identity, so we went with the Three Prophets." They hired a back-up band, who took Scott a song they had written called "I Think I Really Love You." "I liked it and agreed we needed to record it, and so we went to a studio and put it on tape. I had a friend named Roy Callaway, and when I played it for him he said "The production's not good enough on this thing, nor is the arrangement," but he was involved with an Atlanta outfit called Together records. Together was excited about the song, so we went in and recorded it, and Janet came up with a vocal arrangement that was awesome." Scott says that to his surprise however, "the song did absolutely nothing! But that song was one of the best songs I think we recorded."

Nevertheless, Together Records apparently felt good enough about the group that they wanted an album. They said, "you've got a lot of good material, and we've got a good producer, so let's record an album." The producer they'd hired was Norman Whitfield, who had produced and co-written a number of Motown hits such as "Ain't Too Proud to Beg," "I Heard It Through the Grapevine," "War," and many others. "We were really excited," Scott said. "We had an album deal, a well-known producer, everything was great. Then two to three weeks before production, the FBI charged the owner of the company with racketeering and murder. They shut the record company down and that cut our legs right out from under us. Nothing happened after that. That was our last opportunity for an album."

In 1974 the group would go on to record one more highly regarded beach song, "So Glad You Happened to Me," but like its predecessors it did not chart nationally. Eventually the group broke up, but Scott would enjoy continued success over the years as a solo artist, singing duets, and with his band the Party Prophets until his death in 2012.

Jim Gilstrap

BEACH MUSIC DISCOGRAPHY: "Swing Your Daddy" (Roxbury 2006, 1975: Billboard Pop #55).

Pittsburg-born James Earl Gilstrap got his start with a group called the Duprells who had just been signed to backup Sam Cooke on tour when Cooke was killed in 1964. A talented singer who was not afraid to be part of an ensemble as opposed to a headline act, in the late '60s Gilstrap joined the Doodletown Pipers, who played the Frontier Hotel in Las Vegas six months a year and who also appeared on the *Ed Sullivan Show*. By the late '60s he had become friends and eventually roommates with Stevie Wonder, and he had the opportunity to do session work on some of Wonder's productions. "We were at Jimi Hendrix's Electric Lady Studios in the Village, and it was about 3 o'clock in the morning when we recorded 'You Are the Sunshine of My Life'" Gilstrap told the author. "Stevie asked me to sing the opening lines, and my girlfriend at the time, Lani Groves, sang the next few lines." The song went all the way to #1 and netted Wonder a Grammy, and a thankful Wonder also gave Gilstrap a gold record for his contribution to the song. Gilstrap would later work with Wonder on *Talking Book* and *Inversions*, two of Wonder's most highly acclaimed albums.

By the mid 1970s, friends were encouraging Gilstrap to go out on his own, and Carolyn Willis, who was with the group Honey Cone, told him they were looking for new solo acts at Chelsea Records, owned by Wes Farrell. The label signed Gilstrap (label credits say Jimmy Gilstrap), and they offered him "Swing Your Daddy." "Swing Your Daddy" was written by Kenny Nolan, who'd written #1 songs such as "My Eyes Adored You" for Frankie Valli and "Lady Marmalade" for LaBelle already that year, and would later write and sing his own song, "I Like Dreamin,'" which went to #3 in 1977. Gilstrap knew it was a good opportunity for him, and the label thought it had the potential to be a hit as well. "They brought the song in and told me they wanted an Eddie Kendricks/Smokey Robinson kind of sound. So I did it, but I honestly did not expect it to do what it did. It was big all over Europe and I even went to England and did *Top of the Pops*" (it reached #4 on the UK charts). Gilstrap says "the Top Ten on the R&B charts here in the States, but the record did what it did due to Kenny Nolan, because he also produced it, and even sang background

on it too." Though the record peaked at #55 on the pop charts, Gilstrap seemed poised to make a big breakout, but a miscalculation may have caused his career to lose the momentum it had gained. "Then we did an album called *Love Talk*," he said. "I really had no input as far as what they put on the album cover, and unfortunately they put a nude couple, back-to-back, on the front of album. Well, back in those days, they wouldn't even put the album in stores in some parts of the country, and so it didn't sell. By the time they revamped the album and put a picture of me on the cover, the album had played itself out."

Gilstrap was beginning to sense that he was just as happy being in the background as he was being a headline act however, and says that "After *Love Talk*, I got away from solo recording. It had been a lot of fun, and I got to know a lot of the artists at Chelsea, and 'Swing Your Daddy' had been a real blessing. But I started to do some other things." From that point on Gilstrap built one of the most impressive resumes of anyone in the recording industry. During his years as an artist in a supporting role he worked with Quincey Jones, The Temptations, Boz Scaggs, Joe Cocker, the Four Tops, Barbara Streisand, Rod Stewart, Leo Sayer, Whitney Houston, Dolly Parton, and with Michael Jackson on the *Thriller* and *Off The Wall* albums. He did movie vocals on films such as *Grease*, *The Matrix*, and *Rocky*, and television work on *Cheers*, *The Simpsons*, and of course, as the singer on the well-known theme for *Good Times*, where his voice sings "Temporary layoffs.... Ain't we lucky we got 'em–Good Times!" "The royalties for that alone have paid very, very well" he told me.

"I have had fun working throughout the industry—it's been a wonderful career" Gilstrap said. Despite his many accomplishments, he's appreciative of the regard his song has in the Carolinas; "I feel blessed that even today people such as beach music fans remember 'Swing Your Daddy.'"

The Globetrotters

BEACH MUSIC DISCOGRAPHY: "Rainy Day Bells" (Kirshner 63–5008, 1970; Did Not Chart).

In the late 1960s and early 1970s, Hanna-Barbera was developing into a frontrunner in the Saturday morning cartoon market, and they developed a cartoon based on the touring basketball team the Harlem Globetrotters. The Globetrotters, who had originated in the 1920s, had evolved over the years and had included some of the most proficient basketball players in America, including Wilt Chamberlain and Connie Hawkins. Perhaps the height of their fame was in the 1970s, and CBS liked the concept of building a Saturday morning cartoon around the team's fictitious exploits. As a result, from 1970 to 1972, twenty-two episodes featured characters based on real Globetrotters "Meadowlark" Lemon, "Curly" Neal, "Geese" Ausbie, "Gip" Gipson, Bobby Joe Mason and Pablo Robertson, along with several fictional counterparts. In these cartoons, much like the "gang" in Hanna-Barbera staples such as *Scooby Doo, Where Are You?* and *Josie and the Pussy Cats*, the team would find themselves up against evildoers but would reign supreme in the end, despite some hilarious misadventures. Also like other car-

toons at the time, the main characters would sing and perform (ala the Archies) so that Hanna-Barbera could cash in on the cartoon's popularity by having the characters release an album and a few singles.

Hanna-Barbera decided to have the Globetrotters release an album, and to that end they brought in producer Jeff Barry and involved series music supervisor Don Kirshner. One of the songs recorded for the album was the Neil Sedaka and Howie Greenfield tune "Rainy Day Bells." "When we recorded 'Rainy Day Bells' for the album I thought it was a nice, catchy little tune, but that's it. I didn't think it would be as popular as it is or do what it's done" Meadowlark Lemon said. "Rainy Day Bells" was indeed a good song, and it was rumored that it was the team themselves singing it. That was partially true, and Lemon says that though he was "not the best background singer, I did sing background, but they had some great professional studio singers and musicians there to put that thing together, and they, not the team, sang it." Instead of the other members of the team, the other singers were vocalists such as Sammy Turner (who had charted with "Lavender Blue" in 1959), J.R. Bailey (formerly of the Cadillacs of "Speedo" fame), Robert Spencer (also of the Cadillacs and Crazy Elephant) and Rudy Clark (singer and also writer of such hits as "The Shoop Shoop Song"). The song had a late '50s/early '60s doo-wop sound, and when released as a single it was not a big seller, perhaps because that type of music had faded from popularity a decade earlier. One other single from the album fizzled too, and as the cartoon itself only lasted 22 episodes. After one album the experiment was over.

As for the song, Lemon was impressed by its longevity. "I think 'Rainy Day Bells' has remained popular because it has an infectious melody," he says. "It's one of those songs that when you hear it, over and over and over, you begin to like it even more. Neil Sedaka did the song before we did, though his version didn't catch on like ours. Now why, I have no idea. But I realize that our version is still a hit up and down the East Coast. People talk to me about it all the time. It's amazing." Lemon told me he even considered re-recording it, but he passed away in 2015 before doing so.

Rosco Gordon

BEACH MUSIC DISCOGRAPHY: "Surely I Love You" (Vee-Jay 348, 1960: Did Not Chart).

Born in Memphis, Tennessee, Rosco Gordon learned to play the piano as a child and by the time he was a teenager he had formed his own band. Gordon lived about 30 minutes from the famed Beale Street, and after playing a number of early gigs there, he became one of a group of musicians often referred to as the "Beale Streeters." This group, which would include the likes of Johnny Ace, B.B. King, Junior Parker, Bobby "Blue" Bland, and others, often played together in impromptu performances acting much like session men for one another. By 1951 he landed a recording contract, and as Roscoe Gordon he recorded some sides for Sam Phillips that were leased to RPM records including "Roscoe's Boogie," "Saddled the Cow (And Milked the Horse)," and "Dime a Dozen." However, it was the release of "Booted" on RPM in 1952 that marked the first in a series of controversies that Gordon would be embroiled in with record labels. RPM felt that Gordon was under contract to them, but Phillips had sent the song to Chess who released it on their label. After some legal maneuvering, both labels ended up releasing the song, which went to #1 on the R&B charts.

His next RPM release, "No More Doggin,'" was a #3 hit on the R&B charts, but after several more recordings on RPM in 1952, disputes between RPM and Gordon regarding the payment of royalties saw him sign with the Duke label, though he released songs on both labels in 1953, now as Rosco Gordon. That contract was up in 1955, so he signed with Sam Phillips and released several singles on Sun and Flip. In yet another confusing turn of events, Gordon sold some tapes back to Duke, which caused a problem between him and Sam Phillips. Despite that, he continued to record at Phillips' Sun Studios, and his 1958 release on Sun, "Sally Jo," is cited as one of the few examples of a black artist doing rockabilly. Also, some of his songs were done in a style known as "Rosco Rhythm," often cited as an early form of Ska, which helped him build an audience in South America. Gordon signed with Chicago's Vee-Jay label in 1959, where his third release was the catchy "Surely I Love You" in 1960. Though it was not a hit and did not chart, the song was very popular in the Southeast; it was later covered by Colin James and Huey Lewis and the News.

For the remainder of the 1960s he recorded for a number of labels including ABC-Paramount, Calla, and his own label, Bab-Roc. After five singles for Bab Roc in the early 1970s, he recorded very infrequently. He made a recording comeback of sorts in 2000, began performing more frequently and even appeared in documentaries about the history of rock and roll before passing away from natural causes in 2002.

The Happenings

BEACH MUSIC DISCOGRAPHY: "See You in September" (BT Puppy 520, 1966: Billboard Pop #3); "I Got Rhythm" (BT Puppy 527, 1967: Billboard Pop #3).

Paterson, New Jersey, natives Bob Miranda, Harry Arthur, Ralph DiVito, and Thomas Giuliano formed the singing group the Four Graduates after graduating from high school. Although some sources say the four of them met while in the Army at Ft. Dix, Miranda confirmed for the author that the four of them in fact met at "a St. Leo's Church dance in East Paterson." The group worked in the Tri State area and especially the Catskills, and Miranda says after working for a while he and Tom Giuliano did spend six months at Fort Dix before returning to the group. They spent some time working as session singers, most notably for Bob Crewe who was working with the Four Seasons at the time: "We were just doing background vocals to tracks mostly," Miranda said. "I don't think we ever did any Four Seasons tracks that I know of, because most of the time there were no lead vocals on the tracks yet so we didn't always know who or what group it was for. I know we did some vocals for Mitch Ryder, but don't know who else."

The group's first break as a featured act came when they signed with the Laurie label's Rust subsidiary, releasing an updated cover version of the Ink Spot's 1944 recording "A Lovely Way to Spend an Evening" in 1963 and "Candy Queen" in 1964. Neither record made the national charts, but while at Rust they came to attention of the Tokens, who had hit #1 with "The Lion Sleeps Tonight" in 1961. By this point the Tokens were producing for some other acts on Laurie and Rust, and although they did not produce anything for the Four Graduates at the time, Miranda had been writing music and they did ask him to pass along any songs he might have for their Bright Tunes Music company. One song he wrote, "Girl on a Swing," would go on to be a Top 40 hit for Gerry and the Pacemakers in 1966, and later Miranda would record it himself.

When the Tokens formed their own label, Miranda opined that they should sign the

Four Graduates to the label. They auditioned, and while the Tokens liked their sound they felt they should change their name because it seemed dated. From a number of possibilities that included the Cordoroys and the Bitter Lemons, they chose the Happenings because "What's happening?" was a popular phrase at the time. Harry Arthur left the group at this time, and David Libert, who "was our piano player at first and was not one of the Grads until Harry decided to leave" then became a member of the regular line-up Miranda said. The newly constituted and renamed Happenings signed with B.T. Puppy.

Their first release, "Girls on the Go," did not chart, but their second, "See You in September," was a smash. The song was a Sid Wayne and Sherman Edwards composition that had originally been recorded by the Tempos in 1959, when it went to #23 on the national pop charts. The Happenings had been performing the song for a while, and while they had always felt it was a good song they also thought the Tempos' version was a bit lackluster. They put their own twist on it and turned it into an uptempo number, and recorded it that spring. By July 1966 their Bob Crewe-produced version was on the National charts, reaching a peak of #3 in September. By the end of the year they'd sold more than a million units and received a gold record. They followed with "Go Away Little Girl" (Pop #12) and "Goodnight My Love" (Pop #51) before releasing another updated cover version, "I Got Rhythm." The 1930 George Gershwin composed tune was originally from the musical *Girl Crazy* and had been featured in movies and recorded many times since, but as usual the Happenings put their own spin on it and with their updated sound they landed another Top 10 hit; the record peaked at #3 in April 1967.

Six of their next nine singles would chart, but most were covers such as "Why Do Fools Fall in Love," "Sealed with a Kiss," and others; 1967's "My Mammy" (a song Al Jolson had made famous) was their last Top 40 hit, peaking at #13. By the late '60s the group who had changed their name because it sounded dated found that their music was starting to sound dated and they felt doing covers was getting old, although their producers reasoned that since the formula had worked there was no reason to change it. The group thought that they needed to go in a different direction to stay relevant, and at this point group members started to leave. They changed to the Jubliee label, and afterwards did a few singles for different labels but had no more chart hits.

Libert would go on to be a well-known music executive who worked with George Clinton, Alice Cooper, Sheila E, and others. Miranda tours with a new group of Happenings and still performs today.

Harmonica Fats

BEACH MUSIC DISCOGRAPHY: "Tore Up" (Darcey 5000, 1963: Did Not Chart).

Born Harvey Blackston in McDade, Louisiana, the performer who would come to be known as "Harmonica Fats" grew up laboring in his grandfather's cotton fields. Hard work and poverty provided him with only a second grade education and an appreciation for music, especially blues by Blind Lemon Jefferson, Peetie Wheatstraw, and Sonny Terry. By the mid 1940s he had set out to Los Angeles to see if he could improve his fortunes, and while recovering from an auto accident in the early 1950s he started perfecting his technique on the harmonica. By that time he and his band were playing in the Los Angeles area as Heavy Juice, a name taken from jazzman Tiny Bradshaw's 1953 release of the same name. But it wasn't until the early 1960s when Blackston was performing as Harmonica Fats that he had his first successful recording, 1962's "Tore Up." First released on the small Skylark label, "Tore Up" was a song written by Hank Ballard and recorded by Ballard and the Midnighters in 1956 (as "Tore Up Over You") on Federal. The Midnighters' version failed to chart, but the Harmonica Fats version sold well enough that it was picked up for release by the larger Darcey label in 1963. Despite the song's popularity in some parts of the country, it was not a big hit and did not make the charts. In 1963 he recorded one more unsuccessful single for Darcey, "Mama Mama Talk to Your Daughter for Me."

Subsequently, a series of one or two off releases on labels such as Dot, In-Sound, Masai, Kris, Normar, and Duplex during the '60s and early '70s failed to generate many sales. He did frequent work as a studio musician, playing behind the likes of Lou Rawls and Ringo Starr, and he also worked as a travelling solo act for a number of years. In the 1970s he married civil rights and welfare activist Johnnie Tillmon (Blackston), the first chairperson of the National Welfare Rights Organization. While his wife's career as a civil rights activist blossomed, Blackston entered one of the most productive periods of his career, teaming up with blues guitarist Bernie Pearl. They frequently played at Ash Grove, a blues bar run by Pearl's brother, and they released several blues albums in the 1990s, including *Two Heads are Better*, *Blow, Fat Daddy, Blow!*, and *I Had to Get Nasty*. While that big hit record always remained elusive, his reputation in blues circles far surpassed his records sales; upon his death in 2000, the *Los Angeles Sentinel* eulogized Blackston as a "kind and gentle man known as Harmonica Fats, 320 pounds of rhythm and blues."

Peppermint Harris

BEACH MUSIC DISCOGRAPHY: "I Got Loaded" (Aladdin 3097, Did Not Chart 1951).

Texarkana, Texas-born Harrison Demotra Nelson became a professional musician in the late 1940s after serving in the army. He acquired the stage name "Peppermint" in order to better fit into the late '40s blues scene, where many of the top performers such as "Gatemouth" Brown, "Juke Boy" Bonner, "Blind Boy" Williams, "Lightnin'" Hopkins and others had nicknames, and so it was as "Peppermint" Nelson that he recorded "Peppermint Boogie" for the Gold Star label in 1948. In 1949 he began to record for the Sittin In With (SIW) label, one of the earliest East Coast labels to feature Southern R&B. There his name changed once again when after a recording session someone accidently wrote "Peppermint" *Harris* down as the artist instead of "Peppermint" Nelson. The record was released with the "Peppermint" Harris name on the label, and the name stuck when the record became a hit. He would go on to release a number of popular blues records

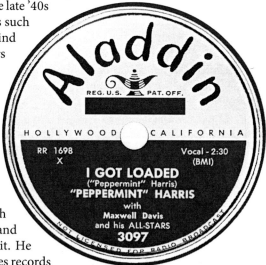

on the SIW label in 1950 and 51, and he then moved to Aladdin Records, where his first recording for the label in 1951 was a song he wrote, the classic "I Got Loaded."

Harris' song was perfectly in keeping with the times. By the early 1950s, drinking songs were making more than just an occasional appearance on the R&B charts. Songs about the evils—and joys—of whiskey, women, and gambling had always been a mainstay of R&B music, and perhaps one of the earliest of these songs which would find its way into the beach music canon was Stick McGee's "Drinkin Wine Spo-Dee-O-Dee," which had reached #3 on the pre–Billboard R&B charts in 1949. Harris' contribution to the genre featured the backing of Maxwell Davis and his band, and the song about the "juice really flying" where Harris says "I got loaded, oh I sure got high" went all the way to #1 on the R&B charts and stayed in the top ten for six months. The song became Harris' biggest hit, and though today it is appreciated as a slow, rhythmic shagger, the song set in motion the recording industry's penchant for recording the countless drinking songs that would come out over the next few years; tunes such as The Clovers' "One Mint Julep"(1952) and "Nip Sip"(1955), Jimmy Liggins' "Drunk" (1953), and The Checkers' "I Wasn't Thinkin' I Was Drinkin'" (1954) and others soon flooded the airwaves. Aladdin, too, felt they needed to continue this trend, and so Harris' next release for the label was another drinking song, "Have Another Drink and Talk to Me." The song did not do well, nor would any of his subsequent Aladdin recordings, whether about drinking or not. Unbeknownst to Harris at the time, he would never again record a song as popular as "I Got Loaded," and his failure to match the success of his hit would culminate in Aladdin failing to renew his contract.

Even though he would later record on a number of labels, including Modern, Cash, "X," Money, Combo, Dart, Duke, and many others, he would never have another big hit. Many regard his mid–60s stint with Jewel records as the most prolific of his career, and the Louisiana-based company not only recorded up-and-comers like John Fred and the Playboy Band, but also more established acts such as John Lee Hooker, Charles Brown, and Harris' old friend Lightnin' Hopkins. None of his songs were commercially successful however, but Harris was able to supplement his recording income as a writer, writing songs for Junior Parker, B.B. King, Etta James, Bobby Bland, Amos Milburn, and Guitar Slim. While he retained the rights to many of his compositions, in other cases he reportedly sold the songs for cash and waived all future rights to any royalties. Harris would record until 1980, retire from the business, then once again begin recording in the 1990s. He died in 1999, leaving a legacy as a good bluesman whose biggest hit just happened to be a crossover beach music hit as well.

Wynonie Harris

BEACH MUSIC DISCOGRAPHY: "Good Rocking Tonight" (King 4210, 1948: Billboard Pop Did Not Chart, R&B #1).

Wynonie Harris was born in Omaha, Nebraska, to a single mother, and it was after his mother Mallie Hood Anderson married Luther Harris when he was five that Wynonie was given his stepfather's last name. After teaching himself to play the drums, he dropped out of high school when he was 16 and formed a song and dance team with Omaha native Velda Shannon. Harris moved to Los Angeles in 1940 where he earned the nickname "Mr. Blues" for his strong vocal performances, and he moved to Chicago where he joined Lucky Millender's band. Harris and the band went to New York in 1944, and while Harris was quickly becoming the star of Millender's act, because of scarcity of materials used to make records during World War II he was unable to release any recordings. Eventually Harris left Millender's band, and with the end of the War the embargo on record production was lifted and a song Harris had recorded called "Who Threw the Whiskey in the Well" was released on Decca.

Credited to Lucky Millender and his Orchestra with "Vocal Chorus by Wynonie 'Mr. Blues' Harris," the song went to #1 on the R&B charts and made Harris a star. Because he wasn't under contract to Decca, has was able to release recordings on several labels, including Apollo, Aladdin, and King. It was in 1948 that he released his first #1 as a solo artist, "Good Rocking Tonight."

"Good Rocking Tonight" was one of the first songs a marginally successful (to that point) singer named Roy Brown had written. Brown was a fan of Harris,' and when Harris came to New Orleans and was performing at the Dew Drop Inn Brown offered him a song he'd written on a brown paper bag in 1947 called "Good Rocking Tonight." Harris declined to record the song, and Brown offered it to another singer who suggested Brown do it himself. Brown recorded it on Deluxe and it started getting some airplay, and which point Harris reconsidered and recorded it for King in 1948. Harris' version is lyrically quite different from Brown's, mainly because Harris would forget lyrics and improvise, which ultimately made the song sound much more raucous and off-the-cuff. The song also included references to a number of popular songs, hence the shout-outs to Sweet Lorraine, Sioux City Sue, Caldonia, Sweet Georgia Brown, and others. The song was a massive hit, and Harris' version went to #1 and stayed in the Top 10 for six months, and his loud, clapping, shouting style is credited with kick-starting the jump-blues movement as well. Harris' cover actually revitalized Brown's career too, and he had more than a dozen chart hits afterwards. "Good Rocking Tonight" was covered many times thereafter, including a release on the Sun label by Elvis Presley. The song is often considered among the top candidates for the first rock and roll record ever recorded.

"Good Rocking Tonight" made Wynonie Harris a major star, and his next #1 record, 1949's "All She Wants to Do Is Rock" cemented his reputation. He lived a lifestyle that we now associate with rock stars but that at that point was far less commonplace; he was a hard-drinking, sharp-dressing ladies' man with a big house, and a Cadillac and a chauffeur. Because the word "rock" was also euphemism for sex in R&B music at the time, it wasn't a big leap to his more deliberately ribald songs such as "Sittin' on It All the Time" and "I Like My Baby's Pudding." Between 1945 and 1952 Harris had sixteen straight Top 10 releases on the R&B charts, but after that his career went into decline as R&B and rock and roll underwent a number of changes. His last recordings were in the 1960s for Chess, and he died of cancer in 1969.

Wilbert Harrison

BEACH MUSIC DISCOGRAPHY: "Don't Drop It" (Savoy 1138, Did Not Chart 1954); "Kansas City" (Fury 1023, Billboard Pop #1 1959).

Born in Charlotte North Carolina, Wilbert Huntington Harrison was a multi-talented artist who could not only sing but play the piano, guitar, and harmonica. After he left the military in 1950, he was performing in Miami when he came to attention of Henry Stone, who signed him to the Rockin' label, and for whom he then recorded "This Woman of Mine" in 1952. The single would also be released on the Deluxe label a year later, but neither it or his next Deluxe release would find much of an audience. Harrison would move to New Jersey and sign with Savoy Records, now seen as one of the seminal jazz, R&B, soul, and blues labels of the early 1950s, and home to artists such as Cannonball Adderley, Charlie Parker, John Coltrane, and others. Harrison's first Savoy release would be the beach music classic "Don't Drop It."

"Don't Drop It" was originally written as a country song for Terry Fell, who had released his version on the "X" label in April 1954. That version, which hit #4 on the country chart hit to become Fell's biggest hit, sounds drastically different from the version Harrison would record, and in fact one could say that it took a genius to mold Fell's hillbilly hit into a creditable

R&B record. The music on Harrison's cut was far superior to Fell's original, led by arranger Leroy Kirkland (who had worked or would work with Tommy and Jimmy Dorsey, the Five Satins, The Everly Brothers, and Jimmy Ricks and The Ravens) directing New York area musicians such as Buddy Lucas on saxophone (who recorded with Big Joe Turner, Frankie Lymon and the Teenagers, Lavern Baker, Aretha Franklin) and Mickey Baker (played with The Drifters, Ray Charles, Ruth Brown) and Kenny Burrell (played with Dizzy Gillespie, Billie Holiday, and Duke Ellington) on guitar. Even today, the resonance and quality are obvious and in stark contrast to many R&B records from the period. However, it wasn't just that the music was superior, nor was it just Harrison's strong vocals, but also that a few of the lyrics had been slightly changed from Fell's version in keeping with the more risque types of lyrics predominant on R&B records of the early 1950s. For example, while Fell's version had said "I said I won't mend it till the day I am wed, but each time I kiss you I forget what I said," Harrison's said "I said I wouldn't lay me 'til the day we were wed, but each time I kiss you I forget what I said. I'll let you keep it tonight if you hold it real tight…." Later, while Fell told his girl to "cuddle up close" so he could tell her what he would do to fix the relationship, Harrison tells his girl to "Huddle up real close, I'll tell you what I will do…." While these types of subtle changes mean little in relation to song lyrics today, at the time it was somewhat suggestive—which was clearly in keeping with the R&B music of the period.

But Harrison's song failed to find much of an audience, although the label apparently felt strongly enough about "Don't Drop It" that they released it once again in 1959, this time backed with a different song ("Baby Don't You Know"); yet again, it did not chart. However, just two releases later (still in 1959), he would record "Kansas City" for the Fury label, and Harrison would become a household name overnight. The song would shoot to #1 on the pop and R&B charts and become a million-seller. And though millions know this tune as Harrison's, it was a cover version of a Jerry Leiber and Mike Stoller original that had been recorded by Little Willie Littlefield in 1952, "K.C. Lovin.'"Though it would go on to be covered by several other artists, including the Beatles, Harrison's version would be the highest charting and best known.

Unfortunately, despite repeated quality recordings, Harrison's successful periods would be brief and intermittent. After "Kansas City" he would move from label to label, recording for Neptune, Sea Horn, Constellation, Port, Sphere Sound, Vest, Roulette and others. None of his releases after "Kansas City" would break the top 100 until 1969 when "Let's Work Together," an original composition by Harrison, was released on the Sue label. It had first been released on the Fury label in 1962 as "Let's Stick Together" and had done nothing, but on its release on Sue, with Harrison himself playing harmonica, tambourine, guitar, and drum, it would go to #32 on the pop charts. But just as Harrison had successfully covered songs by other artists, ironically Canned Heat's 1970 release of the song as "Let's Work Together" would be their highest charting hit at #26 on the pop charts; it would go to #2 in England and reportedly to #1 in thirty-one countries.

Despite several releases in the early 1970s, after "Let's Work Together" Harrison would have only one more charting record, and when he died of a stroke in a North Carolina nursing home in 1994 he was reportedly destitute. And while today he is best known for "Kansas City" (named by the Rock and Roll Hall of Fame as one of the 500 Songs that Shaped Rock and Roll), it is "Don't Drop It" which is his greatest beach music recording.

Leon Haywood

BEACH MUSIC DISCOGRAPHY: "It's Got to Be Mellow" (Decca 32164, 1967: Billboard Pop Did Not Chart, R&B #63).

Houston-born Otha Leon Haywood started playing the piano as early as age three, and by the time he was a teenager he was putting his musical abilities to work in a band. He moved to Los Angeles to further his musical career, and there as an organist he worked with sax player Big Jay McNeely. McNeely recorded for Swingin' Records, and though it is often reported that Haywood recorded a song he wrote called "Without a Love" for the label, the single is under the name "Big Jay McNeely and Band," though the label credits Haywood and McNeely as co-writers, and the flipside, "The Squat," does say "featuring Leon Haywood at the Organ." Haywood went on to play with Sam Cooke until the singer's death in 1964, and then recorded a dizzying array of singles on various labels over the next few years, including "A River's Invitation" on Convoy, "Whiplash" (as Leon and the Burners) on Josie, "The Truth About Money" on Fantasy, and many others. Alathough at the same time he was writing for and sitting in on sessions for the Packers, the Hideways, Dyke and the Blazers, and the Romeos, during this whole period he had just one successful record on his own, 1965's "She's with Her Other Love" on Imperial, which went to #13 on the R&B charts and #92 on the pop charts. When signed with the Fat Fish label around 1966 he settled in to a more stable routine, but despite five singles on the label none made the charts.

Other than his two singles with Imperial, to this point Haywood had been recording largely on small, impermanent labels, and in 1967 he left Fat Fish and started his own label, Evejim (named after his mother Evelyn and his father Jim Ed). He recorded a song he had written called "It's Got to Be Mellow," and it sold so well in Los Angeles that Decca picked it up for nationwide distribution. Finally with a company with the distribution power to bring his music to a broader audience, the results were obvious almost immediately, as "It's Got to Be Mellow" rose to #21 on the R&B chart and #63 on the pop charts. The single's success prompted Decca to offer him an album deal, but because Haywood was on the road at the time and Decca was impatient he cut the *It's Got to Be Mellow* album on the road in New Orleans. Haywood wasn't happy with the final product because of the way the label rushed it, and indeed the album didn't produce any other hits. Unfortunately, there would be only more chart record over the next seven years, 1968's "Mellow Moonlight," but it didn't do as well as "It's Got to Be Mellow."

After several more failed releases with Decca, he started label jumping again, but at least now they were large labels with solid reputations. Singles at A&M, Capitol, and Atlantic all did nothing. In 1972 two singles at 20th Century met a similar fate, and just when it looked like Haywood was going to be known for his writing and session work more so than his solo recording, his third release on 20th century, "Keep It in the Family," hit #11 on the R&B charts in 1974. This kicked off a string of nearly 20 chart hits over the next decade, the most successful of which was the 1975 funk hit "I Want'a Do Something Freaky to You" (#7 R&B, #15 pop), and 1980's "Don't Push it, Don't Force It"(#2 R&B, #49 pop). In 1981 he wrote Carl Carlton's huge Top 40 pop and R&B hit "She's a Bad Mama Jama," and by the late '80s he had forged out a career as a producer as well. More recently, Haywood's music reached a whole new audience through rap music, as his songs have been sampled by Dr. Dre, Snoop Dogg, Aaliyah, 50 Cent, Common and others. He died on April 5, 2016, aged 74.

Bobby Hebb

BEACH MUSIC DISCOGRAPHY: "Sunny" (Philips 40365, 1966: Billboard Pop #2).

Nashville, Tennessee born Robert Von Hebb was the son of blind musicians, and he and his bother Harold grew up playing with their parents' band, Hebb's Kitchen Cabinet Orchestra. Hebb was viewed as somewhat of a musical child prodigy, and after a performance on a local television show he was invited to play with country singer Roy Acuff's Smokey Mountain Boys around 1952. Over the next decade, he'd do a stint in the U.S. Navy where he played trumpet in the Navy jazz band, sing with the doo-wop group the Hi-Fis, work as an occasional session musician, and record several non-charting singles on the Rich and Fm labels under his own name between 1959 and 1961. By this time he had moved to New York, and during Mickey Baker's on-again/off-again musical relationship with Sylvia Robinson during the late '50s and early '60s in their duo Mickey and Sylvia, Hebb actually recorded with Robinson as the one off duo Bobby and Sylvia. Their sole single, 1962's "You Broke My Heart and I Broke Your Jaw" on the Battle label, did not sell and quickly dropped from sight.

After recording several more one shot records on Smash, Boom, and Scepter, Hebb seemed to be on a path shared by legions of unheralded artists who cut a few singles without ever really having any sustained success. Hebb, however, had written a song after the assassination of John F. Kennedy followed by the murder of his brother a few days later in November 1963 called "Sunny," which reportedly came to him as he left a jazz club one dawn after a long night of performing and drinking. Hebb later claimed "Sunny" wasn't about a girl as many believed, but one's disposition, and he had so little faith in the song that he was actually the third person to record it, following versions in 1965 by Japanese singer Mieko Hirota and vibraphonist Dave Pike. When Hebb signed with Philips Records in 1966 he was working with producer Jerry Ross, and Ross convinced Hebb to record his own version toward the end of a recording session. Hebb did so, and when released the song went to #2 on the pop charts and sold more than a million records. This led to Hebb touring with the Beatles in 1966, and ultimately the song became so famous that it was covered by Frank Sinatra, Marvin Gaye, Dusty Springfield, Stevie Wonder, Ella Fitzgerald, James Brown, the Four Tops, and many other artists.

After "Sunny," Hebb had a few low charting singles, but none made much of an impact. Perhaps his greatest achievement after "Sunny" was the success of a song he co-wrote for Lou Rawls, 1971's "A Natural Man." The song won Rawls a Grammy, but after this Hebb more or less faded from the public consciousness. In 2004 he moved back to Nashville, played the Grand Ole Opry, and received his due as an important person in the Nashville music scene. His later years were marred by health problems, and he died of lung cancer in 2010.

Eddie Holland

BEACH MUSIC DISCOGRAPHY: "Jamie" (Motown 1021, Billboard Pop #30 1962).

Detroit, Michigan-born Edward Holland met future Motown Mogul Berry Gordy in 1958 when both were around 20 years old, and both were struggling in the music business. Holland had recorded one single for Mercury, "You," and Gordy was just about to start his first record label, Tamla. Holland recorded a single on Tamla before going on to a brief and unsuccessful stint at United Artists, before returning to Berry's Motown label in 1960. In 1961, another Motown singer, Barrett Strong, was starting to suspect that despite some early success perhaps his future did not lie in a career as a vocalist. Although he had charted with "Money" in 1960 (Billboard #23, R&B #2), a song which would go on to be recorded by numerous artists including the Beatles and the Rolling Stones, Strong's post-"Money" success was nil. After recording four failed singles in a row, he was quickly becoming the earliest, and one of the only, "one-hit-wonders" Motown would have. Consequently, though Strong had already recorded his fifth single, "Jamie," a song he had written with Mickey Stevenson, it may be that he sensed that it, too, would fail to find an audience, and he departed the label before the record was released.

Holland had a fairly strong voice, good looks, and charisma, and not being one to pass up a potential hit record simply because Strong had left the label, Berry Gordy had Holland record his vocals over Strong's. Holland's version used the same backing tracks, and in this case the backing vocals were handled by the Andantes (Louvain Demps, Jackie Hicks and Marlene Barrows), Motown session singers extraordinaire, who would go on to sing backup on five #1 songs and dozens of singles by the Four Tops, Supremes, and Marvin Gaye. "Jamie" was also one of the first Motown records to incorporate strings, using eight members of the Detroit Symphony to handle those duties. Add to this that Holland is doing his best Jackie Wilson sound-alike (whether intentional or not), and the components were there for a sure-fire winner.

A one-sided promo version of the song, which clocked in at 2:15, was released to deejays in October 1961, and Motown released a second version of the song in January 1962. The second single version is nearly identical to the first except that at 2:21 is just a few seconds longer, not from a surfeit of words, but due to different pacing. The song is poppy, and peppy, and not at all as soulful as the dozens of great Motown classics that would follow it. But even if the song wasn't a harbinger of the greatness that was to come from Motown, it was appropriate at the time, and it went on to reach #30 on the pop charts and #6 on the R&B charts; it was a solid, if not spectacular, hit.

Holland would go on to release nine more singles on Motown over the next three years, and while three would make the lower reaches of the pop charts, none would even equal the moderate success of "Jamie." Perhaps it's just as well: Holland suffered from stage fright and really did not like performing live, so his career as a singer was becoming problematic. However, by the mid–1960s Holland, with his brother Brian and friend Lamont Dozier, formed the famed songwriting team of Holland, Dozier, and Holland and penned more than twenty-five #1 songs and many other hits over the next decade including "Baby I Need Your Loving," "I Can't Help Myself," "Stop in the Name of Love," "This Old Heart of Mine," "Jimmy Mack," and "Give Me Just a Little More Time," as well as many other songs that have become beach music classics.

The Impressions

BEACH MUSIC DISCOGRAPHY: "Gypsy Woman" (ABC Paramount 10241, 1961: Billboard Pop #20); "It's All Right" (ABC Paramount 10487, 1963: Billboard Pop #4); "Woman's Got Soul" (ABC Paramount 10647, 1965: Billboard Pop #29).

Curtis Mayfield and Jerry Butler met as teenagers when both were members of The Northern Jubilee Gospel Singers in Chicago, but both also sang with other groups in the '50s, Butler with the Quails and Mayfield with the Alphatones. In Chattanooga, Tennessee, Sam Gooden and later Fred Cash were in the Southland Jubliee Singers, and they later teamed up with Arthur Brooks, Emanuel Thomas and Catherine Thomas to form Four Roosters and a Chick. After Catherine left, Richard Brooks joined and they became simply the Roosters. Gooden and the Brooks brothers took the act to Chicago, where Mayfield and Butler joined them to complete the Roosters new line-up. There are conflicting stories about how they signed with a label. One story is that they were doing a gig at a fashion show where they sang an original composition called "For Your Precious Love," and someone saw them and arranged an audition for them at Vee-Jay Records. Curtis Mayfield later said that first they actually went to Chess Records to try and get an audition and a secretary wouldn't let them in the building, so they walked across the street to Vee-Jay. There they auditioned for Calvin Carter while standing in the hall, who not only signed the group but was also responsible for changing their name to The Impressions.

Their first release was "For Your Precious Love," which peaked at #11 in 1958. Despite the fact that the song was successful, its release was fraught with complications. Some releases were on Vee-Jay, while others were on a label Vee-Jay distributed named Falcon, a label in which Vee-Jay general manager Ewart Abner reportedly had a financial interest. Apparently Falcon was threatened with a lawsuit, and so changed the name to Abner Records, though retaining the same label design. Furthermore, all three labels read "Jerry Butler and the Impressions," though the group had never actually designated him as the frontman. This was mitigated a bit when their next releases, "Come Back My Love," was issued as The Impressions featuring Jerry Butler, and the next, "Gift of Love," was credited simply to the Impressions. Despite the internal conflict this may have caused, Vee-Jay saw Butler as a sure fire solo act and after a few more singles they broke him off to do solo work. After one more single and the release of another recorded with Butler earlier, Vee-Jay dropped the Impressions from the label.

Mayfield took over as lead and former Rooster Fred Cash came to Chicago and joined the group. After a couple of small-label releases the group went to New York and signed with ABC Paramount. Their first single for their new label was 1961's "Gypsy Woman," a Mayfield-penned story-song with a smooth sound featuring Mayfield's falsetto and utilizing castanets, which was unusual for a pop song. It went to #20 on the pop charts and #2 on the R&B charts. The next few follow ups didn't do much however, and the Brooks brothers left the group and Mayfield, Gooden and Cash returned to Chicago and performed as the Impressions as a trio. At this point Mayfield was becoming more and more diversified, writing hits for other artists such as "Mama Didn't Lie" for Jan Bradley and "The Monkey Time" and "Um, Um, Um, Um, Um, Um" for Major Lance. A song he wrote for his own group however, 1963's gospel-influenced "It's All Right," would become the group's next big hit. I sold more than a million copies, and went to #1 on the R&B chart and #4 on the pop charts.

144   The Intrigues

This would kick off a long string of Impressions hits, but as the 1960s progressed and music was becoming more diversified, Mayfield's music was no exception. From the socially conscious "Keep on Pushing" to the religious "Meeting Over Yonder" the Impressions music ran the gamut. Oddly enough, one of their finest efforts in the minds of beach music audiences, 1965's "Woman's Got Soul," was one of their first songs not to break into the pop Top 20, stalling at #29 though it did go to #9 on the R&B charts. Two releases later, "I Need You" also gained a bit of traction in the beach clubs, though the cover ("I Need a Love") by Gene Barbour and The Cavaliers is actually now better known to beach music audiences. The Impressions version did not break the Top 40, going only to #64 and #26 on the R&B charts.

Increasingly, the group's music was making the R&B charts but faltering on the pop charts, and they left ABC after 1967. Mayfield was diversifying to the extent that he was doing less and less with the group, and he founded two short-lived record labels and then the better-known Curtom label, where the group would sign next. Mayfield would finally leave the group in 1970, and though the group would still chart occasionally they started to undergo a number of personnel changes and after 1976 they were no longer charting. Mayfield would become extremely successful as a solo artist with hits such as "Freddie's Dead" in 1972 and "Superfly" in 1973, and he would continue to be a force in music until a lighting unit fell on him before a concert in New York in 1990 and he was paralyzed for the rest of his life; he died in 1999. An Impressions group still performs to this day; they were inducted into the Rock and Roll Hall of Fame in 1991 and the Vocal Group Hall of Fame in 2003.

The Intrigues

BEACH MUSIC DISCOGRAPHY: "In a Moment" (Yew 1001, 1969: Billboard Pop #31).

The Intrigues were a group of Philadelphians consisting of Alfred Brown, James Lee, James Harris and Ronald Hamilton. Their first recording was the obscure "Soul Brother" for Toot Records, a small label that existed only for a year or two before folding. Their next single was "In a Moment" on the tiny Philadelphia label Bullet in early 1969. Despite Bullet's limited distribution, "In a Moment" was a big song regionally, bolstered by the arranging and production skills of Bobby Martin and Thom Bell. Martin would later work with Lou Rawls, LTD, the Manhattans, and Tavares, and Bell had produced for

the Delfonics and would later do the same for the Stylistics and the Spinners, among others. "In a Moment," with its fast-paced, almost anthemic chant-like refrain was a big enough hit that it was eventually picked up by the slightly larger Yew Records as the second 45 the label distributed. Released nationally it rose to #31 on the pop charts and #10 on the R&B charts. Their next 1969 release, "I'm Gonna Love You," was also produced and arranged by Martin and Bell, and charted at #86. On the strength of these singles, Yew Records released the group's sole LP, *In a Moment*, in 1970.

In 1970 and 71 they released four more singles on Yew, including "Just A Little Bit More," "Tuck A Little Love Away," both of which were under the guidance of Martin and Bell, but neither charted. Their next single, 1971's "The Language of Love," was co-produced and arranged by Van McCoy, and it had some success, peaking at #100 on the pop charts and #21 on the R&B charts. One more McCoy-arranged single on Yew, 1971s "Mojo Hannah," would fail before they signed with the larger up-and-coming label Janus, who had recently released singles by The Whispers, Cissy Houston, Mungo Jerry, Johnny Nash, and others. Two releases on Janus would fail, and other than a comeback attempt in 1985 with the song "Fly Girl," the Intrigues' recording career was over.

The Intruders

BEACH MUSIC DISCOGRAPHY: "Together" b/w "Up and Down the Ladder"(Gamble 205, 1967: Billboard Pop #48); "A Love That's Real" (Gamble 209, 1967: Billboard Pop #82); "Cowboys to Girls" (Gamble 214, 1968: Billboard Pop #6); "Love Is Like a Baseball Game" (Gamble 217, 1968: Billboard Pop #26); "I'll Always Love My Mama" (Gamble 2506, 1973: Billboard Pop #36).

The Intruders originated in Philadelphia in the late 1950s and originally consisted of Sam "Little Sonny" Brown, Eugene "Bird" Daughtry, Phillip Terry and Robert "Big Sonny" Edwards. By the early 1960s they had recorded with the Philadelphia-based Gowen label, but their single releases "I'm Sold On You" and "This Is My Song" didn't find an audience outside of their region. In 1964 they did "But You Belong to Me" for Musicor, and though not successful they did have the opportunity to work with Leroy Lovett, who was also producing Patty & the Emblems with songwriter Frank Bendinelli through their B & L Productions group. Nothing else followed for the next couple of years, but in 1966 they began working with Kenny Gamble and Leon Huff who had started their own label, Excel, where the Intruders recorded "Gonna Be Strong," which didn't chart. After just a few Excel releases in 1966 Gamble and Huff changed the name of Excel to Gamble, and their very first release was the Intruders' 1966 single "(We'll Be) United," which peaked at #78 on the pop charts and #14 on the R&B charts.
Having a chart record for their first Gamble release was significant, and would create a bond between the group and Gamble and Huff that would endure for many years.

Four of the Gamble label's first five releases were by the Intruders, and their second, "Devil with an Angel's Smile" also made the R&B charts, going to #29. Two singles later, their first release of 1967 was "Together," which was written and produced by Gamble and Huff.

The song climbed to #9 on the R&B charts and #48 on the pop Hot 100, and both Gladys Knight and the Pips and the Three Degrees recorded the song later, and the one-off group Tierra had a big hit with it in 1981, taking it to #18 on the pop charts and #9 on the R&B charts. On the original by the Intruders, listeners were able to flip the 45 over and find a song they had originally released on the flip side of 1966's "We'll Be United" called "Up and Down the Ladder," which also became a favorite in beach music circles. These releases were followed by "Baby I'm Lonely" (#70) and the fine "A Love That's Real" (#82), another song that was popular with beach music audiences.

"A Love That's Real" made a reference to Jack and Jill fetching a pail of water together, and this would be the first of several Intruders hits to make reference to the innocence and simplicity of childhood crushes. The most successful of these would be 1968's "Cowboys to Girls," which referred to childhood innocence once again. The Gamble and Huff–penned classic that sold more than one million records, earned an RIAA-certified Gold Record and went all the way to #6 on the pop charts and #1 on the R&B charts. By this time, it was apparent that Gamble and Huff's faith in the group had paid off, and the Intruders would have a string of fourteen chart hits over the next few years, including "(Love Is Like A) Baseball Game" (#26), a song that, like "Cowboys to Girls," played on the idea of the relationship between childhood memories, games, and love. Kenny Gamble's mother Ruby was the inspiration for, "I'll Always Love My Mama," a #36 hit in 1973 which, although it had a more electric '70s Philadelphia soul sound than their older R&B, was a beach favorite in some circles.

Around 1970 "Little Sonny" Brown, who had been the lead singer on all of their hits, would leave the group, and Bobby Starr would step in as lead singer, though Brown would rejoin the group once again in 1973, the group's last year on Gamble. Two further releases on TSOP made the lower reaches of the R&B charts, but after 24 R&B chart hits, including six in the Top 10, and 14 singles on the Billboard Hot 100, the Intruders would disband in 1975. Eugene Daughtry died of cancer in 1994, while "Little Sonny" Brown committed suicide in 1994, an act precipitated by years of drug problems as well as the deaths of his wife and mother.

The Isley Brothers

BEACH MUSIC DISCOGRAPHY: "This Old Heart of Mine (Is Weak for You)" (Tamla 54128, 1966: Billboard Pop #12); "I Guess I'll Always Love You" (Tamla 54135, 1966: Billboard Pop #61).

Lincoln Heights, Ohio natives The Isley Brothers got their start when the four oldest of six brothers—O'Kelly, Jr., Rudolph, Ronald, and Vernon—formed a singing group in 1954. Within the year 12-year-old Vernon was hit by a truck and killed while riding his bike to school, and the remaining brothers temporarily decided to suspend their plans to perform as a musical group. Encouraged by their parents to pursue their dreams despite the loss of their brother, O'Kelly, Jr., Rudolph, and Ronald once again began singing R&B and doo-wop, and after honing their craft they went to New York in 1956. There they auditioned for several record labels, and recorded singles for the Teenage, Mark-X, Cindy, and Gone labels in 1957 and 1958. None were very successful, but their family was encouraged enough to move to Englewood, New Jersey, so the boys could be close to the New York music scene. Their performances caught the ear of executives at RCA, who signed them in 1959. While their first single for the label was forgettable, their next one was not, as the raucous "Shout" has gone on to become a classic. While today the song is well known and seen as a seminal rock-and-roller, it only reached #47 on the charts, though eventually it would sell more than one million copies and become their first gold single. Because they weren't able to follow it up with another hit, however, RCA dropped them from the label. They went to Atlantic and then Wand, where they did a cover of the Top Notes' "Twist and Shout" in 1962. The song went to #17 on the pop charts and #2 on the R&B charts and was their first big hit, although the Beatles' cover version went to #2 in 1964 and is now better known.

The brothers next signed with United Artists, then formed their own label, T-Neck Records, named for Ronald's hometown at the time, Teaneck New Jersey. They released just one song on their label before they returned to Atlantic, before finally signing with Motown mogul Berry Gordy in 1965. They first recorded the Holland, Dozier, and Holland penned "I Hear a Symphony" on the V.I.P. subsidiary, and though it didn't register on the charts it would go on to be a #1 record for the Supremes. Nevertheless, Gordy recognized the group's potential and moved them up to his Gordy subsidiary label. He gave them another Holland, Dozier, and Holland (with Sylvia Moy) song to record called "This Old Heart of Mine (Is Weak for You)," which, oddly enough, had been intended for the Supremes. With the Funk Brothers providing back up and Ronald Isley on lead, the single raced up the charts to #12 on the pop charts and #6 on the R&B charts, the Isleys' biggest hit to that point. Ronald Isley's anguished cry for his girl to return his love would resonate with listeners then and later; Tammi Terrell, Rod Stewart and others would also record the song, and Stewart and Ronald Isley would record a duet in 1989 that would top the adult contemporary charts.

Despite this powerful and very promising start, after "This Old Heart of Mine" they had six more charting releases at Tamla, but another Holland, Dozier, and Holland-penned song, "I Guess I'll Always Love You," was their highest subsequent pop charter in the U.S. at #61. The group also recorded a fine version of Holland, Dozier, and Holland's "Take Me In Your Arms," which Eddie Holland had recorded in 1964 but had not been released. It was then covered by Kim Weston in 1965, and her version went to #50 on the pop charts and #4 on the R&B charts; the Isley's version topped out at #22 on the R&B charts.

The group would leave Tamla and reactivate their own T-Neck label, and in 1969 brothers Ernie and Marvin joined the group at long last, along with their brother-in-law Chris Jasper. From that point they went on to their greatest success with records such as "It's Your Thing" (which won them a Grammy), "That Lady," "Fight the Power," and others. They began undergoing changes in their personnel in the 1980s,

Paul Jabara

BEACH MUSIC DISCOGRAPHY: "Trapped In a Stairway" (Casablanca TGIFS3, 1978: Did Not Chart).

Paul Jabara was a New Yorker who got his start as a teenager modeling in both print and visual media. From this he moved into acting in musicals (he was offered parts in *The Sound of Music*, *Jesus Christ Superstar*, and *Hair*), and thus for Jabara acting and music would always be inextricably intertwined. He was also an important songwriter, eventually going on to write "The Main Event" for Barbra Streisand, the Donna Summer/Barbra Streisand duet "No More Tears (Enough Is Enough)," "It's Raining Men" for The Weather Girls, as well as songs for Diana Ross, Julio Iglesias, and others. Jabara would also appear on numerous television shows throughout his career, such as *The Tonight Show*, *American Bandstand*, *Starsky and Hutch*, and *Mary Hartman, Mary Hartman*, and he would also appear in films including *Midnight Cowboy*, *The Lords of Flatbush*, and *Legal Eagles*.

His greatest acclaim for beach music aficionados, however, would come via the 1978 film *Thank God it's Friday*, which was about clubbing and the disco scene. As Jabara told Dick Clark in 1978, in the movie "I play a kid named Carl, who goes to a disco looking for action…. This girl says 'Will you go downstairs and get my sweater for me?' I go downstairs and I get stuck in the stairway…." While he's locked in the stairway, "Trapped in a Stairway" provides the backdrop for that experience. Of the many songs recorded in the 1970s that walk the fine line between disco and beach music, few do so more tenuously than Jabara's offering; it was even recorded on disco-label-mainstay Casablanca, home to the Village People, Donna Summer, and Parliament. Despite these elements which could be perceived as drawbacks, "Trapped in a Stairway" was quickly adopted by beach music lovers as a first-rate shag song. It is one of two songs he performed in the film, and though it is a catchy tune, when released as a single it failed to chart, and few listeners at the time appreciated the song.

What listeners did appreciate, however, was another song that he wrote for the movie, though he didn't perform it. His composition "Last Dance," which Donna Summer sang in the film, was a monster hit, and for it Jabara earned a Grammy Award, a Golden Globe, and the Academy Award for Best Original Song. Though these awards would be the high point of his career, Jabara would go on to write many songs for other artists, continue his acting career, and in addition, Jabara has been credited with co-founding the red-ribbon project which distributed ribbons to raise awareness of AIDS. Jabara himself would die of AIDS in 1992.

Chuck Jackson

BEACH MUSIC DISCOGRAPHY: "I Don't Want to Cry" (Wand 106, 1961: Billboard Pop #36); "Any Day Now" (Wand 122, 1962: Billboard Pop #23).

One of five children of a single mother, Charles Jackson was born in Latta, South Carolina. When he an infant his mother left him with his grandparents and moved to Pittsburgh to find work. As a child Jackson began singing in the church choir, and when he was 12 his singing won him a scholarship to South Carolina State College. Not long afterwards he moved to Pittsburgh to attend high school, and by the time he was 14 he was sneaking into nightclubs to hear jazz musicians perform. In 1955 he joined the doo-wop group the 5 Mellows, and he would join the Ray Raspberry Gospel Singers before returning to South Carolina State in 1956 to take advantage of the college scholarship he had earned as a child. There he studied music, but due to intense racial strife in the area at the time he returned to Pittsburgh later that year.

In 1957 Jackson joined the Del Vikings right after they'd scored a million-selling, Top 10 hit with "Come Go With Me." The group had just split into two factions, and one stayed at Pittsburgh's Fee Bee label and the other group went to Mercury. Jackson signed with the faction at Fee Bee, and adding an L to their name to become the Dell Vikings they had several chart hits including "Whispering Bells" and "Cool Shake." After several years of litigation between record companies, the Fee Bee group changed their name and became Chuck Jackson and the Versatiles. In 1959 he went solo, releasing several singles on the Clock label as Charles Jackson. After performing with Jackie Wilson at the Apollo Theater he joined the Jackie Wilson Revue in 1960. Working as Wilson's opening act brought him to the notice of several large record labels, and ultimately he was signed to the Scepter subsidiary Wand in 1960 after owner Florence Greenberg and producer Luther Dixon saw him perform. Although Scepter had one big act at the time in the Shirelles, the artists signed to Wand included Bette Watts, The Titones, and the Leeds, none of whom had scored a single chart hit.

Jackson's very first release would change that. "I Don't Want to Cry" was co-written with Luther Dixon, and arranged by Carole King, who at the time was a little-known musician and writer working in New York's Brill Building. The song went to #5 on the R&B charts and #36 on the pop charts, and seemed to indicate that Jackson was going to have the chart success that many had anticipated. Of his next five single releases however, none surpassed "I Don't Want to Cry" on the pop or R&B charts, and in fact three didn't make either chart. A couple of these singles had been written by the up-and-coming songwriting team of Burt Bacharach and Hal David, and Bacharach and Bob Hilliard were also the co-writers of his next big hit, "Any Day Now." The song peaked at #23 on the pop charts and went to #2 on the R&B charts. It would be Jackson's biggest pop hit, and several artists would later cover the song, including Elvis Presley and Ronnie Milsap, whose 1982 cover would actually surpass Jackson's, going to #14 on the pop charts and #1 on the country music charts.

Jackson would have twenty-five records make the pop, adult contemporary, and/or R&B charts right up through 1970 not only on Wand but also Motown, ABC, EMI and other labels, but only three after that. As a producer, writer, and arranger he worked with many artists such as The Impressions, Natalie

Cole, Aretha Franklin, and The Dells, so while his chart success was somewhat limited his abilities in all facets of the recording industry led to his nickname "Mr. Everything." In 1992 he was given the Rhythm and Blues Foundation Pioneer Award, and in 2009 he inducted into the Carolina Beach Music Hall of Fame.

Deon Jackson

BEACH MUSIC DISCOGRAPHY: "Love Makes the World Go Round" (Carla 2526, 1965: Billboard Pop #11).

Ann Arbor, Michigan-born Deon Jackson studied clarinet and drums as a child, and in high school started a vocal group called The Five Crystals while he also performed as a solo act in talent shows. In 1962, producer Ollie Mclaughlin heard Jackson and his group singing at a local concert, although the group really only knew McLaughlin as a DJ and not as the successful producer who worked with Barbara Lewis, the Capitols, Betty Lavette, and others. Mclaughlin decided to sign Jackson as a solo act because not only was he writing music but he also seemed to be serious about singing as a career whereas the others did not. Mclaughlin became Jackson's manager and got him a deal with Atlantic, but two 1964 releases for the label, "You Said You Love Me" and "Come Back Baby" did nothing.

McLaughlin decided to release Jackson's next single on a label he had just founded, Carla, one of four labels he'd own (with Karen, Moira and Ruth), all of which—other than Ruth—were named after his daughters. Jackson's first release on Carla, and the very first release for the label, was 1965's "Love Makes the World Go Round."

Oddly enough, in the *Billboard Book of One-Hit Wonders*, Wayne Jancik says Jackson told *Goldmine*'s Bill Dahl, "I would cringe every time the song came on the radio. I'd think' 'God' I don't like that.' And I wrote it, too. I just don't like that song." Jackson says he wrote the song during a period of massive riots during the Civil Rights Movement, because he thought the world just needed love. It was a beautiful day, and he thought about the difference between the weather outside, his sister singing (whom he could hear in the kitchen), contrasted with the ugliness happening across the country. He said he wrote the song in four minutes. He did a demo of the song backed up by the then all-but-unknown, but later very famous, Edwin Starr, as well as Telma Hopkins and Joyce Vincent Wilson—who would be the voices of Dawn behind Tony Orlando. The demo, however, was promptly shelved and forgotten.

Then a year later, McLaughlin released it. When it hit it caught Jackson by surprise because he'd forgotten about it—and he still just didn't like it much. "'I mean it bugged me-because wrote it so fast and put it aside so fast and then it sat around for a year before it was released" he told Dahl. "I guess I figured it shouldn't be worth anything–it was too easy." Radio listeners did not share that sentiment. It went to #11 on the pop charts while going to #3 on the R&B charts. Deon Jackson was a star.

Unfortunately, in six more singles on Carla and one on Shout he couldn't land another Top 40 hit, though 1966's "Love Takes a Long Time Growing" made it to #77 on the charts and 1967's "Ooh Baby" clocked in at #65. Within a few years he had become a keyboard player in New York City nightclubs, and then moved back to Chicago where he played in clubs and performed in musicals until 2000. That year he started working at the Wheaton Warrenville South High School as a student supervisor until his death in 2014.

J.J. Jackson

BEACH MUSIC DISOGRAPHY: "But It's Alright" (Calla 119, 1966: Billboard Pop #22).

Born Jerome Louis Jackson in Gillet Arkansas in 1941, he recorded with a group in the '50s known as the Jackaels, who cut a song called "Oo-Ma-Liddi" which failed to chart. He also worked as an arranger and songwriter, and his songwriting credits from the early '60s include songs such as the Shangri-Las' "It's Easier to Cry," the flip side of their hit "Remember (Walkin' in the Sand)." This song still lists him as merely J. Jackson, but when the Pretty Things charted in England with another Jackson creation, "Come See Me (I'm Your Man)," in 1966, he was by that time taking label credit as J.J. Jackson. A big, nearly three-hundred-pound man in the physical mold of Billy Stewart and with a soulful "belter" voice like Otis Redding, his talent as a singer was recognized in the mid–1960s, and he was signed by the Calla label.

His first release for Calla was a big one, a song he wrote with Pierre Tubbs and recorded in England, "But It's Alright." Rock critic Don Waller claimed that with "two notes, then four and then two notes, then four," it had an opening riff "strong enough to levitate a bloc of communists." Arranged and conducted by Jackson and produced by Lew Futterman, this rocking 1966 soul number rose to #22 on the Billboard charts and #4 on the R&B charts and spawned an album, *But It's Alright,* before stalling. His next Calla recording, "I Dig Girls," only charted at #83, but nevertheless two consecutive records, both charters, seemed to bode well for the singer. His next song, on Calla 133, "Four Walls," didn't chart, and unbeknownst to anyone at the time, Jackson would never have an original issue chart again. "But It's Alright" *would* chart again, however, when Warner Brothers bought the Calla catalogue and re-released the song in May 1969 and it climbed to #45.

Jackson's chart fame had passed, though he continued to perform in England and cut albums and singles into the early '70s. Perhaps the question most often asked is if this is the same J.J. Jackson who was an MTV VJ in the 1980s. He is not; as of this writing, the MTV Jackson had passed away, while the "But It's Alright" Jackson still performs occasionally.

Millie Jackson

BEACH MUSIC DISOGRAPHY: "Ask Me What You Want" (Spring 123, 1972: Billboard Pop #27); "My Man, a Sweet Man" (Spring 127, 1972: Billboard Pop #42).

Born Mildred Jackson in Thompson Georgia, her mother died when Millie was 2. Her father was a sharecropper who at times ran a juke joint, and when she was about 12 he moved to New Jersey, leaving Millie behind with her strict grandparents. At 14 she ran away to join her father up north, and ended up living with her aunt in Brooklyn. For a while she worked as a model and appeared in magazines such as *Sepia* and *Jive*, but her life would change when in 1964 she was at the Palms Café, a Harlem nightclub. On a dare she took the stage after claiming she could sing better than the act being paid to perform, and after singing a version of Ben E. King's "Don't Play That Song for Me" the club owner was so impressed with her performance that he hired her that night. For the next few years she worked daytime as an assistant supervisor at a clothing manufacturer and spent her nights singing in bars throughout the area before finally recording a single on MGM ("A Little Bit of Something") that didn't chart. At about this same time she was briefly married, and had daughter Keisha in 1965.

She next signed with Spring records, and her first Spring release was 1971's "A Child of God," which bubbled under at #102 on the pop charts and went to #22 on the R&B charts. Her next release was a song she co-wrote with Billy Nichols, "Ask Me What You Want." The song is an excellent slice of early '70s soul boosted by Jackson's strong voice. However, like much of her early music, she dismisses it today. In an interview for TV One's program *Unsung*, she said, "it's just some lyrics put to a Motown groove. I didn't feel that song at all … it's just a huge lie, one of the biggest lies I ever sang in my life. You can tell I was not in control of my career at the time." Apparently those in control of her career knew what the public wanted however, and it would be her second biggest hit, peaking at #27 on the pop charts and #4 on the R&B charts.

Her next release was 1972's "My Man, a Sweet Man." Now a beach music and Northern Soul favorite, it's also a song Jackson dismisses today, and even at the time she was aware she didn't want a career singing songs like it—despite the success she was having. "I couldn't picture me singing 'My man is a sweet man/my man is a kind man/I know he's a fine man/and he's mine all mine' [forever]. Who cares?" Jackson apparently felt that the pop/soul sound about adoring relationships just wasn't the type of music she wanted to be known for. "You know, to me it was just a nothing song" she said. "I mean, who walks around and says 'my man is a sweet man/my man is a kind man/my man is a fine man/ he's mine, mine, mine.' … And the person next to you is going, 'So?'" Yet despite her own misgivings about the subject matter of the song, once again the public was appeased, and the catchy single went to #42 on the pop charts, #7 on the R&B charts, and #50 in England, making it her first transatlantic hit.

Jackson continued to have success, and 1973's "It Hurts So Good" would not only be featured in the film *Cleopatra Jones*, but would also be the biggest chart hit of her career, going to #24 on the pop charts and #3 on the R&B charts. 1975's "If Loving You Is Wrong I Don't Want to Be Right" would also perform well, going to #42 and earning two Grammy nominations, and the album it was on, *Caught Up*, would earn a gold record. Yet Jackson still wasn't really happy with the work she was producing. "A gold record didn't mean too much to me because I found out it wasn't gold, it was just gold colored" she told TV One. "I couldn't pawn it." Ironically, it was the success of this mainstream music that she didn't like that allowed her to finally take control of her career. By the late '70s she was recording more risqué material with increasingly provocative titles. The 1977 album *Feeling Bitchy* was the first to cross the line, and later albums such as *Back to the S__t*, featuring a cover picture of Jackson sitting on the toilet, saw her branded as a very adult, sexually explicit singer—a reputation she has done much to foster, and nothing to dispel.

Her daughter Keisha recorded albums in the late '80s and 1990s, and has remained in the music industry, now working primarily as a backup singer. Millie Jackson continues to perform well into her '70s.

Etta James

BEACH MUSIC DISCOGRAPHY: "Pushover" (Argo 5437, 1963: Billboard Pop #25); "Tell Mama" (Cadet 5578, 1967: Billboard Pop #23).

Los Angeles born Jamesetta Hawkins was the daughter of 14-year-old unwed mother Dorothy Hawkins. Though the identity of her father was never established, later in life James's mother and others told her she was the daughter of Rudolf Walter Wanderone, Jr., also known as pool shark Minnesota Fats, with whom her mother had a relationship. Jamesetta would go on to be raised mainly by James and Lulu ("Mama Lu") Rogers, and while in their care she began singing in the choir at St. Paul's Baptist Church at age five. It was there that she developed her strong singing voice, though unfortunately it was because the choir director would punch her in the chest to force her to sing using her diaphragm. There was apparently some abuse in the Rogers home as well, and after Lulu Rogers died 12 year old Jamesetta went to live with her mother.

Jamesetta was drinking, ditching school, and on the verge of becoming just another problem teenager when her talent allowed her to turn her life around. She had formed a singing group called the Creolettes with friends Abbye and Jean Mitchell. Working in low-end nightclubs for as little as $10 a night, the girls were discovered by Johnny Otis, who would also discover Jackie Wilson, Hank Ballard, and others. Otis signed 15-year-old Jamesetta and the Mitchell sisters to Modern Records, and in the process had Jamesetta flip her name to Etta James. The group was known as The Peaches due to James's childhood nickname "Miss Peaches," as she was so-called due to her light complexion.

Their first recording was 1954's "Roll with Me Henry." The song was an answer record to the Hank Ballard and the Midnighters' "Work with Me Annie," but because the word "roll" still had strong sexual connotations in the early '50s it was retitled "Dance with Me Henry." Though the group had been singing it before they met Otis, songwriting credit went to both James and Otis, and by the time it was released the title had become "The Wallflower." Under that title the song went to #1 on the R&B charts in 1955, although later 45 reissues and compilation albums would use both the "Roll" and "Dance" titles. Soon James broke off from the Peaches, and of her next dozen or so releases on Modern and Kent only 1955's "Good Rockin' Daddy" would be a hit.

By this time James was in a relationship with Harvey Fuqua of the Moonglows, and he introduced her to Leonard Chess, who signed James to record on his Argo (later Cadet) subsidiary label. This would be the most prolific period of her career, and highlights included her debut album *At Last!* in 1960, Grammy nominations in 1960 and 61, and her first Top 40 pop hit, "Trust in Me" in 1961. As a result, James had become a regular chart presence by the time she released "Pushover" in 1963. Co-written by Roquel "Billy" Davis, who had written "Lonely Teardrops" and who would write songs such as "Rescue Me," and Tony Clarke, who would not only write another James hit, "Two Sides (To Every Story)," but also have his own hit, "The Entertainer" in 1965, the song would reach #7 on the R&B charts and #25 on the pop charts, making it her biggest pop hit to that point.

Over the next four years James would have very little chart success, largely due to her personal demons. She had become an alcoholic and a heroin addict, and was in and out of rehab. In 1967 she underwent a rejuvenation of sorts after Chess sent her down to Muscle Shoals and she recorded the smash hit "Tell Mama." Written by Clarence Carter, the song was originally called "Tell Daddy" and Carter himself recorded it at Muscle Shoals in 1966. Retitled and produced by Rick Hall, the song brought her another Grammy nomination and was her biggest pop hit, going to #23. Despite the fact that James told her biographer David Ritz that she never really liked the song, Leonard Chess apparently thought it would allow James to make some headway in Aretha Franklin's audience and indeed for a while it seemed her career was back on track. Her songs were once again charting, but "Tell Mama" would be her biggest pop hit.

After the death of Leonard Chess in 1969 James's career went into a slow decline. She'd stay with the label until 1976, though she'd have few chart records. Her addictions would become more problematic and would plague her for many years, but in the 1980s she'd start to have a resurgence in popularity and by the 1990s she'd regain her rightful place in the pantheon of American music. She was inducted into the Rock and Roll Hall of Fame in 1993, received a star on the Hollywood Walk of Fame, and many other accolades before her death from Leukemia in 2012.

Jimmy James and the Vagabonds

BEACH MUSIC DISCOGRAPHY: "Come to Me Softly" (Atco 6551, 1968: Billboard Pop #76); "I'll Go Where the Music Takes Me" (Pye 71068, 1976: Did Not Chart).

Kingston, Jamaica-born Jimmy James started writing music when he was in his teens, but it wasn't until he joined the pre-established Jamaican group The Vagabonds in 1964 that he turned to music as a fulltime career. They moved to England, where they were one of the earliest groups to bring Ska music to mainstream European audiences. Their recording "Ska Time" brought the group some notoriety and got them on the bill with the Who, Jimi Hendrix, Sonny and Cher, the Rolling Stones, and others.

Having signed with Pye records in 1966, the group released the album *The New Religion* in 1966. *The New Religion* largely consisted of cover versions of songs by American writers and artists such as Curtis Mayfield, Sam Cooke, Smokey Robinson, and Holland, Dozier, and Holland, and the album also included covers of songs that were beach music mainstays; The Radiants' "It Ain't No Big Thing" and Tony Clarke's "The Entertainer" and "This Heart of Mine." The only original song on the album was a song James had penned, "Come to Me Softly."

James had actually written the song and recorded it on Tip Top's Gaydisc subsidiary label when still in Jamaica, and it was the success of that and other local hits that had encouraged him to go into the music business full time. The original version actually sounds somewhat different, with a steel drum accompanied Jamaican sound, and the version from the album, which was released in America on Atco in 1968, is actually lusher and more orchestral. The song rose to #76 on the pop charts and #44 on the R&B charts, and was the group's first American chart record. Their growing popularity saw the group touring around the world in the late '60s, and they released a second album, *Open Up Your Soul*. Their next chart record, a 1969 cover of Neil Diamond's "Red, Red Wine" from the album, rose to #36 on the UK charts, though it didn't chart in the U.S.

The group disbanded in 1970, and James recorded some solo efforts before reforming the group with a new line-up in 1974. This new version of Jimmy James and the Vagabonds recorded "I'll Go Where the Music Takes Me" in 1976, which rose to #23 on the U.K. charts but did not chart in the U.S. As it was a somewhat fallow time in beach music circles in the mid '70s, coming after the great R&B songs of the '50s and '60s and before the advent of "new beach music" in the late '70s, the song's danceable beat saw it gain acceptance in beach music circles, though its popularity has not endured. One other song from the group, "I Am Somebody," made the U.S. pop charts at #94 and R&B #62; it would be the group's last U.S. chart appearance.

Janice

BEACH MUSIC DISCOGRAPHY: "I Told You So" (Fantasy 748, Did Not Chart 1975).

Although the public first came to know the name Janice Barnett as a teenage beauty queen and as a *Jet Magazine* model, her greatest success would come as a singer. She had her first chance when she became the lead singer for Reggie Saddler's band, which would work under a variety of names in the late '60s and early 1970s, including Janice and the Jammers. Though they recorded several singles on the Dee-Lite label, none charted and the group seemed destined for a career as an opening act for better-known groups. By 1974 she and Saddler were married and they decided to head to California, agreeing that if they hadn't made it within 30 days they'd return home at least secure in the thought that they had tried to achieve their dreams.

It was a chance encounter with Richard Pryor that led to the group getting an audition at a club called the Total Experience—the Soul Train headquarters—which ultimately led to a recording contract and their working with the legendary Harvey Fuqua, who had developed talent at Motown including the Spinners and Marvin Gaye. Fuqua was also developing acts for Fantasy Records in Los Angeles, and, struck by Janice's strong voice he suggested the group call themselves simply 'Janice.' Fuqua decided the group needed to put together an album, and so they went into the studio to record. "We were in the studio at the top of the RCA building with Marvin Gaye and a couple of other people like Smokey Robinson who were always around Harvey. We were just playing around and Reggie started playing something on the guitar, and when he did I started putting lyrics to it and so did he. Harvey heard us and said 'What's that you're messing with? What are you working on?' We played it for him and he really liked it. That song became 'I Told You So.'"

Barnett said it was funny that "We had all these songs we'd worked on for years, and this one we wrote in just 12 minutes went on to become our signature song. We didn't sit down and plan to write it or anything. It just came out. It was just Reggie and me going back and forth talking about how our relationship had developed. 'I told you didn't I, that I was going to be your wife'—there we were playing around with each other and that kind of thing." Even though the song wasn't originally supposed to be on the album, "Harvey was an old Motown veteran and he always tested the records. The test audience loved it, so we put it on the album." And though the song never charted, live audiences have always loved it. "Everybody liked 'Wake up Smiling' and 'Goody Two Shoes,' but 'I Told You So" was the one they really went nuts for. It just amazed us at the way people loved it—how the women sang it and how it brought people together and how we could see the love in the room."

Unfortunately, while their 1975 album sold well in some areas of the country, neither it nor the single releases were ever big hits. Fuqua moved on to other projects, and while the group played clubs for many years eventually Janice and Reggie divorced and the group came apart. Janice went on to do both television and stage work, and eventually she turned to the ministry while also continuing to work in beach music, recording and performing duets with notables such as Maurice Williams and Billy Scott. Her association with beach music led to her winning a beach music award as female vocalist of the year, as half of duo of the year (with Billy Scott), and her induction into the Beach Music Hall of Fame. Ultimately, these awards and a number of other nominations led to her being hailed as the "Queen of Beach Music, " she says "because I started out as teenager and as a female singing in a man's arena, and that opened the door for other women in Carolina beach music." Certainly Janice Barnett has made an incredible impact on beach music, both in the past and today as well.

Jay and the Techniques

BEACH MUSIC DISCOGRAPHY: "Apples, Peaches, Pumpkin Pie" (Smash 2086, 1967: Billboard Pop #6); "Keep the Ball Rollin'" (Smash 2124, 1967: Billboard Pop #14).

Jay Proctor was an Allentown, Pennsylvania, singer who had cut a few unsuccessful singles in 1960 and 61, and who by the mid–60s was still trying to find direction with his musical career. Proctor and his friend George "Lucky" Lloyd were sitting in a bar when a friend came in and asked them to audition for a new group he was putting together. Proctor and Lloyd did audition, and along with Chuck Crowl, Karl Landis, Ronnie Goosley, Jon Walsh and Dante Dancho they formed their own group, The Techniques.

In 1966 they came to the attention of Philadelphia producer Jerry Ross, who was riding a string of pop-star discoveries such as Dee Dee Warwick, Keith, Spanky and Our Gang, and Bobby Hebb. Ross had offered Hebb a song called "Apples, Peaches, Pumpkin Pie" as a follow up to his smash "Sunny," but Hebb refused it and Ross gave it to his new group instead. "Actually several people and groups had tried recording the song–I think even Jerry Butler" Proctor told me. "Jerry Ross didn't like the way any of them did it, and so he gave it me. I'm raw off the street, I don't know anything about music, so I just opened my mouth and whatever came out, came out. Well whatever came out pleased him, so we got to release it." The "we" in this case comes with a qualifier, because Proctor was the only member of the group to actually attend the recording session. "Jerry used session musicians on everything we did. The band was the road group and they never went in the studio. I asked Jerry to use them, but he just felt they weren't good enough because they didn't read music well."

Jay and the Techniques, circa 1967–68 (photograph courtesy Jay Proctor).

But to his credit, Ross chose top-notch session musicians and singers, including backup singers who would later go on to have their own hits: Melba Moore and Nick Ashford and Valerie Simpson. But as for the song, "I didn't like 'Apples, Peaches, Pumpkin Pie'" Proctor told me. "I'm a very soulful singer and there wasn't any soul in that song at all. I didn't want to sing about no damn fruit!"

When the record was released the band was surprised to see that Ross had changed the group's name to in Jay and The Techniques, and Proctor says "I think Jerry changed it because there was Smokey Robinson and the Miracles, and Martha and the Vandellas, and he just didn't like that single-name thing. It wasn't that I was the leader of the group, just the lead singer on the song. Then it didn't make sense to change it back after the song was a hit." The song went to #6 on the pop charts, sold a million copies, and earned a gold record, and so despite the fact that the group hadn't actually played on the song, and their name had been changed without their being asked, and even though Proctor says he "didn't even like the song," they had a hit on their hands nevertheless.

To follow up on the success of "Apples, Peaches, Pumpkin Pie," Ross had a song written just for them, "Keep the Ball Rollin." "Jerry Ross picked the song, and I didn't do anything but go in and perform what I was told or asked to. But I wasn't crazy about 'Keep the Ball Rollin' either—that wasn't soulful to me. But of course I did it and I'm glad I did." Ross clearly had a better ear for a hit than his lead singer, as 'Keep the Ball Rollin" soared to #14 on the charts, sold a million copies, and earned them yet another gold record.

Their next recording, "Strawberry Shortcake," was by the same writers who had composed "Apples, Peaches," and in fact sounded so much like it that "we never did it live but once because it was too close to 'Apples, Peaches.' It was by the same writers and used the same musicians. It was okay, and it had a nice beat, but those kinds of songs, you hear them once and you don't want to hear them no more." "Strawberry" peaked at #30, and in fact after just one more Top 100 record in 1968, the group's charting days were over as quickly as they had begun. "The music was all way too bubble-gummy—they even called it bubble gum soul. You look back at it and it was kind of ridiculous" Proctor said. "It was way far from what I thought my career would be like. I never really had the chance to do anything soulful like I wanted to do." Perhaps it was inevitable that with Proctor being the sole focus of the group, and with Proctor himself unhappy about the music they were offered, before long dissension started to set in and they broke up. Eventually Proctor re-formed the group with new members, and though they released a few singles in the '70s nothing really connected with audiences. Proctor continues to perform, and plays the beach music circuit as well.

Jewell and the Rubies

BEACH MUSIC DISCOGRAPHY: "Kidnapper"(La Louisianne 8041, 1963: Did Not Chart).

Little Rock, Arkansas-born Jewell Douglas moved to Gary Indiana as a child, and learned to play trombone in the high school band. After serving in World War II he attended Xavier College in New Orleans, and then Southern University in Baton Rouge, and as a result he was close to the New Orleans music scene and able to immerse himself in Louisiana music. After college he worked in a mill for a while, but eventually he was able to get a job teaching music at the James Stephens High School in Ville Platte, Louisiana. He taught music to a number of students over the years, and in the early 1960s he recruited a number of his current and former students to form his group, Jewell and the Rubies. The group, which would have a slightly fluctuating membership over the next few years, first consisted of Douglas and Sylvester Weatherall, Ralph Frank, Milton Lazar, Rogers Thomas, Lannis Fontenot, Leroy Alfred, and keyboardist Hershey Deville. After practicing for a few months, the group started playing local gigs all over Louisiana, pounding out R&B influenced by the Cajun sounds so well known in the area.

Deville says they started writing their own music, and "we'd sit down and I'd play the chords, Jewell would plot them and we'd go from there. When we came up with 'Kidnapper,' Doug and I were sitting there and he said, 'How does this sound?' He hummed, 'Da-da-da-da-da-dah, da-da da da-da,' I played it on the piano and he started singing the chorus, 'Kidnapper, bring my baby back to me.' We filled in the rest later." But even early on, they knew "Kidnapper" was something special, "so we went to the [La Lousianne] studio in Lafayette. We spent a couple of weeks, going back and forth, adding, deleting, until we got it right and we liked it. But when we recorded it, we had no idea it would be such a hit."

Some of the intricacies of the song are probably lost on listeners today because the song is so era-appropriate. The lyrics mention '60s legal and detective shows such as *Route 66, Perry Mason, Hawaiian Eye, Peter Gunn, The Untouchables* and others. Television references aside, "It just had that beat," Deville says. "After we recorded it everybody wanted us to play it. Out of twenty songs, we'd play 'Kidnapper' for what seemed like two hours. People would say, 'Play that again,' and we would." The song was in such demand in the South that ABC records became interested, and they released it on ABC Paramount 10485. The song didn't sell nationally, but even though it wasn't a national hit, the group was still in demand. Deville said, "A guy heard us play at a club in Lafayette, and he wanted to sign us up and take us out on the road." Although touring behind a single on a national label might have positioned them to break into the big time, it was not to be. "We were all still in school—I was a junior in high school—but my mother said, 'No, you're not quitting high school to go on the road to travel.' All of our parents said the same thing. So there was no national tour."

Deville says that they did write some more songs, and David Rachou, son of Carol Rachou, owner and founder of La Lousianne Records, said that though the group "did come back to the studio to try a follow-up recording session, but the material wasn't very good, so that was pretty much it." La Louisianne did release two more Jewell and the Rubies singles—"Our Love Is Here" and "Days Go By"—but nothing else really clicked with listeners like "Kidnapper" had.

The group's inability to travel to support their records, coupled with the failure to record that big follow-up single to "Kidnapper," meant that though the band played together for a few more years locally, they never got another shot at the big time. When the members graduated from high school and started to go off to college or joined different bands, the group just ceased to exist. Jewell Douglas later moved to Chicago, where he passed away some years ago.

The Jewels

BEACH MUSIC DISCOGRAPHY: "Opportunity" (Dimension 1034, 1964: Billboard Pop #64).

Sandra Peoples Bears, Grace Ruffin, Margie Clark and Carrie Mingo originally came together in Washington, D.C., in the late 1950s as the Impalas. Ruffin was the cousin of the then relatively unknown Billy Stewart, who was a piano player for Bo Diddley's band, and under Diddley's tutelage the Impalas recorded for "For the Love of Mike" on Checker in 1961. Perhaps to avoid being confused with the Impalas who had charted with "Sorry, I Ran all The Way Home" in 1959, they changed their name to the Four Jewels in 1962 and signed with the tiny Start label. They recorded three of the label's six releases in 1962 and 63 before the label folded, and then signed with Chess Records. On the Checker subsidiary they recorded two singles, but after six releases on three labels, none of their recordings had charted.

By this time Ruffin's cousin Billy Stewart was emerging as a star in his own right, and between recordings the girls did a few stints as backup singers, and according to Bears they "sang backup on many songs with Billy," including vocals on "Fat Boy." Martha Harvin joined the group to replace the departing Carrie Mingo, and their potential finally paid off for them on the Dimension label in 1964. "Our manager was Smokey McCallister, who we'd met previously while we were performing at the Howard Theater" Bears told me. "He asked about managing us, but we didn't get together until later because we were under contract with someone else at the time." When McCallister came on board, they changed their names to simply the Jewels (Clarke wasn't touring with the group, so appearing as the Four Jewels didn't seem appropriate), and then "Smokey McCallister took us to New York and let us hear some songs before we decided on 'Opportunity.'" With Sandra Bears' dynamic lead vocal, the record started to pick up steam—but it didn't happen overnight. "Well, when we recorded it, it didn't come right out—it was a few months—and we were hoping it would come out sooner," Bears said. Released in October 1964, to song climbed the charts slowly, peaking at #64 in the first week of December but dropping off the charts altogether just two

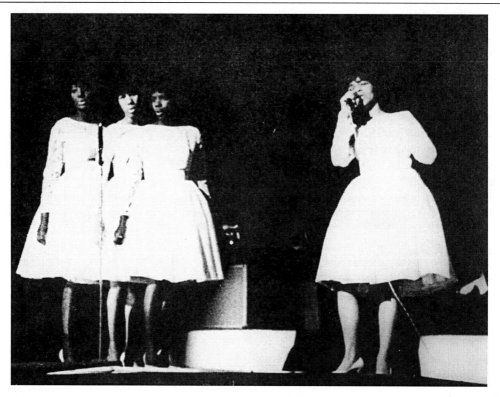

The Jewels, circa 1964 (photograph courtesy Sandra Peoples Bears and Beverly Johnson).

weeks later, despite its riveting sound. "I thought, personally, it could have been promoted a little more," Bears said. "I think when it started taking off on its own they started to push it more, but I think that had it been promoted more from the beginning it may have done even better."

Bears said the group "recorded some other songs around that time also, but 'Opportunity,' that was the big one." The group did "But I Do," a remake of the Clarence "Frogman" Henry hit, but it didn't break the top 100, nor did "several songs we recorded around the same time, like 'Smokey Joe'" and some others. Not long afterward, the Dimension label folded, and then post-"Opportunity" recordings by the group on the Federal and Dynamite labels stalled as well. "After that, we toured backing up James Brown," Bears said, "and we're on one of his albums of the show with James Crawford, Bobby Byrd and some others." After backing up Brown for a few years they disbanded about 1968, having had only "Opportunity" as their one moment in the spotlight.

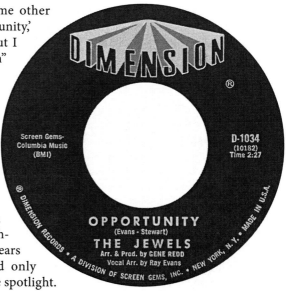

The Jive Five

BEACH MUSIC DISCOGRAPHY: "I'm a Happy Man" (United Artists 853, 1965: Billboard Pop #36).

The Jive Five got their start in Brooklyn, New York, when founder Eugene Pitt and Jerome Hanna, Billy Prophet, Richard Harris, and Norman Johnson renamed themselves after having been together under various names such as the Top Notes, Zip-Tones, Akrons, and Genies. The group finally settled on the name The Jive Five, and signed with the newly-established Beltone label in 1961. The label's second release had been the immensely successful "Tossin' and Turnin'" by Bobby Lewis, and the label's sixth release would be the Jive Five's first recording, "My True Story," a song Pitt had written. Despite the fact that the harmonizing vocal group/doo-wop sound was slowly winding its way down by the early '60s, nevertheless listeners warmed to the song as it reached #3 on the pop charts. With but a single release, the group was suddenly popular and very much in demand. Unfortunately, that success did not translate into hits on subsequent Beltone recordings, and although "Never, Never" went to #74 later that year, and "What Time Is It?" went to #67 in 1962, five other Beltone recordings didn't make a dent in the pop charts and by 1964 they had left the label.

Jerome Hanna had passed away in 1962 during their stay with Beltone, and by 1964 the group consisted of Pitt, Johnson, and Andre Coles, Casey Spencer, and Beatrice Best. They signed with the small Sketch label, but two releases there failed to generate any sales. They then signed with United Artists, and their first release, a doo-wop song called "United," had been a Sketch release that was ultimately unsuccessful for both labels. Their first original recording for the label was 1965's "I'm a Happy Man," which was a national hit. Though the label claimed the recording was by "Eugene Pitt and the Jive Five," in reality the five was only four–Pitt on the lead backed by Spencer, Harris, and Best. The song reached #36 on the pop charts and #26 on the R&B charts, and this led to the release of their only album, appropriately titled *I'm a Happy Man*. Their next single for United Artists, "A Bench in the Park," bubbled under the Top 100 pop charts at #106, and four further releases on United Artists did nothing at all. Recordings on Veep, Double R, and Cameo failed to impress listeners as well, with only 1967's "Crying Like a Baby" (#127) and 1968's "Sugar (Don't Take Away My Candy)"(#119), both on Musicor, coming close to the pop charts at all. By 1970 the group had changed their name to the funkier "Jyve" Five, and despite this and shift in personnel (the group now consisted of Pitt, Spencer, Richard Fisher and Webster Harris), releases on Avco, Brut, and Beltone all failed, though "I Want You to Be My Baby" on Decca did make the low end of the R&B charts in 1970. The group changed their name to Shadow for one failed recording on Chess, took the name Ebony, Ivory, and Jade for a single on Columbia, and even performed as Sting before retaking their original 1960s name as the Jive Five with the classic line-up of Eugene Pitt, Casey Spencer, Richard Harris and Beatrice Best around 1980. Another half dozen singles and several lineup changes followed, but no chart hits, and as it turned out 1965's "I'm a Happy Man" had been and would be their last pop Top 40 chart record.

Though the lineup of the group would often change, their most memorable post '60s work would come in interesting milieus. They sang background for Gloria Gaynor on her hit "Never Can Say Goodbye" in 1974, and they arguably reached their widest audience ever singing the jingle "Nic-Nic-Nic Nickelodeon" for the Nickelodeon children's network in the 1980s and '90s. "I'm a Happy Man," however, stands as their lone significant contribution to the annals of beach music.

Little Willie John

BEACH MUSIC DISCOGRAPHY: "Fever" (King 4935, 1956: Billboard Pop #24); "Heartbreak (It's Hurtin' Me)" (King 5356, 1960: Billboard Pop #38).

William Edward John was born in Cullendale, Arkansas, one of ten children born to Mertis and Lillie John. When Willie was four his father moved his family to Detroit to take a job at the Dodge factory, and while he worked Willie's mother, a former nightclub singer, tended to the children. Willie and his brothers and sister formed an amateur gospel group but it was when he was taking singing lessons at age 14 and came to the notice of Johnny Otis during a talent competition that people started to see that Willie had real talent. Otis told King Records mogul Syd Nathan he should sign John, but Nathan refused due to John's age. Instead, for his first single John (recording as Willie John and the Three Lads and Lass) laid down "Mommy, What Happened to the Christmas Tree" on the tiny Prize label in 1953, and after that he handled lead duties on "Ring a Ling" on the Rama label in 1955 backed by Paul Williams and his Orchestra. Though neither of these songs were a hit, working with Williams was prestigious enough that it should have been a solid foundation for his career moving forward. Unfortunately, John was already displaying the type of disruptive and erratic behavior that would ultimately be his undoing, and Williams fired him in 1955.

John finally signed with King Records, and his first recording was "All Around the World," which spent four months on the R&B charts in 1955 and climbed to #5. He was now going as "Little" Willie John (he was 5 feet 4 inches tall), but he was insecure about his height and fueled by a fondness for drink his personality was becoming more volatile. Nevertheless, his next release on King was a song his brother had written, "Need Your Love So Bad," and it too was a Top 10 R&B hit in 1956. Although his next release did not chart, his fourth single was his biggest yet, "Fever." Written by Otis Blackwell (as Joe Davenport) and Eddie Cooley, John did not want to record it but was convinced to do so by Nathan and Henry Glover. In a recording session that was reported to have taken six hours, the sax-and-finger-snap-driven song was a #1 R&B hit in 1956, and crossed over onto the pop charts as well, hitting #24. It was later covered by Elvis Presley, Peggy Lee, and others, but nevertheless, John's is considered the definitive version.

He had two more R&B chart records in 1956 before a streak of six releases over the next year that didn't chart at all. In 1958 his personal life appeared to be stabilizing as he got married and had a child and then a second child in 1960. He was back on the charts in 1960 with "Heartbreak (It's Hurtin' Me)." John's version was a cover of his friend Jon Thomas' 1960 release on ABC-Paramount. Written by Thomas, John's version is a bit more of a screamer than Thomas's slightly more laid back rendition, though the instrumental tracks on both are nearly identical. Thomas' version would go to #3 on the R&B charts but only #48 on the pop charts, while Little Willie John's version would peak at #11 on the R&B charts but would break into the Top 40 (#38) on the pop charts. John's next release, "Sleep," would be his biggest pop record, peaking at #13 and #10 on the R&B charts.

Sadly, it was at this time that his world started to unravel. After "Sleep" he only had four chart records, all in 1961, and he was drinking frequently and also using drugs. After he started missing recording sessions, his unreliability soured his relationship with King to the point that although he was under contract with them the label simply stopped recording him by 1963. No longer recording he found himself in financial difficulties, which exacerbated his other problems. By this time he had moved to Miami, and his behavior became even more volatile and he was carrying a gun and a knife at all times. In 1964 he was charged with assault in Miami but jumped bail and wound up across the country in Washington, where he killed a man named Kendall Roundtree in a Seattle nightclub. John had gone to the restroom only to return find Roundtree had taken his chair, and after Roundtree refused to move John stabbed him to death. He was convicted of manslaughter and sentenced to eight to twenty years in the Washington State Penitentiary in 1966, though he was able to make a few recordings (unreleased at the time) for Capitol before he went behind bars. His wife and sons moved back to Detroit when he went to prison, but he never served out his sentence. In 1968 he died in prison from causes that have at various times been attributed to a heart attack, asphyxiation, or pneumonia, although many people believe he was beaten to death by either the prison's guards or inmates. In any event, by age 30 Little Willie John was dead; he was inducted into the Rock and Roll Hall of Fame in 1996.

Robert John

BEACH MUSIC DISCOGRAPHY: "If You Don't Want My Love"(Columbia 44435, 1968: Billboard Pop #49); "When the Party Is Over" b/w "Raindrops, Love, and Sunshine" (A&M 1210, 1970: Billboard Pop #71); "You Don't Need a Gypsy" (Atlantic 2930, 1972: Did Not Chart).

Even when he was a child, it was obvious that Brooklyn—born Robert John Pedrick had an extreme vocal range and a voice well suited for singing. He had taken music lessons at the New York School of Music, and by the time he was twelve years old he had signed with manager Henry Tobias who landed him a contract with Big Top records. As Bobby Pedrick, Jr., he recorded "White Bucks and Saddle Shoes," written by Doc Pomus and Mort Shuman, which peaked at #78 in 1958. He had two more releases on Big Top, and now marketed as a teen-idol type singer he recorded "School Crush" for Shell and "That Girl Is You" for Dual records. After Dual changed their name to Duel he released "Dining and Dancing," followed by a spin as a frontman for the group Bobby and the Consoles who in 1963 released "My Jelly Bean." It made some noise regionally but not nationally, and recording as Bobby Pedrick again but now singing in what would become his trademark falsetto, he did a cover of the Chantels' "Maybe," for Verve, which, like everything he had done since 1958, was unsuccessful as well.

In 1966 he decided to try his hand as a songwriter. This came about when he met Michael Gately, a writer for MGM Records, who had co-written an MGM release for Pedrick called "(I Have To) Teach Myself How To Cry." Although the recording was not a hit, the two of them began writing together and composed a song called "If You Don't Want My Love." CBS producer David Rubinson heard the song and thought it was a black artist and also that the tape had been sped up to achieve the high falsetto, and he asked to hear Pedrick sing the song in person. After being convinced that Pedrick did in fact sing the song without technical trickery, CBS signed him to do the one recording, and retired the name Bobby Pedrick in favor of "Robert John" in the process. The record gave John the opportunity to show off his full vocal range as the song built to a climax that clearly demonstrated that John's voice was as strong and versatile as contemporaries Frankie Valli and Lou Christie, and after the song almost broke the Top 40 by reaching #49, CBS asked him to do an album. However, rather than give John and Gately a chance to exhibit how their songwriting skills could take advantage of John's vocal abilities, the *If You Don't Want My Love* album that Columbia released to capitalize on the single contained mainly cover tunes. Predictably the album failed, and after John recorded four more singles on Columbia and only one, 1968's "Don't Leave Me," "bubbled under" the Top 100 at #108, he left Columbia.

John and Gately were now writing for other artists as well, including Lou Rawls, Blood, Sweat, and Tears, and the Whispers. John recorded a song they had written for A&M Records, 1970's "When the Party Is Over," which broke the Top 100 but only stayed on the charts five weeks, topping out at #71. Both that song and its flipside, "Raindrops, Love, and Sunshine," though not as highly regarded as "If You Don't Want My Love," would come to be moderate beach music hits. After two more non-charting releases on A&M in 1971 and 72, John left the label. Without a contract with a record company he recorded a cover of the Tokens' "The Lion Sleeps Tonight" despite the fact that he really didn't want to do the song. The song was produced by original Tokens singer Hank Medress, and Lou Christie had given it a try before contractual obligations prevented it from being released. Christie's vocals were erased from the master and John's overdubbed, and Atlantic picked it up. It resulted in his most successful record up to that point, as it went to #3, sold more than one million copies and was awarded an RIAA gold record in 1972. Despite its success, Atlantic would not let him do an album, and John told Steve Pond of *Rolling Stone* that since Atlantic "didn't have enough faith to let me do an album…. I decided that if that's what happens after a [hit] song, then I just wasn't going to sing anymore." Nevertheless Atlantic still had masters of a few songs he'd already recorded for them, and they released his cover of the Mystics' "Hushabye" which charted at #99. The label also released the beach classic "You Don't Need a Gypsy" in 1972, a song that he and Gately had written and that once again featured his full vocal range as well as background singers Daryl Hall and John Oates, who had signed with Atlantic that same year. "Gypsy" did not chart, Atlantic had no more recordings in the vault, and so less than a year removed from a Top 10 hit he was no longer singing and in fact he wouldn't have another release as a vocalist for five years.

In 1978, after John had held an assortment of jobs (including carrying bricks at a New Jersey construction site) while he scraped by as a songwriter, producer George Tobin found him and got him recording again. John recorded about ten songs, and after a series of failures to place them EMI picked them up and released a song he had written called "Sad Eyes." After recording for almost twenty-two years, John finally had a #1 chart-topper. John would stay with EMI and would continue to do originals as well as covers of many songs that required a unique sound or a falsetto. He would chart with Eddie Holman's "Hey There Lonely Girl" (#31), and his cover of the Four Seasons' "Sherry" (#70) would make some noise. He would then move to Motown and do another cover, this time of the Newbeats' 1964 #2 hit "Bread and Butter" (#68) in 1983. It would be his last chart record, capping off what was all in all a relatively successful career.

Ben E. King

BEACH MUSIC DISCOGRAPHY: "Spanish Harlem" (Atco 6185, 1960: Billboard Pop #10); "Stand By Me" (Atco 6194, 1961: Billboard Pop #4).

Benjamin Earl Nelson was born in Henderson, North Carolina, and moved to Harlem when he was nine years old. As a child he started singing in church and as a teen sang with a doo-wop cover group called the Four B's, but it was while working at his father's restaurant in 1956 that he took the first step towards singing as a professional. Talent scout and manager Lover Patterson lived across the street from the restaurant, and after hearing Benjamin singing he asked if he could bring over four singers he was managing to see if they could gel as a group. They sounded good together, and Patterson signed King to join Sy Palmer, Charlie Thomas, Dock Green, and Elsbeary Hobbs to perform as the Five Crowns. Not long afterwards Palmer left and was replaced by James Clark, and with this line up the group recorded a few sides and landed a performance at the Apollo in 1958. It was there while opening for The Drifters that Drifters' manager George Treadwell saw them perform. Clyde McPhatter had left The Drifters and the group was having some internal issues (see the entry for The Drifters), and Treadwell decided to fire his Drifters and transform the Crowns (other than James Clark) into a new group of Drifters. Despite some early growing pains, by 1959 the group was recording new material, including a song King had written called "There Goes My Baby," which went to #2. The King–led group recorded a number of hits including "Dance with Me," "This Magic Moment," and the #1 smash "Save the Last Dance for Me."

Despite their success, once again the group was having internal strife, and after King (he changed his name around 1960) confronted Treadwell about the group's salaries and was rebuffed, after only roughly a dozen recordings with the group he decided it was time for him to go out on his own. Patterson did manage to ensure that King stayed on the Atlantic subsidiary Atco however, and though his first single failed, his second solo release was 1961's "Spanish Harlem." Written by Jerry Leiber and Phil Spector and produced by Leiber and Mike Stoller, the song was slated to be a B-side of the single "First Taste of Love," but soon both sides were getting airplay and eventually "Spanish Harlem" went to #10 on the pop charts while "First Taste of Love" stalled at #53. King followed this up with 1961's "Stand By Me," written by King and Leiber and Stoller, and inspired by a spiritual written by Sam Cooke. King originally wrote it for The Drifters, who declined to record it (though they later covered it), and after recording "Spanish Harlem" there was some left over studio time and Leiber and Stoller encouraged King to record "Stand by Me" then. It would be King's biggest hit, peaking at #1 on the R&B charts, #4 on the pop charts, and then going to #9 again in 1986 when the movie *Stand By Me* was released; it hit #1 in England in 1987. The song would be ranked by *Rolling Stone* as one of the Top 500 songs of all time, and BMI declared it #4 on its list of the Top 100 Songs of the (Twentieth) Century and estimated that the song was played more than 7 million times. Because King was the primary songwriter, the royalties from this song and others he had written would provide financial security for him for his whole life.

King would go on to have a number of chart hits in the ensuing years, such as "Amor"(#18 Pop, 1961), "Don't Play that Song" (#11 Pop, 1962), "I Who Have Nothing" (#29 Pop, 1963). The latter song would get some play in the beach clubs in the mid–60s, and would in fact be included on Atlantic's seminal *Beach Beat Vol. 2* album released in 1968, although the song would not endure as a popular beach song probably due to its slow pacing. His songs would continue to chart, though it would not be until 1975's funky "Supernatural Thing" (#5 Pop) that King would have another Top Ten hit. It would also be his last Top 40 pop hit other than re-releases of "Stand By Me."

In 1988 King would be inducted into the Rock and Roll Hall of Fame as a member of The Drifters, he would win a Rhythm & Blues Foundation Pioneer Award, and in 2012 "Stand By Me" won The Songwriters Hall of Fame's Towering Performance Award. He passed away in 2015.

The King Pins

BEACH MUSIC DISCOGRAPHY: "It Won't Be This Way Always" (Federal 12484, 1963: Billboard Pop #89).

When brothers Robert, Andrew, and Curtis Kelly and their family relocated to Chicago in the late 1940s, the boys had already been in a Gospel group in their home state of Mississippi. As members of the Little Delta Big Four, they, along with their cousin Robert Pittman, had been singing at churches in Mississippi and Arkansas. In Chicago, they came under the guidance of William Adair, who persuaded them to re-form their quartet as the Kelly Brothers. Adair sang lead until an old friend of theirs from Mississippi, Offe Reese, moved to Chicago and joined them. The group recorded a few unreleased sides before adding member Charles "T C" Lee. They signed with Vee-Jay where in 1956 they rerecorded two songs they had laid down a couple of years earlier, "God Said He Is Coming Back Again" and "Prayer for Tomorrow." Though the songs were not commercial hits and did not chart, the recordings did lead to solidifying the Kelly Brothers' reputation in Gospel circles and resulted in radio appearances and increased bookings. Nevertheless, Vee-Jay dropped them, and they then recorded a few sides on Nashboro, which did nothing. By 1959 when Nashboro dropped them their future as recording artists did not look promising.

In 1960 they met with King Records' Alphonse "Sonny" Thompson, who initially wasn't interested in recording the group but reconsidered and signed them to the Federal subsidiary. There they recorded a number of gospel songs, some of which garnered considerable airplay. This led to more releases and an album, *The Kelly Brothers Sing a Page of Songs from the Good Book,* in 1962. Sales were not good, however, and eventually Thompson convinced them the real money to be made was recording popular music. Redubbed the King Pins, in 1963 they first recorded and released "Believe In Me" on Federal, which did nothing, followed by "It Won't Be This Way (Always)," which did quite well. Written by Robert Kelly and Sonny Thompson, the song went to #89 on the pop charts and rose all the way to #13 on the R&B charts. That led to an album, *It Won't Be This Way Always,* and at least four more Federal releases in 1963 and 1964, including "The Monkey," "Hop Scotch," and "I Got the Monkey Off My Back." None of those records charted, and eventually they left Federal and label jumped to Sims and then Excello. Nothing else they recorded charted, and in the early 1970s the group returned to recording Gospel as the Kelly Brothers, their career as the King Pins now behind them.

Robert Knight

BEACH MUSIC DISCOGRAPHY: "Everlasting Love" (Rising Sons 705, 1967: Billboard Pop #13).

Franklin, Tennessee-born Robert Peebles started his musical career singing in church when he was 7, and his first solo performance was actually at a funeral that same year. His first high school band was called the Cheers, and after high school along with Clarence Holland, Richard Sammonds, Neil Hooper and Kenneth Buttrick he formed the Paramounts. That group signed a contract with Dot Records, and in 1961 released two singles, "Congratulations" and "When You Dance," neither of which were successful. The group's producer, Noel Ball, felt that Knight would do better on his own, and arranged for Knight to record a couple of solo sides on Dot as Robert *Knight*. Ball had Peebles change his name "because disc jockeys were always pronouncing my name wrong, saying 'Pebbles' and things like that" Knight said. Those singles, 1961's "Because" and 1962's "Free Me," were no more successful than the Paramount sides, and the group broke up while Knight rededicated himself to working on a degree in chemistry at Tennessee State University and later at Vanderbilt.

The lure of singing was great, however, and while in college in 1964 he formed another group, the Fairlanes, along with Danny Boone, Lehman Keith, Jack Jackson, Tommy Smith, and Jim Tate. The idea was to keep it simple and just play in nightclubs in the area while making sure school was his main focus, but by the time Knight finished his degree he had been "discovered" once again while singing in a nightclub. "Buzz Cason had worked for Noel Ball, and Buzz was working with Mac Gayden. Cason was starting his new Rising Sons label and working on some material with Mac" Knight said. In 1967 they approached Knight about signing with them and put together a few tunes for him to record. In his autobiography Cason said the idea behind "Everlasting Love" (its name taken from Jeremiah 31.3 which says "Yea, I have loved you with an everlasting love") was to do a Motown-type song, and Cason and Gayden cobbled together some material they already had to complete the song. It didn't get a lot of thought because it was going to be used as the flip side of a track called "The Weeper,"

Robert Knight, circa early 1970s (photograph courtesy Chikena Peebles).

and in fact Knight wouldn't have access to the completed version of the song until the actual recording session.

According to Knight though, the song wasn't exactly popular radio-ready. "Buzz and Mac were country artists, and I was R&B, and so I had to make it more of an R&B song" Knight said. "I practiced and practiced on it—it was a hard song to sing because at the time it was hard to sing a fast song slow. I didn't sing it the way they had written it. I made some changes to fit my voice, and I didn't do it note for note. They had the melody going too fast, and it was jamming, it wasn't doing right, it wasn't sounding right. So I started what you call a steady step. I start singing a beat and a half: 'hearts-go-a-stray'—like that. It wasn't like that in the beginning, and I think that's what got 'Everlasting Love' off the ground." Even with the modifications, Knight wasn't convinced it was a great song, and nor were Gayden or Cason. "Everlasting Love" was supposed to be the B-side for "the Weeper," but by the time it was released it had been paired with "Somebody's Baby"—still intended as the B-side—until "somebody turned it over and started playing 'Everlasting Love' and that's what we went with." As a result, the record that was twice destined to be a B-side before being flipped would be a classic. "Everlasting Love" would go to #13 on the Billboard pop charts during its 12 week run, and it would also reach #14 on the R&B charts. Unfortunately its follow-ups would barely chart or not chart at all. Knight would go on to be very successful in England on the Northern Soul scene however, and when re-released in 1973 his 1968 effort "Love on a Mountain Top" was a major UK hit and reportedly sold 400,00 copies in the UK. That prompted a re-release of "Everlasting Love" in England, and though it had originally only gone to #40 in 1968, in 1974 it went all the way to #19. Covers of "Everlasting Love" by other artists have been popular as well, with Love Affair's version going to #1 in England in 1968, while versions by Carl Carlton, Rex Smith and Rachel Sweet, Gloria Estefan, and others have all performed well. It is one of only two songs to reach the U.S. Top 40 in the 1960s, '70s, '80s, and '90s.

By the mid–1970s Knight had moved away from recording, but unlike many artists, he had a career and a college education to fall back on. He went on to work at Vanderbilt University as a chemical lab technician and worked there until he passed away in 2017.

Gladys Knight and the Pips

BEACH MUSIC DISCOGRAPHY: "Baby Don't Change Your Mind" (Buddah 569, 1977: Billboard Pop #52).

Atlanta-born Gladys Maria Knight showed an ability for singing from an early age, and by the time she was eight years old she had taken first place and a $2000 dollar prize on the nationally renowned *Ted Mack's Original Amateur Hour* in 1952. Using that win as a springboard for success, she formed a vocal group with her brother Merald, sister Brenda, and her cousins William and Eleanor Guest. Another cousin, James Woods, whose nickname was "Pip," acted as their manager, and as a result the group adopted his nickname to become "The Pips." Their first record came when they released "Ching Chong" on Brunswick in 1958, but it was not successful and did not lead to a long-term contract with Brunswick. Brenda and Eleanor finally decided to leave the group at this point to raise families, and their cousin Edward Patten and their friend Langston George replaced them. They next recorded a cover of The Royals' "Every Beat of my Heart" on the tiny Atlanta based Huntom label in 1961, and it was picked up for wider distribution by Vee-Jay. The group subsequently went to New York and recorded the song in stereo on the Fury label, which credited them for the first time as Gladys Knight and the Pips. Both versions debuted on the charts on exactly the same day, although the monaural Vee-Jay version was the bigger hit, going to #1 on the R&B charts and #6 on the pop charts.

Over the next few years, the group would have releases on the Fury, Everlast, Vee-Jay,

Enjoy, and Maxx labels, but only 1961's "Letter Full of Tears" was really noteworthy. Members of the group changed, and Gladys Knight herself left for a while, but by 1964 Gladys rejoined Bubba, Edward and William, and in 1966 they signed with Berry Gordy who put them on his Soul subsidiary label. 1967's "I Heard it Through the Grapevine" would go to #2 on the pop charts and #1 on the R&B charts, and would actually garner them a Grammy nomination. The song would be their biggest hit, although Marvin Gaye's 1968 version went to #1 on both charts and is in fact the better-known version today.

Between 1966 and 1973 the group would have a number of chart records on Soul, including "If I Were Your Woman" and "Neither One of Us (Wants to Be the First to Say Goodbye)," but like a number of artists on Motown subsidiaries during the 1960s the group felt like they weren't getting the attention that headliners such as the Supremes, Temptations, Four Tops, and others got. In February 1973 they signed with Buddah Records, oddly enough just as they won their first Grammy for their last Motown release, "Neither One of Us."

In the same way that Motown had let the Spinners get away just as they were finding their musical niche, the same thing that happened with Gladys Knight and the Pips as well. Their second Buddah release was 1973's "Midnight Train to Georgia," which topped the pop and R&B charts and won them another Grammy. Their next twelve releases on Buddah included classics such as "I've Got to Use My Imagination," "Best Thing That Ever Happened to Me" and "I Feel a Song in My Heart," all of which went to #1 on the R&B charts. Their first release of 1977 was "Baby, Don't Change Your Mind," a song written by Van McCoy. McCoy was of course famous for having the #1 hit "The Hustle" in 1975, but had also written such beach music favorites as Chris Bartley's "The Sweetest Thing This Side of Heaven," Barbara Lewis's "Baby I'm Yours," and Jackie Wilson's "I Get the Sweetest Feeling," among others. Although the record wasn't a big hit in the U.S., going only to #10 on the R&B charts and #52 on the pop charts, it was popular in England with Northern Soul audiences, reaching #4 on the UK charts and becoming the last big hit the group ever had in England.

Not long after the release of was "Baby, Don't Change Your Mind" the group had a falling out with Buddah and contractual obligations prevented them for recording for a few years. They signed with Columbia in 1980 and thereafter continued to record quality music for most of the decade before disbanding, though Gladys Knight had a successful solo career as well. Despite a catalog that included nearly 70 charts records well into the 1990s, "Baby, Don't Change Your Mind" was the group's only song that really took root in the beach clubs along the East Coast. In 1996 they were inducted into the Rock and Roll Hall of Fame, and they were later inducted into the Vocal Group Hall of Fame and received a Lifetime Achievement Award from the Rhythm & Blues Foundation as well.

Bob Kuban and the In-Men

BEACH MUSIC DISCOGRAPHY: "The Cheater" (Musicland 6548, 1965: Billboard Pop #12).

Born in St. Louis, Bob Kuban graduated from Washington University and the St. Louis Institute of Music and in 1963 started teaching music at Bishop DuBourg Catholic High

School. In 1964 he had a band called the Rhythm Masters when he met a lead vocalist Walter Notheis, aka "Sir" Walter Scott," who was singing with the Pacemakers. Notheis joined Kuban's band, and as The Bob Kuban Band they cut a couple of songs on the regional Norman label—"I Don't Want to Know" and "Jerkin Time." Though regionally popular they were not national hits, and it wasn't until 1965 as the newly christened Bob Kuban and the In-Men that Kuban, Scott, John Michael Krenski, Gregory Hoeltzel, Patrick Hickson, Harry Simon, Paul Skip Weisser, and Emil Ray Schulte established themselves as a feature act. Krenski had written a song called "The Cheater," which was recorded in St. Louis on the Musicland label. Originally the song was written in the first person ("Look out for me, I'm a Cheater"), but Kuban says "I wanted to do a song that had excitement to it, had some energy and had a good driving tempo, so we added a bridge, and put it in the third person." These alterations made the song a winner, and nationally, the record took off. It peaked at #12 on the Billboard charts and earned a gold record in the process. Bookings across the nation followed, and the group played with the Turtles in San Francisco and with Otis Redding at Whiskey a Go Go and appeared on television on programs such as *Where The Action Is* and *American Bandstand*. Internationally, the song did well too, and it went all the way to #1 in Australia. They were so big in Australia, in fact, that they were scheduled to do a nine-week tour there, and it seemed that with a Top 40 hit and international appeal, the group's ship had finally come in.

All of this happened at the height of the Vietnam War, and just being in a popular band wasn't enough to keep you out of the draft so in order to qualify for their deferment most of the members of the band were also college students. While teaching or going to college kept them out of the army, it also meant they couldn't tour for too long or too far away from home, but as a regional act early on that wasn't much of a problem. Touring for months on end or going overseas was a different situation altogether, however. The group discovered they couldn't go to Australia because if they weren't working as teachers or weren't in school they'd lose their deferment. Kuban says that the draft board told him that if they went, they would immediately be classified 1-A and be drafted, and that effectively put an end to any plans the group had for traveling abroad. So instead of the planned tour, they headed back to the studio and recorded the follow-up to "The Cheater," "The Teaser." Kuban says, "I hated the song, and even today I have never played it live. I fought with our manager about releasing it after 'The Cheater' because I knew a hit record needed a strong follow-up, and 'The Teaser' wasn't it." Over Kuban's objections, their manager released the song anyway, and despite its clear inferiority to "The Cheater," "The Teaser" actually climbed to #70 on the charts, followed by a cover of the Beatles' "Drive My Car," which went to #93. No matter how one looked at it, three chart records in a row in one year did seem to promise great things ahead for the band.

But trouble was brewing, and unbeknownst to Kuban, their manager, of all people, was trying to break up the group. "Mel Friedman was the manager at the time…. He started causing a lot of problems because he saw the advantage of Wally breaking away for his own purposes. Wally was a very good lead singer, and he was like a Fabian or Frankie Avalon, a good showman, a good-looking guy, and Mel obviously wanted to pull Wally away from the band." The next thing Kuban knew, "despite the fact that we had a hit record, all of a sudden, the band was breaking up, and guys were leaving. At the time I was completely blown away, I was in shock really, because I didn't know why this was happening." Lead singer Walter Scott left and opted for a solo career, though neither he nor the other members of the group matched the magic they had held collectively. "It was only years later that Wally told me what had happened, because by then he realized what an opportunity we had and that Friedman had blown it for all of us. He got hold of good talent and screwed it up."

Despite the acrimony of the group's split, nearly twenty years after their dissolution, the band was preparing for a big reunion concert when Walter Scott was murdered in December

1983. Kuban continues to perform to this day, and he has a band that is highly regarded and plays a variety of venues across the Midwest. All of the other members of the band have gone on to be successful in their fields as well.

The Lamplighters

BEACH MUSIC DISCOGRAPHY: "I Used to Cry Mercy, Mercy" (Federal 12176, 1954: Did Not Chart).

Willie Ray Rockwell, Matthew Nelson, and Leon Hughes of South Central Los Angeles' Jordan High School were a group who sang at talent shows in the L.A. area. One night they lost to Indianapolis-born Army veteran Thurston Harris, and afterwards they asked Harris to join their group and take over lead singing duties in the spring of 1952. They had been joined by Al Frazier, a veteran of several other groups, when they were discovered by talent recruiter Ralph Bass of Cincinnati's Federal-King Records. Some sources say it was actually singer Johnny Otis who tipped Bass to the group's potential, and it's also not clear whether it was Bass or Otis who dubbed them the Lamplighters, but the name stuck—for the time. Hughes left the group when they signed with Federal, and the quartet's first release "Part of Me" did nothing, though their next, "Bebop Wino," did apparently get some airplay in the Los Angeles area. The group toured some, sang back up for bluesman Jimmy Witherspoon on a single, and even released another single, "I Can't Stand It," all to no fanfare.

In February 1954 the group released their fifth single, "I Used to Cry Mercy, Mercy." The song is a thinly disguised reworking of the Dominoes' 1952 hit "Have Mercy Baby," which had also been released on Federal. This was not a new idea, and as the Dominoes were one of the label's most successful groups, Federal had already copied the Dominoes successful formula by having groups such as the Four Jacks record their homage to "Sixty Minute Man" with "Last of the Good Rocking Men" in 1952. Like the Four Jacks release, the Lamplighters song was an exceptional effort and became a favorite with shaggers in the Carolinas, although it failed to register on either the pop or R&B charts.

Although at this point the group hadn't registered a chart hit, they seemed right on the cusp of making it big. Unfortunately, by 1954 the group was encountering almost every type of personality and behavioral disorder that was humanly possible. They were literally getting into fistfights with one another and drug and alcohol use was rampant; Rockwell's drinking was so bad that it would lead to his death in a motorcycle accident. Harris had become so overbearing and controlling that the other group members rebelled, and he left the group in 1955 to go solo. Although they released eight more singles as the Lamplighters thorough 1956, over time the group underwent other personnel changes, and more importantly, name changes. They changed to their name to and recorded as the Tenderfoots briefly, then the Lamplighters again, then the Sharps. They actually backed their old groupmate Thurston Harris on his hit solo effort, "Little Bitty Pretty One," and sang backup on a Paul Anka single as well. They changed personnel and their name several more times after that, to the Four After Fives, the Crenshaws, and finally became the Rivingtons of "Poppa Ooh Mow Mow" fame in 1962, although

Major Lance

BEACH MUSIC DISCOGRAPHY: "The Monkey Time" (Okeh 7175, 1963: Billboard Pop #8); "Um, Um, Um, Um, Um, Um" (Okeh 7187, 1964: Billboard Pop #5); "Follow the Leader" (Dakar 608, 1969: Billboard Pop #125); "You're Everything I Need" (Osiris 001, 1975: Billboard Pop Did Not Chart, R&B #50).

"Major" was actually Lance's given name when he was born in Mississippi in 1939. His family moved to Chicago, where he attended Wells High School along with soul greats Jerry Butler and Curtis Mayfield, and in fact Mayfield would go on to have a major impact on Lance's career. In high school Lance worked at a drug store, sang with several soul groups including the Five Gospel Harmonaires and The Floats, and trained as a boxer. His footwork would serve him differently than expected when he became a dancer on Chicago television show called *Jim Lounsbury's Record Hop*. Lounsbury heard Lance sing and arranged for him to get an audition at Mercury Records, where he had a single release titled "I Got a Girl." The single failed to chart, and a for few years Lance did odd jobs while his friend Mayfield's career as a songwriter was taking off. Eventually Okeh records apparently felt Lance had something to offer, and though his first single did nothing his next release, a song Mayfield had written called "The Monkey Time," would be an enormous hit. Gene Chandler, who had taken "Duke of Earl" to #1 in 1962, had heard the song and wanted to record it, and reportedly even had his dance steps down and was ready to perform it as well as sing it. However, Mayfield gave the song to Lance and backed by the Chicago group the Artistics, "The Monkey Time" went to #8 on the Billboard chart and #2 on the R&B charts. His next release, "Hey Little Girl," went to #13 on the pop charts, followed by 1964's "Um, Um, Um, Um, Um, Um," which went to #5 and climbed to #1 on the R&B charts. Both were written by Mayfield as well.

Lance had nearly a dozen chart hits over the next few years, but of his Top 40 chart records only one was not written by Mayfield. When Mayfield moved on to focus on his own group, The Impressions, Lance's records stopped charting; Lance never again had a Top 40 record on the Billboard Pop Charts after 1965. Lance's last single for Okeh was in 1968, and thereafter he signed with Dakar, where his second release for the label, "Follow the Leader," garnered some attention in beach music circles and became his only chart release on Dakar, peaking at #125 on the "bubbling under" Billboard Pop Chart and registering a respectable #28 on the R&B charts. Subsequent releases on Curtom, Volt, and Playboy all failed, and Lance moved to England for a couple of years where he saw a resurgence in popularity due to the burgeoning Northern Soul scene before moving back to the U.S. He formed his own record label with friend Al Jackson, the drummer for Booker T. & the M.G.s, who was a songwriter and producer in his own right. For the label's first release they decided to record a song

Frederick Knight had written, "You're Everything I Need." Though Knight's biggest hit would come a few years later with Anita Ward's #1 smash "Ring My Bell," the smooth soulful sound of "You're Everything I Need" was a good tune for Lance's vocal range, and with its updated instrumentation it had more of a '70s sound than Lance's earlier work. Unfortunately, though, audiences didn't connect with the record, and although it did reach #50 on the R&B charts, it failed to make the pop charts at all; it would unfortunately be Lance's last chart record of any type in this country. Lance would release one more record on Osiris, 1975's "I've Got a Right to Cry," but before Osiris really had a chance to establish itself, Al Jackson was murdered in his Memphis home, and without his partner Lance was forced to fold the label that same year.

Lance would only record two singles between 1976 and 1978, and neither charted. His career was clearly faltering, and this was exacerbated by his arrest for cocaine possession 1978 which would lead to a three-year prison sentence. Though he would record a couple of singles after his release from prison his recording days were essentially over, and after a heart attack in 1987 his career as a live performer was over as well. In 1994 he died of heart disease, his body obviously weakened by his years of drug abuse.

Barbara Lewis

BEACH MUSIC DISCOGRAPHY: "Hello Stranger" b/w "Think a Little Sugar" (Atlantic 2184, Billboard Pop #3 1963); "Baby I'm Yours" (Atlantic 2283, Billboard Pop #11 1965); "Make Me Your Baby" (Atlantic 2300, Billboard Pop #11 1965); "Make Me Belong to You" (Atlantic 2346, Billboard Pop #28 1966); "I Remember the Feeling" (Atlantic 2361, Did Not Chart 1966).

Salem, Michigan, native Barbara Lewis was born to musical parents who both played instruments and performed when Lewis was a child. She started writing music when she was 9, and in high school—where she was reportedly the only black student in the school—she was competing in a talent show where she finished second to two tap dancers. This brought her to attention of disc jockey and producer Ollie McLaughlin, who mentored her and arranged for her to cut her first record, her self-penned "My Heart Went Do Dat Da," in 1962. Released on the Karen label, the record was a regional hit that didn't register nationally. McLaughlin worked out a deal with Chicago's Chess Records to get Lewis some studio time, and even arranged for Lewis to arrive a day early to see Etta James record. The next day Lewis recorded a song she had written herself called "Hello Stranger," the single that would be her first hit. Lewis claimed that idea for the record came from touring with her father, and people would tell him, "Hello Stranger ... it's been a long time." The song was arranged by Riley Hampton, who was at the time also working with Chess standout Etta James, and McLaughlin was able to get the Dells, who like James recorded for a Chess subsidiary Argo, to do the "chew-bop, chew-bop, my baby" background vocals on the record (see the entry for The Dells).

With the five Dells and Lewis in the recording booth at the same time crowded around two microphones, after 13 takes they felt they had a winner, so much so that Dell Chuck Barksdale was telling Lewis and the others "It's a hit, it's a hit." McLaughlin thought so too, as he went to New York and sold "Hello Stranger" and some other sides to Atlantic. Atlantic wasn't as sure about "Hello Stranger" as McLaughlin was, and first released "My Momma Told Me" in 1963. It failed, but they next released "Hello Stranger" and it rose to #3 in the summer of 1963 and went to #1 on the R&B charts. Perhaps surprisingly, though "Hello Stranger" was a hit on the beach music circuit, the flipside of the record, "Think a Little Sugar," is probably bigger. Also written by Lewis, produced by McLaughlin, arranged by Hampton, and with the Dells on backup, this song gives the single a one-two punch that is perhaps unparalleled in the beach music milieu. As a flipside it did not chart, but both songs were included on the Atlantic album of Lewis-penned songs, appropriately titled *Hello Stranger*.

Two of Lewis's next four singles on Atlantic would break the Top 100, but it was 1965's Van McCoy–produced "Baby I'm Yours" that would be her next standout hit. Recorded in New York at Atlantic studios and produced by McLaughlin, the song featured McCoy and Shirelles touring member Kendra Spotswood on backing vocals. McCoy wrote the song with Lewis in mind, though when Lewis heard the demo she didn't like it. This was reportedly apparent at the recording session, where Lewis gave less than a full effort. Unsatisfied, Lewis did several re-takes back in Detroit before Lewis found the sound McCoy wanted. After it was released in April 1965, the single went to #11 on the pop 100 and #5 on the R&B charts.

At just about the time that "Baby I'm Yours" was peaking, Lewis would record her next single, "Make Me Your Baby." Written by Helen Miller and Roger Atkins, Atlantic actually wanted to offer the song to Patti Labelle and the Bluebelles to lure them to Atlantic, but after "Baby I'm Yours" hit big it was given to Lewis instead. It had already been recorded by a group called the Pixies Three, who had released four Top 100 sides in 1963 and 1964. But Lewis's single was released first and would rise as high as its predecessor, #11 on the pop charts and #9 on the R&B charts. The Pixies Three version would remain unreleased.

Lewis would have just one more pop Top 40 hit, 1966's Billy Vera and Chip Taylor penned "Make Me Belong to You" which would peak at #28 on the pop charts and #36 on the R&B charts. The song would find an audience in beach music and Northern Soul circles, as would "I Remember the Feeling," which did not chart at all. From 1966 through 1968, Lewis recorded five more singles for Atlantic, including her last two Top 100 chart records. She did an album for Stax, three singles for Enterprise in 1969 and '70 and one for Reprise in 1972. Despite the fact that her songs have been covered multiple times since then, by the early '70s she opened her own jewelry store and pursued other jobs unrelated to the music business. In the 1990s she started performing once again; she received the Pioneer Award from the Rhythm and Blues Foundation in 1999.

Jimmy Liggins

BEACH MUSIC DISCOGRAPHY: "Drunk" (Specialty 470, 1953: Billboard Pop Did Not Chart, R&B #4); "I Ain't Drunk I'm Just Drinkin" (Aladdin 3250, 1954: Did Not Chart); "Boogie Woogie King" (Aladdin 3251, 1954: Did Not Chart).

Jimmy Liggins was born James L. Elliot in Newby, Oklahoma, and when he was about 8 he and his brother Joe adopted their stepfather's surname, Liggins. When Jimmy was 10 his family moved to San Diego, and Joe, seven years his elder, was already into music at that point. Initially Jimmy had no such ambitions, and he worked as a disk jockey and pursued a career in professional boxing. Although he trained with light heavyweight champion Archie Moore and fought professional bouts as Kid Zulu, by the time he was 18 he had decided boxing would not suit him as a long term career. By this point his brother Joe and his band The Honey Drippers had already had a #1 R&B hit, "The Honeydripper," followed by several other Top 10 R&B chart hits, and Jimmy took a job as the band's driver—a job that often required him to load and unload the car and carry their luggage and equipment as well. As the Honeydrippers continued to rack up hit singles, despite the fact that he had no musical experience at all Jimmy decided that he too wanted to pursue a career in music. The brothers parted amicably, Jimmy bought a guitar, learned to play and started writing music. By 1947 he had formed his own band, the Drops of Joy, and they signed with Los Angeles' Specialty Records. While their first release, 1947's "I Can't Stop It" was not a hit, their second, 1948's "Teardrop Blues" backed with "Cadillac Boogie" made the R & B Top 10.

Thereafter, between 1948 and 1952 he would release thirteen more singles, although only "Careful Love" (#15) and "Don't Put Me Down"(#9) made the national R&B charts. During this period, however, Liggins ran into a number of pitfalls that no doubt kept him from enjoying the same continued success that his brother had. The band was constantly touring, but apparently he ran afoul of the unions, had some cancelled engagements, and a bad car accident. During a performance in Jackson Mississippi skating rink on April Fools' Day 1948 one member of the band was slashed with a razor and Liggins was shot in the mouth; the band broke up afterwards. They reformed with some new members, a despite their previous mishaps, in 1953 the band recorded the biggest hit of their career, "Drunk." The song, penned by Liggins, went to #4 on the R&B charts, and the one-chord anthemic song was a long-time quick-step shag favorite on the beach music circuit. He released just one more single on Specialty before leaving the label, apparently because of a disagreement about the amount of royalties he was receiving, though Liggins later admitted it may not have been a wise decision. He jumped to the Aladdin label where he released just two singles, but in 1954 the answer record "I Ain't Drunk" was well-received in beach music circles, though it didn't make the national charts. Another Aladdin release recorded the same day, "Boogie Woogie King," also found listeners in the Carolinas. By this point he was being pigeonholed as yet another artist who was primarily recording songs about alcohol and drinking, and even the flipside of "Boogie Woogie King" was "No More Alcohol." Those types of songs were on the way out by 1954, so perhaps not coincidentally, Liggins' recording career at this point was essentially over.

Aladdin let Liggins go and he became a record distributor for a while and in 1958 formed his own record label, Duplex Records, where he released a few non-charting sides under his own name from 1959 to 1964. The label sporadically released singles into the 1970s, and eventually Liggins moved to Durham, North Carolina, where he ran a record store, recording studio, and a nightclub. He died in July 1983 in Durham.

Little Willie John *see* John, Little Willie

The Love Committee

BEACH MUSIC DISCOGRAPHY: "Cheaters Never Win" (Gold Mind 4003, 1977: Billboard Pop Did Not Chart, R&B #57)

The Love Committee got their start as the Philadelphia-based Ethics in 1967, with group members Ron Tyson, Joe Freeman, Carl "Nugie" Enlow, and Andrew "Bike" Collins. As the

Ethics they recorded some local hits such as "There Will Still Be a Sweet Tomorrow" on Wale in 1967, and songs such as "Look at Me Now," "Sad Sad Story," and "Standing in the Darkness," on Vent between 1967 and 1970. Despite the fact that some of their sides had even been arranged by future Sound of Philadelphia superstar Thom Bell, none of these songs were national hits. By 1970 it appears the group had splintered and gone their separate ways when Vent folded, at which time the owner of Wale subsequently claimed ownership of the Ethics name. Tyson and Freeman reformed the group as the Love Committee, adding members Norman Frazier and Larry Richardson; Richardson's death would bring on the addition of Michael Bell, formerly of the group Sly, Slick, and Wicked.

The group continued to label hop, recording for Golden Fleece, Philadelphia International, TSOP, and Ariola, yet still finding no national chart success. They next moved to Salsoul's Gold Mind subsidiary, and in 1978 they released their album *Law and Order,* a type of concept album which featured songs co-written by Tyson revolving around the rights, wrongs, rules and "Law and Order" of relationships. The titular song would go on to be a minor R&B hit, but the album's most important song in regard to beach music was "Cheaters Never Win," co-written by Tyson, T.G. Conway, and Allan Felder. Though most of the songs on the album fit the mid–70s disco format, "Cheaters Never Win" is more of a standard R&B song. Surprisingly, when Gold Mind released extended disco versions of several of the songs on the album, "Cheaters" was one of them. The song never made the national pop charts in any form, and stalled at #57 on the R&B charts. As result, the song has been far more popular on the beach music circuit than it ever was when released, and the various cover versions by regional bands have been popular as well.

After one more self-titled album in 1980, the band would break up for good. Tyson had been earning a reputation as a songwriter and producer for quite some time, working with The O'Jays, The Trammps, Harold Melvin and the Blue Notes, Archie Bell and the Drells, among many other others. He worked with the Temptations as the producer of their 1977 album *Hear To Tempt You,* and in 1983 joined the group as a regular member, singing the parts Eddie Kendricks once performed.

Carrie Lucas

BEACH MUSIC DISCOGRAPHY: "It's Not What You Got" (It's How You Use It) (Solar YB-12085, 1980: Billboard Pop Did Not Chart, R&B #74)

Carmel, California-born Carrie Lucas was the daughter of an Army officer and as such spent much of her childhood moving around throughout the U.S. and Europe. As a result, in many areas there weren't soul radio stations, so she was raised primarily listening to pop music. By the time she was in high school in Monterey, California, she was singing in the chorus and the glee club, and in the early 1970s she moved to Los Angeles to pursue a career singing. While attending a party with friends she was introduced to Dick Griffey, who was the manager for the group the Whispers. Lucas mentioned that she was a singer, and he asked if she was a songwriter as well. Griffey challenged her to write a song, and she did and recorded a demo of her song "Fairytales." When Griffey and Don Cornelius founded Soul Train Records in 1975 one of the label's first releases was Lucas's song recorded by the Soul Train Gang. While Lucas would go on to write songs for Shalamar, the South Shore Commission, and others, she was still primarily working as a backup singer, and sang back up on the Whispers' 1976 album *One For The Money*. As a result of her involvement in that project Griffey apparently decided to give her a shot as a solo act.

In the mid–1970s disco was ruling the airwaves, and Lucas should have been a natural with her connections to soul and the influence of pop music on her early life. Her 1977 debut album, *Simply Carrie*, featured a number of soul luminaries including George Bohannon, and background vocals by Carolyn Willis of The Honeycone and Walter Scott of The Whispers, but although the single "I Gotta Keep Dancin'" did break into the pop and R&B Top 100, overall the album was a disappointment. By this time Griffey and Lucas were dating and would soon marry, and Griffey was having her open for the Whispers in concert to increase her exposure. By this point Griffey had founded a new label, SOLAR (the Sound of Los Angeles Records), and he released Lucas's next album, *Street Corner Symphony*, on the new label. It didn't make the album charts and produced no chart singles.

Despite these setbacks, her next album, 1979's *Carrie Lucas in Danceland*, seemed to justify the efforts that had been spent promoting her to that point. With another power-packed roster of back-up artists, including Jody Watley of Shalamar and Walter and Wallace Scott of The Whispers, the single "Dance With You" went to #70 on the pop charts, #27 on the R&B charts, and #6 on the dance charts; the album also peaked at #37 in the U.S Dance Album chart. In 1980 she released her fourth album, *Portrait of Carrie*, which included "It's Not What You Got (It's How You Use It)" a crossover disco-beach music hit. While not as successful as her previous album, it did include two chart singles. "It's Not What You Got (It's How You Use It)" was produced by Leon Sylvers and arranged by John Roberts, former Duke recording artist who released the beach classic "To Be My Girl" in 1968. The single peaked at #74 on the R&B charts but did not make the pop charts.

Lucas would go on to record two more albums, 1982's *Still in Love* and 1984's *Horsin' Around*. The latter would be released on Griffey's newest label, Constellation, and would include a cover of Barbara Lewis's beach classic "Hello Stranger" which would be her biggest R&B hit, peaking at #20. By this time Lucas had tired of the music business, and in the 1980s she decided to retire to concentrate on her family and raise horses.

Barbara Lynn

BEACH MUSIC DISCOGRAPHY: "You'll Lose a Good Thing" (Jamie 1220, 1962: Billboard Pop #8).

Born Barbara Lynda Ozen in Beaumont, Texas, as a child she stated writing poetry and initially she aspired to set those poems to music—specifically piano music. After taking lessons, she realized she didn't like the piano and switched to guitar. She learned to play on a ukulele, and by the time she graduated to a full sized guitar she was, oddly enough, playing left handed and on a right handed instrument. She formed her first band, an all-girl group called Bobby Lynn & The Idols, and they were playing at a club called the Palomino Lounge when a country singer named Joe Barry saw her and told manager Huey Meaux about this young black girl who played guitar left handed and had an incredible voice. After hearing her Meaux decided to sign her, but as a minor she needed her parents' approval, and they wanted her to go to college. Her father agreed to let her record on the condition that if her first release wasn't a hit she had to head to college.

After signing her Meaux heard her sing a bit of a song she had written called "If You Lose Me, You'll Lose a Good Thing,"—which was later shortened to "You'll Lose a Good Thing." The song was based a poem she had written about her own experiences losing someone she loved when she was 16. She had heard her boyfriend was running around with another girl, and she confronted him and told him, "You know what? If you lose me, you're gonna lose a good thing." She said the title stuck in her head, and the next day she wrote the song.

Three years later, Meaux had her cut the record at Cosimo Matassa's studio in New Orleans, and once released on the Jet Stream label in Houston it was a regional hit. Philadelphia-based Jamie Records picked it and released it nationally, where it went to #8 on the pop charts and beginning in May 1962 spent three weeks at #1 on the R&B charts, where it ended a ten week stay at the top of the charts for Ray Charles' "I Can't Stop Lovin' You.'" As a result, her parents agreed to let her pursue her singing career after all.

Over the next two years she'd have several R&B charts hits on Jamie, including "You're Gonna Need Me," "Oh! Baby (We Got a Good Thing Going)," "Don't Spread It Around," and "It's Better to Have It," and although a couple of them broke into the pop Top 100, none made the Top 40. After her contract with Jamie ran its course, she had one R&B charter on the Tribe label, then two on Atlantic, the last being 1971's "Until Then I'll Suffer. " It was her best-selling record since "You'll Lose a Good Thing," although it peaked at just #31 on the R&B charts; it was her last chart record. During the 1960s she had married (and become Barbara Lynn Johnson) and had three children, so although after leaving Atlantic in 1973 she recorded on Copyright, Jamstone, Starflite, Ichiban and other labels, she mainly focused on her family during this period. She received a prestigious Pioneer Award from the Rhythm and Blues Foundation in 1999.

The Magic Lanterns

BEACH MUSIC DISCOGRAPHY: "Shame Shame" (Atlantic 2560, Billboard Pop #29 1968).

Founded as the Sabres in 1962 in Warrington, England, members Jimmy Bilsbury, Peter Shoesmith, Ian Moncur, and Allan Wilson mainly played clubs in the Manchester area, and eventually took on the psychedelic-sounding name the Magic Lanterns in the mid–60s. They recorded "Excuse Me Baby," a pop tune that landed them a contract with the English division of CBS records. CBS released the record in 1966, and it rose to the modest #44 position in England, though it didn't make the charts in the U.S. After a few more largely unsuccessful singles and an album, and ever-changing personnel, they left CBS and signed with Atlantic records in 1968.

Their first Atlantic release would be their biggest hit, "Shame, Shame." With an intro that features first a twangy guitar, then a cantina piano, drums, and then a brass section (arranged by John Paul Jones, of Yardbirds and Led Zeppelin fame), initially it seems an unlikely song to be adopted by beach music audiences as a shag tune. Once the vocals begin, however, and especially during the chorus, it's easy to hear the song's appeal and why it was quickly adopted in beach music circles. The song did well nationally in the U.S., going to #29 (although it did not chart in England). After a non-charting follow-up single and an album, the group changed labels again in 1970, then going to Big Tree. A couple of low charting records, "One Night Stand" (#74) and "Country Woman" (#88) followed in 1971 and 72 respectively, but this point even Bilsbury had left the group that by 1972 was now known as the Magic Lantern, singular; they folded shortly thereafter.

Despite a U.S. chart legacy that included only one Top 40/beach music hit, a number of notable names passed through their often-changing lineup. Kevin Godley and Lol Creme were early members of the group, though both would find greater fame as members of 10cc in the 1970s and as the duo Godley and Creme in the 1980s. Albert Hammond was also a member in the early '70s, and he would go on to find fame as a solo artist ("It Never Rains in Southern California") and songwriter. Perhaps the person most often claimed to be the group's most famous member is Ozzy Ozborne, but while Mike "Oz" Osborne *was* a member of the Lanterns, and though pictures of the group from the 1960s show an individual who does in fact look remarkably like a young Ozzy Ozborne, he is *not* the same Ozzy who was the famous frontman for Black Sabbath. Nevertheless, the group was for a brief time an important presence on the British rock scene, and contributed one moderate hit to the genre of Carolina beach music as well.

The Main Ingredient

BEACH MUSIC DISCOGRAPHY: "Everybody Plays the Fool" (RCA 74–0731, 1972: Billboard Pop #3); "Just Don't Want to Be Lonely" (RCA 0205, 1974: Billboard Pop #10).

The group that became The Main Ingredient originated in Harlem and consisted of Donald McPherson, Luther Simmons, and Tony Silvester. The three of them grew up together, served in the army together, and after their service they formed a singing group called the Poets (*not* the Poets who sang the beach classic "She Blew a Good Thing") in 1965. They recorded as the Insiders on the Red Bird label, and in 1967 released a couple of singles on RCA. Their career wasn't taking off, and after a brief hiatus that changed their name to The Main Ingredient (taken from the wording on a Coke bottle) and from 1969 to 1971 released nine more singles. Several of these records "You've Been My Inspiration," "I'm So Proud," "Spinning Around," and "Black Seeds Keep on Growing," made the R&B charts and the lower reaches of the pop charts, but none were Billboard Top 40 pop hits.

Cuba Gooding had been singing backup with the group occasionally, and when Donald McPherson contracted leukemia and died not long afterwards, Gooding moved up front as the new lead vocalist. The group had been given a song, "Everybody Plays the Fool," that was written by Ken Williams, J.R. Bailey (formerly of the Cadillacs), and Rudy Clark, who'd also written hits such as "Good Lovin" and "The Shoop Shoop Song"; Bailey and Clark had also actually been two of the singers on the Globetrotters "Rainy Day Bells." Gooding said "'Everybody Plays the Fool' was actually written for Charlie Pride, who listened to it and decided it wasn't country enough for him to sing. He said 'I'll never be able to sell this as a country song. It's more like a pop song.' So we gave it to our arranger, put an orchestra behind it and recorded it ourselves. But we never liked it—we never believed 'Everybody Plays the Fool' was going to be a hit record. We wanted to be more like the Temptations or the Four Tops, and that's what the rest our album was about. But they sent us on a European tour for two weeks, and when we came back 'Everybody Plays the Fool' was the hottest record on pop radio." The song went to #3 on the pop charts, sold more than a million copies, was awarded with a gold record, and was nominated for a Grammy as best R&B song of the year. It elevated the group from the status of an also-ran soul group to pop stars.

Their next three releases—all in 1973—made the R&B charts but did not do much on the pop charts before they released 1974's "Just Don't Want to Be Lonely." "The song had been recorded by three or four artists before we did it" Gooding said. "Blue Magic did a good version, and Ronnie Dyson did it and almost had a hit record with it" (#60 on the pop charts). "Well, we were on the road as usual going to a gig on what used to be called the chitlin circuit, and we turned on the radio and someone was singing it—maybe Blue Magic. And we said 'Let's put that on the next album.'" Although they decided the song was worthy of a single release, they knew that in order for it to be a hit they'd have to offer up a take on the song that other groups hadn't. "'Just Don't Want to Be Lonely' was always done as a slow ballad" Gooding said, "and it always crashed and burned. When we put the grooves on it, like at the beginning–'dum-dum, dah dah dumm dum…' it just took off." The song went to #8 on the R&B chart and #10 on the pop chart, sold over a million copies, and even charted in England, going to #27.

Their next few singles did moderately well but were not big hits, and 1975's "Rolling Down a Mountainside" would be their last pop charter, though they would have seven or eight more songs make the R&B charts. Soon the members of the group were ready to move on to other projects; first Tony Silvester left and was replaced by Carl Tompkins, then Gooding left in 1977, then Simmons who became a stockbroker. They reunited in 1979 and did two albums, split and reunited again and yet again. Silvester passed away in 2006, and Simmons decided to quit the group. Gooding, who was the father of Oscar winner Cuba Gooding Jr., performed with a different Main Ingredient line-up until he passed away in 2017.

The Manhattans

BEACH MUSIC DISCOGRAPHY: "I Wanna Be (Your Everything)" (Carnival 507, 1965: Billboard Pop #68).

Edward "Sonny" Bivins, Winfred "Blue" Lovett, and Kenny Kelley lived in Jersey City, New Jersey where they attended Lincoln High School. Bivins was older than Kelly and Lovett, but once they discovered their common love of music they would sing at school, and on street corners, and in amateur contests. Across town George "Smitty" Smith and Richard "Ricky" Taylor were friends at Snyder High School. Bivins met Smith at a dance for teens at the YMCA in 1953 when he heard him playing piano and singing, and as a result the five became friends due to their musical interests. All entered the service after high school, with Bivins, Lovett, Smith, and Taylor serving in the Air Force while Kelly served in the Navy.

After their discharge Kelly went to college and would graduate from Morgan State University in 1963. Smith, Bivins, Lovett and two other singers formed the Dulcets, and in 1961 the group recorded a single for the Asnes label, "Pork Chops" (the label credited the Dorsets due to a misspelling). The record did nothing and the group disbanded, but Bivins and Smith decided to start another group, adding both Kelly and Taylor when other members left. Finally, they brought Lovett in and became the Manhattans, taking their name from either the Manhattan skyline or the famous alcoholic drink depending upon whom you asked. They saw themselves as a group in the mold of the Impressions or Temptations, featuring Smith on lead vocals, while Lovett served as songwriter for many of their songs. The group decided to compete in the Apollo Theater's Amateur Night, and though they only placed third Joe Evans of Carnival records was in the audience that night. As a musician Evans had once played with Charlie Parker, Louis Armstrong, Cab Calloway, Dizzy Gillespie and Lionel Hampton, and had partnered to run a small, largely unsuccessful R&B label called Cee-Jay records. After it folded he had worked for Ray Charles' Tangerine label before going to Motown. Though still working with Motown, in 1962 he decided to start his own New York–based Carnival label with Paul "Hucklebuck" Williams. One of the label's artists had heard the Manhattans and suggested Evans see them perform at the Apollo. Evans signed them, and had them demo a few songs that he took to Motown to see if they were interested in a national distribution deal. The terms weren't agreeable to Evans, so he quit Motown and the Manhattans released their fist two singles on Carnival in 1964, "For the Very First Time" and "There Goes A Fool," neither of which was successful.

At this point the group had no hits, and they had another problem as well—their name. There were several groups known as the Manhattans, including Eli & the Manhattans, Ronnie & the Manhattans, and scores of groups called simply the Manhattans. Recording on labels such as Dootone, King, Colpix, Golden World, Atlantic and Avanti, and many others, none were this group, who did not have a record deal after Asnes until signing with Carnival. Apparently there was a dispute and the musicians union ruled that whoever had the first chart hit got to keep the name. The outcome was in the balance until "I Wanna Be (Your Everything)" came out in 1964, and the group became the one and only Manhattans.

Recorded at Talent Masters Studios in Manhattan, "I Wanna Be" was a Blue Lovett composition, and as result although Smith usually handled lead vocals, Evans decided to have Lovett sing lead on his own song although in a higher register than he normally sang. Session musicians included Bernard Purdie on drums, Jimmy Tyrell on bass, Robert Banks on piano, "Snaggs" Allen and Eric Gale on guitar, and the Lovettes singing backing vocals, and going forward this grouping would do background on all of the Manhattans' records. Evans reportedly knew the song was a winner and worked DJs such as Murray the K to make sure it got airtime. The song would climb to #68 on the pop charts and #12 the R&B charts, and the group went from hopeful part time singers to full blown professionals. The college-educated Kelley had been working in a laboratory and singing part time, and Lovett actually worked for the Muscular Dystrophy Association—and reportedly wrote the song at work. After the song charted they all quit their jobs and became full time singers.

The Manhattans would have seven more R&B Top 40 records for Carnival before moving to Deluxe in 1969 where they had more than a half dozen chart records. In 1970 George Smith fell down a flight of stairs and would die later that year. He was replaced Gerald Alston, who would take over lead vocal duties, and eventually the group moved to Columbia, where after almost two dozen chart records they'd hit #1 on both the pop and R&B charts in 1976 with "Kiss and Say Goodbye." Taylor left in 1976 and the group performed thereafter as a quartet, and in 1980 they'd have another big hit with "Shining Star," which went Top 10 on the pop and R&B charts. They recorded for Columbia until almost the end of the decade, and from 1965 to 1990 they'd have nearly 50 chart records. The group continued until 1988, when Columbia dropped them and Alston left for a solo career. Roger Harris became the new lead, and thereafter members came and went as Bivens and Lovett kept a touring group together for many years. Taylor, Bivens, Lovette, and Kelly have now all passed away.

Martha and the Vandellas

BEACH MUSIC DISCOGRAPHY: "Come and Get These Memories" (Gordy 7014, 1963: Billboard Pop #29); "Jimmy Mack" (Gordy 7058, 1967: Billboard Pop #10).

Alabama-born Martha Rose Reeves and her family moved to Detroit when she was an infant, and as a child she grew playing in her grandfather's church choir. After graduating from Northeastern High School in 1959, she co-founded a group called The Sabre-ettes, which eventually evolved into the Fascinations. In 1960 she formed the Del-Phis along with Gloria Williamson, Rosalind Ashford and Annette Beard, and the group worked as backup singers in the Detroit area. In 1960 they sang backup and for J.J. Barnes on "Won't You Let Me Know," released on both the Rich and Kable labels (both labels credit the group as The Dell Fi's) and on the Mah's label for Mike Hanks on "I Think About You" and "When True Love Comes to Be" (the label on the latter single reads the Del-Fis) in 1961. Later that year they recorded their own single as the Del-Phis on the Chess subsidiary Check-Mate, an answer record to the Barnes release called "I'll Let You Know," but at this point session work and a single release weren't paying the bills. The Del-Phis broke up, and after landing a solo gig singing at a club Reeves was spotted by Motown A&R man Mickey Stevenson who wanted her to audition for the label. Though she wasn't brought in as a solo act, she was hired to do secretarial work and sub in as a singer when needed. One of her first opportunities came when Mary Wells had to miss a session and Reeves recorded "My Baby Won't Come Back" in her stead. Later, when the Andantes couldn't back up Marvin Gaye at the session for "Stubborn Kind of Fella" Reeves called the other Del-Phis and they sang back-up instead. After more back-up work Berry Gordy decided to bring them on full time, but they had to change their name from the Chess-owned Del-Phis and chose the Vandellas as homage to Detroit's Van Dyke Street and singer Della Reese.

The group began recording under a confusing series of names and labels as Motown tried to find a working combination. On Tamla they backed up Saundra Mallet (later with the Elgins) as Saundra Mallet the Vandellas and on "Stubborn Kind of Fella" as simply The Vandellas, while on Gordy as Martha and the Vandellas they had their own release "I'll Have to Let Him Go" and the song Reeves recorded in place of Mary Wells "My Baby Won't Come Back"(the other girls voices were later dubbed in). To further confuse the issue on the short-lived Motown subsidiary label Mel-o-dy they recorded "There He Is" as The Vells. Their own singles still failed to find an audience, and they continued to sing back up, notably on Gaye's "Hitch Hike" and "Pride and Joy."

A few line-up changes resulted in some stability at last, and now as Martha and Vandellas, Reeves, Rosalind Ashford and Annette Sterling backed by the fabulous Funk Brothers had their first chart hit in 1963 with their second release, "Come and Get These Memories," which peaked at #29 on the pop charts and #5 on the R&B charts. This song was especially notable because it was the very first big hit by the soon-to-be-famous songwriting team, Holland, Dozier, and Holland. This was followed by "Heat Wave" (#4), "Quicksand" (#8), Dancing in the Street" (#2), "Nowhere to Run" (#8) and other hits up through 1966. Throughout this period, the group's lineup would fluctuate, with Reeves being the one constant. But the group was popular, surpassed only by the Supremes as a girl group Motown draw, and they performed on *The Ed Sullivan Show, Shindig!, Ready Steady Go, American Bandstand* and others.

Around the same time "Dancing in the Street" was recorded, the group also recorded "Jimmy Mack," another song written by Motown's famed Holland, Dozier, and Holland writing team. Lamont Dozier attended a dinner where the late songwriter Ronnie Mack was being honored, and Dozier wrote the song with him in mind. In the song the group pleads for Jimmy Mack to come back, especially since there are now other boys in the picture. It was a good song with a good sound (as its chart status would eventually prove), but nevertheless, Motown decided not to release it. Apparently the label felt that the song might be too controversial if audiences thought the group was pleading for Jimmy to return because it could be interpreted that he was in Vietnam, and that might make people edgy. Consequently, the recording was stuck in the vault, and in 1967, with the condemnation of the Vietnam War more vogue than taboo, the single was finally released. It shot up the charts, peaking at #10 and #1 on the R&B charts.

In fact, the song was the last Top 10 song the group would ever have. After "Jimmy Mack," the group would have only two more Top 40 hits, both in 1967. In the late '60s Holland, Dozier, and Holland left Motown, and this coupled with the fact that internal strife led to a number of line-up changes by this point, they'd break up and then re-form, but nevertheless the hits had stopped coming. 1972's "Tear It on Down" would peak at #37 on the R&B charts, their last chart record of any type. Martha Reeves and the Vandellas were inducted to the Rock & Roll Hall of Fame in 1995, the Vocal Group Hall of Fame in 2003, and received a Pioneer Award by the Rhythm & Blues Foundation, among other accolades.

The Marvelettes

BEACH MUSIC DISCOGRAPHY: "Playboy"(Tamla 54060, 1962: Billboard Pop #7) "Beachwood 4–5789"(Tamla 54065,1962: Billboard Pop #17) "Don't Mess With Bill"(Tamla 54126, 1965: Billboard Pop #7).

In 1960 Inkster, Michigan, natives and schoolmates Gladys Horton, Georgeanna Tillman, Katherine Anderson and Juanita Cowart sang together in their high school glee club, and fifteen-year-old Horton decided to form a girl group in the mold of the Shirelles. They added high school graduate Georgia Dobbins and called themselves The Casinyets, an allusion to the fact that they jokingly stated they "Can't Sing Yet." They were spotted at a talent show by Robert Bateman of the Satintones, who knew Berry Gordy of the up-and-coming Motown label. Now performing as the Marvels, in 1961 Bateman got the girls an audition with Gordy and Smokey Robinson. The audition went well, and the group was told to come back if they could come up with a decent song to record, and through a connection Dobbins had with a bluesman named William Garrett they repurposed a song of his into a doo-wop tune called "Please Mr. Postman." Gordy liked the song and signed the girls as the Marvelettes, but at this time Dobbins left the group and was replaced by high-school friend Wanda Young. It would be the first of many personnel changes the group would undergo.

"Please Mr. Postman" was issued on Gordy's Tamla label, and reached #1 on the pop charts in December 1961. It was Motown's first #1 hit, though the group's next release, "Twistin' Postman," was a blatant attempt to capitalize on both their first hit and the twist craze. The forgettable song peaked at #34 in 1962, but its follow-up, "Playboy," did far better song. The song was composed by Brian Holland (soon to be part of the famous songwriting trio Holland, Dozier, and Holland), Bateman, Robinson, and the group's own Gladys Horton. Horton sang lead on the song backed by Young, Tillman, Anderson, and Cowart with instrumentation by the Funk Brothers, and the group had their second big hit, going to #7 on the pop charts. Their next release, "Beachwood 4-5789," was written by Marvin Gaye, Mickey Stevenson, and George Gordy. Horton again sang lead, again backed by the other girls, the Funk Brothers, but also Gaye on drums. The song went to #17 on the pop charts, and like "Playboy," it had some traction in beach clubs as well. The song's flipside, "Someday, Someway," made the R&B charts as well, peaking at #8.

Although having four Top 40 releases emerge from their first four releases should have had the group on top of the world, success was having a very different effect on the group. First off, they'd never finished high school, and though they supposedly had tutors, the constant touring prevented them from finishing their educations. Touring led to exhaustion, and perhaps due to this after Cowart had a simple slip of the tongue on *American Bandstand* and declared that Detroit was a suburb of Inkster instead of the other way around, she was apparently teased so much that she cited it as a reason for leaving the group. In addition, despite being Motown's first really successful act, they were already starting to feel as if the Miracles, Supremes, Martha Reeves and the Vandellas, and others were getting more of the label's attention. One reason for the Supremes' ascendency was actually due to a mistake by the Marvelettes; given a choice between recording "Where Did Our Love Go" and "Too Many Fish in the Sea" the girls chose the latter song and the Supremes were given the one they passed on. "Too Many Fish" only went to #25, while in 1964 the Supremes' recording became their first #1 record. In addition, Wanda Young married the Miracles' Bobby Rogers (and took his name) and Georgianna Tillman married Billy Gordon of The Contours, and then Tillman was diagnosed with lupus and left the group in 1965. Consequently, at that point the group was down to Wanda Rogers, Horton, and Anderson.

The group had been in a slump, chart-wise, as well. After "Beachwood 4-5789" had charted, from 1962 to 1966 they had released at least eleven singles and only "Too Many Fish" had broken into the pop Top 30. That was remedied to some degree when "Don't Mess with Bill" went to #7 in 1966. The Smokey Robinson-penned song featured Wanda Rogers singing lead, once again with instrumentation by the Funk Brothers. The song was also popular in the beach clubs, and in an interview with Linda "Quig" Quinlan of the Monzas she remembered it being one of the hottest songs in venues such as the Pawleys Island Pavilion and in the beach clubs in Ocean Drive in general.

Unfortunately, instead of marking a resurgence for the group, it would be their last Top 10 hit even though they would have two more records that would make the pop Top 40, "The Hunter Gets Captured by the Game" (#13, 1967) and "My Baby Must Be a Magician" (#17, 1968). In 1967 founder Gladys Horton left the group, and Ann Bogan joined in her stead. The only original member left, Katherine Anderson, had a disagreement with Wanda Rogers after Rogers recorded an album as being by the group but that did not actually include Anderson. The group finally called it quits not long afterwards.

In 1995, the group was honored with a Pioneer Award at the Rhythm & Blues Foundation, in 2004 they were inducted to the Vocal Group Hall of Fame, and in 2013 they were inducted into the R&B Hall of Fame. They have twice been nominated for induction into the Rock and Roll Hall of Fame.

Cash McCall

BEACH MUSIC DISCOGRAPHY: "When You Wake Up" (Thomas 307, 1966: Billboard Pop #102); "That Lucky Old Sun" (Thomas 311, 1966: Did Not Chart).

Born Morris Dollison, Jr., in New Madrid Missouri, McCall served in the U.S. Army in the early 1960s and upon discharge moved to Chicago. His first professional musical experience was in gospel, as he sang and played with the Gospel Songbirds and later with another gospel group, the Pilgrim Jubilee singers. The Gospel Songbirds recorded "Let Jesus Lead You" and "Do You Ever Call Jesus?" in 1964 on Ernie Young's Nashboro label (Young also founded Excello, which has led to some confusion about the group's label over the years), and McCall sang and played guitar on the record while future blues great Otis Clay sang lead. That same year he recorded one unsuccessful single on the M-Pac! label under the name Morris Dollison and the Turnkeys, "Earth Worm."

For the next few years he spent most of his time composing music, and during the remainder of the '60s he would write for the likes of Etta James, Pigmeat Markham, Little Milton, Muddy Waters, and Irma Thomas, among others. However it was a song he co-wrote with producer Monk Higgins, "When You Wake Up," that brought him his first recognition as a solo artist,—albeit with a new name. He had done a demo of the song and Thomas records released it in 1966 under the name Cash McCall, a name that had surfaced in a 1960 James Garner film, which in turn was based on a 1955 Cameron Hawley novel of the same name. The song peaked at #19 on the R&B charts, though it only bubbled under the Billboard pop 100 at #102. Even though it was not a major seller, it was enough to secure the newly christened McCall a place touring with Lou Christie and others on Dick Clark's "Caravan of Stars."

His next Thomas release that year, "You Can't Take Love," did nothing, and was followed by "That Lucky Old Sun," his final release of 1966. "That Lucky Old Sun" had been written in 1949 and the song's most successful version had been done by Frankie Laine, who had logged a #1 hit with it. Others, including Louis Armstrong, Frank Sinatra, Pat Boone, Ray Charles and many others had also recorded the song, and though McCall's version became a hit with beach music audiences, it did not sell well nor did it chart. Though McCall would record one more record for Thomas, a couple for Checker, and a variety of singles for a number of labels over the next twenty years, as it turned out "When You Wake Up" would be his only chart record.

Over the years McCall would continue to write music and work as a session musician, but he would continue to record though he ultimately became known as a blues singer and musician. He worked with many of the most influential names in blues music, including Willie Dixon, Phil Upchurch, Jimmy Dawkins, Les McCann, and others. In 1988, he helped produce Dixon's Grammy winning album *Hidden Charms*, and has gone on to be regarded as one of the most influential and prolific artist in blues.

Gene McDaniels

BEACH MUSIC DISCOGRAPHY: "A Hundred Pounds of Clay" (Liberty 55308, Billboard Pop #3 1961); "Tower of Strength" (Liberty 55371, Billboard Pop #5 1961).

As a child in Omaha, Nebraska, Eugene McDaniels sang in the church choir and formed his own gospel group when he was eleven. After graduating from the University of Omaha Conservatory of Music, McDaniel ended up in California singing on the club circuit, where he came to the attention of Liberty Records. He signed with them in 1959, and his first two releases, "In Times Like These" and "Green Door," did not chart.

In an effort to turn McDaniels' million-dollar voice into a million record sales, Liberty offered him the song "A Hundred Pounds of Clay," a song about how God created the human race. Though it may have been an odd topic for a popular song, Liberty teamed him with producer Snuff Garrett who they thought could get the most from McDaniels. McDaniels, however, initially resented Garrett, telling me he was "bean counter" and a front office type who didn't know anything about music. "He didn't like the way I was singing the song," McDaniels told me, "so he asked me to clip the lyrics.... I didn't understand; nobody explained to me that there's a specific sound out there that the audience wants to hear. He told me, 'You're singing too much, clip the lyrics.' I clipped them, and he thought I was responding angrily to his request. And I was! Well, he went to Al Bennet, who asked him, 'How'd he do?' and Snuff said, 'He blew it.' Al said, 'We're putting it out anyway. I'm not gonna spend $1,500 and not put this thing out.'" So Garrett didn't like the final product, nor did McDaniels, but put it out they did, and with backing vocals by the Johnny Mann singers and McDaniel's strong lead "A Hundred Pounds of Clay" went all the way to #3 on the pop charts, earned a gold record, and became McDaniels' first big hit.

The success of "A Hundred Pounds of Clay" "taught me a lesson," McDaniels said, "and that lesson is that you can always learn something. Snuff had a golden ear and produced Top 10 hits for a lot of Liberty artists." With a more open attitude towards Garrett, the two of them collaborated on a number of hits, and while McDaniels' next single, "A Tear," would only go to #31, he would end 1961 with a third straight Top 40 song in "Tower of Strength" which would go to #5 and become a favorite among shaggers in the Carolinas. In 1962 after "Chip Chip" (#10), four of his next five singles would make the Top 100. Unfortunately, though McDaniels had registered eight Top 100 hits between 1961 and 1963, over the course of his next seven singles up through 1967 none of them would make the popular charts.

McDaniels would continue recording into the 2000s, however by the late 1960s he had transitioned in to being a songwriter and penned a number of songs including Les McCann's 1969 #1 jazz hit "Compared to What" and Roberta Flack's 1974 #1 hit "'Feel Like Making Love," which earned platinum status and a Grammy Award. Eventually he retired to his home in Maine, where he died in 2011.

Stick McGhee

BEACH MUSIC DISCOGRAPHY: "Drinkin' Wine Spo-Dee-O-Dee" (Atlantic 873, 1949: Billboard #26); "Six to Eight" (King 4783, 1955: Did Not Chart).

Knoxville, Tennessee born Granville Henry "Stick" McGhee was not a drummer, as some might think given his nickname, but a guitar player and a singer. His nickname wasn't "Sticks," plural, either, but "Stick." "Stick" got his nickname by pushing his polio-stricken brother Walter ("Brownie") McGhee around in a wagon with a stick. Before World War II "Stick" McGhee was already working toward a career in the music business, playing smaller venues and working up his guitar-playing act. He entered the army in 1942, and after his discharge in 1946, McGhee, along with brother Brownie and friend Dan Burley, laid down a track Stick used to sing in the army, retitled "Drinkin' Wine Spo-Dee-O-Dee," on Mayo Williams' small Harlem label. (Spo-dee-o-dee is reported to be the leftovers and dregs of many wine bottles, poured together and passed around.) However, Stick's army version had been quite different, and quite profane ("Drinkin' wine motherfucker, Godamn!"), so it was a drastically sanitized and slower version that was released for radio play. The song did not sell well and did not chart.

Despite the fact that it was unsuccessful, one of the founders of Atlantic Records, Ahmet Ertegun, heard about the song and was told that it was getting significant airplay in the South around New Orleans. Ertegun got hold of a copy and liked it, so in February 1949 he tracked down Stick and with Brownie on guitar and "Big Chief" Ellis on piano he set up the studio time for them to rerecord it. Though they initially tried to reproduce the Harlem single's sound, it wasn't working for them so they recorded it with a new uptempo rhythm. Released on Atlantic 873 and backed with "Blues Mixture (I'd Rather Drink Muddy Water)," the record was Atlantic's first big hit, going all the way to #2 on the R&B charts and #26 on the pop charts, a rare crossover hit for a black artist in the early 1950s. McGhee followed up with releases such as "Drank Up All the Wine Last Night," "I'll Always Remember," "My Baby's Comin' Back," and others, but only 1951's "Tennessee Waltz Blues" charted, and though it also made #2 on the R&B charts it did not register on the pop charts.

After a few more releases he left Atlantic records for King, where he cut such living-on-the-edge singles as "Whiskey, Women and Loaded Dice," "Double Crossin' Liquor," and "Dealin' from the Bottom." In February 1955 he had his last session at King, and with Jimmy Wright on tenor sax, Duke Parham on piano, Prince Babb on bass, and Gene Brooks on drums, he recorded several sides, including another beach music favorite, "Six To Eight"; the King label erroneously credits "Sticks McGhee." No hits followed, and McGhee now jumped to Savoy records, where he recorded a few sides as Sticks McGhee & The Ramblers, with, again, the label crediting the incorrect plural form of his nickname. His last stint was with Herald Records, where he recorded "Sleep in Job" in 1960; this time the label had both his first and last name wrong, crediting the song to "Sticks Mcgee." As a result, the repeated variations of his name from his post–Atlantic years right up until his last recording have subsequently led to considerable confusion, and his credits on 45 re-pressings and album compilations run the gamut.

Not long afterward the Herald session McGhee fell ill,

and he died of cancer a few months later in 1961. Although "Drinkin' Wine Spo-Dee-O-Dee" and "Six to Eight" were originally his principal songs that were popular on the beach music circuit, others such as "Jungle Juice," "Head Happy With Wine," and "One Monkey Don't Stop No Show" have garnered attention over the years as well.

Clyde McPhatter

BEACH MUSIC DISCOGRAPHY: "Ta-Ta (Just Like a Baby)" (Mercury 71660, 1960: Billboard Pop #23).

Clyde Lensley McPhatter was born in Durham, North Carolina to George McPhatter, a minister, and Beulah, a church organist. Clyde sang soprano in the Mount Calvary Baptist Church choir, and after his family moved first to New Jersey, then to New York City, in New York he joined the Mount Lebanon Singers of the Mount Lebanon Church. Although they were one of the most popular gospel groups on the East Coast, McPhatter's interests eventually moved him towards rhythm and blues, and he entered an amateur contest at the Apollo Theater. There he was spotted by Billy Ward, who was forming a new singing group. In 1950 McPhatter joined Ward, Charlie White, Bill Brown, and Joe Lamont to form the Dominoes (see entry this book), and while it was Brown's bass voice that was featured on their early smash "Sixty Minute Man," soon it was McPhatter's voice that was attracting the notice. He sang lead on a number of their hits, and really came into this own on the phenomenal "Have Mercy Baby."

By 1953 however, McPhatter was no longer happy as a member of the Dominoes. McPhatter was disturbed because despite the fact that he was really the voice of the group—Ward himself only occasionally sang or played on their songs—he was a virtual unknown often passed off as Ward's younger brother. He wanted more money and lead billing, and Ward was unwilling to give him either so he left the group. Stories differ as to what happened next. Some accounts claim that McPhatter formed his own group, named The Drifters, and then went to Atlantic seeking a contract, while other accounts say Atlantic Records President Ahmet Ertegun heard McPhatter had left the Dominoes and approached McPhatter about starting a group. In any event, The Drifters signed with Atlantic in May 1953. Although the original line-up was a mis-fire, Atlantic formed a second group behind McPhatter, and this time things clicked. With Clyde's distinctive voice singing lead, the group reeled off a series of hits, including "Money Honey" and "Honey Love," before McPhatter was drafted and sold his controlling share of the group to manager George Treadwell. Eventually Johnny Moore took over lead duties for the most part, and the group moved on without McPhatter (see the entry for The Drifters).

All indications are that McPhatter was ready for a solo career in any event, and being drafted facilitated a clean break. When he was discharged in 1955, he returned to Atlantic as a solo act, although ironically his first recording was a duet with Ruth Brown, "Love Has Joined Us Together." On his own in 1956 he released "Seven Days" (Pop #44, R&B #2), "Treasure of Love" (Pop #16, R&B #1), "Thirty Days" (did not chart), and "Without Love (There Is Nothing)" (Pop #19, R&B #4), but releases in 1957 and 1958 performed just moderately well until his last release of 1958. "A Lover's Question," which he co-wrote with Brook Benton, made the Top 10 on the pop charts and went to #1 on the R&B charts. However, instead of finally hitting his stride and compiling a string of big hits afterwards, once again his next few records only performed moderately well, and when his Atlantic contract was up he moved to MGM. His five releases there did even worse than his Atlantic sides, none made the pop Top 40 and only one made the R&B charts at all. He returned to Atlantic in 1960, and his second stint there was even worse; only one release charted at any level, and even then it barely broke the Top 100.

Later that year he signed with Mercury, and with his first release "Ta Ta," he seemed to return to winning form. For this record he re-teamed with his old friend Jimmy Oliver, who had been the guitarist for The Drifters, and their co-written hit went to #23 on the pop charts and #7 on the R&B charts. His next releases on Mercury were hit and miss, some not charting at all, and others, such as 1962's "Lover Please" (Pop #7, R&B #4) and "Little Bitty Pretty One" (Pop #25) doing well. Unbeknownst to anyone at the time, "Little Bitty Pretty One" would be his last Top 40 hit on the pop charts, and only his last Mercury release, 1965's "Crying Won't Help You Now," would make the R&B charts (#22). Thereafter he'd record for Amy, Deram, B&C, and Decca up through 1970, but there would be no hits.

McPhatter's decline would be linked largely to alcoholism, which resulted in missing performances and increasingly erratic behavior. He seemed to be unable to handle the drop-off in popularity that all but a select few performers find to be inevitable, but like many soul performers in the mid to late 1960s he discovered he had quite a following in England, and he moved there from 1966 to 1970. He wasn't content just as an oldies act however, and he once made the claim that by the 1970s that he had no fans, feeling they had let him down by abandoning him. Alcoholism, depression, and poor health (he had heart, kidney, liver disease) led to his death from a heart attack in 1972 when he was just 39 years old. He was inducted into the Rock and Roll Hall of Fame in 1987.

Mel and Tim

BEACH MUSIC DISCOGRAPHY: "Backfield in Motion" (Bamboo BMB 107, 1969: Billboard Pop #10); "Good Guys Only Win in the Movies" (Bamboo BMB 109, 1970: Billboard Pop #45).

Cousins Melvin McArthur Hardin and Hubert Timothy McPherson started writing songs when they were teenagers growing up in rural Holly Springs, Mississippi. They first sang with a gospel group known as the Welcome Travelers, but left their native Mississippi and headed to St. Louis, where Mel's mother Yolanda Hardin worked for Bamboo Records. Leo and Mamie Hutton, owners of St Louis's Bamboo Lounge, had founded the label in 1968 and hired producer and songwriter Andre Williams to run it. Williams, who had worked with Mary Wells, Carl Carlton, the Contours, and others, and who had also co-written the Five Du-Tones "Shake a Tail Feather," saw the label through its first few releases but by 1969 the label had moved to Chicago where it was run by new label President Gene Chandler. Hardin and McPherson had written some songs they were hoping Bamboo would use when Chandler asked them to record the songs themselves.

Mel and Tim's first release was just Bamboo's sixth single release, a song they had written called "I've Got Puredee." It did nothing, but their next single, the playful "Backfield in Motion," was smash. Co-produced by Chandler and Karl Tarleton, the single, which was also a Hardin and McPherson composition, reached #10 on the pop charts and #3 on the R&B charts in 1969. The million seller gave Mel and Tim a gold record in just their second ever release. 1970's "Good Guys Only Win in the Movies," a song they did not write, was their next release. Also produced by Chandler, he was attempting to follow up the lighthearted nature of their first hit with another somewhat playful song. The formula wasn't quite a successful the second time around, and the single rose to #17 on the R&B charts but didn't quite break into the Top 40 on the pop charts, stalling at #45. Nevertheless, the success of two chart records in a row prompted Chandler to release Mel and Tim's and Bamboo's first album, *Good Guys Only Win in the Movies.*

Unfortunately for Bamboo, Mel and Tim was really the only thing the label had going. Their entire stable of artists in addition to Mel and Tim consisted of Sylvia Thomas (one release with the label), The Voice Masters (three releases), The Profiles (three releases), and Lee Charles (four releases). The Voice Masters and the Profiles each had one R&B chart record but neither broke into the R&B Top 40 and neither made the pop charts at all. Consequently, Mel and Tim's two chart records surpassed the efforts of every other artist the label had signed, and when their subsequent Bamboo releases–"Feeling Bad," "Mail Call Time," "We've Got a Groove to Move You," and "I'm the One"—stiffed, the label was history, and folded in 1971 after releasing just 18 singles and one album.

Mel and Tim's record of success, though limited, was such that another label was bound to take a chance on them, and Stax did. They signed in 1972 and immediately had another big hit with their first release, "Starting All Over Again," which peaked at #19 on the Hot 100 and #4 on the R&B charts and was another million seller. Unfortunately, although Stax had a reputation as a solid label for R&B, by the early 1970s they were having distribution problems which of course led to financial shortfalls. None of Mel and Tim's other four releases on Stax in 1973 and 74 made the pop charts and only two made the lower reaches of the R&B charts, although they did release two albums on Stax and appeared at the famed Wattstax concert. By this time the label was insolvent, and went the way of Bamboo and shut down in 1975. Mel and Tim did not record as a duo thereafter. Tim McPherson passed away in 1986.

Harold Melvin and the Bluenotes

BEACH MUSIC DISCOGRAPHY: "The Love I Lost" (Philadelphia International ZS7 3533, 1973: Billboard Pop #7).

There were several groups using the name the Bluenotes in the 1950s, but the group that would eventually become Philadelphia's Harold Melvin and the Bluenotes started as the Charlemagnes. They changed their name to the Blue Notes in 1954, and over the next decade they would record a number of non-charting singles for a variety of labels starting with the 1956 release "If You Love Me" on Josie. Releases on Instant Action, Gamut, Twentieth Century, 3 Sons, Arctic, Uni, Dash and others failed to find much of an audience, with only 1960's "My Hero" (#7 R&B charts, #78 pop) and 1965's "Get Out (and Let Me Cry)" (#38 R&B charts, #125 pop). As with many groups with limited chart success there were a number of defections over the years, and by the early 1970s the group consisted of Harold Melvin, Bernie Wilson, Teddy Pendergrass, Lawrence Brown, and Lloyd Parks. Parks had been with the Episilons and sang back up on Arthur Conley's "Sweet Soul Music," and Pendergrass had been a former member of a Philadelphia group named The Cadillacs—though not the Cadillacs of "Speedo" fame. Pendergrass had been recruited to play in the back-up band but replaced lead singer John Atkins when he left the group.

It was this line-up that signed with Melvin's old friend Kenny Gamble's Philadelphia International records in 1972, and their first release for the label was "I Miss You." With Pendergrass singing lead, the long slow ballad went to #7 on the R&B charts although it only peaked at #58 on the pop charts. Their next song however, "If You Don't Know Me By Now," topped the R&B charts and went to #3 on the pop charts, and would be the group's big breakthrough at long last. Their next release, 1973's "Yesterday I Had the Blues," going to #12 and #63 on the R&B and pop charts respectively, but the follow-up was "The Love I Lost."

"The Love I Lost" was written by label owners and producers Gamble and Leon Huff, and though originally written as a slow ballad it was updated to meet the musical tastes of the burgeoning dance music (soon-to-be-disco) market of the early 1970s. Some critics have proclaimed it the first disco song, a sweeping piece with excellent backing by Philadelphia International's in-house MFSB group of studio musicians, who were still a year away from their own Top 40 hit "TSOP." The record was a smash, peaking at #7 on the pop charts and #1 on the R&B charts, and was released on the group's *Black & Blue* album in late 1973. It was one of the earliest 1970s dance songs to find a crossover audience with beach music audiences, despite the fact that it clearly wasn't like the Philadelphia-generated hits of just a few years earlier.

From that point on the group would have another twenty R&B chart records over the next decade, although the bulk of their success would come between 1973 and 1976 when they were recording for Philadelphia International. They would have several more R&B number one songs, and songs such as "Bad Luck" and "Where Are All My Friends?" would get some spins among shaggers. Unfortunately, although they were successful, the group's membership became more fluctuating and unstable than ever. In 1974 Parks was replaced by Jerry Cummings, vocalist Sharon Paige was added, and most importantly Pendergrass felt that although he was handling lead on most songs he wasn't being paid accordingly. Despite the fact that he was given separate billing, he left the group and after his departure the label seemed to understand that no matter what the name of the group was, Pendergrass was the star, and they retained Pendergrass and let what was left of Harold Melvin and the Bluenotes go to ABC. As a solo act Pendergrass was extremely successful on the charts, while Melvin's Blue Notes had only very limited success. Ironically, their late 70s+ career was much like their pre–70s career, and saw them recording for a succession of labels such as Glades, Fantasy, Source, MCA, Philly World, and others.

Harold Melvin kept the group together with a rotating membership until he passed away in 1997. Teddy Pendergrass died in 2010.

See also Teddy Pendergrass

Bob Meyer and the Rivieras

BEACH MUSIC DISCOGRAPHY: "Behold" (Casino 103, 1964: Did Not Chart).

Charlotte, North Carolina, teenagers Nat Speir and Charles Van Wagner formed the Rivieras in 1958. The 1958 lineup also included Joe Harris, Smitty Flynn, Bill Bolen and Dwight Stephens, and though like many regional acts the lineup would vary over the next few years. In late 1962, the group added a new lead vocalist in Bob Meyer, a former soloist with the Charlotte Boys' Choir and after that a vocalist for The Catalinas, and their sound moved more towards a '60s "blue-eyed soul" group similar to the Righteous Brothers and others. The group, now consisting of Meyer, Nat Speir, Bobby Speir, Eddy MacAleer, Bud McNeely, and Doug Neal, were working as Bob Meyer and the Riveras. They recorded "Behold" in a garage in Charlotte in 1963, a song written by Meyer and Speir. It was produced by Harry Karras, who would also later produce the Swingin' Medallions' "Double Shot," and the tune acquired an instant audience along the East Coast. Released on the Casino label, it was also released on the slightly more prestigious Lawn label, a subsidiary of Swan. Swan, of course, was the label where the Beatles had previously gone to #1 with "She Loves You," and perhaps through the connection between the two labels, legend has it that the Beatles heard and liked "Behold" and even considered recording it for a while during the period when they covered a number of songs such as "Money," "Please Mr. Postman," "You Really Got a Hold on Me" and "Anna." By late 1964, however, Lennon and McCartney had come into their own as songwriters and had essentially quit doing covers, which may have led to them changing their minds about recording "Behold." Neither the Lawn nor the Casino release charted, though the flip side, "You've Got to Tell Me," would later go on to be a Northern Soul classic; in fact, in England the 45 is highly collectible today for the flip and not "Behold."

Although the group played with an opened for a number of famous acts over the years, including Stevie Wonder, The Impressions, The Four Tops, The Temptations, The Platters, Wilson Pickett, and others, they never had any chart success nationally. Meyer didn't stay with the group long, though with some personnel changes the group would go on to record a number of singles such as "My Girl Stormy" (1965), "Caring for You" (1967) and "I Only Get This Feeling" (1968) on a variety of labels. There would continue to be many personnel changes throughout the '60s until the group folded in 1970.

Amos Milburn

BEACH MUSIC DISCOGRAPHY: "Chicken Shack Boogie" (Aladdin 3104, 1948: Billboard Pop Did Not Chart, R&B #1); "One Scotch, One Bourbon, One Beer" (Aladdin 3197, 1953: Billboard Pop Did Not Chart, R&B #2).

Joseph Amos Milburn, Jr., was born in Houston, Texas, one of twelve children. Just five years old, in less than a day he apparently taught himself to play "Jingle Bells" on a piano rented for his sister's wedding, prompting his parents to pay for him to take lessons. Milburn also danced in amateur shows, and as he got older he spent his free time hanging around outside of bars and honky tonks in Houston listening to piano players hoping to pick up pointers. He quit school in the 7th grade, and when he was fifteen he lied about his age in order to enlist in the navy. During World War II he served in the Pacific Theatre for three years, serving in the Philippines, at Bougainville, and Guadalcanal. When discharged he returned to Texas and played boogie-woogie piano at house parties and in speakeasys, and while playing a gig at San Antonio's Key Club he met Lola Ann Cullum, who would go on to be his manager and the co-writer of several of his songs. When they had a few songs penned they cut demos and headed to Los Angeles where they talked to Jules Bihari of Modern Records, who apparently made them an offer. Cullum felt they could do better, and Milburn auditioned for and signed with Leo and Eddie Mesner's Aladdin Records.

One of the songs Cullum and Milburn had written back in Houston was "After Midnight."

His first release for Aladdin, it sold a solid 50,000 copies, and was followed by "My Baby's Boogie," "Down The Road A Piece," "Amos' Boogie," "Operation Boogie," "Money Hustlin' Woman," "That's My Chick," "Pool Playing Blues" and others. He had begun working with saxopohonist Maxwell Davis, who became his arranger, and they became one of the most productive teams in music. However, it wasn't until he released another of those old songs written in Houston, the jump boogie tune "Chicken Shack Boogie," that he became a star.

Recorded in November 1947, Milburn told *It Will Stand* magazine that "Chicken Shack Boogie" was inspired by the fact that "there were a lot of places in Houston called somebody's Chicken Shack. Jack's Chicken Shack and so and so's Chicken Shack. And usually most of 'em were just a hole in the wall. But it was somebody's Chicken Shack." In 1948 "Chicken Shack Boogie" went to #1 on the R&B charts and stayed there for five weeks. Miburn became known as the "Chicken Shack Boogie Man," and his band at that time—Donald Wilkerson, Willie Simpson, Johnny Brown, Calvin Vaughn, and Harper Cosby—as the Aladdin Chickenshackers. Over the next two years Milburn was selling records at a frantic pace, and *Billboard* named him the Top R&B artist two years in a row in 1949 and 50 and *Downbeat* named him Best Blues & Jazz Star of 1949.

"Chicken Shack Boogie" started a streak of 19 Top 10 R&B hits between 1948 and 1954, and "Bewildered" and "Roomin' House Boogie" also hit #1. In 1950 Davis wrote a song for Milburn called "Bad Bad Whiskey," which also went to #1, and it had 100,00 in sales in less than four weeks. It's success kicked off a string of charting drinking songs such as "Thinking And Drinking" (# 8), "Let Me Go Home Whiskey" (# 3), "One Scotch, One Bourbon, One Beer" (#2) and "Good Good Whiskey" (# 5), as well as a few non-charters such as "Vicious Vicious Vodka," "Let's Have a Party," "House Party (Tonight)." "One Scotch One Bourbon One Beer" (written by Rudy Toombs, who also wrote "One Mint Julep" for the Clovers and later "Thinkin' and Drinkin'" for Milburn) had advance sales of more than 50,000 units, the largest ever for the Aladdin label. A number of other artists would later record it, including Champion Jack Dupree, John Lee Hooker, and George Thorogood, making it the best known song he'd ever record. Unfortunately, as is so often the case, life was imitating art, and Milburn had a drinking problem, exacerbated during performances of "One Scotch One Bourbon One Beer" when he'd consume a jigger of each while playing the piano.

By 1955 the music scene was changing, and Milburn's records had stopped charting. Drinking songs were no longer popular, and his music was seen as old fashioned compared to the emerging rock and roll scene, despite the fact that Little Richard, Fats Domino, Jerry Lee Lewis and others all acknowledged Milburn as having influenced their styles, and his songs such as "Let's Rock a While" (1951) and "Rock, Rock, Rock" (1952) obviously anticipated the revolution in music taking place in the late '50s. He went solo for a while, Aladdin dropped him in 1957 after more than 50 singles, and he played with a variety of labels over the next few years including Ace, King, and even a short stint at Motown in 1962. By the late '60s he was living in Ohio, and years of alcoholism had taken a toll on his body. In 1969 while playing in a Cincinnati club called Satan's Den he noticed his left hand wasn't working when he tried to play the piano and he learned he'd had a stroke. Just a few months later while at home in Cleveland his wife noticed his arm wasn't moving and he discovered he'd had a second stroke. Now an invalid, he moved back to Houston and finally stopped drinking. By that point he also suffered from high blood pressure and epileptic seizures, and in 1979 he had to have his leg amputated. He died in 1980, aged 52. He was inducted into the Blues Foundation Hall of Fame in 2010.

Percy Milem

BEACH MUSIC DISCOGRAPHY: "I Slipped a Little" (Goldwax 201, 1964: Bootleg, Unreleased).

Percy Milem grew up singing in the church, and formed his first group, the Nighthawks, in his hometown of Memphis, Tennessee, when he was fifteen. At about the same time Memphis-born Cornethers "Kirk" Kirkwood had formed a singing group and he invited Milem to join him and William Glenn, Lavern Edwards, and Fonnie Harley as a member of the Lyrics. Milem soon took over lead vocal duties, and after the group entered a local talent contest and won first prize they decided to hire local DJ Rubin Washington to manage them. They approached the new Memphis-based Satellite Records label (Kirkwood's distant cousin was Booker T. Jones, later of Booker T. & the M.G.s), and managed to get a recording session with Chips Moman. Though they cut several sides, Satellite (whose name would be changed to Stax in 1961) didn't release them at the time. Eventually Kirkwood took copies of the tapes and sold them to Ronald 'Slim' Wallace at the Memphis-based Fernwood label. The label released "Let's Bee Sweethearts Again" ("Bee" was a misprint) backed by "You and Your Fellow" in 1961, but the record was not successful. The Lyrics sang backup on releases for some other Fernwood acts such as Bill Black and Bobby Lee Trammell but would see no more singles released under their name at Fernwood.

At this point Stax finally decided to release two songs from those earlier Lyrics' sessions, and to do so they created the Mid-South label, whose one and only release was "Crying Over You." Milem's wailing lead kept the song on the charts for most of the year in Memphis but it didn't break nationally. Fortunately for the Lyrics, Quinton Claunch and Rudolph "Doc" Russell had formed yet another Memphis-based label, Goldwax, and they signed the group for the label's very first release in 1963, "Darling." The song did nothing, but their next Goldwax release, "The Side Wind," got enough regional play that it was picked up by ABC-Paramount for national distribution, but it too flopped.

Frustrated by a lack of success, it was at about this time that the Lyrics disbanded. Goldwax offered Milem a recording contract as a solo artist however, and he released two singles, 1966's "Crying Baby Baby Baby" and 1967's "I Don't Know What You Got," but neither single charted. By the late '60s Claunch and Russell were disagreeing on a number of business issues, and despite the fact that Goldwax artists such as the Ovations and James Carr were fairly successful, the label folded not long after it produced its last singles in 1969.

After the label folded Claunch leased the Goldwax masters to a company in Japan, and among them was a song Milem had recorded in 1964, "I Slipped a Little." Goldwax never released it on an album or single, but the song found its way from the masters to Canada where it was pressed as a bootleg. A great deal of trouble was made to make it appear as an authentic "lost" record from Goldwax, as the label was similar in color and design to one Goldwax used for a few singles in 1968 and 1969, and the label number, 201, would have come between the last single the label released in 1965 and the first they released in 1966, although if real it would have been the only number in the 200 sequence. Over the years the bootleg eventually it made its way to the Carolinas, and by 1990 the record was being widely played as a shag song and became quite popular.

Claunch did relaunch Goldwax in the 1980s, and Milem and James Carr recorded for the label again. Milem's last recording appears to have been an album on the label in 1994, *The Many Moods of Percy Milem*, which contained "I Slipped a Little," no doubt to capitalize on the song's newfound popularity. Milem has had no further releases since that time.

Garnet Mimms and the Enchanters

BEACH MUSIC DISCOGRAPHY: "A Quiet Place" (United Artists 715, 1964: Billboard Pop #78).

Born "Garret" Mimms in Ashland, West Virginia, Mimms had a strong background in the church and gospel music, and early on he sang with groups such as the Evening Stars and the Harmonizing Four after his parents moved to Philadelphia. He did a stint in the military, and then returned to Philadelphia where he sang with the Deltones for a while before forming the Gainors with Howard Tate, Sam Bell, Willie Combo, and John Jefferson in 1958. The group's first recording, 1958's doo-wopper "The Secret," was a regional hit, and Cameo picked up and released the first two Gainors' regional recordings hoping for a little national chart action that was nevertheless elusive. The Gainors had a few more singles before Mimms left to form another group, Garnet Mimms and The Enchanters. The Enchanters were Sam Bell (from the Gainors), Charles Boyer and Zola Pearnell, and the group moved to New York.

But almost from the start, the Enchanters weren't always the group backing up Mimms on those Garnet Mimms and The Enchanters singles, despite what the record label said. For example, on "Cry Baby," the group's biggest single, which went all the way to #4 in 1963 and reportedly sold more than one million copies, the actual backing group was the Gospelaires, whose members included Dionne Warwick and Dee Dee Warwick. On the flip side of the record, however, "Don't Change Your Heart," it was indeed the Enchanters singing backup. "Baby Don't You Weep" (#30) and a cover of the Impressions' "For Your Precious Love" (#26) both made the Top 40, though the singles billed as just "Garnet Mimms," sans Enchanters, "Tell Me Baby" (#69) and "One Girl" (#67), did not. On the flip side of "One Girl" the real Enchanters *were* billed and *were* singing backup on the beach music classic, 1964's "A Quiet Place." Mimms's wailing song of a man is the beach song with perhaps the three most famous opening words—"Johnny, Johnny Dollar"—of all time. As a national record, it only went to #78, so it was not a big performer for the band.

Despite the confusion over who was and was not singing backup, the group was off to a good start, but perhaps the question over whether this was a one-man show or not led to

Mimms decisively going out on his own in 1964 right after "A Quiet Place" charted. The Enchanters stayed together, but without Mimms they didn't seem to have the magic, and they folded in 1966. Mimms, meanwhile, continued to record, sometimes using the Enchanters as uncredited backup singers. With his wide vocal range and wailing soul style, he remained a hot act over the next few years. He cut eight more records for United Artists, though only three charted, and only one, "I'll Take Good Care of You" (#30), broke the Top 40. After his career as a solo artist appeared to have peaked, he worked with Jimi Hendrix in 1967. By the early '70s, Mimms found that he was still very popular on the growing UK Northern Soul scene, so he moved to England and continued to record well into the 1970s.

Eventually Mimms retired from the music industry and became a minister. He founded the New Jerusalem Prison Ministry and later the Bottom Line Revival Ministries. In 1999 he received a Pioneer Award from the Rhythm and Blues Foundation.

The MOB

BEACH MUSIC DISCOGRAPHY: "I Dig Everything About You" (Colossus 130, 1971: Billboard Pop #83).

James "Jimmy Soul" Holvay and Gary Beisbier were first part of a group known as the Maybees, then the Chicagoans, who, as the Livers, who had cut the single "Beatle Time" on Constellation in 1963. They played with The Executives, but ultimately decided to form a band that was more horn-based and play the clubs and other venues in the Chicago area, and Holvay said he got the idea for the group's name watching a late-night movie called *The MOB*. "I thought, 'What a perfect name for group. A bunch of guys with pinstripe suits, black shirts,

The MOB, circa early 1970s (photograph courtesy Jim Holvay).

white ties, carnations, white suspenders and spats, playing R&B music.'" Holvay and Beisbier formed the MOB in 1966 along with Al Herrera, Tony Nedza, Bobby Ruffino, James Franz and Michael Sistak. With their distinctive look and sound in place, the band became one of the premier regional bands in and around Chicago in the 1960s. They had such a strong following that a record deal was inevitable, but singles such as the 1966 release "Wait" on Cameo and 1968 releases "Disappear" on Mercury and "Unbelievable" on Twinight did not break onto the national charts.

Oddly enough, although their own singles weren't charting, Beisbier and Holvay were writing music for another Chicago-based band, the Buckinghams, and those songs had taken the national charts by storm. Holvay's song for the Buckinghams, "Kind of a Drag," hit #1, and Holvay and Beisbier together wrote "Don't You Care" (#6), "Hey Baby (They're Playing Our Song)" (#12) and "Susan" (#11), which were all chart hits. As a result, even though their own band couldn't produce a chart record, Beisbier's and Holvay's writing helped crosstown rivals the Buckinghams earn Billboard's title of "The Most Listened to Band in America" in 1967.

After failing to produce a chart record, the band made a few alterations and developed their act into more of a Vegas-style club band sound. While playing at a hotel in Puerto Rico, Jerry Ross, a well-known producer who had worked with Jay and the Techniques, Jerry Butler, and others, caught their act and decided to sign them to his newly-formed Colossus label. "Colossus had a few hits under their belt," Holvay said, "so we thought that this would finally be our ticket to success." In fact, the fledgling Colossus label had recently released Top 10 hits such as "Venus" (#1) by Shocking Blue and "Ma Belle Amie" (#5) by the Tee Set, and it seemed to follow that the new sound, the proven writing ability and the up-and-coming label were the perfect recipe for the group to be successful at long last.

In 1971 the band's first release on Colossus was song Holvay and Beisbier had written one night while they were waiting on their girlfriends to get dressed so the four of them could go out. "Gary and I were sitting in the living room, and a week or so earlier I'd come up with the verse, 'Baby I need your sweet, sweet lovin', baby. Ooo baby.' That's all I had. I got out my acoustic guitar and played it for Gary. He said, 'Hey—I like that—I've got an idea.' I handed him the guitar, and he wrote the chorus. Songwriters say that the really good songs just flow out naturally—you don't struggle with it. We probably wrote that song in fifteen minutes." The song was, of course, "I Dig Everything About You," now a beach music classic. Surprisingly, given Holvay and Beisbier's track record as writers, the song really didn't do much on the charts. Holvay was shocked, especially since of all the hit songs he'd written, "I'd say that 'I Dig Everything About You' is on the top of my list" as a personal favorite. But soon the problem came to light:

> Unbeknownst to us, Jerry Ross was having financial difficulties at the time. Radio stations were playing the record, but after hearing the song our fans were going to the stores to buy the record and lo and behold ... no records in the rack. The way you move up on the radio station rotation playlist and get more spins every hour is that the station calls the local record stores in the area every week and asks how many singles were sold. As you sell more records, they increase your airplay. No record sales, you

move down on the playlist. Watching that happen just killed me. I was heartbroken. Had I known then what I know now, I would've been on the phone hourly, screaming at Jerry to get records in the stores. I would've driven to the record distributor or pressing plant and taken the records to the stores myself, just to keep that airplay going.

Despite its superior quality, the song peaked nationally at #83 on the Billboard charts.

Their next single, "Give It to Me," went a little higher, peaking at #71 in 1971, but the problem of not having their product on the shelves persisted. The group released two more singles and an album on the label, but Colossus was in dire straits financially and despite a promising beginning the MOB's records were the label's last charters; Colossus folded in 1971. After the collapse of Colossus, the group was picked up by MGM where they released four singles in 1972 and 73, then moved to Private Stock for four singles and an album in 1975 and 76. The band stayed together a while longer through several personnel changes before folding, though they occasionally still play together today. Though not native South Dakotans, they frequently played there in the early '70s and were inducted into that state's Rock and Roll Hall of Fame in 2011.

The Monzas

BEACH MUSIC DISCOGRAPHY: "Hey! I Know You" (Wand 1120, 1964: Did Not Chart).

The Monzas were formed when UNC student Nelson "Salty" Miller decided to put together a band. He recruited drummer Ward May, pianist Bing Greeson, singer Skippy Hin-

The Monzas, circa 1964 (photograph courtesy Linda Quinlan James).

shaw. Hinshaw's sister Sharon and her friend Linda "Quig" Quinlan would sometimes come out to hear the band practice, and eventually they were asked to provide backing vocals for a song the group was trying to perfect. Pleased with the results, they added the two girls their lineup, even though the girls were just sixteen at the time.

It was Linda who was indirectly responsible for the group's name. She drove a Corvair Monza Spider, and said that as "there were many other bands with car names at the time, and my friend Rodney Carden suggested the name Monzas for the band and it stuck." Starting in 1962, the Monzas toured the Carolinas making their own special brand of beach music.

They became more than just another band playing frat parties and dances after they wrote and recorded their original beach music hit, "Hey! I Know You." "Nelson Miller wrote the song on a porch in Ocean Drive," Quinlan (now James) told me, "and I helped with a word here and there." Once completed, "there were two cuts of 'Hey! I Know You. The first was done at Copeland Studios in Greensboro, and the second was done in Charlotte at the Arthur Smith Studios" about a year later. "The first cut was much faster than the second, but there were no major differences other than that one was faster than the other." With Mickey Combs singing lead and Linda and Sharon's haunting backing voices, "Hey! I Know You" was a regional hit. Originally released on the Pacific label, it was picked up for national release by Wand. According to James, what really gave the record a boost was the playtime it received from DJ Charlie Brown (Ed Weiss) of WKIX radio in Raleigh. "Charlie Brown was very instrumental in the song going as far as it did. Back in the day, WKIX was a huge and very popular radio station. He played it a lot and told other DJs about it." And though the record never did much nationally, regionally it was a bona fide hit.

The Monzas post–1965, after the departure of Sharon Hinshaw (photograph courtesy Linda Quinlan James).

Although the group had a few more releases on Pacific, such as "Where is Love" and "Instant Love," there were no more national releases after "Hey! I Know You" appeared on Wand. The group's lineup would continue to change however, despite the fact that it appeared they had at least taken a small step toward the big time. Sharon left the group in 1965, and although Linda had stayed on as the only female in the group after Sharon's departure, she, too, left in 1968. The guys kept recording as the Monzas, and other members were added (and subtracted), but they were never again able to equal the magic of "Hey! I Know You."

Jackie Moore

BEACH MUSIC DISCOGRAPHY: "Sweet Charlie Babe" (Atlantic 2956, 1973: Billboard Pop #42); "Both Ends Against the Middle" (Atlantic 2989, 1973: Billboard Pop #102); "Personally" (Columbia 10779, 1978: Billboard Pop Did Not Chart, R&B #92).

Jackie Moore got her start in Jacksonville, Florida, and in 1968 she moved to Philadelphia. Her first recording there was "Dear John," which was released on the Shout label but debuted to little fanfare. A second single on Shout in 1968, and one on Wand in 1969, appeared with much the same results. At this point she went to Atlantic records in New York, where her first release was the 1970 single "Willpower." That song failed to generate much play, but after it was released someone (reportedly a hometown DJ in Jacksonville) flipped the record to the B-side and started playing "Precious, Precious." Within the next few months that B-side had climbed to #30 on the pop charts and #12 on the R&B charts and had sold more than a million records; it was awarded a gold record in March 1971.

Four singles on Atlantic followed, but none cracked the Billboard pop Hot 100. Perhaps Atlantic didn't know how to market her to a crossover market, although at the same time they *were* doing a good job with The Spinners, Roberta Flack, and Aretha Franklin. But Moore's records weren't selling to pop audiences, and they sent her back to Philadelphia to record at Sigma Sound Studios where the great Philadelphia International soul sounds of the '70s would be recorded.

The move seemed to pay off. "Sweet Charlie Babe," a song written by Phil Hurtt (who wrote the Spinners' "I'll Be Around" that same year) and Bunny Sigler (who wrote several songs for the O'Jays) had a far more sophisticated sound than some of her earlier efforts. Though it probably should have been a solid Top 40 hit, it stalled at #42. The very next release was "Both Ends Against the Middle," which was co-written by Hurtt and Tony Bell. This song had a bouncy clean feel that categorized so many of the tracks that were popular in England on the Northern Soul scene, but it did no better than "bubble under" the Top 100 at #102. In a 1979 interview with David Nathan, Moore admitted that the poor chart performance of those two singles was perplexing. "I've got some mixed feelings about the time I spent with Atlantic" she told Nathan. "I felt like some of the records could have been bigger—especially sides like "Both Ends Against The Middle." But then I'd have to say quite a bit of the blame lay on me. I didn't surround myself necessarily with the right business people—you know, managers and attorneys and so forth." Perhaps it's telling that though Moore was with Atlantic for four years the only album the label released was *Sweet Charlie Babe*, which basically contained the A- and B-sides of every one of her singles up to that point, going all the way back three years to "Precious, Precious"; "Sweet Charlie Babe" led off side one, and "Both Ends" led off side two. The album did not do well, not doubt because the expanse of time represented different directions in her music, multiple producers and songwriters, and no cohesion whatsoever. Besides, anyone who had bought her singles didn't need to buy the album—there were no unreleased songs on it. In this case, it was pretty clear Atlantic dropped the ball.

By this time no doubt Moore and Atlantic had envisioned greater success than they had had, and Moore left. By 1975 she was on the Kayvette label, where her first release there was a big R&B chart hit, "Make Me Feel Like a Woman." None of the five Kayvette singles she released did anything on the pop charts, though all made the R&B charts. By 1978 she had moved to Columbia, and her first release there was a very fine song, "Personally," which Karla Bonoff would cover and take to #19 on the pop charts in 1982. Not only did this song not make the pop charts, it only went to #92 on the R&B charts. An album followed, as did several singles; her last R&B chart hit was in 1983, and no new releases have appeared since the 1990s.

Bobby Moore and the Rhythm Aces

BEACH MUSIC DISCOGRAPHY: "Searching for My Love" (Checker 1129, 1966: Billboard Pop #27); "Try My Love Again" (Checker 1156, 1966: Billboard Pop #97).

Bobby Moore and the Rhythm Aces, 1966 (photograph courtesy Booby Moore Jr.).

New Orleans-born Robert "Bobby" Moore's first experience in a band came when he was serving in the army in the early 1950s. A tenor sax player, his first group consisted of members of the Fort Benning, Georgia army marching band. After leaving the army, he decided to make music his profession and formed the Rhythm Aces in 1961. When the group's lineup solidified, "there were six of us: Dad, me, Chico Jenkins, Joe Frank, Clifford Laws and John Baldwin," Bobby Moore, Jr., said. As a unit, the Rhythm Aces quickly gained a reputation as a first-class ensemble, and as a result, they had the opportunity to back up singers such as Ray Charles, Sam and Dave, Etta James, Kim Weston, Wilson Pickett, Sam Cooke and Otis Redding.

They didn't want to be just a backup band, however, and in 1965, they got their first real shot as a feature act at the legendary Muscle Shoals studio in Alabama. There they recorded "Searching for My Love," which Moore himself had written. "We were playing the song in clubs for a long time before we ever recorded it, and Dad and Chico decided it would be a good one to record because people liked it when we played it—I think the response there had a lot to do with it." Moore said "we went to Muscle Shoals and were one of the first Chess groups to record there. We cut the record, and it took off." The song was a begging-and-pleading-type soul song that featured Chico Jenkins's plaintive vocals, which convey a sense of loss far better than many songs designed to impart a very similar message. The record executives at Chess Records in Chicago heard the tune and thought so too, and released it on their Checker label in 1966. The group watched the song soar into the Top 40 before finally settling in at #27, where it eventually sold more than one million copies. The benefits of having a hit record were immediately obvious, Moore said: "Before the record came out, we had been making like $25 to $30 a night, and after the record, we were making $300 a night." They even performed on television's *Where the Action Is* as a follow-up to the single and were hoping their next release would sustain that momentum.

That next release, "Try My Love Again," though a very solid beach music classic, "didn't do that much though" nationally, Moore said, peaking at #97. Their next single, 1967's "Chained to Your Heart," did not make the Top 100 at all, though it did make the R&B charts. Despite the promise shown by their early singles, Checker didn't seem to have much faith in the group's ability to produce long term, and after they released two more non-charting singles, Checker dropped them from the label.

Bobby Moore, Sr., died in 2006. "Dad kept the band going even after the label released us, and we have been playing for four decades now," Moore said. "Dad was a class act, and today I'm still trying to carry on the legacy." Considering that they cut only five singles, having had two emerge as sizeable beach music classics is a testimony to the quality of their music, even if their limited chart success means they aren't as well known today as some other national acts from the period.

New York City

BEACH MUSIC DISCOGRAPHY: "I'm Doin' Fine Now" (Chelsea 0113, Billboard Pop #17 1973).

New York City began as a group called Tri-Boro exchange, so-named after a New York City bridge linking three boroughs in the Big Apple. Members John Brown, Eddie Schell, Claude Johnson and lead singer Tim McQueen had varying musical backgrounds, with Brown reportedly having sung with in various incarnations of '50s doo-wop groups such as the Five Satins, the Cadillacs, and the Moonglows. Johnson was no less experienced, having performed with the Genies and as "Juan" in a featured role as one half of Don and Juan on their big hit "What's Your Name?" (#7, 1962). Though McQueen and Schell had less-illustrious musical pedigrees, they, too, were accomplished vocalists.

The group landed its first recording contract with Buddah Records, and did a one-off single in 1972, "Seven Lonely Nights" that went nowhere. However, the record was produced by Wes Farrell, who had published and would publish songs such as "Hang On Sloopy" by the McCoys, "Knock Three Times" by Tony Orlando and Dawn, and "It's A Beautiful Morning" by the Rascals, and had written songs such as "Come a Little Bit Closer" by Jay and the Americans and Partridge Family hits including "Doesn't Somebody Want to Be Wanted." With an eventual 100 gold records to his name and 300 million records sold, Farrell knew a winning sound when he heard it, and despite the failure of their first single, Farrell knew Tri-Boro Exchange had that special something. When Farrell founded his own Chelsea label that year, he would sign the group to his stable of artists that included or would include Rick Springfield, Hall and Oates, and Jim Gilstrap (see the entry for Gilstrap).

Farrell's first move was to change the group's name to New York City, and in order to best capitalize on their potential he brought them together with Thom Bell, who had produced the Delfonics and the Stylistics, and who was working with the Spinners on their Atlantic recordings. Bell's idea was to record all the instrumental backing tracks for the group's songs, *then* have them come in and overdub the vocals—which was not the normal procedure. Then the vocalists added their tracks and the result would be a quick single recording that was supposedly easier and quicker to produce.

Initially, it seemed like the methodology was a success, as the group's soulful side "I'm Doin' Fine Now," written by Bell and Sherman Marshall (who himself would co-write songs such as "Lady Love" for Lou Rawls and "Then Came You" for Dionne Warwick and the Spinners), soared before stalling at #17 on the Billboard charts in 1973. However, with success comes touring, and so a back-up band had to be hastily assembled so the group could follow-up the single with personal appearances. The band, known as the "The Big Apple Band," would include two members, Nile Rodgers and Bernard Edwards, who would eventually find great success after renaming themselves Chic in 1977. New York City and the Big Apple Band toured extensively, even opening for the Jackson 5 throughout the U.S. in 1973. New York City was an overnight sensation.

But like many groups, their success evaporated overnight as well. They followed "I'm Doin' Fine Now" with two singles, "Make Me Twice the Man," which only went to #93, and "Quick, Fast, in a Hurry," which topped out at #79 in early 1974. All three of the singles were included on their debut album, also called *I'm Doin' Fine Now*, and despite their faltering singles sales, Chelsea backed them for another album in 1974, *Soulful Road*. Despite the fact that the album cover was homage to the Beatles' "Abbey Road," there was no comparison with that album in terms of sales, and in fact no singles from the second album charted. The group disbanded shortly thereafter.

Billy Ocean

BEACH MUSIC DISCOGRAPHY: "Love Really Hurts Without You" (Ariola 7621, 1976: Billboard Pop #22).

Born Leslie Sebastian Charles in Trinidad, the man who would become Billy Ocean moved to England with his parents and five brothers and sisters around 1960. His father was a singer, and after a friend of his mother's bought him a ukulele when he was young he started to entertain the idea of becoming a musician. He had started writing lyrics when he was 13, and by the time he finished school he joined a band, despite the fact that his parents hoped he'd be an engineer. He did session work, and in 1971 he had the chance to record a single on Spark, "Nashville Rain," under the name Les Charles; neither that record nor his next release on Spark, 1972's "Reach Out a Hand" did anything on the charts. Ocean had started working with a producer named Ben Findon when he doing session work, and Findon called him in to sing lead on a single, 1974's "On the Run." While it didn't chart either, it got the two working together and writing together. When he was signed by the GTO label in 1975, he and Findon collaborated on "Love Really Hurts Without You," his first release as Billy Ocean and his first release for the label.

Written by Ocean and Findon, the song was as close as anything in the '70s came to sounding like a '60s Motown production. Though an upbeat dance track, the vocals expressed love and loss in a bold uncompromising way. The song was released by Ariola in the United States and went to #22 on the pop charts, although it was in the Top 10 in most countries around the world. Like mid '70s releases by the O'Jays, Jerry Butler, The Trammps, and others, "Love Really Hurts Without You" was released at a time when those solid beach hits of the '50s and '60s were no longer being produced and a good dance R&B song that could be shagged to—even if it was a little fast—was a commodity. The record took off in beach clubs in the South and was one of the biggest of the new wave of beach songs of the '70s.

Ocean's follow-up, "L.O.D. (Love on Delivery)," did have some chart life, even if it was not as significant as "Love Really Hurts Without You," and was another song on which Ocean and Findon worked together. In the late '70s however his releases were sporadic, and after a few years of very little chart action despite eleven post "Love Really Hurts Without You" releases, Ocean was in danger of going the way of many artists who after a little chart success flame out never to be heard from again. He signed with the Jive label in 1983, and suddenly the hits started coming. He started working with producers such as 'Mutt' Lange and Keith Diamond, and starting with 1984's "Caribbean Queen" he had seven top-10 pop hits in the U.S, including three #1's—"Caribbean Queen," "There'll Be Sad Songs (To Make You Cry)," and "Get Outta My Dreams, Get into My Car." He won a Grammy for Best Male R&B Vocal in 1985, two American Music Awards in 1986, performed at the American Live Aid Concert.

By the end of the 1980s, Ocean decided to go into semi-retirement for a few years to concentrate on spending time with his family. He has only recorded sporadically since then.

Lenny O'Henry

BEACH MUSIC DISCOGRAPHY: "Across the Street" (Atco 6291, 1963: Billboard Pop #98).

Buffalo New York native Danny Cannon began his career as a founding member of the Vibra-Harps in 1955, and along with Donnie Elbert, Charles Hargro, and Donald Simmons (some sources list Douglas Gibson as a founding member as well), the group recorded the group their first single, "Walk Beside Me," for the New York based Beech label in 1958. Apparently the group had a disagreement right before they recorded the song and Elbert opted not to sing on the record. Elbert soon left the group, and would go on to record eight singles as a solo artist on Deluxe in the next two years alone and would eventually find fame as a songwriter ("Open the Door to Your Heart" for Darrell Banks) and performer in his own right. In the meantime the remaining group members recorded the singles "The Only Love of Mine" for Fury and "It Must Be Magic" for Atco, though neither release was successful on the national charts.

Failing to find any sustainable success, the group would break up and reunite several times. Occasionally Hagro would work as Elbert's driver, and one occasion Cannon and Simmons performed as a duet called "Danny and Donnie." But when they re-formed to perform as a group their sound was improving, and eventually Berry Gordy, Jr., heard about them, auditioned them, and attempted to sign them to Motown. Apparently contractual obligations their management had entered into prohibited this, and so instead they signed with ABC-Paramount. Just as it seemed they were finally clicking as a group, ABC apparently decided that Cannon should be billed as frontman, his name should be Lenny O'Henry, and the backing group (i.e. The Vibraharps) would be called The Short Stories. Though the group cut the single "Cheated Heart," a song Cannon had written, it would be their last recording together.

The producer for "Cheated Heart" was Bob Crewe, who would become a mentor of sorts for the newly christened performer Lenny O'Henry. O'Henry and Crewe co-wrote O'Henry's next release, "Mr. Moonlight," for the Smash label (on some copies the recording is credited to Lenny O. Henry), but the name didn't seem to matter as the record did nothing. O'Henry signed with Atco in 1963, and in 1964 he released "Across the Street," his claim to beach music fame. By this time Crewe was producing the Four Seasons, who by 1963 had already had three #1 hits produced and co-written by Crewe and Bob Gaudio. "Across the Street" was co-written by Crewe and Charlie Calello, who arranged many of the Four Seasons big hits. Calello also arranged "Across the Street," and perhaps the pièce de résistance was that they had the Four Seasons to do the male backing vocals. The song was a fantastic recording, so much so that in his book *The Heart of Rock & Soul: The 1001 Greatest Singles Ever Made*, rock critic Dave Marsh lists "Across the Street" at #782—not a bad all-time listing for record which was under the radar nationally. Marsh says the record's appeal lies in O'Henry's unexplained banishment from the party across the street where his girl is dancin' and romancin' and his mournful promise to get her back.

Yet for all the talent assembled, and the accolades that followed, the recording barely registered nationally. The single stalled at #98 during its one week stay on the charts, and then disappeared from sight. Sadly, it would be O'Henry's most successful record, though not for lack of effort by Crewe and company. His next release on Atco in 1964 would be "Sweet Young Love," co-written by Crewe and his partner on so many Four Seasons hits, Bob Gaudio, and once again arranged by Calello. Even with the hottest producing, writing, and arranging ensemble in the business, the record didn't chart. It would be O'Henry's last original recording; a 1967 re-release of "Across the Street" backed with "Saturday Angel" wouldn't even fare as well as it had the first time.

O'Henry wasn't around to promote the second release in 1967, as he retired from the music business in 1965. He died of cancer in Buffalo in 2014.

The O'Jays

BEACH MUSIC DISCOGRAPHY: "Lonely Drifter" (Imperial 5976, 1963: Billboard Pop #93); "I Dig Your Act" (Bell 691, 1967: Did Not Chart); "Deeper (In Love with You)" (Neptune 22, 1970: Billboard Pop #64); "Used to Be My Girl" (Philadelphia International 3642, 1978: Billboard Pop #4).

Eddie Levert, Walter Williams, William Powell, Bobby Massey and Bill Isles were students at McKinley High School in Canton, Ohio, when they formed a group called the Triumphs in 1957. They changed their name to the Mascots in 1960, and it was under this name that they recorded a couple of non-charting singles in 1960 on the King label. They next did "Miracles" for the Apollo label in 1961, a single which reportedly impressed Cleveland DJ Eddie O'Jay enough that he advised the band about their music and how to get their name out there. After a couple more releases as the Mascots on the Little Star label, they decided to rename themselves the O'Jays in his honor. Apollo folded in 1962, and Little Star in 1963, so the group signed with Imperial that year. After re-releasing an earlier Little Star release called "How Does it Feel" which failed to make any noise, their next single, 1963's "Lonely Drifter," was the spark they were looking for. The Levert and Williams-penned song opened with an intro similar to that the Tymes had used on their earlier 1963 release, "So Much in Love" (see the entry for the Tymes) with the sound of seabirds and waves crashing on the beach. The O'Jays' version, led by Levert's mournful singing, was not as successful as the Tymes' ocean-intro release, which had gone to #1, but it did make the Hot 100 at #93 and as such was the group's first chart record.

The group followed up with four more non-charting singles over the next two years on Imperial until they released another single that had ties to beach music, a 1965 cover version of Benny Spellman's "Lipstick Traces." This record was actually more successful than "Lonely Drifter," going to #28 on the R&B charts and #48 on the pop charts, and as such charted slightly higher than Spellman's original release; these singles both appeared on their 1965 debut album, *Comin' Through*. They had two more low charting releases on Imperial, and they also released a cover of the Commands' beach favorite "No Time for You" in 1966 which did not chart.

Bill Isles left the group, and as a quartet the O'Jays left Imperial and moved to Bell records. There the group scored their first top ten hit on the R&B chart, a song called "I'll Be Sweeter Tomorrow (Than I Was Today)." It was the flipside, however, "I Dig Your Act," which would become one of the biggest beach music hits of the classic era. Written by Robert and Richard Poindexter, who wrote the Persuaders' hit "A Thin Line Between Love and Hate" and many other songs, on this single Levert once again sings lead on a classic that is also considered a Top 500 Northern Soul song as well. Four more releases on Bell failed to equal their first release however, and they moved to songwriters and producers Kenny Gamble and Leon Huff's new Neptune label in 1969. Though the label would only release a little more than 20 singles in two years, the O'Jays would be their most successful act, recording such mainstays as "One Night Affair," "Looky Looky," "Christmas Just Ain't Christmas," all of which at various times have been embraced by shaggers. The most successful of their Neptune efforts on the pop charts was 1970's "Deeper (In Love with You)." Written by Gamble and Huff, it reached #64 on the Billboard pop charts and #21 on the R&B charts.

Having failed to have any real sustainable chart success in more than a decade and having not once made the pop Top 40, the group was reduced to a trio in the early 1970s when Massey left. Levert, Williams, and Powell signed with Gamble and Huff's new Philadelphia International label in 1972 and their first release, "Backstabbers," brought them the success that had long eluded them. It went to #1 on the R&B charts and #3 on the pop charts, and after "Love Train" topped both the R&B and pop charts in 1973 the group was soon considered one of R&B's biggest acts. Five more singles topped the R&B charts over the next four years, followed by a sixth in 1978, "Used to Be My Girl." Written by Gamble and Huff, the song was a departure from the more raucous, funk-infused O'Jays hits of the '70s, and no doubt it was the single's throw back, doo-wop influenced sound that made it one of the biggest beach music hits of the decade. The single sold more than a million copies, was #1 on the R&B chart for five weeks and was #4 on the pop charts, and it helped propel their *So Full of Love* album to platinum status. Three years later the Four Tops followed the O'Jays lead and recorded the very similar sounding "When She Was My Girl," which was predictably big in beach music circles as well.

"Used to Be My Girl" was the group's last super hit, though nearly three dozen chart records followed. The group had faced a serious setback when William Powell was diagnosed with cancer in 1975, and after he passed away in 1977 he was replaced by Sammy Strain (of Little Anthony & the Imperials). Strain remained with the group until 1992, when he was replaced by Nathaniel Best, who was replaced by Eric Grant. Grant. Levert and Williams continue to perform together to this day. The O'Jays were inducted into the Vocal Group Hall of Fame in 2004, and the Rock and Roll Hall of Fame in 2005.

The O'Kaysions

BEACH MUSIC DISCOGRAPHY: "Girl Watcher" (ABC 11094, 1968: Billboard Pop #5); "Love Machine" (ABC 11153, 1968: Billboard Pop #77); "Little Miss Flirt" (Album Cut, 1968: Did Not Chart).

The O'Kaysions started in Wilson, North Carolina, in the '60s as The Kays, though by 1968 Donnie Weaver, Wayne Pittman, Ron Turner, Jim Spiedel, Jimmy Hinnant and Bruce Joyner had changed their name to the O'Kaysions because "in order to play in the clubs up north, you had to become a union member," Pittman said. "You had to register your band's name, and there was a DJ in New York named Murray the K, and we couldn't register our name because it was too similar to his. So we coined the name O'Kaysions so we could try to maintain our identity in North and South Carolina, Georgia and Virginia where we played, so people would still know who we were."

Their first recording under the new name was "Girl Watcher," the Pittman-penned tune they would record for the tiny North State label in 1968. According to Pittman, "We used to play down at Atlantic Beach a lot, and when we got back home people would say, 'Did you meet any girls this weekend?'" O'Kaysions founder Wayne Pittman told the author. "I'd say, 'I didn't meet any, but I sure do like to watch them.'" It was from this simple concept that "Girl Watcher," the O'Kaysions' 1968 million-selling hit, was born. Eventually one of the band members said, "'Wayne, you're the writer, why don't you write a song called "I'm a Girl Watcher."' What was funny was that about a month before I had written a tune and I hadn't even thought about putting any words to it yet. But when he made that comment, it was like a lightbulb went off in my head. I said, 'Okay, I will, I'll go back and write it, and I'll be back next week,' and that's exactly what I did. I wrote it in two nights that week. There was this great-looking girl that ran by my house every afternoon after work, and I'd be at home, and she'd go by when I was writing. That helped a lot too."

The catchy tune was played regionally almost nonstop, and soon it came to the attention of ABC Records, which decided to pick up distribution. Despite a story that circulated that someone at North State had lost the master tapes and so the ABC single had to be dubbed from the original 45, Pittman says "The ABC people flew down from New York, met the owners of NorthState and took the tapes back. They had and still have the master tapes." The song

The O'Kaysions, circa mid–1960s (photograph courtesy Wayne Pittman).

did well, going to #5 on the charts, and eventually it reached gold record status with one million sales by December 1968.

ABC rushed them into the studio to do an album, but Pittman says it wasn't as good as it could have been because "ABC wanted something quick and something fast, and we had to do the whole album in two days. It just wasn't a good product." One album cut that garnered some notice on the beach music scene was "Little Miss Flirt," which was not released as a single at the time though it saw a regional release in 1984. "Love Machine," from the same album, was released as a single, and it did chart at #76. But nothing else the group recorded registered on the charts, and Pittman believes this may have been partly due to Atlanta promoter Bill Lowery:

> The North State people thought they had the right to sign us to any booking agency they wanted to. They signed us with Lowery without our knowledge, and he was supposed to book us, and this was even before "Girl Watcher" charted. But Lowery just wasn't booking us enough, and we cancelled our agreement with him. We then signed with Associated Booking in New York City. Well, Lowery had a lot of power and contacts in the industry, and the word we got was that he put the kiss of death on us. So we promoted the record and made it a hit, but ABC wouldn't put a lot of money behind us after that.

Consequently, after those little-heard singles on ABC and then a couple on Cotillion, by the early 1970s the group was done.

Eventually, Pittman decided it was time to get out of the music business. "That period was the beginning of the psychedelic and acid rock scene, and 'Girl Watcher' had been an anomaly. Everywhere we played, the acid rock groups would go on, with all the noise and distortion, and there were the drugs all around, and I just didn't want to go in that direction. I knew I'd burn myself out if I stayed in it, so I just stopped performing." But by the 1980s he had re-formed the group, and The O'Kaysions are active to this day and perform throughout the South.

Patty & the Emblems

BEACH MUSIC DISCOGRAPHY: "Mixed Up, Shook Up, Girl" (Herald 590, 1964: Billboard Pop #37).

Though often categorized as a "girl group" due to the fact that Patty & the Emblems peaked when true girl groups such as the Ronettes, Dixie Cups, the Shirelles, Sapphires and others were popular, only strong voiced lead singer Patty Russell was a female. Patty & the Emblems were a Camden, New Jersey act formed by lead singer Russell who was backed by Eddie Watts, Vance Walker and Alexander Wildes.

After signing with Herald records, their first release was a song co-written by fellow Camden native Leon Huff. Huff, who in a few short years would partner with Kenny Gamble and would go on to write "Cowboys to Girls" for the Intruders, "Love Train" and "Backstabbers" for the O'Jays, "Only the Strong Survive" for Jerry Butler and many, many more, was at the time a struggling artist who was more or less unknown. Cranking out songs

while working primarily as a pianist, he wrote "Mixed Up, Shook Up, Girl" which would be his first songwriting credit to chart. It would also be Patty & the Emblems first and only Top 40 record, peaking at #37 on the charts. Their next two releases were 1964's "The Sound of Music Makes Me Want to Dance" (another Huff-penned tune) and "And We Danced," and neither record did anything, nor did a couple of the flipsides Huff had written. The group then did one single for the Congress label in 1966 before signing with Kapp for four releases including their 1968 release "I'm Gonna Love You a Long, Long Time." Like many '60s soul artists, their work actually found more of a following in England, and Northern Soul expert Kev Roberts ranks "I'm Gonna Love You a Long, Long Time" as the #38 record on his Top 500 Northern Soul records of all time. The song was also the last single the group ever recorded.

Patty Russell got married, and the group dispersed and went its separate ways though all but Russell apparently stayed in the music business. Listening to the group's music today, it's apparent that though Russell had a good voice and Watts, Wildes, and Walker were competent backups, the group really never found their sound. Their recordings all sound very different from one another, and perhaps record buyers were looking for a definable consistency that the group's records simply didn't offer. Russell passed away in 1998.

Freda Payne

BEACH MUSIC DISCOGRAPHY: "Band of Gold" (Invictus 9075,1970: Billboard Pop #3).

Freda Payne's career in entertainment started when she won several amateur singing contests in her hometown of Detroit when she was in her early teens. When she was 14 her talent brought her to the attention of a young Berry Gordy, who Payne says "had seen me on television on Ed Mckenzie's *Dance Hour*, Detroit's equivalent to *American Bandstand*. The show had teenagers dancing to top records, and he also had guests who would perform a couple of songs. I'd also been singing with the Jimmy Wilkins Orchestra, and I'd been singing on the radio on Don Large's *Makeway for Youth* show. So Berry heard about me, and that drew his attention to me."

Payne notes however that although when you think of Berry Gordy, Jr., "you think of a pioneer in the recording industry, Motown founder and a very prosperous man, but back then Berry didn't have substantial funding or a record company, just a lot of ambition to manage artists and to get his own record label." Gordy wrote some songs for Payne, and he took her to the United Sound studios were they recorded the songs. "Then he, my mother and I all drove to New York. He wanted to get a deal on Roulette records, and because he got a positive response he wanted to sign me to a managerial contract. My mother, who was not a pushover, was not receptive—they couldn't agree on terms. I think had he been more modest in his demands she would have said okay." Without a record deal Payne continued to perform locally, and when she turned 18 she moved to New York and signed with ABC-Paramount. Between 1962 and 1966 she released two singles on ABC–Paramount, one on Impulse, and one on MGM, and none made the charts.

But things were soon to change:

> In 1968, a friend called me and said "an old friend of yours from Detroit, Brian Holland, is sitting here with me and he wants you to come over." I had gone to high school with Brian, but by that time he was part of the Holland, Dozier, and Holland songwriting team and they were famous. When I got there, he asked me if I was under contract or anything. Well as it happened my contract was just up and so was my management contract, so I was literally free of any contractual obligations. So Brian said, "Would you like to come with us? We just left Motown and formed our own label called Invictus." I flew to Detroit and that was it.

Her second single for Invictus was "Band of Gold," and "to be honest, I thought the lyrics were a little strange," Payne said. "I mean, why would a young girl on her wedding night want to stay in another room? The lyrics say 'that night on our honeymoon/we stayed in separate rooms.' What's up with that?" Though it has been reported that Payne didn't want to do the song, she said "I was going to do it whether I liked it or not. I just told them, 'This is for a fifteen-year-old or something—it's so immature.'"

The song benefited not only from Payne's dynamic vocals and the writing of Holland, Dozier, and Holland but also from the presence of Motown's famous Funk Brothers on backup, the then relatively unknown Ray Parker, Jr., on lead guitar and backups Joyce Vincent Wilson and Telma Hopkins, both of whom would be the "Dawn" in Tony Orlando and Dawn less than a year later. Also, Payne's sister Scherrie and several members of the Originals were there, so it was a veritable who's who of talent in the studio. It all paid off, as "Band of Gold" climbed to #3 on the Billboard charts and went to #1 in the UK. "My career took off," Payne said. "I started getting requests for interviews, getting booked on TV shows, my salary went up, everything was suddenly better." "Band of Gold" was followed by a number of Invictus singles, the highest-charting being "Bring the Boys Home," which reached #12 in 1971. She continued to record, but at the same time with her considerable talent she diversified and branched out into television, movies and Broadway too. Over the years she has hosted her own television show called *Today's Black Woman*, acted in movies, and even appeared on *American Idol*. "Regardless of what else I've done, I was educated on a musical basis by singing standards and jazz and show tunes, so what sustained me after the hit records faded out was the fact that I could still work and do other things like Broadway and theater. I've reinvented myself. But 'Band of Gold' started all that."

Teddy Pendergrass

BEACH MUSIC DISCOGRAPHY: "I Don't Love You Anymore" (Philadelphia International 3622 1977, Billboard Pop #41).

Theodore DeReese Pendergrass, Jr., was born in Kingstree, S.C., and moved to Philadelphia while an infant. He was raised by his mother and both attended church frequently, and consequently he was singing in church before he was three years old. He started a youth ministry when he was 10, but it was his vocal abilities led him to join the Philadelphia Boys Choir and later the All City School Choir. When he was 13 he taught himself to play the drums, and while working as a waiter when he was 18 he joined his first band. From that point on he played in several R&B groups, the last of which was a Philadelphia group named The Cadillacs (though not the Cadillacs of "Speedo" fame). Pendergrass was recruited by another local group, the Blue Notes, to play in their back-up band, but founder Harold Melvin had Pendergrass replace lead singer when John Atkins when he left the group. At this point the group consisted of Pendergrass and Melvin as well as Bernie Wilson, Lawrence Brown, and Lloyd Parks, and soon renamed Harold Melvin and the Bluenotes they signed with Melvin's old friend Kenny Gamble's Philadelphia International records in 1972. Their first release for the label was "I Miss You," and with Pendergrass singing lead the ballad went to #7 on the R&B and #58 on the pop charts. Their next song however, "If You Don't Know Me by Now," topped the R&B charts and went to #3 on the pop charts, and would be the group's big breakthrough at long last (see the entry for Harold Melvin and the Blue Notes). The group would have a number of hits with Pendergrass singing lead, including "The Love I Lost" and "Bad Luck," but by 1975 Pendergrass felt that although he was handling lead on most songs he wasn't being paid accordingly. He left the group, and Pendergrass signed with Philadelphia International as a solo act while the Blue Notes signed with ABC; Melvin's Blue Notes had only very limited success thereafter.

Pendergrass was extremely successful on his own. His first four albums as a solo artist went platinum, and his first album, *Teddy Pendergrass*, included his debut single release "I Don't Love You Anymore." Written by Kenny Gamble and Leon Huff, the single surprisingly stalled at #41 on the pop charts, though it did go to #5 on the R&B charts. Though extremely uptempo for a beach song, it did find an audience with collegiate shaggers in the late 1970s.

While Pendergrass would go on to have nearly three dozen chart records, his music would always perform better on the R&B charts than the pop charts. He'd have ten Top 10 R&B hits, including the #1s "Close the Door" (1978), "Joy" (1988), and "It Should Have Been You" (1991), but "Close the Door" would be his highest pop chart record, coming in at #25. In 1982 he was paralyzed from the waist down in an automobile accident, and at the time he arguably the biggest male solo act in R&B. He already had two albums recorded for Philadelphia International which were released in 1982 and 1983, and neither did particularly well and he parted ways with the label at that point. His next album was 1984's *Love Language*, and released on the Asylum label it went gold. He would continue to chart before retiring from the music business in 2006. In 2009 he was treated for colon cancer, and in 2010 he passed away from respiratory failure at the age of 59.

The Penguins

BEACH MUSIC DISCOGRAPHY: "Ookey Ook" (Dootone 353, 1954); "Baby Let's Make Some Love" (Dootone 362, 1954)

The Los Angeles–based group got their start when Curtis Williams, Dexter Tisby, Bruce Tate, and Cleveland Duncan came together to form the Penguins, so-named after Willie the Penguin, the advertising mascot for Kool cigarettes. Curtis had been working on a song he had written called "Earth Angel" and the group decided that they needed to find a label and record the track. They signed with Walter "Dootsie" Williams' Dootone records in 1954, and Williams released a demo track by the group before they recorded "Hey Senorita" backed by "Earth Angel," which was released in September of 1954. Though "Hey Senorita" was originally the designated A side, "Earth Angel" started to get played and began to climb the charts.

"Earth Angel" would eventually rise to #8 on the pop charts and #1 on the R&B charts, but as was the tendency in the 1950s, because the song was by a black group, it was also covered by a white group, the Crew Cuts, and their version went to #3 on the pop charts. Despite that, the Penguins version is considered the standard, and one of the classic songs of the 1950s.

Already the group was becoming increasingly frustrated with Dootone over royalty payments, and so they decided to let Buck Ram manage them and find them another label. Although Dootsie Williams told the group they'd lose the "Earth Angel" royalties if they went with Ram, they figured they would be successful enough that losing those royalties wouldn't make much of a difference in the long run. As one of the hottest groups in the country, Ram had no problem signing the group with Mercury, and in a package deal he also leveraged Mercury to sign the Platters who were at the time unknown and hitless. In the meantime "Earth Angel" was moving up the charts (on Dootone), the Penguins were playing all the big venues including the Apollo, and seemed poised for even greater success.

Almost forgotten in all the controversy were four more tracks they had recorded for Dootone, including two that have been embraced by the beach music community, "Ookey Ook" and "Baby Let's Make Some Love." "Ookey Ook" was designed to be a dance craze tune along the lines of the Stroll, the Twist, and the Harlem Shuffle, all of which came later. The idea was for the group to waddle like Penguins, and though there was even a Dootone-sponsored dance contest in Los Angeles, the Penguins weren't there. After the falling out with Dootone, the label seemed disinclined to put a great deal of effort into promoting a record by an artist now signed to another label. The same applied to their next release and the last on Dootone during this period of their careers. Neither record was a hit.

From this point on, the Penguins story was one of lawsuits, squabbling, and controversy. The group actually re-recorded "Ookey Ook" on Mercury, but it was never released due to lawsuits. Curtis Williams sued Dootsie Williams over the copyright of "Earth Angel," and shortly afterwards Dootsie Williams sued Mercury and Buck Ram for coercing the Penguins into breaking their Dootone contract. Singer/songwriter Jessie Belvin sued Dootsie Williams saying that he (Jessie) had actually written "Earth Angel" and asking for royalties. It would take years to straighten it all out, but in the end the Penguins never had another pop chart hit despite recording more than fifty songs and recording for not only Dootone and Mercury, but later Atlantic, Sun State, and Original Sound. Though the group never officially disbanded, after 1962 they ceased to record for any label and existed as performers only.

The Platters

BEACH MUSIC DISCOGRAPHY: "I Love You 1,000 Times" (Musicor 1166, 1966: Billboard Pop #31); "With This Ring" (Musicor 1229, 1967: Billboard Pop #14); "Washed Ashore" (Musicor 1251, 1967: Billboard Pop #56).

After several personnel changes, by the mid–1950s The Platters (formerly The Flamingos) consisted of Tony Williams, David Lynch, Herb Reed, Paul Robi and Zola Taylor. While that group had cut a number of early singles, none of them really did much on the charts although "Only You" did make some noise regionally. They got their first break when manager Buck Ram took the group to Mercury as a condition to signing the then-better-known Penguins (see the entry for the Penguins) in 1955, and so Mercury decided since they had the group they'd try "Only You" as a national release. Once released nationally, it soared to #5 on the pop charts and #1 on the R&B charts, and their next single, "The Great Pretender," became their first #1 pop hit. With Williams on lead, between 1955 and 1960 the group churned out some of the greatest hits of the 1950s, including "My Prayer" (#1, 1956), "Twilight Time" (#1, 1958), "Smoke Gets in Your Eyes" (#1, 1958) and many, many more.

After a period of sustained success, Williams, who as early as 1954 had tried to get Ram

The Platters, 1966 (photograph courtesy Sonny Turner).

to manage him as a solo act, decided to go out on his own in 1959. Ram brought in Sonny Turner, formerly of the Metrotones, as the group's new lead. The group tried to weather the departure of other key members over the next few years but the hits stopped coming, and by 1963 their records were no longer even making the charts. Mercury seemed determined, however, to keep trying to have them do the same type of material that had worked for them in the '50s, and for a while it looked like the Platters were destined to become just another oldies act. Nevertheless, Turner says the group knew they needed to update their sound. "We felt the change coming" Turner told me. "The Beatles hit and then they had Motown, and we felt the whole format of the rhythm and blues era was changing. The soul mixed with the R&B and pop music—the writers were beginning to combine the sounds. The music scene was shifting." Fortunately Turner had the voice and charisma to make it all work, and along with Lynch and Reed, and new members Nate Nelson and Sandra Dawn, the group reinvented itself to adapt to the changing music scene. They left Mercury in 1965 and went to Musicor, where in 1966 they released the smooth and soulful "I Love You 1,000 Times."

"Inez Foxx and Luther Dixon came up with 'I Love You 1,000 Times,'" Turner told me. "They felt we needed another hit, and they asked Buck to give it me." The group worked on the song, though initially not everyone agreed on how the song should be sung. Luther Dixon told Turner, "'Just sing it like you feel it,' but Buck wanted me to sing it a different way. Luther said, 'Buck, you're thinking old school, old fashioned, the music's changing—Sonny has a feel for it—let him sing it the way he feels it.' So I sang it my way and from the heart. Afterward, Luther told me, 'That's it—you nailed it.' And sure enough—bam!—hit record." The song reached #31 on the charts and was the group's first hit in years. A couple of releases later, 1967's "With This Ring" was another bona fide hit. "Richard 'Popcorn' Wylie came up with 'With This Ring,' and this was yet another move toward that new sound," Turner said. "On this song I came into my own—I didn't have to mimic Tony Williams. We wanted a brassy song and sound and bam!— another hit record." Charting at #14, it was their first Top 20 tune since 1960, and suddenly they were a hot national act once again. Their very next release was the classic "Washed Ashore," and Turner said that when Wylie wrote it "He was thinking in terms of summertime and the beach, and we took the song into the studio and we nailed it. I said, 'Hell yeah! I like this. Another hit.'" And though it didn't make a huge impact on the charts, stalling at #56, as one of those "beach music about the beach" songs it has been a fan favorite for decades.

But the group's resurgence was brief, and after a couple of additional minor chart "hits," the group once more faded into the background. It wasn't so much because of the group, however, and Turner thinks it was due more to their management. "Buck Ram had a few hits under his belt, and he thought he was Svengali. I always feel like had Buck stayed out of the way, we might have had four or five more hits, but as it was, that was it." Soon the group splintered again, with Turner himself leaving eventually. But despite their long and storied chart history, beach music audiences consider those Musicor tunes the Platters' greatest achievements, no matter what they might have done in the years before.

The Poets

BEACH MUSIC DISCOGRAPHY: "She Blew a Good Thing" (Symbol 214, 1966: Billboard Pop #45); "So Young (And So Innocent)" (Symbol 216, 1966: Did Not Chart).

The Poets who sang "She Blew a Good Thing" and "So Young (And So Innocent)" were Ronnie Lewis, Melvin Bradford, Paul Fulton, and Johnny James, a Brooklyn-based group who would eventually sign with Charleston, South Carolina born Henry "Juggy Murray" Jones's Symbol records in New York. Although Fulton had been the bass singer with the Chips of "Rubber Biscuit" fame and would also sing with the Invitations, Blue Chips, and the Velours, the rest of the group doesn't seem to have had extensive experience in the industry. In 1966 the Poets would release three singles on Symbol, and the first, "She Blew a Good Thing," co-written by Ronnie Lewis and Murray, was their only chart record, topping out at #45 on the pop charts and #2 on the R&B charts. Another well-loved song along the Carolina coast was "So Young (And So Innocent)," though it did not chart. After their third 1966 release, "I'm

Particular," a *Billboard* magazine article of May 28, 1966, says the group followed with a tour of Baltimore, Pittsburgh, Memphis, Richmond, and other venues, to culminate in an appearance at the Apollo Theater in New York. But aside from those three 1966 releases and the subsequent tour, very little is known about the group or what happened to them after that. It seems the group simply dissolved.

The song was released in England as by The American Poets, to avoid confusion with another Poets group from England. Further adding to the confusion was that there was also another American group known as the Poets who cut one single on Flash, and this Los Angeles–based group consisted of Roy Ayers, James Bedford, Sherman Clark, Robert Griffett, and Frederick Nance. *Another* Poets group was from New York was recording on Leiber and Stoller's Red Bird label. Tony Silvester, Luther Simmons and Donald McPherson would later change their name to the Insiders, and later re-emerge as the Main Ingredient. After McPherson's death in 1971 they would add Cuba Gooding, Sr., and would go on to have hits such as "Just Don't Want to Be Lonely" and "Everybody Plays the Fool" (see the entry for the Main Ingredient). None of these groups were the Poets who recorded "She Blew a Good Thing" however, though they have often been confused. In short, other than some superficial information about the group and the song much about their identity is still a mystery—and after the passage of almost 50 years is likely to remain so.

Tower of Power

BEACH MUSIC DISCOGRAPHY: "This Time It's Real"(Warner 7733, 1973: Billboard Pop #65); "You Ought to Be Havin' Fun" (Columbia 3–10409, 1976: Billboard Pop #68).

Detroit-born Emilio Castillo moved to Freemont, California when he was 11, and his entrance into the world of music came as the result of a mistake he made as a child when he, his brother, and a friend got caught shoplifting. After getting the situation straightened out with the store manager their father told the boys they had to come up with some way to occupy their time and stay out of trouble—or else. They chose music, and Castillo says he picked his instrument because "I'd noticed that the guy who always seemed to get all the attention [in a band] was the guy who played the sax. So when he took us to the store and told us we could have any instrument we wanted, I pointed to the sax. We started the band that day, and I've had a band ever since. But it's not like we practiced for years and joined a band; we started the band, *then* learned to play the instruments." Their father's investment in his children's future would pay off well. They started out covering soul and R&B songs and called themselves The Motowns, but when Castillo added Doc Kupka to the band, Kupka said he believed they could do more than cover tunes. "He said 'what you're doing with these soul tunes is amazing, and I like how you make them your own. But you need to write your own songs.' I don't think that ever would have occurred to me, but I thought we could give it a try, and the first song we wrote was "You're Still a Young Man." We had an audition at the Fillmore, where everyone was trying to get signed by Bill Graham, who had two labels, and he decided to sign us, and that's where it all started."

Tower of Power, circa 1973 (photograph courtesy Emilio Castillo).

"You're Still a Young Man" would go to #29 on the charts in 1972, and in 1973 they'd release their biggest hit, "So Very Hard to Go" (#17). Lenny Williams was by then lead vocalist for the group, and his contributions made not only "So Very Hard to Go" a big hit, but in fact the album it was taken from, *Tower of Power*, went to #15 on the album charts and earned a gold record. The album's sales were also helped by another chart record, the now classic "This Time It's Real." "David Bartlett was the main guy who wrote the song. David had an amazing aptitude for writing, but when he brought it to us he had less than half of the tune written. He had the chorus, the chords, and the first verse. He brought it to us, and we sat down and wrote that tune quick. We added the modulation—the way it goes (singing)—"And I know, I can feel it, this time it's real. And I know, I can feel it…" You know the way it goes up, and it goes down, and it goes up? And so we finished it, and were really happy with it" Castillo said. While the single only charted at #65 on the Hot 100, it did hit #27 on the R&B charts, and like many other beach music classics it found an audience in the southeast despite its failure to climb high on the national charts.

Several more big albums and hit singles would follow, and in 1976 the group would record another song that many beach music lovers have since adopted as a party-time anthem, "You Ought to Be Havin' Fun:"

> It was mainly written by Hubert Tubbs, who had replaced Lenny Williams in the group. He came to us started clapping his hands and singing "You ought to be havin fun," but that was really about all he had other than the line "put your troubles on the run" and the chant, "You ought to be, you ought to be! You ought to be, you ought to be!" So I wrote the tune, was really excited about it gave it to the band. The intro, that bass line, was directly inspired by the bass line intro on "Bad Luck" by Harold Melvin and the Blue Notes. I mean we didn't steal their line, we made up our own, but it was the inspiration.

Like "This Time It's Real," "You Ought to Be Havin' Fun" didn't chart very high either, going only to #68, and #62 on the R&B charts. "That song was one of my heartbreaks," Castillo says. "As a record producer, I felt like I missed the mark on that song. I'm usually good at getting to that place. I have the picture, and I get it there. But in that case, I felt like it fell short."

While "You Ought to Be Havin' Fun" would be the group's last chart single, today they still tour and play to packed houses everywhere, although they have frequently changed their lineup and have had at least 60 different members at one time or another. Though they primarily perform in the west and northeast they are "*very* aware of [beach music] now" according to Castillo, and are probably as popular today in the Carolinas as they ever have been.

Lloyd Price

BEACH MUSIC DISCOGRAPHY: "Stagger Lee" (ABC Paramount 9972, 1958: Billboard Pop #1).

Lloyd Price grew up in Kenner, Louisiana, and learned to play his mother's piano and his brother's flugelhorn in high school. His brother Leo formed a band and had Lloyd singing as frontman, and one of the group's most popular songs was one Lloyd had written, "Lawdy, Miss Clawdy," based on a catchphrase used by a New Orleans disk jockey. Fats Domino's songwriting associate Dave Bartholomew caught Price's act and suggested that Art Rupe of Specialty Records check him out; he did, and signed him to the label that day. Price recorded the Bartholomew produced "Lawdy Miss Clawdy" for Specialty with Domino on piano and by July 1952 it was #1 on the R&B charts and stayed there for seven weeks. His very next release on Speciality, "Oooh-Oooh-Oooh" went to #4 on the R&B charts that year, and even the record's flip side, "Restless Heart" charted as well, going to #5. In 1953 his next release, "Ain't It a Shame," entered the charts and rose to #6, dropped off the charts, reentered, and rose to #4 the second time around. By the time he was 20 Price had become a star.

When it seemed as if nothing could slow Price's momentum, the U.S. government drafted him for a tour of duty in Korea. Upon his return to the states he formed his own KRC label, setting up a distribution deal with ABC records whereby he leased his songs to ABC-Paramount while retaining control of the music and the rights to his songs. It was one of these ABC releases, "Stagger Lee," that would become his biggest hit and a favorite in beach music circles for decades to come. It was a remake of a "Stack-o-Lee"(also sometimes referred to a "Stagolee"), a song that had long been in the public consciousness and of which to date there are reportedly more than 400 recorded versions. The origins of the song are extensive, but the fundamental story is that in 1895 "Stag" Lee Shelton, a pimp in St. Louis, shot Billy Lyons to death while the two were drinking in a bar. Apparently versions of the song were being performed as early as the late 1890s, and it was first recorded in 1923 by a group called Waring's Pennsylvanians. Price had been performing the song long before he ever recorded it, and apparently enjoyed acting out the events of the song on stage. The song detailed Billy and Stagger Lee playing cards, and then Stagger Lee shooting Billy to death with a .44. With the more pop-like-than-normal backing vocals provided by the Ray Charles Singers, this time the song not only climbed high on the R&B charts, where it went all the way to #1, it climbed to #1 on the pop charts as well and became one of the biggest hits of 1959; it even spawned an "answer record" that year, "Return of Stagger Lee," released by Titus Turner which peaked at #29 on the R&B charts. The song was so big that Dick Clark asked Price to appear on *American Bandstand*, and in what seems a ridiculous case of censorship today, he asked Price to remove the gunplay from the lyrics for the television performance. Price did, with the result that Lee and Billy simply had an argument then patched up their differences (though that version was not a radio release, it did appear on an album years later). The result was a classic now considered the definitive version of the song, and Price's "Stagger Lee" is included in *Rolling Stone*'s list of the 500 Greatest Songs of All Time.

Price followed up with a series of impressive hits. "Where Were You (On Our Wedding Day)" (#4 R&B, #23 pop), "Personality" (#1 R&B, #2 pop), "I'm Gonna Get Married" (#1 R&B, #3 pop) and two more chart records followed in 1959; "Personality" was so successful that he gained his nickname "Mr. Personality" from the song. At that point Price was one of the best known performers in the music industry.

Few artists have ever had a year like Price had in 1959, and fewer still were able to maintain that momentum going forward; Price was no exception. He had four singles that performed moderately well in 1960, but from 1961 to 1976 he only had a total of five records make the R&B charts, only one of which made the pop charts. One of the cuts from his 1961 album *Lloyd Price Sings the Million Sellers* was "C'est Si Bon," a song written in 1947 and recorded almost as many times as "Stagger Lee" by artists such as Eartha Kitt, Louis Armstrong, Josephine Baker, Benny Goodman, and others. Price's English language version had that jazzy cocktail music sound in common with other versions, while retaining a hint of Price's R&B roots as well. The song was never released as a single and consequently was not regarded as beach music at the time, but in the late 20th century it gained some traction in the beach clubs as a shag song.

Price founded another record label, Double-L, but it folded in 1966. As time went on his recordings were selling fewer copies, and he moved in to the realm of investments and finance and became a successful businessman. With Don King he promoted boxing matches such as 1974's "Rumble in the Jungle" between Muhammad Ali and George Foreman, and 1975's "Thrilla in Manila" between Joe Frazier and Ali, and in the 1980s he developed low income housing for underprivileged families. As a result, despite his immense success as a singer, he was able to remain successful long after his initial success in music. Price was inducted into the Rock and Roll Hall of Fame in 1998.

Louis Prima and Keely Smith

BEACH MUSIC DISCOGRAPHY: "Just a Gigolo/I Ain't Got Nobody" (Capitol Album Cut, 1956: Did Not Chart).

Louis Prima was the second of four children born to Italian immigrants living in New Orleans. His mother arranged for each of the children to learn to play an instrument, and although Louis learned to play violin, as he grew older he became more interested in jazz and learned to play the coronet as well. He formed his first band when he was 14, and within a few years he was playing in New Orleans nightclubs. Eventually he set out for New York City, and now married he enjoyed some success recording as Louis Prima and His New Orleans Gang on some sides for Brunswick in the early 1930s, including his first chart record, "Chasing Shadows" which peaked at #14 in 1935. He followed up with three more chart records that year before setting out for Los Angeles to work as a headliner. Already divorced from his first wife, he married again in 1936, and he and his band toured the country trying to bring a new big-band style to audiences. By the 1940s he was recording for RCA, and exempt from the draft due to an injured leg he became more popular than ever during World War II. Prima divorced his second wife and remarried again, and despite his inability to maintain a successful marriage he was successful as an entertainer; during the 1940s he was one of the best-paid musicians in show business. By the late 1940s Big Band music was going out of style, but Prima was not against experimenting and he adapted his music to fit audience tastes rather than hold steadfastly to one style.

Although he was now in his 40s and had been immensely successful on the big band scene, the 1950s would be the period of his greatest success. He added then seventeen-year-old singer Keely Smith (born Dorothy Jacqueline Keely in Norfolk, Virginia) to his act in 1948, and by 1953 he had divorced this third wife and he married Smith that same year. He added saxophonist extraordinaire Sam Butera and his group The Witnesses to his act, and in Las Vegas they became the hottest performers in town, playing at the Sahara and the Desert Inn.

Prima signed with Capitol Records in 1955 and released his album *The Wildest!* in 1956. One cut from the album was a song Prima had written, "Jump, Jive, an' Wail," which would win Brian Setzer a Grammy for his cover version in 1999. But it was another cut from the album, "Just a Gigolo/I Ain't Got Nobody (And Nobody Cares for Me)," that would go on to be Prima's signature song and the one for which he is best known today, despite the fact that it was not released as a single at the time. The song was actually a combination of two old songs, "Just a Gigolo," adapted in 1929 from two even older songs, and "I Ain't Got Nobody," written in 1915. Prima had experimented with a combination of the two songs as early as the 1940s, but it was updated with his new '50s sound for his stage show. The song was so popular that thereafter many people assumed that songs were always actually just one song, and the success of David Lee Roth's version in 1985, which went to #12 on the charts, solidified the song's place in popular music.

Prima and Smith had a few more charts records and remained immensely successful in Las Vegas, but Prima's gambling, drinking, and womanizing led to the dissolution of their marriage and their act in 1961. Prima married again, and he continued to record and tried to make his music remain relevant throughout the 1960s and '70s, although perhaps his most notable success in the 1960s came as the voice of King Louie in Disney's animated *The Jungle Book* in 1967. After undergoing surgery for a brain tumor in 1975, he fell into a coma, and passed away in 1978.

James & Bobby Purify

BEACH MUSIC DISCOGRAPHY: "I'm Your Puppet" (Bell 648, 1966: Billboard Pop #6); "Wish You Didn't Have to Go" (Bell 660, 1967: Billboard Pop #38); "Let Love Come Between Us" (Bell 685, 1967: Billboard Pop #23).

In 1963 Robert Lee Dickey dropped by a Florida nightclub to see a performance by his cousin James Purify's group, the Dothan Sextet. The group's guitarist had quit that night, and Dickey joined them on stage to get them through their set. They asked him to join the group on a permanent basis, and by 1965 they were touring with and backing up the likes of Otis Redding, Wilson Pickett and James Brown. In 1966 producer "Papa Don" Schroeder heard the group and offered Purify and Dickey recording contracts. Schroder took them to Muscle Shoals to get some studio time, and he gave them a song called "I'm Your Puppet," written by Muscle Shoals mainstays Dan Penn and Spooner Oldham. Penn had released the song the year before and it had done nothing, but Schroeder felt it would be a good song for Dickey: "I don't think either one of them liked the song, because it wasn't R&B enough to suit [them]," Schroder told Bill Dahl in an interview. Furthermore, Dickey couldn't sing the song correctly, but when Purify took lead everything clicked. Nevertheless, the trial and error and experimentation made for a grueling session. Schroeder noted, "it was a twenty-something-hour session, 'cause we were cutting mono. You had to get it all in one time. I mean, it was just incredible. Then you've got to come back and do your overdubs." In a 2000 interview with the *Florida Democrat*, Dickey said of the song, "I hated it. It was originally intended to be the B-side. But things got changed…. I sang it for 23 hours straight (in the studio), that's why

I hate it. And the last one, the last take was the one they decided to go with." The two men had a song, and despite the fact that they hadn't signed to be a duo, they were rechristened James and Bobby Purify by Schroeder and released "I'm Your Puppet" in September 1966. It peaked at #5 on the R&B charts and #6 on the pop charts.

For their second single, they recorded "Wish You Didn't Have to Go," another Penn and Oldham song. Schroder said "It's a nice little record," but it "wouldn't have been my choice as the follow-up of 'I'm Your Puppet.' It's not on my 'Favorite records that I produced' list." The record was a moderate hit, climbing to #38 on the pop charts. For their next release, they covered the Five Du-Tones raucous hit "Shake a Tail Feather," which had hit #51 for that group in 1963. Schroeder says, "I thought I could cut a good record on it, and we did ... what a great, fun record. Melba Moore and Ellie Greenwich and I were out there in the studio beating our beer cans on a table ... screaming and having fun. I wanted to create a party environment." The record climbed to #25 on the pop charts. The group's next release didn't break into the Top 40, but their subsequent record, "Let Love Come Between Us," would be their second-biggest hit. Schroder said when heard the song he knew it was right for the duo and he chose it because "I was cutting a beach song." The original version had been recorded by an Alabama group called the Rubber Band, whose frontman, John Townsend, would later go on to fame with the Sanford Townsend Band (see the entry for the Sanford Townsend Band). The Rubber Band had recorded a demo of the song for CBS, but CBS didn't promote it, and Townsend said "some months later, James and Bobby Purify [did it]. When I heard their version on the radio, we knew it was us that should have had the big record." The Purifys' version went to #23 on the pop charts, and Schroder said he had achieved his goal of cutting "a real good beach hit. It's one of my favorite records that I cut on the Purifys."

It would be James and Bobby Purify's last Top 40 hit. The group would go on to record some moderately successful songs after that, but Dickey to quit by 1972. James Purify eventually brought in Ben Moore to sing as Bobby Purify, and though their re-recording of "I'm Your Puppet" in 1976 went to #12 in the UK, it was their last chart record. Dickey passed away in 2012.

The Radiants

BEACH MUSIC DISCOGRAPHY: "Voice Your Choice" (Chess 1904, 1964: Billboard Pop #51); "It Ain't No Big Thing" (Chess 1925, 1965: Billboard Pop #91); "Baby You Got It" (Chess 1954, 1966: Did Not Chart); "Hold On" (Chess 2037, 1968: Billboard Pop #68).

The Radiants had perhaps the most variable line up of any group in the annals of soul music. They got their start as youth choir singers in Chicago. Maurice McCallister not only put the group together but would also serve as one of two constants throughout most of the group's recordings—Wallace Sampson being the other. Other members at the start were Jerome Brooks, Elzie Butler and Charles Washington. They realized their future probably wasn't in gospel recordings, however, and they started trying to edge into the R&B market by 1961. They were turned down by a number of labels before Chess finally signed them, but even before they had their first recording, they had a personnel change, as Washington was replaced by Green McLauren.

Their first release, the 1962 single "Father Knows Best," did not chart, nor did the subsequent single "Heartbreak Society." On the next release, 1963's "Shy Guy," in another of many personnel changes Frank McCollum replaced Green McLauren, who had been drafted. From this point on, the lineup changed so often it is nearly impossible to accurately pin it down for more than a one-year period. After recording another failed single as Maurice and the Radiants in 1964, the group broke up. They almost immediately re-formed with just Sampson and McCallister from the previous group, and in 1964, with Leonard Caston, Jr., they recorded "Voice Your Choice" as a trio. It went to #51 on the Billboard Top 100 and #16 on the R&B charts. However, they finally seemed to have found the right blend of talent, and the result was their first chart hit. Chess also realized this trio had the perfect blend of voices and used them as backup singers on Tony Clarke's "The Entertainer" as well as Billy Stewart's "Sitting in the Park." "The Entertainer" was Chess catalogue #1924, and the Radiants' next single, "It Ain't No Big Thing," was the next record the label released at #1925. "It Ain't No Big Thing" was a mellow, harmonious-sounding song, with McCallister and Caston alternating as lead and Maurice White (later of Earth, Wind & Fire) on drums. The song has long been considered a canonical beach song, and although it only went to #91 on the Billboard charts, it actually outperformed "Voice Your Choice" on the R&B charts, getting as high as #14.

Changes were in store for the group yet again however, and after releasing one more single as a trio, in 1965 Caston left the group, then later McCallister left to pursue a solo career and record duets with Green McLauren beginning in 1967 as Maurice and Mac. McCallister, Sampson, and James Jameson made the next Radiants' recording as a trio, a song McCallister co-wrote, 1966's "Baby You Got It." This single had a sound quite different from previous single releases, with more of a hard driving Motown-like beat. With string accompaniment, a strong bass-line, and distinctive backing vocals by Minnie Riperton (who would eventually become a star in her own right), it may actually be the finest overall recording the group ever produced. It did not make the charts, however, and would be McCallister's last effort with the group. Subsequently, Chess decided to take "Don't It Make You Feel Kinda Bad," a single recorded by another group that had split up, the Confessions, and release it as a Radiants disc in 1966, and then the lead singer of that group, Mitchell Bullock, was teamed with Sampson, Jameson and Caston's brother Victor to create a new incarnation of the Radiants. The record did moderately well, and although it didn't make the pop chart, it did go to #47 on the R&B chart. At this point the group started working with Chess's Charles Stepney, who had just arranged two successful singles for the Dells, "There Is" and "Wear It On Our Face" (see the entry for the Dells). He arranged "Hold On" for the Radiants in much the same upbeat frenetic style. A great record that shows the group had moved a long way musically from their early recordings, it did a little better in 1968 by hitting #68 on the pop chart, but that was the end of their chart success, and they left Chess the next year. They broke up for good in 1972.

In a ten-year career that produced nearly twenty single recordings, the Radiants never released more than two consecutive records that were produced with exactly the same lineup of personnel singing. Based on the quality of their single recordings, perhaps had they been able to overcome their compatibility issues their history might have been more successful as a group. Unfortunately, that was not to be.

Lou Rawls

BEACH MUSIC DISCOGRAPHY: "You'll Never Find" (Philadelphia International 3592, 1976: Billboard Pop #2); "Lady Love" (Philadelphia International 3634, 1977: Billboard Pop #24); "Sit Down and Talk to Me" (Philadelphia International 3738, 1979: Billboard Pop Did Not Chart, R&B #26).

Louis Allen Rawls was born on the South Side of Chicago and started signing in the choir at the Greater Mount Olive Baptist Church when he was seven. In high school he and classmate Sam Cooke began singing together, and eventually they sang in the gospel groups the Teenage Kings of Harmony and then the Holy Wonders. By the early '50s Cooke had migrated west to Los Angeles, and Rawls followed a few years later where he sang with two different gospel groups before serving a three year stint in the Army as a sergeant in the 82nd Airborne. After his discharge he returned to Los Angeles and joined the Pilgrim Travelers (by then simply known as the Travelers), and it was while touring with this group that he was in an automobile accident that first saw him pronounced dead, then resuscitated and falling into a coma for almost a week. It took Rawls a year to fully recover.

By the late 1950s he was playing clubs in Los Angeles and performing at the Hollywood Bowl with Dick Clark's line up of entertainers. In 1960 and 61 he recorded several non-charting singles on the Shar-Dee and Candix labels before landing a contract with Capitol Records in 1962. His first release for Capitol was "That Lucky Old Sun," (the better-known version by beach music audiences is Cash McCall's), which did not chart. Seven more non-charting solo singles and five albums followed, but the only Top 40 release he was associated with during this period was when he sang backup on Cooke's #13 pop hit "Bring It on Home to Me" in 1962. Finally, in 1965 he broke the pop Top 100 with "Three O'clock in the Morning," which went to #83. Thereafter he had some success on the pop charts, but despite recording 27 singles on Capitol up through 1970, only three, "Love is a Hurtin' Thing"(#13, 1966), "Dead End Street" (#29, 1967), and "Your Good Thing is About to End"(#18, 1969) would make the pop Top 40, though "Love Is a Hurtin' Thing" would also top the R&B charts. Despite a tangible lack of chart success, he was one of the most respected entertainers in the recording industry; he opened for the Beatles on their American tour in 1966, "Love Is a Hurtin' Thing" was nominated for two Grammy awards, and his "Dead End Street" won him his first Grammy for Best R&B Vocal Performance.

In 1971 he'd sign with MGM, and his first release, 1971's "A Natural Man" would peak at #17 and win him a second Grammy. He would not have any sustained chart success with MGM however, and after releases on Bell and Arista, in 1975 he'd sign with Philadelphia International. His first release for the label was "You'll Never Find (Another Love Like Mine)" in 1976, which would become Rawls' biggest hit. Written by Kenny Gamble and Leon Huff, the single came at a time where disco ruled the airwaves and as a result was welcomed not only by listeners nationwide but also by beach music audiences hungry for more mainstream R&B that could be shagged to. The song peaked at #2 on the pop charts, #1 on the R&B and Adult Contemporary charts, and made the Top 10 in the UK (his only chart record in England). Releases such as "Groovy People" and "See You When I Git There" did well on the R&B charts but not the pop charts, but the two songs from this period that resonated most with beach music audiences were 1978's "Lady Love" and 1979's "Sit Down and Talk to Me." "Lady Love" was written by Von Gray and Sherman Marshall; Marshall had co-written or would co-write beach music hits such as "I'm Doin Fine Now" by New York City, "Swing Your Daddy" by Jim Gilstrap, and "Party Time Man" by the Futures. The song went to #24 on the pop charts and #21 on the R&B charts. The Gamble and Huff-penned "Sit Down and Talk to Me" was not as well known, making only the R&B charts (it went to #26). Oddly enough, both songs would be significant in that "Lady Love" was his last Top 40 pop hit, and "Sit Down and Talk to Me" was the highest he would ever chart on the R&B charts from that time forward.

Although Rawls continued to record, by the late 1970s his interests had diversified into acting in movies and on television and doing voice work for television. With a career that garnered three Grammys and 13 nominations, a platinum album and five gold albums, a Star on the Hollywood Walk of Fame, he continued to release music right up until his death from lung and brain cancer in 2006.

Jimmy Ricks and the Ravens

BEACH MUSIC DISCOGRAPHY: "Green Eyes." (Jubilee 5203, 1955: Did Not Chart).

James Thomas Ricks was born in Adrian, Georgia, and moved to Jacksonville, Florida, when he was 13. He sang in the church choir on Sundays, and his strong bass voice was evident by the time he was an adolescent. During World War II he moved to New York City, and there he joined a group called the Melodeers for a short time. Ricks soon met Warren Suttles, and because they shared a common interest in music they decided to form a vocal group. They enlisted Leonard "Zeke" Puzey, who had won first prize in an amateur show at the Apollo Theater, and then Henry Oliver "Ollie" Jones. Taking the name The Ravens, they signed with Hub records, releasing their first single, "Lullaby" in 1946. They followed this with a couple of other releases on Hub, but none sold well. All the while they were performing on the radio and in clubs, and in order to improve their sound in 1947 they hired Maithe Marshall (whose real name was Maithe Williams) to replace Ollie Jones; Jones went on to form the Blenders.

In 1947 the Ravens signed with National Records, and although their first recording, "Mahzel," did not sell, their second, the standard "Ol' Man River" went to #10 on the R&B charts. Two releases later, "Write Me a Letter" went to #5 on the R&B and crossed over to the pop charts, peaking at #24. The group was constantly recording and performing and they were considered one of the most popular vocal groups of the late 1940s.

The group had become so popular that King Records actually bought and released some of their old Hub master recordings when that label folded, and "Bye Bye Baby Blues" went to #8 on the R&B charts. Their National releases continued to chart as well, but like many groups during this period, success bred discontent which in turn meant personnel changes. In 1948 Suttles and then Maithe quit, and were replaced by Joe Medlin and Richie Cannon. Medlin didn't stay long, and Maithe returned, then Suttles returned and Cannon was dropped; Biggs left by 1950 and was replaced by Bill Sanford, then Suttles left again.

In 1950 the group left National to sign with Columbia, and while National continued to release their records they also sued Columbia saying that the label had encouraged them to breach their contract. After a year they jumped to Mercury, but now the group consisted of Ricks backed by all new members. This began a revolving door of personnel, with members old and new coming and going, and in the spring of 1954 Jimmy Ricks himself left. The Ravens' contract with Mercury ran out, and at that point they signed with Jubilee and Ricks rejoined them. In the spring of 1955 they recorded "Green Eyes," with Ricks and Jimmie Steward trading off lead vocal duties. The song had been written in 1929 and had previously been a #1 hit for the Jimmy Dorsey Orchestra in 1941, but the Ravens' version did not chart. Interestingly, not long after the group toured in the Carolinas and Georgia, and no doubt many people heard the song that would become a beach music classic when it was the group's most current single.

In 1956, Ricks left the group for the last time. Since leaving National they'd had only one chart record, and music was changing and after more than a decade together Ricks was tired of the group dynamic. The group struggled on before splitting up in 1958. Ricks would do solo work on a variety of small labels, and some duets, most notably the classic "You're the Boss" with Lavern Baker in 1961 which peaked at #81 on the pop charts.

Ricks died in 1974; all other members of the group are now deceased as well. They were inducted into the Vocal Group Hall of Fame in 1998.

John Roberts

BEACH MUSIC DISCOGRAPHY: "To Be My Girl" (Duke 429, 1968: Did Not Chart).

Houston-born John Edward Roberts' first real success in the music business came as the co-writer of the Jackie Wilson song "Watch Out," the flip side of Wilson's 1964 Brunswick release "She's All Right" which "bubbled under" the pop charts at #103. He signed with Don Robey's Duke Records in 1966 as singer/songwriter, and at the time Duke was home to artists such as Bobby "Blue" Bland, Ernie K. Doe, and Junior Parker. His first release with the label was "The Hurricane" backed with "Cold-Hearted Woman" in 1967, and was attributed to John Roberts and the Hurricanes. The record failed to chart, but his next release, "Sockin 1-2-3-4" backed with the instrumental "Sophisticated Funk" broke onto the R&B charts, going to #19 in 1967; it also broke into the Billboard Pop Hot 100, rising to #71.

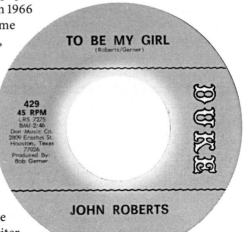

Fresh off of the success of a Top 20 R&B record, the very soulful "To Be My Girl," his next Duke release, should have been a hit. Produced by co-writer Bob Garner, the song failed to find an audience although it was popular in the beach clubs in the Carolinas. Between 1968 and 1970 he had four more single releases on Duke, "I'll Forget You," "Baby I Need Somebody," a cover of Johnny Ace's "Pledging My Love," and "Come Back and Stay Forever," but none of them charted. These would apparently be his last single releases for Duke or any other label.

Over the course of the next nine years, Roberts would emerge as a frequent arranger for 20th Century Records, particularly for Barry White. In 1979 Roberts surfaced as performer once again, now as "Sir" John Roberts, releasing an LP on Venture called *Sir John Roberts and The Sophisticated Funk Orchestra*. Accompanied by his wife, the former Patience Valentine who had recorded sides for SAR and Thrush in the 1960s, this seven-track album was for disco lovers, heavy on a sound suited for dancing. It was the last time Roberts would be featured as performer, as he afterwards returned to producing, writing, and arranging. He continued to work with Barry White up through the 1990s, and also Carrie Lucas, arranging her 1980 beach music hit "It's Not What You Got It's How You Use It" (see the entry for Lucas). His last appearance of note seems to have been as the writer of George Duke's 2013 song "Burnt Sausage Jam," on which he also played drums. Roberts reportedly retired from the music business and became a music teacher at Centennial High School in Compton, California.

Smokey Robinson and the Miracles

BEACH MUSIC DISCOGRAPHY: "More Love" (Tamla 54152, 1967: Billboard Pop #23); "I Second That Emotion" (Tamla 54159, 1967: Billboard Pop #4); "If You Can Want" (Tamla 54162, 1968: Billboard Pop #11); "Yesterlove" (Tamla 54167, 1968: Billboard Pop #31); "Special Occasion" (Tamla 54172, 1968: Billboard Pop #26); "The Tears of a Clown" (Tamla 54199, 1970: Billboard Pop #1).

Nicknamed "Smokey Joe" by an uncle due to his light skin, Detroit, Michigan-born William Robinson, Jr., was influenced by singers such as Sarah Vaughn and most particularly by Clyde McPhatter. At the time McPhatter was with the Dominoes, and McPhatter's non-traditional high voice was relatable to the aspiring singer. In high school, Robinson formed a group called the Five Chimes with Northern High School classmates and over time they evolved into the Matadors, which included Robinson, Sonny Rogers, Ronnie White, Warren Moore and Bobby Rogers. They auditioned for Brunswick Records and although failed to get a contract they soon teamed up with Berry Gordy, who had them record "Got a Job" on the End label. By this time the group was recording as the Miracles, and Robinson's girlfriend Claudette Rogers had replaced her brother Sonny. "Got a Job" did well locally, but more importantly the collaboration between Robinson and Gordy was the foundation of one of the most successful relationships in the history of music.

At Robinson's urging Gordy decided to start his own company and borrowed money to establish Tamla Records. The first Miracles release, "Bad Girl," was actually released nationally by Chess Records due to distribution issues at Tamla, but it was a success and broke into the Billboard Hot 100 at #93. The group had another release that barely broke into the Top 100 at #94, "Way Over There," before they released "Shop Around" in 1960. It topped the R&B charts, went to #2 on the pop charts, and was the Miracle's and the label's first smash hit. Over the next five years the group would have a number of chart records, including "You've Really Got a Hold on Me," "Mickey's Monkey," "I Gotta Dance to Keep From Crying," and others. Robinson was also writing hits for other artists, including "My Guy "for Mary Wells, "The Way You Do the Things You Do" and "My Girl" for the Temptations, and "Don't Mess with Bill" for the Marvelettes. As a group the Miracles were also writing more collaboratively, working together to write their own hits such as "Ooo Baby Baby," "The Tracks of My Tears," and "My Girl Has Gone."

Though the Miracles' mid '60s ballads such as "Ooo Baby Baby" and "The Tracks of My Tears" generated some interest among beach music aficionados, it was during the late 1960s that their more upbeat music found an audience. One song that found many listeners in beach music circles as 1967's "More Love," a song Robinson considered one of his most personal as he wrote it for his wife, former group member Claudette Rogers. At the time Claudette Robinson had quit travelling with the group after having had a number of miscarriages, and Robinson wrote the song to express his love for her. The song peaked at #23 on the pop charts. Their next release, "I Second That Emotion," was written by Robinson and his friend Al Cleveland. The two were shopping when Robinson saw some pearls and commented that he should by them for Claudette, when Cleveland said "I second that *emotion*" instead of "motion." The two wrote a song around the phrase, which went to #1 on the R&B charts and #4 on the pop charts. Their next release was 1968's "If You Can Want," the first of three charting singles from their 1968 album *Special Occasion*. Of their songs that appealed to beach music audiences, "If You Can Want" may well have been the most popular as it had the right beat to make it an often-requested hit in beach clubs. It peaked at #11 on the pop charts and #3 on the R&B charts. Their next two single releases from the same album, "Yesterlove" and "Special Occasion," were also collaborative efforts by Robinson and Cleveland, and they didn't fare quite as well on the pop charts as other recent releases, peaking at #31 and #26 respectively.

"Special Occasion" would be followed by five more Top 40 singles before the release of "The Tears of a Clown," one of the group's best known efforts and their first song to hit #1 on the pop charts. The song was written by Robinson, Stevie Wonder, and Hank Cosby, and the group had originally recorded it for their album *Make It Happen* in 1967. The song wasn't issued as a single at the time, but when the song was released as a single in 1970 in Great Britain and hit #1 Motown issued a new mix of the song in the U.S. as well. It became the group's only #1 hit on the pop charts up to that time, and went to #1 on the R&B charts as well.

By 1972 Robinson had grown tired of touring and decided to leave the group to concentrate on other aspects of his career, which would include solo work. Billy Griffin took over lead singing duties, and though they several hits after Robinson's departure the group had a different sound thereafter. The group is in every major hall of fame, including the Rock and Roll Hall of Fame, the Vocal Group Hall of Fame, and the Rhythm and Blues Hall of Fame.

Rose Colored Glass

BEACH MUSIC DISCOGRAPHY: "Can't Find the Time" (Bang 584, Billboard Pop #54 1971).

Larry Meletio and Roe Cree met in high school, when Cree was a member of a band called the Sensations. At about the same time Bobby Caldwell, Mary Owens, and Bob Penhall formed a folk group called Rose Colored Glass in 1969. When Penhall left the group, Caldwell and Owens reached out to Cree (the Sensations had disbanded and he was a student at Texas Tech), and he suggested they bring in Meletio as their drummer. This new version of Rose Colored Glass played harmonic vocal covers by groups such as the Byrds, the Association, and Crosby, Stills, and Nash. Their manager booked them time at a recording studio, where they tried out a few different songs for producer Jim Long. According to Caldwell, Long told them they should record "Can't Find the Time," a song Long said "a guy had written and his group recorded but it just didn't go anywhere." The song was written by Bruce Arnold and recorded by his band Orpheus, and Caldwell says, "We'd never heard of them … and when we heard the song we thought it kind of just droned along. One night about 2:30 in the morning we'd just gotten off playing at one of the local clubs, and we were asked if we wanted the recording time. We got in there and started working on 'Can't Find the Time.' When it was

Rose Colored Glass, 1971 (photograph courtesy Bobby Caldwell).

done, we thought 'You know, we just might have something here.'" Bang records signed them, and when released the song climbed the national charts. Meletio said that as a result "We got the call to go to LA to be on *American Bandstand*, and we were told Dick Clark had requested us because 'Can't Find the Time' had really taken off—it had been in the Top Ten in Chicago for like six weeks or something and people just loved it. We get out there and they met us at the airport in a limo. They took us to the studio and the Jackson 5 was there, as were Paul Revere and the Raiders."

Soon afterwards their manager quit, telling the group that he felt they needed someone with a big firm to represent them because he wasn't sure he could get them to the next level. With new management, and acting under the dictates of the failing Bang record label, things weren't running as smoothly as they had previously. They had recorded "If It's All Right with You," which peaked at #95 on the Billboard pop charts in October 1971, but Caldwell also notes that the label was starting to come apart, even as the group was scheduled to release some songs they'd recorded for an album. "By that point I don't think Bang had the money to promote an album. They didn't even have any singles left—they didn't have the right financing. Believe it or not we never saw one dime in royalties from 'Can't Find the Time,' and they wouldn't even let us listen to the tracks we'd recorded for our album." Indeed, Bang Records was in turmoil and by 1971 had lost their two biggest acts in Neil Diamond and Van Morrison, and the label would eventually be bought out by CBS Records. In the meantime, the label foisted other individuals on the group, thinking they needed a new frontman to move them away from their folksy sound. They brought in Bill Tilman, who was "more of a Vegas-type entertainer. He was a big guy, and he had charisma, and the new management thought he'd be a good fit. The problem was that all that charisma was only on stage, and it was never off stage. He kept to himself a lot. He was an interesting study, but he never let you 'in.'" Tensions arose and Meletio and Cree quit, and after a while Caldwell and Owens decided to end it as well.

The various members of the group went on to different things, and for a while most of them stayed active in the music business in one way or another. Though the group no longer actively tours, occasionally they still get together and "play four or five times a year, and of course we play 'Can't Find the Time' every time we get together. We play to have fun now."

Jackie Ross

BEACH MUSIC DISCOGRAPHY: "Selfish One" (Chess 1903, 1964: Billboard Pop Did Not Chart, R&B #11).

Jackie Ross was born in St. Louis, and as the daughter of ministers she got her start singing gospel music on the radio. After her father died in 1954, her family moved to Chicago, and she was signed by Sam Cooke's SAR records. She only issued one single on SAR, and billed as "Jacki" Ross she recorded the Cooke-co-penned "Hold Me" backed with Ross' own "Hard Times." The record was not successful, and after a period as a back-up singer with Syl Johnson she signed with the Chess label in 1964. At the time Chess had been successfully recording a number of blues, R&B, and rock artists such as Bo Diddley, Chuck Berry, Dale Hawkins, and Howlin Wolf for more than a decade, but other than Etta James on their Argo subsidiary, the label hadn't had an array of popular female singers, other than some mildly successful work by Jan Bradley and Mitty Collier. Ross' first release was "Selfish One," which soared to #11 on the pop charts and #4 on the R&B charts, and at the time it appeared Chess had found the female solo pop act they'd been searching for.

Unfortunately, Ross's subsequent recordings were less successful. She released an album, *Full Bloom*, as well as the singles "I've Got The Skill" which stalled at #89, followed by "Haste Makes Waste" which did not chart, and her first release of 1965, "Jerk And Twine," which would only climb to #85. Oddly enough, while Ross' success was diminishing, Chess was hitting stride with its Chicago sound that appealed to audiences in the Southeast. During the same period, the label released The Radiants' "Voice Your Choice" and "It Ain't No Big Thing," Billy Stewart's "I Do Love You" and "Sitting In the Park," and Tony Clarke's "The Entertainer." Ross was becoming increasingly dissatisfied with the label due to her lack of royalties, and her dissatisfaction reached a peak when she recorded "Take Me for a Little While" in 1965. In New York, up-and-coming singer Evie Sands had recorded "Take Me for a Little While" for the Blue Cat label, but ahead of its release a test pressing was stolen and offered to Ross. Ross and her producers thought it was a standard demo, and she recorded and released the record before Sands' version was released. After the fact Ross learned that the demo she heard was a stolen pressing, and in the meantime lawsuits ensued. Chess stopped pressing and selling the record, but the damage was done. Neither artist's version charted, Sands' was denied a hit many thought was rightfully hers (she wouldn't have a chart record for another four years), and a disgusted Ross decided she'd had enough of Chess. After an argument with Leonard Chess, she left the label.

Ross did a single for USA, then signed with Brunswick, followed by recordings for Mercury, Scepter, GSF, and Sedgrick. She'd record into the '80s, but was never able to recapture the success she had with Chess.

Diana Ross and Marvin Gaye

BEACH MUSIC DISCOGRAPHY: "My Mistake (Was to Love You)" (Motown 1269, 1974: Billboard Pop #19).

Prior to the 1970s Diana Ross's fame was primarily as the lead singer for the Supremes, who had had twelve #1 singles, including "Where Did Our Love Go," "Baby Love" and "Stop! In the Name of Love" (see the entry for The Supremes). Ross left the group to become a solo artist, and in the early 1970s she had scored nine Top 40 singles including "Ain't No Mountain High Enough" (#1) and "Touch Me in the Morning" (#1), songs that were largely pop influenced and more in the genre of adult contemporary music. During the 1960s, Marvin Gaye (see the entry for Gaye) had been one of music's most popular solo artists, and he'd recorded hits such as "I Heard It Through the Grapevine" (#1), "How Sweet It Is to Be Loved By You" (#6) and "Too Busy Thinking About My Baby" (#4). His music had changed by the 1970s, and he was producing songs such as "What's Going On" (#2), "Mercy Mercy Me" (#4) and "Let's Get It On" (#1). In light of early successful pairings Berry Gordy had orchestrated with Gaye and Mary Wells, Kim Weston, and Tammi Terrell during the 1960s, he paired his two biggest '70s solo stars for an album to be titled, *Diana and Marvin.* Gaye had originally vowed never to record a duet again after the death of his favorite singing partner, Tammi Terrell. Terrell had collapsed on stage in Gaye's arms during a show in 1967, and after being diagnosed with a brain tumor she would eventually die in 1970. Gordy had entertained the idea of a collaboration between Gaye and Ross as early as 1970, and by 1972 Gaye and Ross finally began recording the album at the Motown studios in Hollywood California.

Gaye, who had been depressed since Terrell's illness and death, had begun smoking marijuana constantly, and when recording began for the album that was to become *Diana and Marvin*, Ross was pregnant and consequently worried that Gaye's smoking in the studio would have an adverse effect on her health and the health of her unborn child. Ross apparently begged Gordy to make Gaye stop the smoking in the studio, Gaye refused, and as a result the songs were recorded with each artist in a different studio and mixed together and overdubbed later.

The album was released in 1973, and the first single from the album, "You're a Special Part of Me," reached #12 on the charts. The second single, "My Mistake (Was to Love You)," was written by songwriters Gloria Jones (writer of the Four Tops' "Just Seven Numbers" and Gladys Knight and the Pips' "If I Were Your Woman") and Pam Sawyer (cowriter of the Supremes' "Love Child" and later of Ross's #1 hit "Love Hangover") and had instrumentation by the Funk Brothers. With its sweet, meaningful vocals, it *sounds* like Gaye and Ross have the perfect chemistry, despite the real-life friction in their relationship that forced the recording to be done in separate studios. Nevertheless, "My Mistake" only reached #19 on the charts, and two subsequent singles from the album would not do even that well in the U.S. Though the album sold more than one million copies, it only went as high as #25 on the album charts, so in the United States it was viewed as somewhat of a failure—especially given the talent assembled for it.

Both artists would go on to have subsequent #1 hits on their own, and as such the *Diana and Marvin* album and "My Mistake" are somewhat of an afterthought on the résumés of both Ross and Gaye in the 1970s. Despite this, in the Carolinas "My Mistake" is considered a beach music classic.

David Ruffin

BEACH MUSIC DISCOGRAPHY: "My Whole World Ended (The Moment You Left Me)" (Motown 1140, 1969: Billboard Pop #9); "Walk Away From Love" (Motown 1376F, 1975: Billboard Pop #9); "Everything's Coming Up Love" (Motown 1393F, 1976: Billboard Pop #49).

Born in Whynot, Mississippi, David Eli Ruffin was the fourth child of Elias and Ophelia Ruffin. His mother died not long after giving birth to David, and as a result he and his brother Jimmy (who was five years older) were raised by their father and stepmother. The family had a gospel group and traveled throughout the South, but by the time David was a teen he went to Memphis intending to become a minister. His plans changed after he began singing in talent shows, and he soon started singing with his brother Jimmy in the gospel group the Dixie Nightingales. He sang with several other groups, including the Soul Stirrers, the Womack Brothers, and the Staple Singers.

He moved to Chicago and in the early 1960s he recorded a couple of sides on Chess' Check-Mate subsidiary, including 1961's "You Can Get What I Got" and "Mr. Bus Driver," neither of which was successful. Chess had a national distribution deal with Detroit's Anna Records, founded by Berry Gordy's sisters Anna and Gwen along with Roquel Davis, and Ruffin did some work for the label with the Voice Masters and also recorded a solo single on Anna called "I'm in Love." The single was not successful, but by this point he had come to the attention of Berry Gordy. Though he longed to perform as a solo act (as his brother Jimmy would), he was growing more amenable to the idea of being in a group, especially after joining the Temptations onstage for a live performance. When the Temptations fired Eldridge Bryant in late 1963 they brought in David Ruffin to replace him. Though the group had a few moderately successful singles early on, when Ruffin took the lead for the first time on "My Girl," the record raced to #1. From that point forward the group members would still occasionally share lead vocal duties, but it was Ruffin's strong gravelly voice that handled lead duties on their biggest hits between 1964 and 1968, including the R&B #1's "Ain't Too Proud to Beg," "Get Ready," "Beauty is Only Skin Deep," "(I Know) I'm Losing You," and "I Wish It Would Rain." Unfortunately, Ruffin was heavily into drugs by the late '60s, and his demands on the group for front-man billing and special privileges became more and more unreasonable. The band fired him in June 1968 and replaced him with Dennis Edwards (see the entry for the Temptations).

Because he had started as a solo artist Ruffin had always had a separate contract from the other members of the Temptations, and consequently he was still signed to Motown though he was no longer with the group. Though by now his relationship with Motown had become strained, he was required to honor his contract and for his first solo release he was given a song that had been intended for the Temptations, "My Whole World Ended (The Moment You Left Me)" in 1969. Written by Harvey Fuqua, Johnny Bristol, Pam Sawyer and James Roach, the song was very much in the mournful/heartbroken mode of Temptations songs such as "(I Know) I'm Losing You" and "Since I Lost My Baby," and Motown pulled out all the stops to make it successful. With instrumentation by the Funk Brothers and backing vocals by the Originals, the song went to #9 on the pop charts and #2 on the R&B charts.

While this initial success seemed to bode well for Ruffin, after this he would have a series of misfires and wouldn't have another pop Top 40 single until "Walk Away from Love" in 1975. Written by Van McCoy and Charles Kipps, the song would actually surpass all of his previous solo efforts by hitting #1 on the R&B charts and #9 on the pop charts. Because of its soulful easygoing style it garnered considerable play time in the shag clubs, as would another single release in 1976, "Everything's Coming Up Love." Although "Everything's Coming Up Love" would not break into the pop Top 40, it would hit #8 on the R&B charts. In fact, between 1975 and 1980, Ruffin would have nine singles make the R&B charts, though only "Walk Away from Love" would make the pop Top 40. Still, as a solo artist, it was Ruffin's most productive period.

Unfortunately, Ruffin's personal demons were never far from the surface nor far from the public eye. Although later in life he mended his relationship and toured with some former members of the Temptations, he remained a troubled man. He was jailed for jailed for tax evasion in 1982, charged with receiving stolen property in 1986, and arrested for parole violations due to cocaine use in 1987. In fact, cocaine use would lead to his death in 1991. Though his solo career was only moderately successful, he was inducted into the Rock and Roll Hall of Fame as a member of the Temptations in 1989.

Jimmy Ruffin

BEACH MUSIC DISCOGRAPHY: "What Becomes of the Brokenhearted" (Soul 35022, 1966: Billboard Pop #7); "I've Passed This Way Before"(Soul 35027, 1966: Billboard Pop #17); "Hold on to My Love"(RSO 1021, 1980: Billboard Pop #10).

Collinsville, Mississippi-born Jimmy Ruffin was the son of a Baptist minister and as such grew up singing gospel music in the church. After a childhood stint with his brother David in the group the Dixie Nightingales, in 1961 he recorded one solo side on Motown's Miracle label, but "Don't Feel Sorry for Me" didn't make any chart noise before Ruffin was drafted. After his enlistment was up, he was a recorded a few failed sides before receiving an offer to join the Temptations in 1964. Feeling that he was better suited for a solo career he turned them down but recommended his brother David instead.

As a solo artist for Motown's Soul subsidiary, he recorded a couple of unsuccessful tracks before hearing about a tune William Witherspoon, Paul Riser and James Dean had written for another Motown group, the Spinners. At the time, the Spinners had recorded several songs but had still not had a breakout, as only "I'll Always Love You" had made the Top 40. Ruffin convinced the powers at Motown to let him have the song, and thus it was Ruffin, and not the Spinners, who recorded "What Becomes of the Brokenhearted" in 1966.

The song seemed to appeal to anyone who had ever loved and lost before. Interestingly, the song originally had a spoken introduction, which resulted in a version was about twelve seconds longer than the later-popular version. However, the decision was made to remove the intro and begin the single release with the powerful Funk Brothers instrumentals, which now seems an indispensable part of the song. With backing by both the Adantes and the Originals, listeners certainly liked it as released; it went to #7 in the Top 40 and #6 on the R&B charts. It went to number #10 in the UK, and like many quality songs rereleased during the Northern Soul explosion in England, it charted even higher the second time around, reaching #4 in 1974. The song would go on to be recorded by many groups, and Robson & Jerome would later take their version of the song to #1 in the UK. The Isley Brothers also did a version in the 1960s called "Smile," with different words set to the exact same backing tracks. One group who didn't have a hit with it was the group who was supposed to record it, the Spinners. They would have to wait four more years for their first big hit, "It's a Shame" in 1970.

Ruffin became a Motown superstar almost overnight. His next release was another Dean and Witherspoon composition, the fine "I've Passed This Way Before" (1966). Oddly enough, this time the song kept the spoken word intro, and it went to # 17 on the pop charts and broke the Top 10 on the R&B charts. These two big hits were followed by 1967's "Gonna Give Her All the Love I've Got"(#29) and "Don't You Miss Me a Little Bit" (#68). Though each American release was less successful than the previous one, in England, his records were doing increasingly better. While "I'll Say Forever My Love" (1968) only reached #77 in the U.S., it went to #7 in the UK. "I've Passed This Way Before" was reissued in England in 1969 and went to #33, and "Farewell Is a Lonely Sound" (1969) went to #8 in the UK even though it didn't chart at all in the States.

In the 1970s Ruffin continued to have success in England, but almost none in the U.S. In 1980, when American audiences had all but given up on him, he charted with a song Bee Gee Robin Gibb had written, "Hold On to My Love" for RSO. Though with its Gibb-influenced sound it had a bit of a disco feel, in 1980 it was popular with shaggers looking for quality R&B hits that weren't straight-up disco recordings. It made the Top 10 in the U.S., but as usual it would chart even higher in England (#7). That seemed to be the writing on the wall for Ruffin, and in the 1980s he actually moved to England where his work was clearly much more popular and where his music continued to chart well into the late 1980s. He passed away in 2014.

The Sandpebbles

BEACH MUSIC DISCOGRAPHY: "Love Power" (Calla C-141, 1967: Billboard Pop #22)

Originating in New York City, the Sandpebbles consisted of Calvin White, Andrea Bolden, and Lonzine Wright. White had been a member of the Gospel Wonders, and from 1957 to 1965 that group had recorded sides for Chess, Scatt, Gospel, J&S, and Revelation. Bolden, Wright, and White came together to form the Sandpebbles, and New York producer Teddy Vann, who had worked with the Bobettes and Johnny Thunder, liked White's gospel influenced sound and they signed with Calla Records. The group's first release was a song Vann and White wrote, "Forget It," which climbed to #10 on the R&B charts and broke the Billboard Hot 100 at #81 on the pop charts. In late 1966 they recorded a Vann composition, "Love Power," which would become their second release and rise to #14 on the R&B charts and #22 on the pop charts in 1967. The song, featuring White's vocals, would be the group's signature hit and their only song to climb into the Top 40 on the pop charts. The song would not only have an extended life while being played in the beach clubs in the Carolinas, but would go on to be re-recorded by the likes of Dusty Springfield, the Bay City Rollers, and Luther Vandross, whose 1991 recording would go to #4 on the Billboard Hot 100 and #1 on the R&B charts.

The group's third release was yet another Vann composition, 1968's "If You Didn't Hear Me the First Time," and it would also chart and rise to #42 on the R&B charts, but would fail to make the Top 100 on the pop charts, stalling at #122. Nevertheless, with their first three records having charted, it would have seemed that the group would have sustained some momentum, but three more 1968 releases on Calla would fail to chart. They would leave Calla and sign with the Cotillion label, and adopting the name C and The Shells in 1968, under the tutelage of producer Jerry Williams they would have a minor hit with a song he penned called "You Are the Circus," which rose to #28 on the R&B charts in 1969. Their next release on Cotillion, a cover of Oliver's "Good Morning Starshine," would chart at #46 on the R&B charts in 1969, and a third, a cover of Judy Clay and William Bell's classic "Private Number," failed to chart at all. The group would leave Cotillion in 1970, and eventually sign with the Zanzee label, where they released several singles in 1972 and 73 before disbanding that year.

The Sanford Townsend Band

BEACH MUSIC DISCOGRAPHY: "Smoke from a Distant Fire"(Warner 8370, 1977:Billboard Pop #9).

John Townsend decided to start a band while in school at the University of Alabama after being influenced by bands such as the Swingin' Medallions, who he'd seen at clubs and fraternity parties. His group, The Magnificent Seven, eventually branched out beyond campus parties to become part of the Gulf Coast club scene. There Townsend met Ed Sanford of The Rockin Gibraltars, and after Townsend spent time with a group called the Rubber Band, he, Sanford, and a few others eventually went on to found a band called Heart (no relation to the '80s band of the same name). They moved to California, and then a few years later Townsend and Sanford went out on their own.

In California, Sanford and his friend Steve Stewart were living together, and one morning when Townsend popped in Sanford was in a bad mood because he'd been kept up by Stewart playing his guitar all night in the next room. According to Townsend, an angry Sanford told Stewart the next morning "'When are you going to knock that off and write something that's gonna make you some money?'" Townsend says Stewart, who still had his guitar around his neck, said, "Anybody can write that crap!" and started playing a riff he'd made up. "Ed and I looked at each other and said 'Hey, that's pretty cool!' We sat down at the piano and started the song using Steven's riff, and Sanford said 'I think this will fit a poem I wrote in college—check out these lyrics and see if they work for you.' This poem he'd written when he was at Auburn was actually called 'Smoke from a Distant Fire.' He'd had this girl friend who was fooling around on him, and I thought it was a great image. I don't remember anything else about the poem—we just took the title from it."

The Sanford Townsend Band–Sanford, Townsend, Otis Hale, Jerry Rightmer, Jim Varley,

The Sanford Townsend Band, circa 1977 (photograph courtesy John Townsend).

and Roger Johnson—recorded the song with producer Jerry Wexler, who was famous for working with artists such as Ray Charles and Aretha Franklin. After the record started getting a lot of airplay it went national, and was a smash hit. The song went to #9 on the Billboard Pop charts and #1 on *Cash Box*, and was one of the biggest songs of the year. Soon beach music lovers picked up on it because it had just the right beat for shagging, and so it quickly became a mainstay of the shag-club circuit. Townsend says that makes sense, because "Most definitely old R&B and beach music influenced the sound of the song. We had started as a band playing Otis Redding, Little Anthony and the Imperials, Sam and Dave, the New Orleans music, the Muscle Shoals stuff, mostly by black artists. It was the music of the day, and when it came time to do our own songs they came out of the music we were really in love with."

Although they were never able to follow up that one really big hit, the band toured with Fleetwood Mac, Jimmy Buffett, Foreigner, and a number of other top acts. Ed Sanford would later co-write "I Keep Forgettin" with Michael McDonald, and though Sanford and Townsend have since gone their separate ways, Townsend says he still gets a thrill out of playing "Smoke From a Distant Fire." "I've never stopped playing it, and it always gets a great reaction. I remember when we played in Myrtle Beach and there was a great crowd. After we played the song people came up and said, 'You sound just like that guy who sang that song,' and I'd say 'Well, that's because I *am* that guy!' Other people would say 'I never knew you guys were white!' For someone with my musical roots, that's one of the greatest compliments I could ever have. When I was playing the Carolinas I found out what a big beach music record 'Smoke From a Distant Fire' had been, and that's pretty special." "Smoke From a Distant Fire" has now been considered classic beach music for decades.

The Sapphires

BEACH MUSIC DISCOGRAPHY: "Who Do You Love?" (Swan 4162, Billboard Pop #25 1964); "Gotta Have Your Love" (ABC-Paramount 10639, Billboard Pop #77 1965).

The Sapphires hailed from Philadelphia, and consisted of Carol Jackson, Joe Livingston, and George Garner (often misidentified as George Gainer). They were signed to the Swan label by producer Jerry Ross, and though he would go on to find great fame working with a number of acts such as Bill Deal and the Rhondels, the MOB, Jay and the Techniques, and Jerry Butler, at this point early in his career he was still trying to establish himself as a force in the music business. He liked the sound of the Sapphires however, and in 1963 they released their first single on Swan 4143, "Where Is Johnny Now." Despite the musical accompaniment of future Philly soul luminaries such as Thom Bell and Leon Huff, the song failed to find an audience and did not chart.

Ross had discovered a 17-year-old songwriter named Kenny Gamble, and for the Sapphires' next release the group would record Ross and Gamble's composition, "Who Do You Love." With a haunting sound that was slightly akin to the Jaynett's "Sally Go Round the Roses," "Who Do You Love" was one of Gamble's first successful compositions, going to #25 on the pop charts and #9 on the R&B charts. The Sapphires followed up with two more singles for Swan in 1964, "I Found Out Too Late" and "Gotta Be More Than Friends," neither of which charted, and an album, *Who Do You Love,* before moving to ABC Paramount later that year. Though their first two singles for ABC, "Let's Break Up for a While" and "Thank You for Loving Me" (written by another great songwiritng team, Tommy Boyce, Bobby Hart, and Wes Farrell), did not chart, their third, 1965's "Gotta Have Your Love," seemed to suggest a new Motown-like-sound for the group, and it took off. With a smooth, Marvelette's-like sound, and bolstered by backing vocals by Nick Ashford, Valerie Simpson, and Melba Moore, the song went to #77 on the Billboard pop charts and #33 the R&B charts. But just as it seemed the group was going to establish a chart presence, further releases did not chart and by 1966 the group broke up for good.

Despite being surrounded by enormously talented people, the Sapphires never seemed to find a definitive sound of their own. Gamble's greatest fame as a songwriter would come later when he paired with Leon Huff, the backup musician on the first Sapphires single (and who would write 1964's "Mixed Up, Shook Up Girl" by Patty & the Emblems). Their compositions would eventually include hits such as "Cowboys to Girls" for the Intruders, "Love Train" and "Backstabbers" for the O'Jays, "Only the Strong Survive" for Jerry Butler and many, many more. Ross would produce a number of successful acts, Boyce and Hart would be successful songwriters and performers, and even backup singers Ashford, Simpson, and Moore would go on to acclaim as headline acts. The Sapphires, however, despite the quality displayed on "Who Do You Love?" and "Gotta Have Your Love," tend to be remembered as a group who never found success despite enormous potential, even though they had the benefit of working with some of the greatest singers, songwriters, and producers of the 1960s.

Boz Scaggs

BEACH MUSIC DISCOGRAPHY: "It's Over" (Columbia 10319, 1976: Billboard Pop #38); "Georgia" (Columbia 01023, 1976: Did Not Chart); "What Can I Say" (Columbia 10440, 1976: Billboard #42); "What Do You Want the Girl to Do?" (Columbia Album Cut, 1976).

Canton, Ohio, born William Royce Scaggs moved to Oklahoma as a child, then later his family moved to Plano Texas. He first learned to play the cello, then he was later taught guitar by classmate Steve Miller. In high school he was affectionately called "Bosley" (which was ultimately shortened to Boz), and he joined Miller's group the Marksmen in the late '50s. He and Miller both attended the University of Wisconsin where both played in various bands, before Scaggs returned to Texas in the early '60s. There he joined another band called the Wigs, who primarily played R&B. They moved to England, disbanded, and Scaggs stayed in Europe a while and even recorded *Boz,* an unsuccessful album. In 1967 he returned to America to hook up with his old friend Miller who was now fronting the Steve Miller Band. While he would stay with the group to record two albums—*Children of the Future* and *Sailor*—Scaggs wanted to move in a more soulful direction and left the group in 1968.

Scaggs landed a contract with Atlantic records, and in 1968 he went to Muscle Shoals to record the album *Boz Scaggs* backed by studio musicians including a young Duane Allman. Like previous efforts, the album was not a commercial success, and he next signed with Columbia where he recorded the albums *Moments, Boz Scaggs and Band, My Time,* and *Slow Dancer,* before he finally had a commercial success equal to the critical accolades he had been receiving, 1976's multi-platinum album *Silk Degrees.*

With the album, whose title Scaggs said didn't really mean anything but came from an image he had in his head, he brought his blue-eyed soul sound to a new level. Assisted on the album by David Porcaro, David Paich, and Jeff Hungate, who would go on to form Toto, and background singers such as Jim Gilstrap (see the entry for Gilstrap), he brought his music to the attention of listeners in the Carolinas, as several of the album's cuts were adopted by beach music listeners during the somewhat barren period for beach music in the mid to late 1970s. The album's first single, a song Scagg's had written called "It's Over," was extremely popular with beach music crowds, and rose to #38 on the national charts as well. "What Can I Say" was also popular, reaching #42 on the charts. Two songs from the album that were not released as singles yet also found an audience with shaggers were "Georgia" and "What Do You Want the Girl to Do?." The latter was written by Allen Toussaint and included on his R&B album *Southern Nights* in 1975, but was not a hit for either artist. Ultimately, *Silk Degrees* reached #2 on the album charts, produced four Top 40 singles, and won Scaggs a Grammy in the R&B category.

Scaggs would go on to record a number of albums and have several Top 40 hits, but none resonated with beach music lovers quite like his masterpiece *Silk Degrees.* Today Scaggs owns and operates a California vineyard, and also continues to perform and record.

Peggy Scott and Jo Jo Benson

BEACH MUSIC DISCOGRAPHY: "Lover's Holiday" (SSS International 736, 1968: Billboard Pop #31).

Born Joseph M. Hewell in Phenix City, Alabama, the man who would gain fame as Jo Jo Benson started singing by sneaking into nightclubs when he was 14. For a large part of his early career he was destined to be a back-up performer, working with the likes of the Enchanters and the Upsetters, and he also landed a job as a backup singer with Chuck Willis, who would rocket to fame with the #1 R&B hits "C.C. Rider"(1957) and "What am I Living For" (1958). Willis died just before "What am I Living For" topped the charts, and so throughout the early 1960s Benson spent time picking up singing work in clubs and even selling cars for a while. Like many soul singers Peggy Stoutmeyer's musical roots were in Gospel; her mother was a Gospel music promoter, and in high school in Pensacola, Florida, Peggy formed a group called the Gospel Harmonettes. Later her interests became more secular, and she sang with Ben E. King for a year and also embarked on a career singing in nightclubs.

Benson was working just across the river from Phenix City in Columbus, Georgia, when he came to the attention of local DJ Ed "Dr. Jive" Mendel. Mendel had started his own record label,

Men-Del, and after having Hewell change his name to Jo Jo Benson and then signing on as his manager, he had him record the label's first release, Benson's 1967 cut "Kiss Tomorrow Goodbye." The record garnered some local attention, and at about this time Mendel also started managing Peggy (whose name was soon changed to Scott) after hearing her singing in a local club. Mendel had formed another label, Peggy Sue, and a release by Johnny Barfield and the Men from S.O.U.L called "Mr. Starlight" had been picked up for national release by Shelby Singleton's SSS Intl. Label. Mendel told Singleton about his two other singers and took Benson and Scott to Jackson Mississippi to record some solo demo efforts for SSS. Producer Huey Meaux (who had also managed and produced Barbara Lynn of "You'll Lose a Good Thing" fame—see entry this book), suggested that they record a song as a duet called "Lover's Holiday" which they did in one take. When Singleton heard their duet he decided to release it instead of their solo recordings, and it was released nationally on SSS in 1968. The duo's debut went to #8 on the R&B charts and #31 on the pop chart, sold more than a million copies and earned a gold record.

As a duo Scott and Benson had achieved the fame that eluded them as solo acts. Their next release was 1968's "Pickin' Wild Mountain Berries," which also went to #8 on the R&B charts and #27 on the pop chart, and which was nominated for a Grammy for Best Rhythm & Blues Performance. By this time they were the label's hottest act, and Singleton himself took on producing duties for the two. He took them to Nashville to record 1969's "Soul Shake," which also went to #13 on the R&B charts and #37 on the pop charts and garnered them another Grammy nomination for Best Rhythm & Blues Vocal Performance. In the meantime the duo was touring, performed on *American Bandstand*, and released two albums in 1969.

Unfortunately, their next single in 1969, "I Want to Love You Baby," only barely broke into the Hot 100 at #81, though it did moderately well on the R&B charts at #24. Though no one could have expected it given the success they'd had in just a year's time, as a chart presence the duo was done. Four more SSS releases and even a solo effort by Scott went nowhere, and by 1970 they had signed with Atco. Two releases on that label failed to generate any interest, and Scott and Benson parted ways in 1971.

Over the next three decades both of them would work both inside and outside of the music business, and in 1984 they actually reunited for an album but the reunion was short lived. Benson spent most of his time as a nightclub owner, and in 1979 he was wounded in a shooting at a card game. In 1999, he released an album called *Reminiscing in the Jam Zone* which was critically acclaimed but failed to yield any chart hits, and in 2001 he released another, *Everybody Loves to Cha Cha Cha*. In his later years Benson suffered from a number of health problems and had a pacemaker installed; he passed away in 2014.

Scott got married to Robert L. Adams Sr., a City Commissioner in Compton, California, and was out of music for a while. In the early 1990s she recorded with Ray Charles on a number of efforts, and in 1996 Jimmy Lewis persuaded her to record once again as a solo act. She released a number of singles on the Miss Butch label, and her album *Help Yourself*, made the Billboard Top 200 albums chart and actually topped the Blues Album chart for seven weeks. Her career revitalized, she went on to release a number of singles and albums that did well. She has now returned to her Gospel roots, and still performs today.

Shades of Blue

BEACH MUSIC DISCOGRAPHY: "Oh How Happy" (Impact 1007, 1966: Billboard Pop #12).

The Detroit–based group The Domingos consisted of high school friends Dan Guise, Bob Kerr, Ernie Dernai, and Nick Marinelli. The group played dances and clubs singing doo-wop and R&B songs, and after high school Guise left the group and they added Linda Allen in his place. They attempted to land a recording contract, and fortunately they were friends with some members of the Reflections, who had gone to #6 on the charts with 1964's "Just Like Romeo and Juliet" on the Golden World label. The Reflections recommended them to Golden World owner Ed Wingate, and though he liked their sound he didn't sign them because he told them he didn't want to sign another white vocal group. Fortunately, their recordings caught the ear of producer John Rhys, and the first thing he did was rename the group; "he said the name of the group wasn't going to cut it, that it sounded too much like Dominoes. So we all hashed out possible names, and being that we were a blue-eyed soul group, we wanted 'blues' in our name so we settled on Shades of Blue" Marinelli said.

Shades of Blue, circa 1966 (photograph courtesy Nick Marinelli).

With a new name, they needed a song to record, and at this time they met a songwriter and performer named Charles Edwin Hatcher. Hatcher had been recording for the Golden World subsidiary Ric-Tic as Edwin Starr, but he had produced only one Top 40 pop single. He'd written and co-written some songs, including his own "Stop Her on Sight," and Marinelli said "While we were working doing backup vocals and demos at Golden World, he heard us sing and liked our sound." Marinelli says Starr "had an idea for a song he hadn't finished called 'Oh How Happy,'" and that Starr and the Shades of Blue "all sat down together and finished it, and we even contributed some of the wording and the chorus." Rhys took the record to Harry Balk at Impact records, who signed the group to a contract. "Oh How Happy" was released in March 1966 and almost immediately shot to #1 in several local markets, and would eventually ascend the national charts as well, going to #12 on the pop charts and #7 on the R&B charts. Unfortunately, the nature of their impromptu songwriting session didn't become apparent until later; "we never got co-writing credit because at the time we were young and stupid, and didn't know that we could have and should have." Consequently, Starr was credited as the sole songwriter.

With a Top 40 hit the group's fortunes changed overnight. They played on *Where the*

Action Is and several other television shows, and so expectations were high for their follow-up single. But Marinelli says the next release, another song Starr had written called "Lonely Summer," didn't perform well because "it was released late in August, but it should have been released in June right as 'Oh How Happy' was staring to move back down the charts." "Lonely Summer" lacked the cohesive sound of "Oh How Happy," and peaked at #72. They followed this with a song John Rhys wrote for the group called "Happiness," which peaked at #78 in 1966. Even though the follow-ups to "Oh How Happy" weren't big hits they had all charted, and the group also released an album in September 1966 to cap off a very successful year.

Unfortunately, like many young groups during the 1950s and '60s, success wasn't taking quite the tangible form that it should have. "At Impact we were the big money maker in the company at the time, and of course they started seeing residuals coming in. But we were out on the Dick Clark tour, and we were hearing the other artists talking about the royalty checks they were getting, and we're going 'Wait a second, we haven't gotten any royalty checks.' Though we were making money on the road, the company was sucking up our royalties and using them to promote other Impact artists." The group felt they were being taken advantage of, and they were further incensed when subsequent singles weren't well promoted. The deathblow came when Motown bought up Impact and its catalog, and then didn't seem interested in giving them new songs or promoting the group. "After Motown bought out Impact in late '67, we saw the handwriting on the wall," Marinelli said. "Motown was like any other big corporation, and they'd buy up record companies, take the stable and get rid of the competition. They kept booking us in shows, but they weren't really interested in developing anything new for us or promoting us as a group. But music was changing too, and that's when we decided to hang it up." By the late '60s the great harmonizing and vocals that had been a mainstay of the group's repertoire were not as fashionable as they once had been. As a result, they called it quits as performers about 1970.

The group reunited for a while in the mid-70s, and recorded some new songs that have never been released. The group broke up again, and the other original members got out of show business while Marinelli did television production work. He eventually went back into the music with the Valadiers, though after they saw how crowds reacted when Marinelli sang "Oh How Happy," they started working as Shades of Blue. Eventually Marinelli went out on his own and today he performs as a solo act.

The Showmen

BEACH MUSIC DISCOGRAPHY: "It Will Stand" (Minit 632, 1961: Billboard Pop #61); "39–21–40 Shape" (Minit 662, 1963: Did Not Chart); "In Paradise" (Swan 4213, 1965: Did Not Chart).

Norfolk, Virginia natives The Showmen began as The Humdingers in the early 1950s. The group, consisting of General Norman Johnson (his given name), Milton Wells, Gene Knight, Dorsey Knight and Leslie Felton, recorded a few unreleased early sides for Atlantic in 1956, but when they took on manager Noah Biggs, he had the ambition to make the group more than just a competent local act. The group did a few demos and sent these to New

Orleans-based producer Joe Banashak. Banashak agreed to work with them as long as they changed their name, and beginning in 1961 the newly christened Showmen recorded a number of sides on the Minit label with an up-and-coming talent in the recording industry named Allen Toussaint. Minit artists included Ernie K. Doe, Irma Thomas and Benny Spellman, so the Showmen were squarely in the middle of the burgeoning New Orleans R&B scene of the early 1960s. (In fact, Ernie K. Doe's beach music favorite "Mother-in-Law" would be released just before the Showmen's first single, and Spellman's "Lipstick Traces" would be released just afterward.)

The first of the Showmen's records released was "Country Fool" on Minit 362, but it was the record's flip side, "It Will Stand" (originally written with the title "Rock and Roll Will Stand"), that got the bulk of the airplay and charted. The homage to rock-and-roll went to #61 on the Hot 100 and #40 on the R&B charts. Considering how this song has become such an anthem for beach music *and* rock-and-roll, in retrospect it wasn't a very significant showing. Nevertheless, as their first chart record and first record for Minit, it was a promising start. Their next three Minit releases in 1961 and 1962 would all fail to find an audience, as would their fifth Minit release, the now classic "39–21–40 Shape." General Johnson told writer Jim Newsom in 2007 "I was only about 14 years old when I wrote that song," and he said he didn't actually know any girl with a 39–21–40 shape. "I don't know," Johnson said, "maybe it rhymed with 'ape-itty ape.' That came from a young teenager's brain!" But the exact title depends on who you listen to and what you read. Minit released the single with the much more provocative measurements "39–21–46" on the label, and Johnson stated that though Minit claimed it was a clerical and printing error, he didn't believe it. He told Newsom, "I think they did it as a ploy because it was more commercial, it aroused curiosity." As a result, though the label says "39–21–46," the lyrics of course always say "39–21–40 Shape." Even if listeners were curious, however, they didn't buy the record, and it failed to chart.

A failure to sustain any chart success soon led to the group and the label parting ways, and most of the Minit recordings were eventually purchased by Imperial. Perhaps feeling that "It Will Stand" had the potential to do better than its first release indicated, Imperial rereleased the song in 1964, and this time it rose as high as #80 during its three weeks on the chart. The group eventually moved to BB Records in 1965, and there they recorded a song Johnson had written that had would get some traction in beach music clubs, "In Paradise." Primarily based on its popularity in the southeast Swan picked it up as well as a couple of other songs they had recorded; none of the Swan releases made the national charts.

In 1968 Johnson would leave to form the Chairmen of the Board (see the entry for the Chairmen on the Board) and The Showmen continued recording with Felton on lead vocals but no further chart records were forthcoming.

The Skyliners

BEACH MUSIC DISCOGRAPHY: "Pennies from Heaven" (Calico 117, 1960: Billboard Pop #20).

The Pittsburgh-based Skyliners were formed in 1958 when a group Joe Rock managed called the Crescents had two members quit, leaving high school students Jimmy Beaumont, Wally Lester and Jack Taylor as a trio. Rock recruited local teenagers Joe Versharen and Janet Vogel from a group called The Eirios to join his trio, and as a five-member group once again the Crescents played local dates in the Pittsburgh area.

Rock gave the group a song he had written called "Since I Don't Have You," and asked Beaumont to set it to music. Supposedly the song was about a girl Rock was dating who had broken up with him, and in despair he wrote the lyrics while sitting at a traffic light. Beaumont wrote the music, and the group sensed it could be a hit and cut a demo. After being rejected by more than a dozen labels they learned that a new label, the Pittsburgh-based Calico records, was holding auditions looking for new artists to sign. Although they arrived too late to audition, a tearful Vogel convinced Calico founders Lennie Martin and Lou Guarino to listen to them anyway, and after hearing "Since I Don't Have You" Martin and Guarino felt the song had hit potential. They decided to have the group record the song, and after Beaumont suggested a backing string arrangement they recorded the song in New York with a full string section. It was at this time that they changed their name from the Crescents to the Skyliners.

"Since I Don't Have You" was released in December 1958, and by March 1959 it was #12 on the Billboard Pop chart. The group appeared on *American Bandstand*, played at the Apollo, and toured with Dick Clark's Caravan of Stars. They released "It Happened Today" in 1959, which disappointingly peaked only at #59. They released an album, *The Skyliners*, in 1960, as well as another single, "This I Swear," which gave them their second Top 40 record, peaking at #26. In 1960 they released "Pennies From Heaven," a song that had originally been written in 1936 as the title song for the movie *Pennies from Heaven*. It was sung by Bing Crosby, whose version was #1 on the charts for ten weeks that year, and it was later covered by Dinah Washington, Big Joe Turner, Louis Prima, Frank Sinatra, Billie Holiday, and many others. Beaumont later said the group recorded it because they realized that the teen market was ever changing and Doo Wop was fading, and they felt a more traditional hit song would help them build an older audience and find success on the nightclub circuit.

Although the song was a success, it would be the Skyliners' last Top 40 single. By 1961 the wear and tear of constant touring was taking its toll on the group, who had dropped out of high school when "Since I Don't Have You" had become a hit. They broke with Calico and signed with Colpix, and by 1961 Vogel decided to leave the group. After singles on Cameo, Original Sound, and Atco, the group broke up in 1963. Beaumont and Vogel (as Janet Deane) later released solo efforts, and the group reformed a couple of times over the ensuing decade. One release, "Where Have They Gone," hit #100 in 1975; it was their last chart record.

Suffering from clinical depression, Janet Vogel committed suicide in 1980; Rock, Verscharen, and Lester have all passed away. Beaumont formed Jimmy Beaumont and the Skyliners in the 1990s and performed until he passed away in 2017. The Skyliners were inducted into the Vocal Group Hall of Fame in 2002.

Percy Sledge

BEACH MUSIC DISCOGRAPHY: "Sugar Puddin'" (Atlantic 2342, 1966: Did Not Chart).

Percy Tyrone Sledge was born in Leighton, Alabama, and as a child in the 1940s and '50s his primary exposure to music was in church and through the country music he heard on Alabama radio stations. Influenced by early country singers as well as by Elvis Presley, despite the fact that he loved to sing he worked standard laboring jobs in construction and as a farmhand before landing a job as an orderly at the Colbert County Hospital in Sheffield

Alabama. He left the hospital for a factory job, but when he was asked to join a group called the Esquires Combo he quit to pursue a career in music. Early on this mainly consisted of gigs at nightclubs and fraternity parties, but at one such party at the University of Mississippi he met DJ and aspiring record producer Quin Ivy, who arranged for the group to cut a record at his studio back in Sheffield. Sheffield was also home to the Muscle Shoals Studios, and so it was with backing instrumentation by the Muscle Shoals musicians that Sledge recorded 1966's "When a Man Loves a Woman," produced by Ivy and Marlin Greene. The song was based on a composition that Sledge had written along with Esquires bandmates Cameron Lewis and Andrew Wright called "Why Did You Leave Me, Baby?," and though most of the writing had been done by Sledge and the Esquires Combo didn't even play on the song, Sledge generously gave the writing credit to Lewis and Wright; he would later call it the greatest mistake he ever made as he lost a lifetime of royalties. The song went to #1 on the pop and R&B charts, and Atlantic Records picked up Sledge's contract.

Sledge's next release that year was "Warm and Tender Love," another pop hit going to #17, and the record's b-side was "Sugar Puddin.'" Written by Greene and Bruce Gist and again produced by Greene and Ivy, the song was not in the mold of Sledge's traditional, heartfelt soul ballads filled with anguish and pain, but was instead more upbeat, as his Sugar Puddin' is a love who is "dandy." The song never gained any traction with Sledge's core audience, but beach music audiences found it a passable dance tune and perhaps the only song in Sledge's catalog appropriate for shagging.

Sledge would go on to have another dozen or so songs over the next six years that would meet with varying degrees of success, but nothing would ever come close to "When a Man Loves a Woman." Because he had given away the writing credits to the song he was never able to reap the financial rewards that many songwriters enjoy, and continued to rely on performing in the U.S. and abroad for the rest of his life. In 1989 he won the Rhythm and Blues Foundation's career achievement award, and he was inducted into the Rock and Roll Hall of Fame in 2005. He passed away in 2015.

Soul Inc.

BEACH MUSIC DISCOGRAPHY: "What Goes Up Must Come Down" (Emblem 101, 1967: Did Not Chart).

The beach music version of Soul Inc. (not to be confused with the psychedelic group Soul Inc. from Louisville, Kentucky) was a Columbia, South Carolina–based band whose founding members included Freddy Pugh and Perrin Gleaton. Gleaton was originally from Columbia, and was with the Greenwood-based Medallions (later the Swingin' Medallions) in 1963 when band leader John McElrath needed a couple of horn players for a Labor Day weekend gig in Florida. According to Fred Pugh, "Perrin said 'let's get in touch with my friend from high school, Fred Pugh.' After we played in Panama City, John said 'I like it with eight instead of six, so let's keep Fred and Rick Godwin,' who played trumpet. So we stayed with the band."

That arrangement worked for a while, but Gleaton said that by the fall of 1965 he, Pugh, and Godwin "all lived in Columbia, but the rest of the members lived in Greenwood. Because of the physical separation, the members from Greenwood just decided me, Fred, and Rick didn't need to be in the band anymore, and they had a lot of friends from Greenwood who did want to join." So, the band split, and Godwin moved on to other things while Pugh and Gleaton played for a few months with a thirteen piece big-horn band out of Columbia, the Singin, Swingin Counts. Then they decided to form Soul Inc. with Eddie Zomerfield and Skip Davis; they were joined a few months later by Billy Jackson. "Jackson just walked up one day and said, 'Hey, can I sit in with you guys?' He was a tremendous singer and put on a good show, and joined the group." Not long after that, in June of 1966, Gleaton went back to school at Clemson and got out of the music business, and Edgar Smith took his place on guitar. Over the next two years, other members who would join were Robbie Robinson, Pete Toglio, Donnie Rhodes, and Jackson Woods.

Known for their popular live act at venues such as the Pawleys Island Pavilion and the Cellar in Charlotte, the group released "What Goes Up Must Come Down" in 1967 on the Emblem label. "We played at the Cellar in Charlotte one Sunday night and it was recorded live on one of those old reel to reel machines" Pugh said. A regional release, it did not make the national charts, but Emblem also released an album *Live at the Cellar* from which the single was taken and it sold fairly well in the South. Pugh says they also recorded a studio version of "What Goes Up Must Come Down" "at Moses Dillard's studio in Greenville," but it has been the live, rawer version that has long been most popular with beach music audiences.

Soul Inc., circa 1967 (photograph courtesy Fred Pugh).

Strangely enough, a few years later a few members of Pugh and Gleaton's old band from Columbia, the Singin, Swingin Counts, renamed themselves The Charms Unlimited and rerecorded yet another version of "What Goes Up Must Come Down" on Emblem.

By 1968 Zomerfield and Davis decided they wanted to move away from R&B and pop and start doing hard rock. "So I got out," Pugh said, "and they changed the name to Freeway and then Fire and Rain. They were sure enough hard rock by then." By 1974 Pugh decided to get back into music and helped start a beach music group called Mama's Home Cookin, a beach music band that Pugh stayed with for a decade. Pugh and Gleaton are retired but still stay in touch today; the rest of the members of Soul Inc. are now deceased.

The Spaniels

BEACH MUSIC DISCOGRAPHY: "People Will Say We're in Love" (Vee-Jay 342, 1960: Did Not Chart).

Gary, Indiana native Thornton James Hudson, who acquired the name "Pookie" from an aunt, was from strong musical stock as the cousin of both Josephine Baker and Thomas "Fats" Waller. While still in junior high, Hudson formed a group called the 3 Bees, and when the other members graduated in 1952 Hudson teamed up with Ernest Warren, Willie C. Jackson, and Gerald Gregory to sing in a talent show as the 4 Buddies. After bringing home the win, they decided to stay together, added Opal Courtney, Jr. and performed as the Hudsonaires. Gregory was married, and after his wife joked that the group sounded like a bunch of dogs, the group adopted the name the Spaniels when Hudson graduated from high school.

In 1953 Vivian Carter and Jimmy Bracken had just set up Vee-Jay records and were looking for talent to record when they heard the Spaniels perform; they were the first group to sign with the label. At their first recording session they recorded several songs, and one, "Baby It's You," was their first release. The song was so popular that the fledgling label couldn't handle national distribution, and instead Chance released the song nationally and saw it climb to #10 on the R&B charts by September 1953. A substantial amount of live performing followed and they recorded some more songs, one of which was their fourth release, "Goodnite, Sweetheart, Goodnite." It was a song Hudson wrote for his girlfriend, and although the other members of the group didn't like it all that much they released it and saw it climb to #4 on the R&B charts and #24 on the pop charts. The song was covered by several other artists, and has come to be seen as one of the most representative recordings of the 1950s.

The record's success really vaulted the group into the spotlight, allowing them to play top rank venues such as the Apollo, and perform with the likes of Big Joe Turner, The Drifters, Lavern Baker, and others. Opal Courtney eventually left the group and was replaced by James Cochran, and they also added Jerome Henderson for a brief time. In 1955 their song "You Painted Pictures" reached #13 on the R&B charts, but as they were building momentum Warren was drafted and then Jackson quit as well. In fact, the revolving door of group members was a situation exacerbated by the fact that although they had a few hits and were performing fairly often, the paychecks weren't steady or reliable. When the now-married Pookie Hudson opted for a steady job drawing a regular paycheck, replacements were brought in and by the fall of 1956 only Gerald Gregory of the original group remained.

Oddly enough, it was Hudson's disintegrating marriage that drove him back to the group and got them in the studio again. In 1957 they released their first album, *Goodnite, It's Time To Go,* featuring the now oldie "Goodnite, Sweetheart, Goodnite" under a new title to match the album. In 1957 "Everyone's Laughing" charted at #13 on the R&B charts and #69 on the pop charts, and Ernest Warren rejoined the group. In 1958 they appeared on *American Bandstand,* and they returned to the studio in August 1959 and recorded eight new sides, one of which was "People Will Say We're In Love" with Gerald Gregory singing lead. Written by Rogers and Hammerstein, the tune was from the 1943 musical *Oklahoma!* While a cover of a show tune might seem an odd choice for an R&B group, the Spaniels were more or less grasping at straws as they saw their popularity fading fast—they hadn't had a single make any chart in two years. Though the song would become popular in beach music circles during the late 20th Century among shaggers, at the time it garnered little notice and did not chart.

From this point the group's membership changed frequently, and they had just one more chart record for Vee-Jay, "I Know," which became the group's first real success in three years, hitting #23 on the R&B charts in 1960. But the group's relationship with Vee-Jay had disintegrated irreparably by this point, and they didn't feel like the label cared about them anymore. Gregory left in 1961 to join Sonny Til's new Orioles, and the remaining members recorded for several different labels, including Neptune, Parkway and Double-L, and then broke up in the summer of 1963. In December 1969, Pookie started his own label, North American, and pulled together a group for a new Spaniels release "Fairy Tales." Surprisingly, it did so well that Calla picked it up for national distribution, and it reached #45 on the R&B charts in 1970. The group recorded some other sides but nothing else sold well, but did get attention once again when "Goodnite, Sweetheart, Goodnite" was used in the 1973 film *American Graffitti*. Most of the original members of the group started performing together again in the 1990s, but at time of his passing in 2015 Willie C. Jackson had been the group's last living member.

Benny Spellman

BEACH MUSIC DISCOGRAPHY: "Lipstick Traces" (Minit 644, 1962: Billboard Pop #80).

Pensacola, Florida-born Benny Spellman's entrance into the music business was atypical of many R&B artists, in that he didn't grow up with an eye towards becoming a singer. Instead, he was interested in sports, and it wasn't until he was in college on a football scholarship at Southern University in Baton Rouge, Louisiana, that he became interested in singing. Spellman joined a singing group in college and won a few talent contests, but his career as an entertainer was interrupted by a stint in the army. After his enlistment he returned to Pensacola to find work, but a chance encounter with Huey "Piano" Smith and his group the Clowns in 1959 changed his life. Smith's bus had been wrecked and Spellman offered to give them a ride back to New Orleans. Smith eventually invited Spellman to join the Clowns, and Spellman performed with that group and then later went out on his own after positive reaction at an impromptu live performance in New Orleans. He did a lot of studio work and backup work, and became a regular at the Dew Drop Inn where he'd sit in with Edgar Blanchard and the Gondoliers, the house band. Eventually he signed to Minit records, which would be home to artists such as Ernie K. Doe and the Showmen. His first records for Minit, "Life Is Too Short" and "Darling No Matter Where," both recorded in 1960, failed to generate any substantial sales.

Minit artists often backed each other on their recordings and on one occasion Ernie K. Doe was making a record and Spellman was enlisted as a background singer. The song was "Mother-in-Law," which skyrocketed up the charts to #1. Spellman's bass voice can be heard echoing Doe by singing the words "mother-in-law" throughout the record, so oddly enough his first brush with chart success was for another artist. Deacon John Moore, who played on many of the Minit sessions including "Mother-In-Law," said that after K. Doe's hit "Benny believed his bass voice was so instrumental in making 'Mother-in-Law' a hit, he worried Allen Toussaint to death to write him a song that sounded similar to it." Moore said Benny "kept hounding Allen and hounding him. 'Please write me a song,' Benny would say. He wanted a song that would work with his bass vocals. So, Allen did write him his own song—'Lipstick Traces,'" Moore said.

Moore said he felt like it just had to be a hit, because

> if you listen, "Lipstick Traces" is almost identical to "Mother-in-Law," with the same chord changes but a different story line. If you listen to the melodic line, "Don't leave me no more," it's the same as "Mother-in-Law." He used that little hook to construct "Lipstick Traces." Allen was able to write around people's personalities and vocal styles, and he successfully did it with Benny and K. Doe. And though the songs, construction-wise, were similar, they had their own identity because of the personalities of the different singers. Benny was a baritone bass, and K. Doe was a tenor. So Allen knew how to write for both of them and yet give them individuality at the same time.

With Moore and also Minit recording artist Irma Thomas on backup, "Lipstick Traces" climbed to #80 on the pop charts and #28 on the R&B charts in June 1962; although it didn't chart as well as "Mother-in-Law," "Lipstick Traces" is just as big, if not bigger, on the list of all-time greatest beach music hits.

Perhaps unfortunately, Spellman's second biggest hit happened to be the flip side of "Lipstick Traces," a song called "Fortune Teller." It was a minor hit in its own right, and it was later recorded by the Rolling Stones, the Hollies and the Who, among others. "In New Orleans, 'Fortune Teller' was more popular than 'Lipstick Traces,'" Moore said, "because it had that Latin rhythm to it, and it was a huge song, with that bass line that was Benny's trademark." It was also apparently the key to Spellman's popular live performances. "He had a stage show that was unbelievable. The audience would sing along with him. He'd do all these crazy antics, pull off his coat and throw it out in the audience. And because he was an ex-football player, he'd roll up his shirtsleeves and show them his muscles. He'd get down in the crowd, put a rag around his head and dance like a fortuneteller, like a swami. He had the whole audience eating out of the palm of his hand. He was a fabulous entertainer."

Spellman was never able to replicate the success of "Lipstick Traces," however, despite three more singles on Minit. When Minit was sold to Imperial Records in 1963, he recorded a few sides on Watch, then Alon, and lastly Sansu in 1967. By that time the hits had dried up for Spellman, and he retired from the music business in 1968 to work for a beer distributorship for many years. He made a comeback attempt in the 1980s and performed for a while, but a stroke in 1996 caused him to spend the remainder of his life in an assisted living facility. Spellman was elected to the Louisiana Music Hall of Fame in 2009; he passed away in 2011.

The Spinners

BEACH MUSIC DISCOGRAPHY: "I'll Always Love You" (Motown 1078, 1965: Billboard Pop #38); "Truly Yours" (Motown 1093, 1966: Billboard Pop #111); "It's a Shame" (V.I.P. 25057, 1970: Billboard Pop #14); "I'll Be Around" (Atlantic 2904, 1973: Billboard Pop #3); "Could It Be I'm Fallin' In Love" (Atlantic 2927, 1973: Billboard Pop #4); "One of a Kind (Love Affair)" (Atlantic

2962, 1973: Billboard Pop #11); "Mighty Love" (Atlantic 3006, 1974: Billboard Pop #20); "Wake Up Susan" (Atlantic 3341, 1976: Billboard Pop #56).

The Spinners got their start in Ferndale, Michigan, in 1954 as the Domingoes, and originally consisted of members Billy Henderson, Henry Fambrough, C.P. Spenser, Pervis Jackson, and James Edwards. Edwards was soon replaced by Bobbie (sometimes listed as Bobby) Smith, and Spencer would leave and be replaced by George Dixon. By 1961 they had renamed themselves after those spinning car hubcaps, and had their first real shot at success on Tri-Phi with "That's What Girls Are Made For" which went to #27 on the charts. Other than one more low-charting single, further success eluded them on Tri-Phi, but Motown bought out the label and so the group began a new phase of their career. "We went to Motown in 1964" the late Bobbie Smith told me, and he noted that though they had a couple of moderate hits there—"I'll Always Love You" went to #35 in 1965, and "Truly Yours" went to #111 in 1966—none of their other releases charted in the 1960s, despite the fact that he felt that they were high quality songs. Both songs were written by Mickey Stevenson and Ivory Jo Hunter, and both featured Smith on lead vocals with the rest of the group backed by the Andantes and the famous Funk Brothers:

> We had some real good stuff at Motown that wasn't getting promoted, songs like "Truly Yours." In Detroit we knew a lot of the DJs, and we'd take our records out ourselves and do the promotion and interviews at the radio stations. They played "Truly Yours," and then all of a sudden they weren't playing it any more. We called and asked why and they said "Marvin Gaye has a new song, and we got orders from Motown to take yours off and put his on." So they'd play Marvin's or whoever else's Motown was pushing and take ours off. I thought we did some great songs at Motown, as good as a lot that was being recorded there, but we seemed to get lost in the shuffle.

In fact, the group ended up doing a lot of odd jobs for other acts at Motown, working as chaperones, chauffeurs, and even shipping clerks, among other things. But the label didn't seem willing to invest the time or effort in the group that was being given to other acts. Smith says that he thought they weren't appreciated at Motown may have been due to his lead vocals, which wasn't in the same mold as many other Motown artists. "I had a soft smooth voice, and at Motown they seemed to go for a raspier voice, like David Ruffin of the Temptations on 'Ain't Too Proud to Beg' or Levi Stubbs on the Four Tops' 'Bernadette.' My voice was soft and smooth, and I started to feel like I wasn't strong enough as we kept getting overlooked. That's when we brought G.C. Cameron in 1967. He had the ability to sing Motown style."

The Spinners, circa late 1960s (photograph courtesy Lorraine Smith).

When Cameron joined he did bring a different sound to the group, and he had some close connections as well. "After I signed with Motown and joined the group, Stevie Wonder and I became very good friends," Cameron told me. "We'd hang out together, and he knew that because I'd been thrown in the midst of all these great Motown singers like Marvin Gaye, David Ruffin, Levi Stubbs and Diana Ross, I needed to catch up. So one night we were out and he told me, 'I wrote a song for you.' I asked him what it was, and he had me take him to his house and he started playing this song on his electric piano. The song was 'It's a Shame.'" After Wonder played the song for Cameron that night, "the next day Stevie went in and recorded the track and three or four days later I went into the studio with the rest of the Spinners to record the vocal track." Cameron sang "both leads" on the song, and he explained, "that means that I not only sang the part when it says 'It's a shame, the way you mess around with your man,' but the higher chorus when it says 'why do you use me, try to confuse me' and so on. We did the song in one take, and Stevie and everyone else was really excited. That's how 'It's a Shame' came about." But after so many songs that went nowhere at Motown, the group was unprepared for the song's success: "I didn't think much of anything about 'It's a Shame' being special when it came out," Cameron said. "There was too much music, too many hits. I felt like anything coming out of Motown had the chance to be a hit, but I wasn't paying any particular attention to it. I just hoped at the time that we would have the opportunity to have a hit record like so many of the great acts at Motown." Though by now the group had been "sent down" from the main Motown label to the lesser V.I.P. subsidiary, "It's a Shame" was that hit, and as it raced to #14 on the pop charts it not only indicated the Spinners' potential, but as the first song Wonder produced for another group, it was an indication of his marketability as more than just a singer as well.

Despite the hit, the group was ready to leave Motown. "We left Motown because they had a lot of groups of the same caliber as the Spinners," Smith told me:

> They had a staff of writers, and naturally the writers had a choice about who to work with. If you were an artist with a hit, like Marvin Gaye or the Temptations, that's who the producers wanted to work with. When you had a hit you needed to follow a hit with another record, but at Motown, even if we had a hit, it might be another year before we had another record. It was like starting all over. So when our contract was up we decided to leave. Aretha Franklin was a good friend of ours and she thought Atlantic would be a good place for us because they didn't have a lot of groups playing the kind of music we were.

So the group changed labels, minus Cameron, who stayed at Motown to pursue a solo career. Phillipe Wynne joined the group to handle some of the lead singing chores in Cameron's stead:

> When we went to Atlantic, we had already recorded four songs, and one, "Oh Lord I Wish I Could Sleep" was about to be released. But at the last minute they called us and said "Do you guys want to go with your song, or do you want to do another session?" We asked why, and they it was because we had a chance to have Thom Bell produce us. They gave Thom a choice to work with anyone there, and he chose us. He said he used to be the piano player at the Uptown Theatre, and he remembered hearing

us do "That's What Girls Are Made For" and the song stuck in his mind because he liked the harmony. So when he saw our name on the Atlantic roster he said "I'll take them." It was a great marriage that brought us our great success.

So Bell joined the group in Detroit, and they went into the studio and recorded "I'll Be Around," "How Could I Let You Get Away," "Could It Be I'm Falling in Love," and "Just You and Me Baby." Smith says at the end Bell said, "'Well I'm going back to Philadelphia, and when I come back you'll be #1.' Of course we'd heard that before! But to make a long story short, three of the songs were million sellers."

They almost misfired on their first effort for Atlantic, however. "'I'll Be Around' was actually the B-side of the first record" Smith said. "'How Could I let You Get Away' was the A-side, but it was moving up the charts slowly, and I said 'We've got to turn this record over.' We did, and it shot right to the top." The decision paid off, and while "How Could I Let You Get Away" did go to #77 and #14 on the R&B charts, "I'll Be Around" went to #3 on the pop charts and #1 on the R&B charts. They followed that with Smith singing lead on "Could It Be I'm Falling in Love," which went to #4 on the pop charts, but also went to #1 on the R&B charts. Despite having two straight hits, after twenty years in the business Smith really wasn't convinced they had made it:

> I had gotten a job because I was getting to the point where I was thinking "It ain't gonna happen" and was thinking about giving up music. In show business you can't hold a steady job, but you had to have one because you have one of those mediocre hits and you go out of town and work for a while with the band and then you're back to zero. So I always tried to have part time jobs in between. I had just gotten a good job at the GM building with good benefits, so I had to make the decision after we recorded those songs with Thom. I had to decide if I wanted to keep that job or try one more time. I asked GM for a leave of absence, and they wouldn't give it to me. So I decided to take one last chance, and it was the right one.

Their next song, "One of a Kind (Love Affair)," was released, went to #11, and became their third straight #1 record on the R&B charts. But for the first time the group, who'd had a squeaky clean image up to that point, faced controversy. Philippé Wynne sang lead on the tune, and some listeners thought he sang "One of a kind love affair/Makes you want to love her/You just got to f**k her, yeah…" Atlantic felt like they needed to make sure that the song was radio-worthy, so they sent the group back into the studio. "What a difference a day makes" Smith said. "Just because some DJ thought that, we had to go back into the studio and clean up that one line. When we were coming up, you did everything you could to protect your career, because one scandal could end it all. So we didn't think anything about being told to do it—we just went in and cleaned it up. If a disk jockey said he thought it said that, we wanted to clear it up for everybody."

The controversial moment over, the group would go on to an unbelievable level of success with songs such as "Mighty Love" (Wynne and Smith alternate lead vocals; the song went to #1 R&B, #20 pop), "Ghetto Child," "Rubberband Man" and their #1 song with Dionne Warwick, "Then Came You." A song they would release right before "Rubberband Man" in 1976, "Wake Up Susan" also became very popular on the beach music scene, even though it peaked at #56 on the pop charts. "We used to do 'Wake Up Susan' in our act, and I really liked it" Smith said. "When you put a song out and you want it to be a nationwide hit, and sometimes it surprising that songs are big in the Carolinas but not in other places. But 'Wake up Susan' was a great song." Late '70s audiences hungry for shaggable songs also took an interest in disco-influenced, pop-crossover hits such as "Love or Leave"(#36), "Working My Way Back to You/Forgive Me Girl" (#2), and "Cupid/I've Loved You For a Long Time" (#4). Smith notes that 1983's "'City Full of Memories' was big in the Carolinas though it didn't make any noise anywhere else." But for all the hits on all the levels, Smith believes it was the group's chemistry that led to their success:

> We were always the type of group who didn't let success go to our heads—we learned a long time ago that you can't take an ego to the bank. Phillipe was the strongest voice and had a lot of charisma on stage, so sometimes he sang lead. You'll hear some smooth ballads that Henry was singing lead on, because that the type of voice he had. Then you'll hear one I'm lead on, or G.C when he was with us, and so on. We never looked at any one person as the lead—it was whoever the song fit. We don't care who is singing lead on the song because we're all the Spinners. We didn't let those egos get in the way.

The Spiral Starecase

BEACH MUSIC DISCOGRAPHY: "More Today Than Yesterday"(Columbia 44741, Billboard Pop #12 1969); "She's Ready" (Columbia 45048, Billboard Pop #72 1970).

The group started as the Sacramento-based combo the Fydallions, and evolved into a five-piece group consisting of Harvey Kaye, Dick Lopes, Bobby Raymond, Vinnie Parello and lead vocalist Pat Upton. After cutting a few sides for the Crusader label, they signed with Columbia Records in 1967. Although Columbia liked their sound, they hated the group's name and their conservative appearance. The group's name was changed to The Spiral Starecase (though it was deliberately misspelled to avoid copyright infringement of the movie *The Spiral Staircase*), and their hairstyles and clothing were updated to reflect a more late-60s-appropriate fashion.

Their first record, "Baby What I Mean," didn't go anywhere, and Upton said "when we were in Las Vegas in '68, Columbia suggested that someone in the group should write our songs, so I was the one who did." "I'd already had the title in my mind for a couple of years and when I was jamming with a friend he showed me a passing chord that I loved. I knew I would never use that chord with the stuff we were doing and decided the only way was to write a song and use it, and I did. When the chorus came around those words 'I Love You More Today than Yesterday' just fell right into place." The group recorded it and it raced to #12 on the charts, and would sell more than a million copies and earn the group a gold record.

Though the group should have been riding high with their new-found chart success, the reality of the situation was that things were bad—so bad, in fact, that the group members had started to go their separate ways. "We were breaking up and were not together as a band when 'More Today than Yesterday' came out and became a hit" Upton said.

The Spiral Starecase, 1969 (photograph courtesy Candy Kaye).

The problem was that the group's manager had been mis-appropriating funds, people weren't getting paid, and it was directly affecting the group's ability to perform. "Once we were flying out to do a performance and we got to LAX and all of our gear was out on the street because our manager bought our tickets with a stolen credit card," Upton noted. "Another time we were working at the Flamingo Hotel and we bought a PA system, and then we found out that the money we were giving our manager every week to pay for the PA was not being paid and so they came to repossess it. It was one thing after another. But the incident with the PA system was the final straw, and a couple of members said 'I'm done,' and we were dead in the water, so-to speak."

But when "'More Today' started playing on the radio everybody jumped back on board" he said. The group toured with Three Dog Night, Creedence Clearwater Revival, Sly and the Family Stone, and the Beach Boys, and did *American Bandstand*. They cut an album to showcase "More Today Than Yesterday," and released "No One for Me to Turn To" as a single. Because it only charted at #52, the group looked for another big single that would take them back to the heights they had reached with "More Today," and that's where "She's Ready" came into the picture. The song had been recorded by girl-group The Poppies as "*He's* Ready" in 1966 but had stalled at #106. It was a good choice for a cover version, and though the Poppies had released a vocal-heavy version with very little backing instrumentation, they added horns and lush orchestration combined with Upton's always vibrant vocals made the Starecase version a superb track. Unfortunately, "She's Ready" only reached #72 on the charts, and after that the problems with management and internal disagreements because of it, coupled with the group's failure to find another follow-up hit, forced the group to finally call it quits in 1970. The guys all went their separate ways, and Upton regrets that things went down like they did; "the band would have probably stayed together if [the manager] would have taken care of things." Upton "stayed around LA and did song commercials, sang demos for people, and worked in a trio called Old Friends for few years. I released one single on RCA and it didn't do anything." Kaye kept the band's name alive by touring for many years afterwards before he passed away in 2008. Upton passed away in 2016.

Edwin Starr

BEACH MUSIC DISCOGRAPHY: "Stop Her on Sight (S.O.S.)" (Ric-Tic 109, 1966: Billboard Pop #48).

Edwin Starr was Nashville-born Charles Edwin Hatcher, and as a high school student in Cleveland he joined a group called the FutureTones. This successful group appeared on a local television show called *The Uncle Jake Show*, backed up Billie Holiday at a nightclub, and even cut a single called "I Know" for Tress records. Hatcher was drafted in 1960, and after returning to civilian life he joined the Bill Doggett Combo as a singer. It was there that the group's manager, Don Briggs, suggested that he change his name to "Starr" (with the extra 'r') since Briggs was convinced that he was destined to be a star.

Starr had been doing some songwriting by this point, and based on the popularity of the James Bond movies, he'd written a song called "Agent Double-O-Soul." He told Doggett he wanted to record it, and Doggett, probably reluctant to have his singer go out on his own, downplayed the idea. Starr was persistent, however, and landed an audition at Ed Wingate's Ric Tic Records in Detroit. In 1965 he was able to record his single, just the fourth release for the new label. In order to get the best sound possible, the backup music was provided by the famous Funk Brothers, the studio musicians who of course provided the music on the great hit records by the Supremes, Four Tops, Temptations, and other acts at crosstown rival label Motown. The musicians would moonlight from time to time, unbeknownst to label founder Berry Gordy, and so by contributing their pulsing rhythms to Starr's distinctive vocals they helped the song rise to #8 on the R&B charts and #21 on the pop charts. He followed up "Agent" in 1966 by not only charting with his own songs "Back Street" (#95 pop) and "Headline News" (#84), but he also did a vocal accompaniment on the Holidays' "I'll Love You Forever" (#63), and wrote "Lonely Summer" for The Shades Of Blue (#72). Most famously, he also wrote "Oh How Happy," Shades of Blue's biggest hit, which went to #12 (see the entry for Shades of Blue). Then came one of his most brilliant moments, a song he had co-written with Albert Hamilton and Richard Morris, "Stop Her on Sight (S.O.S.)."

Rock critic Dave Marsh compares "Stop Her On Sight" to Starr's other early recordings by noting that of his early releases, "it's this one that's got the goods, one of the greatest non–Motown Motown discs ever cut, with the same booting backbeat, the same thunderous baritone sax riffs, and a vocal as tough and assured as any of the early Marvin Gaye's." Of course the reason for that Motown sound was the presence, once again, of the Funk Brothers—but they weren't there because Berry Gordy was a team player willing to share his musicians with others in the music industry, and in fact far from it. Gordy had learned after the session for "Agent Double-O-Soul" that the Funk Brothers had moonlighted at Ric Tic and had fined the musicians $100 each. Ric Tic owner Eddie Wingate caught wind of this, and, incensed, reportedly showed up at Motown and paid each of them back $200 each. Consequently, the guys were a lot more agreeable about backing up Starr again, and did so on "Stop Her on Sight." Oddly enough, the beach music classic was originally titled "Sending out Soul," about a DJ playing soul music. However, while watching an episode of *Voyage to the Bottom of the Sea* Starr had the idea to make it about Morse code, and so a new title was born. The combination of Starr's powerful voice and the Motown instrumentation drove the record up to #9 on the R&B charts and #48 on the pop charts. It was so popular in England that it not only went to #11 on the British charts in 1966, but would chart again in 1968. The song was dynamite.

By this point Berry Gordy was seeing Ric Tic as a threat, and to get rid of the competition he bought Impact and several other Detroit labels in 1968. The buyout came as a surprise to Starr; as he noted in a 1994 interview on Palace FM, "I was co-starring at the Apollo Theater with the Temptations and one of the Temptations informed me that I had been signed with Motown. I didn't think that that was possible because no-one had told me that Motown bought the company that I was with.... I instantly became a Motown artist." Gordy apparently saw Starr as too valuable a property to let him languish, and a number of hits ensued such as 1969's "25 Miles," which went to #6 on the R&B and pop charts, and of course what would become his signature hit, 1970's "War," which went all the way to #1.

Starr would continue to record throughout the '70s and would eventually move to England. In 2003, at the age of 61, he would die of a heart attack, having left a legacy of many great songs that were loved the world over.

Billy Stewart

BEACH MUSIC DISCOGRAPHY: "Fat Boy" (Chess 1820, 1962: Did Not Chart); "I Do Love You" (Chess 1922, 1965: Billboard #26); "Sitting in the Park" (Chess 1932, 1965: Billboard #24);

"Summertime" (Chess 1966, 1966: Billboard Pop #10; "Cross My Heart" (Chess 2002, 1966: Billboard Pop #86).

Born William Larry Stewart, "Billy" Stewart was involved in music at an early age as a member of his family's group, the Stewart Gospel Singers, performing with his Uncle Hound Dog Ruffin's Orchestra, and later in the Four Stewart Brothers along with his brothers Johnny, James, and Frank. Billy won a talent show singing the George Gershwin tune "Summertime" when he was a teenager, but his first real break came in 1955 when Bo Diddley heard his piano playing skills and asked him to join his band. Stewart became more diversified as he learned to play a variety of instruments, including the bass and the drums, and he recorded his first song, "Billy's Blues," with Diddley on guitar, on Chess in 1956. Though the record met with some success, it wasn't a national hit and nor were subsequent singles, and Stewart would spend the next five years as a background singer and player with Diddley and not as a featured act.

Chess hired a new A&R man, Roquel Davis, and he encouraged Stewart to record solo once again. His first recording was 1962's "Reap What You Sow," which went to #18 on the R&B charts and #79 on the Billboard Hot 100. During the session, he enlisted the services of his cousin Grace Ruffin and her group the Four Jewels, who within a short time would change their name to simply the Jewels and have their own hit "Opportunity" (see the entry for the Jewels). Perhaps more importantly, the flip side of the record was a song Davis had asked Stewart to write and record based on his nickname, "Fat Boy." This song exists in two versions: the original mono version starts with a guitar and a calliope opening the record, while the stereo version features the guitar only. Though "Fat Boy" did not chart, it got a fair amount of airplay and would become Stewart's signature song. Stewart had a couple of other releases before his next single, "Strange Feeling," went to #25 on the R&B chart and #70 on the pop chart in 1963. He had his first really big hit in 1965 with a song he had written called "I Do Love You," which also exists in two versions with the single release and album release being slightly different. With his brother Johnny on the backing vocals, the single went to #6 on the R&B charts and #26 on the Top 40 and stayed on the charts for twenty-one weeks; suddenly Stewart was a hot commodity. His very next release was also from his *I Do Love You* album and was a hit that same year, "Sitting in the Park," which did even better than "I Do Love You," going to #4 on the R&B charts and #24 on the Top 40. That record featured the backing vocals of another Chess act, the Radiants, who had charted with "Voice Your Choice" in 1964 and had just recorded "It Ain't No Big Thing" in 1965 (see the entry for the Radiants).

Stewart would release several more records before Davis convinced him to do a whole album of standards, *Unbelievable*. Stewart would first go back to his roots and record "Summertime" again. The song had made the rounds since it was written by Gershwin in 1934 for *Porgy and Bess*, and versions by Billie Holiday (1936, #12), Sam Cooke (1957, #81), The Marcels (1961, #78), and others had charted before Stewart's release. Nevertheless, Stewart's trademark tongue stutter lifted the song higher on the charts than it had ever been, rewarding him with a #7 record on the R&B charts and #10 in the Top 40 in 1966. His next release was his 1967 cover of a song composed by Sammy Fain and Paul Francis Webster had written for the 1953 musical

Calamity Jane, "Secret Love." Taken from his album *Billy Stewart Teaches Old Standards New Tricks,* Doris Day's classic version had topped the charts at #1 in 1953, and Stewart's version would go to #11 on the R&B charts and #29 on the pop charts.

After 1967, the Top 40 hits quit coming, although "Cross My Heart" did reach #86 on the pop charts and #34 on the R&B charts in 1968 and was popular in beach clubs. After one last R&B charter in 1968 it appeared that Stewart's days as a viable chart presence may have ended, but by this time he was having more serious issues than just failing to have a chart record. His weight was causing increasing problems, he developed diabetes, and in 1969 he had a motorcycle accident. In January 1970, Stewart was killed while on tour when the car he and three band members were in plunged off a bridge and into the Neuse River near Smithfield, North Carolina. He was just short of thirty-three years old.

Sunny and Phyllis

BEACH MUSIC DISCOGRAPHY: "If We Had to Do It All Over" (Uni 55091, 1968: Did Not Chart); "I've Got Something On My Mind"(Soft 1023, 1969: Did Not Chart).

Sunny and Phyllis, circa late 1960s (photograph courtesy Sonny Threatt).

Greenville, South Carolina native Sonny Threatt formed his first group, the Swinging Tangents, while a student at Greenville High School. The group consisted of Threatt and Murray Judy, Lang Ligon, Ross Boland, Andy Mckinney, Tommy Compton, and Carrol Cox, and after winning a talent show they had the opportunity to record a single on Mastertone records called "Why Today," and the small-label release did not chart. In 1967 Threatt moved on to Mars Hill College and the change of venue meant he needed to form a new group. This second group, the Nomads, consisting of Darrel McClenden, Hugh Martin, Tony Waldrop, and Baker Scott, cut a few sides and their second release on Mo-Groove records, "Somethin's Bad," is highly collectible and a popular tune on the English Northern Soul scene. Threatt transferred to Clemson in 1969, and Threatt, McClendon, and Martin were joined by Andy Mckinney, Carrol Cox and Phyllis Brown (who was co-lead singer). As Sonny and Phyllis and the Nomads, they recorded "I've Been Lost" for the Texas based Soft label. Major Bill Smith, the owner of Soft, would sometimes take recordings and sell them to larger labels, and he sold "I've Been Lost" to Los Angeles–based UNI records. UNI liked their sound, but they wanted the group to make a few changes before releasing the record. First, they wanted to change the backup band's name from the Nomads to the Danes, and Threatt told me this was because "UNI had the copyright on the name Danes, so we agreed to change the band's name." Also, Sonny's name was changed to "Sunny" at UNI's request to avoid confusion because "Sonny and Cher had split up" that year and apparently UNI feared audiences might think Sonny was Sonny Bono, re-teamed with another female co-lead—which could get complicated.

The newly-christened Sunny and Phyllis and the Danes released "I've Been Lost," and Threatt remembers that though it wasn't a national hit it was big on the Carolina coast, and was #1 at WTGR in Myrtle Beach for six weeks in 1969. Their next release was a song UNI gave them, the now classic "If We Had to Do It All Over." In the Carolinas it was huge because "'If We Had to Do It All Over' was a good shag record" Treatt said. "Guerry Sample told me it stayed on the jukebox at the Pad at OD for over twenty years and on the jukebox at the Tally Ho in Columbia (which he owned) for longer than that. It was played in both places until it literally wore out." Despite its popularity in the Carolinas, the song did not sell nationally and UNI dropped them after two singles.

The next song the group recorded was one Threatt had written, "I've Got Something on My Mind." Sunny and Phyllis recorded the song and released it on Soft, but unbeknownst to them, Bill Smith released the exact same song on the Karat label as being by Paul and Paula, who'd had a #1 hit in 1963 with "Hey Paula." Threatt told Jim Davis in *It Will Stand* that Smith still had the rights to their name, so he released it hoping it would get airplay. It did not, but it was as well-received in beach clubs as its predecessor had been.

Because UNI owned the rights to the name Sunny and Phyllis, the group recorded a number of subsequent singles under different names such as Johnny and the Mark V, Berry Street Station, San Diego, Gulf, and Jessie and Jessica. Phyllis did some solo work as Phyllis Brown as well, but Threatt says that "eventually the band dispersed, most of us going back to school. We had always worked the music in between school, playing live mainly in summers and weekends." Sunny and Phyllis got married, and though they settled down and did work in advertising,

> we really never stopped the music. I guess nobody who's been in it ever does. Back then the larger radio stations (like WTOB Winston Salem or WTGR Myrtle Beach) would have promotion shows once a year or so. They would bring in six or eight acts to a stadium or auditorium and each of us would do our record and maybe one more song. Phyllis and I would come out and sing our records with the stage bands for a while. It was great money, but the sound was not as good as having your own band. I do miss those shows though because the audiences were great and it was fun to meet other entertainers from all over the country.

Although they had fun doing those shows just a few years removed from their days as performers, "we've never wanted to do oldies shows—we've always thought that would spoil a great memory." Most of their musical output during their post-performing years was done in advertising, singing commercial jingles and the like.

The Supremes

BEACH MUSIC DISCOGRAPHY: "Where Did Our Love Go?" (Motown 1060, 1964: Billboard Pop #1); "Baby Love" (Motown 1066, 1964: Billboard Pop #1).

Mary Wilson and Florence Ballard were Detroit junior high school students when they joined with Betty McGlown and Diane Ross to form the Primettes. They were formed as a counterpart to the Primes, whose members included Paul Williams and Eddie Kendricks, whose group would eventually evolve into the Temptations. Ballard and Wilson were friends, McGlown was Willams' girlfriend, and Ross was Wilson's classmate. As a quartet starting out they often performed for free, but after winning an amateur talent contest they decided to audition for the new Motown label. Auditioning first for Smokey Robinson, then Berry Gordy, for whom they sang The Drifters "There Goes My Baby," they impressed both men but Gordy told them to finish high school and then come back and see him. They recorded one failed single on the Lu Pine label, "Tears of Sorrow," but continued to hang around the Motown offices and actually earned a spot singing back up on a few sides for Mary Wells and Marvin Gaye. McGlown left the group to be replaced by Barbara Martin, and at about this time Gordy relented and signed the group to his label. He didn't like their name, however, and from a list of suggestions they chose The Supremes. It was also at Gordy's suggestion that Ross changed her name from Diane to Diana, and thereafter Martin, Ross, Wilson, and Ballard were in place as The Supremes.

Their first Motown release was 1961's "I Want a Guy" on the Tamla subsidiary. Neither this song nor their next charted, and in 1962 Martin left the group and they moved forward as a trio. In 1962 they had their first chart single, "Your Heart Belongs to Me," which barely snuck into the Billboard Pop Top 100 at #95. Their next three releases performed in much the same fashion, the highest charting being the Smokey Robinson-penned song 1963's "A Breath Taking Guy," which stalled at #75. That same year they had their first Top 40 hit, the Holland, Dozier, and Holland-penned "When the Lovelight Starts Shining through His Eyes," which climbed to #23. Though it would seem they had turned the corner, their next release, 1964's "Run, Run, Run" peaked at #93.

With six straight singles, only one of which broke the Top 40, by early 1964 the group seemed destined to be Motown's first big failure, and in fact it is well known that they were often referred to as the "The No-Hit Supremes." Still, when the songwriting team of Holland, Dozier and Holland offered them "Where Did Our Love Go" they weren't sure they wanted it. Conflicting stories have emerged in the years since the song's release, but apparently the Marvelettes may have been offered the song first, but felt it was a bit slower than their normal style and passed. The Supremes, however, wanted something faster, too—in the Marvelettes style, oddly enough—and were not thrilled about "Where Did Our Love Go." Having had no big hits themselves however the group felt obliged to record it.

The next problem that arose was who would sing it. It seemed to fit Mary Wilson's voice better, but Ross had handled lead duties on all of their chart singles. Eventually Ross was instructed to sing in a lower key than normal and did so. Yet despite all of the issues prior to recording the song, they seemed to know as soon as they heard it that the song would be a hit. Not long after the record's release the group was touring with the Dick Clark Caravan of Stars, and ironically they were only on the bill because Clark wanted Brenda Holloway and Gordy offered the Supremes as a take-it-or-leave-it package deal. When the song reached #1 the Supremes, who were almost an after-thought on a bill featuring Major Lance, the Dixie Cups, Bryan Hyland, and the Shirelles, suddenly became the headline act. The song was #1 for two weeks and spent nine weeks in the Top 10.

One of the song's most characteristic sounds is the footstomping in the background, which was done by Mike Valvano. He had originally pursued a career in music as the lead of his group the Modifiers (and later the Hornets), but soon he was performing all type of odd jobs at Motown on recordings and behind the scenes. After the success of "Where Did Our Love Go," Gordy instructed Holland, Dozier, and Holland to find the Supremes a song that was very similar to their #1 recording, and the result was "Baby Love." It had the same musicians (the Funk Brothers), and even had Valvano keeping time once again. The song also went to #1 and remained there for four weeks, and was nominated for a Grammy for Best R&B Recording in 1965.

"Baby Love" was just one in a long string of hits. Their next three singles—"Come See About Me," "Stop! In the Name of Love," and "Back in My Arms Again," all hit #1, followed by "Nothing But Heartaches," which peaked at #11, followed by another #1, "I Hear a Symphony." By the end of the decade, the Supremes would have a total of twelve #1 hits, more than any American group, and surpassed only by the Beatles among all groups, who had 20. In terms of beach music however, while many of their mid-60s recordings were danceable, like many Motown acts their bigger hits were not embraced by beach music audiences as hard core beach music.

Like several other Motown acts, the group's name was changed to feature their lead singer, and so they became Diana Ross and the Supremes. Also not unlike other groups, over the years the Supremes had personnel changes. Ballard was having problems with alcohol, and after a number of incidents, Cindy Birdsong replaced her in 1967. Ross left the group to go solo in 1970, and the group replaced her with Jean Terrell and took the name The Supremes once again. Their first single, "Up the Ladder to the Roof," made the Top 10, and in fact was fairly popular in shag clubs. Their next, "Stoned Love," hit #7, but although they didn't know it at the time it would be their last Top 10 hit on the pop charts and their last R&B #1. Cindy Birdsong left the group and was replaced by Lynda Laurence, who then left and Birdsong came back. Terrell left in 1973 and was replaced by Scherrie Payne, Freda Payne's sister, Birdsong left again and was replaced by Susaye Greene in 1976. They had their final Top 40 hit that year, "I'm Gonna Let My Heart do the Walking," before disbanding in 1977.

Mary Wilson had remained the one constant over the years. Ross went on to be immensely successful as a solo artist, while Ballard had a couple of underperforming singles but died in poverty in 1976 at the age of 32. Wilson and Ross are both still living at the time of this writing. The group was inducted into the Rock and Roll Hall of Fame in 1988, the Vocal Group Hall of Fame in 1998, and received a star on the Hollywood Walk of Fame in 1994.

The Swallows

BEACH MUSIC DISCOGRAPHY: "It Ain't the Meat" (1951, King 4501: Did not chart).

The Swallows started out in the 1940s as a group of Baltimore teenagers calling themselves the Oakaleers. They were a typical streetcorner group, singing where they could and looking for a break. One of the members lived across the street from Sonny Til, who would eventually go on to lead the Orioles and have a #1 R&B hit in 1948 with "It's Too Soon to Know," and later their biggest crossover hit, 1953's "Crying in the Chapel." The Orioles were reportedly the first of a plethora of groups (including the Cardinals, the Wrens, the Robins, and the Ravens) to name themselves after birds in the late '40s and early '50s, and certainly their proximity and success contributed to the Oakaleers eventually renaming themselves the Swallows (reportedly the name was suggested by one group member's mother, whose favorite song was "When the Swallows Come Back to Capistrano" by the Ink Spots). Eventually the group came to attention Maryland DJ Jack Gale, who contacted a man named Bill Levinson, who would, along with Ike Goldstick, manage and book the group. Eventually King

The Swallows, circa 1951 (photograph courtesy Todd Baptista).

Records signed them to a recording contract, and in April 1951 they recorded four songs with Eddie Rich singing lead; one of them, "Will You Be Mine," peaked at #9 on the R&B charts. Though the group's releases sold, none were big hits. On September 19th, 1951, in a New York session they recorded two songs with bass singer Bunky Mack on the lead, "It Ain't The Meat" and "Roll, Roll, Pretty Baby." Rich said the decision to feature Mack on the song, though unorthodox, was almost natural: "Bunky had a voice where he could sing by himself. I'd put him in a class with an artist like Brook Benton. He was damn good, a real strong bass."

In December the record company released the slow ballad "Eternally" with the raucous "It Ain't The Meat" on the flipside. The *Billboard* Rhythm and Blues record review for December 22, 1951, lists the "It Ain't the Meat"'s position at #84, and commented that "The vocal group has a winner in a rhythmic hand-clapper with an intriguing lyric. This one could follow the 'Sixty Minute Man' success story. Could meet with difficulties at radio censors." "Sixty Minute Man" was in fact at #9 that same week, and had been on the charts for 30 weeks. Ultimately, the song wasn't a big hit, and the censors probably did hurt it. Rich said "Everybody liked it everywhere, no doubt about it. But if it came out now with the stuff that they allow on T.V. and the radio, it would have been a million-seller. But you couldn't play it. The people blackballed us on that." While certainly it's mild by today's standards, it's still edgy, and so even today it comes off as extremely risque (indeed, when the Poor Souls released the song in on the Surfside label in 1982 their version changed the title to "It Ain't The *Beat*, It's The Motion"). Consequently, though this was a great rhythmic song, with superb harmonies, piano, and a pulsating beat set off by handclapping, is was a bit too overtly sexual for most people at the time, and as a result it was not a big seller.

The Swallows would go on to record dozens of tracks, but they would never have that one really big hit they were looking for. They would disband in 1956 (Mack had left by 1953), then Eddie Rich reformed them in 1957. This group would record a few records but no big hits, disband again, and then reform again with the result that, as of this writing, there is still a Swallows group performing led by Eddie Rich, the last living original member.

The Swingin' Medallions

BEACH MUSIC DISCOGRAPHY: "Double Shot (Of My Baby's Love)" (Smash 2033, 1966: Billboard #17); "She Drives Me Out of My Mind" (Smash 2050, 1966: Billboard #71).

The Medallions got together in 1962 at Lander College in Greenwood, South Carolina. Group founder John McElrath and his friends formed the band to make extra money to help pay for school. Their act was based in rhythm and blues, and like many regional bands during the 1960s they made their living lining up gigs to play across the South. After a few years in

The Swingin' Medallions, circa 1966 (photograph courtesy John McElrath).

the clubs and on the campus party circuit, McElrath and the group—by that time consisting of Carroll Bledsoe, Steve Caldwell, Jim Doares, Brent Forston, Charlie Webber, Jimmy Perkins and Joe Morris—wanted to record "Double Shot," a huge regional hit that had been originally recorded by Louisianan Dick Holler and his group the Holidays. "I had heard it played in Columbia in the 1950s," McElrath said. "It was a local hit when I was a teenager, and when we put our band together we started playing it too."

Eventually, the group was encouraged to record the song: "We were with Bill Lowery in Atlanta, and they kept trying to have us record it with different arrangements and in different ways with horns and so forth that didn't fit the song. We wanted to play it live like we did at shows, so we just took off and went to Arthur Smith Studios in Charlotte. We actually pulled in people off the street and had a big crowd in the studio to make background noise, and that party atmosphere gave us the sound we were looking for." With that version, everything clicked. Initially the record was released on their For Sale label, and they sold them at their performances, but the record got some airplay and really started to take off. Soon they added the "Swingin'" moniker to the Medallions name, and history was made.

Smash records liked what they heard, but before distributing the record nationally they wanted the song altered a bit and wanted Holler's original lyrics changed for the Medallions version. McElrath said, "They didn't like some lines, like 'Woke up this morning, my head hurt so bad/ The worst hangover that I ever had,' and made us change it to 'worst morning after that I ever had'—which was stupid, I thought." But even with the changes it worked, and the single was released and became a million-seller, going all the way to #17 on the charts. "It was strange, really, because it had moved up on the charts before it got played up North and out West and became a hit. It helped us as far as our touring went because it was so popular."

The group next released "She Drives Me Out of My Mind." "Freddie Weller, a friend of ours with Bill Lowery, wrote the song. They wanted it to be as close to 'Double Shot' as we could make it." Despite—or maybe because of—the similarities, the record stalled at #71, and their next release was another party track, a version of Bruce Channel's "Hey! Baby" called "Hey, Hey Baby." It did not chart but has become a southern party staple nonetheless.

Eventually, band members went their separate ways, some going on to form the group Pieces of Eight, most going back to college to finish their educations. "We had a lot of fun," McElrath said. "I think we just lucked into it." The band and their music have become legendary in the Carolinas, and play in the Carolinas to this day. As for "Double Shot"'s writer, Dick Holler would go on to pen a number of hits for other artists, including "Abraham, Martin, and John" for Dion, and he'd co-write "Snoopy vs. the Red Baron" by The Royal Guardsmen.

The Tams

BEACH MUSIC DISCOGRAPHY: "Untie Me" (Arlen 711, 1962: Billboard Pop #60); "Find Another Love" (Arlen 729, 1963: Did Not Chart); "What Kind of Fool (Do You Think I

Am?)/Laugh It Off" (ABC-Paramount 10502, 1963: Billboard Pop #9); "You Lied to Your Daddy/It's All Right (You're Just in Love)" (ABC-Paramount 10533, 1964: Billboard Pop #70/79); "Hey Girl, Don't Bother Me" (ABC Paramount 10573, 1964: Billboard Pop #41); "Silly Little Girl" (ABC-Paramount 10601, 1964: Billboard Pop #87); "I've Been Hurt" (ABC-Paramount 10741, 1965: Did Not Chart); "Riding for a Fall" (ABC-Paramount 10770, 1966: Did Not Chart); "It's Better to Have Loved a Little" (ABC-Paramount 10825, 1966: Did Not Chart); "Be Young, Be Foolish, Be Happy" (ABC 11066, 1968: Billboard Pop #61); "Too Much Foolin Around" (1–2–3 1726, 1970: Did Not Chart); "The Tams Medley" (Capitol 3050, 1971: Did Not Chart); "This Precious Moment" (Sounds South 14098, 1978, Did Not Chart).

The Tams got their start around 1952 as students at David T. Howard High School in Atlanta, Georgia. As the Four Dots, Brothers Joe and Charles Pope, Robert Lee Smith, and Willie James "Frog" Rutherford played in Atlanta area clubs in the 1950s, although after Floyd "Little Floyd" Ashton joined to make the group a quintet they decided they needed a new name. Rutherford had purchased red sweaters and blue tam o'shanter hats for the group to perform in, and as Charles Pope told the author this was "because we really couldn't afford anything else." Taking their cue from their stage wear, they became The Tams.

The Tams, circa early 1970s (photograph courtesy Charles and Diane Pope).

After Rutherford ran into to some legal trouble he was replaced by Horace "Sonny" Key, and by 1960 the group's line-up of the Popes, Smith, Ashton, and Key would remain the same for the next four years. They recorded one non-charting single for Heritage before they came to the attention of Atlanta song publisher and entrepreneur Bill Lowery, who arranged for the group to record a song written by Joe South, "Untie Me." Sold to Philadelphia's Arlen records and released in 1962, the song was recorded at Rick Hall's FAME Studio in Muscle Shoals, Alabama. One of the studio's first recordings had been Arthur Alexander's hit "You Better Move On," and the studio magic that worked for Alexander as well as Tommy Roe, Etta James, The Rolling Stones, Paul Simon, Wilson Pickett and others later, worked for The Tams as well. The song featured led singer Joe Pope's gravelly lead vocals and piano work by the then-unknown Ray Stevens. "Untie Me" climbed to #62 on the Hot 100 and #12 on the R&B charts, and the group followed it with four more releases on Arlen in 1962 and 1963, only one of which, 1963's "Find Another Love" has a had much of a shelf life and is well known today.

Several things happened which would take The Tams' music to a whole new level. Perhaps most importantly, they'd start working with a young songwriter who was a protégé of Lowery's, Ray Whitley. The Columbus Georgia native was just 20 years old, and would go on to write for Brian Hyland, Tommy Roe, The Swingin' Medallions and others. The first song he wrote for The Tams was called "What Kind of Fool (Do You Think I Am?)," which the group also recorded at Hall's FAME Studios. ABC-Paramount picked up the song and it went #9 on the Billboard pop charts and #1 on the *Cash Box* R&B chart, even though, Charles Pope said that he "was surprised by 'What Kind of Fool.'" because he didn't like it much and "didn't even want that song to be our second release." Nevertheless, the combination of Whitley's songwriting and The Tams voices seemed to be a recipe for success, and even the song's flip side, another Whitley composition called "Laugh It Off," went on to become a beach classic as well.

This led to a long series of national and regional hits. Their next release was the Whitley-penned "You Lied to Your Daddy," which went to #70 on the charts, while it's flipside, "It's All Right (You're Just in Love)" made the charts as well, peaking at #79. This was followed by another Whitley composition, "Hey Girl Don't Bother Me," which went to #41 on the pop charts, and "Silly Little Girl," which went to #87. Charles Pope recalled that "Silly Little Girl" was his brother "Joe's favorite song. He especially liked to perform it live and would ad-lib a lot of lines that weren't in the song originally. He'd add 'I'll even beg you girl' and things like that." "Silly Little Girl" was the first single release written for the group by Joe South since "Untie Me," and interestingly its flipside, "Weep Little Girl," was by an up-and-coming songwriter named Mac Davis.

Although The Tams' songs weren't charting high—only one had broken the Billboard Pop Top 40—their records were selling quite well and the group was developing a huge regional following. Unfortunately by this point Floyd Ashton was having problems with alcohol, which was affecting his performances, and he was replaced by Albert Cottle. After two largely forgettable single releases in early 1965 (though "Concrete Jungle" does have its fans), their third release of 1965 was another Ray Whitley composition, "I've Been Hurt." Despite the fact that the song didn't chart, Pope said it was "a favorite with the college kids," so it became a monster regional hit and was reportedly the best-selling and most often played Tams song of all time—despite the fact that it never made the Hot 100. Their next single release, 1966's "Riding for a Fall," was another Mac Davis composition, and it was followed by the Joe South- penned "It's Better to Have Loved a Little." Though neither of them charted, they were hits in the South, and it was becoming apparent that almost anything the group released had a strong appeal for beach music audiences.

In 1968, they released the anthemic "Be Young, Be Foolish, Be Happy," which for many beach music lovers epitomizes the beach music experience. "Be Young" was written by Whitley along with J.R. Cobb, and had actually been first recorded by the Columbia, South Carolina–based Sensational Epics. Although Pope said "Bill Lowery chose all the songs for us," that did not apply in the case of "Be Young, Be Foolish." "It had been recorded by another group, who hadn't had a hit with it, but Joe wanted to do the song, so Bill let us do it" Pope says. While "Be Young" would only hit #61 on the pop charts, it would go to #26 on the R&B charts and would eventually sell more than one million copies and be a RIAA-Certified Gold Record.

After nearly a decade, regionally The Tams were as popular as ever, but after a few more releases on ABC the group and the label parted ways. In 1970 the group released another song by Whitley, "Too Much Foolin Around," which Pope said they "recorded in Mississippi on Bill Lowery's own 1–2–3 Label." Though the song didn't make the pop charts, it was another big regional beach music hit. But things were not going well in terms of the relationship between the group and Lowery by this time. Pope says though the group was selling a lot of records, very little money was trickling down to the members of the group, and that was causing unrest. The group honored their contract with Lowery nevertheless, and they next released "The Tams Medley" in 1971, a compilation of Whitley-penned hits by the group, including "Hey Girl, Don't Bother Me," "What Kind of Fool (Do You Think I Am)," "You Lied to Your Daddy," "I've Been Hurt," "Laugh It Off," and "Be Young, Be Foolish, Be Happy." "We had all wanted to do a medley of our songs, so we talked to Bill Lowery and he had the writers put together 'The Tams Medley'—and we loved it" Pope said. Released by Capitol records in 1971, though it failed to chart nationally, it became yet another popular regional hit and would go on to be one of their most popular numbers on the beach music circuit.

At about this same time, the group would have a huge chart hit—but not in the United States. Due to the Northern Soul boom in England, 1964's "Hey Girl Don't Bother Me" had found a whole new audience, and upon its re-release in England it went all the way to #1, stayed there for three weeks, and was song of the year in the UK. Pope noted that this was a pleasant surprise, and a highlight of the song's popularity was that "we went over and performed at *Top of the Pops* with Rod Stewart in 1971." Hoping to capitalize on this success in the States as well, ABC Dunhill re-released the song in the U.S. in 1971 in a sleeve that said "It's Number ONE in England and the Biggest Selling Record in the U.K. this Year." The song didn't re-connect with audiences here as it had in England, and the U.S. re-release failed to chart.

Despite a decade of success, by the early 1970s their relationship with Bill Lowery had finally reached a breaking point. Like many R&B artists during the 1950s and '60s, The Tams saw very little of the profits from their music. "Lowery just seemed to get all of the money—he always did," Pope said. "I have paperwork about all kinds of money we were supposed to get for record sales, but we never saw it." The group split with Lowery as their manager, but even then they couldn't make a clean break. "We left Bill sometime in 1972, and even though he stopped managing us, he still did some of our bookings. He and Cotton Carrier had an agency and booked all of our acts. Everyone called them to book the Tams, so he still had control of the booking money." Eventually the group "went with Harold

Thomas from Charleston, and he was the one that put out 'This Precious Moment'" in 1978. The group returned to Muscle Shoals to record it, and the result was that "This Precious Moment" was a lushly orchestrated number with a late '70s dance beat; the flip was actually a reworking of "Hey Girl, Don't Bother Me," also in a late-70s danceable format. Though the song didn't chart, it was another regional favorite.

The group recorded into the late 1980s, and would find more chart success in England with both "There Ain't Nothing Like Shaggin'" going to #21 on the British charts in 1987, and "My Baby Sure Can Shag" going to #91 in 1988. "What Kind of Fool" was one of the songs featured in the 1989 film *Shag*, and it reintroduced their music to new audiences everywhere. A new group of The Tams still actively performs today, even though both Joe and Charles Pope are now deceased. "My son Little Redd started with me and my brother Joe when he was seven years old, and he'll be taking over the Tams. That's why I say the Tams will never die" Pope told me before he passed away in 2013. With multiple national and regional hits, The Tams stand alone as the premier homegrown beach music group who bridged the two milieus, and who are regarded as beach music royalty even today.

Tavares

BEACH MUSIC DISCOGRAPHY: "Bein' With You" (Capitol album cut, 1976: Did Not Chart).

Providence, Rhode Island-born John, Ralph, Arthur (nicknamed "Pooch"), Antone ("Chubby"), Victor, Feliciano Jr. ("Butch") and Perry Lee ("Tiny") were the sons of Feliciano and Albina Tavares, both of whom were active singers and musicians. By the late 1950s John, Ralph, Chubby, Pooch and a cousin formed a doo-wop group called the Del Rios, and were offered a recording opportunity by producer Juggy Murray. Their 1962 release on Murray's Crackerjack subsidiary, "Come On, Let Me Try," paired them with Providence singer Linda Steele but nevertheless the single failed to chart and the group broke up. Chubby, Pooch, and Butch then formed a group called Chubby & The Realities, and by the late '60s the group had expanded to include a back-up band. In 1967 they were signed by producer Marvin Holzman, who thought he could take the group beyond the six-night-a-week schedule of nightclubs and small venues they were playing in the Northeast. Holzman had the group record a couple of sides which Capitol agreed to release on the condition that the group, once again, change their name. As Chubby & the Turnpikes they released "I Know the Inside Story" in 1968, which failed to chart. A 1969 single released as being by The Turnpikes, "Cast a Spell," failed as well, and once again the group found themselves without a label.

Over the next few years their line-up changed several times, and the band morphed into more of a show band than a mere vocal group. They changed their name to Tavares, and covered a Friends of Distinction B-side called "Check It Out." Capitol Records liked what they heard and signed the group once again, though this time it would be the start of a continued and productive relationship at long last. The single went to #5 the R&B charts and #35 on the pop charts, but surprisingy at that point their brother Victor decided to leave the group to go solo. Capitol paired the rest of the group with Johnny Bristol to produce their first album, *Check It Out*, in 1974. A second single for the album, "That's the Sound That Lonely Makes," also made the R&B charts.

From their next album, 1974's *Hard Core Poetry*, three singles charted, including "She's Gone," written by the also then-unknown duo of Hall & Oates. The song went to #1 on the R&B charts for Tavares, prompting Hall & Oates to re-release it in when it went to #7 on the pop charts. Their next album, 1975's *In The City*, again offered up three chart hits, of which "It Only Takes a Minute" went to #10 on the pop charts and received a good bit of play in the beach clubs.

With their next album, 1976's Freddie Perren produced *Sky High!*, they reached the pinnacle of their success. Perren had worked with the Jackson 5 at Motown, then the Miracles, and most recently had worked with the Sylvers on their biggest hits. On the *Sky High!* album, Perren not only produced but co-wrote the two biggest chart hits from the album, "Heaven Must Be Missing an Angel," which hit #15 on the pop charts, and "Don't Take Away the Music," which went to #34 on the pop charts. Both were crossover hits in more than the traditional sense, in that both received a great deal of play in the beach clubs, the former especially. Perhaps the most astounding achievement on the album was a song not released as single in the United States, "Bein' With You." The song, also produced and co-written by Freddie Perren, was one of the best songs written during the 1970s that fit into the beach music genre, and was perfect for shagging. Its play as an album cut in the southeast gained it and the group an even broader audience than their disco-styled dance cuts, despite the fact that the song was never released as a single. In 1978 Capitol did release the song as a single in the UK however, as the B-side to "The Ghost of Love." "The Ghost of Love" made its way to #29 on the British charts, and as with a few other songs that connected with beach music audiences but were not single releases in the U.S., a number of copies eventually found their way to jukeboxes in the southeast.

The group's next big success came with the inclusion of their version of a song written by the Bee Gees, "More Than a Woman," on the soundtrack to the movie *Saturday Night Fever*. Both the Bee Gees and Tavares recorded it for the soundtrack, though the Bee Gees never released it as a single. Tavares' version went to #32 on the charts, and earned them their only Grammy when the fifteen-times-platinum album won the 1978 Album of the Year award. It would also be the highest pop chart record they have from that point on, as their popularity began to fade as disco and dance music was soon on the wane. The group's membership has fluctuated since, with the brothers at times performing together and doing solo work as well. As of this publication, Pooch, Chubby, Butch, and Tiny were performing as Tavares.

Gloria Taylor

BEACH MUSIC DISCOGRAPHY: "You've Got to Pay the Price" (Silver Fox 14, 1969: Billboard Pop #49).

Gloria Ann Taylor was born in West Virginia though her family moved to Toledo, Ohio, when she was two. She was diagnosed with rheumatic fever as a child, and Taylor's mother was told Gloria would not live past her teenage years. After three years at the Feilbach School for Crippled Children she was able to attend public school and lead a normal life, and that included singing in church. When she was 18 she started singing in nightclubs with a repertoire that was heavy in the music of Aretha Franklin and other strong-voiced soul singers from the period.

Taylor was discovered by promoter Walter "Whiz" Whisenhunt, who worked with James Brown, and who had produced for the Larks, Doris Troy, and others. After meeting Taylor he worked with her almost exclusively, the two were married, and he took her from the Toledo nightclub circuit to the vibrant Detroit music scene. Taylor released three singles on the King Soul label (the only three records released on King Soul), and a couple on Glo-Whiz (also the only two releases that label seems to have produced), including a song that would be picked up and released by the Silver Fox label in 1969, "You've Got to Pay the Price." The song was a B-side instrumental written by Al Kent and Hermon Weems and performed by Kent with Dennis Coffey on guitar on the Ric-Tic label in 1967. Kent had written and produced songs while working with artists such as The Drifters, and had produced Edwin Starr's "Stop Her on Sight" as well. Kent's instrumental version of "You've Got to Pay the Price" had peaked at #22 on the R&B charts and #49 on the pop charts, while Taylor's vocal version went to #9 on the R&B charts and #49 on the pop charts. Despite the fact that it wasn't a big chart hit, "You've Got to Pay the Price" was nominated for a Grammy for Best R&B Vocal Performance, but lost to Aretha Franklin—no surprise given that Franklin won every Grammy in that category from 1968–1975 and three after that as well. Despite the loss, Taylor seemed to be on the cusp of a successful career.

Taylor had one more R&B chart hit in 1970 "Grounded" (R&B #43), and she and Whisenhunt moved to California to sign with Columbia, where she only had the low charting "Deep Inside You" (R&B #96) in 1974. Whisenhunt and Columbia disagreed with the way Taylor's music was being released, and he took her away from the label and she signed with Mercury for a few sides. Whisenhunt was also having her record for his own Selector Sound label (yet another label for which she was the sole act, with just a half dozen releases), but after the Columbia release nothing charted at all. Taylor and Whisenhunt ended their marriage and working relationship not long afterwards, and Taylor moved back to Toledo and got out of the music business.

Willie Tee

BEACH MUSIC DISCOGRAPHY: "Teasin' You" b/w "Walking Up a One-Way Street" (Atlantic 2273, 1965: Billboard Pop #97); "Thank You John" (Atlantic 2287, 1965: Did Not Chart); "Please Don't Go" (Nola 737, 1966: Did Not Chart).

Willie Tee was born in New Orleans' Central City District as Wilson Turbinton, where he was surrounded and influenced by the vibrant New Orleans music scene. His father played the trombone and his older brother Earl played saxophone while Willie learned to play the piano. Willie and his brother put together their first band, the Seminoles, who played local gigs and even cut a demo. In junior high Willie's music teacher was none other than Harold Batiste, who in 1961 would form the first all-black-owned record label in New Orleans, A.F.O. (All For One) records along with New Orleans music scene luminaries such as Allen Toussaint and Melvin Lastie. As a producer and arranger for the label Batiste would work on songs such as Barbara George's "I Know," Joe Jones's "You Talk Too Much," Lee Dorsey's "Ya Ya" and others. In 1962 Wilson, though still in high school, recorded his first single, "Always Accused," on A.F.O. Although the song got some airplay locally, it was notable in that the recording was attributed to Willie Tee, a name given to Turbinton by A.F.O.'s Red Tyler. Willie Tee recorded one more single on A.F.O before the label folded, and he next recorded on the Cinderella label in 1963. None of the songs were hits.

Tee next signed with his cousin Julius Gaines' New Orleans–based Nola records. The label's eighth single release was "Teasin' You," a song that apparently Tee was reluctant to record because he felt it was too great a departure from the jazz-like sound he was seeking to be known for. But the song quickly found an audience, and after the Righteous Brothers sang "Teasin' You" on the popular music showcase program *Shindig!*, suddenly Tee was a hot property. Atlantic picked up the rights to distribute the song nationally, and it just barely charted at #97 though it did reach #12 on the R&B charts. Almost unnoticed was the flip side of the record, the now popular "Walking Up a One-Way Street." That song, in which Tee laments being left alone and almost tortured by his lover, puts into perspective the one-sidedness of their relationship. Plaintive and soulful, Tee's song, though it did not chart, nevertheless touched a nerve with beach music lovers and has remained a classic since its release. Like many beach music songs, its failure to make the national charts has not been an impediment.

The Top 100 Billboard slot "Teasin' You" earned was apparently encouraging enough that Atlantic gave Tee another shot, and his next recording for the label was 1965's immortal "Thank You John." "Thank You John" is an odd song, or at least the subject matter is. It seems to be about deception, infidelity, physical abuse, pimping, lying—any and all of the above. Though "Thank You John" failed to connect with fans nationally, it was popular enough that Tee began touring on the famed "Chitlin Circuit." Despite a failure to consistently connect with fans nationally, in the Southeast the record became a beach music staple in a very short time indeed.

After "Thank You John" and his next single, "I Want Somebody," both failed to chart, Atlantic didn't renew Tee's contract. His next single was for Nola, 1966's great "Please Don't Go," now regarded as a good beach tune in its own right. Of his subsequent singles on Nola, Hot Line, and Bonatemp, none really did much outside of the New Orleans area, although a contract with Capitol in 1970 did produce a fine cover of Burt Bacharach and Hal David's "Reach Out for Me." Dissatisfied with his contract with Capitol, he created his own label, Gatur, in 1971. Founded with old friend Julius Gaines, "Gatur" was derived from the names *Gaines* and *Tur*binton, Tee would release singles on the label throughout the decade. While many were popular in the New Orleans area, none made the national charts. Though he'd never again have a record make the popular charts, he remained a mainstay of the New Orleans music scene for the rest of his life, performing, producing and recording a variety of music until his death from cancer in 2007. He was inducted into the Beach Music Hall of Fame in 2005.

The Tempests

BEACH MUSIC DISCOGRAPHY: "Would You Believe" (Smash 2094, 1967: Did Not Chart).

The Tempests originated in Charlotte North Carolina in the early 1960s when high school student John Roger Branch founded a cover band called the Larks, though Branch later changed the group's name to The Tempests after reading the *The Tempest* by William Shakespeare. The band met James Arp, who already had a record deal with Vellez Records, and as James Arp and The Tempest they cut "Let it Rock" though it failed to chart. They then signed a management deal with Charlotte DJ "Chattie" Hattie Leeper, who already managed lead singer Mike Williams. Williams had signed a record deal with Atlantic, but he needed a band to back him. As The Tempest Band they recorded "Love Have Mercy" and the record failed to chart. Williams fronted the band for a short time but eventually went solo, and he had a minor hit with "Lonely Soldier."

By 1966 the band consisted of Roger Branch as well as Roger's brother Mike, Nelson Lemmond, Van Coble, Tom Brawley, Gerald Schrum, Rick White, Ronnie Smith and Jim Butt. They continued to do back up work as they searched for a new lead, and they heard about a singer named Hazel Walker who sang with the Pastels and decided to invite him to join. Through a series of mix ups they ended up finding singer Hazel *Martin* instead, who would become the group's lead during their most productive period. They cut some demos at Edgebrook Studios in Washington and Arthur Smith Studios in Charlotte, and then while backing up Little Sonny Warner they met his manager Ted Bodnar, who agreed to manage and produce them as well. Bodnar got them a recording deal with the Smash label, who had also signed the Swingin' Medallions and for whom the Georgia Prophets would also record "I Got the Fever."

The group was still playing fraternity parties and clubs in the South when their first single for Smash, the 1967 classic "Would You Believe" was released. While the song performed well in the Southeast and even in New York, it made little impact west of the Mississippi and did not break into the Hot 100 though it did manage to "bubble under" at #127. Smash followed up with an album of the same name, but their next two singles—"What You Gonna Do" in 1967 and "In the Cold Light of Day" in 1968—failed to chart. The group was touring extensively during this period, having signed with New York's Premier Talent Agency, and found themselves on the bill with acts such as the Four Tops and Jay and the Techniques. By this point Hazel Martin had come to feel that he should receive billing as the frontman, and so for a while the group performed as Hazel Martin and the Tempests though it did lead to some dissension. They also signed Otis Adams to share vocal duties during some performances, and though Martin sang lead on their last single for Smash, 1968's "Out of My Life," Adams sang lead on the flip side, "The Way to a Man's Heart." Though not released as a single, the album cut "Someday" would be a big hit on the Northern Soul scene in England.

From this point on the group changed personnel frequently, and after Martin left they enlisted Allan Waldman as a lead singer and then he was replaced by Buddy Hawks, who handled the vocal chores on "Georgia Woods" on Polydor. Changing lead singers yet again, this time Bruce West joined the group to sing lead on 1971's "Rockin' Pneumonia and Boogie Woogie Flu" on Polydor, an old Huey "Piano" Smith song from 1957. The Tempests' version did not chart, but the Johnny Rivers version released on UA peaked at #6 in 1973. Changing personnel once again, by this point Roger Branch had reduced the group from what had once been a high of ten members in the late 1960s to a four piece band with a female, Nan Mason, singing lead. Mason left in 1974, the group recorded their last two singles, "You Are Always on My Mind" and "Boogie Woogie USA" on the Southern Wing label in 1974 before breaking up in 1975. Mike Branch would go on to form Surfside records in 1979 with General Johnson, and the label would be home to "new" beach music hits by the Chairmen of the Board, the Poor Souls, the Band of Oz, and others. The Tempests were inducted into the Beach Music Hall of Fame in 1996.

The Temptations

BEACH MUSIC DISCOGRAPHY: "I Want a Love I Can See" (Gordy 7015, 1963: Did Not Chart); "The Way You Do the Things You Do" (Gordy 7028, 1964: Billboard Pop #11); "The

Girl's Alright With Me" (Gordy 7032, 1964: Billboard Pop #102); "Girl (Why You Wanna Make Me Blue)" (Gordy 7035, 1964: Billboard Pop #26); "My Girl" (Gordy 7038, 1965: Billboard Pop #1); "Since I Lost My Baby" (Gordy 7043, 1965: Billboard Pop #17); "My Baby" (Gordy 7047, 1965: Billboard Pop #13); "Ain't Too Proud to Beg" (Gordy 7054, 1966: Billboard Pop #13); "Beauty Is Only Skin Deep" (Gordy 7055, 1966: Billboard Pop #3).

The original Temptations were formed in Detroit as the Elgins in 1960 and consisted of Otis Williams, Eldridge Bryant, Melvin Franklin, Eddie Kendricks and Paul Williams. Williams and Kendricks had been singing together since childhood, and were involved in several groups such as the Cavaliers and the Primes. Williams and Bryant were members of Otis Williams and the Siberians, and after a series of changes they all, along with Franklin, became the Elgins. They auditioned and signed with Motown in 1961, but Berry Gordy had them change to their name to the Temptations. Although they released seven singles in the early '60s, nothing made the Top 40 on the pop charts. The group tried various leads during this period but remained unsuccessful, even though the quality of their music was exceptional, such as their 1963 single "I Want a Love I Can See." The song was written and produced for them by Miracles lead singer Smokey Robinson and featured Williams on lead vocals, but the song did not make the pop or R&B charts. At that point in 1963 the group had yet to have a single break the Top 100 on the pop charts and had had only one low-charting R&B single, and it was only when Eldridge Bryant left and David Ruffin (brother of Motown solo artist Jimmy Ruffin) joined the group in 1964 that things started to gel. They made some progress towards stardom with "The Way You Do the Things You Do," which featured Kendricks on lead and was their first Top 20 hit. Kendricks also sang lead on their next two releases, and "Girl (Why You Wanna Make Me Blue)" and "The Girl's Alright with Me." "Girl (Why You Wanna Make Me Blue)" was produced by Norman Whitfield, who co-wrote the song with Eddie Holland. "The Girl's Alright with Me" was on the flip side of "I'll Be in Trouble," which went to #33, but "The Girl's Alright with Me" charted as well although it only bubbled under the Top 100 at #102.

Kendricks had been singing lead to that point, but Smokey Robinson felt that with Ruffin on lead the group might be able to get to the next level. In fact, it was Ruffin's strong, gravelly, distinctive voice on his first lead performance that brought the group their first #1 hit, the unforgettable "My Girl." Smokey Robinson had written the song about his wife, Claudette, and as an answer to Mary Wells' hit the previous year "My Guy"—a song Robinson had also written. Robinson felt it would be perfect for Ruffin's vocal abilities, so he let the Temptations have it instead of giving it to his own group. The elegant orchestration of the background music gave the song an airy, romantic feel and made it one of the all-time great classic love songs. The song has remained so popular that artists as diverse as Otis Redding, Al Green, the Rolling Stones and Stevie Wonder, as well as many others, have recorded their own versions.

With Ruffin now taking over lead duties the group started to rack up the hits. Among them, "Since I Lost My Baby" and "My Baby" both became popular shag songs and both made the pop Top 20. He also sang lead on "Ain't Too Proud to Beg," a song which, though it only peaked at #13, has gone on to be one of their best-known hits. Again produced by Whitfield who, again, co-wrote it with Eddie Holland, the song would be topped by yet another Whitfield/Holland composition which followed, "Beauty Is Only Skin Deep," which went to #3.

In truth, almost every Temptations hit from this period seemed suitable for shagging, as songs such as "All I Need" and "You're My Everything" were popular as well. But although with Ruffin's distinctive voice as lead the group seemed to have found their sound at last, disagreements with Ruffin stemming from his desire for special treatment and featured status and his drug use would eventually lead to him being fired from the group in the summer of 1968. Dennis Edwards, formerly of the Contours, stepped in, and though the Temptations would continue to be successful, times were changing and the very nature of the songs changed. By the late 1960s, those feel-good, love-themed songs were few and far between, and more socially conscious songs were prevailing.

Consequently, the group was no longer recording those beach-music-type songs and so interest in the group's music in the beach clubs remained tied to those 1960s hits. The group went through a number of personnel changes in the ensuing years, but overall racked up four #1 pop hits and fifteen #1 hits on the R&B charts. Of the hit making line-up of the early and mid–1960s, only Williams is living. The group has been inducted into the Rock and Roll Hall of Fame, the R&B Music Hall of Fame, has a Lifetime Achievement Grammy as well as many other accolades.

The Trammps

BEACH MUSIC DISCOGRAPHY: "Hold Back the Night" (Buddah 507, 1975: Billboard Pop #35).

In the 1960s Philadelphian Earl Young formed a group called the Volcanos, along with Gene Faith, Steve Kelly, John Hart, Stanley Wade, and Harold "Doc" Wade. They signed with the Artic label and their second record, "Storm Warning," peaked at #33 on the R&B charts. Despite the promising beginning, their next five efforts on Arctic were unsuccessful on a

The Trammps, circa 1976 (photograph courtesy Ed Cermanski).

national level. They recorded a single on Harthon as the Body Motions, and by the early '70s they were recording as the Moods, releasing the unsuccessful single "Rainmaker" for Wand in 1970 and singles on the obscure Red Dog and Volare labels. Gene Faith was in and out of the group in pursuit of a solo career, and ultimately Young re-formed the group in 1972 with longtime members Hart and the Wades, as well as Michael Thompson, Jimmy Ellis, Ron Kersey, and Dennis Harris. They considered names such as "Bummie & the Bums" and "The Hobos" before settling on The Trammps, which Young said he chose because "they were kind of raggedy when I first got them together, so the Trammps was a pretty appropriate name." Initially the group even wore old blue jeans to fit their name, but quickly dropped that gimmick before donning glitzy '70s-appropriate show costumes.

As the Trammps, they cut "Zing Went the Strings of my Heart" on Buddah in 1972, and as their first chart record it went to #64 on the pop charts and #17 on the R&B charts. Their next release, "Sixty-Minute Man," just bubbled under the Hot 100 at #108 in 1972. "Pray all You Sinners" went to #34 on the R&B charts, but at this point Thomas decided to partner with Norman Harris and Ronnie Baker to form Golden Fleece Records. The group left Buddah for Golden Fleece, and while two releases—"Love Epidemic"(R&B #75) and "Where Do We Go From Here"(R&B #44)—made the R&B charts, only 1974's "Trusting Heart" (1974) made the pop charts, just bubbling under at #101. Golden Fleece was having problems, and the group started thinking that the label might not have the marketing ability to get their songs to crossover for pop success, so they signed with Atlantic in 1975.

Before their relationship with their new label could come to fruition, Buddah released a song which had garnered a little attention in 1973 when just an instrumental, "Hold Back the Night." Written by Young, Baker, Harris, and Allan Felder, the 1975 release charted this time around, coming in at #35 and becoming the group's first Top 40 pop record and Top 10 R&B hit. The song was an obvious reworking of an instrumental called "Scrub Board" they had recorded as the B-side to "Sixty-Minute Man" in 1972. With lyrics added to the instrumental and Jimmy Ellis singing a powerful lead, "Hold Back the Night" not only broke into the U.S. Top 40, but like so many beach music hits, it was even better appreciated in England, where it moved into the Top 10 to #5.

The group was just getting started, though subsequent tunes would more disco-based. From that point on they would go to even greater fame, recording dozens of singles, including "That's Where the Happy People Go" (1976, #27) and their mega-hit "Disco Inferno." When first released, "Disco Inferno" only climbed to #53, but when rereleased in 1978, it shot to #11. The group would have more than a dozen further releases on Atlantic, Venture, and Philly Sound through 1983, but as disco fell to the wayside so, too, waned the group's popularity. By the 1990s the group had split up, though the original members did reunite for a performance in 2005 when "Disco Inferno" was inducted into the Dance Music Hall of Fame. Although there are currently a couple of groups touring as the Trammps, lead singer Jimmy Ellis died in 2012.

Doris Troy

BEACH MUSIC DISCOGRAPHY: "Just One Look"(Atlantic 2188, 1963: Billboard Pop #10).

Born Doris Elaine Higgenson in New York City, she got her start in the music business working as an usher at the Apollo Theater in New York at age sixteen. It was at the Apollo that she was reportedly discovered by James Brown, and her first active role as a singer was as a part of the Gospelaires (with Dionne and Dee Dee Warwick), then a group known as the Halos, and she then recorded a solo side on Everest as Doris Payne (her grandmother's surname) in 1960. She followed this with a duet with Doc Bagby on the Shirley label that same year as half of Jay and Dee on Arliss in 1961, and recorded with Pearl Woods and the Gems on the Wall label in 1962.

All this time she was writing, however, and her song "How About That" had been a hit for Dee Clark in 1960. But it was when she recorded a demo of her own song, "Just One Look," in 1963 that everything changed. Atlantic's Jerry Wexler loved the record so much that they released it straight off the demo she'd made without rerecording it, although she did change her name again, this time to Doris Troy in honor of Helen of Troy. The single raced to #10 on the charts and became a bona fide hit, and although subsequent sides on Atlantic failed to find an American audience, "Whatcha Gonna Do About It," made the British Top 40 and a number of her songs would be smashes in England as part of the Northern Soul scene. England would in fact show a greater appreciation for her talents than her homeland, and after frequent visits to the UK she eventually moved there in the late 1960s. In 1969, she signed with Apple records, which would allow her to work with Beatles George Harrison and Ringo Starr, but she would never find further stateside success as a solo artist.

She cut a few singles into the 1970s, but even toward the end of her career as a solo artist, Troy was also doing session work as a background singer. She sang on a number of very famous recordings, including the Rolling Stones' "You Can't Always Get What You Want," and along with Clare Torry she provided the haunting backing vocals on the 1973 Pink Floyd album *Dark Side of the Moon*. Other artists she would do backup work for during her career included Dee Clark, Dusty Springfield, Jackie Wilson, Chuck Jackson, Solomon Burke, The Drifters, James Brown, Tom Jones, Stephen Stills and many others. In the 1980s, *Mama, I Want to Sing!*, a musical based on her life, ran for 1500 performances off Broadway and was eventually made into a film. She moved back to the States for her health, first to New York, then to Las Vegas, where she died from emphysema in 2004.

Big Joe Turner

BEACH MUSIC DISCOGRAPHY: "Honey Hush" (Atlantic 1001, 1953: Billboard Pop Did Not Chart, R&B #1—1959 remake hit Pop #53); "Shake Rattle and Roll" (Atlantic 1026, 1954: Billboard Pop Did Not Chart, R&B #1); "Flip, Flop, and Fly" (Atlantic 1053, 1955: Billboard Pop Did Not Chart, R&B #2); "Morning, Noon, and Night" (Atlantic 1080, 1956: Billboard Pop Did Not Chart, R&B #8); "Corrine, Corrina/Boogie Woogie Country Girl" (Atlantic 1088, 1956: Billboard Pop #41); "Lipstick Powder and Paint" (Atlantic 1100, 1956: Billboard Pop Did Not Chart, R&B #8); "Wee Baby Blues" (Atlantic 1167, 1957: Did Not Chart).

Kansas City-born Joseph Vernon Turner Jr. started singing on street corners as a child in an attempt to help support his mother and sister, who had lost Joe's father in a train wreck when Joe was four years old. After breaking both legs while jumping from a second story window during a fire when he was 12, through sheer determination Joe had to learn to walk again after being told he would be crippled for life. He dropped out of school when he was 14, and although he was underage he was able to get in various nightclubs to listen to bands because he was tall and disguised himself by wearing his father's old shirts and hats and drawing on a mustache with his mother's eyebrow pencil. Before long he was working in some of those same jazz clubs, first as a cook, later as a singing bartender. It was at the Backbiter's Club that he first met Pete Johnson, who would become one of music's most famous boogie-woogie pianists, and the two formed a friendship that would result in their performing together on and off in the ensuing years. Johnson got Turner a singing job at the Sunset Café, and in 1936 they headed to New York City in search of their big break. They played a few clubs there, but after a disastrous appearance at the famed Apollo Theater they went back to Kansas City.

In 1938 record producer and talent scout John Hammond was in Kansas City to hear Count Basie, and after hearing Turner and Johnson he promised them that if he they came to New York again he would help them get established. After an appearance at the "Spirituals to Swing" concert at Carnegie Hall in December 1938, where Turner impressively belted out his vocals without the use of a microphone, they signed with Vocalion Records. Their first release for the label, credited to Turner and Johnson, was 1938's "Roll 'em Pete," a boogie woogie number that some claim was a prototype for what was to become rock and roll. The Vocalion recordings led to a contract with Decca, where Turner would record early versions of later boogie woogie hits "Wee Baby Blues" and "Corrine, Corrina" in 1941. He was dropped from Decca in 1945, and afterwards recorded with several labels such as National, Stag, Dootone, Downbeat, Aladdin, Okeh, and at least a half dozen others.

The 6-foot-2 inch 300-pound singer was now performing as "Big" Joe Turner, but by 1951 his career could not be summed up using the same superlative. He'd had just three R&B chart records in his career—"S.K. Blues"(#3) in 1945, "My Gal's a Jockey"(#6) in 1946, and "Still in the Dark" (#9) in 1950—and consequently though he was a remarkable talent he had never had a major, sustained string of hits. In 1951 he appeared with Count Basie at the Apollo after agreeing to fill in for another performer who had to cancel, but because Turner couldn't read music he was out of sync with the orchestra and was jeered by the crowd. Among those in the audience that night was Ahmet Ertegun, founder of Atlantic Records, and he tracked Turner down after the concert and found him drowning his sorrows in a local bar. Ertegun paid Turner $500 to do a couple of sides for Atlantic, and though nothing of note emerged from that session, in 1952 Turner was back with Atlantic for what would become the most productive period of his career.

Turner's fifth single for Atlantic was "Honey Hush," a song Turner wrote himself and recorded in New Orleans in 1953. The song was #1 on the R&B charts for eight weeks, and though it didn't make the pop charts, a sanitized version was released again in 1959, and this version went to #53 on the pop charts. "Honey Hush" and many of Turner's other hits during the early 1950s were somewhat risqué for the time, and while for R&B stations that was acceptable, that was not true of mainstream "white" pop stations. This was especially true of his next big record, the 1954 classic "Shake, Rattle, and Roll." Turner's extremely suggestive version did not make the pop charts of course, but topped the R&B charts for a staggering eight weeks. Though he was now 42 years old, he became a star and one of the voices of a new generation's music. Bill Haley and the Comets and Elvis both recorded "clean" versions of "Shake, Rattle, and Roll," and the song is considered a prototypical rock and roll classic.

Turner became one of Atlantic's biggest stars, and many of his songs, including "Flip, Flop, and Fly" (1955), "Morning, Noon, and Night"(1956) a remake of "Corrine, Corrina" backed with "Boogie Woogie Country Girl" (1956), "Lipstick Powder and Paint" (1956), and the aforementioned "Wee Baby Blues" (1957) became shag classics. In the 1960s he moved towards jazz and the chart hits stopped coming, but as many critics have noted Turner was one of the few musicians to have success in almost every 20th century musical movement, from big band/swing, to boogie woogie, R&B, to rock and roll, to jazz. Doc Pomus has been credited as saying "Rock and roll would have never happened without him," and certainly Turner's contributions to beach music are noteworthy as well. Turner, who died of heart failure in 1985, is a member of both the Blues Hall of Fame and the Rock And Roll Hall of Fame.

The Tymes

BEACH MUSIC DISCOGRAPHY: "So Much in Love" (Parkway 871, 1963: Billboard Pop #1); "Wonderful! Wonderful!" (Parkway 884, 1963: Billboard Pop #7); "The Love That You're Looking For" (Columbia 44799, 1969: Did Not Chart)"; You Little Trustmaker" (RCA 10022, 1974: Billboard Pop #12); "Ms. Grace" (RCA 10128, 1974: Billboard Pop #91).

Philadelphians Donald Banks, Albert Berry, Norman Burnett, George Hilliard, and late addition George Williams actually started out as "the Latineers because we thought the name sounded good, like we had a Latin sound" Burnett told the author. "About that time there was a radio station contest for Tip Top bread. The deal was that you'd do your song, they'd play it on the radio and people would send them the end wrappers of the bread telling them who they liked in the contest. Well, we were nervous, and we didn't sing our best. But a promoter heard our audition when we were doing our tape for the radio program, and he told us to go to Cameo-Parkway records and he gave us the number. We called and set up an audition with Billy Jackson, the A&R man." For the audition, the group sang a song they had written called "As We Strolled," which would eventually be retitled "So Much in Love." "Well, a few weeks went by, and nobody called us, so we called them, and they were happy we called because they had lost the phone number!" Burnett said the group signed with Cameo-Parkway, but "Bernie Lowe, the owner of Cameo-Parkway, didn't like our name, so he named us the Tymes. I don't know where he got it, but that's how our name came about."

With a new name, the newly titled "So Much in Love" was released in June 1963 and went all the way to #1. Burnett says the sounds of the seabirds and waves crashing at the beginning of the song were to give it a romantic feel, and after the song became successful, two other songs released that year, The O'Jays' "Lonely Drifter" (released in September) and Robin Ward's "Wonderful Summer" (released in November) used similar sound effects but neither charted as high as the Tymes' disk. Almost overnight the group went from being unknowns who just happened to be on the same label with Chubby Checker, Dee Dee Sharp, Bobby Rydell, the Orlons, and the Dovells, to having a #1 record: "The song was bigger than

The Tymes, circa early 1960s (photograph courtesy Norm Burnett).

us—we were really unprepared. We did a tour with Dick Clark, but our inexperience showed. Len Barry was with the Dovells at the time, and he came up and said, 'You guys perform like you just met right here on stage!' We really had to grow into the song."

"So Much in Love" was followed by a cover of a Johnny Mathis standard written in 1957, "Wonderful! Wonderful!" (#7), but after a few poorly performing records through 1964, they left Parkway. At this point they they were singing backup for other artists, even providing the background vocals for old labelmate Len Barry on his #2 smash "1–2–3," and they also tried a release on their own Winchester label that failed. Next they signed with MGM who dropped them after two non-charting releases before they signed with Columbia. At Columbia their first release was their first pop Top 40 record since "Wonderful, Wonderful," 1968's cover of the song "People" from the musical *Funny Girl*, which stalled at #39. Their next release, and their first of 1969, was "The Love That You're Looking For (Ain't Gonna Find It Here)."

Though not a hit at the time, eventually beach music and Northern Soul audiences took to the song which even led to its inclusion on a beach compilation album, Epic Records' *Endless Beach* (Epic 37915) in 1982. Three more releases on Columbia through 1971 failed to chart and found them without a label once again by 1971.

It was at about this time that Hilliard left and was replaced with Charles Nixon. Still searching for a label, the group's producer, Billy Jackson, had them cut some demos he hoped Kenny Gamble and Leon Huff would find suitable for their fledgling Philadelphia International label, but they passed and Jackson took the tapes to RCA. RCA signed the group and took the very song Gamble and Huff had passed on, "You Little Trustmaker," and released it in 1974. The song shot up to #12 on the Billboard pop charts and broke the Top 20 at #18 in the U.K., and the group was suddenly hot once again. They followed that with the release of what many people consider the greatest all-time beach music classic, 1974's "Ms. Grace." "Ms. Grace" was written by husband-and-wife team John and Johanna Hall (John would be a member of the group Orleans, which would later chart with hits such as "Still the One" and "Love Takes Time"), and despite the chart impetus provided by the success of "You Little Trustmaker," "Ms. Grace" only reached #91 on the Billboard charts. In England, however, it soared all the way to #1. "It's a nice song, a different type of song," Burnett says, "a really beautiful song." Yet surprisingly, the Tymes' newfound success was short-lived, and after charting once more with "It's Cool" in 1976 (#68), there were no more chart records. A number of personnel changes followed, and today the living members of the group continue to perform in England and the U.S.

The Van Dykes

BEACH MUSIC DISCOGRAPHY: "You're Shakin' Me Up" (Mala 549, 1966: Did Not Chart).

Though the Van Dykes claimed they modeled themselves after the Impressions, in their origins they were very much like another Texas group, the Commands. Like the Commands, who originated in San Antonio and were founded by a lead singer in the military at Randolph Air Force Base, the Van Dykes were founded at Fort Hood, Texas, where frontman Rondalis Tandy was stationed in the Army. Tandy, along with Charles Puryear, Lafayette Williams, and Lawrence Spikes, performed together a bit in the early '60s, but after Tandy was discharged he moved to Ft. Worth and formed a new Van Dykes group consisting of himself and Eddie Nixon, Wenzon Mosley, and James Mays. Nixon eventually left the group, and Tandy decided to keep the group together as a trio.

As a way to break into the business the group would play local talent shows, and through this eventually they met Charles Stewart, who would sign them and in 1965 produce their first record on his own regional HUE-CSP label, a song Tandy had written called "No Man Is an Island." Stewart liked the group's sound, and convinced Larry Utall, president of Mala Records (and Bell and Amy as well), to release "No Man" nationally on Mala. In late 1965 the record made the pop charts, and though it only rose to #94 it fared better on the R&B charts where it hit #24. Following that winning formula, subsequent Van Dykes releases would be overseen by Stewart in Texas and sold to Mala, and in 1966 their Mala releases "I've Got to Go on Without You" (#109 pop charts, #28 R&B) and "Never Let Me Go" (#25 R&B) would enjoy limited chart success.

Their next 1966 release, "You Need Confidence," would make the R&B charts at #24, but is today best known because the flipside was "You're Shakin' Me Up." Tandy also wrote this song, and backed by a group called the Rays the song is the only Van Dykes recording that Tandy did not sing lead on. Though Tandy and James Mays sometimes shared lead duties on the same song, for the first and last time Mays handled the lead vocal alone. The song was never promoted as a featured song, and languished as a flip side until discovered by beach music enthusiasts.

Though early on the Van Dykes had largely performed only in Texas, with four chart records they were soon performing up and down the East Coast. They played the Howard in Washington with the Four Tops, and at the Apollo with the Marvelettes, Billy Stewart, the Spinners, and Percy Sledge. Throughout 1966 and 1967 they would perform at venues such as Regal in Chicago, the Uptown in Philadelphia, and did repeat performances at the Apollo, playing with the likes of Mary Wells, the Artistics, the Intruders, Martha and the Vandellas, and Jimmy Ruffin. Bell Records finally released an LP in 1967, *Tellin' It Like It Is,* which contained their singles to that point including "You're Shakin' Me Up."

In 1967 they released two more singles from the album, "A Sunday Kind of Love" and "Tears of Joy," but neither of those registered on any chart. By this point Mays and Wenzon were tired of the road, and although Tandy recruited two other singers to perform with him after a short tour the Van Dykes broke up. Tandy eventually moved to California and became a technician for Paramount Studios. The group re-formed in 1984 for a reunion album on Marquee, *Return Engagement,* and after that broke up for good.

The Videos

BEACH MUSIC DISCOGRAPHY: "Trickle, Trickle" (Casino 102, 1958: Did Not Chart).

Few groups had a shorter tenure, fewer recordings, or a more tragic and clouded history than the Queens, New York–based Videos. Ronald Cuffey, Clarence Bassett, and Johnny Jackson had been members of the Five Sharps, who in 1951 had recorded the now ultra-collectible "Stormy Weather." The group wasn't together long (there are reports that Bassett joined the service, and that Cuffey may have as well) and it wasn't until 1957 that Cuffey, Bassett, and Jackson added Charles Baskerville and Ron Woodhall to form the Videos. After a second place finish at an amateur night event at the Apollo Theater, where they sang the Orioles' "At Night," audience member Sid Wick offered to manage them and the group accepted. Wick introduced the group to big-time Philadelphia DJ Doug "Jocko" Henderson, who helped them land a contract with Philadelphia-based Casino Records. Their first single was 1958's "Trickle Trickle," a song the label's songwriting credits attribute to the group and Henderson. The song was popular regionally but did not make the Billboard charts though it did register at #90 on *Cash Box*. Casino released a follow up, "Love or Infatuation," but it failed to chart as well.

Before they could record and release any further singles Cuffey was diagnosed with leukemia (he would die in 1960) and the group broke up. Bassett and Baskerville then joined James Sheppard to form Shep & the Limelites. Some reports say Woodhall may have passed away at about the same time as Cuffey, though it cannot be substantiated. It is not known what happened to Jackson, but it is a certainty that by 1959, after just two singles, the Videos no longer existed. The song, however, would finally garner some national notice when covered by the Manhattan Transfer in 1980 and it peaked at #77 on the pop charts.

Jr. Walker & the All Stars

BEACH MUSIC DISCOGRAPHY: "What Does It Take?" (Soul 35062, 1969: Billboard Pop #4); "Gotta Hold on to This Feeling" (Soul 35070, 1970: Billboard Pop #21); "Do You See My Love (For You Growing)" (Soul 35073, 1970: Billboard Pop #32).

Although various accounts list the birth name of the man known as Junior Walker as Autry DeWalt II, Autry Dewalt Mixon, Jr., and Oscar G. Mixon, and that he was born in Blythesville, Arkansas in 1931, census records indicate that he was born in Blytheville in 1932 as simply Autrey Dewalt; he was later nicknamed Junior by his stepfather, whose surname was Walker. His family moved to South Bend, Indiana, where he learned to play the saxophone as a teenager. After graduating from high school he played sax in jazz and R&B nightclubs, and in 1954 he formed his first group, the Jumping Jacks. He later joined The Rhythm Rockers, led by drummer Billy 'Stix' Nicks, and the group also included Fred Patton and Willie Woods. After Nicks was drafted, Walker, whose sax solos had increasingly become the focus of the group's performances, took over, and moved the group to Battle Creek, Michigan in the late 1950s. Now known as the All Stars, the group went through some personnel changes before becoming the house band at Battle Creek's El Grotto Club, where they were discovered by Johnny Bristol in 1961. Bristol was recording for Harvey Fuqua's Tri-Phi label, and he brought them to the attention of Fuqua who signed them to another of his labels. Having performed as both Autry DeWalt and Oscar Mixon at various times, he was convinced to change his name to Junior Walker, and thus Jr. Walker & The All Stars were born.

The group recorded three singles for Harvey in 1962 and 1963, and though none made the national charts "Cleo's Mood" was popular regionally in the Detroit area. During this period soon-to-be-Motown-mogul Berry Gordy was buying out small labels in the Detroit area in order to build his own brand, including both Tri-Phi and Harvey. Often this included signing the acts associated with the label, and as a result the All Stars found themselves signed to Gordy's Soul subsidiary. Their first release as Jr. Walker & The All Stars, 1964's "Satan's Blues," did not sell nationally, but their next, "Shotgun," featuring Walker doing vocals, was a huge hit, going to #1 on the R&B charts and #4 on the pop chart, and earning a Grammy nomination for best R&B recording of the year. What followed over the next four years was a string of sax-heavy R&B (and to a lesser degree pop) chart successes, including "(I'm A) Road Runner," "How Sweet It Is (To Be Loved By You)," "Pucker Up Buttercup," "Hip City," and others. In 1969, he started heading in a new direction, releasing the first of a series of more soulful romantic songs with "What Does It Take (To Win Your Love)." He had continued to work with Harvey Fuqua and Johnny Bristol occasionally over the years, but this time everything came together to produce his biggest hit in four years. Written by Fuqua, Bristol, and Vernon Bullock (who had also teamed with the two to write "If I Could Build My Whole World Around You" for Marvin Gaye & Tammi Terrell), the record took him to #1 on the R&B charts once again as well as to #4 on the pop charts and a second Grammy nomination.

At this point Walker seemed to have found the formula, and so began a series of songs in the same romantic vein as "What Does It Take." He did a version of the Guess Who's "These Eyes" which did well on the R&B charts, followed in 1970 by two songs, "Gotta Hold On to This Feeling" and "Do You See My Love For You Growing," both of which were done in the same fashion as "What Does It Take" and both of which were co-written by Bristol. "Gotta Hold On to This Feeling" went to #2 on the R&B charts and #21 on the pop charts, and "Do You See My Love For You Growing" went to #3 on the R&B charts and #32 on the pop charts. Considering that in late 1969 and 1970 Diana Ross was leaving the Supremes, the Four Tops sales were in a decline and they would soon leave Motown for ABC, and that Marvin Gaye had a brief period of lesser chart hits before his more socially conscious music of the 1970s, for a brief moment Walker was one of the labels most productive and best-selling acts.

As is frequently the case, however, it would not last. "Do You See" would be his last record to break into the Top 40 on the pop charts, and only one more release would make the Top 10 on the R&B charts. He would release records on Soul up through 1977 before he went solo in 1979, and he'd have a few releases on various labels after that. In 1981 he would reach a whole new audience playing saxophone on Foreigner's Top 10 hit "Urgent." He died of cancer in 1995, and was inducted into the Rhythm and Blues Foundation that same year.

Billy Ward and the Dominoes

BEACH MUSIC DISCOGRAPHY: "Sixty-Minute Man" (Federal 12022, 1951: Pre Billboard Pop #17); "Have Mercy Baby" (Federal 12068, 1952: Billboard Pop Did Not Chart, R&B #1); "Can't Do Sixty No More" (Federal 12209, 1955: Did Not Chart); "Give Me You" (King 1502, 1955: Did Not Chart).

Savannah, Georgia–born Robert L. Williams moved to Philadelphia when he was a child, and like many R&B singers his introduction to music came in the church choir. Because his father was a minister and his mother sang in the choir, in addition to singing he learned to play the organ as well. He was also trained in classical piano, winning his first award for a piece he had written called "Dejection" when he was 14. After military service, he went to the Julliard School of Music, and having adopted the name Billy Ward his career plans were to work as a vocal coach and Broadway arranger. Instead, Ward soon formed his own vocal group called the Dominoes, so-called because the group consisted of white and black singers. He disbanded the group in 1950, and this time formed an all-black group called the Ques. This group, which was made up of music students, never really even got going before he discovered how undisciplined they were and disbanded the group. While this was indicative of the degree of professionalism with which he'd approach all of his groups, it was also a foreshadowing of the rigidity and tendency to micromanage that would cause problems later on.

Later that same year he would form another group consisting of Clyde McPhatter, Charlie White, William Lamont and Bill Brown. All had a background in gospel, and along with Ward they made up the second incarnation of the Ques. They won a contest at the Apollo and appeared on Arthur Godfrey's Talent Scouts Show in 1950, which caught the attention of King Records, and the powers at King convinced Ward that his group should try their hand at R&B. Soon Ward—who did the promotional work, wrote the songs and basically oversaw every aspect of the group now known as the Dominoes—had written several new songs, which the group recorded in 1950. Their first chart record was "Do Something for Me," which in 1951 went to #6 on the R&B charts, and though their next release did not do well, next came "Sixty-Minute Man"—and everything changed almost overnight. Brown sang lead on "Sixty-Minute Man," and the double entendre lyrics and the song's rocking beat captured the ears of audiences everywhere. Because of the risqué nature of the song, it was banned by many radio stations, though some simply saw it as a novelty record. Today, many claim it was the first rock-and-roll record, though Ward himself admitted he wasn't sure what it was exactly and that the song's distinctive sound came about almost by accident. Whatever Ward was trying to do, it was a hit with listeners. "Sixty-Minute Man" was voted the year's #1 record in the jazz and blues field by music writers and by the national jukebox operators and was #1 on the R&B charts, where it was in the Top 10 for months. It even crossed over and hit #17 on the early pre–Billboard pop charts—a significant and almost unheard of accomplishment for a black group at the time. It sold more than one million records, but perhaps most importantly, it bridged the gap between black music and white music, which was extremely significant not only in where pop music was at the time but in where beach music would later be as well.

All was not well within the group, however, and some members resented Ward's almost total control over most aspects of their lives. Ward wouldn't let members have mustaches, they had to drink a glass of warm milk at night, and leaving one's hotel room at night while on tour would result in a $50 fine—and if you failed to tell Ward someone else had left, it was a $100 fine. White had had enough and was the first to leave the group, and he was replaced by James Van Loan. With Van Loan the group had a two more chart records before releasing 1952's "Have Mercy Baby." The song was number one on the R&B charts for ten weeks, and has often been lauded for being the first hit record to use a gospel format. McPhatter's lead voice and his own background in gospel that made the record successful, but by this point people either thought Billy Ward was singing lead since it was his group, or in other cases they believed it was Clyde "Ward," Billy's younger brother—because that's how Billy Ward was billing McPhatter. By this point McPhatter was tired of Ward's controlling ways, especially since he was really the voice of the group and Ward himself only occasionally sang or played on their songs. Consequently, in early 1953 McPhatter left to form The Drifters, and he would later have a successful solo career as well. By this point Brown had left too and formed the Checkers, where interestingly enough, he would reprise the role of Lovin' Dan on "Don't Stop Dan" in 1954 (see the entry for the Checkers).

As was the case with many groups, the membership started fluctuating, and it wasn't helped that the fact that Ward was more rigid than ever. The Dominoes were lucky, however, in that despite the fact that they had lost the great Clyde McPhatter, waiting in the wings was another superior talent: Jackie Wilson (who at that point was still known as "Sonny" Wilson). Wilson and the group (now consisting of Ward, Wilson, Prentice Moreland, Milton Merle, and Cliff Givens) did a session in January 1955 where they recorded two songs that would go on to be big with beach music audiences, "Can't Do Sixty No More" and "Give Me You." "Can't Do Sixty No More" was the next entry in the "Lovin' Dan" saga, but by this point the Dominoes records weren't selling and it did not chart. "Give Me You," with Wilson's strong resonating voice in full force, was likewise not a success. In fact, after 1953, the group had just one song to make the R&B charts, 1957's cover of "Star Dust," which hit #5 and #12 on the pop charts. 1957's cover of "Deep Purple" would also make the pop charts, coming in at #20.

Wilson wasn't the lead on either of these however, having been fired by Ward for "misconduct." As the '50s wound down, the group's heyday was clearly behind them. There were frequent and numerous personnel changes in the ensuing years, and though Ward tried to keep the group together into the late '60s, by then they were relics of a bygone age. Billy Ward died in 2002; the group was inducted into the Vocal Group Hall of Fame in 2006.

Dionne Warwick

BEACH MUSIC DISCOGRAPHY: "Then Came You" (with the Spinners) (Atlantic 3029, 1974: Billboard Pop #1); "Do You Believe in Love at First Sight?" (Warner Brothers 8419, 1977: Did Not Chart).

East Orange, New Jersey-born Marie Dionne Warrick was born to Mancel Warrick, who had once worked with gospel distribution for Chess Records, and Lee Drinkard Warrick, who was a member and later manager of the gospel group The Drinkard Singers. Dionne and several other family members were involved in her mother's group, including her aunt Cissy Houston (mother of Whitney Houston), and her sister Delia Warwick, who later found fame as Dee Dee Warwick during the 1960s and early 1970s. Judy Clay, who would go on to do "Private Number" with William Bell was also a member of the group at one time, and after Dionne, Dee Dee, and Cissy broke off to form their own group, The Gospelaires, Clay occasionally appeared with them as did their friend Doris Troy, who would later have her own hit with "Just One Look." In the early 1960s Dionne went out on her own and ended up doing back-up work as a session singer. In 1961, while singing back-up on The Drifters' "Mexican Divorce," she was spotted by the song's co-writer Burt Bacharach, who signed her to sing demo records for some songs he was writing for other artists to be recorded for Scepter Records.

It was while recording a demo of a song by Bacharach and Hal David that was to be given to Jerry Butler, "Make It Easy on Yourself," that her career moved into overdrive. She felt she had the potential to make the song a hit as her debut single, but after Bacharach told her it was being released by Butler, she angrily retorted "Don't make me over, man ... accept me for what I am" as she left the studio. Inspired, Bacharach and David wrote "Don't Make Me Over" just for her and in 1963 the song peaked at #21 on the pop charts and #5 on the R&B charts. Her name was misspelled on the label as "Warwick" instead of Warrick, a name she chose to retain and that her sister Dee Dee also adopted when she began recording solo as well. For the rest of the decade and into the early 1970s, Warwick and Bacharach and David would churn out hit after hit, producing some of the best songs of the period including "Anyone Who Had a Heart," "Walk on By," "Do You Know the Way to San Jose," "I'll Never Fall in Love Again," and many others. Along the way, she picked up a couple of Grammys, but in the early 70's she was offered a multi-million dollar contract by Warner Brothers and left Scepter.

Bacharach and David parted ways with her soon after she left Scepter, and having now terminated that productive relationship and having changed labels (while also having added an "e" to her last name), Warwicke found herself without the support system that had allow her to flourish during the previous decade. Few of her subsequent recordings made the charts until 1974 when she was able to work with legendary producer Thom Bell. Bell later said that Warwicke asked him to work with her, but he initially declined because he was too busy with the Spinners, who at the time were riding a wave of very impressive chart hits. But because The Spinners were signed to Atlantic, a sister label of Warner Brothers, Bell was able to get them to collaborate on "Then Came You." Bell brought them together to record in California at the Beach Boys' studio due to scheduling issues that wouldn't allow them to meet in Philadelphia, and there they recorded two songs, "Just as Long as We Have Love" being the second. According to both Pervis Jackson of the Spinners and producer Thom Bell, Warwicke thought "Just as Long" was the better track and should be released as the A-side, even making a sour face after they completed their take of "Then Came You." Bobbie Smith told the author that Bell bet her a dollar that "Then Came You" was the hit, and after it indeed hit #1, she apologized. It would be her first #1 and the only one the Spinners would have, and would see both nominated for a Grammy.

Based on the success of the single, their labels wanted an album, but some speculate that Warwicke felt the Spinners were getting a bit too much credit for giving her what was her first #1, and she decided against it. Instead, Warwicke went back to her solo work, which was largely uninspired, but one song she did for Warner Brothers did strike a chord with beach music lovers, that being the 1977 release "Do You Believe in Love at First Sight?" The song was a cover version of a recording by British songstress Polly Brown, who had also charted in America in 1975 with "Up in a Puff of Smoke." Arranger Gerry Shury told *Black Music* magazine in 1975 that Brown's voice was a cross "between Diana Ross and Dionne Warwick," so when Warwicke heard Brown's version of "Do You Believe," which Brown had sung at the 1976 Eurovision Song Contest, it seemed logical that it was a good fit for her vocal stylings. Despite its appeal in the southeastern beach clubs, the song did not make any major charts.

After leaving Warner Brothers, Warwick (she had now dropped the "e" from the end of Warwicke) signed with Arista, and in the 1980s regained and bolstered her star status once again. Hits such as "I'll Never Love This Way Again," "That's What Friends Are For," "Heartbreaker," and others propelled her up the charts again and again. As a result, Warwick has nearly 70 chart singles, has sold more than 25 million albums to date, and is considered one of the biggest stars in American music.

Dinah Washington

BEACH MUSIC DISCOGRAPHY: "September in the Rain" (Mercury 71876, 1961: Billboard Pop #23).

Born Ruth Lee Jones in Tuscaloosa, Alabama, the woman who would be known as Dinah Washington and "the Queen of the Blues" moved to Chicago with her mother when she was a child. She learned to play the piano but it became obvious early on that her greatest gift was her voice. She won an amateur singing contest when she was 15, and this helped land her a spot with the Chicago gospel group the Sallie Martin Singers. Eventually, however, she found the allure of being a jazz singer a proper outlet for her talents, and it was while playing at the Garrick Lounge in Chicago that she was discovered. Lionel Hampton asked her to join her band, and it was at this time that she changed her name to what she thought was the more appropriate stage name Dinah Washington.

In 1944 she released a pair of songs that made the Top 10 on the R&B charts, "Salty Papa Blues" and "Evil Gal Blues," and in 1946 released "Blow Top Blues" with Hampton, which not only peaked at #5 on the R&B charts but also made the popular music charts as well. Over the course of the next decade, she released more than three dozen chart records, including a pair of #1s on the R&B charts, 1948's "Am I Asking Too Much" and 1949's "Baby Get Lost," and in all 27 recordings made the R&B Top 10. At this time she was arguably the biggest female singing star in the United States.

In 1959, Mercury Records began promoting her not just as a "black" artist, but as a crossover star. The first song to benefit from crossover charting was "What a Diff'rence a Day Makes," a cover of a song done by several groups previously, which hit #8 on the pop charts for Washington and won her a Grammy. Next up was a cover of a song Nat King Cole had released in 1951, "Unforgettable," which made the Top 20, and then she paired with singer Brook Benton for the spectacular "Baby (You've Got What it Takes)," which hit #5 on the pop charts and spent ten weeks at #1 on the R&B charts. They followed with "A Rockin' Good Way (To Mess Around and Fall in Love)," which went to #7 and then #1 on the R&B charts. Unfortunately, she didn't think Benton was very professional, and openly criticized him; the two of them never worked together again. "This Bitter Earth" hit #1 R&B in July 1960, followed by "Love Walked In" which peaked at #30 on the pop charts, but of her next five releases, none broke the Top 40 on the pop charts and none made the R&B charts at all.

In 1961 she released "September in the Rain" on Mercury, a cover of a song written by Harry Warren and Al Dubin in 1937 that was featured in the film *Melody for Two*. With an orchestrated opening in the style of many of The Drifters hits of the period, it became a favorite with shaggers and its appeal resonated around the country. Peaking at #23 on the pop charts and #5 on the R&B charts, it would be the highest charting song she'd have from that time on.

After a nearly 20 year career Washington's popularity was at last starting to fade, but her personal life had long been in shambles. Married seven times, her last husband was NFL superstar Dick "Night Train" Lane, who woke up to find her dead in December 1963. Washington had long had a dependency on drugs and alcohol, and her death was attributed to a lethal combination of barbiturates; she was 39 years old.

Mary Wells

BEACH MUSIC DISCOGRAPHY: "Bye Bye Baby" (Motown 1003, 1960: Billboard Pop #45); "You Beat Me to the Punch" (Motown 1032, 1962: Billboard Pop #9); "Two Lovers" (Motown 1035, 1962:, Billboard Pop #7); "My Guy" (Motown 1056, 1964: Billboard Pop #1); "Dear Lover" (Atco 6392, 1966: Billboard Pop #51).

Detroit, Michigan-born Mary Esther Wells was one of three children of an impoverished single mother. She started singing in church when she was four, and was helping her mother do cleaning work by the time she was twelve. While attending Northwestern High School, which would produce such notable alumni as Florence Ballard of the Supremes, Melvin Franklin of the Temptations, and Norman Whitfield, she joined the choir. She realized that her musical ability could provide her with an opportunity to improve her life, and was singing in nightclubs when a friend arranged for then 17-year-old Mary to meet Motown/Tamla founder Berry Gordy. Wells's intention was to pitch him a song she had written as a poem called "Bye, Bye, Baby" because she knew Gordy had been working with Jackie Wilson and she wanted to get the song to him. Gordy was no longer working with Wilson, however, but he was so impressed when she sang the song for him that rather than give it to another singer he decided to sign her to record it herself. With the backing of the soon to be famous Funk Brothers, it reportedly took Wells more than two dozen takes before Gordy was satisfied. The song went to #45 on the pop charts and #8 on the R&B charts and catapulted Wells into to the spotlight as one of Gordy's first stars.

After a few middling releases Gordy had Smokey Robinson write some songs for Wells including "The One Who Really Loves You," which went to #8, followed by "You Beat Me to the Punch" which went to #9 and became her first R&B #1 record; as a result, she was the first Motown artist nominated for a Grammy for Best Rhythm and Blues Recording. She followed this with another Smokey Robinson tune, "Two Lovers." Robinson based the song on an old movie he saw where a woman was in love with two men, though he adapted the concept to reflect two lovers in one person. It went to #7, and three more Top 40 records followed before she recorded the Robinson–penned 1964 hit "My Guy," which went all the way to #1. Though she was just 21 years old, Wells was the biggest Motown star of all. She toured with the Beatles, who unabashedly declared her to be their favorite American singer. Though no one knew it at the time, "My Guy" would be her last release for Motown.

Wells was unhappy with Motown. As the label's first female star, by 1964 she felt she was being neglected while the label spent more time promoting up-and-coming acts such as the Supremes. In addition, there were rumors that she was eager to break into movies, although Wells later denied it. As a result, although Wells had a number of Motown recordings ready for release, she left Motown acrimoniously by revealing that her contract with them had been signed when she was a 17-year-old minor. Motown cancelled her unreleased 1964 follow-ups to "My Guy," and it was alleged that an incensed Gordy told DJs *not* to play her records. Seizing the opportunity to sign a bankable star, 20th Century–Fox stepped in to sign for an amount that has been reported to be anywhere from $200,000 to $500,000, which would allow her to record and make movies. Unfortunately, neither the hits nor the movie roles materialized. Other than 1965's "Use Your Head," which peaked at #34, and her performance of the song title song "Never Steal Anything Wet" for the movie *Catalina Caper*, her time at 20th Century–Fox was unproductive. Wells later said that while labels such as Motown were receptive to new ideas proposed by artists, 20th Century–Fox had a more rigid hierarchy-based approach where artists were there to perform, not to make suggestions. Within a year she was out at Fox, taking with her but a small part of her massive contract earnings.

Wells was scooped up by Atco, where she was able to work with the very capable Carl Davis, Gerald Sims, and Sonny Sanders, and together they created "Dear Lover," her first and most successful single for the label. Cleary a departure from her Motown recordings with just the right amount of strings and brass, the song was not supposed to be a featured single. The flip side of the record, "Can't You See," co-written by Barrett Strong, was more of a Motown-type record initially promoted as the hit side of the single, but DJs on the East Coast felt "Dear Lover" had more potential and started pushing and playing it instead. While "Can't

You See" did make it to #94 on Billboard charts, "Dear Lover" peaked at #51 on the Hot 100 and to #6 on the R&B charts; both positions would be the highest her recordings would ever attain on either chart thereafter. The song is probably her most popular song in beach music circles as well.

Unable to sustain any momentum at Atco, she moved to Jubilee, then Warner Brothers-Reprise, and then Epic, and with no further chart success other than that her 1979 release "Gigolo" registered on the dance charts. By this point Wells had suffered through two divorces, a failed suicide attempt, and cocaine addiction, and during the 1980s she became addicted to heroin. A chain smoker, in 1990 Wells was diagnosed with laryngeal cancer, and though treatment forced it into remission, it returned in 1992. Having struggled with health issues her entire life—she'd had both meningitis and tuberculosis previously—she died in 1992 after contracting pneumonia at the age of 49. In 1989 Wells was celebrated with a Pioneer Award from the Rhythm and Blues Foundation, and in 1999 "My Guy" was inducted into the Grammy Hall of Fame.

The Whispers

BEACH MUSIC DISCOGRAPHY: "Needle in a Haystack" (Dore 794, 1967: Did Not Chart): Rereleased (Soul Clock 1004, 1970: Did Not Chart).

Watts natives Nicholas Caldwell and Marcus Hutson started the Eden Singers, and after meeting Gordy Harmon and twin brothers Walter and Wallace Scott at a talent show they agreed to combine forces and start a new vocal group. Harmon had already signed with Los Angeles' Dore Records, and after signing the five of them as a group in 1964 label owner Lew Bedell renamed them The Whispers. Unfortunately for the group, though their time with Dore would result in eleven single releases up through 1969, none of their records would chart. When they signed with the fledgling Los Angeles label Soul Clock in 1969, however, they would begin to experience some chart success. Soul Clock was originally owned by Ron Carson, the group's producer at Dore, and their second release for the label, "The Time Will Come," rose to #17 on the R&B charts. After two more Soul Clock releases in 1970 they issued "Seems Like I Gotta Do Wrong," which went to #6 on the R&B charts and was their first record to crack the pop charts, peaking at #30. The B-side of the record was an updated version of a song written by Harmon and Caldwell called "Needle in a Haystack" that they had originally recorded as an A side on Dore in 1967. The original Dore version of "Needle in a Haystack" was slower, clocking in at 2:31, whereas the 1970 version was more uptempo and lusher, and clocked

in at 2:14. It was this second version that became a hit with shaggers along the east coast, although it was not a chart hit.

The group had just one more release on Soul Clock before the label folded, and after the group released a one-off on the similarly unstable Roker label (which went under after just five releases), Janus bought the rights to the group and their catalog. It was with Janus that the group's fortunes would finally begin to change, with eight R&B chart records between 1970 and 1974. In 1971, Harmon injured his throat in a car accident and the four remaining original members added Leaveil Degree, who had briefly appeared with the Friends of Distinction. The group signed with Soul Train records, where they had six R&B chart singles through 1977. They then moved to Solar, where they had 22 R&B chart records, seven of which placed in the Top 10. This included their first #1 "And the Beat Goes On" which was also their first Top 40 single on the pop charts, and another #1 "Rock Steady," which was their first Top 10 record on the pop charts. In 1990 they signed with Capitol, where they'd have eight more R&B chart records and three in the Top 10.

The Whispers are now considered one of the most highly regarded R&B acts in music, with two platinum albums, seven gold albums, and nearly fifty chart hits. They have been inducted into The Vocal Group Hall of Fame and the R&B Hall of Fame.

Wild Cherry

BEACH MUSIC DISCOGRAPHY: "1–2–3 Kind of Love" (Epic 6497, 1978: Did Not Chart).

Mingo Junction, Ohio born Rob Parissi started playing guitar professionally when he was 14, and after graduating from high school in 1968 he formed the band that would become Wild Cherry in Steubenville Ohio in 1970. They coined their name when Parissi jokingly told the band that maybe they should call themselves Wild Cherry after a box of coughdrops he

Wild Cherry, 1976 (photograph courtesy Rob Parissi).

had on hand during an illness. The band liked it, though Parissi himself was less than wild about it. "I just gotten out of the hospital with a week to go to rehearse for our first gig" he told me. "I had had tubes stuck down my throat and still had a sore throat. In the middle of rehearsal one day the guys said 'What are we going to call ourselves?' I picked up the cough drops I had on our keyboard player's B-3 and said: 'You can call it Wild Cherry if you want; the band's going to make the name famous if it's good.' They stopped dead, and said 'That's a great name!' I said, 'No, there's no way we're going to name this band Wild Cherry.'"

The name stuck, however, and the band played throughout the Ohio, Pennsylvania, and West Virginia corridor. Soon they landed a recording contract and cut several singles in the early '70s before disbanding. Parissi then became the manager of some Bonanza steakhouses, but the lure of music was too strong and so before long he reformed the band as a quartet, now consisting of Bryan Bassett, Rob Beitle, and Allen Wentz. The band a had a great local following in the Pittsburgh area, and though they were a rock band, with the emergence of disco, audiences were calling more and more for dance music. As the now legendary story goes, at the 2001 disco in Pittsburgh, black fans kept asking them "are you going to play some funky music, white boys?" In between shows one night Beitle made the comment that they had to "play that funky music, white boy," and Parissi said "I wrote out the song on a bar order pad in about five minutes." The group recorded the song, Epic picked it up and released it, and in 1976 the song went to #1 on the pop and R&B charts. The album went platinum, but oddly enough despite the fact that the group had a #1 record no one knew what the band looked like; the record company wanted to maintain the illusion that the group was black.

The group had bigger problems however, as they had scored a #1 song with music that was far from their rock and roll roots, and they weren't happy. Parissi said "The members of the band hated everything, even 'Play That Funky Music,' and getting them to do anything at all was a day to day challenge, as they constantly complained about everything that I wrote, but never contributed anything progressive regarding material they thought was better or what they thought was 'cool' enough for them…. It was like dragging three people you need to cut a track toward getting on the gravy train, constantly. I had to push everything out of all of them." Despite Parissi's pushing, and his skill as writer, after "Play That Funky Music" subsequent singles didn't come close to reaching the success of their #1 record. 1977 saw the group release three singles that charted; "Baby Don't You Know"(#43), "Hot to Trot" (#95), and "Hold On" (#61), and then in 1978 they released "1–2–3 Kind of Love." "The idea for '1–2–3 Kind of Love' came from thinking that it's like seeing someone attractive you have an eye for" Parissi told the author. "First, the attraction, second, you imagine and fantasize about them, then, when you get to know them and the two of you fall in love with each other, you think about it being a lasting thing" he said. "I was just thinking 'Motown' when I wrote it. Nothing more, nothing less." Perhaps the very same throwback-sound that made it a beach music hit during a time when disco was king was why national audiences didn't take to the song and it didn't chart. "I haven't performed that song live since 1978, but as far as how I feel about how '1-2-3 Kind Of Love' ranks among all the songs I wrote, it's not about me after I write and record whatever tune, it's about how people like it and what they think. Obviously, people in 'beach music country' like that song, and for that I'm grateful."

Parissi says that by 1979 the rifts within the group had reached the point where they couldn't even bear working together any more. "Actually, I'm amazed we got all the way through the '1–2–3' of that tune. It might have only got as far as being a 1 or 2 Kind Of Love if they had their way back then" he said. But he does feel the song does a good job of delivering its message about the nature of relationships "in three and a half minutes or so." You "tell a story in three verses, and have one good chorus and a bridge within 3½ minutes, fade it out and call it a good day." Parissi was fed up with having to fight to motivate the band, they finally disbanded. "I wish I had a rosier picture to paint for you," he told me, "but the whole Wild Cherry debacle is not a warm and fuzzy memory for me, and I'm quite glad it's a done deal that I don't need to revisit or live over again." Parissi lives in Tampa and continues to perform and record today.

Lenny Williams

BEACH MUSIC DISCOGRAPHY: "Shoo Doo Fu Fu Ooh!"(ABC 12300, 1977: Billboard Pop #105).

Leonard Charles Williams was born in Little Rock, Arkansas, though his family moved to Oakland, California, when he was a child. In school he learned to play the trumpet and honed his vocal style singing in gospel groups. Like many aspiring singers entered and won some talent contests, which led to a contract with Fantasy Records where he released several songs between 1968 and 1970. After a brief stint with Atco in 1972, he joined Tower of Power (see the entry for Tower of Power) and was the lead vocalist on many of their greatest hits. Their first album with Williams on lead, 1973's *Tower of Power*, included their biggest hit, "So Very Hard to Go," which reached #17 on the Billboard pop charts. The album also featured Williams' lead vocals on their most popular entry in the genre of beach music, "This Time It's Real."

But Williams still wanted to be a solo artist, so he left Tower of Power in 1975. He had a brief relatively unproductive stint at Motown, and only 1975's single "Since I Met You" sold well, but even at that it topped out at #94 on the R&B charts. He signed with ABC in 1977, and his first single to chart was "Shoo Doo Fu Fu Ooh!" Written by Williams and Bernard Thompson and from his album *Choosing You*, Williams said that he came up with "Shoo Doo Fu Fu Ooh!" as the hook, but when the song was finished he still didn't have a title and ultimately really couldn't think of any else to call it. Even with the odd title, the song peaked at #31 on the R&B charts in 1977 although it only bubbled under the pop Hot 100 at #105. It was popular in beach music circles at a time when similar less-traditional sounding songs from artists such as Tavares and Lou Rawls were deemed suitable for shagging.

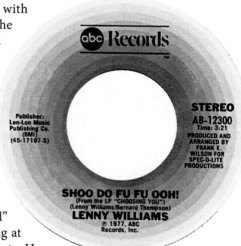

Williams would go on the make the charts with a total of nearly twenty singles right up through the 1990s, though 1978's "Midnight Girl" would be his most successful solo effort, peaking at #20 on the R&B charts and #102 on the pop charts. He did vocals on Kenny G's multi-platinum album *Duo Tones*, and Williams and Kanye West were honored with a BMI Songwriter's Award for the song "Over Night Celebrity" by Twista. He continues to perform as of this writing.

Maurice Williams and the Zodiacs

BEACH MUSIC DISCOGRAPHY: "Stay" (Herald 552, 1960: Billboard Pop #1); "I Remember" (Herald 556, 1961: Billboard Pop #86); "May I" (Dee-Su 304, 1967: Did Not Chart).

Lancaster, South Carolina native Maurice Williams was interested in music from an early age. Like many Southern R&B singers his first experiences were singing in church, starting when he was just six years old. He and his friend Earl Gainey formed a gospel group called the Junior Harmonizers, but by the age of thirteen they decided to focus on popular music and so he, Gainey, William Massey, Norman Wade, Mac Badskins and Willie Jones made up the reinevented Royal Charms while still in high school. The group went to Nashville to record a song Williams had written for Ernie Young's Excello records in 1957, and that song about a Lancaster girl Williams had dated was called "Little Darlin.'" Young suggested they adopt a new name for the group, and as the newly dubbed Gladiolas they released "Little Darlin'" which did extremely well, reaching #41 on the pop charts and #11 on the R&B charts. Soon Williams discovered that a white cover group, the Diamonds, wanted to do a version of the song. As he told Marion Carter, "At first I was against it, but Mr. Young gave me some very sound advice that I've always remembered: 'Don't let your ego get between you and your money. You wrote the song and the more copies you sell, the more money you make.'" He followed Young's advice, and the Diamonds' cover version went all the way to #2 on the charts.

After a few more singles the group left Excello, and because Young owned the Gladiolas name the group had to rename themselves yet again. They encountered a car made by Ford in the 1950s for the European and Australian market called a Zodiac, adopted the name, and as the Zodiacs they recorded a couple of singles on small labels. In the meantime Gainey left, and Henry Gatson joined Wiley Bennett, Charles Thomas, Albert Hill, Willie Morrow, and Williams. More shuffling followed; with the additions of Calvin McKinnie, Harold Alexander and Mac Badskins they became a nine-piece band. In 1960 they signed with Herald Records in New York, and working with producers Phil Gernhardt and Al McCullough they recorded another song Williams had written, "Stay." "Stay" was a song he had written years earlier about that same Lancaster girl and the night she had to leave because she had to be home by 10:00 p.m. He apparently didn't think as much of the song as he did the girl, however, and he told Carter, "I had never thought too much about 'Stay' and had thrown the lyrics in the trash. However, I still had a demo tape and one night we were playing demos and my girlfriend's sister heard it and went crazy over it. That changed my thinking, and we used the song as a demo for Al Silver at Herald Records." Williams did change the original lyrics, however, and a line that referred to smoking cigarettes was changed because it was likely to offend parents. Herald released "Stay," and audiences loved hearing about Williams's efforts to persuade his girlfriend to remain past her curfew as he assures her that her parents won't mind if she stays for just one more dance—not one more smoke. By November, the record had reached #1, and at one minute and thirty-seven seconds the record is well known for being at the shortest #1 record in the history of the Billboard Pop charts. It is estimated that the record has sold more than ten million copies.

Five Herald singles followed, and while "Come Along" reached #83 on the pop charts only one other, "I Remember," saw any chart action. The song, which was enormously popular in the Carolinas, reached #86 on the pop charts. The group left Herald after 1962 and started label jumping before ending up with Vee-Jay where in 1965 they recorded "May I." The label was in serious financial trouble and the times and would in fact declare bankruptcy, and as a result it probably didn't get promoted like it should have been. Williams had faith in the record however, he contacted Marshall Sehorn and Allen Toussaint and arranged for the song to be and rereleased on their New Orleans–based Dee-Su label in 1967. It still wasn't a national hit, but it became one of the greatest beach music classics of all time, even more so than "Stay." It was a favorite all along the East Coast and was so popular that Bill Deal and the Rhondels recorded it and had a Top 40 hit with it in 1969—mainly because everywhere they went people wanted to hear it. Amazingly, though "May I" never charted for the Zodiacs, due largely to the beach music and R&B crowds in the South it would sell over one million copies over the years and earn a gold record as well.

The group continued to release occasional singles on different labels right up into the 1980s. Williams still performs today, and was inducted into the North Carolina Music Hall of Fame in 2010.

Jackie Wilson

BEACH MUSIC DISCOGRAPHY: "Lonely Teardrops" (Brunswick 55105, 1958: Billboard Pop #7); "Whispers (Getting' Louder)" (Brunswick 55300, 1966: Billboard Pop #11); "(Your Love Keeps Lifting Me) Higher and Higher" (Brunswick 55336, 1967: Billboard Pop #6); "I Get the Sweetest Feeling" (Brunswick 55381, 1968: Billboard Pop #34).

Detroit-born Jack Leroy Wilson, Jr., began singing at an early age, and although his first group, the Ever Ready Gospel Singers, sang religious tunes, Wilson didn't form the group because he was spiritual but because he saw it as a way to make money instead. Wilson was drinking by age nine, joined a gang, was sent to a youth detention facility twice, and frequently skipped school before dropping out altogether in the ninth grade. He briefly tried his hand at boxing, and by 17, he was married after fathering a number of children out of wedlock. As a way to make a living he finally turned to singing professionally, first as a solo act in nightclubs and then as a member of the 4 Falcons. He was eventually discovered by Johnny Otis (who discovered Etta James and Hank Ballard, among others), and Otis put him in the R&B group The Thrillers. He was able to record a couple of solo efforts for Dee Gee records as "Sonny" (his nickname) Wilson in 1952, but neither "Rainy Day Blues" nor "Danny Boy" charted.

Wilson's big break came when he was hired by Billy Ward to join the Dominoes as a replacement for Clyde McPhatter, who left the group to form The Drifters. Ward changed Sonny's name to Jackie Wilson, and under Ward, Wilson developed the stage moves and showmanship that would lead to his eventual moniker as "Mr. Excitement." Although Wilson sang on more than twenty Dominoes recordings on Federal, King, Jubilee, and Decca before leaving the group in 1957, his tenure took place well after the group's most significant beach music contributions, save 1955's very fine "Give Me You."

As a solo act, Wilson was fortunate to sign with Brunswick and work with songwriters Berry Gordy and Roquel Davis, who wrote a number of hits for him including "Reet Petite," "To Be Loved," "That's Why" and the Top 10 hit "Lonely Teardrops." It was the first Top 10 hit Gordy wrote, and was reportedly one of a handful of his early songs successful enough to provide seed money for him to later establish the Motown label. As for Davis (whose label credit is listed as Tyran Carlo), the song apparently drew the notice of Chess Records and allowed Davis to sign with that label as the head of A&R. These moves were precipitated, however, by disagreements between Gordy and Davis and Wilson's manager Nat Tarnopol regarding royalties. Once Wilson was without their songwriting genius most of his post "Teardrops" early to mid–'60s recordings are less dynamic. This brought about a lull in his career, and from 1962 through 1965 he only made the pop Top 40 once, with "Baby Workout."

His personal life was similarly complicated during this period. Though married, he was reputed to have been seeing a number of women, and one woman who was reportedly in a jealous rage shot him in 1961. Wilson had to have a kidney removed, another bullet was permanently lodged near his spine and he was in the hospital for a month and a half (to this day, the story that she was a crazed fan, and not a spurned lover, continues to circulate). He was also out of money (despite reportedly making roughly $250,000 a year by this point), though much of this turned out to be due to Tarnopol's mismanagement of his funds. His wife divorced him in 1965, and in 1967 he and a friend were arrested on moral charges in South Carolina after being discovered in a motel with two twenty-four-year-old white women. But just as it appeared Wilson was about to become more famous for making the tabloids than hit records, he started working with producer Carl Davis and his career was rejuvenated. Under Davis's tutelage, in 1966 he recorded "Whispers," a song co-written by Barbara Acklin and David Scott (see entries for Acklin and the Five Du-Tones). As would be true on a number of Wilson's later hits, Davis enlisted underpaid Motown session musicians The Funk Brothers, as well as Motown backing vocalists the Andantes, to perform behind Wilson on the song, giving it a Motown-like sound. The recording was Wilson's most successful in three years, going to #11 on the pop charts and #5 on the R&B charts.

After two more singles, Wilson released "(Your Love Keeps Lifting Me) Higher and Higher." The song had originally been recorded by the Dells but wasn't released, and Brunswick acquired a slightly altered version for Wilson. Davis once again had some of Motown's legendary Funk Brothers play the backing tracks and a couple of the Andantes do vocals in Chicago, and Wilson added his vocals in New York. In an interview with Bill Dahl, Davis said, "I remember I brought the track into New York. And we went into the studio, and Jackie started singing it, and it was completely different from what I thought it should sound like. And I told him, 'No, no, no, no. I don't like that.' He told me, 'Well, come out here and sing it how you want it sung!' So I came out and I told him, 'This is the way it needs to go.' He said, 'Oh, that's what you want?' I said, 'Yeah.' He went back in there and in one take he did it." Davis apparently knew the magic formula, because the song went to #1 on the R&B charts and #6 on the Top 40. The song would actually chart three times in England, hitting #11 in 1969, #25 in 1975 and #15 in 1987. Ultimately, the record would reach four million in sales and would be named to *Rolling Stone*'s list of "The 500 Greatest Songs of All Time."

Wilson followed "Higher and Higher" with another twenty-plus singles, including the Davis-produced 1968 beach favorite, "I Get the Sweetest Feeling," written by Van McCoy and Alicia Evelyn, with accompaniment by the Funk Brothers and Andantes once again. It went to #34 on the pop charts and #12 on the R&B charts; it would be his last record to register on the pop Top 40.

Wilson continued to record, but over the next seven years his success would be limited to another ten singles that only made the R&B charts. Living up to his Mr. Excitement nickname until the end, he had a heart attack on stage during a performance of "Lonely Teardrops" at the Latin Casino in New Jersey in 1975. After singing the lines "My heart is crying" he collapsed, and initially the audience thought it was part of the act and cheered and applauded. When Wilson didn't move Dick Clark stopped the show and Cornel Gunter of the Coasters resuscitated him while they waited for the ambulance. He never fully recovered, and remained in a semi-comatose state for the rest of his life before passing away in 1984 at the age of forty-nine.

The Winstons

BEACH MUSIC DISCOGRAPHY: "Color Him Father"(MMS 1117, 1969: Billboard Pop #7).

The Winstons were a Washington, D.C., based band consisting of Richard Spencer, Phil Tolotta, Quincy Mattison, Ray Maritano, Sonny Peckrol, and Gregory Sylvester "G.C." Coleman. When they came together to form a soul group in the 1960s they already had extensive musical pedigrees. Spencer, Mattison and Coleman had worked in Otis Redding's band, and Mattison had also worked with Arthur Conley and had in fact played on "Sweet Soul Music." Coleman had worked for a couple of years playing drums for Tamla, particularly for the Marvelettes, and Maritano had graduated from the Berklee School of Music and had played in the U.S. Air Force Band. They named themselves the Winstons after the brand of cigarettes Spencer smoked, and once they started booking gigs in the D.C. area they were discovered by Curtis Mayfield and the Impressions, who happened to catch their act at a club. After working for a while as the Impressions' back-up band, Mayfield had them back up singer Wayne Lagadeece on his single "I Need A Replacement" on the Mayfield-owned Curtom label in 1968. The song was not a hit, and on their own they went out and signed with Atlanta-based Metromedia Records.

For their debut single in 1969 they released a song Spencer had written, "Color Him Father." The record was an instant hit, and rising to #7 on the pop charts and #2 on the R&B charts it sold more than a million copies and earned a gold record, eventually winning a Grammy for Best Rhythm and Blues Song. The treacley-sweet song about the love of a boy for his stepfather had a beat that made it easy to shag to, but perhaps the same subject matter that made it a hit also ensured it would never take root as a beach classic and consequently it is not a record normally categorized as beach music today.

Just as beach audiences lost interest in the record after a while, the group faced a similar fate in the world of popular music. They released just four more singles and an LP in 1969, and only "Love of the Common People" charted, peaking at #54 on the pop charts and not breaking onto the R&B charts at all. The group broke up and apparently went their separate ways thereafter, and while Cameron would go on to play with Brick, Spencer went back to school and eventually earned several advanced degrees and became a teacher. Over the course of the last twenty years the group has become even better known for the controversy that has arisen of the illegal sampling of a drum solo by Cameron on the B-side of "Color Him Father," "Amen, Brother." The solo has come to be referred to as the "Amen break," and has apparently been sampled, uncredited and without having royalties paid, on more than 2000 recordings, primarily in hip hop.

Sadly, Cameron, the creator of the break, would eventually die homeless and broke in Atlanta. Today Spencer is the only surviving member of the group.

Robert Winters and Fall

BEACH MUSIC DISCOGRAPHY: "L-O-V-E"(Casablanca Album Cut, 1982: Did Not Chart).

Robert Winters was stricken with polio as a child as a child growing up in Detroit, and as a result he was confined to a wheelchair for life. Nicknamed "Budda"[sic] by his friends for his tendency to sit cross-legged in order to rest comfortably, he developed an early love for music while singing Gospel music with his sister, and he taught himself to play the piano as well. By the mid–60s he had met Ron Murphy, and Murphy noted that though they started recording in 1966, "we didn't release anything until 1968." "Soul Motivation" was in fact released twice on the Ron record label, though neither effort charted. Murphy noted that although "The songs were the quality that Robert wrote in the 80's" and Decca showed a slight interest in his music, Winters was not able to land a national recording contract.

Winters decided that he had a greater chance at success in California, and headed for the west coast. He performed with a Hispanic/African American group called "Spic and Spade"—Winters, Tina Zeno, Bob Belcher, Cliff Dunne, Ernie Mackelway, and Tito Chavez—who eventually bowed to pressure and renamed their group "Highway Robbery." Winters also made a living doing backup vocals, recording children's songs, and doing session work playing the piano as well. Along with Walter Fall Turner and Tony Saunders, they decided to form a new group, settling on the name Robert Winters and Fall as a play on words referencing Winters' and Fall's seasonal-sounding last names. Working with songwriter and producer Jimmy George, who had collaborated with Smokey Robinson, The Commodores, the Temptations, and others, the group recorded "Magic Man," which came to the attention of Clive Davis, leading to the group signing a national recording contract in 1980. The album *Magic Man* was released on Buddah Records, and the eponymous first single would bubble under the pop charts at #101, the highest a Winters record would ever reach on the pop charts. It did well on the R&B charts, however, going to #11, and garnered the group an appearance on *Soul Train*. In a move that seems especially insensitive today, the record company made Winters stay behind his piano during the show so television audiences could not see that he was handicapped.

The label released two more singles from the album, though only "When Will My Love Be Right" charted (#46, R&B charts). The group then moved to Casablanca, a label that the former head of Buddah Neil Bogart was now running. In 1982 the group released the album *L.O.V.E.*, and though it was mainly filled with ballads, by far the best track is the beach music classic "L-O-V-E." The song is a cover of an Al Green recording that peaked at #1 on the R&B charts and #13 on the pop charts in 1975. However, while Green's version has the slow, almost mournful sound for which Green is so well known, Winters' version is a bouncy, energetic song buoyed by Winters' strong, vibrant voice. Why there was no move to release that track as a single is a mystery, and after this album the group's contract with Casblanca was up and it was their last album or national release of any kind.

Winters health started to decline rapidly in the 1980s, and he passed away due to complications from an enlarged heart in 1989.

Brenton Wood

BEACH MUSIC DISOGRAPHY: "The Oogum Boogum Song" (Double Shot 111, 1967: Billboard Pop #34); "Gimme Little Sign" (Double Shot 116, 1967: Billboard Pop #9).

Born Alfred Jesse Smith in Shreveport, Louisiana, Brenton Wood's family moved to California where after high school he attended Compton College. An accomplished piano player, he had already dabbled in singing as a member of the Dootones under his real name. He soon changed his name to Brenton Wood (derived from the exclusive Brentwood section of LA) and sang under that for the first time as a member of the Quotations at Compton and next as a member of Little Freddy & the Rockets, who recorded "All My Love" on the Chief label in 1958. Over the next few years, he cut a number of singles on different labels, including "The Kangaroo" (1960), "Mr. Schemer" (1963) and others.

By 1966 he was using the name Brenton Wood as a performer though as a songwriter he was still going by Alfred Smith, and it was Smith who became friends with Joseph Hooven and Hal Winn. Winn and Hooven founded Double-Shot Records and invited Wood to record for them in 1967. His first recording for the label would become "The Oogum Boogum Song," but it took some work to get it where it ended up.

Brenton Wood, 1967 (photograph courtesy Brenton Wood).

Wood says the song was influenced by "miniskirts and bellbottom pants and all the fashions of the sixties." But he noted that initially the song had a very different sound and feel—and didn't have the "Oogum Boogum" hook. "The record company gave me a song one day called 'Casting My Spell on You.' I didn't like it very much, so I took the song and rewrote it and added the hook 'Oogum Boogum,' which is another word for abracadabra. It took me six weeks, but I laughed all through it. It was a joy."

Listeners found "Oogum Boogum" to be a joy as well. It reached #19 on the R&B charts and #34 on the Billboard Hot 100, so the expectations were high for his next recording. That single was "Gimme Little Sign," and Wood said, "'Gimme Little Sign' came to me after a few breakups with my girlfriend" and is his plaintive plea for his girl to give him some sign that things weren't as they should be. The catchy tune, which at no point in its lyrics ever actually *says* "gimme little sign"—it's always "gimme *some kind of* sign"—raced to #9 on the Billboard charts and #19 on the R&B charts in 1967. After two big hits, it looked like Brenton Wood and Double Shot were a successful combination.

After "Gimme Little Sign," his next 1967 release,

"Baby You Got It," peaked at #34 in November, but despite the slight drop-off after the popularity of "Gimme Little Sign," the string of three consecutive Top 40 songs gave hope for a promising future. But his next single, "Lovey Dovey Kinda Lovin,'" failed to make the Top 40, peaking at #99 in March 1968. This was the beginning of a trend, as his next release, "Me and You" (1968) would "bubble under" the Hot 100 at #121, his next wouldn't chart at all and his next, "A Change Is Gonna Come" (1969), would also "bubble under" at #131. Unfortunately, that was Brenton Wood's last single to make the Billboard pop charts, as subsequent singles on Double Shot all stiffed.

Wood continued to record throughout the '70s on a variety of labels, but other than his 1977 cover of the Fleetwoods' 1959 hit "Come Softly to Me," which barely entered the bottom of the R&B charts, he never charted after 1969.

Works Cited

Abbey, John. "Etta James: 1974 Interview." July 1974. http://www.soulmusic.com/a-z-of-soul-music-artists/.

_____. "The Whispers Are Getting Louder." March 1974. http://www.soulmusic.com/a-z-of-soul-music-artists/.

Abrahamian, Bob. E-mails to author. July 15 and 23, and August 13, 2010.

_____. Interview with Patti Drew. www.sittinginthepark.com/index.html.

_____. "Sitting in the Park." www.sittinginthepark.com/index.html.

Allen, Craig. "Meet Carl Carlton." New Jersey 101.5. 4 May 2013. http://nj1015.com/meet-carl-carlton-photos-videos/.

"Amos Milburn." *Black Cat Rockabilly*. http://www.rockabilly.nl/references/messages/amos_milburn.htm.

Baker, Mike. "Mike Baker and the Forgotten 45s." web.me.com/mikebaker/themob/themob.html.

"Barbara George Remembered." 1 February 2013. http://www.spectropop.com/remembers/BarbaraGeorge.htm.

"Barbara George Remembered." *Home of the Groove*. August 2008. http://homeofthegroove.blogspot.com/2006/08/barbara-george-remembered.html.

Barker, John. "Summertime's Calling Me." Email to the author. 26 September 2011.

Bell, Archie. Telephone interview with the author. 27 September 2012.

Bell, William. Telephone interview with the author. 11 October 2011.

Bellaire, Rick. "Hardcore Poetry and Street Corner Symphonies: The Story of Tavares." *The Official Tavares Website*. 17 November 2016. http://www.tavaresbrothers.com/index.html.

Benicewitz, Larry. "Remembering Willie Tee." *The Blues Art Journal* (November 2007). www.bluesart.at/Neue Seiten/REMEMBERING%20WILLIE%20TEE%20(1944–2007).html.

"Benny Spellman." Louisiana Music Hall of Fame. louisianamusichalloffame.org.

"Black Bubblegum." *Bubblegum University*. www.bubblegum-music.com/blackbubblegum.

Bogdanov, Vladimir, et al. *All Music Guide to Soul: The Definitive Guide to R&B and Soul*. San Francisco: Backbeat Books, 2003.

Bounden, Stephen. "Maurice Williams: A Brief History of This American Singer and Songwriter." SoulMotion. www.soulmotion.co.uk/Maurice%20Williams.htm.

"Box in the Garage—Shades of Blue." MOG. http://mog.com/DashboardDJ856/blog/2844246.

Bradford, Bill. Telephone interview with the author. 17 February 2012.

Bradley, Jan. Telephone interview with the author. August 15, 2010.

Braheny, John. "Interview with Thom Bell." 28 September 2007. http://johnbraheny.com/2007/09/28/interview-with-thom-bell/.

"Brenton Wood's Biography." www.brentonwood.com/html/biography.html.

Brewster, Bill, and Frank Broughton. *Last Night a DJ Saved My Life*. New York: Grove Press, 2000.

Bronson, Fred. *The Billboard Book of Number One Hits*. New York: Billboard, 1988.

Broven, John. *Rhythm and Blues in New Orleans*. Gretna, LA: Pelican, 1978.

_____. *South to Louisiana: The Music of the Cajun Bayous*. Gretna, LA: Pelican, 1983.

Brown, Clyde. Telephone interview with the author. 25 July 2011.

Burnett, Norm. Telephone interview with the author. December 20, 2010.

Burns, Peter. "The Simply Delicious Betty Everett." *Soul Music HQ*. n.d. http://www.soulmusichq.com/earshot16p3.html.

"Buster Brown." *Black Cat Rockabilly*. http://www.rockabilly.nl/references/messages/buster_brown.htm.

Butler, Jerry. Telephone interview with the author. 1 October 2012.

Cameron, G.C. Telephone interview with the author. February 4, 2011.

Cason, Buzz. *The Adventures of Buzz Cason: Living the Rock n' Roll Dream*. Milwaukee, WI: Hal Leonard Corp., 2004.

Castillo, Emilio. Telephone interview with the author. 7 August 2011.

Cermanski, Edward. "The Trammps." E-mails to author. April 15 and 16, 2010.

Channel, Bruce. "Hey! Baby." E-mails to author. August 23, December 19, 2010.

"Chuck Jackson Overcame Southern Segregation to Become Pioneering Soul Singer Who Gave the World the Classic 'Any Day Now.'" *Pittsburgh Music History*. https://sites.google.com/site/pittsburghmusichistory/pittsburgh-music-story/r-b—funk/chuck-jackson.

Cooper, Francis, and Bill Friskics Warren. "Back With the Beat." *Nashville Scene*. 12 October 1995. http://www.nashvillescene.com/arts-culture/article/13000098/back-with-the-beat.

Cooper, Jim. "Robert 'Budda' Winters: A Tribute to One of the Greatest Singers of All Time." 2011. http://cooptekproductions.com/buddha.htm.

Craver, Paul. "Cannonball." E-mails to author. June 8 and 9, August 1, 2010.

Curry, Clifford. Telephone interview with the author. October 31, 2010, February 2, 2011, 31 October 2011.

Dahl, Bill. "Jackie Wilson." Brunswick Records. www.brunswickrecords.com/artists/jackiewilson.htm.

_____. "Papa Don Schroeder Reminisces about Producing

James and Bobby Purify....." Sundazed.com. 18 March 2012. http://www.sundazed.com/scene/exclusives/papa_don_exclusive.html.

Davis, Jim. "The Sonny and Phyllis Story." *It Will Stand* Volume 2 Number 1, 4–5.

Dawson, Jim, and Propes, Steve. *45 RPM: The History, Heroes, and Villains of the Pop Music Revolution.* Milwaukee, WI: Backbeat Books, 2003.

———. *What Was the First Rock and Roll Record?* Faber & Faber, 1992.

Deffaa, Chip. *Blue Rhythms: Six Lives in Rhythm and Blues.* Boston: Da Capo Press, 1999.

Detroit Record Labels. http://www.seabear.se/detroit2.htm.

Deville, Hershey. Telephone interview with the author. November 19, 2010.

DeYoung, Bill. "Clarence Carter, Soul Man." *Connect Savannah.* 9 February 2010. http://www.connectsavannah.com/savannah/clarence-carter-soul-man/Content?oid=2132341.

Driggs, Frank and Chuck Haddix. *Kansas City Jazz: From Ragtime to Bebop—A History.* Oxford: Oxford University Press, 2006.

Edelstein, Andrew. Hank Ballard." *Goldmine*, November 1981.

Elston, Harry. Telephone interview with the author. 21 May 2012.

"Floyd Dixon." *Black Cat Rockabilly.* http://www.rockabilly.nl/references/messages/floyd_dixon.htm.

Fox, Randy. "Nashville R&B Hero Clifford Curry Dies at 79." *Nashville Scene.* 9 September 2016. http://www.nashvillescene.com/music/news/article/20833253/nashville-rb-hero-clifford-curry-dies-at-79.

Freeland, David. *The Ladies of Soul.* Oxford: University Press of Mississippi, 2001.

Gardner, Veta, and Earl Gardner. E-mails to author. July 14 and August 13, 2010.

Gillett, Charlie. "All for One: A Study in Frustration and Black Organization." *Cream.* 5 Sept 1971 p. 22–25, 50–52. http://www.charliegillett.com/bb/viewtopic.php?f=34&t=5038.

———. *Making Tracks: Atlantic Records and the Growth of a Billion Dollar Industry.* New York: Dutton, 1974.

Gilstrap, Jim. Telephone interview with the author. 27 September 2011.

Goins, Kevin. "Remembering the Esquires." http://www.examiner.com/r-b-music-in-milwaukee/remembering-the-esquires-how-they-got-on-up-from-milwaukee-to-the-music-charts. 24 March 2012.

Goldberg, Marv. "Old Town Records." http://www.uncamarvy.com/OldTown/oldtown.html. 2009.

Gore, Jackie. Telephone interview with the author. 17 July 2011.

Grendysa, Peter. "Hello Ruth! The Ruth Brown Story." *It Will Stand* 4–6. 2013.

Hamilton, Andrew. "Roy Hammond." *All-Music.* http://www.allmusic.com/artist/roy-hammond-p338312/biography.

Hammond, Roy C. Telephone Interview with the Author. 22 March 2012.

Hannusch, Jeff. "Obituary: Benny Spellman." *Offbeat Magazine.* https://www.offbeat.com/articles/obituary-benny-spellman-1931–2011/.

Hayes, Bernie. *The Death of Black Radio: The Story of America's Black Radio Personalities.* Bloomington, IN: iUniverse, 2005.

Haynes, Greg. *The Heeey Baby Days of Beach Music.* 2005.

"Hello Stranger." *The Pop History Dig.* 7 August 2016. http://www.pophistorydig.com/topics/tag/barbara-lewis-biography/.

Henderson, Alex. "The Futures." http://www.alexvhenderson.com/arts__entertainment/rb_liner_notes_18_the_futures.

Hinson, Mark. "Boz Scaggs Talks About His Lost Album." *Tallahassee Democrat.* 16 April 2016.

Hobson, Donald. "I Need a Love." E-mails to author. September 7, October 18 and 19, November 10 and 15, 2010; February 3, 2011.

Hogan, Ed. "Artist Biography: Carl Carlton." *AllMusic.* http://www.allmusic.com/artist/carl-carlton-mn0000174034/biography.

Holvay, James. E-mails to author. September 30 and October 2, 9 and 7, 2010.

Hook, John. "Jewell and the Rubies." *Dancing on the Edge Journal.* 1.5 8 March 2010

———. *Shagging in the Carolinas.* Charleston, SC: Arcadia, 2005.

Houston, Keith. Telephone interview with the author. 18 August 2011.

"Interview with 'One Scotch, One Bourbon, One Beer' Guy Amos Milburn." *It Will Stand* 1.3 (4–5).

"Interview with Richard Younger. Get a Shot of Rhythm and Blues: The Arthur Alexander Story." www.allbutforgottenoldies.net/interviews/richard-younger.

"Jackie Wilson." *The History of Rock.* www.history-of-rock.com/jackie_wilson.htm.

Jackson, John A. *A House on Fire: The Rise and Fall of Philadelphia Soul.* Oxford: Oxford University Press, 2004.

James, Gary. Interview with Ben E. King. http://www.classicbands.com/BenEKingInterview.html.

James, Gary. Interview with Nick Marinelli of Shades of Blue. http://www.classicbands.com/vShadesOfBlueInterview.html.

James, Linda "Quig" Quinlan. "Hey I Know You." E-mails to author. June 29 and 30, July 1, 2, 9, 10 and 13, 2010; January 30, 2011.

James-Johnson, Alva. "Jo Jo Benson Dies at Victory Drive Motel." 23 December 2014. http://www.ledger-enquirer.com/news/local/article29376997.html.

Jancik, Wayne. *The Billboard Book of One-Hit Wonders.* New York: Billboard Books, 1990.

"Jimmy Liggins: I Can't Stop It." 25 September 2009. http://bebopwinorip.blogspot.com/2009/09/jimmy-liggins-i-cant-stop-it.html.

Kantor, Justin. "Billy Ocean's Happy Refrain." *Soul Music.com.* http://www.soulmusic.com/index.asp?S=3&T=36&ART=255.

Kaye, Candy. "The Spiral Starecase." Email to author. 14 April 2010.

Kelly, Red. "James and Bobby Purify: So Many Reasons." *The B Side.* http://redkelly.blogspot.com/2007/10/james-bobby-purify-so-many-reasons-bell.html.

Kilgour, Colin. "Gene McDaniels." *Black Cat Rockabilly.* www.rockabilly.nl/references/messages/gene_mcdaniels.htm.

King, Naomi; "Remembering Barbara George: R&B Legend Left Music to Be with God." 17 August 2006. http://www.houmatoday.com/article/20060817/NEWS/608170323?p=4&tc=pg.

King, Peter. "Jimmy Beaumont, Skyliners, a Hometown Success Story." *The Pittsburgh Press*. 23 February 1989: 26.

Kirby, Michael Jack. "Buster Brown." *Way Back Attack*. https://www.waybackattack.com/brownbuster.html.

_____. "Etta James." *Way Back Attack*. http://www.waybackattack.com/jamesetta.html.

Knight, Robert. Telephone interview with the author. 6 July 2012.

Kuban, Bob. Telephone interview with the author. August 23, 2010.

Laszewski, Chuck. "Hello Stranger': Barbara Lewis in Town for 'Taste.'" https://www.minnpost.com/politics-policy/2008/06/hello-stranger-barbara-lewis-town-taste.

Lemon, Meadowlark. Telephone interview with the author. January 11, 2011.

"Leon Haywood at the Organ, 1962–68." *Funky16Corners*. 14 April 2016. http://funky16corners.com/?p=6359.

Leszczak, Bob. *The Encyclopedia of Pop Music Aliases, 1950–2000*. Lanham, MD: Rowman & Littlefield, 2014.

Lewis, Pete. "Eddie Floyd: Stax Lucky Charm." *B&S Online*. http://www.bluesandsoul.com/feature/697/eddie_floyd_stax_lucky_charm/.

_____. "Errol Brown: A Fondent Farewell." *B&S Online*. http://www.bluesandsoul.com/feature/377/errol_brown_a_fondent_farewell/. 17 May 2012.

_____. "The Four Tops: B&S Classic Interview." *B&S Online*. www.bluesandsoul.com/feature/357/the_four_tops_bands_classic_interview.

Lewsiohn, Mark. *The Beatles Recording Sessions*. New York: Hyperion, 1992.

Lockwood, Rod. "After Fading into Obscurity, Toledoan Gloria Taylor's Music Is Hot Again." *The Blade*. 9 November 2014. http://www.toledoblade.com/Music-Theater-Dance/2014/11/09/After-fading-into-obscurity-Toledoan-s-music-is-hot-again.html.

Lollar, Sam. "Jewell and the Rubies." E-mails to author. April 18, 19 and 20, 2010.

"The Manhattans, Part I." *Soul Express*. http://www.soulexpress.net/manhattans_part1.htm. 26 September 2016.

Marinelli, Nick. Telephone interview with the author. 1 February 2012.

Marsh, Dave. *The Heart of Rock & Soul: The 1001 Greatest Singles Every Made*. Boston: Da Capo Press, 1999.

McDaniels, Gene. Telephone interview with the author. November 15, 2010.

McElrath, John. "The Medallions.com." www.medallions.com/index5F/history.html.

_____. Telephone interview with the author. July 19, 2010.

McGarvey, Seamus and Chris Beachley. "From Across the Sea, the Billy Ocean Story." *It Will Stand*. 6.31 1985: 5–7.

Millar, Bill. "Arthur Alexander." The Alabama Music Hall of Fame Website. ww.alamhof.org/arthuralexander.html.

"Millie Jackson is Amazing!" 24 May 2012. http://fourfour.typepad.com/fourfour/2012/02/millie-jackson-is-amazing.html.

Miranda, Bob. Emails to the author. April 4, 5 2017.

"The Mob Pioneered Chicago's 'Horn Rock' Sound—And Wore Dark Pinstriped Suits with Carnations." *The Chicago Reader*. 18 September 2015.

Moore, Bobby, Jr. Telephone interview with the author. November 1, 2010.

Moore, Deacon John. Telephone interview with the author. November 19, 2010.

Morthland, John. "The '5' Royales Hard Rocking R&B." *Wondering Sound*. 21 April 2014. http://www.wonderingsound.com/feature/the-5-royales-tribute/.

Nathan, David. "Lenny Finds His Devil's Advocate." 20 March 2012. http://www.soulmusic.com/index.asp?S=3&T=3&ART=1133.

_____. "Moore or Less on Her Way." 18 April 2014. http://www.soulmusic.com/index.asp?S=3&T=3&ART=7131.

Nations, Opal Lewis. Percy Milem and the Lyrics. *Memphis Blues and Rhythm* #174, 2002, 14–15.

Newsom, Jim. "Beach Music's Five Star General." www.generalnormanjohnson.com.

_____. "Who Put the 'H' in Rhondel?" http://jimnewsom.com/PFW-Billdeal.html.

"The Northern Soul Top 500." Steve Parker Micro Site. http://www.rocklistmusic.co.uk/steveparker/northern_soul_top_500.htm.

Ollison, Rashod D. "Nasty, Sassy Miss Millie Jackson, the Original Bad Girl of Rhythm and Blues, Was Singing About Sex and Sinning Way Before Lil' Kim Was Born. And at 56, the "Queen of Sex 'n' Soul" Is Still at It." *Philly.com*. 5 April 2001.

Owen James Roberts. "Earl Bostic: Up There in Oribit" (2012).

Palmer, Robert. "Roy Brown, A Pioneer Rock Singer." 26 May 1981. *The New York Times* http://www.nytimes.com/1981/05/26/obituaries/roy-brown-a-pioneer-rock-singer.html.

Pareles, Jon. "Teddy Pendergrass, R&B Soul Singer, Dies at 59." http://www.nytimes.com/2010/01/15/arts/music/15pendergrass.html. *The New York Times.com* 14 January 2010.

Parissi, Rob. "Wild Cherry." Emails to the author. 8, 9, and 10 August 2011.

Parker, Steve. "The Northern Soul Top 500." Steve Parker Micro Site. http://www.rocklistmusic.co.uk/steveparker/northern_soul_top_500.htm.

Payne, Freda. Telephone interview with the author. February 5, 2011.

"Peggy Scott & Jo Jo Benson—Here With Me." *The B Side*. http://redkelly.blogspot.com/2009/07/peggy-scott-jo-jo-benson-here-with-me.html.

Penemy, D.K. "The '5' Royales." *The History of Rock n Roll: The Golden Decade, 1954–1963*. http://www.history-of-rock.com/five_royales.htm.

Peoples Bears, Sandra. Telephone interview with the author. November 20, 2010.

Perrone, Pierre. "Bobby Moore: Leader of the Rhythm Aces." *The Independent*. March 18, 2006. www.independent.co.uk/news/obituaries/bobby-moore-470305.html.

_____. "Earl Nelson: Half of Bob and Earl." *The Independent*. www.independent.co.uk/news/obituaries/earl-nelson-half-of-bob-earl-880270.htm.

_____. "Fontella Bass: Singer Famed for Her Powerful Interpretation of the Million-Seller 'Rescue Me.'" *The In-*

dependent. 28 December 2012. http://www.independent.co.uk/news/obituaries/fontella-bass-singer-famed-for-her-powerful-interpretation-of-the-million-seller-rescue-me-8432763.html.

Peters, Ida. "Carrie Lucas Visits *Afro*." *The Washington Afro-American*. 10 August 1982. Page 6.

Pittman, Wayne. Telephone interview with the author. November 3, 2010.

Pope, Charles. Emails to author. 25 June, 11 July and 23, 25, 27 and 28 August 2010.

Pope, Dianne, and Charles Pope. E-mails to author. 12 December 2011; 21 February 2012.

Proctor, Jay. Telephone interview with the author. 20 July 2012.

Pruter, Robert. "Beach Music from Historic Charleston: The Patti Drew Story." *It Will Stand*. Volume 3 Number 20, 1981: 14–15.

_____. *Chicago Soul*. Chicago: University of Illinois Press, 1991.

_____. "The Gene Chandler Story." *It Will Stand*. Volume 8 Number 35, 1985: 6–11.

_____. "Get On Up ... and Get Away: The Esquires Story." *It Will Stand*. Volume 4 Number 26, 1982: 6–9.

Pugh, Fred. Telephone interview with the author. 11 September 2016.

Rachou, David. "Jewell and the Rubies." E-mail to author. April 20, 2010.

Reid, Jeff. "Blacksmith, Shakers, and etc." Email to the author. 14 September 2016.

_____. Telephone interview with the author. 8 March 2012.

Riggs, Carolyn Pennypacker. "Barbara Lynn: Music on My Mind." *L.A. Record*. 26 May 2012.

Ritz, David and Etta James. *Rage to Survive: The Etta James Story*. Boston: Da Capo Press, 2003.

Rizik, Chris. "The Friends of Distinction." 15 May 2012. *Soul Tracks*. http://www.soultracks.com/friends_of_distinction.htm.

Roberts, Kev. *The Northern Soul Top 500*. London: Bee Cool Publishing, 2003.

Robinson, Dino. "Everybody Knows Patti Drew." *Shorefront Journal*. 2003. https://shorefrontjournal.wordpress.com/2013/08/24/now-everybody-knows-patti-drew-in-the-butler/.

Rosalsky, Mitch. *Encyclopedia of Rhythm and Blues and Doo Wop Vocal Groups*. Lanham, MD: Scarecrow Press, 2008.

"Sad Eyes." superseventies.com/sw_sadeyes.html.

Sawyer, Phil, and Tom Polland. *Save the Last Dance For Me: A Love Story of the Shag*. Columbia: University of South Carolina Press: 2012.

Scott, Billy. E-mails to the author. 10 November 2010; 6 July, 30 January 2011; 3, 7, 8, 9,10, 11 March, 14, 17, 19, 26, 27 September and 1, 2, 3 October 2012.

_____. Telephone interview with the author. 1 November 2010; 7 July 2011.

"Shades of Blue History." SOB Entertainment. http://www.sobentertainment.com/history2.html.

Shane, Ken. "Soul Serenade: Clarence Carter, 'Slip Away.'" *Popdose*. 28 March 2013.

Simmonds, Jeremy. *The Encyclopedia of Dead Rock Stars: Heroin, Handguns, and Ham Sandwiches*. Chicago Review Press, 2008.

"The Skyliners: Five Teenagers from Pittsburg Make Pop Music History." https://sites.google.com/site/pittsburghmusichistory/pittsburgh-music-story/doo-wop/the-skyliners.

Smith, Bobbie. Telephone interview with the author. 10 September 2011.

Smith, John. "Edwin Starr's Early Years." http://www.edwinstarr.info/earlybiog.htm.

"Soulful Kinda Music." http://www.soulfulkindamusic.net/discographies.htm.

"Spiral Starecase." Mclane &Wong Entertainment Law. http://www.benmclane.com/spiral.htm.

Sweeting, Adam. "Percy Sledge Obituary." 15 April 2015. https://www.theguardian.com/music/2015/apr/15/percy-sledge.

Tharp, Ammon. Telephone interview with the author. November 10, 2010.

Thompson, Howie. *And the Bands Played On: The History of Beach Music*. Xlibris, 2013.

"Those Hoodlum Friends: The Coasters." www.angelfire.com/mn/coasters.

Threatt, Sonny. "Sunny and Phyllis." Email to author. May 27, 28, 29, 30, August 16, 2010.

Tomlinson, Bobby. Telephone interview with the author. August 1, 2010.

Townsend, John. Telephone interview with the author. 16 August 1, 2011

Trexler, Donny. Telephone interview with the author. 9 March 2012.

Turner, Sonny. Telephone interview with the author. August 10, 2010.

Upton, Pat. "More Today." Emails to author. June 10, 2010 and October 19, 2010.

_____. Telephone interview with the author. 7 July 2011.

Wald, Elijah. *How the Beatles Destroyed Rock 'n' Roll: An Alternative History of American Popular Music*. Oxford: Oxford University Press, 2009.

Walker, Steve. "The Five Royales." *Black Cat Rockabilly*. http://www.rockabilly.nl/references/messages/5_royales.htm.

Warner, Jay. *American Singing Groups*. Milwaukee, WI: Hal Leonard Press, 2006.

Washburn, Mark Lawrence Toppmann, and April Baker. "Beach Music Icon General Johnson Dies." The Charlotte Observer.com. 17 October 2010.

Webb, Robert. "Double Take: 'Hold Back the Night' The Trammps/Graham Parker and the Rumour." *The Independent*. www.independent.co.uk/arts-entertainment/music/features/double-take-hold-back-the-night-the-trammps—graham-parker-and-the-rumour-592563.html.

Weinger, Harry, and Charlie White. "James Brown: Are You Ready for Star Time?" *James Brown: The Hardest Working Man in Show Business*. http://www.jamesbrown.com/Default.aspx.

Weiss, Ed. Telephone interview with the author. August 12, 2010.

The Whispers Page. http://www.soulwalking.co.uk/The%20Whispers.html.

Whitburn, Joel. *Billboard Hot 100 Charts—The Sixties*. Milwaukee, WI: Hal Leonard Press, 1995.

_____. *Bubbling Under the Hot 100, 1959–1985*. Menomonee Falls, WI: Record Research, 1992.

_____. *Top Pop Singles, 1955–1986.* Menomonee Falls, WI: Record Research, 1987.

_____. *Top R&B Singles, 1942–1995.* Milwaukee, WI: Hal Leonard Press, 1996.

Whitsett, Tim. "The Biography of Mr. Eddie Floyd." EddieFloyd.com. http://www.eddiefloyd.com/biography.htm.

Wicker, Ann. *Making Notes: Music of the Carolinas.* Charlotte, NC: Novello Festival Press, 2008.

Williams, Richard. "Bobby Hebb." *The Guardian.* 5 August 2010. https://www.theguardian.com/music/2010/aug/05/bobby-hebb-obituary.

Windle, Mark. "Bob Meyer and the Rivieras." It's Better to Cry. Wednesday, 2 October 2013. http://southern-soulcollector.blogspot.com/2013/10/bob-meyer-and-rivieras.html.

Wood, Brenton. "Brenton Wood Information." E-mails to author. May 5 and October 18, 2010.

Younger, Richard. E-mails to author. October 31 and December 19, 2010.

_____. *Get a Shot of Rhythm and Blues: The Arthur Alexander Story.* Tuscaloosa: University of Alabama Press, 2000.

_____. "The Life and Times of Arthur Alexander." www.richardyounger.com/arthur-alexander.php.

Index

Author's Note: Because of the nature of the material included in this book, if every individual performer on every recording detailed herein were listed in the index, the index itself would be as long as the book. Consequently, groups, as opposed to individual members, are indexed, and individual members are listed only if they were interviewed, went on to fame with other groups or as solo artists, or were especially noteworthy for some other reason. Individual songs are indexed with a similar methodology: featured songs that were identified with beach music, or songs that were especially noteworthy for some other reason have been indexed, but not every song mentioned in each artist's write-up. The same is also true of cities; while cities that were hubs of activity in the music world such as New York, Detroit, and Philadelphia, or cities that were noteworthy on the East Coast for reasons relating to beach music have been indexed, every city where artists were born or lived at some time in their lives has not been included.

On the other hand, every record label, whether large or small, regional or national, and whether referenced twenty times or just once, has been included. Similarly, every name a group performed under has been included, because acts often went through several name changes before and sometimes after the music that justified their inclusion in this work.

A&M (label) 75, 141, 163–164
The A-Sharp Trio 72
Aaliyah 141
ABC/ABC Paramount/Dunhill (label) 4, 40, 43–44, 55, 57, 105, 112, 114, 117, 119, 134, 143–144, 149, 159, 162, 191, 194, 205, 207–209, 210, 212, 218, 236–237, 263–265, 281, 290
Abner (label) 65, 143
Abner, Ewart 62, 143
Abrahamian, Bob 91
Academy Awards 148
Ace (label) 20, 113–114, 193
Ace, Johnny 88, 133, 226
Acklin, Barbara 15–16, 293
"Across the Street" 5, 10, 98, 205–206
Adderley, Cannonball 138
"Adorable" 92–93
A.F.O. (label) 126–127, 268
The Afterdeck (club) 6
"Agent Double-O-Soul" 253–254
"Ain't No Woman (Like the One I've Got) 117–119
"Ain't that Peculiar" 125–126
"Ain't Too Proud to Beg" 130, 232, 249, 271
The Akrons 161
Alabama (band) 107
Alabama (University of) 235
Alabama Music Hall of Fame 57
Aladdin (label) 37–38, 88, 117, 136–138, 174–175, 192–193, 275
Alaimo, Steve 17
Alexander, Arthur 5, 16–18, 80, 264
All Platinum (label) 98–99
Allen (label) 117
Alligator Records (label) 89
Allman, Duane 238
Alon (label) 248
"Along Came Jones" 73
The Alphatones 143
"Am I the Same Girl?" 15
American Bandstand 16–17, 50, 91, 148, 170, 183, 184, 210, 218, 229, 239, 243, 246, 253
American Graffiti 43, 67, 247
American Hot Wax 67, 114
American Idol 211
Amjo (label) 123
Amy (label) 189, 278
"And Get Away" 103–104
The Andantes 100, 126, 142, 182, 233, 249, 293–294
Animal House 67, 81–82
Anka, Paul 72, 171
"Anna" 5, 16–18, 192
Anna (label) 232
"Annie Had a Baby" 23–24
"Annie Kicked the Bucket" 24
"Annie Pulled a Hum-Bug" 24
"Annie's Answer" 24
"Annie's Aunt Fanny" 24
"Any Day Now" 149–150
Apollo (label) 49, 97, 111, 138, 206
Apollo Theatre 18, 19, 38, 45, 54, 70, 87, 93, 104, 108, 120, 127, 149, 165, 181, 188, 213, 216, 224, 243, 246, 254, 273, 275, 279, 281
Apple (label) 273
"Apples, Peaches, Pumpkin Pie" 156–157
Aquarian (label) 21–22
Archibald, Bob 77
Archie Bell and the Drells 10, 21, 33–34, 101, 176
The Archies 133
Arctic (label) 190, 272
Argo (label) 86, 153, 173, 230
Ariola (label) 176, 204
Arista (label) 59, 92, 95, 110, 223, 284
"Arizona" 94
Arlen (label) 262, 264
Armstrong, Louis 181, 185, 219
The Army-Navy Club 107
Arthur Smith Studios 75, 199, 262, 270
The Artistics 10, 18–19, 62, 172, 279
Ash Grove (club) 136
Ashford, Nick 157, 237
Ashford, Rosalind 125, 182–183
"Ask Me What You Want" 151–152
"Ask the Lonely" 117–119
Asnes (label) 181
The Association 227
Astaire, Fred 37
The Astors 19–20
Astroscope (label) 43
"At the Top of the Stairs" 114
Atco (label) 27, 56, 72, 154–155, 164–165, 205–206, 239, 243, 285–287, 290
Atkins, Roger 91, 174
Atlanta, Georgia 21, 27, 46, 47, 57, 129–130, 168, 209, 262–264, 294, 295
Atlantic (label) 7, 22–23, 32, 33–34, 35, 39, 45–46, 49–50, 54, 56–57, 69–70, 71–72, 84, 89, 92–94, 110, 115, 120, 141, 147, 150, 163–164, 165, 173–174, 178, 179, 181, 187–188, 200–201, 203, 213, 238, 241, 243–244, 248–251, 268–269, 273, 274, 275–276, 283–284
Atlantic Beach 101, 208
Auburn University 235
Augusta, Georgia 47, 128
Avalanche (label) 123
Avalon, Frankie 170
Avanti (label) 181
Avco (label) 98–99, 161
The Avengers 25
The Avons 47

B & C (label) 189
Bab-Roc (label) 134

305

306 Index

"Baby (You've Got What It Takes)" 285
"Baby Don't Change Your Mind" 168–169
"Baby I Need Your Loving" 117–119, 143
"Baby I'm Yours" 29, 169, 173–174
"Baby It's Over" 36
"Baby Let Me Bang Your Box" 66–67
"Baby Let's Make Some Love" 212–213
"Baby Love" 230, 258–259
"Baby, Now That I've Found You" 115–116
"Baby Walk Right In" 26, 98; *see also* "Open the Door to Your Heart"
"Baby You Got It" 221–222
Bacharach, Burt 93, 149, 269, 283
Back Beat (label) 55, 76
"Back Door Santa" 56
"Back in Love Again" 49
"Backfield in Motion" 189–190
"Backstabbers" 207, 209, 237
The Bad Habits 20
"Bad Luck" 191, 212, 217
"Bad Time" 11
Bagby, Doc 273
Bailey, J.R. 133, 179–180
Bailey, Rasie Michael ("Razzy") 21
Baker, Anita 121
Baker, Josephine 219, 245
Baker, Lavern 18, 22–23, 35, 139, 225, 246
Baker, Mickey 141
Baldry, Long John 115
Balk, Harry 240
Ball, Noel 167–168
Ballard, Florence 24, 258–259, 285
Baltimore, Maryland 18, 54, 216, 259
Bamboo (label) 62, 189–190
Banashak, Joe 242
"Band of Gold" 210–211
The Band of Oz 9, 25–26, 61, 82, 270
Bang (label) 227–229
Bank (label) 114
Banks, Darrell 26–27, 98–99, 205
Barker, Gary 57–59, 84
Barker, Johnny 57–59, 84, 107
Barnes, J.J. 182
Barroso, Ary 72
Barry, Joe 178
Barry, Len 277
Bartholomew, Dave 218
Bartley, Chris 29, 169
Bascomb, Paul 74
Basie, Count 275
Bass, Fontella 15, 30–31, 91
Bass, Ralph 23, 47, 117, 171
Batiste, Harold 127, 268
Baton Rouge, Louisiana 20, 158, 247
Battle (label) 141
Baughn, David 64
The Bay City Rollers 234

BB Records (label) 242
be-bop music 36
"Be Young, Be Foolish, Be Happy" 10, 263, 265
Beach Beat 26, 71
Beach Beat Vol. 2 71, 165
The Beach Boys 5, 43, 253, 284
The Beach Club 17, 80
The Beach Music Hall of Fame *see* The Carolina Beach Music Hall of Fame
Beachley, Chris 9
"Beachwood 4-5789" 183–184
Beale Street 133
The Beatles 17–18, 42, 48, 63, 64, 112, 139, 141, 142, 147, 170, 192, 204, 214, 223, 259, 286
"Beauty Is Only Skin Deep" 232, 271–272
The Bee Gees 12, 17, 234, 267
Beech (label) 98, 205
"Begin the Beguine" 3
"Behold" 191–192
"Bein' with You" 266–267
Beisbier, Gary 48, 196–197
Bell (label) 50, 92, 94–95, 108–109, 206, 220, 223, 278–279
Bell, Al (aka Alvertis Isbell) 113
Bell, Sandy 8, 38–39
Bell, Thom 84–85, 144–145, 176, 203, 236, 250–251, 284–285
Bell, Tony 200
Bell, William 4, 19, 31–33, 69–70, 113, 234, 283
Beltone (label) 161
Belvin, Jesse 109, 213
Bennet, Al 186
Benson, Jo Jo 238–239
Benton, Brook 63, 188, 260, 285
Berman, Bess 49
"Bernadette" 117–119, 249
Berns, Bert 49
Berry, Chuck 30, 125, 230
Berry Street Station 257
Best, Pete 63
Bet T (label) 31
Big Daddy's Bottom (club) 6
"Big Time Lover" 76
Big Top (label) 163
The Big Track Diner (club) 45
Big Tree (label) 179
Big Wednesday 67
Bihari, Jules 192
Bill Deal and the Rhondels 2, 8, 82–84, 236, 292
Bill Haley and the Comets 276
Billy Smith's Beach Party Volume 2 (album) 43
Billy Ward and The Dominoes 9, 23, 46, 64–65, 92, 96, 102, 117, 171, 188, 226, 240, 281–283, 292
Billy Ward and the Dominoes *see* The Dominoes
The Bitter Lemons 135
Black, Bill 194
Black, Tommy 57
Black and Blue 46
Black Sabbath 179

Blacksmith 107
Bland, Bobby "Blue" 133, 137, 225
Blast (label) 52
The Blenders 34–35, 224
Blood, Sweat, and Tears 163
The Blossoms 90
Blue Cat (label) 230
The Blue Chips 215
The Blue Diamonds 89
Blue Magic 180
The Blue Magoos 20
Blues and Soul Magazine 119
The Blues Brothers 89
Bob and Earl 35–36
Bob Collins and the Fabulous Five 74–75
Bob Kuban and the In-Men 169–171
Bob Meyer and the Rivieras 191–192
Bobbin (label) 30
Bobby and Sylvia 141
Bobby and the Consoles 163
Bobby Moore and the Rhythm Aces 201–202
The Bobettes 234
Boblo (label) 21–22
Bodnar, Ted 270
The Body Motions 273
Bogart, Neil 295
Bonatemp (label) 269
Bonefetti, Carl 48
Bonner, "Juke Boy" 136
Bonoff, Karla 201
"Boogie Down" 121
"Boogie Woogie Country Girl" 274, 276
"Boogie Woogie King" 174–175
Booker T. & the M.G.s 19, 36, 69, 111, 113, 172, 194
Boom (label) 141
Boone, Pat 185
"Born Under a Bad Sign" 31
Bostic, Earl 36–37
"Both Ends Against the Middle" 200–201
Boyce, Tommy 237
Boze, Calvin 37–38
Bradford, Bill 38–39
Bradford & Bell 9, 38
Bradley, Jan 39–41, 143, 230
Bradshaw, Tiny 136
Branch, Mike 9, 60
Branch, Roger 269–270
"Brazil" 72
"Bread and Butter" 164
The Breeze Band 21
"Brenda" 2
Brice Street 53
Brick 294
"Bring the Boys Home" 59
Bristol, Johnny 232, 266, 280–281
"Broken Heart" 109–110
Brooklyn, New York 43, 69, 151, 161, 163, 215
Brothers Unlimited 19
Brown, Bill 64, 188, 281
Brown, Buster 42–43, 124

Brown, Charles 88, 120, 137
Brown, Charlie (Ed Weiss) 12, 199
Brown, Clyde 94–95
Brown, "Gatemouth" 136
Brown, H. Lee 11
Brown, Jack (and Devora) 106
Brown, James 19, 37, 47–48, 50, 54, 68, 112, 141, 160, 220, 267, 273, 274
Brown, Jim 121
Brown, Maxine 43–44
Brown, Phyllis 256–257
Brown, Polly 284
Brown, Roy 138
Brown, Ruth 35, 45–46, 139, 188
"Brown Eyed Girl" 12
Brunswick (label) 15–16, 18–19, 23, 62, 74, 168, 219, 225, 230, 292–293
Brut (label) 161
Brute (label) 68
B.T. Puppy (label) 134–135
The Bubba Suggs Band 80
The Buckinghams 48–49, 197
Buddah (label) 16, 29, 123, 168–169, 203, 272–273, 295
Buffalo, New York 19, 26, 98, 205–206
Buffet, Jimmy 236
"Build Me Up Buttercup" 115–116
Bullet (label) 144
Bunky (label) 103–104
Burke, Solomon 49–50, 80, 274
Burnett, Norman 276–278
Burney, Mac 117
"Burning Love" 17
Burrage, Harold 81
"But It's Alright" 151
Butler, Jerry 40, 50–51, 101, 105, 143, 156, 172, 197, 204, 209, 236, 237, 283
"Bye Bye Baby" 285
Byrd, Bobby 35, 47, 160
Byrd, Roy "Professor Longhair" 97
The Byrds 227

The C&C Boys 56
C and the Shells 234
Cadet (label) 85–87, 153
The Cadillacs 133, 179, 190, 203, 211
Cahn, Sammy 114
Caldwell, Bobby 228–229
Calello, Charlie 205–206
Calico (label) 242–243
"California" 5, 10, 128–130
Calla (label) 134, 151, 234, 247
Calloway, Blanche 45
Calloway, Cab 36, 45, 181
Calvin Lindsay and the Hysterics 52
Cameo/Cameo Parkway (label) 29, 84–85, 124, 161, 195, 197, 243, 276
Cameo Parkway (label) 29, 84, 98, 100, 195, 247, 276–277
Cameron, G.C. 249
CAMMY Award 75

"Can I Change My Mind?" 81
Candix (label) 223
"Candy" 19
Canned Heat 139
Cannon, Danny see O'Henry, Lenny
Cannonball 6, 52
"Can't Do Sixty No More" (Dominoes version) 281–283
"Can't Do Sixty No More" (Du Droppers version) 96
"Can't Find the Time" 227–229
Capitol (label) 90–91, 141, 163, 219–220, 223, 263, 265, 266–267, 269, 288
The Capitols 53, 150
Capricorn (label) 128, 130
The Caps 53
The Cardinals 54, 259
Carla (label) 150
Carlton, Carl 55–56, 76, 141, 168, 189
Carnegie Hall 275
Carnival (label) 180–181
Carolina Beach Music Awards 26, 82
Carolina Beach Music Hall of Fame 33, 84, 108, 150, 156, 269, 270
"Carolina Girls" 59, 61, 108
Carr, James 194–195
Carrier, Cotton 265
Carter, Calvin 105, 143
Carter, Clarence 56–57, 59, 154
Casablanca (label) 119, 148, 295
Cash (label) 89, 137
Cash, Johnny 42, 63
Cash Box 20, 70, 77, 129, 236, 264, 279
Casino (label) 191–192, 279
The Casinyets 183
Cason, Buzz 55, 80, 167–68
Castaways (club) 52
Castillo, Emilio 216–218
Caston, Leonard 30, 222
Cat (label) 88–89
The Catalinas 6, 8, 9, 26, 57–59, 103, 107, 191
The Cavaliers 271
CBS (label) 132, 163, 178, 221, 229
Cee-Jay (label) 181
The Celebrities 68
The Cellar (club) 245
"Certain Girl" 89–90
"C'est Si Bon" 219
The Chairmen of the Board 4, 9, 10, 56, 59–61, 242, 270
Chance (label) 246
Chandler, Gene 15, 18, 56, 61–62, 91, 172, 189
Channel, Bruce 10, 63–64, 262
The Charlemagnes 190
Charles, Lee 190
Charles, Ray 70, 86, 111, 112, 121, 139, 178, 181, 185, 202, 218, 236, 239
Charles, Tina 3
Charleston, South Carolina 91, 215, 266

"Charlie Brown" (song) 73
Charlotte, North Carolina 27, 38, 52, 57, 75, 138, 191, 199, 245, 262, 269, 270
The Charms Unlimited 246
Chateau (label) 118
Chattahoochie (label) 89
"The Cheater" 169–171
"Cheaters Never Win" 175–176
Check-Mate (label) 68, 182, 232
Checker (label) 30–31, 62, 85, 89, 98, 110, 159, 185, 201–202
Checker, Chubby 24, 276
The Checkers 10, 36, 64–65, 137, 282
The Cheers 166
Chelsea (label) 66, 131, 132, 202–203
Cher 12, 44, 105, 110, 154, 257
Chess (label) 7, 30–31, 39–40, 41–42, 43, 52, 67–68, 78, 85–87, 106, 117–118, 125, 134, 138, 143, 154, 159, 161, 173, 182, 202, 221–222, 226, 229–230, 232, 234, 254–255, 283, 293
Chess, Leonard 30–31, 86, 153–154, 230
The Chi-Lites 16, 104
Chi-Sound (label) 61, 63
Chic 203
Chicago, Illinois 15, 18, 22, 30, 31, 39–41, 48, 50–51, 61, 65, 73–74, 81, 85, 89, 91, 97, 103, 104–105, 110, 134, 137, 143, 151, 159, 166, 172–173, 185, 189, 196–197, 202, 221, 223, 229, 230, 232, 279, 284, 293
The Chicagoans 196
"Chicken Shack Boogie" 192–193
Chicory (label) 68
Chief (label) 296
The Chips 19, 215
Chitlin' Circuit 180, 268
The Chords 87
Christie, Lou 163–64, 185
Chubby & the Realities 266
Chubby & the Turnpikes 266
Cincinnati, Ohio 95, 111, 171, 193
Cinderella (label) 268
Cindy (label) 146
C.J. (label) 104
Clapton, Eric 12, 98
The Clara Ward Singers 30
Clarence & Calvin 56
Clark, Dave 35
Clark, Dee 65–66, 105, 274
Clark, Dick 68, 148, 218, 223, 229, 241, 277, 294
Clark, Rudy 105, 133, 179
Clarke, Tony 5, 10, 62, 67–69, 153–154, 222, 230
The Classics 109
Claunch, Quiniton 194–195
Clay, Judy 32, 69–70, 234, 283
Clay, Otis 185
Clayton, Merry 44, 105
Clemson University 6, 245, 256
Clinard, Joe 52–53

Clinton, George 135
Clock (label) 149
"Closely Guarded Secret" 92, 94
The Clovers 10, 34, 39, 46, 54, 64, 65, 70–72, 137, 193
Club (label) 88
The Coasters 10, 19, 39, 71, 72–73, 82, 89, 110, 294
Cobb, J.R. 265
Cobb, Margaret 63
Cobra (label) 104–105
Cocker, Joe 132
"Cocksuckers Ball" 34
The C.O.D.s 5, 73–74
Coed (label) 114
Cogbill, Tommy 55
Cole, Nat King 285
Cole, Natalie 150
Collier, Mitty 230
"Color Him Father" 294–295
Colossus (label) 196–198
Colpix (label) 181, 243
Coltrane, John 138
Columbia (label) 48–49, 66, 81, 118, 161, 163, 169, 182, 200–201, 216, 225, 237–238, 252, 268, 276–278
Columbia, South Carolina 7, 108, 244–246, 257, 262, 265
The Combinations 73
Combo (label) 89, 137
"Come a Little Bit Closer" 203
"Come and Get These Memories" 182–183
"Come Back My Love" 54
"Come Get to This" 11, 125–126
"Come Go with Me" 149
"Come on Over to My Place" 92, 94
"Come See About Me" (Donnie Elbert version) 98–99
"Come See About Me" (Supremes version) 99, 259
"Come Softly to Me" 297
"Come to Me Softly" 154–155
The Commands 75–76, 206, 278
The Commodores 295
Common 141
Como, Perry 101
Compton College 296
Congress (label) 210
Conlee, John 64
Conley, Arthur 190, 294
Constellation (label) 61–62, 66, 103–104, 139, 177, 196
The Contours 106, 184, 189, 272
Convoy (label) 140
Cook, Roger 108
Cooke, Sam 131, 140, 154, 165, 202, 223, 229, 255
"Cool Jerk" 53
"Cooling Out" see "(I'm Just Thinking About) Cooling Out"
Cooper, Alice 135
Copeland Sound Studios 75, 199
Copyright (label) 178
Coral (label) 34, 87
Corbett, Cecil 80

The Cordoroys 135
Cornelius, Don 177
Cornelius Brothers & Sister Rose 6, 53, 76–77
The Corner Boys 115
"Corrine, Corrina" 274–276
The Corsairs 78–79
Cotillion (label) 27, 209, 234
"Could It Be I'm Fallin' in Love" 248, 251
"Could It Be You" 117–118
The Country Sunshine Band 21
"Cowboys to Girls" 145–146, 209, 237
Crackerjack (lable) 266
Crafton, Harry "Fats" 123
Craver, Paul 52–53
Cray, Robert 82
Crazy Elephant 83, 133
Crazy Zacks (club) 6
Cream 31
Creedence Clearwater Revival 253
Creem 127
Creme, Lol 179
The Cremona Trio 47
Crenshaw, Marshall 17
The Crenshaws 171
The Creolettes 153
The Crescents 243
The Crew Cuts 212
Crewe, Bob 101, 134–135, 205–206
Criteria Studios 77
Cropper, Steve 19, 111, 113
Crosby, Bing 37, 72, 101, 243
Crosby, Stills, and Nash 228
"Cross My Heart" 254–255
The Crows 54
Crudup, Arthur "Big Boy" 124
Crusader (label) 252
"Cry Baby" 195
"Cry to Me" 49–50
"Crying in the Chapel" 259
Crystal Caverns (club) 45
Cub (label) 98, 108
Cuca (label) 103
The Cues 35
Cugat, Xavier 72
Culley, Frank 46
Curry, Clifford 9, 17, 79–80
Curtis, Clem 115–116
Curtis, Mann 46
Curtom (label) 62, 74, 144, 172, 294

Dahl, Bill 150, 220, 293
The Daily Telegraph 36
Dakar (label) 81, 172
Dance Hour 210
"Dance with Me" 92–93, 165
"Dancing in the Street" 183
"Dancing to Your Music" 33–34
The Danes 257
Daniels, Jack 81
Danny and Donnie 205
The Darcells 48
Darcey (label) 135
Darin, Bobby 3, 46
Dark Side of the Moon 274

Dart (label) 137
Dash (label) 190
David, Hal 149, 269, 283
Davis, Carl 18, 63, 81, 286, 293
Davis, Clive 295
Davis, Herman 62
Davis, Mac 264
Davis, Mark 82
Davis, Paul 123
Davis, Roquel "Billy" 30, 118, 153, 232, 255, 292
Davis, Sammy, Jr. 115
Davis, Tyrone 15, 81
Day, Bobby 35
Day, Doris 37, 256
"Day in the Life" 48
"Dear Lover" 285–286
Debbie and the Ladds 20
Decca (label) 34, 46, 137–138, 140–141, 161, 189, 275, 292, 295
"Dedicated to the One I Love" 43, 112
Dee Gee (label) 292
Dee-Lite (label) 155
Dee-Su (label) 291–292
Deep Purple (group) 83
"Deep Purple" (song) 283
"Deeper (In Love with You)" 206–207
Deffaa, Chip 46
The Del-Phis/Dell-Fis 182
The Del Rios 31, 69, 266
The Del Royals 90
The Del Vikings/The Dell Vikings 149
Delaney and Bonnie 20
The Delegates 65
The Delfonics 85–85, 124, 145, 203
The Dell-Tones 76
The Dells 85–87, 104, 150, 173, 222, 293
Delphi (label) 128
The Deltones 195
Deluxe (label) 95–96, 98, 124, 138, 182, 205
Deram (label) 108, 189
Derkson, Amie 167
Detroit, Michigan 22, 23, 26, 45, 53, 55–56, 67–68, 92, 105–106, 111, 112, 118, 142, 162–163, 174, 182, 184, 210, 216, 226, 232, 240, 249, 251, 254, 258, 267, 271, 280, 285, 292, 295
Detroit Star (label) 115
The Dew Drop Inn (club) 138, 247
Diamond, Keith 204
Diamond, Neil 155, 229
The Diamonds 291
The Dick Clark Revue 68
Dick Clark's Caravan of Stars 185, 243, 258
Dick Holler and the Holidays 262
Dickie, Robert Lee, aka Bobby Purify 220–221
Diddley, Bo 125, 159, 230, 255
"Didn't I Blow Your Mind This Time" 85
Dillard, Varetta 87–88

Dimension (label) 159–160
Dion 262
Dirty Dancing 50
"Disco Inferno" 273
The Dixie Cups 209, 258
The Dixie Nightingales 232, 233
The Dixieaires 96
Dixon, Floyd 88–89
Dixon, Luther 149, 215
Dixon, Willie 79, 185–186
"Do You Believe in Love at First Sight?" 283–284
"Do You Have to Go Now?" 92, 95
"Do You See My Love (For You Growing)?" 280–281
Dr. Dre 140
Dr. Generosity's 52
Dr. Hook and the Medicine Show 17, 52
Doe, Ernie K. 89, 225, 242, 247
"Doesn't Somebody Want to Be Wanted" 203
Dogget, Bill/Combo 253
The Domingoes 249
The Domingos 240
Domino, Fats 63, 193, 218
The Dominoes 9, 23, 46, 64–65, 92, 96, 102, 117, 171, 188, 226, 240, 281–283, 292
Don and Juan 120, 203
The Don Gardner Trio 124
Donny and the Blue Jets 74
"Don't Drop It" 138–140
"Don't Ever Be Lonely (A Poor Little Fool Like Me)" 76–77
"Don't Fuck Around with Love" 34–35
"Don't Give Up on Us Baby" 115
"Don't Let It Happen to Me" 47
"Don't Make Me Over" 283
"Don't Mess with Bill" 183–184, 226
"Don't Play Around with Love" 34–35
"Don't Play That Song" 152, 165
"Don't' Stop Dan" 64, 282
"Don't You Care" 48, 196
"Don't You Know I Love You" 70
"Don't You Think It's Time" 128–130
"A Donut and a Dream" 11
The Doodletown Pipers 131
Dootone (label) 181, 212–213, 275
The Dootones 296
Dore (label) 287
Dorsey, Jimmy 37, 72, 139, 225
Dorsey, Lee 268
Dorsey, Tommy 139
Dot (label) 16, 136, 167
The Dothan Sextet 220
Dottie (label) 105
Double-L (label) 219, 247
Double R (label) 161
"Double Shot (Of My Baby's Love)" 4, 67, 192, 261–262
Double Shot (label) 128–129, 296–297
Doug Clark and the Hot Nuts 66–67

The Doug Clark Combo 66
The Dovells 276–277
"Down at the Beach Club" 59–61
The Down Home Band 21
"Down in Mexico" 72
Downbeat (label) 275
The Downbeats 100
Dozier, Lamont *see* Holland, Dozier, and Holland
Drew, Patti 90–91
The Drifters 5, 8, 10, 39, 49, 54, 64, 72, 91, 92–97, 101, 102, 139, 165, 188–189, 246, 258, 267, 274, 282, 283, 285, 292
The Drinkard Singers 69, 283
"Drinking Wine, Spo-Dee-O-Dee" 46, 70, 97, 137, 187–188
"Drip Drop" 92–93
"Drive It Home" 70–71
Driver, Harry 27
The Drivers 3, 95–96
The Drops of Joy 175
"Drunk" 174–175
The Du Droppers 96
The Du-Ettes 110
Dual/Duel (label) 163
The Dukays 18, 61
Duke (label) 56, 76, 90, 134, 177, 225–226
"Duke of Earl" 61–62, 172
The Dulcets 181
Dunhill *see* ABC Dunhill
Duplex (label) 136, 175
Dupree, Champion Jack 3, 97–98, 193
The Duprells 131
Durham, North Carolina 175, 188
The Duvalls 91
Dyke and the Blazers 140
Dylan, Bob 16, 18
Dynamic (label) 75–76
Dyson, Ronnie 180

"Earth Angel" 212–213
Earth, Wind, & Fire 30, 104, 121, 123, 222
Earthquake Productions 68
East Orange, New Jersey 69, 283
"Easy Comin' Out (Hard Goin' In)" 4, 31–33, 70
Ebony, Ivory, and Jade 161; *see also* The Jive Five
Eclipse (label) 84
The Ed Sullivan Show 77, 131, 183
Edelstein, Andrew 23
The Eden Singers 287
Edgebrook Studios 270
Edison Lighthouse 115
The Edsels 82
Edward Blanchard and the Gondoliers 247
The Eirios 243
El Doradoes 85
El Grotto Club 280
El Rays 85
Elbert, Donnie 26–27, 98–100, 205
Elf (label) 79–80
The Elgins 100–101, 182

The Elgins (Temptations) 271
Ellington, Duke 37, 45, 139
Ellis, "Big Chief" 187
Ellison, Lorraine 51
Elston, Harry 121–123
Ember (label) 69, 89
The Embers 2, 6, 9, 10, 26, 61, 101–103
Emblem (label) 245
EMI (label) 149, 164
End (label) 108, 226
Endless Beach 278
Enjoy (label) 169
Enterprise (label) 174
"The Entertainer" 5, 10, 67–68, 153–154, 222, 230
Epic (label) 92, 95, 278, 287, 288–289
Epstein, Abe "Abie" 76
Ertegun, Ahmet 45–46, 70, 92–93, 187–188, 275
The Esquires 103–104
The Esquires Combo 244
Estefan, Gloria 168
The Ethics 175–176
Evejim (label) 140
The Evening Stars 195
Everest (label) 273
Everett, Betty 104–105
Everlast (label) 168
"Everlasting Love" (Carl Carlton version) 55–56, 76
"Everlasting Love" (Robert Knight version) 166–168
The Everly Brothers 105, 110, 139
"Every Day I Have to Cry Some" 16–17
"Everybody Plays the Fool" 179, 216
"Everything's Coming Up Love" 231–232
"Everything's Tuesday" 10, 59
Excel (label) 145
Excello (label) 80, 166, 185, 291
The Exciters (aka the X-Citers) 110
The Executives 196

Fabian 170
Fach, Charles 32
Fairlane (label) 56
The Fairlanes 167
Falcon (label) 65, 143
The Falcons 105–106, 112
Fame (label) 56–57
FAME Studios 16, 56, 264
"Fannie Mae" 42–43
"Fannie Mae's Place" 43
The Fantastic Shakers 9, 26, 107–108
The Fantastic Shakers (label) 107–108
The Fantastics 6, 108–109
Fantasy (label) 105, 140, 155, 191, 290
"Far Away Places" 10, 101–103
Farner, Mark 12
Farrell, Wes 131, 203, 237

Fascination (label) 67
The Fascinations 40, 182
"Fat Boy" 10, 159, 254–255
Fat Fish (label) 140
Fat Jacks (club) 6
Federal (label) 7, 23–24, 47, 110, 116–117, 136, 160, 166, 171, 281, 292
Fee Bee (label) 149
"Feel Like Making Love" 186
Fell, Terry 138–139
Felts, Narvel 66
Fernwood (label) 194
"Fever" 162
The Fiestas 109–110
50 Cent 141
The Fillmore 216
"Find Another Love" 262, 264
Findon, Ben 204–205
"Finger Poppin' Time" 24
"Fingertips" 55
Fire (label) 42–43, 124–125
Fire and Rain 246
Fitzgerald, Ella 45, 141
The 5th Dimension 91, 115, 121
The 5 International Gospel Singers of South Carolina 64
The 5 Mellows 149
The Five Chimes 226
The Five Crowns 93, 165
The Five Crystals 150
The Five Du-Tones 67, 110–111, 189, 221, 293
The Five Gospel Harmonaires 172
The Five Pennies 80
The "5" Royales 10, 24, 47, 111–112
The Five Satins 139, 203
The Five Sharps 279
Flack, Roberta 186, 200
Flagstone 52
"Flamingo" 36–37
The Flamingos 86, 213
Flash (label) 216
Fleetwood Mac 98, 236
The Fleetwoods 297
Flick (label) 106, 112
Flip (label) 134
"Flip, Flop, and Fly" 275–276
The Floats 172
Floyd, Eddie 105–106, 112–113
Fm (label) 141
Fogerty, John 12
"Follow the Leader" 172
"Fool, Fool, Fool" 15, 70
"Fools Fall in Love" 92–93
"For the First Time" 128–130
"For Your Precious Love" 50, 143
"For Your Precious Love" 50, 143, 195
Ford, Dee Dee (and Don Gardner) 124–125
Ford, Frankie 113–114
Foreigner 236, 281
The Formations 114–115
Fort Valley College 42
Fort Worth, Texas 35, 63
"Fortune Teller" 248
The Fortunes 108

Forum (label) 120
The Foundations 115–116
The Four After Fives 171
The Four Aims 118
The Four B's 164
The 4 Bluebirds 72
Four Brothers (label) 81
The 4 Buddies 246
The 4 Clovers 70
The Four Dots 263
The Four Eldorados 18
The 4 Falcons 118, 292
The Four Gents 84
The Four Graduates 134
The Four Jacks 3, 116–117, 171
The Four Jewels 159, 259
The 4 Notes 34
Four Roosters and Chick 143; see also The Roosters
4 Sale (label) 4
The Four Seasons 57, 134, 164, 205; see also Valli, Frankie
The Four Stewart Brothers 255
The Four Tops 5, 6, 8, 10, 28, 75, 99, 117–118, 126, 132, 141, 142, 180, 192, 207, 231, 249, 270, 279, 281
Foxx, Inez 215
Frankie Lymon and the Teenagers 139
Franklin, Aretha 23, 30, 50, 91, 121, 139, 150, 154, 200, 236, 250, 267–268
Freak Out (album) 67
"Freddie's Dead" 143
Freeland, David 44
Freeway 246
Freidman, Mel 170
The Friends of Distinction 121–123, 266, 288
The Frolic Club 45
The Funk Brothers 53, 118, 126, 147, 184, 211, 231, 232, 233, 254, 259, 293–294
"Funky Broadway" 55, 106
Fuqua, Harvey 125, 153, 155–156, 232, 280–281
Fury (label) 43, 124, 138–139, 168, 205
The Furys 74
Future (label) 81
The Futures 123, 224
The FutureTones 253
The Fydallions 252

G&G (label) 37
Gaines, Julius 268
The Gainors 195
Galaxie III Studios 84
Galbraith, Rob 80
Gamble (label) 123, 145–146
Gamble, Kenny 33–34, 51, 114–115, 123, 145–146, 190, 191, 207, 209, 211–212, 223–224, 236–237, 278
"The Game of Love" 105
Gamut (label) 190
The Gap Band 123
Gardner, Carl 72–73

Gardner, Don (and Dee Dee Ford) 124–125
Garland, Judy 65, 72
Garnet Mimms and the Enchanters 5, 10, 49, 195–196, 238
Garrett, Bobby 36
Garrett, Snuff 186
The Garrick Lounge 284
Gately, Michael 163–164
Gateway (label) 98
Gatur (label) 269
Gaudio, Bob 204–205
Gayden, Mac 55, 167–168
Gaydisc (label) 155
Gaye, Marvin 4, 10, 11, 82, 121, 125–126, 141, 142, 155, 169, 182, 184, 230–231, 249–250, 254, 258, 281
Gaynor, Gloria 161
The Gaytones 61
"Gee Whiz" 35
Gene Barbour and the Cavaliers 27–29, 144
The Genies 120, 161, 203
George, Barbara 127–128, 268
"Georgia" 237–238
Georgia Music Hall of Fame 57
The Georgia Prophets/The Prophets/The Three Prophets 2, 5, 6, 10, 52, 128–131, 270
Gerry and the Pacemakers 134
Gershwin, George 68, 135, 255
"Get on Up" 103–104
"Get Ready" 232
"Get Up Offa That Thing" 47
"Ghetto Child" 251
Gibb, Robin 234
Gibbs, Georgia 22
Gillespie, Dizzy 45, 139, 181
Gilstrap, Jim(my) 131–132, 203, 224, 238
"Gimme Little Sign" 5, 296
"Girl on a Swing" 134
"Girl Watcher" 207–209
"Girl (Why You Wanna Make Me Blue)" 271
"Girl You're Too Young" 33–34
"The Girl's Alright with Me" 270–271
"Give Me Just a Little More Time" 59, 143
"Give Me You" 281, 283, 292
Glades (label) 33–34, 191
The Gladiolas 291
Gladys Knight and the Pips 124, 146, 168–169, 231
Glasco, Waymon 42
Gleaton, Perrin 244–245
The Gleems 78
Glo-Whiz (label) 267
The Globetrotters 10, 132–133, 180
Godley, Kevin 179
Goffin, Gerry 44, 93
"Going Back to Louisiana" 64
Gold Disc (label) 108
Gold Mind (label) 175–176
Gold Star (label) 136
Goldberg, Marv 64–65

Golden Fleece (label) 176, 273
Golden Globe Award 148
Golden World (label) 53, 55, 181, 240
The Goldentones 65
Goldmine 23
Goldwax (label) 194–195
Gone (label) 108, 146
"Good Guys Only Win in the Movies" 189–190
"Good Lovin'" (The Clovers) 70
"Good Lovin'" (The Rascals) 94, 179
"Good Morning Starshine" 234
"Good Rocking Tonight" 10, 137–138
Good Times 132
Gooding, Cuba 179–180
Goodman, Benny 219
"Goodnite, Sweetheart, Goodnite" 246
Gordon, Rosco(e) 133–134
Gordy (label) 147, 182–183, 270–271
Gordy, Berry 53, 55, 82, 98, 100, 118, 125, 142, 147, 169, 182, 183, 205, 210, 226, 231–232, 254, 258, 271, 280, 285, 292
Gordy, George 125, 184
Gore, Jackie 101–103
Gospel (label) 234
The Gospel Cavaliers 49
The Gospel Harmonettes 238
The Gospel Jazz Singers 77
The Gospel Songbirds 185
The Gospel Starlighters 47
The Gospel Wonders 234
The Gospelaires 195, 273, 283
Gotham (label) 36, 117, 124
"Gotta Have Your Love" 236–237
"Gotta Hold on to This Feeling" 280–281
Gowen (label) 145
Grady (label) 118
Graham, Bill 216
Grammy Awards/Nominations 31, 44, 46, 48, 50, 54, 56, 59, 63, 82, 85, 119, 121, 126, 131, 141, 147, 148, 152, 153, 154, 169, 180, 186, 204, 220, 223, 224, 238, 239, 259, 267, 268, 272, 280, 281, 283, 284, 285, 286, 287, 294
Grand Funk 11–12
Grand Impact 52
The Grand Ole Opry 141
The Grass Roots 91
"Grazing in the Grass" 121–122
"The Great Pretender" 213
Green, Al 19, 295
"Green Eyes" 10, 23, 224–225
Greenaway, Tony 94
Greenberg, Florence 149
Greenberg, Stan 44
Greenfield, Howie 133
Greensboro, North Carolina 52, 75, 199
Greenwich, Ellie 221
Greenwood, Lil 117

Greenwood, South Carolina 244–245, 261
Griffey, Dick 176–177
Groove (label) 88, 97
"Groovy Situation" 61–62
Gross (label) 66
GSF (label) 230
GTO (label) 204
Guarino, Lou 243
Guercio, Jim 48
Guitar Slim 137
Gulf 257
Gwenn (label) 43
"Gypsy Woman" 143

Hall, Daryl/Hall and Oates 164, 203, 266
Hall, Duke 52
Hall, Johanna 278
Hall, John 278
Hall, Rick 16, 56, 154, 264
Hall, Ted 27, 57
Hall, Willie "Drive 'Em Down" 97
Hall and Oates 164, 203, 266
Halo (label) 273
The Hambone Kids 65
Hamilton, Joe, Frank, and Reynolds 119
Hammond, Albert 179
Hammond, John 275
Hammond, Roy C. 119–120; *see also* Little Frankie
Hampton, Lionel 36, 181, 284
"Hang on Sloopy" 49, 203
Hank Ballard and the Midnighters 4, 10, 23–24, 111, 136, 153, 292
The Happenings 134–135
"Hard to Handle" 91
Harlem (label) 187
Harlem, New York 29, 36, 69, 87, 96, 152, 164, 179
The Harlem Globetrotters 132
"The Harlem Shuffle" 35–36
The Harlem Shuffle (dance) 213
Harmonica Fats 135–136
The Harmonizing Four 195
Harold Melvin and the Blue Notes 123, 176, 190–191, 211–212, 217
Harris, Major 85
Harris, Peppermint 65, 136–137
Harris, Thurston 35, 171
Harris, Wynonie 10, 137–138
Harrison, George 36, 274
Harrison, Wilbert 43, 124, 138–139
Harry Deal and the Galaxies 84
Hart, Tommy 237
Harthon (label) 273
Harvey (label) 280
"Have Mercy Baby" 171, 188, 281–282
"Have You Seen Her" 16
Hawkins, Dale 230
Hawkins, Erskine 36
Hayes, Isaac 19
Haynes, Greg 1
Haywood, Leon 55, 140–141
Hazel McCollum and the El Dorados 24

"He Will Break Your Heart" 51
Head, Roy 76
Heart 235
"Heartbreak (It's Hurtin' Me)" 162
The Heartstrings 16
"Heat Wave" 183
"Heaven Must Have Sent You" 100
Heavy Duty (label) 115
Heavy Juice 136
Hebb, Bobby 141, 156
"Hello Stranger" 10, 54, 86, 173, 177
Helm, Janet 129–130
"Help Me Rhonda" 43
Henderson, "Bugs" 20
Henderson, Douglas 29, 279
Hendrix, Jimi 19, 131, 154, 196
Henry, Clarence "Frogman" 160
Herald (label) 187, 209, 291
"Here Come the Girls" 90
"Here Comes That Rainy Day Feeling Again" 108
Heritage (label) 82, 264
Herman's Hermits 20
"Hey! Baby" 10, 23, 63–64, 84, 262
"Hey Baby (They're Playing Our Song)" 48, 196
"Hey Bartender" 88–89
"Hey Girl, Don't Bother Me" 263–266
"Hey! I Know You" 5, 198–200
"Hey It's Love" 75–76
"Hey Laudie Miss Claudie" 38
"Hey Little Girl" (Catalinas) 57
"Hey Little Girl" (Dee Clark) 65
"Hey There Lonely Girl" 164
"Hey Western Union Man" 50–51
The Hi-Fis 141
The Hideaways 140
High Keys (label) 108
Highway Robbery 295
Hit (label) 27
Hit Attractions 27, 57
"Hitch Hike" 36, 125, 183
Hobson, Donald 27–28
"Hold Back the Night" 10, 272–273
"Hold On" 221–222
"Hold on to My Love" 233
Holiday, Billie 45, 139, 243, 253, 255
Holland, Brian 184, 210; *see also* Holland, Dozier, and Holland
Holland, Dozier, and Holland 59, 100, 106, 118–119, 126, 147, 154, 183, 184, 210–211, 258–259
Holland, Eddie 142–143, 147, 271–272; *see also* Holland, Dozier, and Holland
The Hollies 17, 108, 248
Holloway, Brenda 258
Hollywood (label) 120
Hollywood, California 19, 68, 128, 231
Hollywood a-Go-Go 19
The Hollywood Bowl 223
The Hollywood Flames 35
The Hollywood Walk of Fame 48, 119, 154, 224, 259

312   Index

Holman, Eddie 164
Holvay, Jim 48, 196–197
The Holy Wonders 223
Holzman, Marvin 266
Home of the Blues (label) 112
Honey Cone 59, 131, 177
"Honey Hush" 274–275
"Honey Love" 92–93, 188
Honeycutt, Robert 80
Hooker, John Lee 137, 193
Hopkins, "Lightnin'" 136–137
Hopkins, Telma 150, 211
The Hornets 259
Hot Ice 115
Hot Line (label) 269
"Hot Nuts" 66
Hot Wax (label) 115
House of Pain 36
Houston, Cissy 69, 93, 145, 283
Houston, Keith 25–26
Houston, Texas 33, 76, 140, 178, 192–194, 225
Houston, Whitney 132, 283
"How Sweet It Is (To Be Loved by You)" 125–126, 230, 280
The Howard Theatre (Washington, D.C.) 18, 38, 87, 104, 159, 279
Hub (label) 224
The Hudsonaires 246
HUE-CSP (Label) 278
Huey Lewis and the News 134
Huey "Piano" Smith and the Clowns 114, 247, 270
Huff, Leon 33–34, 51, 114–115, 123, 145–146, 191, 207, 209–210, 212, 223–224, 236–237, 278
The Humdingers 241
"A Hundred Pounds of Clay" 186
Hunter, Ivory Joe 35, 249
Huntom (label) 168
Hurtt, Phil 200
"Hushabye" 164
"The Hustle" 29, 169
Hyland, Brian 258, 264

"I Ain't Drunk I'm Just Drinkin'" 174–175
"I Can't Help Myself" (Donnie Elbert version) 98–99
"I Can't Help Myself" (Four Tops version) 98, 117–119, 126, 143
"I Can't Stop Dancing" 10, 33
"I Can't Stop Lovin' You" 178
"I Could Dance all Night" 33–34
"I Count the Tears" 92–93
"I Cried a Tear" 23
"I Dig Everything About You" 6, 196–197
"I Dig You Baby" 50–51
"I Dig Your Act" 5, 206
"I Do Love You" 10, 254–255
"I Don't Love You Anymore" 211–212
"I Don't Want to Cry" 149–150
"I Forgot to Be Your Lover" 31
"I Found Out (What You Do When You Go 'Round There)" 96–97

"I Get the Sweetest Feeling" 169, 292–293
"I Got Loaded" 136–137
"I Got Rhythm" 134–135
"I Got Sand in My Shoes" 10
"I Got the Fever" 10, 128–130, 270
"I Guess I'll Always Love You" 146–147
"I Hate Hate" 21
"I Hear a Rhapsody" 36–37
"I Hear a Symphony" 147, 259
"I Heard It Through the Grapevine" 126, 130–131, 169, 230
"I Just Can't Get You Out of My Mind" 10, 117–119
"I Keep Forgettin'" 236
"(I Know) I'm Losing You" 232
"I Know It's Hard but It's Fair" 111–112
"I Know (You Don't Love Me No More)" 127–128, 268
"I Like Dreamin'" 131
"I Love Beach Music" 9, 10, 26, 59, 101–103
"I Love You 1,000 Times" 10, 52, 213–215
"I Need a Love" 27–29
"I Need You" 27–28
"I Need Your Love" 18
"I Need Your Loving" 124–125
"I Remember" 291
"I Remember the Feeling" 173–174
"I Second that Emotion" 226–227
"I Should Have Known Better" 63
"I Slipped a Little" 194–195
"I Still Love You" 84
"I Think I Really Love You" 128–130
"I Told You So" 155–156
"I Used to Cry Mercy, Mercy" 171
"I Wanna Be (Your Everything) 180–182
"I Want a Love I Can See" 270–271
"I Want to Marry You" 119–120
"I Want You So Bad" 47
"I Want'a Do Something Freaky to You" 140
"I Wasn't Thinkin', I Was Drinkin'" 64, 137
"I Who Have Nothing" 91, 165
"I Wish It Would Rain" 232
The Ice Man Cometh (album) 51
Ice on Ice (album) 51
Ichiban (label) 57, 178
"I'd Like to Teach the World to Sing" 108
The Idle Hour Arcade 52
Idol, Billy 31
"Idol with the Golden Head" 73
"If I Could Be Loved by You" 70–71
"If I Didn't Have a Dime" 74
"If Loving You Is Wrong I Don't Want to Be Right" 152
"If We Had to Do It All Over" 5, 256–257
"If You Can Want" 226–227

"(If You Cry) True Love, True Love" 92–93
"If You Don't Want My Love" 163–164
Iglesias, Julio 148
Ike and Tina Turner 30, 42, 110
The Ikettes 30
"I'll Always Love My Mama" 145–146
"I'll Always Love You" 248–249
"I'll Be Around" 248, 251
"I'll Be Doggone" 125–126
"I'll Go Where the Music Takes Me" 3, 154–155
"I'll Take You Home" 92, 94
"I'll Take You Where the Music's Playing" 92, 94
"I'll Turn to Stone" 117–119
"I'm a Happy Man" 161
"I'm Doin' Fine Now" 202–203, 224
"I'm Going—But I'll Be Back" 43
"I'm Gonna Miss You" 18
"(I'm Just Thinking About) Cooling Out" 50–51
"I'm Never Gonna Be Alone Anymore" 76–77
"I'm the Father of Annie's Baby" 24
"I'm Your Puppet" 55, 220–221
Impact (label) 240–241, 254
The Impacts 52
The Impalas 159
Imperial (label) 76, 114, 140, 206, 242, 248
The Impressions 19, 27–28, 40, 50–51, 63, 103, 143–144, 149, 172, 181, 192, 195, 278, 294
Impulse (label) 210
"In a Moment" 144–145
"In Paradise" 241–242
In-Sound (label) 136
"In the Bad Bad Old Days" 115
The Ink Spots 134, 259
The Insiders 216
Instant Action (label) 190
The Intrigues 144–145
The Intruders 5, 8, 145–146, 209, 237, 279
"Inventory on Heartaches" 74–75
Invictus (label) 59, 210–211
The Invitations 215
"Is You Is or Is You Ain't My Baby" 43
The Isley Brothers 49, 82, 146–147, 233
"It Ain't No Big Thing" 10, 30, 52, 68, 154, 221–222, 230, 255
"It Ain't the Meat" 259–260
"It Could Happen to You" 45
"It Happened in Brooklyn" 114
"It Never Rains in Southern California" 179
"It Will Stand" 10, 241–242
It Will Stand Magazine 9, 11, 193, 257
"It Won't Be This Way Always" 166

"It's a Beautiful Morning" 203
"It's a Man's Man's Man's World" 47
"It's a Shame" 247–250
"It's All Right" 143
"It's All Right (You're Just in Love)" 263–265
"It's Better to Have Loved a Little" 263–264
"It's Easier to Cry" 151
"It's Got to Be Mellow" 140
"It's in His Kiss" *see* "The Shoop Shoop Song"
"It's Not What You Got (It's How You Use It)" 176–177
"It's Over" 237–238
"It's Raining Men" 148
"It's the Same Old Song" 117–118
"It's Your Thing" 147
"I've Been Hurt" (Bill Deal and the Rhondels version) 8, 82–83
"I've Been Hurt" (The Tams version) 10, 263–265
"I've Got Sand in My Shoes" 92, 94, 10
"I've Got Something on My Mind" 256–257
"I've Never Found a Girl (To Love Me Like You Do)" 106, 112–113
"I've Passed this Way Before" 233

J & S (label) 234
Jabara, Paul 148
The Jackaels 151
Jackie Brenston and His Delta Cats 41–42
Jackson, Al 113, 172–173
Jackson, Chuck 17, 149–150, 274
Jackson, Deon 10, 150–151
Jackson, J.J. 151
Jackson, Michael 74, 132
Jackson, Millie 151–152
Jackson, Mississippi 175, 239
Jackson, Willis "Gator Tail" 46
The Jackson 5 74, 203, 229, 267
Jalynne (label) 98
James, Etta 15, 56, 68–69, 137, 153, 173, 185, 202, 230, 264, 292
James and Bobby Purify 55, 111, 220–221
James Brown and the Famous Flames 47
"Jamie" 142
Jamie (label) 177–178
Jamstone (label) 178
Jan and Dean 5
Jancik, Wayne 150
Janice (Barnett) 155–156
Janus (label) 145, 288
The Jarmels 49
Jay and Dee 274
Jay and the Americans 203
Jay and the Techniques 156–157, 197, 236, 270
Jay-Dee (label) 34
The Jaynetts 78, 236
Jefferies, Herb 37
Jefferson, Blind Lemon 46, 136

"The Jerk" 53
Jessie, Dewayne 82
Jessie and Jessica 257
Jet Stream (label) 178
Jewel (label) 137
Jewell and the Rubies 4, 5, 158–159
The Jewels 5, 110, 159–160, 255
"Jim Dandy" 23
Jimmy James and the Vagabonds 154–155
"Jimmy Mack" 141, 182–183
Jimmy Ricks and the Ravens 10, 22–23, 34, 139, 224–225
Jive (label) 204
The Jive Five/The Jyve Five 161
Joe Liggins and the Honeydrippers 174–175
John, Little Willie 80, 162–163
John, Robert 163–164
John Fred and the Playboy Band 20, 36, 137
Johnny and the Mark V 257
Johnny Barfield and the Men from S.O.U.L 239
Johnny Dollars (club) 38–39
The Johnny Mann Singers 186
Johnson, General Norman 9, 26, 56, 59–61, 241–242, 270
Johnson, Paul "Guitar Red" 74
Johnson, Pete 275
The Jokers Three (club) 75
Jokers Three (label) 52, 74
Jones, Booker T. 69, 113, 194; *see also* Booker T. & the M.G.s
Jones, Gloria 231
Jones, Joe 268
Jones, John Paul 179
Jones, Quincey 132
Jones, Tom 274
Jordan, Archie 80
Josie (label) 67, 140, 190
Jot (label) 98
Jr. Walker & the All Stars 280–281
Ju-Par (label) 104
The Jubalaires 96
Jubilee (label) 66–67, 84, 125, 128, 135, 224–225, 287, 282
Judd (label) 16
The Julian Dash Septet 124
The Julliard School of Music 281
jump blues 36, 37, 98, 138
The Jumping Jacks 280
Junior (label) 124
The Junior Harmonizers 291
"Just a Gigolo/I Ain't Got Nobody" 219–220
"Just Don't Want to Be Lonely" 179–180, 216
"Just Like Romeo and Juliet" 240
"Just One Look" 10, 273–274, 283
"Just Out of Reach (Of My Two Empty arms)" 49
The Jyve Five/The Jive Five 161

Kable (label) 182
Kaiser (label) 124
"Kansas City" 43, 138–140

Kansas City, Missouri 274–275
Kapp (label) 210
Kappa Alpha Order 6
Karat (label) 257
Karen (label) 53, 150, 173
Karras, Harry 192
The Kays 53
Kayvette (label) 201
"Keep on Truckin'" 121
"Keep the Ball Rollin'" 156–157
Keith 156
Kellmac (label) 73–74
The Kelly Brothers 166
Kendricks, Eddie 121, 131, 176, 258, 271
Kenner, Chris 53
Kenny G 291
Kent (label) 153
"Kidnapper" 4, 5, 158–159
"Killer Queen" 107
"Kind of a Drag" 48, 196
King (label) 7, 24, 36–37, 47, 64, 96, 97, 111, 112, 137–138, 162, 166, 171, 181, 187, 193, 206, 224, 259, 281, 292
King, Albert 31
King, B.B. 41, 133, 137
King, Ben E. 49, 91, 93, 95, 152, 164–165, 238
King, Carole 44, 93, 149
King, Don 219
King, Freddie 81
The King Pins 166
King Soul (label) 267
The Kingbees 57
The Kings of Rhythm 41
The Kingsmen 111
Kingstree, South Carolina 43, 211
Kirshner (label) 132–133
Kirshner, Don 132–133
"Kiss and Say Goodbye" 182
"Kissin' in the Back Row of the Movies" 92, 94
Kitt, Eartha 219
Knight, Frederick 173
Knight, Robert 55, 166–167
"Knock on Wood" 106, 113
Knox, Ken 60–61
Knoxville, Tennessee 80, 187
The Kool Gents 65
KRC (label) 218
Krefetz, Lou 70
Kris (label) 136
Krupa, Gene 36
The Kruze Band 53

"L-O-V-E" 295
"La-La Means I Love You" 84–85
La Louisianne (label) 4, 158–159
Labelle 131
Labelle, Patti 174
Ladd (label) 20
The Ladies of Soul 44
"Lady Love" 223–224
"Lady Marmalade" 131
"Lady Soul" 2
Laine, Frankie 46, 185
Lamarr (label) 104

The Lamplighters 117, 171–172
Lance, Herb 46
Lance, Major 18, 75, 91, 143, 172–173, 258
"Land of 1,000 Dances" 53
Lander College 261
Lando (label) 55
"Landslide" 68
Lange, "Mutt" 204
Larkins, Milton Orchestra 37
The Larks 53
The Larks (Charlotte, NC) 267
Las Vegas, Nevada 77, 107, 131, 220, 252, 274
"Last Dance" 148
"(Last Night) I Didn't Get to Sleep at All" 115
"The Last of the Good Rocking Men" 3, 116–117, 171
Lastie, Melvin 268
Lathowers, Maury 91
The Latin Casino 294
The Latineers 276
"Laugh It Off" 263–265
Lauretta's Hi-Hat (club) 33
Laurie (label) 84, 134, 178
"Lavender Blue" 133
Lavette (label) 69
Lavette Bettye (Betty) 125, 150
"Lawdy, Miss Clawdy" 218
Lawn (label) 192
Le Cam (label) 63
Led Zeppelin 179
Lee, Dickey 22
Lee, Jackie 36
Lee, Johnny 89
Lee, Peggy 162
The Leeds 149
Leeper, "Chattie" Hattie 269
Leiber, Jerry 23, 46, 71, 72, 73, 88, 93–94, 98, 139, 165, 216
Lemon, Meadowlark 132–133
Lennon, John 17, 63, 192
"Let It Be Me" 105
"Let Love Come Between Us" 220–221
"Let Me Down Easy" 76–77
"Let Me Make Love to You" 61, 63
"Let the Heartaches Begin" 116
"Let's Get It On" 4
"Let's Go, Let's Go, Let's Go" 24
"Let's Work Together" 139
Lewis, Barbara 10, 29, 53–54, 86, 150, 169, 173, 177
Lewis, Bobby 43, 161
Lewis, Jerry Lee 42, 193
Lewis, Russell 62
Lewisohn, Mark 17
Libert, David 135
Liberty (label) 66, 186
Liggins, Jimmy 41, 65, 137, 174–175
Linda Hayes and the Platters 24
Lindsay, Mark 94
"The Lion Sleeps Tonight" 134, 164
"Lipstick Powder and Paint" 274, 276
"Lipstick Traces" 206, 241, 247–248

Little Anthony and the Imperials 207, 236
"A Little Bit of Soap" 49
"Little Bitty Pretty One" 35, 171, 189
"Little Darlin'" 291
The Little Delta Big Four 111
Little Frankie 119–120; see also Hammond, Roy C
Little Freddy & the Rockets 296
The Little Gentlemen 63
Little Milton 30, 185
"Little Miss Flirt" 207–209
"A Little Piece of Leather" 98
Little Richard 47, 65, 193
Little Rock, Arkansas 158, 290
Little Star (label) 206
Little Vincent 49
Littlefield, Little Willie 139
The Livers 196
"Lonely Drifter" 65, 75, 206, 276
"Lonely Teardrops" 153, 292–294
"Long Cool Woman in a Black Dress" 108
Los Angeles, California 36, 37, 38, 72, 74, 88–89, 136, 137, 140, 153, 155, 171, 175, 176–177, 192, 212–213, 216, 219, 223, 256, 287
The Lost Generation 74
Louisiana Hayride 63
Louisiana Music Hall of Fame 20, 248
Love Affair (group) 168
The Love Committee 175–176
"Love Grows Where My Rosemary Goes" 115
"The Love I Lost" 190–191
"Love Is Here and Now You're Gone" (Donnie Elbert version) 98–99
"Love Is Here and Now You're Gone" (The Supremes version) 99
"Love Is Like a Baseball Game" 145–146
"Love Is Like an Itching in My Heart" 53
"Love Machine" 207–209
"Love Makes a Woman" 15
"Love Makes the World Go 'Round" 10, 150
"Love Me Do" 63
"Love or Let Me Be Lonely" 121–122
"Love Potion #9" 71
"Love Power" 234
"Love Really Hurts Without You" 204–205
"The Love That You're Looking For" 276–277
"A Love That's Real" 145–146
"Love Train" 207, 209, 237
The Love Unlimited Orchestra 36
"Lover Please" 189
"Lover's Holiday" 238–239
"A Lover's Question" 188
The Lovettes 181
"Lovey Dovey" 70

Lowe, Bernie 276
Lowery, Bill 21, 27, 209, 262, 264–265
LTD 141
Lu Pine/Lupine (label) 100, 112–113, 258
Lucas, Carrie 176–177, 226
"Lucky Lips" 46
Ludix (label) 124
Lynn, Barbara 177–178, 239
Lynn, Vera 64
The Lyrics 194

M-Pac (label) 185
"Ma Belle Amie" 196
Macaulay, Tony 94, 115–116
Mack, Ronnie 183
Macon, Georgia 21, 47
The Mad Lads 74
Madison Square Garden 83, 119
Maggie Hathaway and the Robins 72
The Magic Lanterns 178–179
The Magnificent Seven 235
Mah's (label) 182
"The Main Event" 147
The Main Ingredient 179–180
Mainline (label) 75
Maisai (label) 136
"Make It Easy on Yourself" 51, 283
"Make Me Belong to You" 173–174
"Make Me Your Baby" 173–174
Makeway for Youth 210
Mala (label) 278–279
"Mama (He Treats Your Daughter Mean)" 45–46
"Mama Didn't Lie" 39–40
The Mamas and the Papas 112
Mama's Home Cookin' 246
The Manhattan Transfer 280
The Manhattans 144, 180–182
Mann, Barry 94
Mann, Johnny/The Johnny Mann Singers 186
Marc (label) 35–36
The Marcels 255
Marchan, Bobby 14
Marinelli, Nick 240–241
Mark-X (label) 146
Markham, Pigmeat 185
The Marksmen 237
The Marquees 125
Mars Hill College 256
Marsel (label) 63
Marsh, Dave 112, 205, 254
Marshall, Sherman 123, 203, 224
Martha (Reeves) and the Vandellas 28, 75, 100, 126, 157, 182–183, 184, 279
Martin, Bobby 144
Martin, Lenny 243
The Marvelettes 125, 183–185, 226, 237, 258, 279, 294
Marvin Johnston Orchestra 37
The Mascots 206
Masekela, Hugh 121
The Matadors 226
Matassa, Cosimo 178

Mathis, Johnny 3, 277
Maurice Williams and the Zodiacs 8, 10, 156, 291–292
Maxx (label) 168
"May I" (Zodiacs version) 8, 10, 291–292
"May I" (Bill Deal and the Rhondels version) 8, 82
The Maybees 196
"Maybelline" 30
Mayfield, Curtis 40, 50, 62, 63, 82, 103, 143–144, 154, 172, 294
Mayfield (label) 103
MCA (label) 191
McCall, Cash 185–186, 223
McCallister, Smokey 159–160
McCann, Les 185, 186
McCartney, Paul 17, 192
McClinton, Delbert 63
McClure, Bobby 30
McCoo, Marilynn 121
McCoy, Van 29, 145, 169, 174, 232, 293
The McCoys 18, 49, 203
McDaniels, Gene 186
McDonald, Michael 236
McElrath, John 244, 261–262
McGhee, Brownie 97, 187
McGhee, Stick 46, 65, 70, 97, 137, 187
McLaughlin, Ollie 53, 150, 173–174
McNeely, Big Jay 140
McPhatter, Clyde 92–95, 165, 188–189, 226, 281–282, 292
Meaux, Huey 178, 239
Medley, Phil 74
Medress, Hank 164
Mega (label) 25–26
Mel and Tim 62, 189–190
Mel-o-dy (label) 183
Mel Walker and the Bluenotes 72
Meletio, Larry 227–229
Mellencamp, John Cougar 82
The Mellotones 54
The Melodeers 224
Memphis, Tennessee 19, 31, 41, 57, 112–113, 133, 173, 194, 216, 232
Men-Del (label) 239
The Men of Distinction 29, 53
Mendel, Ed, "Dr. Jive" 238–239
Mercury (label) 20, 22, 31–32, 50–51, 55, 61–62, 70, 120, 142, 149, 172, 188–189, 197, 213, 214, 225, 230, 268, 285
"Mercy, Mercy, Mercy" 48
"Mercy Mr. Percy" 87
Mesner, Eddie 192
Mesner, Leo 192
Meteor (label) 31
Metromedia (label) 294
The Metrotones 214
Meyer, Bob 57
MFSB 191
MGM (label) 21–22, 50, 101, 108, 114–115, 152, 163, 188, 198, 210, 223, 277
Miami, Florida 34, 77, 138, 162
"Michael, the Lover" 5, 73–74

Mickey and Sylvia 141
Mid-South (label) 194
"Midnight Confessions" 91
"Midnight Train to Georgia" 169
The Midnights 24
"Mighty Love" 248, 251
Milburn, Amos 46, 137, 192–193
Milem, Percy 194–195
Millender, Lucky 45, 137–138
Miller, Bobby 86
Miller, Steve 237
"A Million to One" 74
The Mills Brothers 11
Milsap, Ronnie 81, 149
Milwaukee, Wisconsin 103–104, 121
The Mindbenders 29
Miner, Raynard 31
Minit (label) 59, 89–90, 241–242, 247–248
Miracle (label) 233
Miranda, Bob 134–135
Miss Butch (label) 239
Mississippi (the University of) 243
Mr. Chand (label) 62
"Mixed Up, Shook Up, Girl" 5, 209–210, 237
MMS (label) 294–295
The MOB 6, 48, 196–198, 236
Modern (label) 88, 137, 153, 192
The Modifiers 259
Moira (label) 150
Moise, Warren 26
Mojo (label) 115
Moman, Chips 194
Money (label) 137
"Money (That's What I Want)" 18, 142, 192
"Money Honey" 92–93, 188
The Monkees 111
The Monkey (dance) 104
"Monkey Hips and Rice" 111
"The Monkey Time" 18, 36, 143, 172
The Monzas 5, 184, 198–200
The Moods 273
"Moody Woman" 50–51
"Moon River" 51
Moon Shot (label) 85
The Moonglows 86, 125, 153, 203
Moore, "Deacon" John 90, 247–248
Moore, Jackie 200–201
Moore, Johnny 89, 93–95, 188
Moore, Melba 157, 221, 237
"More Love" 226–227
"More Today Than Yesterday" 252–253
Morgan, Jaye P. 111
"Morning, Noon, and Night" 274–276
Morris, Joe 46
Morris Dollison and the Turnkeys 185
Morrison, Van 12, 49, 229
"Mother-in-Law" 89–90, 242, 247–248
Motown (label) 5, 8, 9, 29, 51, 53–54, 59, 78, 83, 98, 100–101, 112, 116, 117–119, 124, 125–126, 129–130, 142, 147, 149, 152, 155–156, 164, 167, 169, 181, 182–183, 184, 193, 204, 205, 210–211, 214, 216, 222, 227, 230–231, 232, 233, 237, 241, 248–250, 254, 258–259, 267, 271, 280–281, 285–286, 289, 290, 292–293
The Motowns 216
The Mount Lebanon Singers 92, 188
Mouse and the Traps 20
M.S. Records (label) 68
"Ms. Grace" 6, 9, 84, 276–277
MTV 151
Mungo Jerry 145
Murray, Juggy, aka Henry Jones 127, 215, 266
Murray the K 181, 207
Muscle Shoals 16, 56, 154, 202, 220, 236, 238, 244, 264, 266
Musicland (label) 169–170
Musicor (label) 29, 145, 161, 213–215
"My Baby" 270
"My Baby Just Cares for Me" 3
"My Balloon's Going Up" 33–34
"My Girl" 10, 226, 232, 271
"My Guy" 10, 126, 226, 271, 285–287
"My Man, a Sweet Man" 151–152
"My Mistake (Was to Love You)" 230–231
"My Name Ain't Annie" 24
"My Prayer" 213
"My True Story" 161
"My Whole World Ended" 231–232
Myrtle Beach, South Carolina 5, 7, 17, 39, 52, 80, 107, 236, 257
"Myrtle Beach Days" 26, 59, 107–108
The Myrtle Beach Pavilion 7, 52, 57, 84
The Mystics 109, 164
Mystique 74

Nantucket (band) 52
Nash, Johnny 145
Nashboro (label) 166, 185
Nashville, Tennessee 16, 21, 55, 57, 64, 80, 91, 141, 239, 253
Nat (label) 61
Nathan, Syd 112, 162
National (label) 34, 224–225, 275
"A Natural Man" 141, 223
"Needle in a Haystack" 287
Nelson, Earl 35
Neptune (label) 115, 139, 206–207, 247
"Never Can Say Goodbye" 161
"Never Give You Up" 50–51
New Orleans, Louisiana 20, 89–90, 97, 98, 113–114, 126–127, 138, 140, 158, 178, 187, 218, 219, 236, 242, 247–248, 268–269, 275, 292
The New Seekers 108

316   Index

New York City 18, 19, 20, 32, 36, 38, 43, 45, 54, 67, 89, 70, 72, 78, 83, 87, 94, 96, 98, 104, 105, 111, 119, 121, 124, 127, 137, 139, 141, 143, 144, 146, 148, 149, 151, 159, 161, 163, 168, 173–174, 181, 188, 195, 200, 203, 205, 207–209, 210, 215–216, 219, 224, 230, 234, 243, 260, 270, 273–274, 275, 279, 291, 293
New York City (group) 202–203, 224
The Newbeats 110, 164
Newport Jazz Festival 69
The Nic Nacs 72
Nickel (label) 110
"Night and Day" 37
"Night Owl" 20
The Nighthawks 194
"A Nightingale Sang in Berkeley Square" 3
"Nip Sip" 10, 70–71, 137
"Nite Owl" 20, 62
"No More Tears (Enough Is Enough)" 148
"No Time for You" 75–76, 206
"Nobody" 27
"Nobody but You" 65
"Nobody Loves Me Like You" 128–130
Nocturn (label) 43
Noel (band) 20
Nola (label) 268–269
Nolan, Kenny 131
The Nomads 256–257
Nomar (label) 43–44
Norfolk, Virginia 45, 220, 241
Norman (label) 170
Normar (label) 136
North American (label) 247
North Carolina Music Hall of Fame 61, 108, 112, 292
North State (label) 208–209
Northern Jubilee Gospel Singers 143
Northern Soul 66, 68, 75, 94, 98, 100, 101, 152, 168, 169, 172, 174, 192, 196, 200, 206, 210, 233, 256, 265, 270, 274, 278
"Nothing Can Stop Me" 61–52
"Nowhere to Run" 183
The Nu-Tones 24
"Number One Man" 64

The Oak Ridge Boys 110
The Oakaleers 259
Ocean, Billy 204–205
"Ocean Boulevard" 26
Ocean Drive Beach (OD), South Carolina 184, 198, 257
The Ocean Drive Pavilion 7, 11
Ocean Front (label) 81
"Oh How Happy" 240–241
"Oh No Not My Baby" 43–44
"Oh What a Nite"/"Oh, What a Night!" (reissue) 86
O'Henry, Lenny (Danny Cannon) 5, 10, 98, 205–206

The Ohio Express 94
The O'Jays 5, 8, 65, 75, 76, 123, 176, 200, 204, 206–207, 209, 237, 276
The O'Kaysions 53, 75, 207–209
Okeh (label) 18, 65, 97, 125, 172, 275
"Old People" 34
Old Town (label) 109–110
Oldham, Spooner 220–221
Oliver 234
"On Broadway" 92–93
"On the Beach" 9, 59–60, 108
"One Bourbon, One Scotch, One Beer" 46
One-Derful (label) 105, 110
One Hundred Proof Aged in Soul 59, 106
"One Kiss Led to Another" 72
"One Love" 54
"One Mint Julep" 10, 46, 70–71, 137, 193
"One of a Kind (Love Affair)" 248, 251
"One Scotch, One Burbon, One Beer" 192–193
1-2-3 (label) 263, 265
"1-2-3 Kind of Love" 288–289
"One Way Love" 92, 94
"The One Who Really Loves You" 286
"Only Love Can Break a Heart" 74
"Only the Strong Survive" 50–51, 209, 237
"Only You" 213
"The Oogum Boogum Song" 296
"Ookey Ook" 212–213
"Ooo Baby Baby" 226–227
"Open the Door to Your Heart" 26–27, 98–99, 205
"Opportunity" 5, 110, 159–160, 255
Original Sound (label) 213, 243
The Originals 106, 211, 232, 233
The Orioles 23, 45, 247, 259, 279
Orleans 278
The Orlons 276
Orpheus 228
The Orphonics 84
Osborne, Ozzy 179
Osiris (label) 172–173
Otis, Johnny 23, 72, 109, 117, 153, 162, 171, 292
Otis Day and the Nights 67, 81–82
Otis Williams and the Siberians 271–272
The Ovations 194
"Over and Over" 35
"Over the Rainbow" 26, 64–65
Ovide (label) 34

P&L (label) 98
Pacific (label) 199
The Packers 140
The Pad (club) 7, 60, 257
Paige, Hal 71
The Palms Café (club) 152
"Papa's Got a Brand New Bag" 47
The Paradise Theater 23
The Paramounts 167

Parissi, Rob 288–290
Parker, Charlie 36, 138, 181
Parker, Junior 133, 137, 225
Parker, Ray, Jr. 211
Parkway/Cameo Parkway (label) 29, 84, 98, 100, 195, 247, 276–277
Parliament/Parliament Funkadelic 123, 148
Parton, Dolly 132
The Partridge Family 203
"Party Time Man" 123, 224
The Passions 39, 109
"Patches" 56–57, 59
Paterson, New Jersey 134
Patterson, Floyd 119
Patterson, Lover 164
Patty & the Emblems 5, 145, 209–210, 237
Paul (label) 20
Paul, Clarence 112, 125
Paul and Paula 110, 257
Paul Revere and the Raiders 229
Pauling, Lowman 111–112
Pawleys Island Pavilion 184, 245
"Pay to the Piper" 59
Payne, Freda 59, 210–211, 259
Payne, Scherrie 211
The Peaches 153
Peacock (label) 88
Pearl (label) 89
Pearl, Bernie 136
Pearl Jam 17
Pearl Woods and the Gems 274
Peaston, David 31
Peek, Paul 90
Peggy Sue (label) 239
Pendergrass, Teddy 123, 190–191, 211–212
The Penguins 212–213
Penn, Dan 220–221
"Pennies from Heaven" 242–243
"People Will Say We're in Love" 246–247
Perren, Freddie 267
"Personally" 200–201
The Persuaders 206
Petal (label) 84
Peters, Jerry 121
Philadelphia, Pennsylvania 1, 19, 38, 49, 84, 104, 114, 120, 123, 124, 144, 145–146, 156, 175–176, 178, 190–191, 195, 200, 211, 236, 251, 264, 272, 276, 279, 281, 284
Philadelphia International (label) 34, 50–51, 123–124, 176, 190–191, 206–207, 211–212, 223, 278
Philips (label) 46, 141
Phillips, Sam 41–42, 133–134
The Philly Dog (dance) 104
Philly Groove (label) 84–85
Philly Sound (label) 273
Philly World (label) 191
Pickett, Wilson 50, 53, 55, 80, 86, 94, 106, 112–113, 192, 202, 220, 264
Pieces of Eight 75, 262
The Pilgrim Jubilee Singers 185
Pimp Jerk (dance) 53

Index

Pink Floyd 274
Pinkney, Bill 93, 95
Pitney, Gene 74
Pittman, Wayne 207–209
Pittsburgh, Pennsylvania 98, 131, 149, 215, 243, 289
The Pixies Three 174
Platinum (label) 77
The Platters 10, 28, 52, 109, 192, 213–215
"Play That Funky Music" 289
"Playboy" 183–184
Playboy (label) 172
"Please Don't Go" 268–269
"Please Mr. Postman" 184, 192
"Please Please Please" 47
"Please Stay" 92–93
Pocaro, David 238
The Poets, aka The American Poets (Brooklyn) 52, 215–216
The Poets (England) 216
The Poets (Los Angeles) 216
The Poets (New York) 216
Pointer, Bonnie 101
Poitier, Sidney 68
Polydor 270
Polygram (label) 100
Pomus, Doc 93, 163, 276
The Poor Souls 72, 260, 270
Pope, Charles 263–265
Pope, Joe 263–266
"Poppa Oom Mow Mow" 171
The Poppies 253
Poree, Anita 121
Porgy and Bess 68, 255
Port (label) 139
Porter, Cole 37
The Pott Folse Family Band 21
"Pour Your Little Heart Out" 92, 95
The Prairie View Collegians 37
Prann (label) 30
Presley, Elvis 17–18, 37, 42, 63, 138, 149, 162, 243, 276
The Pretty Things 151
Price, Lloyd 38, 218–219
Pride, Charlie 180
Prima, Louis 36, 70, 219–220, 243
The Primes 258, 271
The Primettes 258
"Private Number" 32, 69, 234, 283
Private Stock (label) 198
Prize (label) 162
Proctor, Jay 156–158
The Profiles 190
The Prophets/The Three Prophets/The Georgia Prophets 2, 5, 6, 10, 52, 128–131, 270
Pruter, Bob 15, 73, 92, 104
Pryor, Richard 155
Pugh, Fred 244–245
The Pulsations 48
"Pushover" 68, 153
Pye (label) 154

The Quails 142
Queen 107
The Ques 281
"Quicksand" 183
"A Quiet Place" 5, 10, 195–196
Quinlan (James), Linda "Quig" 184, 198–199
The Quotations 296

race music 7
Rachou, Carol 159
Rachou, David 159
The Radiants 10, 30, 52, 62, 68, 87, 154, 221–223, 230, 255
"Rainbow" 62
"Raindrops" 65–66
"Raindrops, Love, and Sunshine" 163–164
"Rainy Day Bells" 10, 132–133, 180
Raleigh, North Carolina 101, 199
Ram, Buck 212–213, 214–215
Rama (label) 162
Randolph Air Force Base 75, 278
The Rascals/Young Rascals 94, 203
The Ravens 10, 23, 34, 38, 54, 97, 139, 224–225, 259
Rawls, Lou 123, 136, 141, 144, 163, 203, 223–224, 290
The Ray Raspberry Gospel Singers 149
The Rays 85, 124
The Rays (back-up singers) 278
RCA (label) 22, 69, 88, 96–97, 110, 121, 123, 146–147 155, 179, 219, 253, 276, 278
"Reach Out for Me" 269
"Reach Out I'll Be There" 117–119
"Ready or Not, Here I Come" 85
Ready, Steady, Go 183
Rebennack, Mac 20
Recording Industry Association of America (RIAA) 59, 64
Red Bird (label) 179, 216
Red Dog (label) 273
"Red Red Wine" 155
Red Robin (label) 96, 97
The Red Saunders Band 31
Red Top (label) 98, 125
Redding, Otis 32, 49, 50, 56, 91, 113, 151, 170, 202, 220, 236, 271, 294
Redmon, Don 36
Reese, Della 182
Reeves, Martha *see* Martha (Reeves) and the Vandellas
Reflection (label) 52
Reflection Sound 52
The Reflections 240
Regal Theater (Chicago) 91, 279
Reid, Jeffrey Lynn 107–108
Relf, Bobby 36
Relic (label) 108
"Remember (Walkin' in the Sand)" 151
Renee (label) 105
Reprise (label) 174, 287
"Rescue Me" 30–31, 153
Resnick, Arthur 93
Revelation (label) 234
Revilot (label) 26–27

The Revilot Lounge 26
Rhys, John 240
Rhythm and Blues Foundation 46, 48, 89, 105, 119, 150, 174, 196, 244, 281, 287
Rhythm and Blues Magazine 96
The Rhythm Masters 170
The Rhythm Rockers 280
Ric-Tic (label) 240, 253–254, 267
Rich (label) 141, 182
Rich, Eddie 260–261
Richards, Keith 17–18
"Riding for a Fall" 263–264
Right On (label) 29
The Righteous Brothers 20, 191, 268
"Ring My Bell" 173
"Riot in Cell Block #9" 72
Riperton, Minnie 30, 82, 222
Ripete Records (label) 11, 26, 52, 71
Rising Sons (label) 166–167
Rita (label) 57
Rivers, Johnny 17, 118, 270
Riverside (label) 118
The Rivingtons 110, 171–172
Robert Winters and Fall 295
Roberts, John 177, 225–226
Roberts, Kev 68, 101, 210
Robey, Don 55, 76, 88, 225
The Robins 54, 72, 110, 259
Robinson, Bobby 43, 124
Robinson, Smokey / and the Miracles 28, 29, 53, 131, 154–155, 157, 183–184, 226–227, 258, 271, 286, 295
Robinson, Sylvia 99, 141
Rock, Joe 243
The Rock and Roll Hall of Fame 23, 24, 46, 47, 50, 51, 87, 95, 112, 119, 126, 140, 144, 148, 154, 163, 165, 169, 185, 189, 198, 207, 219, 227, 232, 244, 259, 272, 276
Rock 'n' Roll Revue 71
"Rocket 88" 41–42
The Rockin' Gibralters 235
"Rockin' Robin" 35
Roe, Tommy 264
Rogers and Hammerstein 247
Roker (label) 287
"Roll with Me Henry" 153
Rolling Stone 118, 164–165, 219, 293
The Rolling Stones 17–18, 36, 142, 154, 248, 264, 271, 274
The Romeos 140
Ron (label) 295
Rona (label) 108
The Ronettes 209
Ronstadt, Linda 45, 105
The Rooster Tail (club) 68
The Roosters 50, 143
Rose Colored Glass 227–229
Ross, Diana 82, 121, 126, 148, 230–231, 250, 259, 281, 284
Ross, Jackie 91, 229–230
Ross, Jerry 51, 141, 156–157, 197–198, 236
Roth, David Lee 220

318   Index

Roulette (label) 139, 210
Round Robin 36
Rounder (label) 50
Roxbury (label) 131
Roy Acuff and the Smokey Mountain Boys 141
Royal, Billy Joe 21
The Royal Charms 291
The Royal Guardsmen 262
The Royal Sons Quintet 111
The Royal Theatre 18
The Royals 23–24, 111, 168
RPM (label) 133–134
RSO (label) 233–234
"Rub a Little Boogie" 3, 97–98
The Rubber Band 221, 235
"Rubber Biscuit" 215
"Rubberband Man" 251
Rubinson, David 163
"Ruby Baby" 92–93
Ruby Stackhouse and the Vondells 73
Ruffin, David 55, 68, 231–232, 249–250, 271
Ruffin, Jimmy 126, 232, 233, 271, 279
Rupe, Art 218
Rush, Otis 81
Russell, Bert 49, 74; *see also* Berns, Bert
Russell, Patty 209
Russell, Rudolph "Doc" 194
Rust (label) 134
Ruth (label) 150
Rydell, Bobby 276
Ryder, Mitch 134

The Sabre-ettes 182
The Sabres 178
Sack (label) 81
"Sad Eyes" 164
Sadler, Reggie 155–156
"Saffronia Bee" 37
Safice (label) 113
"Safronia B" 37–38
Sain, Oliver 30
St. Lawrence Records (label) 15
St. Louis, Missouri 30, 110, 169–170, 189, 218, 229
The Sallie Martin Singers 284
"Sally Go 'Round the Roses" 78, 236
"Sally Sue Brown" 16
Salsoul 176
Sam and Dave 113, 202, 236
Sam Butera and the Witnesses 220
San Antonio, Texas 75–76, 192, 278
San Diego (band) 257
The Sandpebbles 234
Sands, Evie 230
Sanford, Ed 235–236
Sansu (label) 248
The Sapphires 209, 236–237
SAR (label) 226, 229
Satan's Den (club) 193
Satellite Records (label) 19, 194
The Satintones 183

"Saturday Night at the Movies" 92, 94
Saturday Night Fever 267
"Save the Last Dance for Me" 91, 92–93, 165
Savoy (label) 80, 87–88, 89, 112, 138, 187
Sawyer, Pam 231, 232
Sayer, Leo 132
Scaggs, Boz 132, 237–238
Scarborough, Skip 121
Scatt (label) 234
Scepter (label) 8, 44, 57, 69, 141, 149, 230, 283
Schroeder, "Papa Don" 55, 220–221
Schronce, Bo 57–58, 107
Scott, Barbara 128–130
Scott, Billy 128–130, 156
Scott, Calvin 56
Scott, Gloria 36
Scott, Peggy 238–239
Scott, "Sir" Walter, aka Walter Notheis 170–171
The Scottsmen 128
"Sea Cruise" 114
Sea Horn (label) 139
"Searchin'" 72–73
"Searching for My Love" 201–202
Sedaka, Neil 91, 133
Sedgrick (label) 230
"See You in September" 134–135
Segar, Bob 12
Sehorn, Marshall 292
Selector Sound (label) 268
"Selfish One" 229–230
The Seminoles 268
The Sensational Epics 265
The Sensational Nightingales 24
"September in the Rain" 284–285
Serock (label) 43
Setzer, Brian 220
"Seven Lonely Nights" 117–119
"Sexy Ways" 23
Shad, Bob 120
Shades of Blue 240–241, 254
Shadow (group) 161; *see also* The Jive Five
Shadow (label) 52
"Shag with Me" 9, 79, 81
"Shaggin'" 25–26, 108
Shagtime 53
"Shake a Tail Feather" 36, 67, 110, 189, 221
"Shake, Rattle, and Roll" 274–276
Shalamar 177
"Shama Lama Ding Dong" (Band of Oz version) 26
"Shama Lama Ding Dong" (Otis Day and the Knights version) 82–83
"Shame, Shame" 178–179
"Shame, Shame, Shame" 99
The Shangri-Las 151
Shar-Dee (label) 223
"Sharing the Night Together" 17
Sharp, Dee Dee 276
The Sharps 171

"She Blew a Good Thing" 179, 215–216
"She Drives Me Out of My Mind" 261–262
"She Shot a Hole in My Soul" 79–80
"She Wanna Rock" 16
The Sheiks 109
Sheila E. 135
Shell (label) 163
Shep and the Limelights 280
Sheppard, Bill "Bunky" 62, 103, 104
Sheppard, James 280
Sheppard, T.G. 64
Sherrill, Billy 16
"Sherry" 164
"She's a Bad Mama Jama" 56, 140
"She's Got It All Together" 84
"She's Ready" 252–253
Shindig! 183, 268
"Shining Star" 1823
The Shirelles 42, 44, 112, 149, 174, 183, 209, 258
Shirley (label) 273
Shirley & Company 99
Shirley and Lee 99
Shocking Blue 196
"The Shoop Shoop Song" 104–105, 133, 180
Shore, Dinah 37, 72, 101
The Short Stories 205
"A Shot of Rhythm and Blues" 17
"Shotgun Wedding" 120
"Shout" 146
Shout (label) 150, 200
The Showmen 5, 9, 10, 52, 59, 102–103, 241–242, 247
Shreveport, Louisiana 20, 295
Shuman, Mort 93, 163
"Shut" 82
The Silent Majority 115
"Silly Little Girl" 263–264
Silver Fox (label) 267
Simon, Paul 264
Simone, Nina 3
Simpson, Valerie 157, 237
Sims (label) 166
Sinatra, Frank 37, 72, 114, 141, 185, 243
"Since I Don't Have You" 243
"Since I Found My Baby" 76–77
"Since I Lost My Baby" 232, 271
The Singin', Swingin' Counts 245–246
Singleton, Shelby 239
Singular (label) 49
"Sit Down and Talk to Me" 223–224
"Sitting in the Park" 10, 222, 230, 254–255
SIW (label) 136–137
The Six Teens 74
"634-5789" 113
"Six to Eight" 187–188
"Sixty-Minute Man" 9, 46, 64, 96, 117, 171, 188, 260, 273, 281–282
Ska 134, 154

Sketch (label) 161
Skylark (label) 136
The Skyliners 242–243
"Slauson Shuffletime" 36
Sledge, Percy 243–244, 279
"Slip Away" 56
Sly and the Family Stone 253
Sly, Slick, and Wicked 176
Smalls Paradise (club) 124
Smash (label) 4, 63–64, 112, 119, 128–129, 141, 156, 205, 261–262, 269, 270
Smith, Bill (label owner) 63, 256
Smith, Billy (DJ) 43
Smith, Bobbie (The Spinners) 248–252, 284
Smith, Bobby (Boblo Founder) 21
Smith, Buddy 68
Smith, Carl William 31
Smith, Keely 219–220
Smith, O.C. 2
Smith, Rex 168
Smith, Roy 128–130
"Smoke from a Distant Fire" 235–236
"Smoke Gets in Your Eyes" 213
Smokey Robinson and the Miracles 28, 29, 53, 131, 154–155, 157, 183–184, 226–227, 258, 271, 286, 295
"Smoky Places" 78
"Smooth, Slow, and Easy" 3, 96–97
Snoop Dogg 141
"So Fine" 109–110
"So Glad You Happened to Me" 128–130
"So Much in Love" 65, 206, 276–277
"So Young (And So Innocent)" 52, 215–216
Soft (label) 256
Solar (label) 176–177, 288
"Soldier of Love" 17
"Some Kind of Wonderful" 92–93
"Somebody's Been Sleeping" 58
"Something Old, Something New" 6, 108–109
"Son of a Preacher Man" 55
Sonny and Cher 110, 154, 257; see also Cher
The Sonotones 124
Soul (label) 169, 233, 279–280
Soul, David 115
Soul, Inc. 244–245
Soul Clock (label) 287–288
The Soul Stirrers 232
Soul Train 91, 155, 177, 295
Soul Train (label) 177, 288
The Soul Train Gang 177
The Soulful Inspirations 29
"Soulful Strut" 16
Sounds South (label) 263
Source (label) 191
South, Joe 21, 264
South Carolina Rhythm and Blues Hall of Fame 75
South Carolina State College 149

The South Shore Commission 110, 177
Southern University 158, 247
Southern Wing (label) 270
The Southland Jubilee Singers 143
The Southwest Jubilee Singers 96
The Spaniels 246–247
The Spanish Galleon (club) 6
"Spanish Harlem" 164–165
Spanky and Our Gang 156
Spark (label) 72, 204
Special Agent (label) 15
"Special Occasion" 226–227
Specialty (label) 20, 89, 174, 175, 218
Spector, Abner 78
Spector, Phil 78, 94, 165
"Speedo" 133, 179, 190, 211
Spellman, Benny 90, 206, 242, 247–248
Sphere Sound (label) 139
Spic and Spade 295
The Spinners 85, 123, 124, 145, 155, 169, 200, 203, 233, 248–252, 279, 283–284
The Spiral Starecase 252–253
Spirit (label) 38–39
The Split Tones 77
Spotts, Roger 68
Spring (label) 151–152
Springfield, Dusty 17, 55, 141, 234, 274
Springfield, Rick 203
SSS International (label) 84, 238–239
Stafford, Tom 16
Stag (label) 275
"Stagger Lee" 218–219
Staggerlee 46
"Stand by Me" 164–165
The Staple Singers 232
Starflite (label) 178
Starr, Edwin 53, 150, 240–241, 253–254, 267
Starr, Ringo 136, 274
"Starting All Over Again" 190
Staton, Candi 3, 56
Stax (label) 8, 9, 19, 20, 27, 31–32, 69–70, 106, 112–113, 174, 190, 194
"Stay" 10, 291
"Stay in My Corner" 86–87
Stepney, Charles 86–87, 222, 230
Stepp (label) 67
Stevens, Ray 264
Stevenson, Mickey 118, 125, 142, 182, 184, 249
Stewart, Amii 113
Stewart, Billy 10, 151, 159, 222, 254–256, 279
Stewart, Rod 12, 44, 132, 147, 265
The Stewart Gospel Singers 255
Stills, Stephen 274
Sting (group) 161; see also The Jive Five
Stoller, Mike 23, 46, 71, 72–73, 88, 93, 94, 98, 139, 165, 216
"Stop Her on Sight" 240, 253–254, 267

"Stormy Weather" 279
The Straightjackets 63
Streisand, Barbara 132, 148
"Strokin'" 57
Strong, Barrett 18, 126, 142, 286
"Stubborn Kind of Fellow" 4, 10, 125, 182
Stubbs, Joe 106, 112
Stubbs, Levi 118–119, 249–250
Studio (label) 108
Studio 54 (club) 32
The Stylistics 85, 145, 203
Styne, Jule 114
Sue (label) 127, 139
"Sugar Puddin'" 243–244
The Sugarbabes 90
Sugarbush (label) 57
Summer, Donna 148
"Summertime" 255
"Summertime's Calling Me" 6, 8, 9, 26, 57–59, 107
Sun (label) 41, 134, 138
Sun State (label) 213
Sun Studios 42, 134
"Sunny" 141, 156
Sunny and Phyllis 5, 12, 256–257
Sunset Café (club) 275
"Superfly" 143
Supreme (label) 84, 88
The Supremes 5, 24, 53, 99, 118, 142, 147, 169, 183, 184, 230–231, 254, 258, 281, 285, 286
"Surely I Love You" 133–134
Surfside Records (label) 9, 59–60, 270
"Susan" 48–49, 196
The Swallows 54, 259–261
Swan (label) 192, 236, 237, 241–242
Sweet, Rachel 168
"Sweet Charlie Babe" 200–201
"Sweet Soul Music" 190, 294
"The Sweetest Thing This Side of Heaven" 29, 169
"Sweets for My Sweet" 92–93
Swing 75
"Swing Your Daddy" 131–132, 224, 238
The Swingin' Medallions 4, 67, 192, 235, 244, 261–262, 264, 270
The Swinging Tangents 256
Sylvers, Leon 177
Sylvia 81
Symbol (label) 215
The Syncopators 113

T-Neck 147
"Ta-Ta (Just like a Baby)" 188
Tail of the Fox (club) 52
"Take Me in Your Arms" 147
Talent Masters Studios 181
Tall Tonio with the Mello-Dees 67
The Tally Ho (club) 257
Talty, Don 39–40
Tamla (label) 55, 100, 118, 125, 142, 146–147, 182, 183–184, 226, 258, 285, 294
The Tams 5, 6, 9, 10, 61, 81, 82–83, 103, 262–266

"The Tams Medley" 263, 265
Tangerine (label) 121, 181
Tarnopol, Nat 293
Tavares 144, 266–267, 290
Taylor, Chip 174
Taylor, Danny 24
Taylor, Gloria 267–268
Taylor, LeBaron 68
"Te-Ta-Te-Ta-Ta" 89–90
"The Tears of a Clown" 226–227
"Teasin' You" 268–269
Ted Carrol and the Music Era 75
Ted Mack's Original Amateur Hour 168
Tee, Willie 5, 9, 10, 102, 127, 268–269
The Tee Set 196
Teenage (label) 146
The Teenage Kings of Harmony 223
"Tell Daddy" 56
"Tell Him" 90–91
"Tell Mama" 56, 153–154
The Tempests 269–270
The Tempos 18, 135
The Temptations 2–3, 5, 10, 100, 121, 124, 126, 132, 169, 176, 180, 181, 192, 226, 232, 233, 249, 250, 254, 258, 270–272, 285, 295
The Tenderfoots 171
Terrell, Tammi 126, 147, 231, 281
Terry, Sonny 136
Tex, Joe 80
"Thank You John" 5, 9, 12, 268–269
Tharp, Ammon 8, 82–84
"That Lucky Old Sun" 185, 223
"Then Came You" 123, 203, 251, 283–284
"There Goes My Baby" 92–93, 165, 258
"There Is" 85–87, 222
"There's Gonna Be a Showdown" 33
"(They Call It) Mr. Dollars" 38–39
"Think" 10, 47, 111–112
"Think a Little Sugar" 17
"39-21-40 Shape" 5, 9, 241–242
"This Heart of Mine" (Artistics) 18
"This Heart of Mine" (Tony Clarke) 67–68, 154
"This Magic Moment" 92–93, 164
"This Old Heart of Mine" 143, 146–147
"This Precious Moment" 263, 266
"This Time It's Real" 216–218, 290
Thomas (label) 185
Thomas, Carla 19, 113
Thomas, Harold 265–266
Thomas, Irma 185, 242, 248
Thomas, Jon 162
Thomas, Rufus 19
Thomas, Sylvia 190
Thorogood, George 193
Threatt, Sonny 12, 256–257
The 3 Bees 246
The Three Blazers 88

The Three Caps 53
The Three Degrees 146
Three Dog Night 253
3-P (label) 128–130
The Three Prophets/The Prophets/ The Georgia Prophets 2, 5, 6, 10, 52, 128–131, 270
3 Sons (label) 190
The Thrillers 118, 292
Thrush (label) 266
Thunder, Johnny 234
"Tick Tock" 57
Tiera 146
"Tighten Up" 21, 33
Til, Sonny 45, 247, 259
"Time After Time" 113–114
Tip Top (label) 155
The Titones 149
T.K. (label) 84
"To Be a Lover" 31
"To Be My Girl" 177, 225–226
Todd (label) 112
"Together" 5, 145–146
Together (label) 128
The Tokays 68
The Tokens 134–135, 164
Tomlinson, Bobby 101–103
"Tonight's the Night" 50
Tony Allen and the Champs 20
Tony Orlando and Dawn 150, 203, 211
"Too Busy Thinking About My Baby" 125–126, 230
"Too Late to Turn Back Now" 76–77
"Too Much Foolin' Around" 263, 265
"Too Weak to Fight" 56
Toombs, Rudy 46, 193
Toot (label) 144
The Top Notes 146, 161
Top of the Pops 131, 265
The Toppers 67
The Tops 66
"Tore Up" 135–136
Torry, Clare 274
"Tossin' and Turnin'" 43, 161
The Total Experience (club) 155
Toto 238
Toussaint, Allen 89–90, 238, 242, 247–248, 268, 292
Tower (label) 21
Tower of Power 216–218, 290
"Tower of Strength" 186
Townsend, John 221, 235–236
"The Tracks of My Tears" 226–227
Trammell, Bobby Lee 194
The Trammps 10, 176, 204, 272–273
"Trapped in a Stairway" 148
Treadwell, Faye 94–95
Treadwell, George 93–94, 165, 188
"Treat Her Like a Lady" 76–77
Tress (label) 253
Trexler, Donnie 74–75
Trexler, Susan 75
Tribe (label) 178
Tri-Boro Exchange 203
"Trickle Trickle" 279–280

The Tri-Odds 88
Tri-Phi (label) 125, 249, 280
Triumph (label) 88
The Triumphs 206
The Troubadours 108
Troy, Doris 10, 93, 267, 273–274, 283
"Truly Yours" 248–249
"Try My Love Again" 201–202
"Trying to Love Two" 32, 70
TSOP (label) 34, 146, 176
The TSU Tornadoes 33
Tufano, Dennis 48–49
Tuff (label) 78
Tulsa, Oklahoma 36
"Turn Back the Hands of Time" 81
Turner, Big Joe 35, 139, 243, 246, 274–276
Turner, Ike 41–42
Turner, Sammy 133
Turner, Sonny 213–215
Turner, Titus 218
The Turnpikes 266
The Turtles 170
"Tweedle Dee" 22–23
20th Century/20th Century Fox (label) 55, 63, 141, 190, 226, 286
Twenty Grand (club) 68
"Twilight Time" 213
Twinight (label) 196
"The Twist" 24
"Twist and Shout" 74, 147
Twista 291
The Tymes 6, 9, 65, 102, 206, 276–278

"Um, Um, Um, Um, Um" 143, 172
Unart (label) 105–106
"Under the Boardwalk" 10, 92, 94
UNI (label) 105, 115, 190, 256–257
United Artists/UA (label) 66, 71, 76–77, 100, 105–106, 142, 147, 161, 195–196
"Untie Me" 262, 264
"Up and Down the Ladder" 145–146
"Up on the Roof" 92–93
Up State (label) 98
Upchurch, Phil 185
The Upsetters 65, 238
Upton, Pat 252–253
Uptown Theatre (Philadelphia) 18, 38, 104, 250, 279
"Urgent" 281
USA Records 48, 230
"Used to Be My Girl" 206–207
Utall, Larry 278

Val-ue (label) 124
The Valadiers 241
Valli, Frankie 57, 131, 163; *see also* The Four Seasons
Valvano, Mike 259
The Van Dykes 278–279
The Vandellas *see* Martha (Reeves) and the Vandellas
Vando (label) 29
Vandross, Luther 123, 234

Vann, Teddy 234
Vaughn, Sarah 226
Vee-Jay (label) 50–51, 61–62, 65, 85–87, 98, 104–105, 112, 133–134, 143, 166, 168, 246–247, 291
Veep (label) 161
Vellez (label) 269
The Vells 183
The Velours 108–109, 215
Vent (label) 176
Venture (label) 57, 226, 273
The Ventures 110
"Venus" 196
Vera, Billy 69–70, 174
The Versatiles 121
Verve (label) 163
Vest (label) 139
The Vibra Harps 98, 205
The Vibrations 68
"Victim" 3
The Videos 279–280
The Village People 148
Vincent, Joyce 150
V.I.P (label) 100, 147, 248, 250
Virgil (label) 20
Virginia Beach, Virginia 8, 82, 84
The Vocal Group Hall of Fame 87, 95, 119, 144, 148, 169, 183, 184, 207, 225, 227, 243, 259, 282, 288
Vocalion (label) 275
The Vocals 121
The Voice Masters 190, 232
"Voice Your Choice" 30, 68, 221–222, 230, 255
Volare (label) 273
The Volcanos 272
Volt (label) 27, 172

"Wake Up Susan" 248, 251
Wale (label) 176
"Walk Away from Love" 231–232
"Walk with the Duke" 62
"Walking the Dog" 19
"Walking Up a One-Way Street" 10, 268–269
Wall (label) 274
Wallace, Johnny 46
Waller, Don 151
Waller, Thomas "Fats" 246
Wand (label) 43–44, 66, 104, 111, 147, 149, 198–200, 273
"Want Ads" 59
"War" 254
Ward, Anita 173
Ward, Robin 276
Warings Pennsylvanians 218
Warner, Little Sonny 270
Warner/Warner Brothers (label) 151, 216, 235–236, 282–284
Warrick, Lee Drinkard 69, 283
Warwick (label) 120
Warwick, Dee Dee (Delia) 44, 69, 93, 105, 156, 195, 273, 283
Warwick, Dionne 69, 93, 123, 195, 203, 251, 273, 283–284
"Washed Ashore (On a Lonely Island in the Sea)" 10, 52, 213, 215

Washington, Dinah 38, 86, 243, 284–285
Washington, Rubin 194
Washington, Tuts 97
Washington, D.C. 18, 45, 70, 104, 125, 159, 279, 294
Watch (label) 248
Waters, Muddy 185
Watley, Jody 177
Watts, Bette 149
"The Way You Do the Things You Do" 226, 270–271
Wayne Fontana and the Mindbenders 105
"We Girls" 40
"Wear It on Our Face" 85–87, 222
The Weather Girls 148
"Wee Baby Blues" 274, 276
Weil, Cynthia 94
Weiss, Ed *see* Charlie Brown
Weiss, Hy 109
The Welcome Travelers 189
Weller, Freddie 262
Wells, Mary 10, 62, 126, 182, 189, 226, 231, 258, 271, 279, 285–286
"We're Gonna Hate Ourselves in the Morning" 79–80
West, Kanye 291
Weston, Kim 126, 147, 202, 231
Wexler, Jerry 49–50, 69, 236, 274
"What Becomes of the Brokenhearted" 233
"What Can I Say" 237–238
"What Do You Want the Girl to Do?" 237–238
"What Does It Take?" 280–281
"What Goes Up Must Come Down" 244–246
"What Kind of Fool (Do You Think I Am)" (Bill Deal and the Rhondels version) 8, 82–83
"What Kind of Fool (Do You Think I Am)" (Tams version) 262, 264–266
"What's the Use of Breaking Up" 50–51
"What's Your Name?" 203
Wheatstraw, Peetie 136
"When a Man Loves a Woman" 244
"When My Little Girl Is Smiling" 92–93
"When She Was My Girl" 207, 119
"When the Party Is Over" 163–164
"When You Wake Up" 185
"Where Did Our Love Go?" (Donnie Elbert version) 98–99
"Where Did Our Love Go?" (Supremes version) 99, 118, 184, 230, 258–259
Where the Action Is 19, 170, 202, 240–241
Whisenhunt, Walter "Whiz" 267–268
Whisky a Go Go (club) 170
"Whispering Bells" 149
"Whispers" 15, 176, 292–293
The Whispers 145, 163, 176–177, 287–288

White, Barry 36, 226
White, Maurice 30, 222
"The White Cliffs of Dover" 10, 64
Whitfield, Norman 82, 126, 130, 271–272, 285
Whitley, Ray 264–265
The Who 20, 154, 248
"Who Do You Love?" 236–237
"Why Do Fools Fall in Love?" 117, 135
The Wigs 237
Wild Cherry 288–289
The Wildweeds 52
"Will You Still Love Me Tomorrow" 44
Williams, Andre 189
Williams, "Blind Boy" 136
Williams, Hank 63
Williams, Jerry 234
Williams, Kae 49
Williams, Ken 179
Williams, Lenny 217, 290–291
Williams, Lloyd 82
Williams, Maurice 8, 10, 156, 291–292
Williams, Mayo 187
Williams, Otis 271–272
Williams, Paul 162, 258
Williams, Paul "Huckebuck" 181
Williams, Tony 214–215
Williams, Walter 206–207
Williams, Walter "Dootsie" 212–213
Williams Lake (club) 80
Williamson, Gloria 182
Willis, Chuck 238
Wilson, Brian 43
Wilson, Jackie 10, 15, 18, 23, 101, 118, 142, 149, 153, 169, 225, 274, 282–283, 285–286, 292–294
Wilson, Joyce 211
Wilson, Mary 257–259
Wilson, Nancy 91
Windy C (label) 103
Wingate, Ed 53, 240, 254
The Wingmen Quartet 115
Wings Over Jordan 115
The Winstons 294–295
Winston-Salem, North Carolina 111, 257
Wisconsin (University of) 237
"Wish You Didn't Have to Go" 220–221
Witcher, Tommy 52, 128–130
"With This Ring" 10, 52, 213–215
Withers, Bill 121
"Without the One You Love (life's Not Worthwhile)" 117–119
WKIX 199
Wofford College 58
Wolf, Howlin' 230
The Womack Brothers 232
"Woman's Got Soul" 143–144
Wonder, Stevie 55, 131, 141, 192, 227, 250, 271
"Wonderful Summer" 276
"Wonderful! Wonderful!" 276–277

Wood, Brenton 5, 296–297
Woods, Danny 59–61
Woodshed (label) 79, 81
"Work with Me Annie" 10, 23–24, 153
"Workin' on a Groovy Thing" 91
Wortham, Ted 123
"Would You Believe" 269–270
The Wrens 54, 259
Wright, O.V. 76
Wright, Peter 91
WTGR, Myrtle Beach 257
Wylie, Richard "Popcorn" 215

"X" (label) 137, 138
Xavier University 36, 158

"Ya Ya" 268
"Yakety Yak" 72–73
The Yardbirds 179
"Yesterlove" 226–227
Yew (label) 144–145
"You Are the Circus" 234
"You Are the Sunshine of My Life" 131
"You Beat Me to the Punch" 62, 285–286
"You Better Move On" 16–18, 264
"You Can't Always Get What You Want" 274
"You Don't Miss Your Water" 31, 69
"You Don't Need a Gypsy" 163–164
"You Haven't the Right" 57
"You Keep Tellin' Me Yes" 6, 52
"You Lied to Your Daddy" 263–265
"You Little Trustmaker" 276–278
"You Really Got a Hold on Me" 192
"You Talk Too Much" 268
"You Threw a Lucky Punch" 62
"You'll Lose a Good Thing" 1771–178
"You'll Never Find" 223–224
Young, Ernie 291
Young, Mighty Joe 81
Young, Neil 83
"Young Blood" 72–73, 82
Young Holt Unlimited 16
Young Rascals 94, 203
"Your Cash Ain't Nothing but Trash" 70–71
"(Your Love Keeps Lifting Me) Higher and Higher" 10, 292–294
"You're Everything I Need" 172–173
"You're More Than a Number" 92, 95
"You're No Good" 105
"You're Shakin' Me Up" 278–279
"You're the Boss" 22–23, 225
"(You've Got Me) Dangling on a String" 10, 59
"You've Got to Pay the Price" 267–268
"Yummy, Yummy, Yummy" 94

Zanzee 234
Zappa, Ben 117
Zebra (label) 57
"Zing! Went the Strings of My Heart" 10, 72 73, 273
The Zip Tones 161
Zodiac (label) 74
The Zodiacs 82, 291–292, 10